LIFE AND DEATH IN
EARLY COLONIAL ECUADOR

by

Linda A. Newson

UNIVERSITY OF OKLAHOMA PRESS : NORMAN AND LONDON

Books by Linda A. Newson

Aboriginal and Spanish Colonial Trinidad: A Study in Culture Contact (London and New York, 1976)

The Cost of Conquest: Indian Societies in Honduras under Spanish Rule (Boulder, 1986)

Indian Survival in Colonial Nicaragua (Norman, 1987)

El Costo de la Conquista (Tegucigalpa, Honduras, 1992)

Life and Death in Early Colonial Ecuador (Norman, 1995)

Library of Congress Cataloging-in-Publication Data

Newson, Linda A.
　　Life and death in early colonial Ecuador / by Linda A. Newson.
　　　　p.　cm. — (Civilization of the American Indian series ; v. 214)
　　Includes bibliographical references (p.　　) and index.
　　ISBN 0-8061-2697-3 (acid-free paper)
　　1. Indians of South America—Ecuador—Population. 2. Indians, Treatment of—Ecuador—History. 3. Indians of South America—Ecuador—Economic conditions. I. Title. II. Series.
F3721.3.P76N49　1995
304.6'09866'0903—dc20　　　　　　　　　　　　　　　　　　　94-41571
　　　　　　　　　　　　　　　　　　　　　　　　　　　　　　　CIP

Life and Death in Early Colonial Ecuador is volume 214 in The Civilization of the American Indian Series.

The paper in this book meets the guidelines for permanence and durability of the Committee on Production Guidelines for Book Longevity of the Council on Library Resources, Inc.♾

1　2　3　4　5　6　7　8　9　10

Contents

PART SEVEN
Conclusion

Maps

Tables

Preface

Throughout my academic life my research has focused on one issue, that of explaining the differential survival of native societies in Latin America during the colonial period. The question why some native populations were able to survive colonial rule better than others is straightforward, but each partial explanation I have found has made me increasingly aware of the complexity of the processes at work. Over time more and more questions have emerged, many of which touch on the frontiers of knowledge, not only of early colonial history but also of many other disciplines. Given my own limitations in so many areas, I have sometimes wondered whether I ought to abandon the field altogether. However, it has remained an endless source of fascination and enjoyment to me, and it has brought me many friends. I only hope that some of my forays into other disciplines have not been too reckless and that I have done justice to their scholarship.

My earliest venture into the field was my study of the impact of Spanish colonial rule in Trinidad, which suggested that the differential survival of tribal groups was related to the distribution of Spanish activities and whether Indians were allocated in *encomiendas* or administered by the missionary orders. It was followed by two studies that compared the experience of tribal and chiefdom societies under colonial rule in Honduras and Nicaragua. These studies demonstrated that chiefdom societies subject to the encomienda were more likely to survive colonial rule than were tribal groups who came under missionary control. Also of significance, however, were external demands made on native lands, labor, and production that were related to the intensity of Spanish settlement and the distribution of natural resources. During the 1960s and 1970s there was a growing awareness, apparent in my own research, of the role played by Old World diseases in the depopulation of the Americas.

For my next project, the subject of this book, I was anxious to follow up several themes: the contrast in population decline between the highlands and lowlands, and the impact of different economic activities such as mining, agriculture, and textile manufacture on demographic trends. In order to extend my knowledge of the native colonial experience, I decided to focus on the Andes. My interest in Ecuador in particular was aroused by a comment by Bill Denevan in his book, *The Native Population of the Americas in 1492,* that "especially important, but unexplained, are indications that the Indian population did not decline significantly in the sixteenth century, except locally" (1976:153). Given the experience of other native societies in the early conquest years, this seemed unlikely. Further reading suggested that not only would research on Ecuador fill a gap in the literature and clarify demographic trends, but it would also enable me to explore some of the themes I had developed and wished to pursue.

When I started research for this study in 1980 I did not envisage that it would take over a decade. In my ignorance I was unaware of the extent of the prior impact of Inka expansion in Ecuador. I therefore had to undertake more background work than I had anticipated, but—as will be apparent from the footnotes—I was greatly aided by Frank Salomon's pioneering thesis, since published as *Native Lords of Quito in the Age of the Incas* (1986). From the outset, clear environmental and cultural differences argued for a regional approach, even though I was not certain that sufficient evidence was available. This was particularly the case because previous demographic studies, most notably that by Robson Tyrer, had largely avoided the sixteenth century due to the fragmentary nature of the documentary sources. Fragmentary they proved to be, but I hope that readers will find that my regional approach has been productive and illuminating.

Research for this book has been greatly facilitated by financial support from a number of sources. I would like to thank the British Academy for two periods of extended research in Ecuador in 1981 and 1987, the Central Research Fund of the University of London for research in Seville and Madrid, the Wellcome Trust for research on Old World epidemics in Seville, and the School of Humanities, King's College London, for a grant to work in the Jesuit and Franciscan archives in Rome. In Ecuador, none of my research would have been possible without the assistance of the staffs of the Archivo Municipal, Archivo Nacional de la Historia, and Archivo Histórico del Guayas as well as the aid of Father Tómas Costa, who tended the Franciscan archive, and the late Father José Maria Vargas, curator of the Dominican archive. In Spain, I would particularly like to thank Rosario Parra, former director of the Archivo General de Indias in Seville, and her staff for the help they provided during my numerous visits to the archive.

Special thanks are due to Roma Beaumont and Gordon Reynell, cartographers in the Department of Geography at King's College London, and to Sabine Dedenbach-Salazar Saenz for her patient guidance with Quechua orthography. With the exception of Inka personal names, I have used modern Ayacucho Quechua dialect for Inka terms, since this is very close to the *lengua general* employed by the Inka.

Finally, I am endebted to David Robinson, George Lovell, Christopher Lutz, David Cook, Bill Denevan, Ann Ramenofsky, Cecilia Rabell, and Bob McCaa, who have not only shared with me the excitement of historical demography, but in different ways have encouraged and supported my endeavors.

Linda A. Newson

London

Part One

INTRODUCTION

CHAPTER 1

Explaining Patterns of Demographic Change

The racial and cultural characteristics of these Latin American regions are clearly correlated with variations in the nature of relations of Indians and Europeans in the early period of European colonization.

Elman R. Service, 1955

The size and distribution of native populations today reflect 500 years of demographic and cultural change, but in most cases it was the first century of Spanish rule that was arguably the most formative. During this period Old World diseases reduced most Indian populations to levels from which the majority have never fully recovered. It also witnessed the introduction of new structures and processes that were to have pervasive and persistent effects on the Indian way of life. While these processes had universally disastrous consequences for native peoples, some Indian societies were able to survive to a greater degree than others. In this book I analyze the factors that might account for regional variations in depopulation and recovery. The most commonly cited causes of native depopulation are the introduction of Old World diseases; the systematic slaughter and ill-treatment of the Indians, often referred to as the Black Legend; the methods used by the Spanish to control and exploit native populations; and the impact of commercial forms of production on Indian economies and societies. Spatial variations in the impact of these agents of change were influenced to a considerable degree by differences in the size and character of native populations at the time of Spanish conquest and by the types of resources to be found in the areas they inhabited.[1] Even though these factors exerted influences in all areas, they and the processes they generated varied in relative importance. Furthermore, they did not operate in isolation but interacted to differing degrees. The complexity of the processes operating needs to be stressed, since for practical reasons the following discussion will consider separately the impact of several factors known to have influenced demographic trends. The introductory discussion builds on my previous research on the impact of Spanish conquest on native peoples, most notably those of Honduras and Nicaragua.[2] Many general propositions contained in these earlier works remain pertinent to the present discussion and will be repeated here only in summary form. However, emphasis will be placed on evidence and arguments drawn from more recent research, especially that of epidemiologists and demographers.

3

THE IMPACT OF OLD WORLD DISEASES

Most researchers agree that a major cause of the rapid decline of Indian populations in the New World was the introduction of Old World diseases, to which, because of centuries of isolation, they had acquired no immunity. Among the most notable killers were smallpox, measles, typhus, plague, and influenza. It was not uncommon for an epidemic to carry off one-third, or even one-half, of the population of an area, and in the early colonial period native populations were ravaged by epidemics at almost regular ten-year intervals. Thus Indian populations could be rapidly hammered down to fractions of their original size. Cook has shown how the six major epidemics that afflicted Peru between 1524 and 1615 could have reduced its population by between 79.3 and 91.7 percent.[3] This chronicle could be repeated for the greater part of Spanish America, for even Indian societies in remote areas did not escape devastation. Indeed, as will be shown for Ecuador, epidemics often ran ahead of the invaders, ravaging populations and weakening native resistance.

While the devastation caused by Old World diseases has been increasingly recognized, some authors have further suggested that spatial variations in Indian survival, most notably between the highlands and lowlands, can be explained by the differential impact of disease. Cook and Borah have suggested that in Central Mexico the level of population decline to 1570 was twice as great on the coasts as in the highlands,[4] and Smith has calculated that the level of depopulation on the central Andean coast prior to 1571 was about 58:1, whereas in the sierra it was only 3.4:1.[5] Cook and Borah observed that "the relationship between altitude (climate, of course) and degree of destruction of population is startling."[6] Although they do not go as far as concluding this was due to the greater impact of epidemic disease in the lowlands, it is alluded to on many occasions and is implicit in their focus on altitude and climate as the basis for regional differentiation. Higher levels of depopulation in the tropical lowlands are often attributed to the presence of tropical fevers, initially to malaria and later to yellow fever, which thrive only in climates with a mean monthly temperature exceeding 20°C, or to the greater virulence of other diseases in tropical climates.[7] These propositions need closer examination, but before proceeding, it is important to note that while each pathogen has climatic limits beyond which it cannot survive, patterns of infection also reflect the character and density of human populations and in some cases the availability of vectors to transmit the disease. They are therefore related to cultural as well as environmental conditions.

Malaria and yellow fever are both generally considered to have originated in the Old World. Yellow fever was the more deadly killer, but since the first definitely identifiable epidemic in the New World occurred in

1647–48, it cannot be held responsible for the early decline of lowland populations.[8] Even after the mid–seventeenth century, outbreaks were confined to urban populations capable of sustaining the disease. Malaria probably influenced demographic trends at an earlier date. Although the mortality rate associated with the introduction of malaria to nonimmune populations is lower than for many other diseases (5 to 25 percent), it may weaken infected individuals' resistance to more deadly diseases.[9] Anopheline mosquitoes suitable for the propagation of malaria were present in the Americas, and theoretically all that was needed to begin cycles of infection was a source of infected blood. Once an individual has been infected by malaria and acquired immunity to it, the parasite remains in the blood. In this way it was probably carried to the New World by apparently healthy black slaves. Medical research suggests that only a proportion of mosquitoes feeding on infected persons acquire the parasite, so that to ensure its transmission to awaiting vectors, a large number of carriers would have been necessary. Once transmitted, a mosquito may remain infective for ninety days, but it generally flies less than one mile from its breeding grounds.[10] Hence the spread of malaria would have depended upon the availability of vectors, which was highly influenced by climatic conditions, as well as the population density. During the early conquest period the dramatic decline in the Indian population reduced the number of human carriers and, in areas peripheral to Spanish economic interests, allowed forest regeneration,[11] which created less favorable conditions for the propagation of the sun-loving vectors. In contrast, forest clearance to establish commercial agriculture would have encouraged their reproduction, though the introduction of livestock raising, particularly cattle, would have provided alternative sources of blood for the parasites and reduced the incidence of malaria in declining human populations.[12] In the process of establishment in the New World, the malarial chain from human to mosquito to human must have broken down on many occasions. The question of the presence of malaria in Ecuador in the sixteenth century will be discussed later, but it is worth noting that for the reasons given, its spread is likely have been slower, and probably more localized, than directly transmitted diseases.

While malaria and yellow fever were probably not responsible for higher levels of depopulation in the lowlands in the early colonial period, intestinal diseases, such as dysentery, typhoid, hookworm, and other helminthic infections, many of which are waterborne and more prevalent in the tropics, may have increased the susceptibility of Indians in the lowlands to more deadly diseases. However, a number of other diseases—notably pneumonic plague, typhus, and respiratory infections—were more common in the highlands, where the spread of disease was facilitated by the presence of larger Indian populations concentrated in nucleated settlements. Implicit in the latter observation is the suggestion that the differential impact of disease was related in part to the nature of Indian societies inhabiting different regions. This issue will be explored further by examining the influence of settlement patterns, marriage rules, and forms of subsistence on disease mortality and on the ability of native populations to recover.

The size and distribution of native populations strongly influenced patterns of infection, which in turn affected patterns of mortality and fertility. It is generally recognized that where populations are congregated in large settlements, unhealthy conditions are often created that encourage the concentration of parasites and facilitate the spread of directly transmitted infectious diseases. The size of the population also determines whether or not a disease becomes endemic. In order for a pathogen to survive, it requires new hosts to infect, but most acute infections have a short period of communicability, generally less than two weeks.[13] A large population can produce a sufficiently large pool of new susceptibles in the form of children to maintain acute infections, which as a consequence become endemic and diseases of childhood. Bartlett has calculated that for measles to become endemic, a population of 7,000 susceptibles is required out of a total population of between 200,000 and 300,000,[14] though Black would put the figure higher at 500,000.[15] Where settlements are small and dispersed, such as among tribal groups, the spread of disease is slow, and "fade-outs" are common.[16] This is particularly true in preindustrial societies, where the rate of population increase is too low to maintain a sufficiently large pool of susceptibles to sustain most acute infections. In such circumstances the only diseases that become endemic are chronic infections such as typhoid and amoebic dysentery. Small communities may therefore remain disease-free for relatively long periods, but their lack of exposure to infection leads to a buildup of susceptibles, so that when a disease is reintroduced from outside, it is associated with higher levels of mortality among adults as well as children. As will be shown, losses among the adult population may have particularly adverse effects on small communities.

This discussion suggests that mortality levels associated with the introduction of Old World diseases initially were positively correlated with the size of the Indian society and the degree of nucleation of its settlement pattern. In the longer term, however, their impact was moderated where sufficiently large populations remained to sustain diseases in endemic form, whereas in small communities they continued to take an elevated toll. Generalizations about the overall impact of the introduction of Old World diseases on different-sized communities are impossible to make. Even though in the later colonial period relatively higher levels of mortality were associated with individual outbreaks in small communities, the aggregate impact of epidemics would have depended among other things on the ease and frequency of reinfection.[17] Communities with easy communications, such as those located on the banks of rivers,[18] or those that had more frequent outside contacts, such as those in the missions, are likely to have been exposed to infection more often and to have suffered greater depopulation. Nevertheless, equivalent losses would have been more difficult to sustain in small communities, to the extent that differences in the demographic impact of disease may derive as much from its effects on fertility as on mortality.

Epidemics not only contributed significantly to mortality rates but also affected fertility rates and hence the ability of Indian populations to recover from demographic crises. The most immediate impact of certain diseases, such as smallpox, influenza, malaria, and dysentery, would have been to induce high levels of pregnancy loss and increase mortality among pregnant women, while in some cases smallpox and mumps would have resulted in male infertility.[19] Other effects would have been less direct. An epidemic that results in pregnancy loss or the death of a child may be compensated for within a short time, perhaps within less than a year, but the loss of a spouse generally has a greater impact on fertility, since it results in the loss in valuable reproductive years while a new partner is sought.[20] This process might be prolonged, in some cases indefinitely, especially in small communities, where the number of potential marriage partners is by definition limited and where there are often cultural restrictions on the suitability of marriage partners and remarriage. In addition, the psychological impact of an epidemic derived from the emotional stresses associated with the loss of loved ones and in some cases the disfiguring effects of a disease may have combined with other economic and social stresses produced by colonial rule to induce lower fertility. Given that infant mortality was high and life expectancy low, even limited breaks or restrictions on reproduction would have threatened the high birthrate necessary to maintain the population. The impact of disease on fertility has been underestimated, not only in general terms, but also in explaining the failure of some Indian groups, and particularly small tribal groups, to recover.

Before leaving the issue of disease, it is worth commenting on the relationship between disease susceptibility and nutrition, and the significance of changes to native subsistence patterns. The relationship between poor nutrition and disease mortality is now thought to be less clear, and certainly more complex, than previously envisaged. Present medical evidence suggests that extreme malnutrition is needed to induce a collapse of the immune system and that moderately malnourished persons may even have some advantage over those well nourished. It is also difficult to relate infection directly to poor nutrition, since malnourished individuals are also likely to experience poor living conditions, where crowded accommodation and inadequate sanitation favor the spread of disease. Inasmuch as there is a direct link between disease mortality and malnutrition, the link appears stronger for some diseases than others.[21] Measles and most respiratory and intestinal infections appear to be affected by nutritional status, whereas smallpox, plague, yellow fever, and malaria appear relatively unaffected. Nutritional levels probably had little influence on the initial impact of Old World disease, to which the Indians possessed no immunity, but as microorganisms became endemic, they may have had a more significant influence on mortality, particularly infant and child mortality. Breast-fed infants would have been better nourished and acquired some immunity from their mothers, so that the greatest threat to their survival occurred when they were weaned.

Inasmuch as malnutrition may have affected disease mortality, it is necessary to examine whether there were any regional variations in nutritional levels. Several authors have noted that groups dependent on the cultivation of root crops such as manioc and sweet potatoes, which require protein supplements in the form of fish or meat in order to maintain a balanced diet, suffered malnutrition, as these activities were sometimes suppressed by *encomenderos,* missionaries, and others to prevent fugitivism or, more often, neglected for lack of labor time.[22] More generally, it is assumed that native subsistence patterns were undermined by the alienation of Indian lands, by demands for labor and tribute, and by increased pressures to produce goods for sale. Some authors, notably Cook, Borah, and Super, have argued that nutritional levels did not decline, and that even if they did, they remained adequate largely because of the greater availability of meat.[23] In fact there are likely to have been considerable spatial variations in food supplies related to ecological conditions and the character of colonial economies, among other things. It is important to remember, however, that the nutritional status of individuals would have depended not only on food intake but also on their energy requirements. These would have varied with the climate, work demands, and the need to resist infection.[24] Even if regional variations in food supplies can be demonstrated, therefore, in terms of disease mortality, it is necessary to judge their adequacy in the context of other factors such as climate and work regimes. The latter will be discussed more fully later.

This protracted discussion has served to indicate that variations in the impact of disease were related not simply to climate but to differences in the character of Indian societies inhabiting different regions and, as will be shown, to the mechanisms used by the Spanish to control and exploit them and to the character of the regional economies they established.

THE BLACK LEGEND

The enslavement, ill-treatment, and overwork of Indians was a significant factor in the decline of Indian populations in the New World, particularly in the Caribbean region, which was conquered and colonized before much of the legislation aimed at protecting the Indians from abuse was introduced. Most notable were the New Laws issued in 1542, which among other things banned Indian slavery, introduced official tribute assessments, and regulated the use of Indian labor. Although these laws and others were often infringed, they provided the Indians a degree of protection from exploitation, to the extent that Indian communities in regions colonized at a later date generally did not suffer the same demographic disaster that occurred in the Caribbean and to a lesser extent Middle America. These early changes in Crown policy can partially account for the distinct demographic experience of these regions, but they cannot explain regional variations within them or on the South American mainland. Neither can regional variations be accounted for by the pursuit of different Crown policies in different areas, for laws and institutions formulated in Spain were to be applied uniformly. Colonial action was therefore based on a myriad of individual attitudes and interpretations of the law that are unlikely to have been so consistently different from region to region as to account for long-term spatial variations in demographic trends. Inasmuch as regional variations in the treatment of Indians emerge, they should be viewed as reactions to different local conditions, notably the presence of particular types of Indian societies or natural resources, rather than manifestations of differences in policy or the way that it was interpreted.

COLONIAL OBJECTIVES, NATIVE SOCIETIES, AND NATURAL RESOURCES

The enrichment of the Spanish Crown and its subjects was paramount in the colonization of the New World, to the extent that conquest bore greater resemblance to a large raid. However, the continued operation of a robber economy and the desolation of native peoples were constrained by obligations placed on the Crown by the pope to convert its newly acquired subjects to Christianity. Actions were also tempered by the need to maintain a subordinate labor force to generate wealth and underpin the establishment of a hierarchical social structure that would reward Spanish colonists and ensure the perpetuation of the empire. Policies aimed at achieving these often contradictory objectives did not vary from region to region. However, there were spatial variations in the mechanisms that were employed that were related to the character and size of Indian populations and the presence or absence of particular natural resources.

In order to achieve the objectives of "civilizing" and Christianizing native peoples while exploiting them as sources of direct profit and labor, the Spanish employed three institutions—the *encomienda,* the mission, or slavery—the choice of which depended on the character and size of the Indian societies encountered. The encomienda was considered appropriate for controlling and exploiting populous state and chiefdom societies where often Indians had paid tribute and provided labor for extracommunal purposes in pre-Columbian times. The Spanish could exploit these societies effectively by modifying existing tribute and labor systems and could control them relatively easily through manipulating the native leadership. The encomienda was not appropriate for controlling tribal groups, however, since no organizational structures existed for the exaction of tribute and labor, which were rendered more difficult by the lack of effective native leadership. Since these societies produced small surpluses, if any, and constituted only small sources of labor, generally the imposition of the encomienda was not considered worthwhile. Instead the initial "civilization" and conversion of these Indians was left to the missionary orders, who could supply the closer form of supervision required. Nomadic hunter-gatherers proved even more difficult to control than tribal peoples and represented even less in terms of tribute or labor, so that little effort was expended in bringing them under Spanish administration. Only where they presented an obstacle to the effective economic exploitation of natural resources, particularly minerals, were attempts made to control these intractable groups through slavery or extermination. Although the correlation is by no means perfect, there was a broad correspondence between the size and character of an Indian society and the institution employed to control and exploit it.

The encomienda, the mission, and slavery differed in the degree to which they brought fundamental changes to the Indian way of life and, as such, had different demographic consequences. These have been described in detail elsewhere and will not be repeated here.[25] For this discussion it is sufficient to note that Indian communities subject to the encomienda were able to survive to a greater degree than those subject to missionary and enslaving expeditions. For those Indian communities that survived the devastating early years of conquest and were allocated in encomiendas, the changes they experienced occurred more gradually and did not result in the complete destruction of their culture. Subsistence patterns changed to meet new demands for tribute and labor and as a consequence of the introduction of new patterns of landholding and forms of production. Meanwhile social relations and power structures, weakened by depopulation, gradually adjusted to the new social and political order.

Missionization and enslavement brought more immediate, personal, and fundamental changes to subsistence patterns, settlements, marriage rules, and religious beliefs, the demographic consequences of which posed greater threats to their survival. Other things being equal, state and chiefdom societies had a greater chance of surviving Spanish colonial rule than other native groups, and being concentrated for the most part in the highlands can partially explain the greater survival of Indian populations in those regions. However, highland state and chiefdom societies did not survive equally. The Aztec of central Mexico and the Chibcha of Colombia suffered greater depopulation than the Inka. In this case part of the difference may have been because of the greater incidence of disease in the former regions, which lay in the hinterlands of Veracruz and Cartagena that were most frequently visited by ships carrying infections from Europe. More significant was the relative intensity of Spanish settlement and the degree of penetration of commercial forms of production with which it was associated.

In simple terms, Spanish settlers were drawn initially to areas where there were minerals or large Indian populations from whom tribute could be exacted; later some were attracted to regions where opportunities for wealth creation existed in the development of commercial agriculture. Commercial enterprises generated demands for Indian labor, brought about the alienation of Indian lands, and fostered racial mixing. These processes significantly affected demographic trends to the extent that variations in the intensity of commercial penetration influenced broad levels of Indian survival as well as more local differences.

Spanish economic interests focused primarily on the production for export of minerals and tropical crops, such as sugar, cacao, and indigo, and on the raising of livestock or cultivation of wheat and maize to support expanding domestic markets in the towns and mining areas. Temperate regions that lacked minerals, such as Argentina and Uruguay, attracted few colonists, and their weak commercial economies focused primarily on the domestic market. At the same time, high transport costs to Europe limited the production of bulky tropical crops such as sugar and cacao in ecologically suitable but distant parts of the empire. Hence the colonial economies of the South American mainland remained more closely tied to the production of minerals, such that the demand for labor was more localized and the alienation of Indian lands associated with commercial agricultural production proceeded at a slower pace. Such broad variations in the intensity of Spanish settlement, to a large extent determined by physical geography, were often apparent at the more local scale, given the diverse ecological conditions that prevailed in most colonial provinces, and especially in the Andes. While the degree of commercial penetration strongly influenced demographic trends, and indeed the tempo of change, its impact varied with the types of enterprises established, the level of demand for Indian labor, and the basis on which it was employed.

The link between Indian depopulation and mining has long been recognized. Silver mining was among the most profitable economic activities in Spanish America, and it received preferential treatment in the allocation of forced labor. Mining was by its nature a more hazardous activity than most work in agriculture, and forced labor more arduous than that undertaken by free workers; in addition the varied sources of labor employed and the confined conditions under which mining took place promoted unusually high levels of racial mixing. Mortality rates associated with mining were generally higher than for other activities. Fatal accidents were more frequent, and there was a higher incidence of sickness and disease, particularly respiratory infections, which derived from the unhealthy conditions of work and the employment of workers in different environments from those to which they were acclimatized.[26] Harsh as conditions were, the consensus is that the direct impact on mortality levels of both placer and vein mining was of less demographic significance than the indirect effects produced by fugitivism or migration to avoid forced labor in the mines.[27] It is worth noting that the impact of mining extended beyond the immediate hinterland of the mines to more distant regions from which they drew migrant workers and where agricultural production was stimulated to meet their demands for food, hides, tallow, and mules.

Textile manufacture was another activity that, despite ordinances governing the operation of the *obrajes,* was noted for its unhealthy and harsh working conditions.[28] Mills were often barnlike structures that were poorly lit and ventilated and were bitterly cold in winter. Indians were often chained to looms or locked in to prevent them from escaping, while cramped conditions, the presence of indoor latrines, and poor ventilation combined to encourage the spread of disease and make the mills unhealthful places of work. However, poor working conditions did not inspire most Indian complaints; rather, it was the harsh treatment they received from administrators and overseers, who constantly subjected them to flogging and imprisonment for shortcomings. Why the textile mills developed such harsh labor regimes—to the extent that they were little more than prisons—is not clear. In Mexico it was claimed that employers were unable to provide higher wages because the markets could not bear increased costs. The result was that wages failed to attract voluntary labor, so that various forms of coercion were required and the low profitability of production encouraged overwork.[29] Nevertheless the number of work-related deaths was probably small.

Most other activities probably had little direct impact on mortality levels, either because the tasks themselves were not particularly hazardous, or because workers were employed for relatively short periods. In agriculture the worst excesses probably occurred at periods of peak labor demand, notably at harvest, and in heavy tasks such as sugar milling, which often employed forced laborers illegally. In most cases Indians worked on local estates such that they did not cross climatic zones, although this was not always the case with sugar and cacao production. Conditions for workers in domestic service, who nearly always worked as free employees, probably depended more on the character of the individual employer than on the tasks to which they were assigned. Certainly there were instances of overwork and cruelty, but the more personal nature of domestic service probably moderated the treatment of workers in many cases.

While mining stands out as an enterprise that directly threatened survival, differences in the pressures exerted by other forms of production on Indian lands and labor may have had minor influences on local and even regional differences in population trends.[30] The production of sugar and cacao stimulated the rapid acquisition of Indian lands or, more often in the latter case, control over Indian production. Since both were labor-intensive activities, they also made greater demands on Indian labor than other types of agricultural production. The cultivation of tropical crops was largely concentrated in the lowlands, where labor shortages often necessitated the migration of workers from the highlands. This not only undermined the economic and social viability of home communities, but since workers were often not acclimatized to the regions in which they worked, migrant labor was associated with high mortality rates. Parallel pressures on Indian lands and labor were exerted at more temperate altitudes by the development of commercial maize and wheat production to supply urban markets. In the latter case, however, these pressures were localized in the hinterlands of towns, since access to wider markets was limited by the bulky nature of the commodity and its poor storage qualities. Where labor-intensive forms of production could not be sustained because of labor shortages, more extensive activities such as indigo manufacture or ranching took their place. Ranching was generally less disruptive, since although it might result in Indian lands being overrun by straying livestock and native communities being deprived of access to sources of wood, water, and game, it made fewer demands on Indian labor and in many cases occupied grasslands that had been underutilized in pre-Columbian times. It was not long before Indians adopted livestock and found a new source of food and, in some cases, even a modest income.

Indian survival was related not only to the type of activity in which native peoples were employed, although this may have been of overriding significance in the case of mining, but also to the labor systems under which they worked. In regions where Indians were allocated in encomiendas, during the colonial period there was a general transition from personal service under the encomienda to forced labor under the *reparti-miento* and finally to free wage labor. This transition, which occurred at different times in different places,[31] has generally been recognized as a progressive response to the shrinking supply of labor.[32] But labor systems emerged not only in response to demands for labor and its availability but had formative influences on demographic trends, not only among those employed but also on the communities from which the workers were drawn. Labor systems differed in the degree to which they affected mortality rates, undermined the viability of Indian communities, especially in terms of subsistence and social relations, and were able to provide the basis of alternative livelihoods.

Research has shown that free workers generally enjoyed better wages, improved working conditions, and higher standards of living than did forced laborers. Even within the same enterprise free workers were assigned more skilled and less arduous tasks than forced laborers and were paid wages several times higher.[33] In the short term, improved working and living conditions fostered population increase by reducing adult mortality levels and enabling parents to raise children past infancy. In the long term, however, free labor posed a greater threat to Indian survival than forced labor. Forced labor systems depended on the perpetuation of Indian communities for the maintenance and reproduction of labor, but in their operation they threatened subsistence production, strained marriages, and weakened kinship ties, thereby undermining the viability of the very communities on which they depended. Nevertheless, the degree to which they brought about the disintegration of Indian communities varied with the quota of Indians required and the length and timing of the periods for which they were employed. In general, however, they were less disruptive than free labor, which often required more extended periods of absence and often a permanent change of residence. This was especially true where forced laborers resided in or close to their communities during their tours of duty, as was generally the case with work in agriculture and in obrajes. While free labor offered individuals an escape from forced labor and deteriorating conditions in native communities, by weakening community ties and bringing Indians into more sustained contact with other races, it posed a greater threat to their ethnic and cultural survival. However, this does not apply where Indians remained in their communities and were employed on a daily or seasonal basis, in which case the wages they earned might help to sustain them.[34] Such circumstances prevailed more commonly in economically peripheral regions, where native subsistence production effectively subsidized commercial operations and Indian communities functioned as a reserve pool of labor.

Although the demographic impact of the establishment of Spanish commercial enterprises is impossible to quantify, it can be more fully appreciated if the processes operating are explored in more detail.[35] The direct impact of harsh labor on mortality levels is obvious, and as already suggested, the negative effects of labor demands on native subsistence may have heightened the impact of epidemics. Less clear are the indirect effects of extracommunal labor on fertility levels, which might have resulted from declining nutritional status and disrupted marriages. The relationship between nutrition and fertility is an issue of some debate. Some authors consider that there is a direct link between the two in that malnutrition may shorten childbearing years, result in greater frequency of anovulatory cycles, and prolong amenorrhea following childbirth, as well as reduce sperm quantity and quality and cause a loss of libido.[36] Maternal malnutrition during pregnancy and lactation may also lead to increased infant mortality. Other studies have suggested that such physiological changes have a relatively small impact on fertility and that the amenorrhea reported in famines may be linked as much to stress as to malnutrition.[37] It has also been suggested that social responses to food shortages may be more important in explaining reduced fertility levels. For example, the separation of spouses in search of food or work would disrupt marriages and reduce frequency of intercourse, while in other cases birth control may be adopted. Overwork, stress, depression, and drug or alcohol abuse can also induce subfecundity.[38] Whether physiological or social in origin, it seems clear that circumstances promoting these conditions were commonplace in the early colonial period.

Demands for extracommunal labor also affected fertility levels by disrupting reproduction and encouraging family breakdown. These processes were most commonly associated with forced laborers who experienced temporary but prolonged absences and among whom the permanent loss of a partner either through death in employment or fugitivism was more prevalent. Even though marriage age, generally regarded as the most important determinant of fertility, was universally low,[39] infant mortality was high and life expectancy low, so that high birthrates were essential to maintain the population. Hence even a small reduction in fertility would seriously threaten the ability of a population to maintain itself, let alone recover from demographic crises. A recent study of the impact of seasonal migration on fertility levels has shown that where workers are absent for three months each year, the annual probability of conception might be reduced by 11.2 percent, rising to 43.3 percent for those who are absent for eight months.[40] Although these calculations are based on migration occurring during the same months each year, and would therefore have to be modified for different circumstances, it is clear that extended absences would have an impact on fertility. While birth intervals might be extended as a result of the prolonged separation of spouses or marriage breakdown, they might be reduced where the cessation of breast feeding caused by infanticide or infant abandonment by working mothers resulted in a short-ening of postpartum amenorrhea.[41] While reduced birth intervals had the potential to raise fertility levels, in general any positive effects would prob-ably have been counterbalanced by miscarriages and extended amenor-rhea induced by arduous work and by raised levels of infant mortality resulting from premature weaning.[42] These observations suggest that in understanding fertility trends, more attention should be paid to patterns of employment, and especially female employment.

The arguments presented so far suggest that differences in the types of activities in which Indians were employed and the demands they made on Indian lands and labor may partially account for different demographic trends. It suggests that Indian survival was most threatened in areas of commercial interest, especially mining, where Spanish settlement was intense, and where labor was short, so that there was an early transition to free labor. At the other end of the spectrum Indian communities were able to survive in areas of limited commercial importance, where Spanish set-tlement was sparse, labor was abundant, and most Indians were employed as forced laborers in activities that were not as hazardous or disruptive as mining.

The incorporation of Indian communities into the new economic and social order did not proceed without resistance from individuals and com-munities. Sometimes resistance took the form of migration or flight, which, although it often ensured the survival of individuals, eroded Indian ethnic and cultural identity. In other cases territorial and social bound-aries hardened to resist domination. Recent research suggests that differ-ences in survival may have been at least partially dependent on the role played by native leaders in promoting community cohesion and mobilising their subjects to resist land encroachment.[43] This suggestion provides an added dimension to the previous argument that Indian survival was favored in stratified societies. Nevertheless, the success of the Jívaro in the Amazonian headwaters in resisting Spanish domination throughout the colonial period suggests that resistance did not always depend on the existence of a stratified social structure but could be sustained by ideol-ogy. Although cultural and physical resistance may have been critical in ensuring the greater survival of particular groups, it was effective only in peripheral areas where Spanish interest was minimal and Indian societies were spared the most destructive effects of conquest, intense exploitation, and epidemics, such that their populations remained above the critical biological threshold that enabled them to reproduce themselves and their culture. Elsewhere, where Spanish economic interests required the subor-dination of native societies, fierce resistance, such as displayed by the Chichimec or Araucanian Indians, proved ineffective in ensuring their long-term survival. It was not only the strength of cultural resistance that was important but the degree to which it was compatible with Spanish economic interests.

THE STUDY AREA

The ideas presented above provide the context within which the sixteenth-century demographic history of Ecuador—or more precisely, the *Audiencia* of Quito—will be explored. The book has two basic aims. First, it seeks to document Indian demographic trends during the sixteenth century. It is the first study to consider the entire region and to cover in detail the whole of the sixteenth century. The task is more difficult for Ecuador than for many other parts of colonial Spanish America for several reasons. The usual problems associated with the analysis of documentary sources for the early colonial period are compounded because the period before 1550 was one of political turmoil when the Spanish civil wars prevailed. During this time records were not systematically kept, and many accounts were written to achieve particular political objectives. In addition those records that do exist describe a society already considerably transformed by Inka conquest and the introduction of Old World diseases. Given the general paucity of early documentary materials and the difficulties of interpretation, researchers have shied away from estimating the aboriginal population and from examining its trajectory during the early sixteenth century. Hence even the most comprehensive demographic studies by Tyrer, Larrain Barros, Ortiz de la Tabla Ducasse, and Alchon have concentrated on the northern and central sierra and, with the exception of Alchon, have focused on demographic trends during the latter part of the sixteenth century.[44] Little is known about the early colonial period or other regions. Second, the book aims to analyze regional differences in demographic trends, addressing some of the issues raised above. For these purposes the book is divided chronologically and geographically.

It is obvious that before any analysis of the changes initiated by Spanish conquest can be considered, it is essential to understand the environmental, cultural, and demographic background against which they took place. An additional factor to be taken into account in the context of Ecuador was the conquest of the region by the Inka. At the time of Spanish conquest the Inka had consolidated their control over the southern part of the sierra, but they were still in the process of conquering northern groups. The demographic impact of Inka conquest and the changes it brought to native economic and political structures varied spatially and were to have an influence on the course and impact of Spanish conquest. Hence although discussion of the impact of Inka rule could have been confined to the description of the different ethnic groups on the eve of

Spanish conquest, spatial variations in the types of changes they brought
may be more clearly demonstrated in a separate chapter. Since it is clear
that a number of Old World diseases ran ahead of Spanish settlement,
decimating native populations and weakening their resistance to the new
invaders, no picture of native societies on the eve of Spanish conquest
would be complete without a discussion of their impact. Epidemic disease
was to play a critical role in the depopulation of all regions in Ecuador,
hence in order to avoid repeating the same disease chronology for each
region, the account will be extended to cover their impact in the sixteenth
century. It will not extend, however, to the seventeenth century, since the
low *selva* regions of the Oriente are the only ones for which discussion of
demographic trends to 1700 are considered. Instead, their epidemic history will be discussed in the appropriate regional chapters.

The greater part of the book is divided into regional sections and
chapters. First there is the basic division between the highlands, the
coast, and the Oriente. These broad ecological regions correspond to a
degree with cultural divisions at the time of contact, with the sierra being
inhabited by populous chiefdoms and the Oriente by tribal groups, while
both types of societies were to be found on the coast. Although the distribution, character, and size of Indian societies at the time of Spanish conquest will be discussed separately for each of these broad regions, it is
clear that there were cultural links between them. There is ample evidence for trading contacts and social and political alliances between
groups in the highlands and lowlands, especially between those in the
sierra and outer flanks of the Andes. Nevertheless, the cultural distinctive-
ness of the sierra was reinforced by Inka conquest, which was largely
confined to this region.

The tripartite division into the highlands, coast, and Oriente is particularly useful in examining demographic changes in the colonial period.
First, it enables an examination of differences in levels of depopulation in
the highlands and lowlands. In particular it allows an investigation as to
whether the impact of Old World diseases was greater in the tropical
lowlands, and if so, whether this was due to the nature of the environment,
the settlement pattern, nutritional levels, or proximity to primary sources
of infection. Second, since chiefdoms were to be found in the sierra and,
with the exception of the southern part of the coast, tribal groups inhabited the lowlands, it permits an examination of the importance of the size
and character of native societies in influencing the pattern of Spanish
conquest and the methods used to control and exploit the native population. In Ecuador there was a fairly close correlation between the distribution of encomiendas and chiefdom societies on the one hand and the
employment of missionaries to convert tribal peoples on the other. (See
Map 1.) Only in the *montaña* were attempts made to control and exploit

tribal groups through the encomienda. Most tribes in the Oriente did not come under effective Spanish administration until the seventeenth century, so that in order to compare the demographic impact of missionary activity with other forms of colonial rule, their discussion is extended to about 1700.

The highlands, coast, and Oriente are subdivided into smaller regions. These subdivisions coincide with colonial political jurisdictions, but with a few exceptions, the latter in turn correspond to a reasonable degree with pre-Columbian cultural divisions. A notable exception were the Panzaleo, who in the colonial period were split between the *corregimientos* of Quito and Latacunga. Even so, it was considered preferable to base the regionalizaton on political jurisdictions because the correspondence was generally good and information was most readily available or these units. Any lack of correspondence between ethnic boundaries and political jurisdictions has been recognized, particularly in calculating the levels of depopulation for the individual groups. Not all political jurisdictions are considered separately, however. Some have been combined to produce regions with a common colonial experience, particularly in terms of the types of Spanish economic activities established and the demands made upon Indian communities. For the sierra, five regions are identified on the basis of the particular type of economic activity that predominated. Hence, the Latacunga, Ambato, and Riobamba region was associated with textile manufacture, the Quito Basin with urban activities, Loja with mining, Otavalo with agricultural production, and Cuenca with both mining and agriculture. (See Table 1.) The aim is to examine whether higher levels of depopulation may be associated with particular types of production.

The regionalization of the Oriente is less obvious. A major distinction can be made between groups of the high selva and low selva. The former groups comprised the *gobernaciones* of Los Quijos, Macas, and Yaguarzongo and Pacamoros, where within forty years of conquest eleven Spanish towns and cities had been established, more than in the rest of the Audiencia of Quito put together. Here Indians were allocated in encomiendas and drafted to pan alluvial gold. The towns were used as springboards for expeditions further east, but more remote groups in the low selva did not come into regular contact with Europeans until the seventeenth century, when Jesuit missionaries began work in the region. At this time the Napo-Aguarico region did not form part of the Jesuit province, so that demographic trends in this area are considered separately.

This book focuses on the demographic changes wrought by colonial rule. However, these cannot be understood outside the environmental context or the broader cultural changes that accompanied conquest. To describe the early colonial history for each of the regions defined would have required a much larger volume. What is attempted here is a compromise.

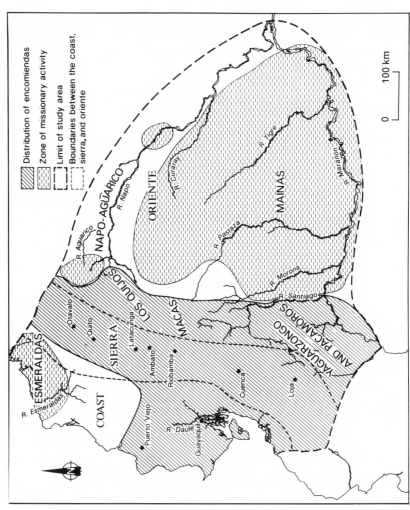

Map 1. Zones of cultural influence

Table 1. Ethnic Groups, Administrative Units, and Economic Activities

Ethnic group	Administrative unit	Dominant economic activities	Regional chapter
Pasto	Corregimiento of Otavalo	Agriculture	Otavalo
Otavalo-Caranqui	Corregimiento of Otavalo	Agriculture, textile manufacture	Otavalo
Panzaleo (Quito Basin)	Corregimiento of Quito	Urban activities, domestic service, textile manufacture, agriculture	Quito
Panzaleo (Ambato-Latacunga)	Corregimiento of Latacunga	Textile manufacture, agriculture	Latacunga-Riobamba
Puruhá	Corregimiento of Riobamba and Chimbo	Textile manufacture, agriculture	Latacunga-Riobamba
Cañar	Corregimiento of Cuenca	Agriculture, mining	Cuenca
Palta	Corregimiento of Loja	Mining, agriculture	Loja

Each regional chapter provides a brief account of the key characteristics of Spanish conquest and colonization but places particular emphasis on the features that, following the introductory discussion, are deemed to have exerted the greatest influence on demographic trends.

Topics receiving particular attention include the brutality of conquest and the demands made on Indian communities to support expeditions. These were clearly important in raising mortality levels and undermining native subsistence and kinship ties. Subsequently the foundation of towns, the distribution of encomiendas, and the establishment of commercial enterprises made different demands on Indian lands, labor, and production. Work in arduous tasks would have directly affected mortality levels, while the alienation of Indians lands and demands for tribute and extra-communal labor placed burdens on native subsistence that may have resulted in reduced nutritional levels and increased susceptibility to disease. These demands, especially for labor, were also critical in influencing fugitivism, migration, and racial mixing. The temporary or permanent absence of individuals undermined the social viability of Indian communities, strained marriage ties, and interrupted reproduction. Overall labor demands are viewed as critical in understanding many of the economic, social, and demographic changes experienced by Indian communities. In discussing demographic trends in the Oriente, attention focuses on different agents of change. Here the main topics discussed are the impact of enslaving expeditions and the establishment of missions.

Finally, each regional chapter considers in detail the documentary evidence for demographic trends during the sixteenth century. The sources are very fragmentary. Few precise references exist to the numbers dying in epidemics, in battles, or on expeditions, and the more subtle effects of the economic and social disruption to native communities occasioned by Spanish rule are almost impossible to quantify. Estimates therefore involve many assumptions about the applicability of experiences derived from other sources and regions. Although the figures presented may appear precise, they must be considered to have a wide margin of error. Similarly, much of the explanation for the decline, including regional variations in depopulation, will necessarily be circumstantial. Furthermore, many links between cultural change and demography are not described explicitly in colonial sources but must be inferred. Although this is far from satisfactory, perhaps it is reassuring to know that even given data of the quality we possess today, many of the processes underlying demographic trends still remain obscure.

Part Two

PRE-COLUMBIAN ECUADOR

CHAPTER 2

Lands and Peoples of the Sierra

> These provinces of Quito and their territories are some of the best
> lands of the Indies both because of the good climate and because
> there are a large number of Indians.
>
> Hernando de Santillán, president
> of the Audiencia of Quito, 15, January 1564[1]

Native life in the sierra was dominated by the Andes. Subsistence patterns, social relations, and even religious beliefs bore their influence. It was an influence that was distinct to Ecuador, for here the Andes are lower and narrower than in the central part of the range and are structurally less complex than their counterparts to the north.[2] In Ecuador the Andes assume their simplest form with two well-defined cordilleras that are capped by snow-covered volcanoes rising to over 4,500 meters, flanking a narrow interandean corridor, or *callejón,* some sixty kilometers wide. The slightly wider and higher Cordillera Oriental (4,000 meters) contains the most active volcanoes, such as Cotopaxi, Tungurahua, and Sangay, and constitutes a more continuous mountain range that is breached only in three places by the Napo, Pastaza, and Paute-Zamora rivers. The lower Cordillera Occidental (3,000 meters), in contrast, is dissected in ten places, and in the south it breaks up into a more complex system of smaller ranges. The lower elevation of the Ecuadorian Andes is reflected in the region's wetter and more temperate climate and its once more extensive forest cover. It is noteworthy that environmental differences between the northern and central Andes have been deemed by some to be of such significance as to explain their distinct cultural histories.[3]

The interandean callejón that separates the two cordilleras is broken up into a series of fifteen basins (or *hoyas*) by transverse knots (or *nudos*) formed by volcanoes, volcanic materials, or erosional landforms that rise to 3,500 meters. The basins, variously located at between 2,000 and 3,200 meters, contain accumulations of volcanic materials or alluvial and lacustrine deposits that have generated fertile soils capable of supporting dense populations. The higher basins to the north of the Nudo de Azuay are covered with recent volcanic deposits, whereas to the south the basins are lower and the volcanic deposits have been eroded away to reveal older Miocene sedimentary rocks, mainly sandstones and clays, which have yielded gold and silver.[4]

In the Ecuadorian Andes the climate is generally wetter, and seasonal differences in rainfall and temperature are less marked, than in the central

25

Andes. However, they vary considerably according to the local topography. Rainfall is heavier on the outer flanks of the mountains and on the elevated perimeters of the hoyas, whereas drier conditions prevail in the middle of the basins and in the deep canyons. Nevertheless, irrigation is necessary only in restricted areas where steep mountains have powerful rain-shadow effects. Although the temperature generally declines with altitude at the rate of about 6°C for each 1,000 meters, aspect can cause marked local differences. Sharp changes in topography that affect altitude and aspect can also produce marked variations in soil, vegetation, and microclimate within a short distance, so that individual valleys may encompass several ecological zones. Even minor differences in slope angle can affect soil fertility, soil drainage, and the incidence of frosts.[5]

Despite the ecological complexity of the Ecuadorian Andes, it has been common practice to distinguish a number of broad ecological zones based largely on altitude.[6] Since temperature is assumed to be the most important factor determining cultivation, by implication particular crops have been associated with different zones. However, it is important to stress that altitude alone does not determine which crops are grown. Even though each crop can be grown only within certain physical limits, within each zone a number of alternatives are generally available, so that social and cultural factors, such as labor availability or a crop's social-ceremonial status, play important roles in determining those raised.[7] Nevertheless, it is useful to examine briefly the agricultural potential of the five broad ecological zones that are generally recognized for highland Ecuador.

The high mountains over 4,750 meters are more or less permanently covered with snow or ice, though on the lower fringes of this uppermost zone some mosses and lichens are to be found. The flanks of the cordilleras and transverse nudos extending down to 3,200 meters are covered with treeless *páramo* composed of coarse bunch grasses intermixed with rosette and cushion plants. Here low temperatures and high humidity combine to give the páramo a constantly overcast and damp appearance, while the boggy, peatlike soils that develop are poor and acidic. To what extent these lands were used for subsistence in pre-Columbian times remains unknown. Tubers can be grown up to 3,800 meters, which, on account of the cold, damp climate, means that the upper limit of cultivation in Ecuador is about 300 meters lower than in the central Andes.[8] However, the cloud cover is too persistent and diurnal variations in temperature not marked enough to permit the drying and freezing of potatoes to form *chuñu* as practiced in the *puna* of Peru.[9] As such, even though some potatoes may have been cultivated at lower levels and some llamas raised in the drier parts of the *páramo,* with the exception of hunting, the greater part of this zone was probably untouched by human activity in pre-Columbian times.

Within the highlands, settlements and cultivation were concentrated in *tierra fría* between 3,200 and 2,000 meters. In fact all the highland basins, with the exception of those of Loja and Ibarra, are located above 2,500 meters, though they are sometimes cut through or bordered by deep valleys and canyons that drop to below 2,000 meters. In Ecuador the tierra fría is often divided into two zones. In classification systems the colder zone above 2,800 meters is often depicted as being dominated by the cultivation of tubers, especially potatoes (*Solanum tuberosum* L.), while the lower warmer zone is viewed as suitable for the cultivation of maize. In reality a greater variety of crops were and are grown in both zones. At higher levels tubers such as oca (*Oxalis tuberosa* Mol.), ullucu (*Ullucus tuberosus* Caldas.), and mashua (*Tropaeolum tuberosum* R. et Pav.) were cultivated, together with cereals such as quinoa (*Chenopodium quinoa* Willd.), lupine (*Lupinus mutabilis* Sweet), and amaranth (*Amaranthus* spp.). At lower levels fruits and vegetables were commonly cultivated along with maize. The tierra fría was once forested, but only a few remnants of forest remain in inaccessible regions. The highest levels over 2,800 meters, known as the *ceja de montaña*, were once covered with elfin forest consisting of stunted trees covered with lichens and bromeliads. It formed a transition zone between the páramo and the more mesophytic forest of the Andean basins, where *chilca* (*Baccharis polyantha* Kunth. and *Baccharis* sp.) and various kinds of willows were common.

Within and bordering a number of the basins, deep sheltered valleys have been cut by headward-eroding rivers such as the Chota, Guayllabamba, Patate, Yunguilla-Jubones, Catamayo, Malacatoes, and Vilcabamba. Semidesert conditions prevail in these warm valleys, which receive considerably less than 1,000 millimeters of rain a year. Here the vegetation is characteristically xerophytic and includes algarrobo (*Prosopis inermis* H.B.K.) and *guarango* (*Coultheria tinctoria* H.B.K.), as well as species of *cabuya* and cactus. These regions were known for the cultivation of fruits, cotton, and coca in pre-Columbian times, but they were generally avoided as unhealthy by sierran groups, who settled there only in small numbers.[10]

The outer flanks of the Andes below the ceja de la montaña are wetter than the interior basins. They receive between 2,000 and 4,000 millimeters of rain a year, and the vegetation is of the classic rain-forest type.[11] At lower altitudes temperatures increase and the topography becomes less rugged as the mountains descend like crumpled cloth into more-rounded foothills. Here in pre-Columbian times native groups practiced shifting cultivation based on maize, manioc, and plantains.[12]

Andean peoples have developed a number of strategies to take advantage of the natural diversity of the mountain environment. Oberem has identified three methods, two of which were commonly used in Ecuador in pre-Inka times.[13] First, Indian communities exploited lands and resources in different environments located within a day's walk or a short distance from their homes. Second, where crops and other desired goods were not available locally, they were acquired through barter or trade. Medium-range trading occurred at the level of the household, while long-distance trade was conducted by *mindaláes* under the auspices of local chiefs. Both forms of trade were probably more extensive in Ecuador in pre-Inka times and were displaced to differing degrees, most notably in the southern highlands, by the vertical archipelago system introduced by the Inka.[14] This system of "vertical control," or "macroverticality" as formulated by Murra, involved highland communities establishing distant, permanent islands (or "archipelagos") outside their territories for the exploitation of desired resources.[15] The inhabitants of these colonies maintained social contact with their native groups in the highlands and were an integral part of their economic organization. Although this system may have been developed on pre-Inka antecedents, its emergence in Ecuador appears to have been associated with Inka rule. Brush argues that today the relative spacing of ecological zones has a important influence on which strategy is used.[16] Where gradients are steep, a variety of ecological zones may be encountered within a short distance, obviating the need to establish extensive trading networks or distant colonies, which are found where gradients are more gentle. While it cannot be denied that environmental factors influenced the strategies adopted, the evidence presented below will show that they were not necessarily alternatives and that their operation was associated as much with social and political developments.

As part of their economic strategies, sierran peoples employed a variety of sophisticated techniques such as drained fields, irrigation, fertilizers, and possibly terracing, all to enhance and maintain production. Using the strategies and methods described, they enjoyed a varied diet that they supplemented by hunting. Communities were fairly small and dispersed, but they were integrated into larger polities, each headed by a chief to whom they paid tribute in labor and goods. These polities might in turn form confederations headed by a paramount chief. As will be shown, these chiefdoms comprised populations running into the tens of thousands.

Most authors distinguish six major cultural-linguistic groups in the sierra at the time of Spanish conquest. From north to south they were the Pasto, Otavalo-Caranqui, Cayambe, Panzaleo, Puruhá, Cañar, and Palta.[17] (See Map 2.) The following account aims to examine the character of native societies prior to Inka rule, even though it is not always easy to distinguish pre-Inkaic cultural elements from later traits. A full discussion of the impact of Inka conquest will follow consideration of ethnic groups on the coast and in the Oriente.

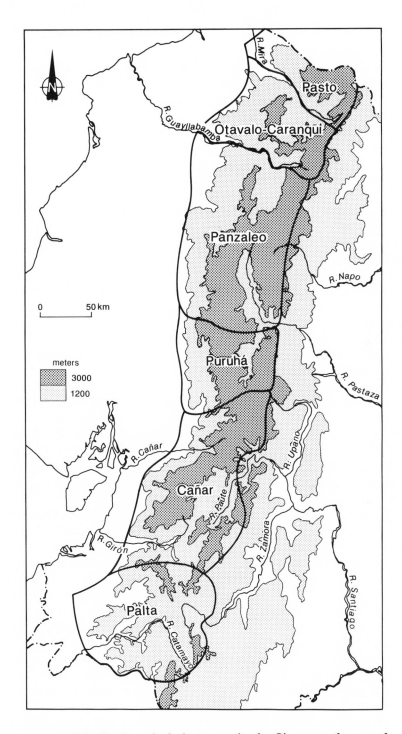

Map 2. Distribution of ethnic groups in the Sierra on the eve of Spanish conquest

PASTO

The northernmost part of the Ecuadorian sierra was inhabited by the Pasto.[18] According to Cieza de León, Pasto territory began at the river Patia and extended south to Tuza (present-day San Gabriel), "which is the last town of the Pasto."[19] Their location in the highlands between the Patia and Chota rivers is confirmed by sixteenth-century *visitas* that reveal that the greater part of Pasto territory fell in what is today southern Colombia.[20]

The Pasto region was only partially conquered by the Inka, and those communities affected experienced only the first stages of Inka domination. The conquest of the Pasto was launched from the Inka's northernmost fort at Rumichaca. Subsequently the main Inka highway was extended north to a point between Ipiales and Guaca.[21] In the aftermath of Inka conquest some Pasto were removed, mainly to the Quito Basin and Lake Titicaca, but there is little evidence that they were replaced by *mitmaq* from other regions.[22] The few who arrived were probably attached to Inka garrisons and played a defensive rather than economic role. Inka influence in northern sierra was therefore slight, and at the time of Spanish conquest Pasto society retained a number of features, such as the employment of mindaláes and the interment of live persons with dead chiefs, which had probably been more widespread in the sierra prior to Inka rule.

The greater part of Pasto territory was located in tierra fría, and its inhabitants therefore grew little maize, although some was grown at lower altitudes, but large quantities of potatoes, quinoa, *jíquimas* (*Pachyrrhizus* sp.), and other roots.[23] Deer, rabbits, and birds were hunted and contributed significantly to their diet.[24] Items that could not be obtained locally were acquired by various forms of trade rather than through the operation of a vertical archipelago system. Although remote Pasto enclaves existed in Abad territory, in present-day Colombia, and at Pimampiro, these colonies differed from classic archipelagos in that they were larger in scale and their members had become assimilated to local social groups retaining contacts with their home territory through trade.[25] In fact the Pasto colonies may represent an earlier and possibly once-widespread form of "vertical control" employed in the Andean region in pre-Inka times. Generally the Pasto obtained items such as cotton, gold, salt, *chaquira,* coca, and capsicum pepper through medium- or long-distance trade. In Abad villages and Yasqual they traded potatoes, maize, and *petates* for cotton and gold,[26] taking the cotton back to their communities to weave into cloth. Similarly, they acquired poorer grades of salt from Yasqual and Mallamas but probably obtained better-quality salt from more distant locations in Anzerma and Cartago.[27] Gold and chaquira were often used as mediums of exchange. The latter consisted of fine bone or shell beads obtained from the Pacific littoral or possibly Amazonia.[28] Chaquira, together with

coca and capsicum pepper, were traded over longer distances by mindaláes. Most Pasto villages had a corps of these long-distance traders who
were sponsored by local lords, to whom they delivered trade goods in
return for exemption from labor service.[29] Within the Ecuadorian sierra,
mindaláes were most in evidence in the Pasto region. As will be shown,
further south in the Otavalo region and Quito Basin only the largest
political units possessed them, and among the more southerly Puruhá
they were absent. While mindaláes enabled the flow of scarce goods in
politically unstable environments, they represented a less reliable means
of obtaining exotic products than the establishment of archipelagos, since
their operation depended on the cooperation of outside groups. At the time
of Spanish conquest mindalá trading had been replaced by the Inka archipelago system, but it persisted on the northern frontier, where Inka rule
was less consolidated and mindaláes could be used to promote political
alliances with otherwise intractable groups.[30]

Cieza de León makes derogatory remarks about the level of "civilization" of the Pasto,[31] perhaps influenced by his acquaintance with the Inka
empire to the south. However, even in pre-Spanish times the power and
status of Pasto chiefs was apparent in their ability to command labor and
sponsor mindaláes. In the sixteenth century a number of Pasto chiefs,
such as Tulcán and Tuza, were able to enhance their power as Spanish
allies by providing support for expeditions aimed at subjugating neighboring territories.[32] In pre-Columbian times these chiefs exercised authority
over several settlements, each with its own leader.[33] Pasto clans appear to
have been exogamous and characterized by parallel descent and patrilocal
residence.[34] Although they sometimes fought each other, the Pasto were
generally regarded as less warlike than their neighbors. This view is supported by the rudimentary character of their weapons, which comprised
hand-thrown stones, wooden clubs, and crude lances.[35] Although relationships between neighboring federations appear to have been good and a
degree of reciprocity was evident in their marriage alliances, burial practices, and trading contacts, nevertheless no evidence exists for the formation of wider political alliances.

Spanish accounts of Pasto religious beliefs are often vague and contradictory. Cieza de León claimed they possessed no idols, temples, or religious beliefs, except that they believed in an afterlife in paradise.[36] However,
a later account claimed that idols were worshiped during drunken festivals
lasting two to three days when they danced, had intercourse without
regard for consanguinity, and even killed each other.[37] Archaeological
evidence has revealed that at death individuals were buried with their
possessions, often in their houses. Chiefs were interred with some of their
wives and female servants, along with two or three persons provided by
neighboring groups. The reputed aim of burying such large numbers of

people was to rebuild a great kingdom in the afterlife. This practice was unknown among the Inka, and it was probably widespread in northern Ecuador in pre-Inka times.[38] Despite its apparent negative demographic impact, its significance for population trends is not easy to gauge.

Pasto territory was highly populated, yet settlements were small. Cieza de León recorded that even though the region was highly populated, it must have formerly contained many more people, since it was impossible to pass anywhere, even in the most rugged parts, without seeing evidence that it had been densely settled and intensely cultivated.[39] Most of the settlements were located a few kilometers apart on high points that dominated the countryside.[40] Archaeological evidence suggests they comprised unordered collections of between twenty and eighty houses, which were characteristically round in form. Some of the larger houses may have been used for religious purposes, and others, often located some distance from the settlement, used as reception houses for *caciques*.[41] Sixteenth-century documentary sources suggest larger settlements containing over 400 tributary Indians, and hence at least 1,000 inhabitants.[42] The large size of the early colonial settlements is surprising, given the demographic decline they experienced in the early colonial period, and it probably reflects the administrative convenience of including small dispersed communities under the name of the largest settlement or possibly the inclusion of inflated estimates in the absence of precise enumerations.[43]

Estimating the size of the Pasto population at the time of Spanish conquest is not easy. During the sixteenth century the extreme north of the Ecuadorian sierra remained a relative backwater, and there are few accounts of the Indian population living there. When Pasto communities in neighboring southern Colombia were enumerated by Tomás López in 1558 and by *Licenciado* García de Valverde in 1570, the visitas did not extend to those in northern Ecuador, which came under the jurisdiction of the *corregidor* of Otavalo. The earliest accounts of the Pasto population in Ecuador date from 1582, and even then they provide estimates rather than accurate enumerations.[44] At that time there were 3,000 tributary Indians living to the north of the Chota Valley. This may be compared with about 5,500 tributary Pasto Indians living in southern Colombia around the same time.[45] Largely based on figures contained in López's visita of 1558, various authors have estimated that the aboriginal population of the province of Pasto in southern Colombia as a whole, which included other groups such as the Quillaçinga and Abad, was about 150,000.[46] This figure is given some credence by Cieza de León, who claimed that the province of Pasto was more highly populated than that of Quito.[47] In 1558 the Pasto represented about 45 percent of the population of the province, and assuming they accounted for a similar proportion at the time of Spanish conquest, their numbers may be estimated at about 67,500.[48] If, as suggested by the estimates for 1582, the latter number represents only 65 percent of the total number of Pasto, the 35 percent living in northern Ecuador may be estimated at about 36,350. This is credible, given the depopulation suffered during Spanish conquest and in epidemics, occurring possibly in 1539 and in 1558, if not before.[49] Prior to the brutal war conducted by Huayna Capac, the pre-Inka population may well have been over 40,000.[50]

OTAVALO, CARANQUI, AND CAYAMBE

The sierra south of the Pasto as far as the Guayllabamba River was occupied by four chiefdoms known as the Otavalo, Caranqui, Cochasquí, and Cayambe. Other small independent polities existed at Pimampiro[51] and on the western slopes of the cordillera. The latter groups included the Caguasquí, Quilca, and Lita, over whom the Otavalo were exerting their influence at the time of Spanish conquest.[52] Since the chief of Otavalo was probably preeminent, at least at the time of Spanish conquest, for convenience the whole area will be referred to as the Otavalo region. In pre-Inka times these northern chiefdoms were not easily distinguishable from groups living to the south in the Quito Basin. There is no evidence for a distinct language being spoken by groups in these two regions; Cieza de León distinguishes only between the Otavalo and Caranqui on the one hand and the Panzaleo on the other.[53] Furthermore, many toponyms in the Quito Basin appear closer to Otavalo than Panzaleo.[54] Indeed place-names with suffixes -pi, linked by Verneau and Rivet to the Otavalo-Caranqui, are found in the Quito region. It is also significant that the Otavalo and Caranqui fought with their neighbors to the east and west, but not to the south. Ethnically, therefore, Indians of the two regions may be related. Nevertheless, it is clear the region between the Chota-Mira and the Guayllabamba was a common culture area.[55] The western limit of this group is unclear, but the bilingual character of the population of Chapi, where some Indians spoke the same language as that spoken at Pimampiro, and others the same as that in the "montaña de Quixos," suggests that the eastern limit was in this region.[56]

Whether or not the Otavalo and Quito regions constituted distinct cultural-linguistic areas in pre-Inka times, they were modified to different degrees by Inka rule. Inka occupation of the Otavalo region was essentially military in character. Two major garrisons were established in strategic locations at Carangue and Quinche-Guachalá, and large numbers of forts were erected throughout the area. However, the region contained relatively few mitmaq colonies, which were common in the Quito region, and there is little evidence for the creation of new political and economic structures.[57] Cultural differences between the Otavalo and Quito regions

at the time of Spanish conquest may therefore reflect different stages in
Inka domination of the northern sierra rather than the presence of distinct
native groups.

Within the Otavalo region the terrain is rugged. There are a number
of large volcanoes, such as Cayambe, Cotacachí, and Mojanda, and only
limited expanses of flat land. In addition several more deeply entrenched,
hot, dry valleys such as those of the Mira, Guayllabamba, and Pisque
border the region, so that the Otavalo had access to "tierra caliente, templada ni [sic] fría."58 The main crops they cultivated were maize, beans,
lupine, potatoes, and sweet potatoes, while fruit trees and garden vegetables were grown in the valleys.59 Many communities, particularly those at
lower altitudes such as those at Caguasquí, Quilca, and Pimampiro, were
able to exploit a variety of ecological niches within several kilometers of
their villages.60 However, with the possible exception of the exploitation of
salt at Las Salinas, the vertical archipelago system does not appear to have
been established in Otavalo region. Here most exotic items were obtained
by trade, though in contrast to the Pasto region, there is evidence that the
Inka were beginning to control the operation of mindaláes.

Various forms of intensive agricultural production were practiced.
They included irrigation and the construction of raised fields, but terracing, so common in the central Andes, was not widespread and may have
performed a defensive rather than productive function.61 Irrigation techniques were employed to water the dry Chota and Guayllabamba valleys
and enable the cultivation of cotton, coca, and fruits in particular. Clear
evidence of pre-Inka irrigation canals has been found at Puntachil to the
east of Cayambe,62 but it is not clear how extensively irrigation techniques
were employed in pre-Inka times. In the sixteenth century, water was
brought over two leagues (ca. eleven kilometers) by canal from the mountain of Chapi to Pimampiro for the irrigation of maize, while cotton and
coca fields in the Chota Valley were irrigated with water from the river
Mira.63 Other sixteenth-century accounts point to irrigation techniques
being employed at Ambuquí, Urcuquí, and Puchimbuela (to the east of
Caguasquí).64 Knapp has estimated that to the north of Quito as many as
seventy square kilometers may have been irrigated. Some irrigation systems were probably constructed by the Inka to extend the cultivation of
coca and maize, but given the short duration of Inka rule, many probably
predated that period.65 Since irrigated lands were used primarily to raise
nonsubsistence crops, their impact on raising the region's carrying capacity was probably minimal.66

The construction of raised fields, known as *camellones,* may have had
greater implications for the population of the region. Raised fields regulate
the supply of water, either facilitating the drainage of easily waterlogged
areas or controlling its loss in areas with a marked dry season. They also

raise the soil temperature and thereby reduce the threat of frost. In addition, the organic matter that accumulates in the intervening ditches may be used as a fertilizer. Archaeological and documentary evidence exists for the construction of camellones around Lake San Pablo and at Paquiestancia, San José de Minas, Pinsaquí (Otavalo), and Sigsicunga, and on the llanos of Cayambe, the last certainly predating Inka times.[67] In addition, Pimampiro was said to have have been established on land created by draining "a large lake" from which it took its name.[68] It is unclear what crops may have been grown in the drained fields. Documentary evidence indicates that in the early colonial period potatoes were grown in camellones, but recent observations at Lake San Pablo suggest that a greater variety of crops may have been cultivated, including totora reeds (*Scirpus californicus* [C. Meyer] Steudel) and edible herbs such as *yuyos* (*Tagetes terniflora* H.B.K.).[69] Knapp and Denevan have suggested that the raised fields in northern Ecuador could have supported 7.5 persons per hectare and that population and economic power were concentrated in those areas.[70]

Most animal protein came from wild sources. Guinea pigs appear to have been widely eaten, but in pre-Columbian times the consumption of llama meat was reserved for Indian chiefs,[71] and most animal protein came from the region's abundant wildlife.[72] There were specialized deer hunters who traded cured venison,[73] and in the sixteenth century deer and rabbits figured among the items paid as tribute by Indians from Otavalo, who also traded "birds" in Quito.[74] Freshwater fish were caught in the lakes using cane traps, and it is possible that fishing was controlled by local chiefs who had privileged access to fishing grounds.[75]

In the Otavalo region, like that of Pasto, middle- and long-distance trading had not been displaced by the development of the vertical archipelago system. Nevertheless, there is evidence that unlike regions to the north, the Inka were beginning to restrict the operation of mindaláes, making them the monopoly of preeminent chiefs. By this means the Inka sought not only to internalize production but also to differentiate among the chiefs, favoring the most powerful, who would ultimately function as administrators within the Inka bureaucracy.[76] From these traders, who were exempt from routine labor, chiefs received tribute in the form of gold, *mantas,* and chaquira, the last possibly being used as medium of exchange.[77]

Traders were concerned with the acquisition of cotton and coca from the river canyons of the Chota and Guayllabamba, salt from salt springs on the slopes of the cordillera, gold from southern Colombia, and salt, fish, and chaquira from the Pacific littoral. Although many of these items could have been obtained from the east, particularly from Los Quijos, easier access to the west through the Chota-Mira Valley favored links with that region, from which marine products could also be acquired. By the time of Spanish conquest these contacts had effectively led to the economic and cultural domination, if not political incorporation, of groups on the western slopes of the Andes, such as the Quilca and Caguasquí, by the Otavalo.[78]

Many Indians from Otavalo became wealthy trading coca and cotton, which they produced on *chacras* located in Mira and Guayllabamba valleys, particularly at Quilca and Pimampiro.[79] In fact the Chota-Mira Valley possessed over 300 "indios forasteros" from Otavalo, Carangue, Latacunga, and Siccho who traded coca, in addition to 80 resident Pasto cultivators.[80] These items were exchanged with highland traders who wove the cotton into cloth before it was resold. Hence many traders from Otavalo were also specialist craftsmen—fine weavers, potters, and carpenters—who traded not only raw materials but also their own manufactures, which they exchanged for gold.[81]

A trade item of particular importance was salt. The most important salt springs exploited were to be found on the western slopes of the cordillera at Las Salinas. Here commoners from Otavalo produced a "dark and bitter" salt that was traded throughout the region.[82] The status of those exploiting the salt is unclear.[83] They may have formed a permanent community specialized in the production of salt or have been temporary workers assigned there for specific periods by different villages within the Otavalo region. The salt deposits at Las Salinas were also worked by Indians from more distant parts of the sierra, including some Pasto, who in the sixteenth century paid two pesos for the privilege.[84] Although some salt was consumed locally, most was traded. Indian traders from other parts of the region converged on Las Salinas to buy salt, but mindaláes from Otavalo also carried it to the Quito Basin and north to the Pasto region.[85]

Apart from trade within the sierra and with its slopes, there is evidence for long-distance trading with the coast and with the lowlands to the east. Indeed, the Otavalo region appears to have been pivotal in relationships between these areas.[86] Gold and copper items found in *tolas* indicate the existence of trading contacts with Indians on the coast of Ecuador,[87] as do chaquira and *Strombus* shells used as musical instruments.[88] Chaquira found its way to the Oriente, where among the Quijo its scarcity encouraged its use as a medium of exchange.[89] From the east the Quijo supplied the sierra and western lowlands with cotton cloth, and highland Indians at Chapi exchanged salt, mantas, and dogs with the Coronado from whom they obtained young men and women.[90]

Four chiefdoms occupied the area between the Mira and Guayllabamba rivers—the Caranqui, Cochasquí, Otavalo, and Cayambe. Each comprised a number of communities or villages each with a leader, who was possibly the head of the most important lineage. These leaders probably formed a hierarchy in which their status was based on the religious prestige of their communities as well as their size.[91] They were subordinate to a paramount chief who was possibly the head of the largest village, or the most powerful and courageous in war.[92] Native chiefs were highly respected for their military prowess,[93] but their power also depended on their access to lands and their control of trade, which enabled them to redistribute goods and maintain the loyalty of their subjects.[94] The power they wielded was judged as considerable. They could command services as required, to the extent that their subjects, with the exception of traders, were said to be treated like slaves.[95] Although the presence of *tolas* and irrigation canals testifies to the ability of chiefs to command labor, there is no evidence they possessed slaves, with the possible exception of the young men and women they acquired from the Coronado. Their status was recognized by the title suffix *-ango* and the possession of multiple wives.[96]

Of the four chiefdoms that occupied the region between the Mira and Guayllabamba rivers, it has often been suggested that the chief of Cayambe was preeminent.[97] This suggestion is based largely on an account by the chief of Cayambe, Geronimo Puento, who in 1579 testified that his father had ruled over "the villages of Cayambe, Cochizquí, and Otavalo." Caillavet argues that other evidence, some of it from the same *probanza,* suggests that the chief of Otavalo may have been paramount.[98] In particular she points to the fact that the chief of Cayambe sent his son to be brought up in the house of the cacique of Otavalo. However, this practice was commonly employed by the Inka to integrate autonomous local communities into the empire and may not have been indigenous. The superior social and political status of the cacique of Otavalo was also evident in marriage alliances and gifts of llamas, but again these practices may not predate Inka rule but perhaps originated as part of Inka policy to integrate smaller independent polities into the empire by creating a hierarchy of chiefs, favoring the most powerful for special privileges at the expense of less important leaders.[99] Nevertheless, it was Inka strategy to reinforce rather than oppose local developments, and Otavalo's preeminence may date from Inka conquest, when the formerly more populous Cayambe and Caranqui sustained much heavier losses.

At the time of Spanish conquest the political integration of the Otavalo region was far from complete, and warfare was common. The Caranqui fought the Indians of Chapi and had wars with those of Otavalo, while Indians from Lita fought those of Caguasquí and Quilca. Often the reason given for warfare was to extend domination over neighboring groups, but in other cases disputes over land and vengeance for wrongs were clearly important. Those defeated were required to recognize the status of the victor in the form of tribute.[100] Expansionist designs were also realized by peaceful means through the establishment of trading links and marriage alliances.[101] Despite such conflicts, chiefdoms did form alliances in the face of more significant external threats, such as when those of Otavalo, Cayambe, Cochasquí, and Piso united together with other villages to oppose Inka domination.[102]

The religion of Indians in the Otavalo region was influenced by the environment in which they lived. The Quilca and Caguasquí worshiped the sky and the highest snow-covered mountains, where many of their *guacas* were located,[103] and many of their gods took the form of animals, such as snakes and "tigers and lions."[104] Indians at Pimampiro possessed idols made of stone and wood, and chicha and coca were widely used in rituals.[105] In common with the Pasto, the Quilca and Caguasquí buried a number of live persons with their deceased chiefs.[106]

The distinctive artificial earth mounds, or tolas, found in the region between the Mira and Guayllabamba valleys indicate that the region was highly populated. The tolas once formed the bases of dwellings and public buildings, and those with ramps have been associated with chiefs and identified as centers of political power.[107] The latter are concentrated at intermediate elevations between 2,000 and 3,000 meters and frequently located in the most productive areas, those of drained fields.[108] Lower elevations were generally regarded as unhealthy, and here settlements were smaller and more dispersed.[109] Over 2,000 tolas have been identified in the highlands to the north of Quito. Although small groups of tolas were once considered to be the remains of small independent villages possessing not more than 200 people,[110] more recent archaeological investigations, especially at Cochasquí and Puntachil, have suggested that settlements with ramp tolas were supported by intensive cultivation and probably averaged 3,000 inhabitants.[111] Archaeological evidence from burials and house sites indicates that settlements were socially differentiated, and this is confirmed by historical accounts that distinguish between the larger houses of caciques, which were built around central posts. Otherwise the form was similar, being round, covered with thatch, and with walls of large interwoven branches plastered on both sides with mud.[112] Small groups of tolas often surround a larger group, suggesting that communities were geographically dispersed, possibly in a manner described for the Caranqui in the sixteenth century.[113] Overall, the settlement pattern was more dispersed than that described in colonial accounts, many of which postdate resettlement programs, which concentrated the remaining population even more narrowly in the zone of maize production between about 2,400 and 2,800 meters.[114]

No precise contemporary estimates exist for the size of the population in the region between the Chota and Guayllabamba valleys at the time of Spanish conquest, but it is clear that it was highly populated. In 1582 the corregidor of Otavalo wrote, "They say that in past times there were many more Indians, and thus it appears from the disposition of the land and evidence from the construction of fields."[115] At that time the Indian population of the sierra north of Quito may be estimated at about 45,000, of which two-thirds were living in the region between the Chota and Guayllabamba valleys.[116] These numbers represented only a remnant of those existing at the time of Spanish conquest. In 1571 President Santillán estimated that since Inka times the population of the sierra in general had been reduced to a quarter of its size as a result of wars, losses on expeditions, and epidemics.[117] This ratio is not inconsistent with *Oidor* Salazar de Villasante's observation in the 1560s that the population of the encomienda of Otavalo had declined by one-half since the first *tasación* in 1549.[118] If a depopulation ratio of 4:1 is accepted, then a pre-Spanish population of at least 120,000 can be suggested.

Recent archaeological evidence from settlement sites and raised fields suggests that this number is not unreasonable. Knapp has estimated that sites with ramp tolas may have averaged 4,700 inhabitants, rather than 3,000 as calculated by Athens, which, applied to the twenty-one sites found in the region, suggests a population of 98,700.[119] He also suggests that the area between the Chota and Guayllabamba valleys could have supported over 210,000 inhabitants.[120] He bases this estimate on an analysis of the types of agriculture practiced in areas above 2,000 meters with an average rainfall of between 600 and 1,300 millimeters, distinguishing between the upper slopes, lower slopes, and flats with camellones. He admits that his estimate for the flats may be too high, since camellones are found in only part of this area and may not have been cultivated simultaneously.[121] Also, part of their product was probably used for nonsubsistence purposes. He also notes that about two-thirds of the area of flats were located in Caranqui and Cayambe territory, which suffered heavy population losses during Inka conquest and may not, therefore, have supported such large numbers at the time of Spanish conquest. With respect to the slopes he also accepts that not all areas suitable for intensive maize cultivation would have been used for this purpose. As a result Knapp prefers an estimate of 155,000, which is midway between that of about 100,000 calculated from evidence for settlements and 210,000 from the estimated carrying capacity of the region. His estimate only includes settlements above 2,000 meters. In 1582 these areas possessed about 16,975 Indians[122] and comprised nearly two-thirds of the population of the region between the Chota and Guayllabamba valleys, the rest being found in settlements located at lower altitudes. These proportions are unlikely to reflect the distribution of the population in pre-Columbian times. In the early colonial period depopulation levels were probably greatest on the flats, where the cultivation of camellones capable of supporting dense populations ceased in the early colonial period,[123] while Spanish interest in developing market gardening in the warm valleys may have resulted in labor being transferred to those regions. However, in estimating the total numbers living in the region at the time of Spanish conquest, some account should be taken of those living at lower altitudes. The previous discussion could be used to justify raising Knapp's estimate of 155,000 to maybe 180,000. However, his estimate is based on the *potential* carrying capacity rather than evidence for the numbers actually supported. Doubts over how much of the land was cultivated at one time, the intensity of the cultivation practiced, and the purposes to which agricultural produce was put also urge caution in raising Knapp's estimate. A figure of 120,000 for the areas above 2,000 meters and 30,000 for the lower altitudes, giving 150,000 for the whole region at the time of Spanish conquest, might be more appropriate, particularly given that it had already lost between 20,000 and 50,000 Indians during Inka conquest.[124]

PANZALEO

Panzaleo language and culture is perhaps the most difficult to reconstruct, since early accounts inevitably describe a society dramatically transformed by Inka rule and Spanish conquest. The Quito region was the most northerly part of the Inka empire to experience political and cultural change as well as military domination. Hence in addition to the roads, forts, and mitmaq found further north, the Inka established an administrative and ceremonial center at Quito, organized the region into moieties referred to as *hurin* and *hanan*, and began to incorporate local lords into the Inka hierarchy.[125] In the southern part of the Inka province of Quito, known as Hanan Quito, the vertical archipelago system was also being developed.[126] The dual division into Hanan Quito and Hurin Quito probably did not reflect major preexisting cultural differences but was an Inka creation that reflected stages in the incorporation of conquered groups into the empire. Prior to Inka rule a variety of cultural-linguistic groups probably existed in the region. Indeed, the greater consolidation of Inka rule to the south of a line running northwest-southeast through the Quito Basin was manifest at the time of Spanish conquest in a greater loyalty to the Inka cause.[127]

One group to be found in the Quito region were the Panzaleo. Cieza de León indicates that the Panzaleo, who spoke a language that was distinct from Otavalo-Caranqui, were to be found in the region between the towns of Panzaleo and Mocha, which encompassed the towns of Mulahaló, Latacunga, Muliambato, and Ambato.[128] However, contemporary sources remain silent as to the language spoken around Quito. The latter area contains mixed toponyms and anthroponyms, which perhaps have greater affiliations with Otavalo.[129] However, the tolas characteristic of the Otavalo-Caranqui region are not found south of Sangolqui in the Valley of Chillo.[130] In addition the cranial form of skulls found in burials in the Quito region is distinct from that found in the tolas. Also, although the pottery found south of Pomasqui is simple and coarse, it is found with finer wares common in the Latacunga-Ambato region. Jijón y Caamaño suggests that the northern boundary of the Panzaleo passed through Pomasqui, Puembo, and Tumbaco and that at the time of Inka conquest the Otavalo-Caranqui were advancing into the Quito region. However, the inhabitants of Uyumbicho and Amaguana, some twelve miles south of Quito, were not Panzaleo, because it was said that they used to fight the Panzaleo, who were described as living two leagues away (presumably to the south).[131] Clearly more research is necessary before the northern boundary of the Panzaleo can be defined with any certainty. Meanwhile the Panzaleo extended south to the Nudo de Sanancajas formed by the Cerro de Igualata. Verneau and Rivet have identified toponyms with suffixes -lo and -alo with the Panzaleo.[132]

The relationship of the Panzaleo to other Indian groups is not clear. To the west was a region known as the Yumbo.[133] The term "Yumbo" was often later applied to any area inhabited by tropical forest tribes and was commonly used to refer to those who lived in the montaña.[134] Nevertheless, Cieza de León clearly distinguished between Yumbo tribes to the west of the Andes and the Quijo to the east.[135] He noted that Indians in the Yumbo were less submissive than those in the Quito region but because of Inka conquest possessed similar customs. Their cultural-linguistic affiliation remains unclear, though Murra regards them as a subgroup of the Panzaleo.[136] During the sixteenth century, Indians living in the Yumbo inhabited the western montaña and foothills of the Andes between the mountains of Lita and the province of Siccho.[137]

To the east were the Quijo, whom Cieza de León describes as being "of the same manner and customs as these."[138] The group to which "these" refers has been variously interpreted as the Panzaleo or, more likely, those of the Yumbo, whose discussion immediately precedes that of the Quijo.[139] Archaeological evidence exists for the westward migration of peoples identified with Cosanga-Pillaro pottery into the highlands about 400 B.C.,[140] and at the time of Spanish conquest trading links existed between the Quijo and the sierra.[141] There is also evidence for marriage alliances between leaders in the two regions in the sixteenth century.[142] Nevertheless, the culture of the Quijo as described by Licenciado Diego de Ortegón in 1577 indicates it was distinct from that of sierran groups, and there is insufficient linguistic evidence to confirm the affiliation of any group in Los Quijos with the Panzaleo.[143]

The fertile basins of Quito and Latacunga-Ambato contain some of the most productive farmlands in Ecuador, and consequently they supported dense native populations. They were noted for the production of maize, even though early native accounts suggest relatively low yields, with Indian estimates in the Valley of Chillo generally well below the maximum estimate of 1:70 and present-day yields of between 1:60 and 1:120.[144] Maize was often intercropped with beans and grown on camellones; there is little evidence for the employment of irrigation techniques.[145] Maize generally took eight months to mature, but in some areas—for example, at Pelileo, located in one of the lower warmer valleys near Ambato—two types of maize were grown that matured in six and eight months, thereby providing two harvests a year. Once harvested, maize could be stored on the cob for six to eight months, and in warmer climates the cobs were smoked to aid preservation.[146] Unlike the Peruvian sierra, the elevation of the Ecuadorian Andes permitted the more extensive cultivation of maize, such that it was not restricted to ceremonial use but was an item of daily consumption.[147] It was eaten as a gruel or as bread baked in the form of a ball.[148]

Early accounts focus on the production of maize, although it is clear that it was only one of a large number of crops that were grown at intermediate altitudes. Apart from the beans already mentioned, other important crops cultivated were potatoes, ullucu, lupine, yuyos, and *jícamas* (*Polymnia edulis* Weddell).[149] Potatoes and ullucu predominated in colder areas,[150] and in the warmer, more humid valleys sweet potatoes (*Ipomoea batatas* [L.] Poir.) and arracachas (*Arracacia xanthorrhiza* Bancroft) were grown.[151] The warmer climate of the Yumbo encouraged the cultivation of cotton, *ají,* and peanuts, in addition to a variety of fruit trees and staples such as manioc and sweet potatoes.[152]

Wild game was the main source of animal protein. Fish made only a minor contribution to the native diet, being obtained in a dried form by trade from the coast.[153] Similarly, the only domesticated animal raised for food was the guinea pig, which was consumed on festive occasions rather than as a daily food.[154] The importance of game to the native diet is indicated by complaints from Indians in the province of Siccho in the sixteenth century that Spaniards were exploiting their hunting grounds, which were essential for their subsistence.[155] Deer, rabbits, and partridges are most commonly mentioned in early accounts, but this emphasis may reflect European interest rather than their importance to the native diet. Undoubtedly a wider spectrum of wild animals was exploited, including insects.[156] There were no restrictions on the exploitation of hunting grounds, but commoners were required to provide game as part of the service they owed to their leaders.[157] Animals were caught with snares, and the meat was dried in the sun. There was an active trade in game, and during the colonial period it became an important item of tribute.

As among the Otavalo-Caranqui and Pasto, exotic products—notably cotton, salt, and coca—were imported from the lowlands. In the Quito region cotton was traded in the Yumbo by individual households and mindaláes. Mindaláes rendered some of the cotton they traded to their sponsoring lords, while the rest, in common with that surplus to household needs, was traded in the market in Quito.[158] Similarly, in pre-Inka times salt was obtained through the same intermediaries from salt springs at Las Salinas in the Mira Valley, from Cachillacta in the northern Yumbo, and from Tomabela in the province of Chimbo.[159] These products not only were traded in Quito and other parts of the highlands but constituted important items of exchange with Indians of the eastern montaña, where cotton was generally in short supply.[160] In return the montaña yielded spices (notably cinnamon), coca, dyes, and gold. This trade involved specialist traders traveling to and from both regions.[161] Traders from Latacunga and Siccho also traded coca at Pimampiro,[162] and the montaña was probably a major source of coca in pre-Inka times.

Although most exotic items were obtained by trade, there is evidence that the Inka were beginning to develop a vertical archipelago system. It was most highly developed in the southern part of the region, which had the longest history of Inka rule. At the time of Spanish conquest *kamayuq* (*camayos*) living in the province of Chimbo also served as channels for acquiring cotton and other goods.[163] Similarly coca was produced by kamayuq to the east and northeast of Ambato, especially around the towns of Pelileo and Patate,[164] where its cultivation may have dated from Inka times. Further north in the Valley of Chillo the vertical archipelago system was only in its infancy,[165] with a few communities possessing small numbers of Indians at lower elevations exploiting wood and cotton. Further north there is no evidence that extraterritorial colonies were established.

The pre-Inkaic settlement pattern of the Quito and Latacunga-Ambato basins is extremely difficult to reconstruct because of changes wrought during Inka rule and Spanish conquest. Inka conquest brought population losses, and Inka attempts to control newly conquered territories witnessed the massive transfer of populations, the foundation of major administrative centers at Quito and Latacunga, and the establishment of a large number of minor settlements along the Inka highway. Still further dislocations occurred in the earlier colonial period as Indians sought to escape Spanish domination and as extensive resettlement schemes were inaugurated. Sixteenth-century accounts of Panzaleo settlements must be viewed against this background of extensive change. At that time the settlement pattern was described as dispersed, with villages located one to four leagues apart. Settlements were generally located on valley slopes, above the most productive warmer valley bottoms, but below those where temperatures were too low to permit the cultivation of maize, and potatoes dominated.[166] Houses reflected the status of their inhabitants. The houses of chiefs were larger than those of commoners, though they were used for receiving guests and drinking, rather than routine residence. Constructed by communal labor, they had some ceremonial significance; there were no separate religious buildings, only guacas. Houses were constructed of lath and mud and roofed with straw, though the walls of larger houses were made of *tapia*. At colder and higher altitudes where wood was not available, houses were round in form and possessed thatched roofs that reached the ground.[167]

Chiefs governed specific territories and were highly esteemed by commoners for the power they commanded and their generosity in the redistribution of food and drink, which they were said to have acquired through hard work. Panzaleo chiefs had formerly possessed power over life and death but had lost this authority under Inka rule.[168] Colonial accounts suggest that a two-tiered political structure existed in which the superior status of chiefs was recognized by *capitanes*, who governed spatially distinct *parcialidades*. The capitanes often resided with the cacique and through messengers, called "*cachas*," conveyed orders, such as demands for labor, to their parcialidades.[169] This organization may not have been native to the region, however, for some of its characteristics, such as the aggregation of vassal lords around a chief and the use of the term "cacha" for a messenger, suggest Inka influence.[170]

The households of chiefs were extensive. In 1559 the largest in the Valley of Chillo was that of Don Amador Amaguana at Anan Chillo, whose household, excluding *yanakuna,* contained forty-three persons, of whom fourteen were his wives. Many of the wives probably undertook domestic chores, and their households were generally supported by the service of commoners, who provided firewood, straw, and game and cultivated their maize fields.[171] The status of chiefs was manifest in distinct forms of dress and adornments of gold and silver jewelery.

Political alliances were strengthened through exogamous marriages and through entrusting the upbringing of noble children to other chiefs. The latter practice has already been noted further north and is documented for the Latacunga chiefdom.[172] Such practices may have also been used to forge and strengthen alliances between communities in different ecological zones, such as between those in the Valley of Chillo and the Yumbo.[173] Nevertheless, there is no evidence for the emergence of an overriding regional authority that was recognized by local chiefs, as appears to have been occurring further north.

Not all contacts between chiefdoms were peaceful. Disagreements arose over land,[174] and probably over the succession of chiefs. Disputes were encouraged by polygamous marriages and the lack of any clearly defined rule of succession, except that positions had to pass to male heirs.[175] For weapons they used lances and clubs of fire-hardened wood, spear-throwers, and, the most deadly of all, slings.[176] Nevertheless, the Panzaleo do not emerge from the literature as a warlike group, particularly compared with their neighbors to the north and south.[177]

At the time of Spanish conquest Panzaleo beliefs had largely been replaced by Inka worship of the sun. Cieza de León recorded that the Panzaleo had formerly possessed "large temples to different gods," but only their guacas remained, where they made secret offerings of gold, silver, and other precious items.[178] He noted that they believed in a creator and the immortality of the soul,[179] but such general descriptions could apply to many religions. The Panzaleo believed they had originated from the foot of the volcano Tungurahua and in their dances and songs repeated this myth, passing it on to their children.[180] They revered the devil called Zupay, whom they appeased with sacrifices.[181] Major fiestas lasting four to six days brought communities together when they did nothing but sing and dance.[182] Other major ceremonies surrounded the burial of chiefs. Chiefs and commoners alike were buried in the sitting position, a cacique being accompanied by his favorite wife. Chiefs were interred with their gold, silver, jewelery, and other precious items, whereas commoners were buried with a cane in their mouths, the significance of which not known, and all burials were accompanied by large amounts of chicha.[183]

Calculating the size of the aboriginal population of the Quito and Latacunga-Ambato basins is not easy. No archaeological surveys of settlements and land utilization comparable to those for the Otavalo region have been conducted in these areas, so that greater reliance must be placed on documentary sources; unfortunately these pose even more problems of interpretation than usual. First, in the immediate conquest period the Quito region was one of political turmoil and intense economic activity, which prompted population movements that the authorities were powerless to control and monitor.[184] Second, most population estimates refer to the audiencia, *provincia, términos,* or *distrito* of Quito, so that figures for the Quito and Latacunga-Ambato basins are often subsumed under those for wider administrative units, and it is not clear what proportions of the totals they may have represented.[185] Calculating the size of the aboriginal population is therefore a highly speculative operation.

During the first half of the century the highlands of Ecuador are likely to have been hit by three pandemics: of smallpox between 1524 and 1527, of measles between 1531 and 1532, and of plague or possibly typhus in 1546.[186] In his excellent analysis of the Indian population of Peru during the sixteenth century, Cook has suggested that these pandemics reduced the Peruvian population by between 60 and 72 percent.[187] It is not clear whether the whole of the gobernación of Quito was affected by each of these pandemics, so that the minimal level of depopulation of 60 percent will be used here.[188] If this ratio is applied to the figures presented in 1561

by the secretary of the Audiencia of Lima, Pedro de Avendaño, for the
gobernación of Quito, this would give a total aboriginal population of
601,675.[189] His summary applies a multiplication factor of 5.0 to a tributary
population of 48,134, but a factor of 4.5 or even 4.0 seems more appropriate.[190] Nevertheless, in the absence of more precise information, the figures for the total and tributary population presented in the Avendaño
summary will be used. An early list of encomiendas in the jurisdiction of
Quito suggests that the colonial corregimientos of Quito and Latacunga
may have contained as much as 60 percent of the population of the region.[191] However, it is clear that this list omitted some encomiendas in the
Cuenca, Otavalo, and Pasto regions; a more realistic estimate of the proportion in Quito and Latacunga might be 50 percent equally divided between the two regions. This would suggest that at the time of Spanish
conquest the Quito and Latacunga-Ambato basins contained about 150,000
Indians each. These estimates take no account of the large numbers who
were lost in wars and on expeditions. If their impact is taken into account
and it is recognized that the Quito Basin was more adversely affected, the
aboriginal population of the region may be estimated at 190,000 and that of
Latacunga-Ambato at 160,000.[192] In this context it is worth noting that
Salomon has estimated that the Valley of Chillo alone possessed an aboriginal population of between 5,000 and 10,000 Indians.[193] Minimal estimates
of the impact of epidemics and of other factor such as wars and expeditions
have been used in the absence of more precise evidence. The true level of
depopulation in the first half of the sixteenth century is likely to have been
much greater and the corresponding aboriginal population probably higher.

PURUHÁ

During the sixteenth century the area inhabited by the Puruhá broadly
corresponded with the corregimientos of Riobamba and Chimbo, or what
today comprises most of the province of Chimborazo and part of the
province of Bolivar. According to Cieza de León, the northern limit of the
Puruhá was at Mocha,[194] an observation that is confirmed in a description
of the corregimiento of Riobamba in 1605 in which San Andrés (Xunxi),
Ilapo, and Guanando appear as the northernmost settlements in the "provincia de los Puruháyes."[195] According to Cieza de León, the eastern
boundary of the Puruhá was marked by Tungurahua and the Cordillera
Oriental, while to the west they were confined by the snow-capped mountains of the Cordillera Occidental.[196] In the sixteenth century Puruhá
kamayuq were present in the Valley of Chimbo, though the area was
dominated by mitmaq from Cajamarca and Huamacucho.[197] Whether the
presence of Puruhá predated Inka rule is not known. Verneau and Rivet

identify the inhabitants of Chimbo as Puruhá because of their cultural affinities and the fact that they allied with them, but Haro Alvear suggests they had stronger links to the west, particularly with the Colorado.[198] To the south the Puruhá bordered on the Cañar. In the sixteenth century Quechua was spoken in Alausí and Chunchi, but since the dominant native language there was Cañar mixed with Puruhá, these towns probably marked the southern boundary of the Puruhá.[199]

Inka rule in the Puruhá region lasted about twenty years longer than in the Quito Basin, and consequently at the time of Spanish conquest native cultures had been transformed to a greater degree. The physical infrastructure of the Inka state in terms of roads and *tampu* was more highly developed, and considerable changes had been made to native political and economic structures.[200] The region had been formally incorporated into the Inka empire as part of Hanan Quito,[201] and a more unified hierarchical political structure had been established. The *mit'a* had also been instituted, and it affected a wider range of activities than in regions further north. Among the Puruhá it extended to the cultivation of maize and herding, not only to household service. At the same time, a fully operative vertical archipelago system involving kamayuq had largely supplanted trading by households and mindaláes.

The region inhabited by the Puruhá broadly corresponds to the Hoya de Chambo, which includes some of the most inhospitable land in the sierra. Its cold, humid climate and extensive páramos discourage cultivation; even today over 45 percent of the land in the province of Chimborazo is natural grassland.[202] Given the cold climate, the main crops grown by the Puruhá were root crops—potatoes, oca, ullucu, and mashua among others. Quinoa, maize, and sometimes beans were also grown. However, maize did not grow well. Yields were reportedly as low as 1:10 or 1:20, and the crop was often destroyed by frost.[203] Better yields were obtained in the warmer valleys, which were irrigated by meltwater from the snow-capped mountains. Here fruits and vegetables were also grown.[204] Like regions to the north, settlements were located on mountain slopes at altitudes that gave easy access to a variety of ecological zones, where a number of smaller subsidiary settlements might be located.[205] During Inka times local lords also farmed more distant lands they had received as gifts from the Inka. For example, chiefs at Guayllabamba possessed fields in the Ambato region,[206] and as late as 1601 the cacique of Chambo owned three coca chacras in Pelileo.[207] The Inka also established archipelagos for the supply of salt and exotic crops such as cotton, ají, and coca, many of which had formerly been obtained by trade. In the sixteenth century some Puruhá, who may have been descendants of kamayuq, were cultivating "gardens" at Penipe, Pallantanga, Chimbo, and the Desembarcadero.[208]

Animals both wild and domesticated played important roles in the

Puruhá economy. Deer, rabbits, and partridges were abundant in the páramos, and guinea pigs were raised widely.[209] Llamas, however, remained few and were owned mainly by caciques and principales, who received them as gifts from the Inka. They were raised for wool and sacrifice; they were not eaten.[210]

Other natural resources were limited. Except at lower latitudes, the water in rivers and streams was too cold to support fish.[211] Similarly, the greater part of the region was covered with grassland, so that there were limited sources of wild food in the form of nuts and berries. The existing patches of forest, such as those at Tungurahua, were heavily exploited for timber, which was worked by specialist carpenters.[212] In the absence of trees, teasels and the roots of bushes and cabuya[213] were used as firewood.[214] Cabuya was also used for both fencing and cordage.[215] In the sixteenth century one of the Indians' main sources of profit was trading cabuya for salt in Guayaquil.[216] This trade may have originated in the early colonial period as demands for cordage emerged with the shipbuilding industry and the use of horses for transport. Indeed at the time of Spanish conquest, with the exception of the purchase of salt in Guayaquil, trade appears to have been limited because exotic items were obtained through the vertical archipelago system. In pre-Inka times these items would probably have been obtained through mindaláes or household trading, as they were further north, such that colonial trade may have developed on pre-Inka antecedents.

The sociopolitical organization of the Puruhá remains obscure. Salomon, using evidence for tribute payments to the cacique of Guayllabamba contained in an account of a visita in 1557, suggests that the cacique possessed about 3,000 vassals who were distributed in five *ayllu*, one presided over by his brother and the other four by principales. These five ayllu were found at distinct locations, though they were clearly within close proximity, since the visita to which they were subjected was conducted within four days.[217] Whether this formal two-tiered structure predated Inka rule is uncertain. However, the payment of tribute by principales to caciques, which was probably instituted by the Inka, appears to have been lapsing at the time of the visita, and it probably represents a reversion to pre-Inka norms, where principales did not recognize a superior authority.[218] Both caciques and principales had the authority to punish crimes.[219] A cacique's position was inherited by a son or, in the absence of a son, a brother.[220] Cieza de León confirms that the position passed to a male descendant, but suggests that in the absence of a son it passed to a sister's son rather than a brother.[221] More likely brothers were favored. Brothers often played an important political role, to the extent that in the case of Guayllabamba the cacique ruled his own ayllu with the help of his brother.[222] Cieza de León also notes that chiefs were buried with their weapons and precious possessions, as well as a number of beautiful women, probably *aklla*.[223] The extent of such live burials is not clear, but most likely the practice was restricted to the most eminent chiefs.

The Puruhá were more warlike than their neighbors to the north. They were said to be constantly at war with the Huancavilca, and they also fought the Cañar.[224] There is no evidence for interethnic warfare, which may have been suppressed by Inka rule. Weapons possessed by the natives of Alausí and Chunchi included clubs, lances, slings, and copper axes.[225]

The provinces of Riobamba and Chimbo were densely settled. Cieza de León described the province of the Puruhaes as "highly populated,"[226] but there is little evidence for the precise size of the population of the Puruhá region in the sixteenth century. Most accounts relate either to particular encomiendas, which are difficult to trace temporally and spatially, or to broader areas such as the términos or Audiencia of Quito, from which it is difficult to disaggregate estimates for the Puruhá region. However, a few sources exist from which it is possible to reconstruct the population in the 1550s and extrapolate the aboriginal population by taking account of the impact of conquest and epidemics. The earliest indication of the size of the Indian population comes from the *Ordenanzas de Minas* of 1549, which assigned encomienda Indians from within the jurisdiction of Quito to work in the Santa Barbara mines of Cuenca. This account plus two others, one probably written in the late 1550s and the other in 1573, suggest that there were nine encomiendas within the jurisdictions of Riobamba and Chimbo.[227] From these nine encomiendas 820 Indians were assigned to work in the Cuenca mines.[228] It seems likely that there was a constant relationship between the numbers drafted for mine labor and the number of tributary Indians in the encomiendas. It is known that about the same time the tribute assessment for encomienda of Chambo by President La Gasca was based on the existence of 1,330 Indians.[229] Since the village of Chambo was ordered to provide 140 Indians for the mines of Cuenca, there is a suggestion that the levy imposed was equivalent to 10 percent. If this was the case, then the total tributary population of the Riobamba and Chimbo regions in 1549 can be estimated at 8,200. Alternatively using the same source and method as employed in the calculation of the aboriginal population of the Quito Basin, a slightly higher tributary population of 12,000 for the Riobamba region may be suggested. This calculation is based on the assumption that the region contained about 25 percent of the Indian population of the gobernación of Quito given in Avendaño's compilation.[230] Although this source uses a multiplication factor of 5, more detailed accounts from the latter part of the century suggest a factor of 4 might be more appropriate.[231] However, to make the total figure comparable with those for other regions, a multiplication factor of 5 will be used, even though it is probably an overestimate. These calculations suggest that the total population in the early 1550s might lie between 41,000 and 60,000.

By the mid–sixteenth century the Indian population may have been reduced by 60 percent as a result of epidemics, in addition to which there were casualties associated with Spanish conquest. Even though Sebastián de Benalcázar met resistance from the Puruhá, the Riobamba region does not appear to have suffered such heavy casualties during conquest and the civil wars as the Quito Basin. Also, poorer access to regions subject to colonizing expeditions meant that fewer were mounted from the Riobamba region. Assuming a 60 percent reduction because of epidemics and 5,000 lost in conquest, the total aboriginal population may be estimated at between 107,500 and 155,000. For calculations of the level of decline during the colonial period, an average of 131,250 will be assumed.

CAÑAR

The Cañar were more profoundly affected by Inka conquest than any other group in Ecuador. The Inka were forced to pacify the Cañar several times before they could establish effective control of the region, and during the process large numbers were killed in battle or transported to other parts of the Inka empire.[232] Subsequently, a major administrative center was established at Tomebamba, and the Inka began to modify native political and economic structures and impose their own language and beliefs.[233] Since Inka rule was longest, and probably harshest, in the Cañar region,[234] by the time of Spanish conquest the culture of its inhabitants had been transformed more profoundly than that of groups further north; as such, less evidence remains of native society in pre-Inka times.

The northern limit of the Cañar appears to have been the Hoya de Chanchan, where the inhabitants of Alausí and Chunchi spoke Cañar but mixed with Puruhá.[235] To the south they bordered on the Palta, whose territory, according to Cieza de León, began at the source of the river Túmbez, where there were remains of Inka tampu. This site is generally considered to have been near Saraguro, where, according to Cabello Balboa, the Palta fortified themselves before being defeated by the Inka.[236] The Cordillera Oriental formed the eastern limit of their territory, and their western boundary was defined by the province of the "Guancavilcas,"[237] though Jijón y Caamaño suggests that the Cañar extended to the coast between the Naranjal and Jubones rivers.[238] In fact other evidence suggests that the southern coastal region was inhabited by the Chono.[239] Verneau and Rivet have associated toponyms with suffixes -cay with the Cañar,[240] the majority of whom lived in the Hoya de Paute.

The region inhabited by the Cañar, although rugged in part, comprised a number of broad fertile valleys, such as those containing the Tomebamba, Challuabamba, Paute, Gualaceo, and Burgay rivers. Here the climate is more temperate than regions to the north, such that the Hoya de Paute is generally warmer and wetter than the Hoya de Chambo, though frost remains a danger between June and August.[241] The main subsistence crops raised were maize, beans, and potatoes, the last assuming greater importance at higher altitudes. In the lower, warmer valleys such as those around Paute, Cañaribamba, and Chunchi, sweet potatoes and manioc were also grown. Valley bottoms throughout the region appear to have been given over to the cultivation of fruit trees, those most commonly mentioned being calabashes (*Cucurbita moschata* Duch.), *guabas* (*Inga* spp.), lucumas (*Lucuma obovata* H.B.K.), and granadillas (*Passiflora ligularis* Juss).[242] There is abundant evidence for the development of irrigation techniques. While their use predated Inka rule, they were probably extended by the Inka in order to increase production.[243] A number of accounts stress that cultivation was a female task, while men were said to be lazy or else employed in cleaning clothes and weapons, weaving, and other, more typical feminine occupations.[244] Cieza de León attributed this division of labor to the marked imbalance in the sex ratio produced by Atahualpa's devastation of the area during the dynastic wars. He implies that the shortage of men gave them greater power over women and enabled them to coerce them into hard labor; equally likely, female employment might have been essential to sustain production in the absence of male labor.

Like other highland groups, the Cañar possessed a variety of strategies for obtaining goods that could not be produced locally. They practiced the system of "microverticality," exploiting different environments within a few miles of their settlements, particularly those located at lower altitudes, where maize, cotton, coca, ají, and even tropical crops were raised.[245] By the time of Spanish conquest, the Inka had also developed a system of archipelagos to ensure access to exotic products, especially cotton and salt, but despite the apparent absence of mindaláes, it had not supplanted trade entirely.[246] Also, despite the greater length and intensity of Inka rule in this region, there is only limited evidence for the establishment of coca archipelagos.[247] Their development together with those associated with cotton is discussed more fully elsewhere,[248] but it is worth commenting in more detail on the acquisition of salt, which the Cañar obtained from local and distant sources. At certain times of the year Indians from Cañaribamba exploited salt springs four leagues away, possibly at Salinas in the canton of Santa Isabel, but their seasonality probably discouraged the establishment of a fully developed archipelago.[249] The inhabitants of Pacaibamba also exploited highland salt springs, but those of Azogues used local salt only occasionally.[250] Most communities, however, obtained their salt from other regions. While the Indians of Paccha obtained salt from springs in the Oriente,[251] the majority obtained it from the west. Salt was imported from the island of Puná through the ports of Bola, Yaguache, Guayaquil, and Machala, though those at Chunchi and Alausí specified that they obtained it from "salinas de Guayaquil"—though they might be referring to the same sources in the island of Puná.[252] While the Cañar probably acquired salt from the coast through long-distance traders, there are hints that more formal and old established economic links may have existed between the Puná and Cañar.[253]

As in other highland basins, hunting was an important subsistence activity. Once again deer, rabbits, and partridges are the game most commonly mentioned in documentary sources. Rabbits were so common that it was estimated that in the páramos of Teocajas one Indian with two small dogs and a club could kill 200 rabbits in four hours.[254] Domesticated sources of meat were probably more important in this region than further north, even though the humid climate of the Hoya de Paute made the area unsuitable for the raising of llamas on a wide scale. Archaeological evidence from Cerro Narrio indicates that some llamas were raised in pre-Inka times,[255] and they undoubtedly became more abundant under Inka rule. Cieza de León observed that at the time of Spanish conquest the Cañar region had possessed a large number of llamas and an even greater number of guanacos and vicuñas.[256] Other sources of protein were freshwater fish from local rivers[257] and, less commonly, saltwater fish obtained by trade from the coast, notably from Machala or through Guayaquil.[258]

Prior to Viceroy Toledo's program of *reducciones* in the 1570s, the distribution of Cañar settlements reflected the pattern of agricultural activities. Previously the villages had been located at intermediate elevations only a few miles from each other, with some community members living at higher and lower altitudes exploiting distinct ecological niches.[259] The cacique's house was located within the village and was clearly distinguishable as a large rectangular residence with a patio where the chief gave orders and administered justice and afterward provided food and drink.[260] Commoners' houses were characteristically round or oval, and although Cieza de León maintained that they were built of stone, this form of construction was probably limited and dated from Inka times.[261] Houses were generally built of lath and mud and roofed with ichu grass. They lasted only six to eight years and could be built by a village in two days.[262]

Each community represented a lineage governed by a cacique. Chiefs were generally polygamous, but only one wife was regarded as the principal one, whose son succeeded to the title.[263] They were supported by the service of commoners, who, among other things, provided firewood and straw, built their houses, and cultivated their fields.[264] Local chiefs in turn recognized the authority of a more powerful chief. The Cañar apparently comprised a number chiefdoms, the most important of which centered on Hatun Cañar and Cañaribamba. Indeed it was said that Huayna Capac named the province of Cañar after Hatun Cañar, where the most powerful chief resided.[265] In Inka times these two chiefdoms formed the cores of the moieties of Hatun Cañar and Hurin Cañar, into which the province was divided.[266]

In essence the Cañar formed a confederation of largely independent chiefdoms whose territories were clearly defined and vigorously defended.[267] The Cañar were said to be "warlike and courageous" and to be constantly at war with each other. Garcilaso de la Vega reported that small chiefdoms often allied together to preserve their independence from more powerful ones.[268] Nevertheless, chiefdoms could overcome their differences in the face of more powerful external threats. They not only formed a strong confederation to oppose Inka rule but even allied with chiefdoms further north in the Quito region.[269] Apart from interchiefdom conflict, the Cañar also fought their neighbors. Indians from Cañaribamba fought Palta Indians from Chaparra.[270] Meanwhile those from Paccha fought the Jívaro to acquire women, and they clashed with Indians from Zamora over access to salt springs.[271] Under the Inka such intertribal warfare was probably partially suppressed in accordance with state policy.[272]

Only fragmentary evidence exists of the religion of the Cañar. According to a number of accounts, their worship of the sun, moon, and natural features, such as mountains and large rocks and stones, predated Inka rule. Bears were regarded as gods, and certain animals such as parrots and snakes may have had some totemic significance.[273] Some authors attribute the worship of natural features to Inka influence, and certainly the Inka encouraged the establishment of guacas, many of which were associated with mountains.[274] Indeed, the Cañar believed they had originated from Mount Guasano.[275] Like their neighbors to the north, Cañar chiefs were buried with their wives and precious belongings.[276] The Cañar were skilled workers of gold and gilded copper; many ornaments, including small plates, disks, headpieces, bells, ear and nose ornaments, and decorations for arms, as well as copper hatchets, have been found in graves, particularly at Sigsig, Chordeleg, and Azogues.[277]

Estimating the population of the Cañar region is particularly hazardous, since by the time of Spanish conquest it had already suffered major losses as a consequence of Inka conquest, the Inka dynastic wars, and epidemics. When the Spanish arrived, the population was only a fraction of the size it had been sixty years previously. In the early colonial period, a Spanish soldier, Alonso Borregán, claimed that prior to the Inka dynastic wars the province of Cañares had possessed 60,000 Indians,[278] while in 1582 Hernando Pablos, a *vecino* of Cuenca, similarly suggested that before Atahualpa's devastation of the region it had contained 50,000 inhabitants.[279] These estimates incorporate losses that were sustained during the prior conquests of the region by Tupa Inca Yupanqui and Huayna Capac. Tomebamba became the center of Inka operations in Ecuador, and local populations were drafted to construct, supply, and service the town, as well as provide conscripts for northern campaigns. These demands raised mortality rates, and the loss or temporary absence of able-bodied males would have affected fertility levels. Even before the smallpox epidemic of 1520s killed Huayna Capac and precipitated the dynastic wars, the Cañar population would have been very much reduced. The smallpox epidemic clearly hit the Cañar region, for Huayna Capac's successor, Ninan Cuyoche, died of it in Tomebamba.[280] There the great pestilence was said to have killed innumerable people,[281] and Cook has suggested that the pandemic may have killed between one-third and one-half of the populations it afflicted.[282] Nevertheless, substantial numbers still remained, since during the subsequent dynastic wars Huascar was able to muster a fighting force of 30,000 Cañar and Palta at Tomebamba.[283] Apart from the battle casualties they sustained, the revenge exacted by Atahualpa on the Cañar region for its support of Huascar was evident in the demographic profile of the Cañar region several decades after Spanish conquest, when there were said to be fifteen women for every man.[284] Hernando Pablos claimed that as a consequence of the dynastic wars the Cañar population had been reduced from 50,000 to 3,000.[285] This level of decline is supported by the parish priest of Pacaibamba who in 1582 claimed that its population had declined from over 10,000 Indians prior to Inka conquest to 500, even though his estimate encompassed the colonial period.[286]

Despite the devastation wrought by wars and epidemics prior to Spanish conquest, it is clear from the size of the earliest encomiendas that the Cañar region contained more than 3,000 Indians, as suggested above, even if it is assumed that they were tributary Indians. In 1539 Captain Diego de Sandoval sent 500 Indians from his encomienda in the province of Cañares to support Sebastián de Benalcázar.[287] Even in the mid–sixteenth century an encomienda in the province of Cañares belonging to Rodrigo Núñez de Bonilla possessed 420 Indians,[288] and that of Cañaribamba belonging to Juan de Narváez contained 1,000 Indians.[289] These encomiendas, although among the largest in the region, accounted for only a proportion of the number assigned; in 1576 there were sixteen.[290] The tributary population at the time of Spanish conquest must have exceeded 3,000. Further support for this conclusion is to be found in the list of Indians from the Cuenca region who in 1549 were assigned to work in the mines.[291] Those drafted totaled 585, which, following previous reasoning, may have represented about 10 percent of the tributary population.[292] This would give an estimated tributary population of 5,850. Since it is clear that shortly before Spanish conquest the dynastic wars severely depleted local populations and created marked imbalances in the sex ratio, it seems preferable to employ a multiplication factor of 4 rather than 5 to estimate the total population, and even this may be an overestimate. This would give an estimated total population of 23,400 for the mid-sixteenth century, which, assuming a reduction of 60 percent as a consequence of epidemics, would suggest a preconquest population of 58,500.[293] In the Cañar region the Spanish encountered a formerly dispersed but dense population much reduced in size.

PALTA

The Palta were relative latecomers to the southern sierra, arriving in the millennium prior to Spanish conquest.[294] Formerly, part of the region may have been inhabited by the Cañar. Toponyms with more northerly affiliations exist in the Palta region, and in the 1570s Juan de Salinas Loyola recorded that Cañar was spoken in the jurisdiction of Loja.[295]

As indicated in the discussion of the Cañar, the northern limit of the Palta was probably at Saraguro. Their western border was probably near Zaruma, leaving the coast inhabited by the Chono, while to the south the Palta probably extended to the river Calvas, or possibly, though less likely, to the river Quiroz.[296] To the east were the Bracamoro,[297] but among them enclaves of Palta inhabited four closely spaced villages near Zamora—Gonzaval, Turocapi, Yunchique, and Capolanga.[298] These were located in colder, wetter lands than those of their neighbors the Rabona and Bolona, who were Jívaro. Some Palta also lived in the province of Xoroca, located in the mountains to the northeast of Jaén.[299] These enclaves suggest that the group may previously have been more widespread.

It is generally assumed that the Palta were related to the Jívaro.[300] The most telling account is that of Hernando de Benavente, who, in referring to the language spoken by some Jívaro to the east of the river Paute, noted that it was like that of the Malacato, who were Palta.[301] Nevertheless, the absence of Palta words makes determination of any precise linguistic affiliation difficult, although Caillavet has noted that many toponyms in the Loja region possess the suffixes -mamá and -numa, which may be related to Palta.[302] Also, it is possible that slightly different languages were spoken in distinct provinces within the Palta region. The provinces that can be identified in the ethnohistorical record include Chaparra and Amboca to the north, Garrochamba to the west, Calva to the south, and, on the right bank of the Catamayo River, the Malacato.[303]

Evidence for Palta culture at the time of Spanish conquest is scant, since it bore the heavy imprint of Inka rule, particularly in the north. From what can be gleaned by reading through this cultural veil, the Palta possessed features in common with other highland groups, but their economy exhibited some distinctive characteristics that were in part related to the distinctive physical geography of the southern sierra. Here the double chain of the Andes breaks down into a more complex mountain system that is generally lower in elevation. While the deep valleys to the southwest are hot and dry and require irrigation, toward the north the rainfall increases as the region comes under the influence of winds bringing moisture from the Pacific and Atlantic. Hence the Palta had access to a wide variety of environments, including valleys that extended below 1,000 meters, where tropical and subtropical crops could be grown.[304] Salinas Loyola observed that because of the variety of lands cultivated, it was impossible for him to give a strict account of the times of sowing and harvest.[305] The main crops cultivated were maize, beans, and potatoes, with maize yields between 1:30 to 1:100, according to the quality of the soil. However, as in other parts of the highlands, the Palta dedicated the lower warmer valleys to the cultivation of fruit trees. A particularly favored valley was that of the Chungacaro, where subsequently Loja was founded. Here lands owned by caciques from different provinces were cultivated by their subjects.[306] Despite the fact that these Indians were referred to as mitmaq, there is no specific reference to them having been established there by the Inka. Translated as "newcomers," these colonists may well represent a pre-Inka mechanism for exploiting extraterritorial lands such as already described for the Pasto. Irrigation techniques were employed, but it was considered that they could be extended.[307] Overall the Palta economy placed greater dependence on agriculture than did groups to the north. Although river fishing was common, and some saltwater fish were obtained from the coast by trade, hunting appears to have been more limited.[308]

Since the Palta enjoyed easier access to lands at lower elevations, they could cultivate exotic crops, such as cotton, which other highland groups were forced to acquire through trade or a variety of other mechanisms. Hence the Inka probably found it unnecessary to establish the vertical archipelago system in this region. The only product that the Palta needed to import was salt.[309] Some salt was obtained from highland springs, but most was acquired by trade from the coast at Paita.[310] In the colonial period the Palta, along with the Cañar, also traded with Indians around Zamora, providing them with bread, cheese, goats, and sheep.[311] Although these goods, with perhaps the exception of bread, are of postconquest origin, trading contacts with the Oriente are likely to have predated Spanish rule. However, trade on the whole was limited. There were no fixed markets; rather, items were bartered, sometimes for gold or silver, and weights were used, a feature that probably dated from Inka times.[312]

Like their highland neighbors, the Palta had a preference for colder altitudes for their dispersed settlements, and this was true not only of sierran communities but also of the Palta enclaves in the Oriente.[313] Their houses, as elsewhere in the highlands, were built of lath and mud and were roofed with straw.[314] The lands of individual communities were well defined by natural features and were a constant source of dispute.[315] In spite of, or perhaps because of, their recent arrival in the region, the Palta were strongly attached to their highland settlements and lands. This is evident from early colonial land disputes and attempts at reducción, which revealed their opposition to the formation of nucleated villages and to valley sites preferred by the Spanish.[316]

The Palta were regarded by the Spanish as less civilized than the Cañar, with the Palta in the province of Xoroca described as "indios de behetría."[317] Early descriptions of the political organization and religion of the Palta reveal the heavy imprint of Inka culture, most notably in its decimal organization, the service owed by commoners, and the sacrifice of llamas.[318] Inka rule imposed a degree of uniformity and even unity on formerly independent chiefdoms. Their independence is revealed in the varied succession of chiefs, for although in all cases it passed through the male line, in some chiefdoms it passed to the son, in others to a nephew, and in others to a brother.[319] Nevertheless, these independent chiefdoms appear to have recognized the higher authority of the chief at Chungacaro.[320] It was said that chiefs were obeyed in everything, but again such extensive authority probably dates from Inka times.[321] Although justice was dispensed, there is nothing to indicate that it was administered by the chief; apparently flogging and haircutting were regarded as the most humiliating of sentences.[322]

The Palta were often at war with each other. In the colonial period it was said that disputes arose over land, women, and livestock, and it has been suggested that population pressure on resources may have underlain interchiefdom conflict.[323] For weapons they had slings, lances, spearthrowers, copper axes, and shields and those who showed courage in war were highly respected.[324] Despite this state of constant conflict the Palta united to oppose Inka and Spanish rule, and a degree of economic cooperation appears to have existed, such as described for the Chungacaro Valley, where the local chief permitted other chiefs to maintain vassals cultivating lands.[325] Indeed as part of Inka policy, interchiefdom conflict would have been suppressed and political unity promoted by the introduction of a new administrative structure.

Most evidence for the religious beliefs of the Palta indicates Inka influence. However, some guacas where offerings of gold, silver, and other items, including coca, were made may have predated Inka rule.[326] Also, like their neighbors to the north, chiefs were interred with their wives and precious possessions, and burials were major ceremonies that were accompanied by much mourning.[327]

In 1544 Cieza de León recorded that around Loja there were many large settlements,[328] but the earliest account of the region's population appears in Pedro de Avendaño's account of tributary Indians in the Viceroyalty of Peru compiled in 1561.[329] This account suggests that the jurisdiction of Loja contained 3,647 tributary Indians and 9,495 Indians of all ages. This account differs substantially from several others from the same period that give the number of tributary Indians as 9,000 and the total number of Indians as 45,000.[330] The same accounts indicate they were paying 14,600 pesos in tribute, which is consistent with the list of encomiendas and their value drawn up at about the same time and attached to the foremost account.[331] This suggests that there was an error in transcription, such that the figure of 9,495 should have referred to tributary Indians. The amount of tribute they were required to pay argues for a larger population. Furthermore, such a small population would have been unable to increase to the level reported in the late sixteenth century within only a few decades. The discrepancy in the accounts is difficult to explain, but the larger figures of 9,000 tributary Indians and 45,000 persons around 1561 seems reasonable. It is assumed that these figures were drawn from records that predate the 1558 smallpox epidemic. For other sierran regions it has been assumed that by the mid–sixteenth century the population had been reduced by about 60 percent as a result of epidemics alone. This would suggest an estimate of 112,500 at the time of Spanish conquest. This estimate may prove to be too high. Taylor argues for much lower pre-Inka population levels on the grounds that descriptions of the sociopolitical organization and warfare of the Palta suggest that they were culturally more akin to the Jívaro.[332] Also, it is not certain that the region was ravaged by each of the three pandemics, although since it was located on the main route between Quito and Lima, it would have been particularly susceptible to the introduction of infections from both areas. Nevertheless, the Palta appear to have suffered less during Spanish conquest than other groups and were not involved extensively in expeditions to the east until the mid–sixteenth century.

CONCLUSION

From the discussion of individual ethnic groups, the aboriginal population of the sierra may be estimated at 838,600. (See Table 2.) This figure takes into account the impact of Inka conquest, to be discussed in a later chapter, but not the devastating effects of the Old World diseases that arrived in the region prior to Spanish conquest. In terms of the distribution of

Table 2. Aborginal Population of the Sierra

Ethnic group	Aboriginal population	Area in km[2a]	Percent of area cultivated[b]	Persons per km[2] for the cultivated area
Pasto (Ecuador only)	36,350	4,641	10	78.3
Otavalo-Caranqui	150,000	7,903	15	126.5
Panzaleo (Quito Basin)	190,000	18,691	25	74.9
Panzaleo (Latacunga-Ambato)	160,000			
Puruhá	131,250	7,276	25	72.2
Cañar	58,500	15,680	10	37.3
Palta	112,500	12,920	10	87.1
Total	838,600	67,111		

[a] Approximate area defined by the location of the ethnic group.
[b] These are very tentative figures based on the proportion of land cultivated in the 1950s and 1960s (Acosta-Solís, *Recursos naturales,* 1:15, 19). The remainder of the area was uncultivable or covered in grassland or forest. Given that the population of the sierra at that time was about three times greater than the aboriginal population estimated here, the area cultivated in pre-Columbian times is likely to have been less extensive than suggested and the population densities correspondingly higher.

population the northern sierra was more densely settled. This probably reflected the more favorable environmental conditions of the region, especially its more fertile soils, as well as the more sophisticated subsistence technology employed by some of its inhabitants. It may also have sustained smaller losses during Inka conquest. In terms of the southern sierra, variations in the impact of Inka conquest were also partially responsible for differences in the size of ethnic groups. The Cañar suffered the greatest demographic disaster, but the Palta were also adversely affected.

Unfortunately there are no contemporary estimates of the aboriginal population of the sierra as a whole with which the figure of 838,600 may be compared. Those for selected parts of the sierra have already been examined in the discussions of individual ethnic groups. The general paucity of early documentary materials and the difficulties of interpretation have meant that researchers have shied away from estimating the aboriginal population and focused on demographic trends during the latter part of the sixteenth century, for which information is more readily available. Hence even the most detailed studies of demographic change in the sierra during the early colonial period by Tyrer and Browne provide only the most general estimates for the aboriginal population of between 1 and 2 million for the audiencia as a whole.[333] In so doing, they follow Phelan's earlier estimate of about 1 million, which assigned between 500,000 and 750,000 to the coast and sierra together.[334] Given the substantial populations living on the coast, this figure is considerably lower than the figure of 838,600 proposed here. However, given the acceptance of a high level of decline from introduced diseases, the latter figure is smaller than might be anticipated from studies of similar societies in other regions. Undoubtedly this reflects the considerable losses of life that accompanied Inka conquest and later their dynastic wars. At least 100,000 were lost in battle, and the economic and social upheavals that accompanied and followed Inka conquest left the population not only depleted but ill prepared to face the new invaders.

CHAPTER 3

Lands and Peoples of the Coast

Just as the peoples and nations included in these provinces [of the coast] are diverse, so they are varied and different in their languages, manners, customs, and ceremonies.

Miguel Cabello Balboa, 1589.[1]

Unlike the dry, desolate coast of Peru, the coastal plain of Ecuador is ecologically diverse. Within a few hundred miles one passes from tropical rain forest in the north to desert conditions in the south. The greater part of the region consists of low undulating lands that are broken up only by coastal mountains, which rise to between 700 and 800 meters. They form a distinct range between Guayaquil, Jipijapa, and Puerto Viejo, but to the north the relief declines to produce a landscape of rolling hills. Most of the region, however, consists of the fertile alluvial floodplains of three major river systems—the Guayas, Esmeraldas, and Santiago. Toward the coast these rivers break up into numerous canals and inlets, creating a landscape of inundated swamps, deltas, and sandbanks.

Because of variations in climate, distance from the coast, and the influence of the Humboldt and El Niño currents, there are considerable differences in the vegetation cover and associated animal life within the coastal region. Temperatures are uniformly high, oscillating around 25°C, but there are marked differences in rainfall that are related to the influence of the Humboldt current. The southern coast as far north as Cabo Pasado in Manabí comes under the influence of a branch of the cold Humboldt current, and the wet season is correspondingly restricted to four months between January and April, when between 200 and 500 millimeters of rain falls. To the north, however, the rainy season lasts longer—from December to June—and the annual rainfall rises to between 1,500 and 2,000 millimeters and more. Superimposed on this there are years of torrential rain caused by the more marked movement south of the warm equatorial current, El Niño. This not only results in heavy rain but has adverse effects on marine life that is adapted to cool temperatures.

Given the higher rainfall in the north, the coast of Esmeraldas and the foothills of the Andes are covered by tropical rain forest, but south of Manabí the forest becomes more deciduous, and in the provinces of Guayas and El Oro the characteristic vegetation cover is deciduous scrub woodland composed of low thorny trees mixed with savanna. In the regions affected by the Humboldt current—that is, the Santa Elena peninsula and parts of the coasts of Manabí and El Oro—semidesert conditions prevail. Here scattered xerophytic shrubs give way inland to savanna areas containing isolated trees such as algarroba (*Prosopis inermis* H.B.K.), guarango (*Acacia flexuosa* Humb. & Bonp.), and guayacan (*Tabebuia ecuadorensis* Standl.). With the exception of this region, the numerous bays that line the coast, including the Gulf of Guayaquil and the stretch of coast between Puerto Bolivar and the Peruvian border, are fringed by mangrove swamps. Marine life is abundant, particularly to the north of Santa Elena. It is noteworthy that although stretches of the coast have been cleared for commercial agriculture, in 1962 about 85 percent of the region was still uncultivated, 72 percent being covered with forest and 13 percent with natural grasslands.[2]

PEOPLES

At the time of Spanish conquest the coast of Ecuador was inhabited by a number of cultural-linguistic groups whose boundaries are difficult to define in the absence of detailed archaeological investigations and the existence of only fragmentary, and sometimes ambiguous, documentary evidence. Nevertheless, most authors indicate the presence from north to south of the Malaba, Esmeralda, Manta, Huancavilca, and Puná, although subdivisions are generally recognized among the Esmeralda, and the last three groups are sometimes considered to be subdivisions of the Manta.[3] Inland in the Guayas Basin and in the headwaters of the Esmeraldas River were the Chono (Colorado). (See Map 3.) The inhabitants of the coast comprised tribes or small chiefdoms that were often closely related. Nevertheless they remained largely independent and often conducted wars against each other. Around Puerto Viejo each village was said to speak its own language, which was the cause of disagreements among them.[4] However, Oviedo recorded that even though there was a great variety of dialects along the coast, they were not so distinct that groups could not understand each other.[5]

MALABA (BARBACOA)

The inhabitants of the coasts of northernmost Ecuador and southern Colombia were often referred to as Barbacoa because they built their houses on stilts. Nevertheless, this house form was common throughout the lowlands of western Ecuador and not restricted to one cultural group.[6] More precisely, the northernmost inhabitants of the coastal region were the Malaba, who extended into southern Colombia. Their name, meaning "the devil," was apparently given to them by the Cayapa, who were their

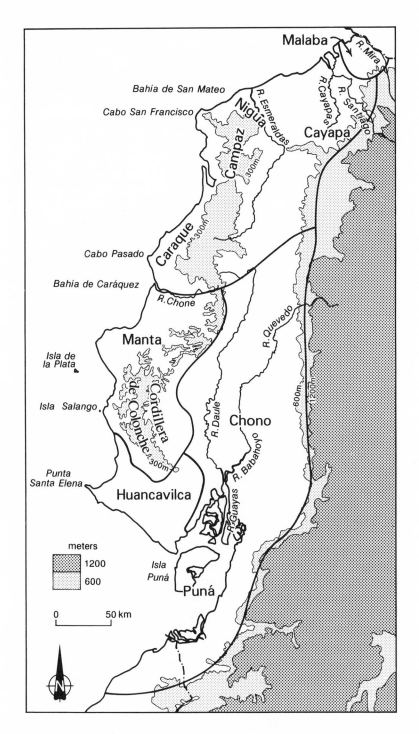

Map 3. Distribution of ethnic groups on the Coast on the eve of Spanish conquest

enemies.[7] According to Father Gaspar de Torres, who was involved in the conversion of the neighboring Cayapa at the end of the sixteenth century, the Malaba, Brispoco, and Cacamal were all "indios de guerra" who lived to the west of the Cayapa toward the coast, to which they had access by canoe and raft via the river Achuacpi.[8] On the map accompanying his account the Malaba are located slightly inland from the coast to the south of the Mira River; whether they had lived on the coast in pre-Columbian times is unknown. In 1611 an *entrada* conducted by Father Pedro Romero among the Malaba confirmed the presence of two groups on the banks of the river Mira. One group was known as Malaba, and the other comprised "Aguamalabas, Espies, Pruces, Nurpes, Mingas, Quamingas."[9] They were said to be constantly at war with each other, employing "darts, a few small axes, and some knives and clubs."[10] A previous entrada between 1606 and 1607 by the corregidor of Ibarra, Cristóbal de Troya, had also encountered Malaba along the Tipulbi River.[11] At the end of the sixteenth century the Cayapa were living inland, having been displaced from the Campi region by some mulattoes and by Ceronda and Soncón Indians.[12] On the sixteenth-century map of the Cayapa region the Ceronda are located near the coast to the south of the Malaba,[13] and being hostile to the Cayapa, it is possible they were a Malaba group. A more southerly extension of the Malaba is also suggested by a Malaba attack on the Spanish fort of San Ignacio de Montesclaros on the Santiago River in 1619.[14] Modern ethnohistorians locate them in the Lower Mira River and Mataje Basin.[15]

The Malaba, like the Cayapa, lived in small settlements, or *rancherías,* subsisting off "plots and fields of maize, game, fish, and native fruits."[16] Father Romero observed more specifically that they cultivated "maize, yuca, plantains, sweet potatoes, calabashes, papayas, and other crops" and that they worked gold, wove cotton, and made blankets of bark cloth.[17]

Few demographic details exist of the Malaba, though even at the beginning of the seventeenth century they were still sufficiently numerous to frustrate Spanish efforts to open a road to the coast and establish a port on the Santiago River.[18] Various members of the expedition led by Captain Miguel Arias de Ugarte aimed at pacifying the warlike Malaba claimed they were numerous. Father Romero reported that on one bank of the river Mira there were 300 Indians headed by five "caciques" and that he had heard that on the other bank there were many others.[19] The 300 may have referred to warriors drawn from a wide area, but given that settlements of between 50 and 60 inhabitants appear to have been characteristic of the area, they may have been drawn from the immediate vicinity.[20] It is not unreasonable to suggest that the Malaba numbered about 5,000. The area they occupied in Ecuador was just over 1,000 square kilometers, giving a population density of just under 5 persons per square kilometer. This is somewhat higher than that suggested below for the Cayapa, and it is consistent with contemporary observations that generally suggested denser populations in this region.

NIGUA, CAYAPA, CAMPAZ, AND CARAQUE

Esmeraldas was inhabited by a number of culturally similar Indian groups that included the Nigua, Cayapa, Campaz, and Caraque. According to Cabello Balboa, the coastal region between the Bahía de San Mateo and Portete was inhabited by the Nigua,[21] but in the late sixteenth century they were recorded as living well inland. In 1582 the village of San Juan de los Niguas was located on the edge of the Yumbos, eighteen leagues from Quito and thirty to thirty-five leagues from the Bahía de San Mateo.[22] In 1601 Nigua and Caravilca were living "next to the province of Canzacoto."[23] Nevertheless, in the late sixteenth century Cabello Balboa was at pains to distinguish the Nigua from the inhabitants of the Yumbos, claiming that the former possessed a distinct language, dress, and customs and that they lived in the lowlands toward the sea rather than in the Andean foothills.[24] Alcina Franch and others have attempted to reconcile these accounts, suggesting that the Nigua were located on the coast between Cabo San Francisco and the Esmeraldas River and extended from there inland into the Esmeraldas Basin as far as the Yumbos.[25]

The Nigua and Cayapa are generally considered to be one group,[26] with the Cayapa more often identified as living further north toward the river Mira. Groups called Lachas, Yambas, and Aguatene, who lived to the south of the river Mira toward Lita, are often referred to with the Cayapa, and most likely they belonged to the same cultural-linguistic group.[27] In the late sixteenth century the Cayapa inhabited the region to the south of the Middle Mira River that separated them from their enemies to the north.[28] At the time of conquest they probably inhabited the coast around the mouth of the Santiago River, for in 1600 Captain Pedro de Arévalo reported he had explored the coast from San Mateo to the Santiago River, where he found "many old plots of plantains and other crops belonging to Indians who had retired inland."[29] On the 1597 map of the region the Cayapa are depicted as living inland in the basins of the Santiago and Cayapas, probably as far south as the Cordillera de Cayapas.[30] Earlier this century Barrett recorded that the Cayapa inhabited the Cayapas Basin while others were living in the Santiago Basin and at scattered points on the coast into southern Colombia.[31] The distribution of Cayapa toponyms, particularly those for smaller rivers, suggests they were formerly more widespread than at present.[32] Modern ethnohistorians locate them in the basins of the Cayapas and Santiago.[33]

Tradition relates that the Cayapa originated in the sierra from which they fled as a result of Inka conquest or the Spanish invasion.[34] Some doubt has been expressed about the basis of this tradition,[35] but given the proposed relationship between the Nigua and the Cayapa, it is worth noting that in the late sixteenth century Cabello Balboa recorded that the Nigua had also descended from the mountains.[36] The Cayapa and Colorado have often been considered to be related and to belong to the Barbacoan linguistic subgroup of Chibcha.[37] However, a recent linguistic analysis by Bernárdez has argued against their relationship and suggested that the Cayapa are not a Chibchan group; their affiliation is unknown.[38]

According to Cabello Balboa, the Campaz inhabited the mountains inland from the coast.[39] Jijón y Caamaño has related the Campaz to the Colorado, but most references to the former group suggest that they were living nearer to the coast than the area commonly considered to have been inhabited by the Colorado.[40] In 1568 Andrés Contero's expedition encountered "Campay" inland from Coaque,[41] while in 1600 Father Juan Bautista de Burgos established San Martín de los Campaces near San Mateo.[42] However, these Indians appear to have been culturally distinct from others at San Mateo[43] and were described by Cabello Balboa as the most warlike group in the region, lacking chiefs and being very superstitious.[44]

Another group to be found in the Esmeraldas region was the Caraque. According to Cieza de León, their northern limit was Colima.[45] The southern limit has been disputed, primarily because of the confused description provided by Cieza de León, which noted that they comprised two groups, one of which possessed tattooed faces and inhabited the region "from Cabo de Pasaos and the Santiago River to the village of Salango."[46] The confusion arises because the Santiago River is well to the north of Cabo Pasado, but the list of villages he provides where men tattooed their faces are all located south of the river Chone, suggesting that the northern limit of this group, the Manta, was not the Santiago River but the Bahía de Cáraquez.[47] In the Regional Development Period between 500 B.C. and A.D. 500, the cultural distinction between the regions inhabited by the Caraque and the Nigua-Cayapa was manifest in two archaeological complexes known as Jama-Coaque (extending from the Chone River to Cabo San Francisco) and Tiaone (on the southern coast of Esmeraldas).[48] At the time of Spanish conquest the Esmeraldas coast between Río Verde and Tonchigüe continued to be a common cultural area,[49] but Estrada has suggested that at that time the distinction between the two areas was less clear. He suggests that Atacames culture, which was derived from Jama-Coaque culture, was common throughout Esmeraldas and Manabí, a proposition that requires further investigation.[50]

Within Esmeraldas, Indian groups shared many features in common, but there appear to have been some distinctive local adaptations. All subsisted by practicing shifting cultivation, hunting, fishing, and collecting, with the emphasis on each activity and the products they yielded varying from area to area. Garcilaso de la Vega claimed that Indians in the province of "Passau" did not practice agriculture,[51] but all other documentary and archaeological evidence is to the contrary. Cabello Balboa's account, probably the most reliable, mentions the cultivation of maize, plantains ("which they grow with great care"), and yuca, from which they made bread and wine.[52] A number of early colonial accounts suggest an emphasis on seed crops, but this may reflect Spanish food preferences and their concern with supplies and hence with crops such as maize, which had greater storage capabilities.[53] Many accounts make reference to the cultivation of root crops, and a seventeenth-century list of crops cultivated in the Yumbos, including the village of San Juan de los Niguas, suggests that although maize was grown, other crops—notably plantains—predominated.[54] Today plantains are by far the most important crop grown by the Cayapa.[55] Archaeological evidence from La Propicia in the form of graters used to process manioc indicates the importance of root crops, though the presence of *metates* and *manos* suggests that maize was cultivated also and around Atacames may have predominated.[56] Overall, the evidence suggests that a variety of crops were grown, the balance of which varied with local ecological conditions and cultural preferences. Agricultural activities were supplemented by broad-spectrum hunting, fishing, and collecting.[57] Cabello Balboa recorded that deer, peccaries, tapirs, rabbits, and many birds were hunted.[58] Fishing was particularly important among coastal groups, who also exploited shellfish, both for food and, in the case of *Spondylus,* for the prized *mullu* shell, which was traded over long distances.[59] Fish were caught with nets rather than hooks, sometimes salted or smoked, and traded inland.

The earliest visitors to the shores of Ecuador explored only the coast, so that few descriptions exist of settlements inland. Coastal settlements were nucleated and contained several thousand inhabitants. Sámanos's account of Bartolomé Ruíz's expedition in 1526 recorded that at the Bahía de San Mateo there were "three large villages next to the sea" and that between there and Tacamez there were "many settlements" that were "very large," with Tacamez itself containing "1,500 houses," not including "other villages next to it where more people were collected."[60] Similarly, Oviedo recorded that the expedition encountered "a very large number of villages and an innumerable number of Indians" and that Tacamez had 1,000 houses.[61] According to Jerez, the expedition arrived at a settlement where it was met by 10,000 "indios de guerra," and he further recorded the presence of a village with 3,000 houses and many others with less.[62] The existence of settlements of this order of magnitude has been confirmed by archaeological investigations at Atacames that have proposed that the town itself possessed a contact population of 2,655.[63] Nevertheless, it appears to have lacked the nucleation and social and political complexity characteristic of a truly urban settlement. Further south, coastal settlements such as Coaque also possessed several hundred large houses.[64] Guinea Bueno suggests that at the time of Spanish conquest the population of the coast was increasing as the trading economy developed, leaving the inland areas as a cultural backwater.[65]

A number of the larger settlements appear to have been focal points in a system of commerce. Here peace prevailed, and otherwise hostile groups could trade. Such a settlement was Ciscala, where, according to Martín de Carranza writing in 1569, "they have fairs or a market, and the Tacamas bring gold and emeralds to sell, and the Campaces and Pidres bring salt and fish, and the Belinquiamas bring cloth and cotton."[66] The site of this settlement is unknown, although the location of groups who were bringing goods suggests that it was probably near Cabo San Francisco.[67] The commercial role of some coastal settlements is attested by the statement of traders from Salango to Bartolomé Ruíz that they had under their control a number of communities including those at Coaque, Atacames, and the Bahía de San Mateo.[68]

Other coastal settlements appear to have performed a ceremonial role, with local groups bringing offerings of gold dust and chaquira to shrines containing idols.[69] Most noteworthy was the site of La Tolita, which was said to have had a guard of 100 Indians drawn from surrounding provinces who ensured that peace prevailed. By the end of the sixteenth century the site had been abandoned, but local inhabitants attested that it had once possessed a substantial residential population that had included many silversmiths.

Apart from these relatively large settlements, there were numerous rancherías, some clustered around major centers, but others more widely spaced along inland rivers. They generally comprised small groups of five or six houses that probably contained related families.[70] Hence each settlement might contain a small lineage of about thirty people, though some were clearly larger. The predominance of female figurines found at the site of La Propicia suggests that these groups may have been matrilineal, though today the Cayapa have a tendency to patrilocality, although it is not marked.[71] With the exception of coastal towns, settlements in Esmeraldas were generally smaller than those of their neighbors to the south, which reflected the less complex culture of its inhabitants, a distinction noted by some early observers.[72]

On the basis of archaeological evidence Guinea Bueno has estimated that at the time of Spanish conquest the total population of the Bay of Atacames may have been between 11,000 and 15,000, rising to between 13,000 and 19,000 if Balao near the mouth of the Esmeraldas is included.[73]

Since further south, coastal settlements such as Coaque also possessed several hundred large houses,[74] a conservative population estimate for the coast from the Santiago River to the river Chone might be 20,000. It might have occupied territory of some 220 square kilometers, which would give a local density of 90.9 persons per square kilometer.[75] These figures are consistent with the documentary evidence already presented for the size of native settlements and are not unreasonable, given that the presence of dense Indian populations on the coast of Atacames was sufficient to dissuade Bartolomé Ruiz from replenishing his supplies there for fear of attack.[76]

Contemporary observations indicate that the interior regions were less densely populated than the coast and probably depended on the cultivation of plantains and root crops rather than maize. An estimated population density of two persons per square kilometer is suggested, which is comparable with population densities calculated for groups of the high selva of the Oriente, whose subsistence patterns and physical environments were broadly similar. It is also consistent with the view that population densities in this region were lower than among groups to the south. The total area inhabited by the Cayapa, Nigua, Campaz, and Caraque may be calculated at 22,049 square kilometers, which excludes the 220 square kilometers for the coast, thereby giving an estimated total population for the interior areas of 44,098. The total population of the Esmeraldas region at the time of conquest may therefore be estimated at about 64,098, which, if anything, is likely to prove conservative.

MANTA

The Manta were distinguished by their tattooed faces, a feature that according to Cieza de León, characterized those Indians living in the region between the Bahía de Caráquez in the north and the island of Salango in the south.[77] Their influence, however, built on their domination of trade along the coast, extended beyond these limits at least as far north as the Bahía de San Mateo. The Manta leader Salangone was said to have under his "sujeción" the Indians of "Tacamez, Bahía de San Mateo, Nancabez, Tovirisimi, Conilope, Papagayos, Tolona, Quisimos, Coaque, Tonconjes, Arampajos, Pintagua, Caraslobez, Amarejos, Cames, Amotopse, Docoa."[78]

The Manta region was described by Cieza de León as very fertile, where a "great quantity of maize, yuca, sweet potatoes, and many other roots" was grown.[79] In addition a great number of fruits was cultivated, including guavas, avocadoes, prickly pears, star apples, melons, pineapples, and red peppers. Maize was probably the most important staple crop, although Cieza de León noted that they also grew "not a small number of plantains."[80] Maize was used to make bread, which was judged by Benzoni to be the best in the Indies.[81] The fertility of the region was echoed in an early seventeenth-century account of the area around Puerto Viejo, which apart from including a similar list of crops raised, estimated that maize yields were as high as 1 to 400 and 500.[82] The productivity of the region was enhanced through the construction of terraces, notably in the Cerro de Hojas and neighboring hills.[83] While this enabled a dense population to be supported, Holm suggests that terracing was not a response to population pressure but was an attempt to maximize the impact of the region's light rains.[84] The land was worked with copper tools[85] and, according to Loor, was communally owned.[86] Although agriculture was well established, the Manta also hunted deer and birds[87] and were skilled fishermen and sailors. An anonymous account of the Manta region written in the sixteenth century recorded that "in Manta there are some Indian fishermen, great divers and swimmers, who live on fish which they also sell."[88] Fish was sometimes salted but often it was eaten raw.[89]

The seafaring abilities of the Manta clearly impressed early observers. Unlike groups to the north who used canoes, the Manta used log rafts, or *balsas,* equipped with sails.[90] These craft may have ventured as far as southern Mexico[91] and were capable of transporting large numbers of people as well as goods.[92] A sailing vessel from Salango encountered by Bartolomé Ruiz was carrying twenty men and thirty tons of merchandise. It included many gold and silver ornaments, emeralds, chalcedony, embroidered and colored cotton and woolen cloth, clothes, black pottery, and a balance for weighing gold and other items.[93] Above all, however, there were large quantities of chaquira or mullu, shells of *Spondylus,* which were highly prized for necklaces and were used as items of exchange. Murra suggests that the presence of woolen cloth and the balance suggests that the impetus for trade may have come from the south.[94] Nevertheless, it is clear that the traders were operating from Manabí and that most of the trade items were manufactured locally.

In pre-Columbian times villages were generally independent to the extent that each had its own cacique and language, and there was often conflict between them.[95] Nevertheless, the fact that Salangone's power extended over four neighboring villages suggests that on the coast at least, integration was taking place and a political hierarchy was emerging.[96] Chiefs were generally polygamous and on death were buried with two or three of their favorite wives, food, weapons, and precious items.[97] Each chiefdom had its own ceremonies that centered on temples, where idols and statues were kept and animal and human sacrifices took place. Idols often took the form of land and marine animals made of gold, silver, wood, clay, and emeralds.[98] The chief at Manta was said to have inherited a very large emerald that was highly revered for its curative powers.[99]

Manta settlements appear to have been more substantial than those of their neighbors to the north. Archaeological evidence indicates that they were the only coastal group to make extensive use of stone for construction, principally for the foundations of houses and temples, as well as for the walls of corrals.[100] Clearly not all houses were built of stone, for Cieza de León described their houses as made of wood covered with straw, the size of which depended on the means of the owner.[101] The settlements as a whole were described as well planned.[102] Benzoni estimated that Manta itself, formerly Jocay, had possessed more than 2,000 inhabitants,[103] but on the basis of archaeological evidence Loor and Estrada have suggested its population may have reached 20,000.[104] Estrada further suggests that Charapotó probably had a similar number of inhabitants, and Cerro de Hojas (Picoaza) slightly more (30,000). Loor asserts that at that time there were some twenty villages in Manabí,[105] and Estrada estimates that at the time of Spanish conquest the whole region occupied by the Manta contained a population of 120,000.[106] This number is credible, given evidence for intensive forms of agricultural production and accounts of substantial populations. Francisco Pizarro claimed to have pacified thirty caciques in the Valley of Charapotó alone,[107] and Cristóbal de Molina estimated that prior to its devastation by Pedro de Alvarado, the area around the Bahía de Caráquez and Puerto Viejo had possessed 20,000 Indians.[108] Although the latter figure may have been exaggerated to condemn the activities of Alvarado, it indicates the presence of a dense population that by that time had already been severely reduced by epidemics. If Estrada's estimate is accepted, the aboriginal population density may be calculated at 10.1 persons per square kilometer. Although this assumes that all of the area was utilized, which is unlikely, it may be too low, given the existence of permanent forms of cultivation and the fact that shifting cultivation may support up to 20 persons per square kilometer.[109]

HUANCAVILCA

The Huancavilca occupied the coast to the south of the Manta as far as the Gulf of Guayaquil. Passing south from Puerto Viejo, Benzoni noted that the first village of the Huancavilca was Colonche.[110] The dividing line between these two groups was preserved in the boundary between the colonial jurisdictions of Puerto Viejo and Guayaquil. The area inhabited by the Huancavilca was arid, and consequently most of their settlements were located on the coast or along the main valleys, where water could be obtained from pits.[111] This settlement pattern is not so discernible today because of a rise in the sea level.[112] Settlement outside of these favored areas appears to have been very sparse. Reginaldo de Lizárraga observed that the Santa Elena Peninsula had "few or no Indians today; and when I saw it and we stopped there, very few people were living there."[113] The main settlements of Huancavilca identified by Cieza de León were "Yacual, Colonche, Chinduy, Chongón, Daule, [and] Chonana," which he claimed were all located in fertile lands that produced an abundance of crops, especially maize.[114] According to Oviedo, they did not use maize to make bread but ate it boiled.[115] However, maize grinders have been found in the region, so that it may have been eaten as a gruel.[116] In any case, the Huancavilca probably lived as much from fishing and trade as from agriculture.[117]

Unlike their neighbors to the north, the Huancavilca did not work stone to any large degree, but in other respects they were culturally akin to them. Bushnell suggests that the Huancavilca may have been an offshoot of the Manta and that they were fisherman who may have arrived by sea, possibly expelling the Colorado from the coast.[118] They appear to have possessed a two-tiered political structure. Chiefs governed small provinces containing a number of villages where different languages were often spoken, but they in turn were subject to the authority of a paramount chief. Benzoni observed that Chief Baltacho "was highly esteemed and had great authority among his vassals" but was subordinate to the chief at Colonche.[119] The Huancavilca possessed idols and conducted human sacrifices to ensure health and the fertility of the fields. The hearts of sacrificial victims were revered as gods.[120] They practiced secondary urn burials, which, unlike the Cayapa and Chono, were unordered and not associated with artificial mounds, or tolas.[121]

Although the Huancavilca were culturally akin to the Manta, the arid conditions of the region meant that settlements were confined to the coast or major valleys. However, it is significant that some of the most valuable, and by implication populous, encomiendas distributed in the jurisdiction of Guayaquil were in the region occupied by the Huancavilca. They included the towns of Chongón, Colonche, Yagual, and Chanduy.[122] In 1581 the province of Huancavilca contained about a quarter of the Indian population of the jurisdiction of Guayaquil,[123] though it is important to note that by the middle of the sixteenth century a significant number of Indians in the Guayas Basin had not been pacified, so that the Huancavilca would have represented a lower proportion than this figure suggests. Nevertheless, estimates for the Huancavilca should be seen in the context of estimates of several hundred thousand for the Chono, who inhabited the latter region. Hence despite the restricted distribution of settlements in the Santa Elena peninsula, the cultural affinity of the Huancavilca and Manta argues for a similar population density of 10 per square kilometer, which would give an estimate for the aboriginal population of 47,970. This figure represents a slight reduction on pre-Inka population levels, for in resisting Inka rule, the Huancavilca sustained losses in battle, and subsequently others were transferred to Peru as mitmaq.[124]

PUNÁ

The Puná inhabited the island of that name and possibly some other islands in the Gulf of Guayaquil. They were closely related to the Manta and Huancavilca, but they were considerably more warlike, conducting constant wars with their neighbors on the mainland, particularly with those at Túmbez.[125] Although the island of Puná was described as very fertile, producing a lot of "maize, yuca, and other roots" and being abundant in game, particularly deer and birds, its inhabitants were essentially fishers and traders.[126] Nevertheless, Volland has suggested that at the time of Spanish conquest, their trading activities may have been under pressure, as the Inka were attempting to break their resistance by isolating them economically through preventing former allies from trading with them.[127] They possessed large numbers of balsas, of a similar construction to those used by the Manta, which it was said could carry up to fifty men and three horses.[128] For weapons they used slings, clubs, axes of silver and copper, and lances with points of low-grade gold.[129] Trading and warfare enabled the Puná to acquire wealth on a scale that clearly impressed early observers.

The island was governed by seven caciques, of whom one was the paramount chief, who was especially feared by his vassals.[130] Chiefs were polygamous, and on death they were buried with precious items and some of their most beautiful wives.[131] Their temples were located in obscure places, where they sacrificed animals, slaves, and prisoners of war.[132] One of their temples that was located on the Isla de Santa Clara was said to contain abundant offerings of gold, silver, jewels, and woolen cloth,[133] but as yet no archaeological evidence of its existence has been found.[134]

The consensus among early chroniclers was that the island was highly populated.[135] Even as late as 1587 Thomas Cavendish's expedition found several Indian towns, each possessing at least 200 houses, one of which was described as larger than Gravesend in England.[136] Oviedo provides the only precise figure for the island's population, estimating that it had possessed about 6,000 or 7,000 "vecinos indios."[137] If Oviedo's estimate is taken to refer to male heads of household and it is assumed that the ratio of tributary to nontributary Indians in the immediate conquest period was probably not more than 1:3 or 1:4, then the total population may be estimated at between 19,500 and 26,000. It is not clear to what date Oviedo's figure refers, but it could reasonably apply to the time of Spanish conquest, except that to take account of the prior impact of epidemics the figures would have to be more than doubled. Despite observations that the island was highly populated and that the economic base of the Puná was extended by trade and warfare, it is doubtful that the island supported 40,000 to 50,000 inhabitants, for this would be equivalent to the total Huancavilca population. This seems unlikely, since although the island of Puná comprised one of the most valuable encomiendas in the jurisdiction of Guayaquil in the early colonial period, it was worth only a fraction of those associated with the Huancavilca.[138] A more reasonable estimate for the island's aboriginal population would be about 20,000, allowing several thousand vassals for each of the seven caciques.

CHONO (COLORADO)

Recent ethnohistorical research has made it increasingly apparent that the greater part of the interior coastal region that comprised the basins of the Guayas, Daule, and Babahoyo rivers was inhabited by the Chono.[139] Lizárraga recorded that two kinds of people lived near Guayaquil—the Huancavilca and the Chono—the latter of which he regarded as "less civilized."[140] The Chono were considered to be more warlike than the Huancavilca, and they had long-standing conflicts with the Puná.[141] Other authors similarly distinguished the Huancavilca from other groups living in the region, who were sometimes but not always identified as Chono.[142] In 1581 a list of tributary Indians in the villages inhabited by Huancavilca indicated that they were all located to the west of the Daule River, whereas those living in the valleys of the Amay, Baba, and Daule rivers were unspecified but were almost certainly Chono.[143] That the Chono also lived on or near the coast is suggested by documentary sources that indicate that just before Spanish conquest the Puná had killed a number of Chono "while they were fishing in the sea."[144] Even though inland groups would have had relatively easy access to the coast by balsa, the fact that in 1536 the Chono destroyed the settlement of Guayaquil established by Sebastián de Benalcázar[145] also argues for their location near the coast.

Espinosa Soriano's detailed analysis of sixteenth-century documents and chronicles concludes that the Chono extended from Quevedo in the north to Tenguel in the south.[146] This region broadly corresponds to that defined by the Milagro-Quevedo archaeological complex, which has been associated with Colorado.[147] The culture of this group is characterized by urn burials whose contents indicate a marked differentiation in social status and well-developed crafts, particularly metallurgy and weaving. Artefacts associated with these activities confirm some of the earliest colonial accounts, which note that Indians in this region went richly adorned with gold jewelery[148] and that they were skilled weavers producing a type of cotton cloth known as chona.[149] The evidence suggests a more highly developed culture than that described in many later colonial accounts and indeed that of the Colorado today.

There seems little doubt that the Chono were ancestors of the Colorado and that the latter, so called because of their red body painting, represent the remnants of a once-widespread group whose distribution since the time of Spanish conquest has become increasingly restricted.[150] Earlier this century the Colorado were living in the northern part of the region in the upper reaches of the Esmeraldas and Daule rivers, their main settlements being Santo Domingo de los Colorados and San Miguel.[151] However, it is clear that they formerly extended further south, for even in the 1920s the group wanderings extended to Babahoyo.[152] The Colorado, as already indicated, are now considered to be linguistically distinct from the Cayapa and are thought to be affiliated to Chibcha.[153]

The basins of the Guayas, Daule, and Babahoyo comprise seasonally flooded grassland plains that are crisscrossed by numerous streams and tributaries. In 1534 Pedro de Alvarado's expedition traversed the region from the Bahía de Caráquez and observed small settlements that were located ten to fifteen leagues apart.[154] This is consistent with an account of Andrés Contero's expedition in 1568, which reportedly penetrated fifty leagues up the Daule River from Guayaquil, where it encountered villages of forty and fifty people. It then retired for reinforcements in anticipation of encountering larger populations two days further upriver.[155] What Chono settlements lacked in size they appear to have made up for in numbers. Artificial mounds associated with Milagro culture occur by the hundreds particularly in the southern Guayas Basin, where the land is seasonally inundated.[156] Many of the mounds were habitation or burial sites. Scattered among the raised fields, these small mounds generally accommodated only one or at best a few *barbacoas*,[157] though a few groups of unusually large mounds existed that were probably centers of administrative or religious activity, or both.

The area inhabited by the Chono was the most productive of the coastal region on account of its seasonally inundated lands, which offered opportunities for the development of intensive forms of agricultural production. Recent geographical surveys and archaeological excavations have revealed the presence of raised fields, or camellones. These were constructed not only to provide well-drained ridges of land in the wet season but also to create moist ditches that could be used to produce a secondary crop during the dry season. Organic matter that collected in the ditches was probably used to fertilize soil on the ridges.[158] The raised fields cover about 50,000 hectares and are testimony to the existence of an intensive farming system and a highly organized society capable of carrying out large-scale community projects.

The economy of the Chono was based on cultivation, fishing, and hunting, with the emphasis on each of these activities varying with the resources of the local area. Maize, manioc, and cotton were widely grown on the raised fields, though plantains were probably more common in the interior as they are today.[159] In the early colonial period deer, peccaries, and various kinds of birds were hunted.[160] Most Chono were probably involved in freshwater fishing in which fish poisons were employed,[161] and some groups participated in marine fishing that they conducted from balsas. There is evidence for trade with the highlands and with groups to the south. Indeed trade was sufficiently active to stimulate the development of a medium of exchange that took the form of copper-ax money. Few minerals existed in the region from which this ax money and their fine jewelery could be manufactured. The copper may have been obtained from the sierra or from Peru, where the Huancavilca or Manta may have acquired it in exchange for chaquira and salt, while the gold was probably imported from Esmeraldas.[162] The Chono appear to have acted as intermediaries in trade between the coast and sierra. In the sixteenth century, traders from Sicchos and Angamarca were exchanging salt for gold, cotton, ají, and dried fish offered by lowland groups.[163]

Largely on the basis of evidence for subsistence patterns, Mathewson has estimated that at the time of Spanish conquest the population of the Guayas Basin was between 400,000 and 500,000. His estimate is based on calculations of population densities associated with areas with and without raised fields. On the assumption that all the fields were used contemporaneously and that about 20 percent of the area was productive, he estimates that the 500 square kilometers of raised fields could have supported 100,00 to 150,000 people.[164] These calculations indicate a population density of between 1,000 and 1,500 per square kilometer for the productive area, which may be compared with a density of 750 persons per square kilometer that Knapp has estimated for drained fields in the sierra.[165] Mathewson then adds a further 325,000 for the rest of the region, assuming a density of 10 persons per square kilometer.

Before modifying the estimates slightly, it is important to discuss the apparent discrepancy between these proposed high population estimates and the relatively few references to the existence of large native populations and raised fields in the early documentary record. While Oviedo described the Guayas River as "bien poblado,"[166] many observers failed to comment on the size of the population. It is possible that the dispersed pattern of single residences in the lower Guayas Basin, still evident in the early conquest period, gave the impression of small populations that were unworthy of note. Similarly the raised fields may not have been easily discernible from ground level; indeed they were brought to scientific attention only in 1965, when they were observed from the air. Furthermore, by the time of Spanish conquest many had probably fallen into disrepair as a consequence of population decline occasioned by the prior arrival of Old World diseases. Nevertheless, the presence of settlements suggests that some fields were still being utilized. Indeed Lizárraga recorded that in the Guayas Basin the Indians possessed "some pieces of high land that are like islands where they have their settlements with an abundance of food and supplies."[167]

Other evidence supports the proposition that the region was highly populated. The existence of a stratified society, attested by archaeological investigations, in which commoners paid tribute to their leaders argues for a high population density.[168] According to a sixteenth-century testimony, in the early 1530s the cacique of Daule possessed 4,000 to 5,000 vassals who paid tribute.[169] Espinosa Soriano interprets this to mean a total population of between 20,000 and 25,000 and takes the reference as pertaining to the Chono as a whole, not just those subject to the cacique of Daule. However, this figure could have referred to one of the small chiefdoms that composed the Chono, for the existence of raised fields in the vicinity of Daule suggests that a population of this magnitude could have been supported locally. Accepting Mathewson's estimate of 10 persons per square kilometer for the area of the Guayas Basin inhabited by the Chono, but excluding the areas of raised fields and the coast south of the island of Puná, which, judging by the numbers of encomiendas distributed there, appears to have been less densely inhabited, the aboriginal population for the interior basin may be calculated at 213,780. For the southern coast a lower population density of 5 per square kilometer is suggested, though this may prove conservative, thereby giving an additional 25,980. The population supported by the 500 square kilometers of raised fields is more difficult to calculate. While the population density proposed by Mathewson is in line with evidence from drained-field agriculture in other parts of the New World,[170] the question remains open as to what proportion of the fields was cultivated at the time of Spanish conquest. The shortage of documentary materials referring to the presence of dense populations urges caution when estimating the aboriginal population. If, at a guess, only half of the area of raised fields was utilized at the time of Spanish conquest, 50,000 to 75,000 may be added, giving a total population estimate for the Chono of between 289,760 and 314,760.

CONCLUSION

Indian groups on the coast comprised tribes or small chiefdoms, with social stratification and political integration being more highly developed to the south of the river Chone and on the coast of Esmeraldas. All groups

Table 3. Aboriginal Population of the Coast

Ethnic group/area	Area in km^2	Persons per km^2	Aboriginal population estimate
Malaba	1,031	4.8	5,000
Esmeraldas (coast)	220	90.9	20,000
Esmeraldas (interior)	22,049	2.0	44,098
Total	23,300		69,098
Manta	11,924	10.1	120,000
Huancavilca	4,797	10.0	47,970
Puná	1,029	19.4	20,000
Chono (raised fields)	500	1,000–1,500	50,000–75,000[a]
Chono (interior)	21,378	10.0	213,780
Chono (southern coast)	5,196	5.0	25,980
Total	44,824		477,730–502,730
Grand total	68,124		546,828–571,828

[a] Population estimate assumes that only one-half of the fields were being utilized at the time of Spanish conquest and that only 20 percent were productive.

practiced agriculture, with the emphasis on different crops varying according to local ecological conditions. Most were grown under a system of shifting cultivation, but more permanent and intensive forms of production appear to have been practiced further south, where terracing and raised fields were constructed. The emphasis on other economic activities also varied with local conditions, with those living near the coast being skilled fishers and professional traders. Many religious beliefs and practices were associated with the sea, and they revolved around temples and idols, to whom offerings and sacrifices were made. As will be shown, the Inka never effectively conquered the coast of Ecuador, and the Huancavilca and Puná were probably the only groups to have come into conflict with them.

These differences in native culture were expressed in variations in population density on the coast as shown in Table 3. It is clear that apart from the coast, Esmeraldas was less densely settled than regions to the south. The accompanying table suggests the northern sector may have contained only about 12 percent of the population of the coast. Most significantly it suggests that the population of the coast exceeded 0.5 million and that the region was much more densely populated than previously thought. Although its population did not match that of the sierra, the coast contained about 34 percent of the total population of what was to become the Audiencia of Quito. While not wishing to detract from the significance of these findings, it is necessary to note that at the time of the Spanish invasion the proportion living on the coast was inflated as a result of losses sustained in the sierra during Inka conquest.

CHAPTER 4

Lands and Peoples of the Oriente

> The number and abundance of Indians in all these provinces [in the Oriente] is so great that according to witnesses and reliable accounts, there are many millions.
>
> Father Francisco de Fuentes, *procurador*
> of the Jesuits, circa 1630[1]

The cloak of forest that covers the Oriente of Ecuador belies its ecological diversity. Variations in relief, climate, river regimes, and soils combine to produce differences in habitat that are almost as diverse as those of the Andes.[2] For most purposes, however, it is useful to distinguish the flanks of the eastern Cordillera from the lowlands proper. The lower slopes of the Cordillera Oriental, the Cordillera de Guacamayos, and the vestiges of the Pre-Andes, or Third Cordillera, reach about 2,000 meters, forming a zone of transition between the high Andes and the lowlands that is more rapid and marked in Ecuador than in the rest of the Andean chain.[3] This transitional zone, often referred to as the montaña, forms a narrow belt of relatively rugged terrain through which the tributaries of the Napo, Paute, Upano, and Zamora have cut narrow canyons and cascade to the lowlands carrying gold deposits weathered from igneous and metamorphic rocks. In contrast the lowlands are composed of sedimentary rocks that are partially overlain by more recent alluvial deposits. They form part of the major sedimentary basin that separates the Andes from the Brazilian Shield, which in Ecuador declines from about 1,000 meters in the north to 200 meters in the south.

The difference between the montaña and the lowlands in terms of topography and geology is paralleled in the climate. At heights of over 500 meters the average temperature falls to less than 25°C, but rainfall reaches its highest levels, especially to the north of the Pastaza, where in some years rainfall exceeds 5,000 millimeters. The lowlands are hotter and receive less rain. There average temperatures surpass 25°C, and the rainfall, although lower, generally exceeds 1,500 millimeters per year. There is no marked dry season, but most of the rain falls between January and July.

The tropical rain forest of the Ecuadorian Oriente contains one of the world's richest floras. A wide diversity of trees tied together by woody climbers and commonly covered with epiphytes rise to thirty meters, forming a canopy that little light can penetrate.[4] As a result the ground flora and fauna are restricted, such that opportunities for collecting are limited, and the animals, being largely arboreal and solitary in habit, are difficult to hunt. Where there are gaps in the canopy, notably where rivers cut through the forest, the ground vegetation and game are more abundant. The rivers also provide opportunities for fishing, and in their lower reaches turtles may be exploited.

The luxuriance of the vegetation cover disguises the fact that the soils underlying the tropical rain forest offer limited opportunities for farming. This is because the nutrients necessary for plant growth are either rapidly absorbed by the forest or washed away by heavy rains, so that once the vegetation cover has been removed, the highly leached soil can be cultivated for only a few years before crop yields decline and the land has to be abandoned to fallow. The exceptions are riverbanks, where the soils are naturally fertilized by floodwaters and can therefore be cultivated for longer periods. While some sediment is deposited on riverbanks in the Amazon headwaters, most of the silt is carried to the floodplains of the Middle and Lower Amazon to the east of Ecuadorian territory. These floodplains, or *várzeas,* are particularly rich in natural resources. Not only are the soils more fertile and, being lightly vegetated, require limited clearance, but aquatic resources are more bountiful. Although food is more abundant, its supply is irregular because of the widely fluctuating river levels. Subsistence activities have to be organized to fit in with river regimes, and food preserved and stored to overcome periods of relative scarcity during high water, when fields are flooded and collecting and fishing are less productive. The greater productive potential of the várzeas, compared with the higher interfluves, or *terra firme,* has been recognized by many, though debate continues as to whether soils or sources of protein are more significant in influencing population density.[5] Denevan has estimated that floodplains constitute only about 2 percent of the Amazonian lowlands, but they are even more limited in Ecuador than downriver. Nevertheless, the banks of most rivers would have been favored sites for settlement, given their greater fertility and the greater abundance of terrestrial and aquatic fauna.

In addition to differences between the floodplains and interfluves, a further distinction needs to be made between the low selva and high selva. Denevan places the boundary between these habitats at about 700 meters, but in Ecuador it ranges from about 800 to 1,800 meters.[6] The high selva has lower temperatures and is a zone of erosion rather than deposition. This means that alluvial soils along the banks of rivers are limited, but soils on the hillsides are more fertile than on the leached interfluves of the lowlands. Upland soils are constantly replenished by new minerals created by weathering, and the cooler climate causes the humus to break down more slowly. In terms of farming, the high selva can support higher population densities, but this habitat offers fewer opportunities for securing sources of protein. Fishing is less productive in the rapid-flowing rivers than in the quiet lagoons and backwaters of the floodplains. Game is no more abundant than in the lowlands, but in the absence of fishing, which is a more reliable source of food, subsistence patterns in the high selva generally placed greater emphasis on hunting and the exploitation of insects.[7] Groups inhabiting this environment included the Cofán, Coronado, Quijo, Macas, and the Bracamoro-Jíbaro branch of the Jívaro. Those inhabiting the low selva comprised the lowland Jívaro and members of the Tucanoan, Kandoshi, Zaparoan, and Panoan cultural-linguistic groups. The Omagua of the Middle and Upper Amazon inhabited the várzea, but this habitat was more limited in Ecuador, and here the Omagua did not approach the population density levels found downriver, though they were more populous than their immediate neighbors. (See Map 4.)

In his original estimate of the population of western Amazonia, Denevan suggested that the population densities that could be supported by these different environments might be 1.2 persons per square kilometer for the high selva, 0.2 per square kilometer for the low selva, with a density of 5.3 per square kilometer being possible on the várzea.[8] He later raised the estimate for the várzea to 14.6 per square kilometer on the basis of new ethnohistorical evidence,[9] and in a further revision distinguished the várzea of the Amazon from its major tributaries, assigning them population densities of 18.2 and 9.1 per square kilometer respectively.[10] Using Denevan's original density estimates, Sweet calculated that the aboriginal population of the low selva area of the Upper Amazon was 151,000.[11] He argued, however, that an intermediate category between the floodplain and interfluvial habitats should be created to take account of the upper reaches of tributaries, where alluvial banks were limited but fishing in small pools was possible. He assigned a population density of 1.0 per square kilometer to this habitat and arbitrarily estimated that it covered 20 percent of the Upper Amazon region. From early descriptions of subsistence patterns of Indian groups in the headwaters, a higher density for those areas seems appropriate, but this habitat may not have been as extensive as he suggests. Sweet's recalculations produced an estimated aboriginal population of 231,000, which is more in line with his estimates of between 187,000 and 258,000 calculated from Jesuit missionary accounts of the province of Mainas in the seventeenth century.[12] All these estimates refer to the province of Mainas, which extended south of the Marañón and east of its confluence with the Napo and hence out of the region being discussed here. They thus exclude groups inhabiting the high selva listed above and the lowland Jívaro, who, with the exception of the latter, according to Denevan's reasoning, should have been more populous than those in the lowlands.

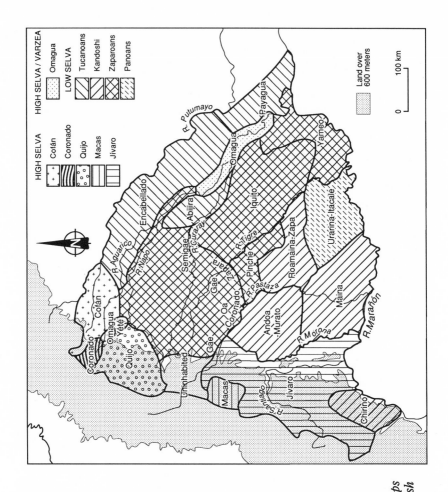

Map 4. Distribution of ethnic groups
in the Oriente on the eve of Spanish
conquest

PEOPLES

The names of Indian groups that lived in the Oriente in pre-Inka times are almost as diverse as the species of the forest they inhabited. However, given the limitations of space, only the distribution and general characteristics of the major cultural-linguistic groups will be discussed. In general the tribes of the Oriente practiced shifting cultivation and to different degrees relied on hunting and fishing for protein. Settlements were small and dispersed. Warfare was common and underlay the power of some leaders, as did their abilities as shamans, but societies were not markedly stratified. They were animistic in their beliefs, and shamanistic practices dominated religious life. Underlying these similarities were differences that may be highlighted by discussing them within a habitat framework—the high selva, the várzea, and the low selva. It is not the intention to adopt a crude environmental deterministic approach but to use these categories to reveal cultural adaptations to different ecological conditions that were realized in the context of their technological skills, needs, and values. These adaptations served to promote or undermine the maintenance and reproduction of the group and its balance with local resources. As such, this framework is considered appropriate for the analysis of demographic change. It is important to recognize, however, that over time, and particularly after European contact, neither Indian groups nor their environments remained constant.

THE HIGH SELVA

Cofán

The most northerly inhabitants of the Ecuadorian Oriente were the Cofán,[13] who inhabited the flanks of Mount Cayambe,[14] probably in the vicinity of the Azuela and Upper Aguarico rivers.[15] Early Spanish contacts in this forested region remain obscure. It is known that the town of Alcalá del Río was established there in 1563,[16] but it was not until the 1590s that more concerted efforts were made to pacify the Cofán. At that time Father Pedro Ordóñez de Cevallos claimed that within two months he had established eight villages containing 4,000 souls. He maintained that they were easy to pacify if well treated but otherwise were indomitable.[17] Unfortunately, his lengthy account of work in the region provides few details of ethnographic interest. What does emerge, however, is that there were numerous "caciques," each with several hundred subjects, from whom the settlements derived their names.[18] They also made chicha from manioc in canoes.

Subsequently, between 1599 and 1611, Jesuit missionaries headed by Father Rafael Ferrer were active in the region. They established three missions—San Pedro de los Cofanes, Santa María, and Santa Cruz—in which it was estimated 6,500 Indians were collected.[19] Their conversion proved difficult because they were widely dispersed and lacked formal settlements.[20] Most likely groups headed by an individual cacique were patrilineal, with component families scattered over a broad area.[21] Polygamy was practiced, but it is not clear whether it was restricted to leaders.[22] Father Ferrer maintained that the Cofán, who included those of Pu and the Ica, numbered between 15,000 and 20,000 *almas*.[23] Some recent researchers have interpreted the figure of 15,000 as referring to tributary Indians and as such have estimated the total population at between 60,000 and 70,000.[24] Given the specific reference to almas in Ferrer's account and the absence of other reports of populations of this size, the total aboriginal population was probably nearer to 15,000.[25]

Coronado

In the early seventeenth century, Jesuit missionaries encountered the Coronado on the banks of the Coca River.[26] These Indians should not be confused with the Coronado to be found on the river Bobonaza; the term "Coronado" was used to describe the head decoration worn by Indians in both areas, although they were probably not related.[27] The Coronado have already been mentioned in connection with trade conducted by the Indians of Chapi in the Otavalo-Caranqui region, with whom they exchanged child slaves, monkeys, parrots, *pita,* and dried medicinal herbs, in return for salt, dogs, and mantas.[28] According to Ordóñez de Cevallos, they were not cultivators but lived by robbing their neighbors and fishing; as such, they were poor and had little to offer as tribute.[29] They were generally regarded as warlike.[30] Ordóñez de Cevallos estimated they numbered 3,000,[31] but in the early seventeenth century Jesuit missionaries considered them to number between 12,000 and 14,000.[32] The latter figure seems high, given the above descriptions of their culture and the absence of other references to this group. It is possible that the Jesuit figures encompassed a number of Quijo groups through whose territory they traveled, though the Coronado would have been easy to identify by their distinctive tonsure. Alternatively the figures may have included neighboring groups of whom the missionaries were aware but had not yet contacted. The discrepancy between the accounts is difficult to resolve, but for the reasons given, the lower figure of 3,000 estimated by Ordóñez de Cevallos is preferred.

Quijo

Within the first fifty years of conquest the Spanish had explored the Quijo region, founded towns, and distributed encomiendas. As early as 1564 the once densely settled region had been "destroyed" by expeditions, excessive tribute exactions, and epidemics;[33] the uprising provoked by Licenciado Diego de Ortegón's visita in 1576 resulted in yet further casualties. By the late sixteenth century, therefore, when the most detailed accounts were written, the Quijo had already experienced significant demographic and cultural changes.

The Quijo region was broadly bounded by the sierra and the Coca and Napo rivers.[34] Most contemporary and recent authors subdivide the Quijo region into four areas that centered on the the Coca Valley and three Spanish towns—Baeza, Archidona, and Avila.[35] These subregions appear to have been largely Spanish creations, for with the exception of those located nearest the sierra in Hatunquijos and around Baeza, who shared some characteristics with groups in the sierra,[36] cultural differences between other Indian groups in the rest of the region were small.[37] The Quijo region as a whole had strong links with the highlands. Even though the Inka never settled there permanently, it was the only part of the Oriente they explored.[38] Quechua was widely spoken during the early colonial period, but its use as a lingua franca probably postdates Spanish conquest.[39] The name "Quijo" is unknown among indigenous languages today, but Jijón y Caamaño argues that the few words noted by Ordóñez de Cevallos as being spoken in the Quijo region suggest the language was related to Colorado and hence with the Barbacoan subgroup of Chibcha.[40] Oberem, however, urges caution in assigning the Quijo language to a particular linguistic group on the basis of such limited evidence, especially since it is clear that many languages were spoken in the region.[41] At the same time, he cites evidence that a language spoken by some Quijo Indians was "in some words" similar to that spoken by Indians around Chapi who were probably Cofán.[42]

A major source of evidence for Quijo culture is the report of the visita conducted by Diego de Ortegón between 1576 and 1577, which is exceptional in the amount of ethnographic information it contains.[43] Despite the fact that its findings have been quoted extensively and were used as a partial basis for the well-known report written by the Conde de Lemus y Andrade in 1608, it is worth noting that Dr. Manuel Barros, commissioned to undertake a subsequent visita in 1587, criticized the conduct of Ortegón's inspection. Among other things, he reported that it had taken only forty days rather than a year, and that the oidor had not visited Indian villages in person.[44] Since Ortegón's description is fairly consistent with ethnographic details found in other accounts, it is assumed that he gleaned information from local encomenderos and other colonists, but some doubt exists concerning its accuracy and particularly the demographic details it contains.

The Quijo lived in small settlements located several miles apart, each comprising three or four houses.[45] Cieza de León noted that their houses were small,[46] but most other accounts suggest that each house contained a large number of people, which could refer to large families created through the practice of polygamy, but more likely it indicates the presence of extended families with each village housing a lineage.[47] Houses around Baeza and Avila were constructed of lath and mud and thatched with straw, but around Archidona, where the climate was warmer, houses were open-sided and roofed with palm leaves.[48]

From the little that is known of Quijo subsistence, efforts were concentrated in cultivation and hunting, rather than fishing, even though some small headwater pools were exploited and special expeditions were sometimes mounted downriver.[49] Manioc, sweet potatoes, and maize were cultivated, and in the cooler climate around Baeza, potatoes were grown.[50] Manioc was roasted and made into cassava bread and chicha.[51] Apart from this reference to cassava, there is no other evidence to suggest that it was the bitter variety of manioc that was cultivated. More likely, as Oberem suggests, the Quijo cultivated sweet manioc and, like the Maina, made from it a type of "pasta."[52] They also cultivated a wide variety of fruits, including lucumas, papayas, and guayabas, but it was the "granadillas de Quijos" that most impressed the Spanish.[53] At the same time, four leagues downriver from Baeza in the Coca Valley, the Quijo harvested coca three times a year. Coca, often masticated with wild tobacco and honey, was used as a stimulant, and dried leaves were traded with the sierra.[54]

Hunting was important, not only for subsistence, but also for trade. Animals hunted included tapirs, peccaries, monkeys, rats, and parrots and other birds.[55] Some were eaten, others kept as pets, and others traded both alive and as dried meat.[56] Around Archidona game was hunted using blowguns and poisoned arrows. Although the Quijo possessed dogs, it is not clear whether they raised them themselves or obtained them by trade from the sierra as did other groups in the Oriente, such as the Coronado.[57] Bees were raised in the Coca Valley, and honey was widely used,[58] but the only locally produced salt was a bitter variety extracted from wild plants;[59] probably some was traded with the sierra. Meanwhile fishing played only a minor role in the economy, although some fish were trapped in small pools and killed with *barbasco* and, like game, were dried and traded.[60]

Compared with many other groups of the Oriente, trade was highly developed among the Quijo, particularly those with easy access to the sierra such as those located on the route through Papallacta, Baeza, and Archidona.[61] Around Baeza there were markets, referred to as *gato,* where fairs were held every eight days. At these fairs clothing, gold jewelery, food, and other items, including slaves, were traded using *carato* as a medium of exchange.[62] Each unit of this monetary system comprised a string of twenty-four pieces of bone, probably from a rare animal, with each string worth the equivalent of one day's work.[63]

It is not clear at what stage trade developed with the sierra. Although the acquisition of trade goods, possibly coca and *canela,* motivated the Inka to explore the region, there is no evidence that they ever established permanent trading contacts there.[64] Nevertheless, trade had become so important, particularly in Hatunquijos, that its caciques, hoping to promote trade, encouraged the Spanish to establish a town there.[65] Apart from the slaves, coca, and food items mentioned, the other major products traded, particularly with the sierra, were canela and cotton. Wild canela was particularly abundant around Avila in the area called *los calientes,* where it was also cultivated.[66] The dried flowers were sold on strings for use in flavoring food and for medicinal purposes. In pre-Columbian times the qualities of canela from this region were widely known in the sierra, perhaps as far as Peru.[67] The region was also known for its textiles, even though, with the exception of the area around Archidona called "los Algodonales," cotton was not cultivated in Los Quijos. Inadequate supplies of local cotton were therefore supplemented by cotton imported from the sierra, and the cotton cloth they manufactured became an important item of trade.[68] Because of local shortages of cotton cloth, many Indians wore bark cloth, and those in Archidona went naked except for a small cotton apron.[69] Cotton clothing was more rudimentary than that worn by the Omagua, but like them, they also practiced head deformation[70] and wore gold jewelry.[71] The latter was manufactured locally from gold obtained from nearby mines, such as those at Cuduceta (Conduceta), located eighteen leagues from Baeza, and the Gabata mine in the Coca Valley, with the gold being refined in small domestic smelteries.[72]

With the exception of Indians around Archidona who lived in the area known as "los calientes" and who possessed no leaders but resided in small kinship groups, the Quijo comprised a large number of "caciquillos." While these groups sometimes formed war alliances, and some had kinship ties with groups in the sierra,[73] there was no overarching political structure that bound them together. Each lineage of about 100 or 200 Indians was headed by a leader, whose position may have been hereditary.[74] Quispa Senacato described himself to Ordóñez de Cevallos as the head of his lineage as all his ancestors had been,[75] but in other cases Ortegón found that the only leaders respected were those who provided the most food and drink.[76] While the superior status of leaders was reflected in the possession of twice as many wives as commoners—four, six, or more[77]—their small number of subjects suggests that the authority they exercised was probably limited. Nevertheless, Ortegón observed that commoners provided their leaders with food and services, such as cultivating their plots and building their houses,[78] and Ordóñez de Cevallos maintained that without their leaders, they were very submissive.[79]

Other leaders included war leaders. Some of these leaders, like Beto and Guami, who led the uprising in 1578, also functioned as shamans.[80] War leaders held office only for the duration of wars, after which they were divested of their positions.[81] Warfare appears to have been fairly common among the Quijo, although it is not known against whom the wars were conducted.[82] They possessed a wide range of weapons including spears, spear-throwers, lances, darts, clubs, slings, shields, and wooden swords and axes. They also hurled stones from precipices or trees and constructed pits and moats.[83] Following victory, the arms and legs of victims were consumed by caciques, and their hands and heads displayed as trophies, while prisoners of war were kept as slaves.[84] Other slaves were obtained by trade, such that slavery appears to have been quite common, although it is not clear whether the ownership of slaves was restricted to those of higher rank. Slaves were commonly employed in cultivation.[85]

Almost all the evidence for life-cycle rites comes from Ortegón's visita. Some social practices he describes clearly functioned to ensure the survival of the group, although it may not always have been their intention. Following childbirth, the father went on a strict fast, consuming only "vino de yuca."[86] This would have favored maternal nutrition and, through lactation, aided infant survival. In the same way, the practice of infanticide, particularly for twins or to achieve child spacing, would have ensured that at least one infant lived, albeit at the expense of others, who in any case might not have survived. Dead infants were often buried in jars, a practice confirmed by archaeological evidence.[87] Interest in ensuring the survival of the group may be inferred from the premarital testing of the ability of individuals to raise children. Males had to pay a bride price in the form of chaquira, and if the woman's family consented to the marriage, the groom had to provide wood, straw, and food before the bride could be taken to his home.[88] The extravagant ceremonies lasting twenty to thirty days that accompanied the birth of a child also suggest that population increase was regarded favorably. Death was not accompanied by mourning; rather, dancing and singing accompanied burials, when bodies were generally interred beneath houses. Sometimes they were embalmed with pitch and then smoked, and gold and chaquira were placed in their intestines.[89]

The Quijo worshiped natural objects, such as trees and birds, and were described as "great witches and fortune-tellers."[90] Their shamans, often called *pendes,* were said to speak with the devil and could bring rain, raise people from the dead, and convert men into fields and vice versa.[91] To aid divination and to cure illness, they made extensive use of herbs and stimulants. The services of a shaman were "bought" through gifts, including clothing. Fiestas were common events, at which large quantities of chicha were consumed and stimulants widely used.[92] They were said to become so drunk that sometimes they killed each other. Among other events, they accompanied life-cycle rites, victory in war, and the divestiture of a leader.

Even though the population of the Quijo region declined rapidly in the early years of conquest, an unusually large number of early colonial accounts provide estimates for the aboriginal population.[93] Even though the earliest accounts lack precise population estimates, they indicate the region was densely settled. The earliest estimate, in 1538 by Gonzalo Díaz de Pineda, claimed that there were some 15,000 Indians in those parts of the region known as Cabi and Guarozta.[94] Later accounts of the pacification of Los Quijos in 1559 by Gil Ramírez Dávalos and others suggest that the population was between 40,000 and 50,000, which included "all the caciques of the provinces of çumaco, and canela, and coca."[95] These figures may have been exaggerated to magnify the achievements of the conquerors, for slightly lower figures for the contact population were suggested in the early seventeenth century.[96] In 1608 the Conde de Lemus y Andrade estimated that when the province was pacified by Gil Ramírez Dávalos, it had possessed 30,000 Indians,[97] and in 1626 the governor of Quijos, Alvaro de Cárdenas, similarly estimated there had been 35,000 Indians.[98] More detailed accounts of the tributary population of the region in the sixteenth century suggest that the latter estimates were probably fairly accurate. Oberem accepts Conde de Lemus y Andrade's estimate of 30,000 for the province of Quijos in 1559 but deducts 4,000 for the Jívaro who lived near Macas in the southern part of the region.[99]

An aboriginal population estimate of 26,000 would give an average population density of 2.0 persons per square kilometer.[100] This is considerably higher than the density suggested by Denevan for other groups who inhabited the high selva such as the Jívaro to the south.[101] Although the culture of the two groups was similar in many respects, hunting appears to have been more productive in the Quijo region, where the subsistence base was also extended by trade. Population estimates for the sixteenth century suggest that the aboriginal population region may well have been even higher, perhaps in the order of 35,000.

Macas

Little is known about the pre-Columbian inhabitants of the region to the south of the river Napo as far as the river Paute, though it appears that

many were related to sierran groups. (See Map 15 in chapter 15 below).
Most is known about the Macas, who lived in the southern part of the region
centering on the Upano Valley and were probably related to the Cañar
living in the highlands to the southwest. In the highlands to the northwest
were the Puruhá, and Taylor suggests that in pre-Columbian times Puruhá groups may have been living in the vicinity of the Palora River. They
may have comprised pre-Inkan lowland colonies exploiting the tropical
environment or have been refugees from Inka rule who settled in this
inaccessible region. It has been suggested they may have been the Huam-
boyas who appear in eighteenth-century documentary accounts of the
region.[102] In the absence of earlier references to them it is impossible to
estimate their numbers, if indeed they inhabited this region at the time of
Spanish conquest. The area to the north between the Pastaza and Napo
rivers appears to have been uninhabited, or at least was not occupied by
any one particular cultural group. The region and its inhabitants came to
be known in the colonial period as Canelos. The consensus is that the
Canelo emerged during the colonial period as a mixed group incorporat-
ing fugitive Indians from the sierra and Los Quijos, as well as some Zaparo
and Jívaro.[103] Whether the region was a zone of refuge from Inka rule in
pre-Columbian times is unknown. In the absence of further information,
the following discussion will consider only the Macas, though it is likely
that at the time of Spanish conquest at least some Indians inhabited the
region between them and the Quijo.

The province of Macas is mentioned in the early literature, very often
in association with Quizna, as having been conquered by the Inka. During
the conquest of the Cañar, according to Montesinos, the Cañar leader
Dumma sought help from the caciques of "Macas, Quizna, and Pumallacta,"
while Garcilaso de la Vega relates that Tupa Inca Yupanqui conquered
"Chanchan, Moca, Quesna, and Pumallacta."[104] Sarmiento de Gamboa,
however, attributes their conquest to Huayna Capac, who entered the
region "conquering the Macas Indians, and the borders of the Cañar and
Quizna."[105] Thus the Macas and Quizna appear to have bordered on the
Cañar, with whom they had close contacts. The former lived at lower
elevations and may have been Cañar who had migrated to exploit the
tropical environment. Equally well they could have been small independent chiefdoms who over a long period had been subjected to Cañar
influence and with whom they traded and allied in war.

Details of early Spanish expeditions to the region are lacking.[106] Vir-
tually nothing is known of Rodrigo Núñez de Bonilla's attempt to conquer
the provinces of Macas and Quizna in 1540,[107] and even the more fully
documented accounts of Hernando de Benavente's expedition in 1549 contain little material of ethnographic interest.[108] Benavente entered Macas
through Zuña, passing to Paira, located eight to twelve leagues away,

where he found 100 houses. From there he passed to Moy and Sumaguallí, where he encountered a few Indians. Subsequently he dispatched an expedition to Chapico, where about 2,000 naked Indians were living in houses dispersed a quarter and a half a league apart and subsisting on fish, maize, and other crops. This brief description suggests the region was densely populated, which might be related to more abundant riverine resources and the cultivation of maize. From there the expedition proceeded to Guallapa, where it was met by a further 800 Indians who also lived in dispersed settlements, after which it entered Xíbaro territory. Slightly later, in 1563, Melchor Vázquez de Avila, governor of Los Quijos, seeking to consolidate his claim to the area, authorized Juan de Salinas Guinea to establish the town of Nuestra Señora del Rosario.[109] It was founded at Sumaguallí in the presence of caciques from the surrounding region who were anxious for Spanish protection against neighboring "indios caribes" from the provinces of Pallique and Xíbaro, as well as from highland raiders and even from other groups of Macas.

In an examination of toponyms and anthroponyms contained in the accounts of these expeditions, Taylor and Descola draw attention to the lack of Jívaro words and suggest that Cañar was widely spoken in the region from Zuña to Guallapa, which included Sumaguallí.[110] Furthermore, names contained in a dispute over encomiendas in the jurisdiction of Sevilla del Oro are not Jívaroan, and some have suffixes -cay, which suggests an association with the Cañar.[111] The relationship between the Cañar and the Indians of Macas is also suggested by a reference to "Cañar Indians from Sumaguallí" in an account of an encomienda in 1630 and by the presence of ceramics in the Middle Upano Valley that have similarities with those in the neighboring highland province of Azuay.[112]

Indians of the Macas region seem to have formed relatively small social groups. Although they could ally together in war or for trade, at times they were hostile to each other; there is no evidence for a supralocal organization such as existed among the Cañar in the highlands.[113] Judging by the accounts of early expeditions and the size of encomiendas distributed in the region, these groups may have comprised several thousand Indians. An early encomienda granted to Rodrigo Núñez de Bonilla included 400 Indians in the "province of Macas" and 350 in "the province of Quizna."[114] In 1643 an encomendero of Sevilla del Oro suggested that when the town was founded in 1575, there had been 3,000 tributary Indians in its jurisdiction.[115] Assuming demographic decline during the sixteenth century, these figures suggest that the region's aboriginal population may have been a conservative 10,000 but was probably higher.[116]

Jívaro

At the time of Spanish conquest the Jívaro constituted one of the most extensive cultural-linguistic groups in eastern Ecuador. They were closely related to the Kandoshi-Candoa, who were more widespread in Peru.[117] In Ecuador two groups of Jívaro may be distinguished. One group comprising the Bracamoro and the Xíbaro inhabited the high selva between 500 and 1,500 meters, while other groups, who will be referred to here as Jívaro, lived in the lowlands.[118]

BRACAMORO AND XÍBARO

The Bracamoro and Xíbaro were culturally similar, but they spoke distinct dialects. The Bracamoro lived to the south of the Xíbaro in the valleys of the Upper Zamora and Chinchipe, though within this broad region there were enclaves of Palta, and possibly Cañar.[119] Tupa Inca Yupanqui and Huayna Capac both attempted to conquer the Bracamoro but were decisively routed.[120] Spanish interest in gold drew early expeditions to the region. In 1535 Alonso de Alvarado, approaching the area from Chachapoyas, explored the borders of the region around the mouth of the Chinchipe, and between 1545 and 1546 Juan Porcel explored the left bank of the Marañón and the Lower Chinchipe, founding the short-lived town of Nueva Jerez de la Frontera.[121] Subsequently in 1548 Diego Palomino was encharged with the conquest of Bracamoros, but he only explored the Lower Chinchipe and the province of Cherinos, the latter being inhabited by the Chirino.[122] It was not until 1557, when Juan de Salinas established the towns of Valladolid in the Upper Chinchipe Valley and Loyola in the Valley of Cumbinama (probably the valley of the river Vergel), that permanent Spanish settlements were founded in the region.[123] The Indians around both settlements were said to be similar in language and customs. Meanwhile further north in the early 1540s Pedro de Vergara had spent two or three years exploring the region around the Upper Zamora, founding a town whose name and location remain unknown.[124] It was not until the end of the decade that the town of Zamora de los Alcaides was founded by Alonso de Mercadillo and Hernando de Benavente.[125] The earliest ethnographic details of the inhabitants of this region, which became known as the "province of Nambija," are to be found in the *relaciones geográficas* written in 1582.

North of the Bracamoro, other Jívaro Indians, referred to in documentary sources as Xíbaro, were living south of the river Paute and north of the river Cuyes-Bomboiza. This region was probably explored by Pedro de Vergara in the 1540s,[126] but no details of this expedition remain. In 1549 Hernando de Benavente's expedition encountered Xíbaro south of the

Paute River. They extended south as far as another major river that he was unable to pass, possibly the Bomboiza or Zamora, on the other side of which were Indians who, in contrast to the naked Xíbaro, wore "camisetas e mantas."[127] However, in 1563 Salinas Guinea encountered "caribes de Pallique" living north of the Paute River. If they were Jívaro, as Taylor and Descola suggest, then the northern boundary of Jívaro territory should be extended further north beyond the Paute River.[128]

The Bracamoro are consistently described in early accounts as "indios de behetría," living in small dispersed settlements, which at most contained several hundred inhabitants, but more often less.[129] Settlements comprised single or several multifamily houses, such as exist today.[130] Around Zamora, houses were built of wooden posts covered with straw, although some larger houses had walls.[131] Barbacoas and hammocks were used for sleeping. Since Jívaro groups lived in a state of constant warfare, their settlements were located on easily defended high points away from riverbanks.[132]

The Bracamoro lived primarily off the products of cultivation. Although fishing and hunting were practiced, they played a less important role in the economy than in the lowlands. Even though shifting cultivation was the norm, around Valladolid the land was plowed, probably with *takllas*.[133] Here in the Upper Chinchipe maize appears to have been more important than around Zamora, where root crops predominated.[134] In the Chinchipe Valley three harvests were possible in fourteen months, but around Zamora even the most fertile riverbanks could yield only two crops a year.[135] Chicha was made from maize and manioc, and drinking bouts were held to celebrate victory in war, the death of a leader, and on many other occasions.[136] Sweet potatoes, *ñames* (*Dioscorea* sp.), peanuts, and beans were also grown,[137] together with fruits such as guabas, guayabas, caimitos, avocados, anonas, granadillas, pineapples, and, around Zamora, plantains.[138]

Hunting and fishing are not mentioned in early documents, and most protein was probably obtained from vegetable sources, notably from seed crops such as maize, beans, and peanuts. Fishing was limited because of the fast-flowing rivers, and the quantity of game available was variable, being absent in very wet or dry conditions and easily depleted, even in areas where it was relatively abundant.[139] Indeed, Denevan suggests that the small size and unstable character of settlements may reflect the dispersal of sources of animal protein. Like other groups of the montaña, the Bracamoro and Xíbaro probably compensated in part for shortages of protein by exploiting insects such as ants, grubs, beetles, and snails. That there was a shortage of protein is suggested by the great esteem attached to domesticated animals, both in pre-Columbian and in colonial times. Llamas and guinea pigs were raised widely and highly sought after as war booty,[140] and in the early colonial period domesticated animals constituted the main items obtained by trade from the Palta and Cañar in the highlands.[141] It has been suggested, however, that the preference for meat protein may be cultural, for today other sources of protein, notably vegetable sources such as maize, peanuts, and wild seeds are widely available, but underused.[142]

The Jívaro were notorious for their warlike character, although those around Loyola were considered to be "algo más domésticos."[143] Feuds occurred between neighboring communities, and conflict was common between groups speaking different dialects or subdialects. Nevertheless, groups often united together to oppose common enemies such as the Cañar, Inka, or Spanish.[144] Warfare was stimulated by the need to avenge wrongs and to acquire social status. The hope of acquiring llamas, guinea pigs, and other booty provided added incentive. An integral part of warfare was the seizure of enemy heads, which were shrunk and kept as trophies.[145] Weapons included lances, shields, and copper axes, the latter probably being obtained through trade with the Cañar in the highlands.[146] The effect of continual warfare on population levels will be considered later.

Most accounts suggest that the Jívaro who lived in the montaña possessed war leaders who were selected only as need required; indeed contemporary observers attributed the state of constant warfare to the lack of effective native leadership.[147] Only around Zamora did leaders other than war leaders command respect, and here the succession passed primarily to a brother, or else to a nephew or son.[148] Similarly most observers considered the Indians to have no religion, though they worshiped the sun as a natural life-giving object; they possessed no idols and held few ceremonies.[149] Only among the Rabona, a subgroup of the Bracamoro, is there mention of a creator of earth and heaven called Cumbanas (Cumbanamas) and of a belief in bird songs as omens.[150]

JÍVARO

Although the lowland Jívaro inhabited the low selva, since they were related to the Bracamoro and Xíbaro they are considered here. They were encountered at a later date than those of the montaña. In 1557 Juan de Salinas passed over the Sierra de Cóndor into the Coraguana Valley, which according to place-names must have been the valley of the Cenepa. Here Indians were different in "language, clothing, and customs" from those around Loyola and Valladolid.[151] From there he passed to the Valley of Giuarra, where he encountered Indians who were the same as those he had met in the Coraguana Valley. The Valley of Giuarra was probably the Lower Santiago River, where in 1557 he founded the town of Santiago de las Montañas.[152] Salinas continued south over the Marañón to the province of Cungarapas, where Indians spoke a similar language and where he founded the town of Santa María de Nieva.

Early accounts of the lowland Jívaro contain few ethnographic details, though it is clear that they differed in a number of ways from those in the montaña. Lowland groups placed greater emphasis on the cultivation of root crops, and on fishing and hunting, from which they derived maybe 80 percent of their protein.[153] It has been suggested that the preference for animal protein may be cultural, since protein-rich crops such as maize, beans, and peanuts can be grown in the region.[154] According to Pablo Maroni, a Jesuit missionary, the area inhabited by the Jívaro was known as the "land of hunger" because the soil was infertile and fish and game more limited than on the Marañón.[155] Peccaries, deer, and tapirs were hunted with lassos and spear-throwers; llamas were relatively scarce. In times of hunger, insects and grubs would have been eaten, as well as chonta palm nuts, as is the case today.[156] They grew cotton, which they manufactured into cloth, but they often went naked.[157] They also extracted salt from rock salt mines and springs and traded it with groups downriver.[158] Indians from the highlands around Loja and Cuenca also traded in this region, quite likely for salt.[159] The lowland Jívaro appear to have been at home on the rivers, traveling in large canoes propelled by forty to fifty rowers.[160]

Like Jívaro groups of the montaña, the only leaders possessed by groups in the lowlands were those who were the heads of their own villages. Leaders were chosen for their military prowess, and their positions were not hereditary, neither did they enjoy any economic or social privileges.[161] Although they banded together to conduct raids and obtain heads, no evidence exists for the presence of a supralocal political organization. Possibly because of their lack of coordinated resistance they were initially considered by the Spanish to be less warlike than those of the montaña.[162] Socially the Jívaro formed a series of endogamous groups that often focused on a major river. Each comprised dispersed households, sometimes in groups of two or three, each containing between ten and thirty individuals. One Jesuit venture into Jívaro territory at the beginning of the seventeenth century encountered eight rancherías with 190 *fogones,* or hearths.[163] The endogamous areas were larger in interfluvial regions than along the rivers and were separated by buffer zones or no-man's-lands. It has been suggested these territorial arrangements functioned to maintain control of resources, especially game.[164] Endogamous groups maintained hostile relations with each other, though exogamous marriages could occur through the capture of women.

Considering the Jívaro population as a whole at the time of Spanish conquest, evidence is biased toward groups living in the montaña. The most extensive account of the aboriginal population is contained in a memorial presented in 1577 by Juan de Estrada, a vecino of Loyola, criticizing the administration of Juan de Salinas.[165] Various witnesses testified that the gobernación of Yaguarzongo and Pacamoros had originally contained between 20,000 and 30,000 Indians. They claimed the region around Loyola (Cumbinama), which had possessed between 8,000 and 10,000 Indians, had been more highly populated than Valladolid, where witnesses testified there had been only 6,000 or 7,000. Unfortunately the memorial provides only sketchy information on Santiago de las Montañas and nothing on other areas within the gobernación. Furthermore, it does not include the jurisdiction of Zamora, which at that time formed part of the corregimiento of Loja. An account by Juan Canelas Albarrán in 1586 claimed that when he had visited the gobernación of Yaguarzongo and Pacamoros in 1576, there were 40,000 Indians. Of those, 25,500 souls were around Valladolid, Loyola, and Santiago de Montañas, with a further 4,000 around Logroño, and 3,000 "Jíbaros."[166] For the area under consideration here, this would give a figure of approximately 32,500 souls, which includes a small number of non-Indians. This figure may appear high, but it was apparently obtained from firsthand observations, and the figures Canelas Albarrán provides are fairly consistent with Governor Aldrete's report in 1580, which indicated that there were 19,627 encomienda Indians around the same cities.[167] The figures given by Aldrete must represent minimum numbers, since it was noted that unpacified Indians had not been inspected.[168] They also exclude the Xíbaro, who, according to Hernando de Benavente in 1549, numbered 1,000.[169] Altogether the figures suggest there were at least 25,000 Indians in the gobernación of Yaguarzongo and Pacamoros in the 1580s, a figure given further credence by witnesses who testified that it contained between 8,000 and 9,000 tributary Indians.[170]

To obtain a total figure for all Jívaro groups, those living around Zamora should also be included. In 1622 the corregidor of Loja, Francisco Mexía Sandoval, claimed that the province of Zamora had once possessed 15,000 to 16,000 Indians.[171] This estimate is fairly consistent with the number of Indians listed for Zamora by the secretary of the Audiencia of Lima, Pedro de Avendaño in 1561. He recorded that the jurisdiction of Zamora possessed 11,222 Indians, of whom 6,093 paid tribute.[172] The numbers listed refer to an unspecified time before that date and probably do not reflect the impact of the 1558 smallpox epidemic. Other accounts drawing on information from the 1560s give Zamora a tributary population of between 5,000 and 8,000 Indians. A list of towns and their Indian subjects in the Audiencia of Quito, possibly drawn up in 1567, recorded that Zamora had twenty-seven encomenderos and 8,000 tributary Indians.[173] López de Velasco suggests that there were 5,000 "indios tributarios." The source and date of his information is unknown, but like most of his other figures, it probably corresponds to a much earlier date.[174] On the basis of these accounts it is reasonable to suggest about 20,000 Indians may have inhabited the province of Zamora at the time of Spanish conquest, an estimate also made by Father Gerónimo de Escobar at the end of the century.[175]

Taylor estimates that at the time of Spanish conquest the Jívaro numbered between 29,000 and 32,000, with the majority (24,000) living in the montaña and the Marañón.[176] It seems likely that her estimate was based on Governor Aldrete's report, in which case it assumes only limited demographic decline between contact and 1580 and implies that the region had escaped the ravages of disease. When Juan de Salinas founded the town of Santiago de las Montañas in 1557, he was accompanied by "many sick people,"[177] who might have been been suffering from smallpox, which raged in the sierra the following year.[178] Even if it is assumed, though unlikely, that epidemics did not reach the region until the late 1580s, the figures presented suggest larger numbers at that time and argue for a higher figure of about 50,000 Jívaro or more at the time of Spanish conquest. Denevan includes the Jívaro among inhabitants of the high selva, to which he would attach a population density of 1.2 persons per square kilometer. His population density estimate would suggest an aboriginal population of about 49,900,[179] indicating that the figure of 50,000 derived from documentary sources might not have been impossible. However, Denevan takes no account of the fact that some Jívaro inhabited the low selva and probably would not have achieved such high population densities. Nevertheless, assuming that one-quarter of Jívaro territory was within the low selva, the estimated aboriginal population would still be about 40,000.[180]

Population levels were said to be low because of continual warfare.[181] Rivet reported that a war between two Xíbaro groups in the Upano Basin in 1889 reduced their combined populations by over half.[182] Even today accidents and feuds inspired by sorcery and violent death may account for over 30 percent of adult deaths.[183] Losses were greatest among men, though women were also slain or captured. Interestingly censuses for fourteen Bracamoro towns in the province of Nambija in 1582 reveal a predominance of men rather than women (100:83).[184] No reason is given for this imbalance in the sex ratio, but it could reflect inaccurate recording, a primary concern with male tributary Indians, or, less likely, the removal of females to work in personal service. Inasmuch as it reflected the sex structure at the time, it is likely to have been a colonial creation.

The excessive mortality among men was compensated for in part by the practice of polygamy.[185] Although the extent of polygamy is not known, it probably enabled most women to bear children. Nevertheless, women in polygamous relationships tend to bear fewer children than those in mo-

nogamous unions, so that although polygamy compensated to a degree for
the shortage of men, the reproductive resources of the group would have
been underutilized. Meanwhile, the seizure of women, while ostensibly
aiding the fertility of a community, probably operated to redistribute
rather than reduce or expand total reproductive resources. Other practices helped to maximize reproductive years. Sexual intercourse probably
began at puberty, and should a woman have lost her husband in conflict,
the requirement of the levirate would have reduced the loss of reproductive capacity.[186] Other practices also helped maintain fertility. Like the
Quijo, infanticide was relatively uncommon, being restricted to twins and
deformed infants. Similarly, prolonged lactation,[187] while controlling fertility, might have ensured the survival of infants in circumstances where
inadequate food supplies might have threatened weaned infants. Modern
studies of nutrition and serological tests among the Jívaro indicate shortages of protein,[188] and although it cannot be inferred that this was the case
in pre-Columbian times, the documentary evidence already presented
supports this proposition. But not all practices promoted population increase. The Jívaro abstain from sexual intercourse on many occasions,
often for prolonged periods.[189] With such heavy losses in warfare that
were only partially compensated for by practices favoring population
growth, the Jívaro must have struggled to reproduce themselves, and
population levels must have been highly variable. Indeed, the small number of children surviving in the sixteenth century was noted by contemporary observers.[190]

HIGH SELVA/VÁRZEA

Omagua

The Omagua, who belonged to the Tupí-Guaraní linguistic stock, were one
of the most extensive and populous Indian groups inhabiting the Amazon
Basin.[191] At the time of Spanish conquest they were expanding westward,
driven by population pressure and/or the desire for war or trade.[192] They
may have reached the Lower Coca River in the twelfth or thirteenth
centuries; certainly they were living there at the beginning of the sixteenth century, when they were encountered by Huayna Capac.[193] This
outlier of Omagua Indians was later known as the Omagua-Yété; two other
groups of Omagua were living downriver on the Napo and Amazon. The
precise location of these three groups is not clear from early accounts,[194]
even though the Omagua can be traced more easily than most groups in
the northern Oriente, since it was the only one to practice head deformation and wear painted cotton clothes. Because of the Omaguas' fine pot-

tery, sophisticated subsistence technology, large populations, and political organization, the Spanish regarded them as more civilized than their neighbors.

Gonzalo Pizarro was the first to encounter the Omagua on the Lower Coca, arriving there in 1541.[195] However, accounts of Francisco de Orellana's subsequent journey down the Napo and Amazon locate the Omagua ("Oniguayal" or "Homagua") below the river Trinidad (probably the Juruá River), which is well downriver and to the east of areas later identified as being inhabited by Omagua. There seems little doubt, however, that the provinces of Aparia menor and Aparia el grande described in the accounts of the journey written by Gaspar de Carvajal and Francisco de Oviedo were also Omagua who lived on the Napo and Amazon respectively.[196] The latter Indians were referred to as Carari and Manicuri (or Maricuri) in reports of Pedro de Ursúa's expedition in 1560. The three groups of Omagua on the Coca, Napo, and Amazon were separated from each other by long stretches of unoccupied territory. Observers reported that these stretches were uninhabited because of wars with neighbors,[197] but some parts that were permanently inundated and of limited agricultural potential were probably bypassed in favor of others with better resources.[198]

Living in different habitats, the subsistence patterns and populations of these different groups of Omagua would have differed to some degree, although colonial sources are insufficiently detailed to confirm this. Fishing and the capture of turtles and manatees were important subsistence activities on the Amazon, but they were more limited in the faster flowing headwaters. Hence the Omagua-Yété probably depended more on game and protein-rich crops such as maize and beans, even though cultivation was probably less productive there than on the extensive floodplains of the Amazon. For reasons already discussed, resources downriver, although more variable seasonally and spatially, were more abundant, providing the basis for larger and more highly organized populations. Since the Omagua living on the Amazon fall outside the study area, they will not be discussed in detail but will be referred to where evidence of their culture can illuminate our knowledge of the other two groups.

Omagua-Yété

Toribio de Ortiguera's accounts of Huayna Capac's and Gonzalo Pizarro's encounters with Omagua-Yété in what was probably the Coca Valley indicate that they wore cotton tunics, had long hair, practiced head deformation, and wore gold jewelery.[199] They cultivated maize, manioc, sweet potatoes, cotton, and calabashes, and they possessed many birds and fished. Their weapons included slings, lances, and clubs. According to

Gaspar de Carvajal, the riverbanks were continuously populated for fifty leagues.[200]

Little is known of the social and political characteristics of the Omagua-Yété. When Diego de Ortegón visited Los Quijos in 1576, he reported that downriver there were Indians called "Tapaca, Magua, and Eguata" who all wore painted clothes and gold ornaments. These groups were probably subdivisions of the Omagua who were headed by distinct leaders.[201] In common with other groups of Omagua, they constantly fought their neighbors to acquire slaves and booty.[202] When Pedro Ordóñez de Cevallos was converting Indians in the Coca Valley in the 1590s, he managed to persuade the Omagua to desist from an incursion into Coronado territory by offering them gifts in compensation for goods they would have acquired.

At the same Ordóñez de Cevallos claimed that there were 5,000 converted "Maguas," and another 200 converted "Omaguas" further downriver.[203] Grohs suggests that these figures were exaggerated, since later accounts indicate much smaller numbers in this region.[204] However, the smaller numbers registered in later accounts would have reflected the impact of epidemics and the dispersion of the Omagua from this area toward the Napo River and later the Amazon, following attempts to involve them in panning gold in the river Sunu at the beginning of the early seventeenth century.[205] Nevertheless, at that time Jesuit missionaries exploring the river Coca were still impressed by their numbers, which they described as "muchísimos," even though it seems unlikely that, as the parish priest of Avila claimed, one Omagua chief possessed 10,000 subjects.[206] An aboriginal population of about 10,000 does not seem unreasonable.[207]

Omagua of the River Napo

In the seventeenth century the Encabellado and Abijira inhabited the Napo Valley between its junctions with the Aguarico and Curaray rivers, as well as the Lower Curaray, but in the sixteenth century the Napo Valley appears to have been inhabited by the Omagua, who later moved to the headwaters of the Tiputini or to the Putumayo or Amazon.[208] When Francisco de Orellana's expedition passed down the river Napo in 1541, Gaspar de Carvajal noted that the first stretch of the river after its confluence with the Aguarico was uninhabited because of wars with neighboring groups, but near its confluence with the Curaray, he encountered a village of Irimara Indians (Irimaraezes) with about 200 "vecinos."[209] This settlement formed part of what was called the province of Aparia menor, which comprised eleven or thirteen leaders who were subordinate to an overall chief. The houses were built on stilts along the river, forming rows of up to sixty houses.[210] By 1619, when Alonso de Miranda initiated entradas in this region, the Omagua, Encabellado, and Abijira were all living there. Unfortunately eyewitnesses on these entradas generally failed to distinguish between them, and descriptions of their cultures do not depart substantially from those already noted for the Omagua.[211] The Spanish were impressed by their painted cotton clothes, which they often wore with gold jewelery and chaquira. One witness claimed they possessed temples of the sun, with offerings of feathers, jewelery, and precious stones, but this may have been little more than wishful thinking. The cotton cloth they produced was widely traded, particularly for gold, and it was probably through the Omagua that groups on the Amazon obtained gold jewelery from the Quijo.[212] They also traded their fine painted and glazed pottery.[213] The Omagua of the Amazon were the river's greatest traders, to the extent that the Spanish claimed that trade ceased once they had passed out of Omagua territory.[214] Leaders were said to be chosen by the head of the province and to have the authority to carry out punishments, including death. As such, they were highly respected. Weapons included lances, clubs, and shields of tapir hide that bore their leaders' insignia.

The Omagua cultivated maize, beans, peanuts, sweet potatoes, and manioc, making the latter into bread and wine.[215] The land was said to be very fertile, and the fruit and fish abundant. Subsistence activities were concentrated in the summer, when the land was cleared and the lowering of the river allowed fish to be caught in pools using barbasco. At this time they collected and stored food for winter. Like groups on the Amazon, they probably stored maize and preserved manioc by burying it for up to several years, apparently preferring to eat it in a half-putrified state. Meat and fish may have been dried or smoked, or even stored in turtle or manatee oil, as they were on the Amazon.[216] Traps, pits, and spear-throwers were used for hunting, which was said to be easy. The climate was described as very healthy, being not too hot or too cold, and free of insects. Hence people lived to an old age and there were many children who grew robust because of prolonged breast-feeding.[217] The same witnesses estimated that the area as a whole, which is taken to be the region around the Coca and Napo rivers, but not east of the confluence of the latter river with the Amazon, possessed 100,000 or 150,000 Indians. These estimates may seem high, but they were firsthand observations and included the Omagua of the Coca and Napo already discussed, the Encabellado and Abijira to be examined below, and many other neighboring groups such as the Iquito and Zapara. Estimates for the Omagua on the river Napo are difficult to extract from these figures. They were more extensive than the Omagua-Yété of the Coca Valley but do not appear to have been as populous as those on the Amazon. An aboriginal population of about 15,000 might be appropriate.

Taken together, the Omagua of the Coca and Napo rivers may have numbered about 25,000. Denevan initially suggested an average density for the várzea of 5.3 persons per square kilometer and is currently arguing for 9.1 for the major tributaries of the Amazon.[218] However, the floodplain was more limited in the headwaters, even though cultivation there would have been more productive than on the interfluves. I am doubtful that such high densities could have been supported in these areas, and the population density of 2.84 per square kilometer estimated here for the Omagua would tend to support this argument. Some researchers have suggested that at the time of Spanish conquest the Omagua were suffering from overpopulation.[219] They have pointed to their westward expansion and warlike stance, as well as their practice of infanticide to achieve child spacing or the desired sex of an infant. Unfortunately the evidence presented throws little light on this proposition.

LOW SELVA

Tucanoan Groups: Encabellado, Abijira, and Payagua

There are no references to the Encabellado and Abijira in the Napo Valley in the sixteenth century, when the region was inhabited by the Omagua,[220] but in the early seventeenth century the Jesuit fathers Rafael Ferrer and Fernando Arnulfini encountered them downriver from the Cofán.[221] The Encabellado and Abijira, although culturally distinct, both belonged to the Tucanoan linguistic stock, and in the late seventeenth century the Abijira apparently understood the Coronado and Gae who spoke Zaparoan.[222] The Encabellado were given their name by the Spanish, who were impressed by their well-kept, long hair; Icajnate was their native name.[223]

During the early 1620s the Encabellado and Abijira were subject to enslaving raids from Alcalá del Río and were contacted by Jesuit missionaries.[224] It was not until 1635 that Franciscan missionaries, headed by Father Pedro Pecador in the company of Captain Juan de Palacios, began working among these two groups.[225] At the end of the same year another five missionaries left Quito to establish a settlement in the province of "Abixiras" but, discouraged by the difficult journey to the area from San Pedro de los Cofanes, they decided to join Father Pecador, who was working among the Encabellado. From there, further expeditions were mounted downriver, and it is assumed they encountered the Abijira, although they are not specifically mentioned. One of the missionaries, Father Laureano de la Cruz, compiled a detailed account of Encabellado culture.[226]

The Encabellado were located to the north of the river Napo as far as the river Putumayo, occupying a strip about thirty leagues wide, which extended from the mouth of the river Aguarico downriver for 150 leagues, which, according to Steward, was as far as its junction with the Tamboryacu.[227] On the north bank of the Napo further east were the Payagua, who were related to the Encabellado.[228] The Abijira were to be found from the southern bank of the river Napo to the Curaray. Originally they were located further downriver, but in the seventeenth century they extended for 50 leagues beginning at the same place in the west as the province of Encabellado.[229] Settlements were distributed a quarter, a half, or a league apart and were located several leagues from the river, suggesting that compared with the Omagua, their subsistence patterns were less oriented toward riverine resources.[230] According to Father Laureano de la Cruz, the settlements of the Encabellado were small, comprising about fifty to sixty people in total. These were contained in four, six, or eight houses, each with one or two Indians and their wives and children. Some Indians were polygamous, but most had only one wife. Houses were built of wood and covered with palm leaves, and hammocks were used. Large houses that could hold 300 or 400 people were used for major feasts. There appears to have been little stratification among the Encabellado, who, it was said, possessed no leaders or government; only the shaman, who was generally an old person, was accorded some respect. They possessed no idols.

The Encabellado cultivated maize, palms, and manioc, which they made into cassava. They currently grate bitter manioc, using thorn-studded graters,[231] but it is not certain that the bitter variety was cultivated in the early colonial period. Today cultivation supplies most of their dietary needs, but in the colonial period they were said to enjoy an abundance of fish, game, and wild fruits. Hunting may have been more important in the past than it is today, when shortages of protein may be critical in limiting the permanence of settlements.[232] Among the Abijira and other groups living on the Curaray, food was regarded as less abundant. They cultivated manioc and plantains, and although they hunted some game, they ate a variety of small rodents, lizards, toads, ants, and various grubs.[233] They probably used various kinds of traps and spears but did not use nets or bows and arrows, as is the case today;[234] they may also have possessed blowguns. Fish poisons were used, and nets may have been used for fishing. Tobacco was smoked.

Juan de Velasco, without citing his source, states that in 1605 Father Rafael Ferrer calculated that the Encabellado on the Aguarico and Napo numbered 50,000 and were divided into ten tribes.[235] Velasco does not provide figures for the Abijira and Payagua, who may have been subsumed in his estimate, but in 1620 the parish priest of Alcalá del Río, who had been working in the area for thirty years, suggested the same figure for the Encabellado alone.[236] Despite the supporting testimony of Father Cristóbal de Acuña, who observed that the province of Encabellado possessed a "multitud grande de gentiles,"[237] the figure of 50,000 seems high, given that Encabellado culture appears fairly typical of the low-density groups that inhabited the low selva. When Father Pecador and Captain Juan de Palacios entered their territory in 1635, they were met by 8,000 Indians.[238] Given the small size of settlements, this large number, if accurate, must have been drawn from a wide area and may well have referred to the tribe as a whole.[239] This figure is given some credence by the fact that following the ill-treatment of an Indian by Captain Palacios, the expedition was surrounded by 5,000 hostile warriors divided into four squadrons.[240] Sweet guesses that their aboriginal population may have been between 6,000 and 8,000, which if anything was probably an underestimate.[241]

In 1620 the parish priest of Alcalá del Río claimed that the province of Abijiras contained more than 10,000 Indians.[242] Later in 1667 Father Juan Lorenzo Lucero claimed he had seen seven distinct rancherías that possessed about 800 people but, after exploring the tributaries of the Curaray, reported that the Abijira were to be found in seventy rancherías.[243] This suggests that they may have numbered about 8,000 altogether, while Father Lucero further claimed that there were 16,000 Payagua.[244] These figures are consistent with claims that following the death of Father Pedro Suárez in 1680, punitive expeditions from Borja pacified the Abijira and Payagua, who between them possessed 5,000 "indios de guerra," here assumed to be Indian warriors.[245] Although this figure may have been exaggerated to magnify the achievements of the expeditions, populations of similar magnitude appear in Franciscan accounts of their efforts to convert the Abijira. They claimed that up to 1689 they had established a number of villages and baptized 6,000 souls,[246] and in 1690 the mission of San Francisco de Abijiras on the Curaray was administering 3,000 souls.[247] Sweet assigns a slightly higher aboriginal population for the Abijira of between 5,000 and 6,000 and suggests between 4,000 and 6,000 for the Payagua.[248] These figures would appear to be underestimates, given the numbers present in the seventeenth century. Although by this time both groups had suffered from enslaving raids and epidemics, there was a relatively long period during the seventeenth century when limited contact may have enabled a degree of demographic recovery. Nevertheless, the Abijira inhabited a fairly restricted territory in which farming was difficult and resources limited, and it is possible that the figure of 16,000 for the Payagua was exaggerated in the absence of detailed knowledge of the extent of their settlement down the Marañón. Precontact estimates of between 6,000 to 8,000 for the Abijira and of 8,000 to 10,000 for the Payagua are suggested, but if anything they are likely to prove conservative.

The individual estimates already discussed for the Omagua, Encabellado, Abijira, and Payagua bordering on the river Napo, but excluding
the Cofán, suggest that the total number of Omagua and Tucanoans living in
this region may have been between 40,000 and 45,000. This figure is considerably lower than the 100,000 to 150,000 revealed by entradas into the provinces of the Encabellado, Abijira, and Omagua between 1619 and 1620.[249]
The region covered by this estimate is not well defined, however, and the
high figure may well derive from contemporary observers, assuming that
the whole area was as densely populated as the more familiar riverbanks or
from the inclusion of many neighboring, but more distant, groups.

Kandoshi Groups: Maina, Chirino, Andoa, Murato, and Roamaina

The affiliations and locations of Indian groups located to the east of the
Jívaro are difficult to determine, not least because of the fragmentary
nature of the early documentary evidence and population movements in
the early colonial period. As the Spanish penetrated the lowlands, many
groups moved eastward, where they adopted the language and culture of
local Zaparoan groups.[250] In many cases this process of "zaparoization"
occurred before Indians came into sustained contact with missionaries,
whose descriptions of their language and culture often appear confused
and give a misleading impression of the extent of Zaparoan groups at the
time of Spanish conquest. Recent research favors affiliating the Maina,
Chirino, Andoa, Murato, and Roamaina to the Kandoshi linguistic family,
which in turn appears to be related to Jívaro, though the dialects are not
mutually intelligible.[251]

MAINA

One of the best-known groups in the Oriente were the Maina, who occupied the northern bank of the Marañón from the Morona River to the
Nucuray, possibly as far as the river Chambira, as well as the lower
courses of the Morona and Pastaza centering on Lake Rumachi.[252] The
lack of vocabulary makes the identification of the Maina with any particular cultural-linguistic group problematic. Steward and Metraux classify
the Maina as Zaparo,[253] but Taylor and Descola argue that the colonial
Maina were more like the present-day Kandoshi in their material culture,
social organization, and mythology.[254]

Alonso Mercadillo's expedition that descended the Huallaga River in
1538 may have encountered the Maina, but it was not until 1557 that twenty-
five leagues below the Pongo de Manseriche Juan de Salinas found Indians
who spoke a different language from that used upriver.[255] At the same time
he explored fifty leagues up the Pastaza around Lake Rumachi. Throughout

the sixteenth century this region remained unsettled, although colonists from Santiago de las Montañas and Santa María de Nieva raided Maina territory for slaves.[256] Finally in 1619 Vaca de Vega founded San Francisco de Borja on the bank of the Marañón,[257] prior to which his expeditions had encountered three groups of Maina. The first was located on the Marañón between the Morona and Pastaza, where 800 Indians were brought under Spanish administration, and a second group of 700 Indians headed by six caciques was found further downriver. Finally, it was rumored that around Lake Pastaza (Rumachi) there were 3,000 Indians. In the event, however, 4,000 warlike Indians from the whole of this region were pacified and settled near the projected site of San Francisco de Borja.[258]

Cristóbal Saavedra, who accompanied Vaca de Vega's expedition, observed that the Maina lived in unstockaded large narrow houses, each inhabited by one to three kin groups, and in which they slept on barbacoas.[259] Each settlement was located one and a half to two leagues apart.[260] The economy was highly oriented toward riverine resources. The Maina were skilled canoeists and used hooks, arrows, and *barbasco* to catch fish and turtles.[261] Hunting, like fishing, was primarily a male occupation. For this purpose the Maina possessed dogs, which they esteemed highly, and which they raised in abundance.[262] While men were involved in fishing and hunting, women cultivated and weaved. Although maize was grown, root crops, which included manioc, sweet potatoes, and plantains, were more important.[263] Plantains were boiled and roasted and, like maize and the fruit of the chonta palm, made into chicha. Locally grown cotton was woven, decorated with colored paint, and made into clothing, and abundant use was made of feathers.[264] The Maina also manufactured polychrome pottery and *cachibangos* (palm fibre mats or cloth), which were used as a medium of exchange. Friendly trading relations existed with the Jevero to the south.

Leadership was more permanent among the Maina than in neighboring groups. Leaders inherited their posts from ancestors who had originally achieved their positions through courage and dexterity in war.[265] While they were not supported by tribute from their subjects, commoners built their houses, worked their lands, and manned their canoes.[266] Polygamy was widespread, with most men possessing two or three wives, but those of higher status had more.[267] The Maina were regarded as being more warlike than their neighbors, conducting raids on the Aguano and Cocama among others, and taking heads as trophies.[268] They fought better in the water than on land, and used lances, blowguns, spear-throwers, and shields. Only a few observations were made about Maina religious beliefs. Like their neighbors, they did not possess idols but believed in dreams and in bird songs as omens.[269]

Only fragmentary evidence exists for the size of the Maina population.

In the mid–sixteenth century Juan de Salinas heard rumors that the area around Lake Rumachi was "poblada de muchos naturales,"[270] but the first quantitative estimate of their numbers was brought back from an expedition in 1616 that had found 8,000 souls waiting to be baptized.[271] As already indicated, Vaca de Vega's expeditions in 1619 resulted in 4,000 Indians being settled near San Francisco de Borja, of whom 1,500 came from along the Marañón and others from Lake Rumachi.[272] According to Figueroa, in 1620 there were 700 tributary Indians in the jurisdiction of Borja and therefore possibly 3,500 souls.[273] However, despite a rebellion shortly after its foundation, other Indians were pacified, so that by 1629 Vaca de la Cadena claimed that 8,000 souls had been baptized and placed in the charge of its forty vecinos.[274] However, these numbers must have represented only a proportion of the region's population, which had already been severely depleted by enslaving raids and possibly epidemics. The aboriginal population could have been about 12,000.

CHIRINO

As already indicated in the discussion of the Jívaro, the Lower Chinchipe was explored by Alonso de Alvarado in 1535 and by Juan Porcel between 1545 and 1546. Subsequently in 1548 the conquest of the region was encharged to Diego Palomino. A few words found in his account and in another anonymous and undated description of the region around Jaén suggest that the Chirino who inhabited the Middle Chinchipe and Chirinos valleys belonged to the Kandoshi linguistic group.[275]

Diego Palomino described the province of Chirinos as "de mucha gente y muy bien poblada," with Indians living in large houses occupied by two or three "moradores," possibly heads of families.[276] They inhabited fertile lands that produced maize, manioc, sweet potatoes, white potatoes, peanuts, and other roots, and around their houses they cultivated fruit trees and palms. Located nearer the sierra than the Maina, they possessed a few llamas, from whose wool they made short shirts.[277] Accounts make no reference to the exploitation of wild food resources, but it seems likely that opportunities for fishing were limited in the swift-flowing rivers and greater emphasis placed on other sources of animal protein. Although the region was rich in gold, it does not appear to have been exploited by the Chirino.

Diego Palomino noted that the Chirino were divided into four parcialidades, by which he probably meant four encomiendas, since the Chirino seem to have recognized only war leaders and were not organized politically.[278] Palomino considered the Chirino to be very warlike, employing lances, spear-throwers, clubs, and wooden shields. Apart from indicating that the Valley of Chirinos was densely settled, early sources are frustratingly silent on the numbers living there. Given that they inhabited a relatively restricted region, they may not have numbered more than 3,000.

ANDOA AND MURATO

In preconquest times the Andoa lived to the north of the Maina between the Pastaza and Morona rivers, centering on the Huasaga River.[279] From an early date Andoa were transported as slaves from the Huasaga Valley to the Marañón, where in 1582 they been incorporated into encomiendas belonging to citizens of Santiago de las Montañas; in the seventeenth century others were to be found in San Francisco de Borja.[280] The Murato, who were also living near the Huasaga River,[281] have been linked, together with the Gae and Semigae, to the Andoa, who Steward and Metraux have suggested were affiliated to Zaparo.[282] However, the Murato appear to be culturally more akin to the Jívaro, and modern linguists have favored a Kandoshi affiliation.[283] Given the cultural similarities between the Murato and Andoa observed by Jesuit missionaries, it seems likely that the Andoa also belonged to the same group. The confusion appears to have arisen because the Andoa and Murato became acculturated to Zaparo as they moved eastward to escape Spanish expeditions, which, purporting to recapture fugitive Maina, indiscriminately enslaved nearby groups.[284] By the beginning of the seventeenth century, a group of Andoa had retreated to an area between the Pastaza, Bobonaza, and Tigre rivers. While recognizing the impact of slave raids, Sweet argues that the restricted territory inhabited by the Andoa suggests they did not exceed 3,000 to 4,000.[285] He does not include an estimate for the Murato, who Costales and Costales suggest were twice the number of Andoa. The latter estimate that both groups together may have comprised 6,000 Indians,[286] and they propose separate estimates for a number of other Andoan groups, notably the Guasaga, Guallpayo or Toquereo, and possibly the Asarunatoa, which would raise the total to 10,000. The territory inhabited by the Andoa was not as restricted as Sweet suggests, and slave raids not only reduced the local population but also encouraged its retreat to the interior. For these reasons the Andoa encountered in the seventeenth century represented only a fraction of those existing at the time of Spanish conquest. An aboriginal population of maybe 8,000 to 10,000 for the Murato, Andoa, and their subgroups seems more appropriate.

ROAMAINA-ZAPA

Jesuit missionaries were probably the first to contact the Roamaina and Zapa in 1641, when it was estimated that they numbered 8,000.[287] Like their neighbors, they were affected by enslaving raids and by that date had already retreated from their original location along the banks of the Lower Pastaza to between the Pastaza and Tigre rivers.[288] The Roamaina and Zapa were regarded as belonging to the same nation, and in 1654 it was said that there had been 9,000 to 10,000 of them.[289] Up to 1686 over 8,000 had been baptized by Jesuit missionaries.[290]

The affiliation of the Roamaina-Zapa is controversial. Steward and Metraux prefer a Zaparoan affiliation on the basis of location and rather slender linguistic evidence. The existence of cultural traits such as head-hunting and the use of shields, which are not found among the Zaparo, suggests that the Roamaina were originally a Kandoshi group who, like the Andoa, became acculturated to Zaparo.[291] Culturally they were similar to the Maina. They subsisted on maize, manioc, plantains, and fruits of the chonta palm, and they conducted wars of vengeance for perceived wrongs. They wore some clothing but used palm-fiber cloth rather than cotton.[292]

Although Jesuit missionaries claimed that the Roamaina and Zapa belonged to the same nation since they spoke the same language, they were culturally distinct. The Zapa went naked and used hammocks rather than beds, thereby showing greater affiliation to Zaparo culture.[293] Nevertheless, the Zapa are included in estimates for the Kandoshi rather than Zaparo, since colonial sources generally refer to the two groups together. Estimates for the Roamaina-Zapa suggest they numbered between 8,000 to 10,000. These figures have been generally accepted by recent researchers[294] and seem reasonable, given that in the mid–seventeenth century they possessed eighteen leaders.[295]

Figures for other Kandoshi groups, excluding the Maina, are little more than intelligent guesses, but Costales and Costales figures for the Andoa (including subgroups), Murato, and Roamaina-Zapa sum to 20,000, while Sweet's (excluding the Murato) total between 11,000 and 14,000.[296] Taylor estimates the total population of Kandoshi groups, excluding the Zapa and Pinche, but including the Chirino and Maina, at not less than 20,000.[297] Accepting a figure of between 16,000 and 20,000 for the Andoa, Murato, and Roamaina-Zapa based on suggestions by Sweet and by Costales and Costales, and adding about 14,000 to 15,000 suggested here for the Chirino and Maina, would give a total more like 30,000.[298]

Zaparoan Groups: Gae, Semigae, Zapara, Zapa, Pinche, Coronado, Oa, Iquito, and Yameo

Zaparoan speakers inhabited an extensive area between the Pastaza and Napo rivers. Steward and Metraux identify a large number of Indian groups as Zaparoan, some of whom—the Maina, Andoa, Murato, and Roamaina—it has been just been suggested originally belonged to the

Kandoshi cultural-linguistic group.[299] Among the most notable Zaparoan speakers were the Gae, Semigae, Zapara, Zapa, Pinche, Coronado, Oa, Iquito, and Yameo. Their early colonial history remains obscure, since they remained outside Spanish administration until the late seventeenth century. However, it is clear that by then they had been subject to enslaving raids and hit by Old World epidemics.

Few details of Zaparoan culture are available from early documentary sources, but from modern ethnographic studies it is evident that it was similar to that of other Indian groups in the Oriente. They practiced shifting cultivation based on manioc; hunted using dogs, pits, and traps; and fished using barbasco. They lived in large communal houses, with settlements consisting of one or two houses. Social stratification was absent except that leaders were chosen in times of war and shamans probably commanded some respect.[300]

The Semigae, Gae, and Zapara were located between the Curaray and Bobonaza rivers. The Semigae were to be found from the southern bank of the Curaray to the Pindoyacu, a tributary of the Tigre River.[301] To the southwest were the Gae, who inhabited higher lands in the headwaters of the Bobonaza.[302] Although Father Lucas de la Cueva claimed to have first encountered Zapara in 1664 below the junction of the Nushiño and Curaray rivers, where Franciscans also observed them in the seventeenth century, most other writers locate them further south and east toward the Tigre River.[303] Little ethnographic information exists for these three groups. Even though they fought their neighbors, they were generally considered to be less warlike, since they did not conduct intratribal wars.[304] Earliest accounts suggest that they lived in dispersed settlements located in interfluvial areas, rather than along the banks of rivers. Given the limited resources of this environment, the numbers reportedly living there in the late seventeenth century seem high. Juan de Velasco describes the Gae as "numerosísimos" and recorded that 7,000 Indians were collected into the mission of San Javier.[305] It is extremely unlikely that such a large number were collected in one mission, but the figure might be more acceptable if it referred to the whole mission field. During a seventeen-year period up to 1686 the Jesuits baptized 4,030 Gae.[306] Velasco does not give estimates for the Semigae and Zapara, though in the case of the former he distinguishes between two groups who lived on the Curaray and Tigre, the former being so numerous it comprised ten tribes and the latter embracing seven large tribes.[307] Costales and Costales, apparently accepting Velasco's account, suggest the Gae and Semigae numbered 5,000 and 7,000 Indians respectively.[308] Sweet estimates their combined numbers at the time of Spanish conquest at between 6,000 and 8,000.[309] Despite Velasco's claims, the small size of Zaparoan settlements suggests that Sweet's figure may be more realistic. There is only limited evidence for the number of Zapara. In 1682 Father Lorenzo Lucero maintained the Zapara and neighboring groups numbered more than 10,000 souls.[310] Although there is no indication of the proportion who were Zapara, the fact that they are specified rather than other groups suggests they formed a substantial proportion of the total. As such, Costales and Costales' figure of 1,000 appears to be low, and an estimate of 3,000 to 4,000 more appropriate, particularly given their cultural similarities to the Gae and Semigae.

The Gae were bitter enemies of the Coronado and Oa, who spoke the same language.[311] The Coronado, so called because of their triangular, crownlike hairstyle, inhabited the Upper Pastaza Valley opposite the mouth of the Bobonaza. They lived in long, dispersed multifamily houses and cultivated maize and peanuts, which they stored.[312] The Oa originally lived in the Aarrabima Valley, possibly near the confluence of the Pindoyacu and Conambo.[313] Driven by wars with the Gae and later by Spanish raids from Los Quijos, they later moved toward the headwaters of the Tigre and to the Nushiño Valley.[314] The fact that they could understand the Encabellado of the Napo has prompted the suggestion that they may not have been Zaparoans, but Tucanoans driven south by Omagua raids or Spanish entradas.[315] When they were encountered by missionaries in the seventeenth century, both the Coronado and Oa had been severely reduced in numbers by raids from Borja, Macas, and Los Quijos, but accounts suggest that both groups had once been very numerous.[316] In 1682 Father Lucero maintained that the Toquereo, an Andoan group, and the Coronado numbered 6,000 souls, though it is not clear whether this was a combined estimate or the size of each group.[317] Recent estimates place their joint numbers at 8,000 to 10,000.[318]

South of the Semigae and Zapara were the Pinche, who were a Zaparoan group that became acculturated to Roamaina.[319] They lived to the north of the Roamaina-Zapa on the interfluves between the Pastaza and the Upper Tigre rivers.[320] In 1700 Father Gaspar Vidal found 500 "indios de lanza" among the Pinche and Pava, a related group,[321] and Sweet estimates that they numbered 3,000 to 4,000.[322]

To the east of the Pinche and Roamaina-Zapa were the Iquito. They lived north of the Yameo in the region drained by the Nanay River, from the river Tigre to the Napo and Curaray.[323] The Iquito were closely related to the Gae. Even though concerted efforts to pacify them date from 1737,[324] they were contacted in 1619, when they were described by the parish priest of Alcalá del Río as forming two provinces of "Yquitos grandes" and "Yquitos chicos" who numbered 20,000.[325] Later in the early eighteenth century Father Carlos Brentano observed that the Iquito were more numerous than the Yameo discussed below.[326] If this observation was also valid for the time of Spanish conquest, it would suggest an aborig-

inal population exceeding 12,000. Costales and Costales, in contrast, estimate they numbered only 2,000, though they would probably add the
populations of a number of subgroups to this figure.[327] The extensive
territory occupied by the Iquito and the numbers collected into missions
in the eighteenth century suggest larger numbers,[328] perhaps of the order
of 5,000 to 6,000, but there is no specific evidence to support the observation that they outnumbered the Yameo. The discrepancy between accounts is difficult to resolve.

The Yameo lived south of the Iquito between the Tigre, Napo, and
Marañón.[329] Steward and Metraux include the Yameo in the Peban cultural-linguistic group, whose culture they describe as being technologi-
cally and socially simpler than their neighbors, though they also note they
had greater affiliations with the Zapara than with other neighboring
groups.[330] According to Father Andrés de Zarate, the Yameo formed one
of the most populous groups in the region, being divided into forty parcialidades, each with its own cacique, whom they obeyed only in times of
war. They lived in large multifamily houses, under which they buried their
dead.[331] In 1682 Father Lucero claimed he had contacted 6,000 Yameo.[332]
As late as the early 1730s Father Pablo Maroni found 3,000 to 4,000 Yameo
living along the banks of the Marañón.[333] These must have represented
only a small proportion of the total, for in 1739 Father Zarate reported that
whereas various people had suggested that the Yameo numbered 4,000 to
6,000 souls, from what he had seen there were 8,000–10,000.[334] The Yameo
clearly formed a populous ethnic group, whose aboriginal population may
have been 10,000 to 12,000, or even more.[335]

Panoan: Urarina-Itucale

The Urarina and Itucale were regarded as being two branches of the same
group, with the Itucale to be found to south of the Urarina. Their culture
was not significantly different from other groups in the Oriente, but they
came to be regarded as a "barbarous" nation because of their cannibalistic
practices.[336] Steward and Metraux have tentatively affiliated them with
the Panoan cultural-linguistic group, of which they were the only represen-
tatives living north of the Marañón.[337] Even though the Urarina-Itucale
were contacted in 1619, there are few early references to them.[338] Permanent missions were not established among them until the eighteenth century, at which time they were living on the Chambira River.[339] The Itucale
were reputedly a "numerous" nation,[340] though Velasco described them as
only a "nación mediana."[341] In 1745 the mission of San Javier de Urarinas
contained over 500 Indians.[342] This suggests a sizable aboriginal population, given that their exposed location along the Marañón made them

particularly vulnerable to enslaving raids and the introduction of disease. Sweet has estimated they numbered between 5,000 and 6,000 at the time of contact, while Costales and Costales suggest 8,000.[343] This range of estimates seems reasonable.

CONCLUSION

In 1967 Phelan guessed that the aboriginal population of the Oriente was about 200,000.[344] He may not have been far wrong. The documentary evidence presented for the size of individual Indian groups, which has been considered in the light of cultural evidence and the capacity of the different environments to support the populations reported, suggests the aboriginal population may have been between 230,000 and 250,000. (See Table 4.) Sweet's estimates for the Upper Amazon are not comparable with these figures, since they do not include groups that inhabited the high selva, but instead encompass the whole of the Jesuit province of Mainas. His estimates for the low selva groups considered in this study may be calculated at between 68,000 and 86,000.[345] These figures are about 25 percent lower than the estimate suggested here for the same groups.

More recently Taylor has suggested that the Oriente possessed between 100,000 and 120,000 Indians. For her the Oriente comprises the region between the Napo and Marañón, but only between the Andes and the river Tigre.[346] This area excludes the Cofán, Coronado, Macas, and Omagua, as well as other groups between the Tigre and Napo, notably the Encabellado, Abijira, and Payagua and a number of Zaparoan groups, such as the Iquito and Yameo. If estimates for these groups are excluded from the total calculated here, her figure of 100,000 to 120,000 is also about 25 percent lower than estimates here for the same groups of between 141,000 to 154,000.

Finally, applying Denevan's estimated population densities for different habitats to the study area produces an aboriginal population of 156,840 (Table 5). This figure is about 35 percent lower than that suggested here. Denevan has recently produced a revised density estimate of 9.1 for the várzea,[347] which would raise his total by 26,262. However, most of the discrepancy derives from differences in estimated densities for the low selva, with documentary sources suggesting population densities in the order of 0.5 per square kilometer rather than 0.2 per square kilometer as proposed by Denevan. This finding supports Sweet's general argument for higher population densities for the low selva on the basis that parts of the region possessed more abundant resources and therefore could have supported higher populations.[348]

The higher estimates suggested here derive from an examination of a

Table 4. Aboriginal Population Estimates for the Oriente

Area and ethnic group	Aboriginal population estimate	Area in km²	Persons per km²a
High selva			
Cofán	15,000	10,146	1.48
Coronado	3,000	2,115	1.42
Quijo	35,000	12,849	2.72
Macas	10,000	3,329	3.00
Jívaro (includes those of the low selva)	50,000	41,570	1.20
Total high selva	113,000	70,009	1.61
High selva/várzea			
Tupians			
Omagua-Yété	10,000	1,555	
Omagua of the Napo	15,000	6,911	
Total high selva/várzea	25,000	8,466	2.95
Low selva			
Tucanoan			
Encabellado	6,000–8,000	28,740	
Abijira	6,000–8,000	6,359	
Payagua	8,000–10,000	11,407	
Total	20,000–26,000	46,506	0.43–0.56
Kandoshi			
Maina	12,000	22,724	
Chirino	3,000	6,658	
Andoa and Murato	8,000–10,000	15,324	
Roamaina (including Zapa)	8,000–10,000	13,555	
Total	31,000–35,000	58,261	0.53–0.60
Zaparoan			
Zapa (included with Roamiana)			
Gae and Semigae	6,000–8,000	⎫	
Coronado and Oa	8,000–10,000	50,400	
Zapara	3,000–4,000	⎭	
Pinche	3,000–4,000	8,075	
Iquito	5,000–6,000	31,130	
Yameo	10,000–12,000	13,337	
Total	35,000–44,000	102,942	0.34–0.43
Panoan			
Urarina-Itucale	6,000–8,000	15,932	0.38–0.50
Total low selva	92,000–113,000	223,641	0.41–0.51
Grand total	230,000–251,000	302,116	0.76–0.83

a Since the areas occupied by individual ethnic groups in the várzea and low selva are very approximate, population densities are calculated only for the major cultural-linguistic groups.

Table 5. The Aboriginal Population of the Oriente, Based on Denevan's
Population Density Estimates for Different Habitats

Habitat	Persons per km[2a]	Area in km[2]	Estimated population
High selva[b]	1.2	61,171	73,405
Várzea[c]	5.3	6,911	36,628
Low selva[d]	0.2	234,034	46,807
Total		302,116	156,840

[a] Denevan, "Aboriginal Population," 78.
[b] Excludes the Jívaro of the low selva but includes the area occupied by the Omagua-Yété.
[c] Excludes the area occupied by the Omagua-Yété. Denevan currently assigns a density of 9.1 per km[2] to the várzea (Denevan, *Native Population*, xxvi).
[d] Includes the Jívaro of the low selva.

broader range of documentary materials. They suggest, as will the suc-
ceeding chapters, that Indian societies were affected by Spanish conquest
to different degrees and in different ways, and that estimates of the aboriginal population projected back from later sixteenth-century figures need
to take greater account of demographic changes that might have taken
place in the intervening period, particularly where the presence of epidemic disease is well documented.

It is important to recognize that early documentary evidence for Indian
populations throughout the region, and particularly for the low selva, is
extremely scant, and it is often not clear precisely which groups are being
included in contemporary accounts. Even though estimates for individual
cutural-linguistic groups are therefore highly speculative, it is possible to
suggest some relative differences in population levels. The estimates proposed here generally support Denevan's proposition that the high selva
was more densely settled than the low selva. Those who lived in the high
selva or on the várzea exceeded densities of over 1 person per square
kilometer, while those inhabiting the low selva only achieved densities of
about 0.5 persons per square kilometer. In the low selva resources were
more limited, and warfare, polygamy, and infanticide functioned to keep
population levels low. The slightly higher densities associated with the
Kandoshi groups may be related to their access to more reliable sources of
food, particularly riverine resources. For the high selva, however, all the
density estimates proposed are slightly higher than those originally suggested by Denevan. While groups of the high selva also practiced polygamy and infanticide, they generally had better access to sources of food.
Variations among them seem to have been most closely related to sources
of protein and warfare. Both the Quijo and Macas appear to have had
access to better sources of protein than the Jívaro, the former to game and
the latter to fish. It is possible that the slightly higher density for the

Macas could be related to the greater reliability of fishing compared with hunting, but the population estimates are too speculative to confirm this. These two groups, together with the Coronado, also had more substantial trading links with the sierra, through which they extended their economic base. The Jívaro, in contrast, suffered from shortages of protein, and their warlike disposition raised mortality rates, both of which contributed to low population levels. While it could be argued that conflict arose from population pressure on poorer resources in this area,[349] equally it could be attributed to the lack of effective native leadership or ideological reasons. The apparent absence of other significant demographic controls, such as widespread infanticide or late marriage, or of attempts to intensify production suggest that conflict may not have been driven by population pressure, though it could easily have gone unnoticed by early observers.

Part Three

INKA RULE

CHAPTER 5

Inka Conquest

The land is depopulated because the Inka fought a cruel war of conquest, and because the people were uncivilized and warlike, they were removed, resettled, and punished, so that it was left deserted.

Licenciado Francisco de Auncibay, 1592[1]

No study of the demographic impact of Spanish rule in Ecuador can ignore the previous conquest of the region by the Inka or the prior arrival of Old World diseases. The Spanish did not encounter a population living in peaceful harmony with its environment, but one beset by wars and in economic and social turmoil because of Inka domination. During the previous sixty to seventy years the Inka had managed, among other things, to build thousands of miles of roads, establish new administrative centers, and adapt local economic and political structures to meet imperial designs, but in terms of its administrative structure and organization, the Inka empire was still in the process of formation.[2] Even though its expansion can be understood more easily if it is assumed that the Inka did not destroy, but modified preexisting economic and political structures,[3] the fierce resistance of native peoples to Inka rule and postconquest rebellions indicate that something new was being created that conflicted with local interests and practice.[4] The expansion of the Inka empire is important in understanding the demographic history of Ecuador, not only because it resulted in battle casualties, but also because it brought about changes to the economic, social, political, and religious life of native groups that were to influence the course of Spanish conquest and colonization.

Inka rule in Ecuador was extremely uneven both in duration and in spatial extent. It probably began during the reign of Tupa Inca Yupanqui, who reputedly left Cuzco with 200,000 men and subjugated the northern Peruvian provinces of Chachapoyas and Cajamarca before arriving in Ecuador.[5] Larrea suggests that this campaign began in 1460.[6] Passing north, Tupa Inca Yupanqui failed to conquer the province of Bracamoros but subjugated the Palta and those in "Guancabamba, Caxas, and Ayavaca."[7] From there he proceeded to conquer the Cañar, although subsequent rebellions meant that it was his successor, Huayna Capac, who brought about their final defeat.[8] Cieza de León maintains that Tupa Inca Yupanqui continued north, conquering the region between Latacunga and Quito, and furthermore established a garrison at Carangue.[9] (See Map 5.) Sarmiento de Gamboa suggests that in fact there were two campaigns, with

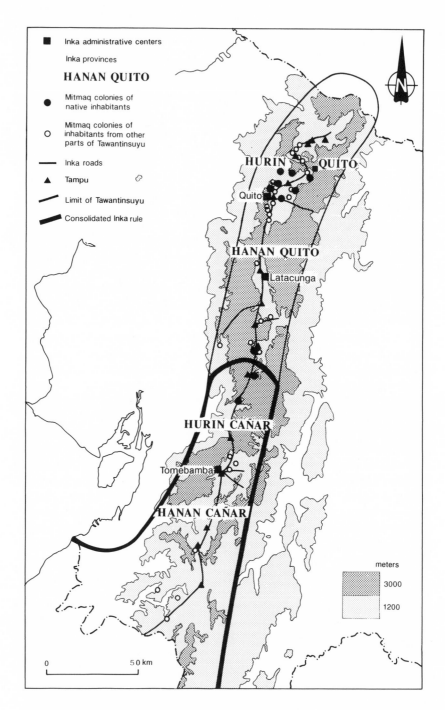

Map 5. Ecuador under Inka rule

Tupa Inca Yupanqui returning to Cuzco between the conquest of the
Cañar and the northern wars; Cabello Balboa and Garcilaso de la Vega
also suggest that Tupa Inca Yupanqui was involved in the northern campaigns.[10] Nevertheless, the consensus among modern researchers is that
while he may have conducted some military incursions north of the Cañar
region, perhaps establishing garrisons there, the final defeat of the Cañar
and effective incorporation of the Quito region into the Inka empire was
brought about by Huayna Capac.[11] The northern campaigns involved the
subjugation of the province of Pasto and a bitter war with the Caranqui;
whether the Quito region was effectively pacified before or after these
campaigns remains a subject of debate.[12] Larrea suggests that the recon-
quest of northern Ecuador by Huayna Capac began in the 1490s. At the
time of Spanish conquest the northern limit of the empire was the An-
gasmayo River, located in the Pasto region, probably just south of Fúnez.[13]

The protracted conquest of Ecuador meant that Inka rule lasted from
sixty to seventy years in the south to between thirty to forty years in the
north.[14] Its impact was greater in the southern sierra, which had a longer
history of subjugation and was located nearer the heartland of *Tawantinsuyu* at Cuzco. Further north, Inka control was weaker, and the imprint of
Inka rule less marked.[15] Even though Inka interest focused on the sierra,
they left little trace of their occupation, while evidence for their expansion
to the west or east is even more scanty.

Even in the sixteenth century contemporary observers were divided
as to whether the Inka had conquered the coast.[16] Some chroniclers suggested that Tupa Inca Yupanqui conquered the Huancavilca and then subjugated the province of Manta, but others recorded that Huayna Capac
conquered the provinces of Manta and Caraque as far north as Passao,
while his captains penetrated as far as the Santiago River.[17] Garcilaso de la
Vega even suggests that Huayna Capac left "teachers and governors" in
the coastal provinces he conquered.[18] Certainly the Huancavilca had been
in contact with the Inka, for some had been transferred to the highland
Peruvian valleys of Pachachaca and Abancay,[19] and it is possible that other
coastal groups, notably those on the island of Puná, paid tribute and
service to them.[20] Even so, there is little evidence for Inka conquest of the
coast. Cieza de León reasoned that the Inka did not establish permanent
buildings or storehouses there because of its unhealthy climate, the small
size of its communities, and its being regarded as "de poca estimación."[21]
However, Borja de Szászdi maintains that the inhabitants of the coastal
region were no less advanced than their neighbors to the south, but that
the Inka accustomed to life in the sierra or the arid coast were unable
to conduct campaigns at sea or in an environment of rivers, mangrove
swamps, and seasonally inundated savannas, through which local inhabitants could move with facility.[22] Meanwhile recent research suggests that

the Huancavilca made a treaty with the Inka in order to forestall an invasion.[23] Whatever the reason, archaeological evidence confirms the failure of the Inka to establish control over the coast.[24] The Inka empire on the coast effectively ended at Túmbez.[25]

The failure of the Inka to expand into the tropical-forested lowlands on a permanent basis has been regarded as an enigma of New World historical geography. Although the Inka conducted a number of expeditions into the region, probably in search of medicinal plants, feathers, and wood,[26] they never settled there permanently. Even though it is unlikely that, as Montesinos suggests, Huiracocha sent six captains from Quito to "los Quijos,"[27] it is clear that at a later date the Bracamoro effectively repelled Tupa Inca Yupanqui's forces and prevented Inka penetration of the southern lowlands.[28] Subsequently, however, Huayna Capac was able to conquer the Macas, Quizna, and the borders of the Cañar[29] and also led an expedition to the provinces of Ique and Antique, which were probably located to the north of the Upper Coca River, where the Omagua were living.[30] Finally, Atahualpa, during a lull in the fighting with his brother Huascar, apparently ordered an expedition to Los Quijos, where his troops subjugated the provinces of "Maspa, Tosta, Cozanga, and Coca."[31] Despite these incursions, in no case was the initial infrastructure of settlement established in the form of forts or roads. The only explanation proffered for the lack of Inka interest in the lowlands relates to Los Quijos, where the provinces were regarded as "so unprofitable and poor."[32] Meggers has argued that ecological limitations on agricultural production militated against their occupation of the lowlands,[33] and more recently Gade has suggested that the Inka were discouraged from settling there because of the presence of the disfiguring disease leishmaniasis, to which lowland groups may have had some hereditary immunity.[34] More recently others have suggested that the difficulties encountered by the Inka in establishing formal political control of groups in the lowlands, because of Indian hostility, weak native leadership, or ecological conditions, may have persuaded them to adopt the alternative strategy of expanding trading relations in order to acquire the goods they desired.[35]

Inka expansion may be divided into two phases—one military, the other cultural. Control over new territories and peoples was achieved by military campaigns, which, in the face of persistent resistance, often had to be conducted several times. Many were highly destructive of human life, with thousands of Indians being killed on both sides. Military control was consolidated and extended by the construction of forts, roads, and storehouses that supported conquering armies. Subsequently political control was realized through the establishment of provincial administrative centers and the creation of colonies of mitmaq who replaced rebellious subjects, who were transported to regions closer to the Inka heartland.

Once hostilities had effectively ceased, the Inka began to modify indigenous political and economic structures to meet state requirements, the acquiescence of local chiefs being bought through gifts and privileges.[36]

MILITARY EXPANSION

Warfare was common in pre-Inka times,[37] but opposition to Inka conquest often united previously independent groups and brought battles on a scale hitherto unknown. Cieza de León suggests that the Inka tried to expand their empire without conflict, but in the face of resistance or rebellion treated those they conquered "with great harshness, and not a little cruelty."[38] Huayna Capac was said to have killed "many thousands" on the island of Puná in revenge for their assassination of a number of Inka *orejones*.[39] The fierce resistance of local populations to Inka rule is reflected in the size of the armies of conquest. Tupa Inca Yupanqui's initial conquest of northern Peru and southern Ecuador involved 200,000 men. For the conquest of the northern sierra the initial force of 40,000 proved inadequate, and another 12,000 soldiers had to be summoned from Cuzco.[40] Resulting battle casualties were high.

The subjugation of the Palta took five "moons," which Cabello Balboa noted involved "the death of many."[41] But this conquest was relatively easy compared with that of the Cañar immediately to the north. The Cañar region was eventually "totally destroyed," and thousands were transported to Cuzco as mitmaq.[42] The fierce resistance they had displayed so impressed the Inka that they later became a mainstay of the Inka professional army. As the Inka moved north, there was almost no place where they did not meet resistance, but undoubtedly the fiercest battles and heaviest losses occurred to the north of Quito. Tradition relates that the wars between the Inka and the Caranqui and Cayambe lasted seventeen years, and although their actual duration may have been somewhat less, it is clear that they resulted in heavy casualties on both sides, not least in the massacre at Yaguarcocha.[43] According to different sources, this massacre involved the slaughter of between 20,000 and 50,000 Indians.[44] Further north, Pasto villages were destroyed, and everyone was killed, "great and small, men and women, young and old."[45]

Inka armies of conquest were drafted from provinces as imperial needs required. For example, 6,000 Indians were recruited from the province of Chucuito to conquer the Cañar.[46] The more able-bodied were chosen, and soldiers served on a rotational basis under their own leaders.[47] As the empire expanded, the demand for soldiers to extend and consolidate political control increased. The mit'a became less able to meet imperial demands, and the Inka began to employ full-time professional soldiers. At first they were recruited from among the Aymara, but later the former rebels from the Cañar region were employed.[48] Similarly, young survivors of the massacre at Yaguarcocha, called "huambracunas," were employed as personal bodyguards by the Inka in Cuzco.[49] As conquest was consolidated, the Inka conscripted local labor as war demanded. Visitas of communities in the Valley of Chillo and of Chilpat in the Puruhá region in the late 1550s reveal that military service, like other services, was levied "by an Inka majordomo with the cacique of the village, equally among the Indians of the village according to the capability of the village and each of the said Indians."[50] The levies were sometimes considerable and had disastrous demographic consequences. Father Pedro Arias Dávila claimed that as a consequence of being employed by the Inka in their northern campaigns and in the dynastic war between Atahualpa and Huascar, the province of Pacaibamba, which had contained over 10,000 people, had been destroyed.[51]

Inka conquest did not bring an end to the bloodshed, since the dispute between Atahualpa and Huascar, initially over the governorship of Quito, eventually led to a civil war into which local communities were drawn as fighting forces. In fact the dynastic wars were probably no less costly in lives than Inka conquest. On the death of Huayna Capac, Atahualpa was left in Quito with the bulk of the Inka army that had been involved in the northern campaigns. In addition he had "many chiefs and mitmaq from the province and lands of that region [Quito]," which with the professional army numbered 40,000 men.[52] Meanwhile Huascar attempted to muster a force of 30,000 at Tomebamba from "the caciques of Tumibamba, and the Chaparras and Paltas and Cañares," at the same time sending to Cuzco for 2,000 trained soldiers.[53] Atahualpa's forces moved south from Quito, and a major battle took place at Ambato, where it has been estimated that 15,000 to 16,000 were killed on both sides.[54] As Huascar retreated, Atahualpa's forces continued south, destroying Tomebamba and devastating the surrounding lands of the Cañar in revenge for their support of Huascar. Oviedo suggests that 1,000 people were killed, but a much larger figure, though not as high as the 60,000 suggested by Agustín de Zarate, seems more likely in the light of other accounts of the devastation.[55] In 1582 Hernando Pablos, a vecino of Cuenca, reported that during the dynastic war "all the Cañares died, that of 50,000 there had been, not more than 3,000 remained."[56] Several decades into the colonial period there were still mounds of whitening bones strewn throughout the region, where there had been large villages, and since Atahualpa had ordered that only men and boys should be killed, there were fifteen times more women than men.[57] As Atahualpa's troops proceeded southward, they increased in size; one account suggests that he had slightly fewer than Huascar, whose army numbered 80,000. These forces met once again in northern Peru at

Cajabamba, where it was estimated that 35,000 were killed, but not before Atahualpa's army had fought Indians on the island of Puná. Here the Indians sided with Huascar, supplying 700 boats and 15,000 men, and although they defeated Atahualpa's troops, 4,000 of them were killed.[58]

The consolidation of military and political control was effected through the establishment of forts, roads, tampu, and public buildings. This massive construction effort is testimony to the ability of the Inka state to command labor. The employment of Indians in public works was not new to highland communities, but the larger scale of Inka projects led to increased demands for labor. Hence, these manifestations of Inka rule are important, not only from the point of view of examining the expansion of the empire, but also in terms of their impact on local communities.

In order to achieve and maintain military control, the Inka built forts and strongholds at passes and on high points that dominated valleys.[59] These fortified sites varied in construction; some were substantial structures comprising three or four stone-wall circles, while others were simple trenches used as overnight quarters for troops.[60]

Throughout Inka conquest Tomebamba acted as the main military base, where troops were mustered for the conquest of the north. The city was protected by a northern line of forts in the Nudo de Azuay.[61] Between there and Quito a number of major forts were constructed that the Inka later used to defend themselves against the Spanish. These included the forts at Riobamba, Mocha, Ambato, Muliambato, Panzaleo, and Uyumbicho.[62] Further north, wars with the Inka were prolonged, and the density of forts increased. Some of the northern forts may have been built during the reign of Tupa Inca Yupanqui,[63] but most were probably constructed following rebellions by the Pasto, Caranqui, Cayambe, and Panzaleo. A major fort was built at Guanguiltagua that dominated the valleys of Cumbaya and Tumbaco. It was an integral part of Quito's defensive system and a stepping-stone for advances further north.[64] To the north of Quito at least forty forts have been identified, of which fourteen formed a strategic cluster in the Pambamarca region.[65] To the south of Quito a line of forts from Puembo to Pifo dominated the Valley of Chillo and acted as a defense against incursions from the east.[66] In addition to those built by the Inka, large numbers of forts were constructed by local Indians to resist Inka advance. Among the most notable were those at Carangue, Guachala, and Cochasquí. In many cases, however, it is difficult to ascertain whether the forts were built by local communities or by the Inka.[67]

An efficient transport and communication system was essential for the extension and maintenance of the Inka empire. Roads facilitated the movement of imperial armies and supplies, enabled the effective administration of conquered territories, and allowed the easy movement of mitmaq, and mit'ayuq. Lateral roads, particularly those that extended from the Quito area, were also used to transport valuable items, such as gold, beads, coca, and cotton from lower altitudes.[68]

The artery of the Inka empire was the major highway, known as the *qapaq ñan*, which ran through the highlands from Cuzco to Pasto in southern Colombia. In Ecuador it followed the interandean corridor, passing through Tomebamba and Quito. Since the Inka never effectively occupied the coast, there was no parallel road in the lowlands as there was in Peru. The coastal road probably terminated on the southern coast of Ecuador; one attempt at building a road further north in the Guayas Valley was a failure.[69] Although ethnohistorical accounts portray the Inka road system in Ecuador as a single road, parallel routes were sometimes constructed, such as between Quito and Panzaleo, and near Chuchishiana.[70] Often a lower, wider road was complemented by a narrower, higher one that negotiated steeper slopes and was possibly used during the rainy season when the former was impassable. There was also a number of lateral routes, particularly to the west of the main artery,[71] but none descended as far as the coast. However, one route did lead through the Chimbo area to the headwaters of the Guayas River, by which it was possible to reach the coast by raft.[72] There is little information on lateral roads to the east, but there may have been one from Papallacta to the Quijos region, another from Mocha to Baños, and finally others from Tomebamba to Chordeleg and Sigsig, where forts were constructed probably for defense against the Jívaro. There was almost certainly a lateral road to Loja.[73] In the north Quito constituted a nexus of long-distance routes. Apart from the road to the east through Papallacta, two other roads descended west to the Yumbos. Another passed north through Guayllabamba and Cayambe. The Inka road system in highland Ecuador was clearly as complex as that in other, better-known parts of the empire further south.[74]

Inka roads often followed indigenous routes, particularly in the more densely populated highland basins. Here the Inka reconstructed, straightened, and widened preexisting paths to facilitate the movement of large armies and supplies. Hernando Pablos recorded that under Tupa Inca Yupanqui the narrow paths around Cuenca, which only permitted the passage of one person at a time, had been widened to two *brazas*.[75] In sparsely populated regions, often of high relief, such as the Nudo de Azuay, where few roads existed and the network was poorly developed, new roads had to be built from scratch. Early travelers recorded the presence of paved roads, but they may have mistaken naturally stony roadbeds for paving or else observed adobe bricks that have since been eroded away. In any case only small stretches of stone-paved road still exist in Ecuador.[76]

An integral part of the Inka road system were tampu. They provided lodgings for individuals or groups traveling on state business and possessed storage facilities where food, fodder, firewood, and other goods might be kept. They varied enormously in size and function; some even had workshops and administrative offices attached.[77] Characteristically tampu were located one-day's travel apart, though the actual distances separating them varied according to the terrain, being shorter on the inhospitable páramo.[78] Their precise location was determined by the availability of water, the proximity of supplies of food and labor, as well as strategic and administrative considerations. However, they were constructed away from Indian communities so that travelers should not make demands upon them.[79] Murra notes that this policy was consistent with the principle that the state should provide the necessary supplies from state storehouses and that local people should be obliged only to provide labor.[80] Hyslop has suggested that the Inka built and maintained at least a thousand tampu in the whole of their empire, some of them probably constructed on pre-Inka antecedents. Although he gives no estimate of the numbers built in Ecuador, probably several hundred were constructed, including the thirty-five or so listed by Poma de Ayala.[81]

Some tampu were used by the relay runners, or chaski, who constituted the Inka courier system, but more often other small posts, or chaskiwasi, were built for their use. They were concentrated on the Quito-to-Cuzco highway and according to the bishop of Quito, they were located between one and one and a half leagues apart.[82]

Apart from tampu and chaskiwasi, the Inka constructed a number of other, more widely spaced larger public buildings, often referred to as *aposentos*, which performed a variety of functions.[83] Many of them were little more than large tampu that were used by armies and royal processions; others, more aptly called palaces, were more elegant and richly adorned and were used as permanent or semipermanent residences of Inka nobles and orejones. The latter were often accompanied by equally impressive temples; that at Carangue was said to house more than 200 virgins of the sun.[84] The palaces and temples were often built of finely sculptured stone and lavishly decorated with gold and silver. Other essential components of these administrative and religious centers were storehouses and garrisons. The major centers that impressed Cieza de León and Garcilaso de la Vega were Tomebamba, the first to be established, Latacunga, and Carangue; Quito, intended to be a second Cuzco, was less impressive, perhaps reflecting its more recent foundation and its strategic rather than political and economic importance.[85]

The construction and maintenance of forts, roads, tampu, and public buildings made heavy demands on local sources of labor. Even though in the late sixteenth century Oidor Alonso de las Cabezas de Meneses claimed that 100,000 Indians had been imported from Cuzco to build roads and public buildings, probably most construction was undertaken by local mit'a labor,[86] even though Cieza de León suggests that prior to the arrival of the Inka, Indians around Quito had not been versed in building techniques.[87] Oidor Cabezas de Meneses claimed that those who had been employed in public works by the Inka had often been ill-treated and killed, and that they had advised the Spanish that if they wanted to extract labor from reluctant local workers, they would have to kill one-third or one-half of them.[88] This statement may have been intended to justify Spanish ill-treatment of local populations, but the labor required for public works was arduous, with much of the stone for the construction of public buildings, notably those at Tomebamba, being brought from Cuzco.[89]

Large-scale building projects required several thousand laborers, but once they were constructed, the maintenance of roads, tampu, and other public buildings and the provision of chaski probably did not impose heavy burdens on local communities, though it was probably higher on those located near the major Inka highways. Indeed Murra suggests that those who guarded, cleaned, and repaired tampu may have been older men and those incapacitated for other labor services.[90] Mit'a labor, however, was used extensively for transporting goods. Although large llama trains emanating from Peru accompanied armies and royal processions, and some llamas were probably raised in the dry valleys of the central sierra, the more humid climate of the Ecuadorian páramo did not favor the raising of large herds. As such, most goods were moved by Indians on their shoulders; humans had the advantage that they could carry heavier loads and move more quickly than llamas, which could cover only about ten miles a day.[91] Oidor Cabezas de Meneses claimed that Indians began carrying loads at the age of two.[92]

In order to establish political control over conquered territories and exploit new lands, the Inka established colonies of mitmaq. (See Appendix 2.) Before discussing their role in detail, it is useful to distinguish them from kamayuq and yana, who similarly resided outside their native villages and were thus exempt from community obligations. The distinctions between these three categories were not always clear, but mitmaq generally lived outside their place of ethnic origin, kamayuq had specialized occupations, and yana provided services for Inka nobles and caciques.[93] A yana might also be a mitmaq. In Ecuador the latter often performed a military role, so they are discussed here; kamayuq and yana are considered later when changes to native political and economic structures under the Inka are discussed.[94]

Mitmaq probably originated under the rule of Pachacuti, though their role was developed under Tupa Inca Yupanqui.[95] Originally mitmaq may have been sent as colonists to exploit desirable lands and resources beyond their immediate home territories, thereby establishing spatially discontinuous "archipelagos."[96] Subsequently, the Inka state adopted the practice to expand production on a large scale and for military purposes. Although there is some evidence that colonies of mitmaq were used to expand production in Ecuador,[97] the majority appear to have performed a military function. Following the conquest of a region, the Inka established garrisons and colonies of mitmaq, transferring them from provinces that were climatically similar and politically reliable. Colonists were provided with lands and house plots,[98] and for the first two years they were supported from state storehouses and aided by mit'a labor.[99] Mitmaq were rewarded with gifts of prestigious foodstuffs and other highly desired goods such as *qumpi* cloth, and they may even have enjoyed the service of one or two yana or aklla.[100] Although these gifts bought the loyalty of many, the allegiance of others remained with their native communities, to which some returned during the turmoil of the Inka dynastic war and Spanish conquest.[101] For this reason, and because some were killed in wars, the numbers of mitmaq recorded by early Spanish observers probably are less than the numbers that actually existed in Inka times.

Those mitmaq transferred to Ecuador replaced large numbers from newly conquered rebellious groups, such as the Cañar and Cayambe, who were moved nearer to the Inka heartland. Although it was Inka policy that more or less equal numbers should be exchanged between newly conquered territories and politically reliable regions,[102] greater numbers appear to have been transferred from Ecuador than arrived from Peru and Bolivia. However, this may reflect inadequacies in the documentary record and reductions in their numbers during the various wars. These major movements of population had important demographic implications. While mitmaq may have been materially better off, their spatial and social dislocation may have restricted their choice of marriage partners, delayed marriages, and reduced fertility levels. Meanwhile as ties with their native communities weakened and their dependence on the Inka state increased,[103] they became more vulnerable to changes in the existing political order than did indigenous groups.

Since the transference of mitmaq followed in the wake of conquest, colonies in the southern part of the country had the longest histories. The hinterlands of Tomebamba, Latacunga, and Quito were singled out by Cobo as being notable for their large numbers of mitmaq.[104] Further north, fewer colonies appear to have been established to replace the large numbers of Cayambe and Caranqui transported to the central Andes.

Passing from south to north, Inka conquest of the Loja region was followed by the transferral of "thousands" of Palta to Collao, near Lake Titicaca, in exchange for settlers from that region.[105] Indians from Cuzco may also have been settled among the Palta at Saraguro, Cariamanga, Nambacola, and Catacocha.[106] One of the most notable exchanges fol-

lowed the conquest of the Cañar. It was notable on account of the numbers
involved and the unusual role the Cañar later played in the Inka army.
Cieza de León claimed that following the conquest of the Cañar, "fifteen
thousand men with their wives" were transported to Cuzco.[107] Initially
they were settled in the Yucay Valley, where they were employed as
farmers; later they became professional soldiers in the Inka army.[108] As
late as 1572 there were still about 300 Cañar in Cuzco who served as
bodyguards for the Inka.[109] Other smaller numbers of Cañar were transported to diverse parts of Peru, namely to Huancabamba, Cajamarca,
Huamacucho, Huamanga, and Lima, as well as to the Yampares region of
highland Bolivia.[110] Espinosa Soriano estimates that the transferral of the
Cañar to Peru and Bolivia resulted in some areas being left with less than
half their populations.[111] In addition to those transferred to Peru, small
numbers of Cañar were moved to multiethnic colonies in the Quito region
at El Quinche, Pomasqui, and Cotocallao.[112] Unfortunately little evidence
exists for the groups who replaced the estimated 15,000 who were exported from the region.[113] When Francisco Pizarro was in Cajamarca, he
observed 4,000 families on their way to resettle the Cañar region,[114] but
this movement was probably linked to the later devastation of the area by
Atahualpa.

In contrast, Puruhá lands to the north seem to have been peppered
with colonies of mitmaq from the south, to the extent that Oviedo claimed
that all the inhabitants of the Riobamba region were either from Collao or
Condesuyo and had been transferred there by Huayna Capac.[115] Although
Oviedo's claim was probably exaggerated, as late as the 1580s mitmaq,
primarily from northern Peru, composed more than one-third of the total
population of the Chimbo Valley.[116] Further east there were colonies at
Achambo, San Andrés (Xunxi), and Quero,[117] and there may have been
another at Salasaca.[118] As yet studies of Indian communities in Peru have
not revealed the presence of Puruhá, but those transferred there must
have numbered several thousand.

Although Cieza de León noted that there had been a great number of
mitmaq around Latacunga,[119] there are few references to specific colonies
in the region. One colony probably comprised Indians from Guayacondo,[120]
and another was established near Saquisilí. Mitmaq from the latter settlement claimed that their ancestors had arrived as soldiers with Tupa Inca
Yupanqui and had been given lands in the Tanicuchi Valley, from whence
the Spanish later moved them to Saquisilí.[121] In 1591 the Latacunga region
still possessed 558 mitmaq.[122]

In addition to the Cañar already mentioned, large numbers of other
mitmaq colonies existed in the Quito region, many composed of Chacha
from Chachapoyas, and Wayacuntu from the provinces of Huancabamba
and Ayabaca in northernmost Peru.[123] Uyumbicho and Urin Chillo both

contained colonies of mitmaq, some from northern Peru,[124] while multiethnic colonies existed at El Quinche and Pomasqui. El Quinche appears
to have been composed largely of settlers from remote regions to the
south, mostly from the central Andes around Cuzco, while those at Pomasqui were mainly from regions to the north.[125] Apart from these centers, it
has been suggested by different authors that there were also colonies of
mitmaq at Carapungo, Yaruquí, Zámbiza, Chillogallo, Añaquito, and Machangara.[126]

Following the long and bloody northern campaigns, the defeated Pasto,
Caranqui, and Cayambe were transferred as mitmaq to different regions.
Most notable was the removal of 1,000 tributary Cayambe to Matibamba in
Angaraes, where they were employed in the cultivation of coca.[127] Other
Cayambe were sent to the Puruhá region and Huánuco,[128] and possibly to
Cuzco, Copacabana, and Chupaico.[129] Meanwhile some Pasto were transferred to the shores of Lake Titicaca, and a Pasto colony was established
near Quito at Tumbaco.[130] Place-name evidence suggests that other Pasto
may have been settled in the Quito Basin at Cayambe, Tocachí, and Malchinguí.[131] Although Ponce claims that Caranqui were also transferred
with the Pasto to Lake Titicaca, Espinosa Soriano maintains that more
likely they were killed.[132]

There is much less evidence for the numbers of mitmaq who replaced
those transferred from northern regions. Santa Cruz Pachacuti Yamqui
relates that mitmaq were moved to the Cayambe-Caranqui region,[133] and
some at least were associated with the major garrison at Carangue.[134]
Nevertheless, Caillavet judges that they were few in number and that most
were rapidly integrated into indigenous societies once their military role
effectively ceased with Spanish conquest.[135] However, Espinosa Soriano
argues for a much larger mitmaq presence in the region, with colonies
existing at Otavalo, Cotacachi, and Cayambe. On the basis of evidence for
"indios tributarios incas" in tasaciones drawn up for the villages of Otavalo,
Cotacachi, Tontaquí, Intag, Tulla, and San Pablo in 1612, he estimates they
numbered about 8,000 and, taking account of the effects of Spanish conquest and epidemic disease, argues that under Inka rule there may have
been 30,000 mitmaq in the region.[136] This suggestion needs further investigation but would clearly indicate a massive Inka presence.

CHANGES IN POLITICAL AND ECONOMIC STRUCTURES

As Inka expansion proceeded and political control was achieved, independent ethnic groups were incorporated into provinces. These provinces
were in turn subdivided into hanan and hurin moieties, the latter being
politically and economically the more important. Rather than correspond

to preexisting ethnic groupings, the newly created provinces incorporated distinct and sometimes hostile groups as separate moieties.[137] What effectively became the province of Quito under Spanish rule encompassed Hanan Quito, which extended from Riobamba to a line passing northwest/southeast through the Quito Basin, and Hurin Quito from there north to Otavalo.[138] Further south the province of Cañar was subdivided into Hurin (Hatun) Cañar and Hanan Cañar, which centered on Ingapirca and Cañaribamba respectively.[139] Although it has been suggested that the river Chota similarly divided the colonial corregimiento of Ibarra into two moieties, the evidence is far from clear.[140] In theory each province comprised 40,000 tributary Indians who were administered by an Inka governor, or *tukrikuq,* nominated by the emperor. Political organization within the provinces was based on a decimal system, whereby the population was arranged in groups of 10, 50, 100, 1,000, and 10,000 tributaries, each subject to the authority of a hereditary *kuraka* of local descent. With the exception of the smallest two groups, the kuraka were exempt from the mit'a and, as payment for their loyalty, received gifts of aklla, yana, land, llamas, and cloth. This decimal organization appears to have been well established in the Loja region,[141] but at the time of Spanish conquest it had not been installed in the Quito Basin.[142] The expansion of the Inka state bureaucracy created new demands for goods and labor to support local leaders, which were met by local communities and redistributed to kuraka through the agency of the Inka state.

Andean economies functioned on the basis of group cooperation and solidarity, which was founded on a common heritage. However, not all members of the group had equal access to goods and resources. Services provided by commoners generated surpluses that supported elites, from whom in return they received "gifts." This traditional system of reciprocity and redistribution was elaborated upon by the Inka to meet state needs. Hence local economies were modified to conform with imperial structures, which were built up concurrently and which they came to parallel.[143] Local elites lost status as they surrendered access to community lands and labor in return for the material benefits of private holdings, retainers, and prestigious foodstuffs distributed by the Inka state. In return for their labor, commoners received lands and sometimes aid in times of famine. The reorganization was designed to produce a surplus to support an Inka elite without alienating local populations and undermining their subsistence base. To aid this process production was expanded and stabilized through the opening up of new lands and the introduction of new crops and animals. The ability of the Inka state to support its members became increasingly problematic, however, as it expanded and a larger number of nonproducers—soldiers, yana, aklla, and mitmaq—were required to extend and maintain it.

When a region was conquered, all lands and resources became the property of the Inka state. Some lands were set aside for state and religious purposes, but probably in most cases the greater part of the land was returned to local communities for cultivation.[144] New lands were also opened up for cultivation through the introduction of irrigation.[145] The Cañar probably constructed irrigation canals in pre-Inka times,[146] but following their conquest by Tupa Inca Yupanqui, the Inka "extended the cultivated fields" and "dug irrigation channels" and transformed the region into an agricultural colony.[147] Garcilaso de la Vega suggests that around Quito the Inka also built irrigation channels and "all other customary benefits for the greater fertility of the soil,"[148] but with the exception of those built in the hot and dry Guayllabamba Valley and around Pomasqui,[149] there is little evidence for irrigation works in the Quito Basin. Further north, however, pre-Spanish irrigation canals exist to the east of Cayambe, in the Chota-Mira Valley, and possibly near Carangue, though there is no evidence to suggest they were constructed by the Inka.[150] The short duration of Inka rule in these areas probably did not permit the widescale development of irrigation systems.

Newly colonized lands composed only part of the land required by the Inka for imperial needs; other lands had to be acquired from native owners. The relative proportions of newly colonized lands to alienated lands remain unknown, though outside the immediate Cuzco area at least most state and temple lands were carved out of the native domain.[151] However, the large-scale alienation of lands was not practicable, since it would have provoked considerable resistance and undermined the local subsistence base. Where possible, therefore, unoccupied lands were probably used. Lands distributed to mitmaq were probably those previously unsettled or vacated by Indians transported elsewhere.[152] The mitmaq moved to Saquisilí received lands from Tupa Inca Yupanqui "leaving the natives in control of their lands."[153] However, some native lands were alienated, and given Inka preference for maize,[154] the lands most at risk may well have been those at intermediate elevations. For example, in Anan Chillo the Indians were required to establish for the Inka "a large chacra of maize on their lands."[155] The amount of land alienated appears to have varied from place to place. Polo suggests that those lands reserved for the state were generally more extensive than those dedicated to the temple or left to the commoners. While this may have been true around Cuzco, it was not the case in all parts of the empire, where lands designated for state and temple purposes were less substantial than those distributed to communities.[156] In the early colonial period Indian accounts probably minimized their dimensions, since the Spanish claimed all lands owned by the Inka, and local communities took the opportunity to reassert their rights to them once Inka rule had ceased.[157] While Inka domination clearly led to a diminution of the productive lands held by native communities, it does not appear to have threatened their subsistence base.[158]

While native lands were being alienated, local leaders received from the Inka gifts of private land that was generally located some distance from their communities. For example, in the mid–sixteenth century the cacique of Guayllabamba in the Puruhá region possessed maize fields at Píllaro in what may have been an Inka irrigation zone.[159] At the same time two of his principales at Chilpat and Chultos had remote fields at Ambato and Pilahaló, which may also have been gifts from the Inka.[160] In effect such lands secured the cooperation of local leaders by compensating in part for the reduced control they exercised over community assets and the loss of status they experienced under Inka rule.

In pre-Inka times commoners were required to provide their leaders with game, firewood, and straw and to farm their lands on a communal basis.[161] During Inka times these types of service continued, but other activities such as llama herding and weaving were added. In the Puruhá region labor for these services was allocated through the mit'a, but in the Valley of Chillo it supplied labor for household service only. Apart from these local demands for labor, commoners were required to work state and temple lands. In the Cañar region the cultivation of Inka lands was undertaken by the community as a whole, but other kinds of labor service were organized through the mit'a.[162] The product of labor on these lands was deposited in storehouses for later distribution.[163] Some communities in the Quito region transported half the produce to central depositories in Quito, keeping the other half in local community storehouses. The distribution of this surplus will be discussed below.

Agricultural production was expanded not only through the colonization of new lands but also through the introduction of new crops and animals. Murra attributes the introduction of oca, sweet potatoes, sweet manioc, and peanuts to the Inka.[164] Ocas were certainly cultivated at higher elevations in the early colonial period,[165] and sweet potatoes may have been cultivated along with maize at intermediate altitudes. Llamas and alpacas (*ovejas de la tierra*) were present in small numbers in Ecuador in pre-Inka times. They were introduced at a relatively late date between A.D. 1000 and 1500.[166] Although their numbers increased in Inka times, the páramo of Ecuador was not suitable for raising of llamas on the same scale as in the central and southern Andes. However, it is difficult to judge how extensively they were raised in pre-Spanish times, given that many llamas were killed in wars and others were appropriated by encomenderos in the early colonial period. By the end of the sixteenth century only a few were left of the "great quantity" that Cieza de León observed around Quito.[167] In pre-Columbian times they were used as beasts of burden and sources of wool, and under the Inka they played an important role in religious ceremonies as sacrificial animals and in providing wool for the manufacture of the cloth that was burned at rituals. Llama meat remained a sumptuary food of the upper classes.[168] Llamas were raised on Inka lands; those owned by the encomendero of Guayllabamba in the Puruhá region in the early colonial period were probably the remnants of state herds, as were those in the Valle de los Chillos.[169] Llamas were often given as gifts to local caciques, and in the colonial period herds continued to be owned by native leaders.[170]

Agricultural production was expanded and stabilized by modifying native subsistence strategies. As as already indicated in chapter 2, in pre-Columbian times a variety of methods were used to exploit the environmental diversity of the Andean region and to buffer communities against the effects of adverse climatic conditions and variable harvests. In many cases, however, it is difficult to tell whether the practices observed in Ecuador were of local or Inka origin. It is clear that Indian communities exploited a variety of ecological zones located within a day's walk or a short distance from their homes and, in pre-Inka times at least, participated in medium- and long-distance trading.[171] At the time of Spanish conquest highland communities also possessed distant colonies located outside their territories for the exploitation of exotic resources.[172] While this vertical archipelago system may have developed on pre-Inka antecedents, in Ecuador it was largely associated with Inka rule, which sought to internalize production and reduce the dependence of highland communities on outside groups.[173] It is not surprising, therefore, that on the eve of Spanish conquest the vertical archipelago system was more in evidence in the south among the Puruhá and Cañar, where Inka rule was longer, but was still being installed around Quito.[174] Its relative absence in the Palta region may be explained by the easier access of local communities to a wide range of ecological zones, which made its introduction less essential.

Under the vertical archipelago system, Indians known as kamayuq (camayos) were delegated by their caciques to form colonies for the exploitation of distant lands or resources. Nevertheless, the colonists retained economic and social links with their home communities and did not become integrated into alien groups, although sometimes they provided service for the local cacique, perhaps to gain access to the resources they controlled.[175] A visita of Puruhá communities in 1557 suggests that in general the products secured by kamayuq were divided between them and their political sponsors.[176] The latter share was probably distributed in turn to those who worked their cacique's lands, while the former is likely to have been traded. The development of this vertical archipelago system seems to have resulted in a decline in medium-range trade conducted by highland households in pre-Inka times.[177]

In Ecuador the exotic items most commonly sought were cotton, salt, ají, and coca, which were all to be found at warmer, lower elevations. Cotton was the most important fiber used for clothing in Ecuador, even though the introduction of llamas by the Inka may have shifted the balance slightly in some drier regions. While highland communities in northern Ecuador obtained their cotton by trade, to the south of Quito cotton was cultivated at lower elevations by highland Indians, particularly the Puruhá. In 1557 about 60 percent of the subjects of the cacique of Guayllabamba who were working outside their communities were cultivating cotton.[178] They were to be found mainly at Chanchan and Chillacoto, but others were living slightly further north at Pallatanga, Chillán, and Telimbela. The Puruhá were not the only group represented in the Chimbo region. At Chapacoto there were up to twenty tributary Indians who had been placed there by the caciques of "Sicho, Latacunga, e Mulahaló, e Puraes e Panzaleos." A small number of cotton cultivators from Uyumbicho were also living in Tungurahua.[179] To the south some Cañar at Alausí and Chunchi culitvated cotton locally,[180] but most cultivated distant fields or obtained it by trade. Caciques at Azogues possessed cotton fields in "tierras calientes" some eight leagues away, and Indians from Paute obtained their cotton from Molleturo, ten leagues to the west.[181]

Another resource exploited by kamayuq was salt. Small numbers of Indians from Otavalo and Quito exploited the salt deposits at Mira,[182] and the Puruhá exploited those at Tomabela.[183] The latter also had a small number of kamayuq cultivating ají at Ypo, the location of which is unknown.[184] Some Cañar exploited local sources of salt, but many communities acquired salt from other regions. Most appear to have obtained it from the Pacific coast by trade,[185] but the kamayuq of Paccha exploited salt springs in the Oriente, access to which was a source of conflict with Indians from Zamora.[186]

Coca was cultivated in Ecuador in pre-Inka times, but demand for it increased under the Inka, for whom it held greater social and religious significance.[187] In pre-Inka times it was probably cultivated in the Coangue Valley, notably around Pimampiro and Ambuquí,[188] and under Inka rule another center of production was developed to the east and northeast of Ambato in the headwaters of the Pastaza. Indeed Atahualpa himself employed kamayuq to cultivate coca in this region, where in the sixteenth century thirty were still cultivating coca for Inka descendants.[189] In 1557 the Puruhá of Guayllabamba maintained Indians cultivating coca at Guambahaló, a parcialidad of Pelileo,[190] and at the same time other Puruhá Indians were cultivating coca in a state archipelago in the "Yumbo."[191] In 1605 there were a total of 690 kamayuq in Pelileo, Patate, Píllaro, and Baños.[192] There are fewer references to the cultivation and consumption of coca in the Cuenca region. Some coca was grown at Alausí and Chunchi, while Indians from Paccha traded coca along with cotton with groups living in the "tierra yunga y caliente."[193] In the seventeenth century some Cañar still possessed coca lands in Xíbaro territory.[194] However, by then the extensive coca fields in the Jubones Valley, more specifically in the deep, dry tributary Valley of Yungilla, which had probably been established under Inka stimulus, had been abandoned.[195]

Exotic products were also acquired by barter or trade. In the Quito region individual households sold foodstuffs in local markets and traded these with communities in the Yumbos for goods such as cotton, ají, and salt; they seem to have had fewer contacts to the east.[196] Individual households or small groups within communities appear to have established trading relations with Yumbo settlements located about three to four days' journey away in ecologically complementary regions.[197] The latter communities in turn may have trading links with the coast and formed part of an extensive network of exchange at the household level. In addition there were specialist merchants known as mindaláes who traded status products such as coca, gold, beads, and cloth over longer distances.[198] Mindaláes, whose activities have been described in detail in chapter 2, were found north of the Siccho region into southern Colombia, but there are no records of status traders to the south. If such merchants had existed, then Inka rule appears to have suppressed or modified their activities.[199] Evidence from northern Ecuador suggests that this process may have involved a reduction in their number and restricting their sponsorship to the most powerful chiefs who played key roles in the Inka bureaucracy.[200] In any case the establishment of the vertical archipelago system in the south effectively displaced long-distance and household trading, creating a system that guaranteed access to exotic products and reduced dependence on shifting, and presumably less stable, alliances with outside groups.[201] Although the development of the Inka redistributive system may have led to a decline in trade and markets,[202] it is clear that in some regions, such as the Quito Basin, they continued to flourish.[203] It is perhaps significant that trade was more in evidence in the northern Andes, where Inka control was weak, and in peripheral lowland regions outside their control, such as Esmeraldas and Los Quijos. In such circumstances the Inka might have allowed trade to persist in the belief that imperial economic and political objectives could be achieved most easily through supporting long-distance traders. Not only could they acquire exotic products, but they could also forge political alliances with outside groups that might later provide the basis for their formal incorporation into the empire.

Under Inka rule agricultural production in Ecuador probably increased through the colonization of new lands, the construction of irrigation works, and the introduction of new crops and animals, while the development of the redistributive system probably made the empire more internally self-sufficient and stabilized overall production.[204] But the costs and benefits were not distributed evenly. Many of the improvements to agricultural production took place on Inka lands and those of native rulers, and their owners largely reaped the benefits. Commoners lost access to some of their lands and were required to work state and temple lands, including those in state archipelagos. Even though local and state storehouses supported those working on the mit'a and alleviated severe shortages, these demands for labor, coupled with other mit'a obligations, especially military service, would have reduced labor inputs that might have proved critical at particular periods in the agricultural calendar.

The benefits of increased production were largely enjoyed by the Inka and those who worked in their service. The surpluses generated from Inka lands and mit'a labor were stored in warehouses, or *depósitos*. Foodstuffs, coca, cotton, wool, and clothing were among the items accumulated. Even in the southern part of the empire, where ecological conditions limited the production of maize, it was the most important foodstuff to enter the storehouses. Because of its semiceremonial status and its better storage qualities, it was generally preferred to chuñu.[205] Most early observers stressed the military, administrative, and religious purposes to which the stored products were put. Produce from state lands supported Inka armies and fed the Inka nobility and their yana, while more prestigious items, such as cloth and coca, were distributed as rewards for services and to buy loyalties. The products from temple lands supported the priests and aklla, while large quantities of chicha were consumed during religious ceremonies when cloth was often ritually burned and animals sacrificed. Community storehouses probably supplied goods for similar but lower-order functions, including the support of those employed on the mit'a and items for religious ceremonies. The Inka empire has been characterized as a welfare state, and even a socialist empire, on the grounds that state surpluses were employed to look after the poor, sick, old, and widowed.[206] However, Murra argues that while central storehouses provided some relief in times of disaster, communities were generally sustained by mutual support systems that predated Inka rule. Indeed, Inka largesse largely maintained and rewarded the elite and bought the cooperation of soldiers, mitmaq, local leaders, and others who extended and consolidated state control.[207] Even though Inka generosity is increasingly being viewed as a myth, it worked to the extent that groups who had been effectively incorporated into Tawantinsuyu generally remained loyal to the Inka cause during the Spanish invasion. Nevertheless, as the empire expanded, the number of "gifts" required to placate supporters multiplied, placing increased burdens on local production, which ultimately may have undermined the subsistence base of native communities.[208]

Part of the costs of expansion were generated by the creation of large numbers of yana and aklla, who were supported by the state. Yana were removed from their communities to provide service for Inka rulers, government officials, or local caciques. In all cases they were exempt from the mit'a and other community obligations. Yana who served the Inka were often moved over long distances, but most of those serving native caciques had a more local provenance.[209] While some were skilled craftsmen, most carried out more routine domestic and agricultural tasks. Yana were employed in the cultivation of Inka coca fields in Pelileo,[210] and others were imported as skilled craftsmen, notably potters and carpenters.[211] In 1557 carpenters from Guayllabamba in the Puruhá region were working in the forest at Tungurahua. Even though they are not referred to as yana, a later document specifies that the carpenters at Pelileo and Quero had been brought in by the Inka.[212]

In contrast to southern Ecuador, large numbers of yana were present in the Quito area in the early conquest period. In 1578 there were said to be "1,500 de yndios yanaconas antiguos naturales y estrangeras" living in mills and chacras within one-quarter of a league of Quito.[213] This number was certainly inflated compared to pre-Spanish times, since in the turmoil of the early conquest period many Spaniards and native leaders acquired household servants, whom they subsequently referred to as yana. Even so, the number of yana in the Quito region is considerably higher than in other parts of the empire where similar conditions prevailed. Salomon's analysis of the 1559 visita of communities in the Valley of Chillo shows that yana in the service of caciques and principales composed about 10 percent of the population. He contrasts this figure with between 2 and 3 percent in Lupaca communities around Lake Titicaca.[214] The higher proportion might be accounted for by individuals being displaced during wars and seeking the protection of political leaders, but the visita records the presence of nuclear and stem families rather than displaced persons such as orphans or widows. Salomon suggests that the larger number of yana in the Quito region may reflect the greater need for the Inka to placate leaders and homesick mitmaq in what was a politically unreliable province.[215]

Beautiful women were also removed from their communities to provide services and perform specialist tasks. These aklla provided services for the Inka himself and were given as wives to deserving nobles and warriors. Some aklla called *mamakuna* performed services for temples, the best known of whom were the virgins of the sun who were designated for sacrifice.[216] Cieza de León recorded that in Inka times the temples at Carangue and Tomebamba housed 200 beautiful women.[217] It seems that most were drawn from communities in their immediate hinterlands rather than brought in from the south.

THE DEMOGRAPHIC IMPACT OF INKA RULE

Inka rule generated contradictory demographic processes. While it inflicted heavy casualties on conquered groups and directly altered their demographic structures, it also introduced policies that promoted population growth. Whether by design or not, these policies would have compensated in part for the effects of warfare and expanded the labor force necessary for the extension of the empire. In Ecuador, however, the balance was probably negative because of the lateness of Inka conquest and the limited time and area over which population growth policies had been operative. In any case Inka rule left a demographic legacy that was clear to the new invaders.

Battle casualties associated with Inka conquest and the dynastic wars took a heavy toll on local populations. The evidence presented suggests that in Ecuador during the sixty to seventy years prior to Spanish conquest, about 100,000 Indians were lost in conflict alone. This is a high figure that overshadows the numbers lost in other parts of the empire and reflects the initial resistance of native peoples to Inka rule.[218] In addition to battle casualties, the loss of able-bodied males also led to marked imbalances in the sex ratio, which were still evident in the colonial period.[219] These losses would have disrupted reproductive lives by creating large number of widows, many of whom did not remarry. These imbalances were mitigated only to a limited degree by polygyny and concubinage, for such practices were restricted to Inka and local elites and would have done little to counteract the widespread effects of high levels of male mortality on fertility. Given that it was Inka policy to promote population growth, the restriction of polygyny to the elite appears contradictory. However, the power structure of the Inka state was predicated on the distribution of women, aklla, to forge political alliances and buy loyalty. To have permitted polygyny among commoners would have undermined existing social and political structures.[220] As a consequence, even though one might ponder on the possible ulterior motives behind Spanish reports of the devastating effects of Inka wars, their direct and indirect effects are likely to have been considerable.[221]

The protracted wars fought by the Inka, which took a heavy toll on local populations, could be interpreted as evidence of population pressure on resources and the need to control population growth. However, the Inka aimed to capture sources of labor and gain access to resources rather than annihilate those they conquered. There were instances of petty vengeance that occasionally resulted in the death of several thousand Indians,[222] but in general the Inka aimed to preserve the population and to deal with rebellious groups by transporting them to other regions. Dangerous war leaders were often put to death and a number of captives sacrificed to give thanks for victory, but there is no evidence that wars were conducted to decimate populations or to obtain captives for sacrifice, as occurred in Mexico, where the Aztec *guerras floridas* ended with the sacrifice of at least 15,000 captives a year.[223] Human sacrifice was less common in the Inka empire, where it was limited to special occasions, such as the coronation of an Inka, and most of those sacrificed were not war captives.[224]

Far from attempting to control population growth, social and religious practices promoted or at least did not actively discourage population expansion. Premarital sexual intercourse was encouraged,[225] and the participation of the state in the arrangement of marriages suggests a concern for the maintenance of populations. Rabell and Assadourian argue effectively that most women were married by their twenties, such that their reproductive capacities were maximized.[226] The importance the Inka attached to population increase is seen in their religious beliefs and practices. The Moon, a major goddess in the Inka pantheon, was the protectoress of childbirth, while midwives played an important social and religious role, and there were guacas that helped women conceive.[227] In fact those who had many children were generally rich,[228] primarily because they provided extra labor, and population growth, rather than being discouraged, was accommodated by the redistribution of community lands or the colonization of new areas.[229] Although there were some restrictions on sexual intercourse at times of religious ceremonies, including those surrounding the life cycle,[230] they were generally of short duration. More prolonged restrictions governed sexual intercourse while women were breast-feeding infants, which was generally until the age of two. While this could be interpreted as a mechanism for controlling population growth, it was practiced in order to prevent premature weaning and ensure infant survival;[231] as such, it promoted rather than discouraged population increase. There is no evidence that abortion or infanticide was practiced. Indeed other customs operated to prevent miscarriages and protect the newborn. Pregnant women were banned from "walking" in the fields,[232] and mothers with infants under one year old were exempt from labor.[233]

Nearly all of the above observations on Inka population policy are drawn from Peru. It is not clear to what extent the Inka altered native practices in Ecuador, but one tradition at least suggests that changes to local customs were far from complete. Acting against population increase was the burial of women, and sometimes children, with deceased leaders.[234] This practice was not common among the Inka, but in the early colonial period it was noted frequently in Ecuador, where it had survived from the pre-Inka times.[235] Consolidation of Inka rule in the region might have resulted in its suppression as being inconsistent with policies promoting population growth. It is assumed that, as with other features of Inka rule, Inka population policies were more effective in the south.

A number of social practices contradicted Inka policies to promote population increase. Polygyny appears to have been become more restricted under Inka rule, where it was limited to Inka and native elites.[236] Among other things, polygyny functioned to increase the size of the dominant class needed for the expansion of the empire. Men often inherited secondary wives who were widows of their fathers or brothers, but others were acquired as military prizes or as gifts from the Inka state for outstanding service, most of the latter being aklla. Other aklla designated as mamakuna were dedicated to the service of the temple and led a life of perpetual chastity, hence their name "virgins of the sun." At the time of Spanish conquest there were probably no more than one thousand mamakuna in Ecuador, so their virgin status would have had a relatively small impact on the fertility rate.

Whether or not the lack of demographic controls promoted population growth, it has been suggested that in pre-Spanish times the Andean area was in a state of chronic overpopulation.[237] The impressive Inka irrigation works, terracing, raised fields, and the colonization of new lands certainly suggest a need to expand production, but these techniques were more common in Peru and Bolivia than in Ecuador. Their more limited development in the northern Andes, however, should not be interpreted as evidence for the lack of population pressure, for it could reflect the later conquest of the region and/or the more limited environmental opportunities for their construction and development. Even if the intensification and expansion of production suggests population pressure on resources, there is little evidence for food shortages or famines in the pre-Spanish times, except those resulting from natural causes such as drought, frost, or hail at high altitudes, as occurred in the Riobamba region.[238] Indeed the variety of crops cultivated in the Andes, the exploitation of different ecological niches, and the redistributive system helped cushion communities against the effects of natural disasters. It is possible that communities in northern Ecuador, where the Inka vertical archipelago system and redistributive mechanisms were less well developed, were more vulnerable. However, given that these systems generally involved nonbasic crops and largely served Inka and local elites, their introduction probably brought little improvement to the subsistence base and economic security of most communities. Indeed, it could be argued that conditions were better where the Inka rule was less consolidated, since a smaller proportion of the surplus produced was siphoned off to support elites. Nevertheless, there is little evidence to suggest that at the time of Spanish conquest the viability of Indian communities was threatened or that the Inka empire was on the brink of demographic disaster. Had the Spanish not arrived when they did, the demands on economic production created by an expanding population and growing numbers of nonproducers needed to extend and sustain the empire might ultimately have put strains on production that would have required fundamental changes in policy and organization that at that time, for ideological or practical reasons, it was not prepared to make.[239]

CHAPTER 6

Old World Epidemics

Some old conquistadores . . . said that the Indians claimed that they would not have been able to conquer them if a few years before there had not been an epidemic of catarrh and pains in the side that carried off the greater part of them.

Father Reginaldo de Lizárraga[1]

No discussion of demographic change during the sixteenth century would be complete without examining the impact of Old World diseases, which ran ahead of the new invaders.[2] In pre-Columbian times diseases were far less prevalent, and epidemics probably nonexistent. Although population densities had been reached capable of sustaining human-to-human disease chains indefinitely, such infections had not become established. Most crowd infections originate as transfers from animal herds, and their absence in the New World can be explained in part by the relative absence of domesticated animals.[3] Although domesticated camelids were present in the Andes, they did not form concentrated herds capable of sustaining diseases. Furthermore, they were generally herded in the puna above settlements located at intermediate elevations, and in Ecuador the wetter environment of the páramo was unsuitable for raising llamas and alpacas on a large scale.[4] In pre-Columbian times the only possible source of infection from domesticated animals was the guinea pig, which was raised in most households for food and ritual purposes.

Diseases native to the Andean area were either spread by arthropods or were parasitic. They were chronic and endemic rather than acute and epidemic. The most common diseases were respiratory and intestinal infections, bartonellosis (Carrion's disease in the form of Oroya fever and verruga peruana), leishmaniasis, Chagas' disease, pinta, and syphilis.[5] Although debilitating, in most cases these diseases would not have been fatal. The presence of typhus, which may have been more deadly, is not proven, although conditions for its propagation existed in pre-Columbian times.[6] In the sixteenth century Indians reported that the main illnesses that had traditionally afflicted them were respiratory and intestinal infections, especially dysentery, and to a lesser extent headaches and fevers.[7] Not only were diseases less well developed in pre-Columbian times, but the isolation of the American continent meant that its inhabitants possessed no immunity to Old World diseases to the extent that common childhood diseases in Europe and Africa became first-rank killers, and deadly diseases became even more fatal. Their arrival prior to Spanish conquest not only weakened native resistance but also indirectly precipi-tated the Inka dynastic wars, which brought heavy casualties and fostered dissension that could be exploited by the new invaders.

The first Old World disease to strike the Inka empire arrived some time between 1524 and 1527. The details of its introduction have been described elsewhere.[8] Various contemporary descriptions of the symp-toms of the disease indicate that it was accompanied by skin eruptions and high fevers, and that it was highly infectious and resulted in high mortal-ity. Some authors have suggested that it was malaria or exanthematic typhus,[9] but neither is likely to have been present in the New World at that time. Most writers suggest that the epidemic was probably smallpox,[10] though a few claim it was measles. It is possible that measles accompanied smallpox, but more likely the disease was hemorrhagic smallpox, which often afflicts nonimmune populations and can be confused with measles, since the virus enters the blood and produces a prodromal rash on the skin.

Circumstantial evidence also points to the disease being smallpox. Smallpox first struck Mexico between 1519 and 1520, from whence it spread south to Guatemala; by 1527 it had struck Indian populations in Honduras and Panama.[11] Whether the disease had passed overland from Mexico to Panama or arrived direct from the Greater Antilles is unknown, but clearly the area was hit in the early 1520s. Panama was used as a base from which the Pacific coasts of Colombia and Ecuador were explored. In 1522 Pascual de Andagoya explored 200 miles along the coast of Colombia, and in 1524 Francisco Pizarro and Diego de Almagro traveled along the same coast as far south as Puerto del Hambre. It was not until between 1526 and 1527 that Bartolomé Ruiz and Francisco Pizarro explored the Ecuadorian and Peruvian coasts as far south as the Santa River.[12] The latter expeditions appear the most likely sources for the introduction of smallpox, but when they reached Ecuador and Peru, they had not had contact with Panama for some time, and there is no evidence that their crews suffered from any infections. Although the virus could have been carried in clothing or dust,[13] the spread of the disease by this means is not common. The normal channel of infection is face-to-face contact. An alter-native source of the disease could have been one of the earlier expeditions that touched the coast of Colombia, from whence it spread overland or along the coast through native population chains.

Since Huayna Capac died of smallpox in Quito some time after a num-ber of his relatives had died in a similar epidemic in Cuzco, it has been suggested that the disease spread from south to north and that therefore it may have been introduced overland through the Río de la Plata region, rather than via the Pacific coast. While the timing of the outbreaks is not in dispute, it seems unnecessary to propose an introduction from Río de la

Plata in order to explain this pattern of occurrence. The source of infection for both outbreaks may have been the southern coast of Ecuador.
Huayna Capac died in Quito immediately after he had returned from the
coast, where he had been punishing the Huancavilca and Puná for their
treachery.[14] At that time the Inka were trying to extend their dominion
over the coast, and they had established a fort at Túmbez.[15] Some of those
involved in coastal campaigns came from the sierra, and it is possible that
the disease was carried back to Cuzco by soldiers some time before
Huayna Capac arrived on the coast to seek his revenge. (See Table 6.)

Other diseases that are likely to have struck the Inka empire prior to
Spanish conquest include plague and measles. Both of these diseases were
probably present in Central America in the early 1530s. In Nicaragua there
was probably an outbreak of bubonic plague in early 1531, followed by an
epidemic of measles in 1533.[16] The dates of the epidemics are significant,
for during this period expeditions were being mounted to Peru. Francisco
Pizarro's third expedition embarked for Peru in December 1530, but in
1531 or 1532 he was reinforced by troops and supplies brought from
Nicaragua by Sebastián de Benalcázar, and in early 1533 expeditions led by
Diego de Almagro from Panama and Francisco de Godoy from Nicaragua
also arrived in Ecuadorian waters.[17] There was therefore contact with
Central America when epidemics were raging, but it does not prove that
the diseases entered Ecuador and Peru at that time. Lizárraga noted that
Indians near Lima claimed that they failed to resist Spanish rule because
"a few years before" they had suffered an epidemic of "*romadizo* and *dolor
de costado* that carried off the greater part of them."[18] Pains in the side are
often a symptom of plague, which, with the presence of a respiratory
infection referred to as romadizo suggests it may have been pneumonic
plague. However, the date of the epidemic is vague, and the symptoms
described could have been the result of pneumonia or another respiratory
complication associated with smallpox. Although it seems likely that measles spread to the Andean region at this time, the only reference to it
relates to the death of Huayna Capac, which it has already been argued
was probably due to smallpox rather than measles.

When Pizarro's third expedition reached the coast of Ecuador south of
the Bay of Coaque in 1531, some Spaniards became ill, according to Friar
Pedro Ruiz Navarro, from "attacks of smallpox and buboes, from which
some died, and from which others were left disfigured and exceptionally
ugly."[19] Other accounts also stress the disfiguring character of the disease, which resulted in "some reddish boils the texture of nuts, which
form on the face, the nose and other places."[20] In some cases victims tried
to excise the swellings, with the result that they bled to death. While the
"buboes" referred to might be symptoms of plague, more likely they were
the result of a form of Carrion's disease called verruga peruana. This is

Table 6. Old World Epidemics in Early Colonial Ecuador
and Neighboring Regions

Date	Epidemic
1524–27	Smallpox epidemic that kills Huayna Capac
1531–33	Possibly plague and measles introduced from Central America
1531	Oroya fever and verruga peruana among Pizarro's troops on the coast
1539	Smallpox epidemic in Popayán, Colombia[a]
1546	Pneumonic plague, or possibly typhus; present in Peru and southern Colombia, and hence probably in Ecuador
1558	Smallpox, measles, and possibly influenza
1562	Smallpox in Cuenca
1566	Smallpox epidemic in Almaguer, southern Colombia[a]
1582	Epidemic in Cuenca, possibly smallpox
1585–91	Smallpox, measles, and possibly mumps, spreading north from Cuzco; typhus moving south from Cartagena
1589	Influenza epidemic in Potosí, Bolivia[a]
1597	Outbreak of measles and "pains in the side" in Lima[a]
1604	Unidentified epidemic in Quito
1606	Diphtheria outbreak in Quito
1611	Outbreak of measles and typhus in Quito
1612	Scarlet fever appears, found with measles and typhus
1614	Typhus and diphtheria present in Quito
1618	Epidemics of measles and *mal del valle* in the province of Quito

Note: The sources of evidence for each epidemic are included in the text.
[a] Epidemic present in neighboring regions but so far has not been identified as affecting Ecuador.

also suggested by the tendency toward severe hemorrhaging. The disease was probably native to the area, for it was said to be worse among Spaniards, who had no knowledge of how to cure it. It was also contracted by Girolamo Benzoni on his visit to the province of Puerto Viejo in 1546.[21]

There are few precise details on the impact of epidemics prior to Spanish conquest. Cieza de León recorded that the epidemic of smallpox that killed Huayna Capac was "general" and was so contagious that "more than 200,000 souls died."[22] Others stress the large numbers killed in terms of "infinite thousands" and "innumerable people."[23] The epidemics were not only devastating but widespread. As already noted, Huayna Capac's relatives died of "a great pestilence" in Cuzco, while he himself died of smallpox in Quito and his successor Ninan Cuyoche succumbed to it in Tomebamba.[24] For this reason, the epidemic was significant not only in the numbers it killed but also because it precipitated the Inka dynastic wars and facilitated Spanish conquest.

For over a decade there is no evidence of new epidemics in Ecuador, though a number were reported in neighboring Colombia.[25] According to Cieza de León, in 1546 a "general pestilence" ran throughout the kingdom of Peru. He made this observation in describing the province of Quimbaya in central Colombia, and it is therefore assumed that the epidemic affected that region and was also present in the interposed province of Ecuador. No documentary evidence has come to light to support this assertion, but this may reflect the turmoil that prevailed in the Quito region during the Spanish civil wars. The epidemic was described as causing a headache and a very high fever, with the pain passing to the left ear and the victim dying within two or three days.[26] Dobyns has suggested that the epidemic may have been an Andean phase of *matlazáhuatl,* which devastated New Spain in 1545.[27] This disease has not been identified, but it has been suggested that it was typhus or pneumonic plague.[28] Typhus is generally accompanied by a rash, and for this reason it is sometimes mistaken for smallpox or measles. While the term "matlazáhuatl" implies the presence of a rash, descriptions of the Andean epidemic make no mention of a rash. Indeed the symptoms of intense headache and fever followed by rapid death suggest that more likely it was pneumonic plague. Furthermore, Polo has noted that at the same time llamas and sheep contracted a disease,[29] and it known that during a plague epidemic these animals may also be attacked. However, the typhus organism, *Rickettsia* sp., appears to infect only monkeys and guinea pigs.[30] The absence of buboes and the rapid death indicate that if plague was present, it was pneumonic rather than bubonic plague. The greater infectiousness of the former, since it is not dependent on a reservoir of infected rats but can be spread by coughing and sneezing, means that the epidemic would have spread rapidly. Since the disease is normally fatal, it would have resulted in very heavy mortality.[31] Cieza de León's observation that "innumerable people died" would fit in with its diagnosis as pneumonic plague. If the disease was pneumonic plague, then the overall mortality rate of 20 percent assigned to the epidemic by Cook, on the assumption that it was typhus, would have to be raised.[32]

The next pandemic in the Viceroyalty of Peru broke out in 1558. Several sources refer to it as smallpox and measles.[33] The virus was said to have been introduced from Hispaniola by black slaves purchased by the bishop of Santa Fé. In Nueva Granada it was said to have killed over 40,000 people.[34] For Ecuador a number of sources indicate that the epidemic was accompanied by catarrh, which occurred mainly at the beginning and end of the summer, and which killed both Spaniards and Indians.[35] Browne suggests that the catarrh was probably a secondary infection associated with smallpox and measles that frequently attacks recuperating victims.[36] Influenza was present in Europe, including Spain, in 1557, and quite likely it was that disease.[37] If it occurred in combination with smallpox and measles, it must have caused considerable mortality. In 1562 the remaining Indians around Cuenca were described as "still some or nearly all ill with smallpox."[38] Whether this was the tail end of the 1558 epidemic or a separate local outbreak is uncertain. Most likely the smallpox epidemic spread into the Oriente. Expeditions to Los Quijos that culminated in the foundation of Baeza in 1559 had departed from Quito the previous year when the epidemic was raging. Further south, meanwhile, when Juan de Salinas founded the town of Santiago de las Montañas in 1557, he was accompanied by "many sick people."[39] The sickness could have been associated with the arduous journey across the Sierra del Condor or been related to the smallpox epidemic, although the date is rather early.

For a period of over twenty years there is no evidence of epidemics in Ecuador, though again there are suggestions of outbreaks of smallpox in Colombia.[40] In 1582 an account of the Cuenca region by Hernando Pablos noted that smallpox and measles were occurring "according to their seasons," thereby suggesting they had become endemic, though in that year "a terrible *peste*," probably smallpox, ravaged villages in the Cuenca region.[41] The latter epidemic was probably a local outbreak, for if it had been more widespread, it would have been recorded by other authors of the relaciones geográficas compiled in that year.

From 1585 to 1591 the Andean peoples were hit by successive waves of epidemics. It seems likely, as suggested by Dobyns, that there were in fact two major epidemics during this period emanating from different regions. One probably spread north to Quito from Cuzco and Lima, while the other clearly moved south through Ecuador. Between 1585 and 1586 the cities of Lima and Cuzco were struck by epidemics of smallpox, measles, and possibly mumps, which appear to have resulted in high levels of mortality comparable with those experienced in New Spain.[42] An epidemic of "high fevers, smallpox, and measles" hit Quito, and within three months it had resulted in 4,000 deaths, especially of children.[43] This epidemic in Ecuador has been variously dated between 1586 and 1589. The second epidemic was accompanied by spots similar to smallpox and measles, and it appears to have been introduced from the Cape Verde Islands through one of two possible channels. In 1585 Drake's fleet touched the Cape Verde Islands, and subsequently several hundred of his crew died. Following the capture of Cartagena, Drake's fleet remained there for six weeks in early 1586, by which time the expedition was so weakened by disease that it returned to England. Other sources suggest that the disease was introduced by black slaves through Cartagena, from whence it spread inland to Mariquita, and subsequently throughout the Andean region. It appears to have arrived in Quito in 1587, from whence it passed to Cuenca, Loja, Paita, and Trujillo.[44] In Lima the epidemic claimed 3,000 victims in three months. The Jesuit provincial, Father Arriaga, described the epidemic there as resulting in boils that covered all the body and blocked the throat, preventing the victims from eating or breathing and thereby causing many deaths. Boils were common around the eyes, causing those affected to lose one or both eyes and to become so disfigured that they could be identified only by their names. They also gave off a fetid smell.[45] Dobyns argues that the disease could not have been smallpox or measles because it would have afflicted a larger proportion of Drake's crew. He suggests that the prolonged mortality on the expedition argues in favor of a disease spread by a vector, but probably not bubonic plague, since it would have been easily identified as the Black Death. More likely it was typhus.[46] This suggestion is backed by observations that it was accompanied by a rash and an unpleasant smell. Moreover, one account indicates the presence of "tabardete pestilencial," from which no one could escape, along with smallpox and measles.[47] The combined effect of these diseases was clearly devastating, not only for Indians, but also for some Creoles. In 1614 the *tabardete* epidemic of 1590 was still alive in the minds of members of the *cabildo* in Quito.[48]

It is clear that between 1587 and 1591 several epidemics afflicted Ecuador, often occurring simultaneously or in the wake of each other. In the city of Quito, Velasco claims that these epidemics carried off 30,000 of its 80,000 inhabitants.[49] Although this figure was undoubtedly exaggerated, it indicates the scale of the devastation, which extended throughout the highlands.[50] The southern sierra appears to have been particularly badly affected, where harsh working conditions, particularly in mining, combined with disease to produce high levels of mortality. In the early 1590s Indians around Cuenca and Loja were said to have been "consumed and finished off" as a result of smallpox, measles, and dysentery.[51] At the same time it was said that around the mines of Zaruma there had been 20,000 Indians, but because of work in the mines and the aforementioned diseases, there were only 500 Indians of all ages left.[52] Further south in the province of Jaén "the sickness of smallpox" had effectively reduced a population of some 30,000 Indians to only 1,000. The province Yaguarzongo and Pacamoros had also been devastated.[53] Some of these epidemics appear to have spread east to the hinterlands of Loyola and Santiago de las Montañas, where, between 1585 and 1586, diseases only vaguely described as "pestilencia" and "enfermedades" caused in a marked decline in the population.[54] From these frontier regions the diseases were almost certainly carried eastward into the Oriente by enslaving raids. The coast also suffered from epidemics at this time. Campos maintains that it was the 1589 epidemic that resulted in the extinction of the Huancavilca,[55] though even before 1574 they had been reduced to a quarter of their numbers by diseases variously referred to as "pestes," "enfermedades," and "pestilencias."[56] Early seventeenth-century references to Indian villages around Puerto

Viejo attributed the depopulation of the region to epidemics of measles and typhus,[57] which probably occurred between 1585 and 1591.

Prior to 1600 two other epidemics occurred in the southern Andes for which no evidence has been found further north. An influenza epidemic broke out in Potosí in 1589,[58] while in 1597 Lima was afflicted by an epidemic of measles and "pains in the side."[59] The latter epidemic is likely to have spread north, given the frequent contact that existed between Lima and Guayaquil. It 1604 the cabildo of Quito requested a doctor from Lima in order to cope with the many sick that there were at the time, but it did not specify the disease responsible.[60] Two years later there was an outbreak of *garrotillo* (diphtheria), which was general throughout the district of Quito and in which many died.[61] This was followed by an outbreak of typhus and measles in Quito in 1611.[62] Arcos suggests these latter two diseases were also present in 1612 along with *scarlatina* (scarlet fever) and that in 1614 typhus appeared again, accompanied by diphtheria.[63] In 1618 an epidemic of measles and *mal del valle* ("valley sickness"), which was described as particularly devastating among children, afflicted the Quito region[64] and was also present in Peru and later Bolivia.[65] These frequent recurrences of diseases and their impact on children suggest that they were becoming endemic.[66]

There is some debate as to whether either yellow fever or malaria was present in Ecuador's tropical lowlands in the early colonial period. Both diseases are generally considered to have originated in the Old World. Yellow fever is a more deadly killer than malaria, but as already indicated in chapter 1, the first definitely identifiable epidemic in the New World occurred in 1647–48.[67] It has been suggested by some that the first outbreak of yellow fever in Ecuador occurred in Guayaquil in 1740, followed quickly by another in 1743,[68] though other writers argue that the city suffered its first epidemic in 1842.[69]

Malaria probably influenced demographic trends at an earlier date. In Ecuador the *Anopheles* mosquito, which acts as a vector for the parasite, is to be found at altitudes of up to 2,400 meters, and malaria may have affected two regions.[70] The coast was probably affected at an earlier date. Elsewhere I have argued that the fevers experienced by expeditionaries on the coast were probably the result of starvation induced by inadequate provisions and the necessity to live off the land, while other fevers associated with the bites of insects probably derived from the activities of sandflies rather than mosquitoes.[71] Even into the seventeenth century the coast was considered to be generally healthy, and in the nineteenth century the major killers there were digestive and respiratory disorders rather than tropical fevers.[72] Nevertheless, malaria was probably introduced during the sixteenth century.

Spaniards may have introduced the benign form of malaria, *Plas-*

modium vivax, direct from Europe, whereas the more acute form *P. fal-ciparum* probably entered with black slaves from Africa, though both parasites might have been carried to the region from other parts of the New World, where they had already become established. It is worthy of note that black slaves were shipwrecked on the coast of Esmeraldas in 1553, and from an early date others were employed in coastal haciendas and towns. The subsequent spread of malaria was probably slow, since the demographic collapse of the region in the early conquest period effectively reduced the number of human hosts. Meanwhile in Esmeraldas forest regeneration that accompanied depopulation would have reduced the num-ber of sun-loving mosquitoes. In the Guayas Basin, however, logging activ-ities for building and ship construction would have maintained a more open environment. Today the more acute form of malaria, *P. falciparum,* accounts for about a half of the incidences of malaria on the coast.[73] In Esmeraldas it is associated with more extensive ecological disturbance, whereas the more benign form, *P. vivax,* is characteristic of regions where an ecological balance is maintained.[74] It is not unreasonable to assume that the more benign form was more common in the colonial period, when population levels were lower and ecologically destructive activities more localized. It is doubtful that malaria had a significant impact on demo-graphic trends in coastal Ecuador in the sixteenth century. More likely, any heightened impact of Old World diseases on the coast derived from the constant introduction of new infections by ships that stopped on the coast for provisions or to trade.

The spread of malaria to the Oriente in the early colonial period is even more problematic.[75] Early missionaries described the region as healthy, even though they often commented on the abundance of annoying insects, though only in some places and at some times of the year.[76] Equally telling is the fact that the expeditions of Francisco de Orellana in 1541–42 and Pedro de Ursúa and Lope de Aguirre in 1560–61 make no comment on the unhealthiness of the region, and even though they were bothered by insects, they did not suffer from fevers. If malaria had been present, it would almost certainly have afflicted some of the expeditionaries during their long journeys across the continent. Fevers are mentioned in many later missionary accounts, but fevers may be associated with many dis-eases and even starvation, which was a fairly common occurrence on expeditions. Serological tests among the Waorani living south of the Napo River to determine antibody prevalence indicate exposure to *P. vivax* and *P. malariae,* but not to the more deadly *P. falciparum.*[77] The earliest candidate for malaria was an epidemic that occurred among the Oa in the mid-1660s, who at that time inhabited the Nushiño River close to the sierra. This area was described as being infected with mosquitoes, which resulted in many Indians and a number of missionaries dying of quartan fevers.[78] Of the three strains of malaria, only *P. malariae* is associated with quartan fevers, as the others produce tertian fevers. Even today the climate of the Oriente, from the point of view of malaria, is regarded as healthy. Although the region's climate favors the *Anopheles* mosquito and malaria is endemic in the high selva area, malarial infection is relatively uncommon because of the low population density and forest cover.[79]

Early accounts of the impact of Old World diseases such as smallpox and measles on Amerindian populations suggest that they often resulted in the death of one-third to one-half of those affected,[80] and the devastating impact of these diseases on previously noninfected populations has been corroborated by historically more recent epidemics.[81] In developing a disease mortality model for estimating the size of the aboriginal population of Peru, Cook suggests that the six major epidemics that afflicted the region between 1524 and 1615 carried off between 79.3 and 91.7 percent of the population.[82] These six epidemics—in 1524–26, 1530–32, 1546, 1558–60, 1585–91, and 1614–15—all affected Ecuador, but whether large areas lost such significant proportions of their populations is a matter for debate. Although the high levels of mortality associated with the impact of Old World diseases on nonimmune populations are generally accepted, most well-documented accounts of their impact, and especially the more recent ones, refer to relatively small areas and populations, and it is debatable whether conditions favoring the spread of these diseases would have prevailed over extensive regions. As already noted in the Introduction, the impact of particular diseases would have depended on a variety of factors, including climate, altitude, population density, the intensity of social contact, subsistence patterns, and sanitation, among other things. Environmental and social conditions on the coast, in the highlands, and in the Amazon headwaters of Ecuador were quite different, and there were further variations within those broad regions. Furthermore, the incidence of diseases would have depended on the frequency of contact with sources of infection and the subsequent ease with which they could spread.

Coastal Ecuador, and especially the region around Guayaquil, was particularly vulnerable to the introduction of diseases because of the frequent contact it had with vessels that stopped there on the way from Central America to Peru. Conversely the Oriente was protected to a degree by its inland location and the physical barrier of the Andean mountains. Although diseases did penetrate this area, being carried by expeditions emanating from the sierra, contacts were less intense, and the cooler climatic conditions of the Andes would certainly have hindered the spread of tropical lowland diseases such as malaria. Within the highlands, diseases could travel along the interandean corridor relatively easily with people, troops, and supplies, but elsewhere the rugged topography would have discouraged contacts, so that not every village would have been hit by every epidemic. Indeed Shea has suggested that in the Andes the impact of disease was moderated by the existence of high mountain ranges, which acted as barriers to its spread. He compares the region with Central Mexico, where disease could spread more easily in a radial fashion, thereby resulting in a higher levels of decline.[83]

In summary, the spatial impact of disease was not uniform, and the large proportions reported as dying as a result of epidemics are likely to have been local maxima. Nevertheless, their overall demographic impact is likely to have been equally as high or even greater during the first century of Spanish rule, since other epidemics apart from the six considered by Cook afflicted the Audiencia of Quito. In addition his disease-mortality model takes no account of their effects on fertility levels, which are likely to have been considerable, although difficult to quantify. As indicated in chapter 1, epidemics often resulted in high levels of pregnancy loss and mortality among pregnant women, while some diseases induced subfecundity. Perhaps more significant was their impact on reproductive capacity, which declined through the breakdown of conjugal unions and psychological stress. The impact of disease on fertility has generally been underestimated and should be considered in any assessment of the overall impact of epidemics. Nevertheless, many of these effects were not felt uniformly but were significantly influenced by the size of the native population and its culture. Spatial variations in the impact of epidemics on mortality and fertility rates will be discussed in greater detail in the following twelve regional chapters.

Part Four

SPANISH RULE: THE SIERRA

CHAPTER 7

Otavalo

The Indians, or almost all of them, leave their villages and flee to distant and remote parts ten, twenty, thirty, and fifty leagues away where neither the *corregidores* nor the *caciques* nor Indian governors nor the appointed tax collectors can collect it [tribute] from them.

Licenciado Melchor Suárez de Poago, 2 May 1634[1]

The corregimiento of Otavalo, established in 1563, comprised the region between the Guáytara and Guayllabamba rivers. The Pasto inhabited the northern part of the region, while to the south of the Chota-Mira Valley were a number of chiefdoms, of which the largest were those of Otavalo, Caranqui, and Cayambe. The corregimiento was named after Otavalo, who at the time of Spanish conquest was the most powerful chief in the region. Even though the corregimiento of Otavalo suffered severe depopulation, throughout the early colonial period it remained one of the most densely populated regions in the Audiencia of Quito.

The greater part of the region was located between 2,000 and 3,000 meters in tierra fría and *tierra templada,* but some communities, such as Lita, Quilca, Mira, and Pimampiro, were found at lower elevations (1,200–2,000 meters) in *tierra caliente.* Although the northern Andes contained rich agricultural lands that were developed for livestock raising and cereal production, its mining activities were limited to the production of salt. Local demands for labor were therefore small, and many Indians were employed outside the region, particularly in the Quito Basin. Some were forcibly transferred there by encomenderos, but increasingly others moved there voluntarily in search of wage labor. Population losses due to migration and epidemics severely undermined the economic and social viability of Indian communities and increased the hardships for those who remained. Unable to meet tribute payments and *mita* levies, many attempted to escape registration. As tribute debts rose dramatically, encomenderos and the Crown sought to recover and sustain their income through the establishment of obrajes. Like the regions of Riobamba, Ambato, and Latacunga to the south, the Otavalo area became an important producer of woolen textiles. (See Map 6.)

The conquest of the northern sierra might have begun after the brutal slaughter of Indians at Quinche, but Sebastián de Benalcázar's attention was distracted south by the appearance on the coast of the rival conquistador Pedro de Alvarado. Once his rights of conquest had been assured,

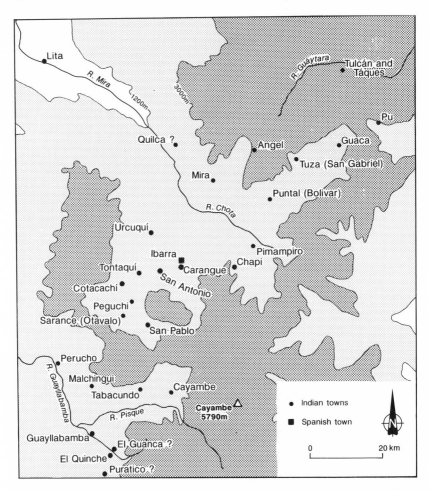

Map 6. The Otavalo region

Benalcázar sent his *teniente,* Diego de Tapia, to explore the northern
sierra. This first expedition met resistance from the Indians at Tulcán,
leaving the effective conquest of the region to Pedro de Añasco and Juan
de Ampudia.[2] By June 1535 Benalcázar boldly claimed that he had pacified
and distributed encomiendas as far north as the Quillaçinga.[3] In fact it was
not until two years later that the Indians of Lita, Quilca, and Caguasquí
were conquered by Pedro de Puelles.[4] Even though the northern sierra
was officially pacified, demands for auxiliaries for expeditions and excessive exactions of tribute and labor kept the region on the verge of rebellion
throughout the century.[5] In 1547 rumors that an armed rebellion was

being organized in the region resulted in the cacique of Otavalo being confined to Quito,[6] and three years later a revolt against the encomendero of Lita and Quilca left five Spaniards dead.[7]

The earliest demands on Indian communities were for auxiliaries for expeditions. Initially they were involved in Sebastián de Benalcázar's expeditions that explored and conquered southern Colombia.[8] Later Indians from the Otavalo region accompanied two notable expeditions to the Oriente. First, in 1538 they were involved in Gonzalo Díaz de Pineda's ill-fated expeditions to Los Quijos;[9] later, headed by the cacique of Cayambe, Gerónimo Puento, they helped Rodrigo Núñez de Bonilla suppress the 1578 uprising.[10] Finally, toward the end of the century, the proximity of the Caranqui and Pasto made them obvious conscripts for expeditions to Esmeraldas. Although the latter expeditions involved smaller numbers and tended to be exploratory rather than military in character, they represented yet another compulsory levy on already overburdened Indians in the northernmost sierra.[11] The numbers involved in these expeditions will be discussed more fully in considering the Quito region, where they had their greatest impact.[12] Suffice it to say that between 43,000 and 53,000 Indians from the northern sierra may have been involved, and possibly about one-third were drawn from what became the corregimiento of Otavalo. Some died in battle, others fell ill on the journey, and many failed to return home. Despite the obvious hardships that expeditions imposed on Indian communities, they were often supported by caciques hoping to enhance their positions and acquire more formal control over lands that produced exotic goods.[13]

Encomiendas, including those in the Otavalo region, were distributed by Sebastián de Benalcázar shortly after the foundation of Quito, but little is known of the number allocated or their recipients. Later accounts suggest that as few as nine may have been distributed in the Otavalo region, though they were substantial in size.[14] Indeed, in the sixteenth century the encomienda of Otavalo itself was the most valuable in the audiencia. It was initially reserved for the Crown, but in 1549 Sebastián de Benalcázar claimed it for himself. At that time he estimated that it contained between 1,500 and 2,000 tributary Indians and the nearby encomienda of Carangue about 500.[15]

Prior to the establishment of royal control after the Spanish civil wars, tribute and labor exactions were unregulated, but in 1549 Licenciado Pedro de La Gasca ordered a visita to be conducted of the repartimiento of Otavalo. The resulting tasación for 1,167 tributary Indians required them to pay 1,400 pesos in cash, with a substantial proportion of the remaining tribute payable in cotton thread and cotton products, plus pigs, chickens, and game. Crops levied were to be cultivated on their encomendero's lands near Quito, and they were to provide domestic service for his household in the city.[16] This early tasación reveals a characteristic feature of encomiendas in the Otavalo region, namely that they supported a nonresident Spanish population. Not only were tributary Indians compelled to work in Quito and on its surrounding estates, but Indian leaders were often forced to reside in the city, where encomenderos felt they could exert greater influence over them. This had important consequences for the protection of community interests and the status of their leaders.[17]

Encomenderos objected to the early tasaciones, maintaining that the Indians had been taxed too lightly. The encomendero of Otavalo, Rodrigo de Salazar, complained that his encomienda had been assessed at only 3,000 pesos, even though the Indians were rich and great traders.[18] Encomenderos expected the tasaciones to be revised in the light of their complaints and in anticipation levied what they thought appropriate. Rodrigo de Salazar exacted 2,000 pesos in cash every three months instead of the stipulated 1,400 pesos a year.[19] Pressure from dissatisfied encomenderos and Indians alike provoked visitas in 1552 and 1559.[20] These revealed 1,300 more tributary Indians than the first tasación, and the discrepancy was attributed to the failure of the first *visitadores* to follow the instructions laid down by La Gasca. Rodrigo de Salazar claimed that as a consequence between 1549 and 1562 he had been defrauded of 13,000 pesos.[21] Unimpressed, the president of the audiencia, Hernando de Santillán, replied that the recent visitas had been a waste of time because, in effect, Indian villages had been assessed by their own encomenderos. However, even the new visita failed to satisfy Rodrigo de Salazar, who managed to persuade his friend Viceroy Conde de Nieva to increase the levy by 1,500 pesos without a new inspection.[22] Oidor Salazar de Villasante commented in dismay that the Indians could not even pay according to the first tasación, for since then more than half had died.[23]

More is known about the encomienda of Otavalo because of the wranglings of Rodrigo de Salazar, whose levies set Indian communities on the path of mounting tribute debts. However, the visitas also affected other communities, although how comprehensive they were is unknown. Evidence exists for the enumeration of Carangue and Pu by Gil Ramírez Dávalos in 1559, but other information is sadly lacking.[24] Fragmentary evidence for tasaciones drawn up in the 1550s and 1560s suggests they followed the same general pattern indicated for Otavalo. The main changes were the exclusion of personal service from tasaciones after 1552 and a slight reduction in the number of items levied, though they remained broadly similar in kind. A major difficulty for communities in this region was that the greater part of the tribute levied was in the form of either cotton or gold, and later silver, pesos. None of these items was produced in the region but was obtained by trade with lowland communities, and increasingly through wage labor. Cotton and gold had been traded in pre-

Columbian times, but Spanish conquest damaged these links and reduced the ability of Indians in the highlands to produce surpluses to trade. Thus in order to acquire the specified items, they had to barter the few goods they possessed outside the region or seek employment as wage laborers.[25] Over time the cash component of tribute payments was increasingly rendered in the form of silver pesos.[26]

Prior to the *visita general* ordered by Viceroy Francisco de Toledo in 1570, some communities in the corregimiento, including Otavalo, were reassessed by Oidor Pedro de Hinojosa. In 1573 the same visitador accompanied by the corregidor, Juan Zarate de Chacón, conducted a comprehensive program of reducciones, but it is not known whether those villages recently visited were reassessed. In 1579 the first visita to assess Indians on an individual basis was undertaken by Licenciados Diego de Ortegón and Francisco de Auncibay. Even though the new tasaciones more closely reflected local production and involved a reduction in the number of items payable, they represented an increased levy.[27] At the same time, the oidores brought charges against Salazar for excessive tribute exactions and for commuting tribute in kind to money payments without license. They calculated that between 1568 and 1578 Salazar had levied over 8,600 pesos in excess of that specified by the tasaciones and ordered it to be returned.[28] This brief and incomplete review of tasaciones for the corregimiento of Otavalo suggests that over time the tribute burden increased, such that by the end of the century Indians in the Audiencia of Quito were paying some of the highest levies in the empire. Assadourian argues that increased tribute levies were an essential part of Viceroy Toledo's policies to increase royal revenue both directly and by encouraging Indians to seek employment in commercial enterprises, particularly mining.[29] This view is supported by evidence from the Audiencia of Quito, where they reinforced and accelerated existing trends.

Another feature of Viceroy Toledo's plan to stimulate the colonial economy was to establish greater control over sources of labor. To this end, programs of reducciones were initiated throughout the viceroyalty. In the corregimiento of Otavalo it generally involved the forcible movement of Indians from small, scattered communities to create larger settlements, though occasionally ayllu were broken up and their members dispersed among a number of villages sometimes located in different regions.[30] The program concentrated Indians at intermediate altitudes, where the majority of the larger settlements were already located.[31] For example the inhabitants of four villages in the Coangue Valley located in tierra caliente, whose unhealthy climate was judged responsible for the failure of the population to increase, were moved to the more temperate climate of Pimampiro.[32] The reorganization left many communities unable to work the now-distant lands they had exploited for generations, which as a consequence became more vulnerable to alienation. Although the newly formed settlements were allocated lands, the subsistence base of many communities was probably adversely affected.

Less evidence exists for tribute assessments at the end of the sixteenth century. Villages paying tribute to the Crown were reassessed by Dr. Moreno de Mera in 1590,[33] and again in 1611 by Oidor Licenciado Diego de Zorilla.[34] While in 1590 each Indian was required to pay 4 pesos, 2 *tomines,* and one chicken, by 1618 the levy had been raised to 5 pesos, 1 *real,* and the price of two chickens.[35] The increased taxes did nothing more than add to the already enormous tribute debts, which by 1620 had reached over 100,000 pesos for the encomienda of Otavalo alone.[36]

The establishment of obrajes was seen as a means by which unpaid tributes could be recovered from dwindling numbers of Indians and a future income ensured. Their establishment was often supported by caciques, who not only received salaries for supervising the mills but hoped the profits would contribute toward tribute payments for which they were personally responsible. Obrajes in the Otavalo region were owned by Indian communities, but since they were attached to encomiendas, each mill was supervised by a royal administrator appointed by the viceroy in Lima. The obraje at Otavalo, which produced coarse cloths—*sayales* and *jergas*—was established by Rodrigo de Salazar prior to 1582, but when he died intestate in 1584, the encomienda reverted to the Crown.[37] Although profits from the mill should have been used to discharge tribute debts, they became a source of royal revenue.[38] Initially 50 Indians were assigned to work in this obraje,[39] but after the Crown assumed control, their number was increased to 180 "tributarios y reservados." Serious shortfalls occurred in the numbers appearing for work, which even the threat of stiff punishments such as flogging, imprisonment, or exile to Guayaquil failed to correct.[40] In 1601, to boost the number of workers, 80 *muchachos* between the ages of thirteen and fourteen were added to the numbers required.[41] However, since workers could only be drawn from distances that enabled them to travel to work daily, instead of the 260 specified, normally only 120 or at best 150 could be recruited, most of them youths. In order to expand the pool of labor, in the early seventeenth century textile workers were ordered to settle in Otavalo so that they could return home at night.[42]

High administrative costs and the corruption and lack of interest of its administrators reduced obraje profits for the Crown and did little to lower tribute debts,[43] which by 1607 had risen to over 20,000 pesos.[44] In 1612 the Crown decided to rent out the mill and use the income to discharge debts. Although it was later claimed that the mill had become more profitable, by 1620 tribute debts had quintupled.[45] Increasing debts prompted the establishment in 1622 of another obraje—San Joseph de Buenavista—at nearby Peguchi.[46]

By the 1620s it had become clear that more fundamental reasons underlay the failure of the obrajes to reduce tribute debts than just the way they
were administered. A major problem was the shortage of workers, partly
due to fugitivism and competing demands for labor. Unlike the obrajes of
Riobamba, Ambato, and Latacunga, those in Otavalo did not have to com-
pete with private mills, which had been banned in the region,[47] but there
were other local demands for labor. Perhaps the most important drain on
sources of labor was the mita discussed below. As far as can be judged,
and the documents are not altogether clear on this point, the numbers of
workers assigned to the mills were not deducted from the *quinto* required
for the mita. Despite labor shortages, the obrajes seem to have been more
successful than other enterprises in securing workers. In 1648 the mills at
Otavalo and Peguchi were employing over 700 Indians and were some of
the largest factories in the New World.[48]

Mounting tribute debts not only stimulated the establishment of obrajes but also encouraged Indians to sell their lands, sometimes before
leaving for regions as far-flung as Lima and Potosí.[49] Land began to be
viewed as a source of capital, and Indians fought more vigorously to defend
their rights. In 1610 the cacique of Cotacachi won a lawsuit against an
alcalde ordinario of Ibarra who had usurped his lands, only then to request
a license to sell it.[50] Community lands and even those belonging to private
individuals were sold by caciques to discharge tribute debts, sometimes in
defiance of the claims of their subjects.[51] Such sales occurred more frequently as Indians left their communities, if only for short periods, as the
program of reducciones took effect, and as commercial agricultural production expanded. The alienation of Indian lands created a footloose population that was seen by the authorities as detrimental to the establishment
of a stable labor force for the obrajes. In 1620 suggested reforms of the
textile industry included measures to discourage migration that would
involve the allocation of lands to Indians and the return of those acquired
by Spaniards.[52]

Tribute in kind or cash formed only part of the Indians' obligations; the
other major burden was the mita. It was gradually introduced after 1552,
when personal service ceased to be included in tasaciones. The mita for
the corregimiento of Otavalo was organized as part of that developed for
the Audiencia of Quito.[53] It required Indian communities to provide one-
fifth of their tributary populations to work in a variety of tasks that included *servicio ordinario,* the collection of wood and fodder, mining, agricultural labor, and the construction and repair of buildings, roads, and
bridges. *Mitayos* were to work within a few leagues of their homes and
were not to cross climatic zones, but as elsewhere, these stipulations were
often infringed. While some mitayos worked in local enterprises, many
were employed in the cultivation of sugar, cotton, and coca in the hot

Chota and Guayllabamba valleys. Unacclimatized to these conditions, many of them became ill and died.[54] The vineyards and gardens of the Dominicans in the Mira Valley earned the reputation of being "fields of blood."[55] Many others worked outside the region.

It has often been noted with validity that Spanish rule brought more profound economic and social transformations to Indian communities located near a major town or economic center than those located at greater distances. It has not always been recognized, however, that distant communities might be put under disproportionate strain. Although Spanish demands for labor generally declined with distance, the longer journeys and periods of absence experienced by mitayos from distant communities may have had equally, if not more detrimental effects. There was no Spanish town between Quito and Pasto until Ibarra was established in 1606, so that mitayos from the corregimiento of Otavalo were ordered to provide services for Quito's citizens. In 1583 some 250 mitayos from Otavalo alone, excluding women and children who usually accompanied them, were providing service for households in the city.[56] Others from more distant communities, such as those from Tuza, Guaca, and Tulcán, traveled up to 160 kilometers across several climatic zones.[57] The exhausting journeys and perpetual labor to which they were often subjected encouraged sickness and raised mortality rates, while their prolonged absence undermined subsistence production and strained kinship ties.

When Ibarra was established in 1606 with about 150 vecinos, a proportion of the mita labor available within the corregimiento was directed to build and maintain the town. For a time this reduced travel distances for some. In 1612 the mita for Ibarra involved 300 Indians from the Pasto villages of Tuza, Guaca, Chuquín, Puntal, Taques, and Tulcán who were to work for six months in three mitas of two months each, while the communities of Otavalo, San Pablo, Cotacachi, Tontaquí, Urcuquí, and Panzaleo were to provide 100 Indians for the months of July to September inclusive.[58] Local *hacendados, obrajeros,* and Quito's citizens objected strongly to the new mita, and in 1625 it was abolished. In 1633 the vecinos of Ibarra were pleading for 50 mitayos to maintain their houses.[59]

Other mitayos were employed in agricultural tasks. The corregimiento of Otavalo became an important cereal- and livestock-raising area, while its warmer valleys produced sugar, vegetables, fruit, and vines.[60] These profitable enterprises, and particularly market gardening, brought large numbers of Spaniards, who generated further demands for labor. In the 1590s Ordóñez de Cevallos observed that while the native population of Pimampiro numbered about 800, the fertility of the surrounding region had attracted so many Spanish and Indian settlers that its total population numbered about 2,000.[61] Similarly, by the end of the sixteenth century between 150 to 200 Spaniards had established estates in the Carangue Valley.[62]

These estates not only competed for mita labor but, by offering an escape from tribute and mita obligations, attracted free labor.

Population decline, fugitivism, and competing demands for labor meant that many Indian villages were unable to meet their mita quotas. In 1604 Otavalo could supply only 85 percent of the numbers required to provide servicio ordinario and to work in construction, and by the time their tours of duty commenced, another 15 percent had fled. The shortfall on this occasion was nearly one-third, but it could reach as high as one-half. In this instance the cacique was imprisoned and given three days to complete the quota or else be deprived of his *cacicazgo*.[63]

Even though there were shortfalls in the numbers required, those who actually worked as mitayos represented more like a quarter than the fifth specified, and this took no account of the numbers employed in obrajes.[64] Persistent demands for labor had a unsettling effect on local communities, which were always thought to be on the verge of rebellion. The demands and rigors of the mita stimulated many to attempt to avoid registration as tributary Indians.[65] While many Indians opted to migrate, some to other provinces, others were concealed by caciques or friends at visitas, and some were continually on the move in order to escape registration.[66] In 1600 President Ibarra, having heard rumors that many Indians had evaded registration in 1590 when the region was inspected by Dr. Moreno de Mera, ordered an investigation by the *contador* Francisco de Caceres, who uncovered 660 absentees.[67] More concerted efforts at locating fugitive Indians meant that by the next visita in 1611 the number of Indians registered since the 1590 visita had risen by 1,452.[68] But the process was never ending, for by 1625 another 300 tributary Indians had fled.[69]

Fugitivism began as a response to colonial abuses, but it was later actively encouraged by the Crown as a means of breaking the power of private encomenderos and increasing its own income. Those who left their natal communities and became *forasteros* were offered the inducements of exemption from the mita and a lower rate of tribute.[70] These Indians were often settled in distinct parcialidades and became the backbone of the wage labor force, which, among other things, supplied the illegal *chorillos* in Quito. Caciques and others seeking to enhance their political and financial positions also attracted forasteros to their protection. A few astute caciques were successful, but many more saw their economic and political power sapped by increased responsibilities and personal hardships. In 1623 Spanish officials considered the Indians of Otavalo to be poorer than elsewhere in the audiencia and their caciques even poorer still, to the extent that they were reluctant to assume office and often fled.[71]

Fugitivism was the survival strategy for which many Indians opted, but most remained. For them daily life was transformed. As Indian lands were alienated and the population declined, vast stretches of land were turned over to livestock raising, and many intensive forms of agricultural production, especially the cultivation of camellones, ceased.[72] The exploitation of lands located in different ecological zones was disturbed by the program of reducciones, as were trading relations with distant communities. Since these strategies were employed primarily to acquire nonessential and often sumptuary items, the changes may have had little effect on subsistence production. Nevertheless, the forced concentration on fewer ecological zones, and hence crops, which was also encouraged by the nature of tribute payments and the demands of the market, may have made communities more vulnerable in the event of harvest failure. Subsistence production was probably more adversely affected by the alienation of intensively cultivated lands in the highlands and new demands for labor and tribute. These losses were compensated for in part by the introduction of new crops and animals, particularly livestock and cereals. Indian communities were quick to adopt chickens and also sheep, whose wool they traded and wove into cloth for sale. In 1582 Indians at Pimampiro owned over 3,500 sheep in common.[73] Although subsistence patterns were profoundly changed by colonial rule, the Otavalo region was generally regarded as fertile, and there is little evidence for food shortages.

DEMOGRAPHIC TRENDS IN THE OTAVALO REGION

Population trends in the corregimiento of Otavalo are difficult to determine because of the fragmentary and confused nature of the evidence available. The relaciones geográficas of 1582 provide comprehensive and fairly detailed accounts of the region, but little quantitative evidence exists, except for the encomienda of Otavalo, with which to chart demographic changes between the time of conquest and 1582. Nevertheless the qualitative evidence makes it clear that the population suffered a dramatic decline, which in 1582 the corregidor of Otavalo, Paz Ponce de León, attributed to conquests by the Inka and Spanish and to epidemics.[74] Expeditions of conquest cost many lives and carried others to alien environments from which they never returned. During the sixteenth century between 14,000 to 17,500 Indians may have been involved in expeditions from the northern sierra, the majority being recruited prior to 1550.[75] Superimposed on this were the effects of epidemics. By 1582 the Otavalo region had been hit by smallpox, measles, and tabardete.[76] In the 1560s Oidor Salazar de Villasante claimed that since the first tasación, probably in 1549, half of the region's Indian population had died.[77] At the same time the population was subjected to unregulated exactions of tribute and labor, which contributed to early death, undermined the viability of Indian communities, and promoted flight on a scale not noted in other parts of the

Table 7. Tributary Population of Otavalo, 1549 to 1665

Year	Tributary population	Source
1549	1,167	RAHM 9/4664 nos. 1–2 fols. 27v–29v, no date
1549	1,500–2,000	LC 1:345–60 Sebastián de Benalcázar 3.11.1549
1552	2,411	AGI EC 922A Tasa de Otavalo 4.9.1579
1559	2,163	AGI EC 922A Tasa de Otavalo 4.9.1579 (plus 411 solteros)
1562	2,548	AGI EC 922A Tasa de Otavalo 4.9.1579 (plus 446 solteros)
1582	2,360	RGI 2:240–41 Paz Ponce de León 2.4.1582 (includes solteros)
1590	1,986	AGI CO 1536 Cuentas reales 1591; ANHQ Real Hacienda 63 fols. 50–83
1591	2,011	CDI 6:41–63 Relación de los indios tributarios 1.11.1591; AGI AQ 19 Testimonio del acrecimiento 7.11.1612
1598	2,800	AGI AQ 9 Licenciado Marañón, no date
1611	3,099	AGI AQ 19 Testimonio del acrecimiento 7.11.1612
1618	2,871	AGI AQ 19 Relación sumaria 22.3.1618
1633	3,725	ANHQ Tierras 2 Carta cuenta for 1632, 27.1.1633; error in the document gives 3,663
1640	2,673	ANHQ Tributos 2 Cartas cuentas de Otavalo 1638–40
1658	3,753	ANHQ Real Hacienda 65 Cartas cuentas de Otavalo 1657–58
1665	4,448	Tyrer, "Demographic and Economic History," 378–79

audiencia.[78] It is surprising to find, therefore, that between 1549 and 1562, according to tasaciones for the repartimiento of Otavalo, the tributary population increased from 1,167 to 2,994. (See Table 7.)[79] This increase, which flies in the face of the qualitative evidence, was attributed to new and more efficient methods of inspection, but more likely it reflects the power of encomenderos to influence assessments and the weakness of royal government.[80] Between 1562 and 1582 the tributary population of the encomienda of Otavalo declined by over 20 percent, a fall that could reflect greater official control as well as real losses.[81] The communities of Pimampiro and Chapi followed the same trend. Between 1570 and 1582 alone the tributary population of these communities fell by 17 percent. This provides some support for contemporary observations that mortality rates were higher at lower elevations, particularly in the Chota and Guayllabamba valleys.[82]

The relaciones geográficas of 1582 are unusually complete for the northern sierra. With the exception of Pasto villages in the far north, for which the corregidor of Otavalo provides only estimates, the returns are based on special enumerations or current *padrones*. Although they contain some arithmetic errors and discrepancies, they are minor, and it is possible to link the figures more firmly to a specific date than is normally the case. From these accounts the total population of the northern sierra in

Table 8. Indian Population of the Otavalo Region in 1582

Ethnic group	Tributary population	Total population	Ratio
Otavalo	2,360	11,252	4.76
Carangue, San Antonio	505	2,891	5.72
Cayambe, Tabacundo	400	2,008	4.67
Perucho, Malchinguí	176	824	4.68
Total	3,441	16,975	4.93
Mira	400	1,961	4.90
Tuza, Puntal, Guaca, Pu, Tulcán	2,600	11,700[a]	4.50[a]
Total	3,000	13,661	4.55
Lita, Quilca, Caguasquí	(677) 700[b]	2,937	4.19
Chapi, Pimampiro	613	2,355	3.84
Guayllabamba, El Guanca	436	1,894	4.34
Puratico	400	1,800[a]	4.50[a]
Total	2,149	8,986	4.18
Grand Total	8,590	39,622[a]	4.61[a]

Source: RGI 2:240–41 Paz Ponce de León 2.4.1582; RGI 2:243 Rodríguez 9.11.1582; RGI 2:245 Aguilar 12.11.1582; RGI 2:252 Borja, no date. The figures for Carangue and San Antonio are calculated by subtracting those for Chapi and Pimampiro given by Borja.

[a] An estimate. Where the total population is not given in the relaciones geográficas, it has been estimated from the tributary population and a multiplication factor of 4.5. This is slightly lower than that of 4.67 calculated for regions for which figures are available.

[b] The figure of 700 is contained in the general account of the corregimiento of Otavalo (RGI 2:241 Paz Ponce de León 2.4.1582), and the figure of 677 is the sum of figures given for the three individual villages found in the other accounts.

1582 can be calculated at 39,622 (Table 8), but it clearly represented only a proportion of the total population of the region, for other evidence suggests that fugitivism was rife.[83] Between 1562 and 1582 the ratio of tributary Indians to the total population in the encomienda of Otavalo fell from 1:4.23 to 1:4.76. In fact the tributary population declined more than the population as a whole—that is, by 21.1 percent compared with 11.25 percent. If the ratio is kept constant at 1:4.23, there should have been 319 (13.5 percent) more tributary Indians in 1582 than were actually enumerated. If this level of fugitivism is assumed for the whole of the northern sierra, the total population may have been about 45,000.[84] The qualitative evidence already presented suggests that fugitivism may have been even more prevalent.

In 1590 Dr. Moreno de Mera conducted a visita of the encomienda of Otavalo, where he registered 2,011 tributary Indians.[85] It is not clear whether other villages in the corregimiento were inspected at the same time. This figure represents a decline of nearly 15 percent since 1582, which could be explained by the smallpox epidemic in the late 1580s, which hit Otavalo particularly badly.[86] However, it was later revealed that as many as 660 fugitive Indians had escaped registration—that is, one-third more than actually recorded and over double the number of fugitives suggested above for 1582.[87] President Ibarra reported that within the audiencia as a whole new inspections were revealing one-quarter, one-third, or one-half more Indians than recorded in previous visitas. Adding 660 to the number enumerated would give a tributary population for 1590 of 2,671, thereby converting the calculated decline into an increase. Because of the smallpox epidemic, an increase in the population during this period is extremely unlikely, and it suggests that the proportion that was absent in 1582 was higher than the 13.5 percent suggested. Indeed, President Ibarra attributed the increase in the tributary population to more effective registration, not population growth.

The visita for 1611 ordered by Licenciado Diego de Zorilla added 1,088 Indians to Otavalo's tribute roll.[88] This marked growth of 54.1 percent since 1590 may include an element of natural increase, but essentially it was due to continued registration of fugitive Indians by the zealous oidor anxious to impress the Crown by increasing its tribute income.[89] By the mid-1660s the tributary population of the Otavalo villages had risen to 4,448 (Table 9),[90] more than double that recorded in 1591.[91] During the same period communities in the southern part of the corregimiento had mixed demographic histories. The tributary population of the village of Cayambe more than doubled between 1590 and 1655, but the population of smaller communities in the same area, such as Malchinguí and Tocache, appears to have stabilized.[92] Although there may have been an underlying growth in the population during the early seventeenth century, the increase cannot be attributed wholly to natural increase, for an increase of 1 percent a year, considered high for preindustrial societies, would only double the population in seventy years, and this would be without taking into account the impact of epidemics, particularly in the 1640s.[93] Undoubtedly part of the increase was due to more effective registration, particularly of forasteros.

The trajectory of what became the corregimiento of Ibarra was not so positive. Morales Figueroa's list of tributary Indians drawn up in 1591 suggests the presence of 2,815 tributary Indians, a figure exceeding that of the encomienda of Otavalo.[94] However, *cartas cuentas* show that by the middle of the seventeenth century their number had been more than halved.[95] While this decline continued established trends, it may have gathered momentum as demands for labor increased. The expeditions to Esmeraldas, the construction of the town of Ibarra, and the establishment of estates particularly in the Coangue and Mira valleys—all forced Indians to work in warmer climates than those to which they were accustomed and that, according to the Indians, were responsible for their continuing decline. In 1622 the caciques of Tuza, Angel, and Puntal claimed that their

Table 9. Tributary Population of the Otavalo Region from 1582 to 1666

Ethnic group	1582[a]	1590[b]	1591[c]	1590[d]	1643[e]	1666[f]
Mira	400	—	454	250	210	141
Tuza, Puntal	ca. 1,100	—	867	1,000	603	404
Guaca, Pu, Chuquín	ca. 800	—	943	500	286	291
Tulcán, Taques	ca. 700	362	551	400	357	293
Total	ca. 3,000	—	2,815	2,150	1,456	1,129
Lita	354	356	354	—	340	304
Quilca	183	146	177	—	127	94
Caguasquí	140	69	118	—	60	ca. 47
Total	677	571	649	—	527	ca. 445
Carangue, San Antonio	505	—	—	500	596	636
Chapi	386	—	—	—	125	89
Pimampiro	227	—	—	—	40	22
Total	1,118	—	—	—	761	747
Cayambe villages	1,412	—	480	—	—	—
Otavalo villages	2,360	1,986	2,011	2,500	2,673[g]	4,448[h]

[a] RGI 2:240–41 Paz Ponce de León 2.4.1582; RGI 2:243 Rodríguez 9.11.1582; RGI 2:245 Aguilar 12.11.1582; RGI 2:252 Borja, no date. The figure for Carangue and San Antonio combined has been calculated by deducting the figures for Chapi and Pimampiro provided by Borja from the total for the four villages of 1,118 given by Paz Ponce de León. There are some arithmetic errors in the latter document, so the summary figures provided have been used rather than the more specific ones for different population categories.
[b] AGI CO 1536 Cuentas reales 1591 and ANHQ Real Hacienda 63 fols. 50–83.
[c] CDI 6:41–63 Relación de los indios tributarios 1.11.1591.
[d] RGI 2:316 Relación de cerro de Zaruma, no date.
[e] ANHQ Residencias 1 Residencia of Pedro de Torres, corregidor of Ibarra 1646.
[f] ANHQ Indígenas 10 Cartas cuentas 1666–69.
[g] ANHQ Tributos 2 Cartas cuentas for Otavalo 1638–40. The total shown is for 1640.
[h] Tyrer, "Demographic and Economic History," 378–79. The total shown is for 1665.

communities had lost more than one-third of the 900 tributary Indians they had possessed in the sixteenth century.[96] Similarly those of Tulcán, Taques, Guaca, and Chuquín reported that one-third of their tributary Indians were missing, working on distant lowland estates.[97]

The evidence presented gives a far from clear picture of demographic trends in the northern sierra. Larrain Barros places the nadir of Otavalo's population between 1545 and 1550, increasing thereafter.[98] I doubt whether the nadir was reached at this time, but given the controversy over the official figures and the high level of fugitivism, the trends are not clear. While the official figures suggest that the population was fairly stable, fugitivism gathered momentum, providing support for the view that the total population was increasing over time. The initial decline, however, may not have been as great as suggested by the early tasaciones, so that the overall trend may have been more stable, if not one of decline. The continued depopulation of Pasto communities seems more certain. Overall,

Table 10. Population Decline in the Otavalo Region
during the Sixteenth Century

Area	Aboriginal population	Estimated population in 1582[a]	Percent decline	Depopulation ratio
Pasto region	36,350	15,505	57	2.3:1
Mira-Guayllabamba over 2,000 meters	120,000	19,267	84	6.2:1
Mira-Guayllabamba under 2,000 meters	30,000	10,199	66	2.9:1
Total	186,350	44,971	76	4.1:1

[a] Includes 13.5 percent for fugitive Indians

the divergent and uncertain demographic trends experienced by Indian communities in different parts of the corregimiento of Otavalo urge caution in asserting that the population of the northern sierra was increasing during the second half of the sixteenth century.

Despite the difficulties posed by the evidence, which reflected the complex trends operating in the region at the time, it is clear that during the first fifty years of Spanish rule the Indian population of the northern sierra declined. My estimates suggest that the Indian population of the corregimiento of Otavalo had fallen from about 186,350 to 45,000, a decline of 76 percent, or 4.1:1 (Table 10).[99] The level of survival was higher among the Pasto, where the decline was 57 percent, while the region between the Mira and Guayllabamba valleys lost 80 percent of its population. (See Table 30.) However, within the latter area the fate of different chiefdoms varied. Archaeological evidence argues for higher population densities in the Cayambe and Carangue regions in pre-Inka times, yet by the end of the sixteenth century Otavalo's villages were about five times more populous. However, this differential decline related to differences in the impact of Inka conquest as well as to the activities of the new invaders.[100]

Other regional variations may relate to altitude. The qualitative evidence points to heavier population losses at lower elevations, although it is contradicted by quantitative evidence for the region between the Chota-Mira and Guayllabamba valleys, where settlements located at altitudes over 2,000 meters declined by 84 percent, whereas those at lower elevations lost two-thirds of their populations (Table 10). It is worth noting, however, that tributary Indians represented a slightly higher proportion of the total population in the warmer valleys (24 percent as opposed to 20 percent), which could be accounted for by the well-documented employment of highland Indians on lowland estates. Migration might therefore conceal the real level of decline in the valleys.

CHAPTER 8

Quito

> Within this district of five leagues there are forty-five Indian vil-
> lages, and most of them are deserted because some are absent with
> their wives and children serving Spaniards . . . and others because
> Spaniards have taken their lands.
>
> Corregidor Sancho Díaz de Zurbano, 13 January 1609[1]

Following the death of Atahualpa, Francisco Pizarro named Sebastián de
Benalcázar as his lieutenant in Piura. Here he learned of the arrival on the
coast of Ecuador of Pedro de Alvarado and 200 soldiers. Benalcázar immediately directed his attention north with the aim of forestalling Alvarado's
claim to the region. In alliance with 300 Cañar he moved north to Tomebamba,[2] but on reaching the pass at Teocajas encountered Atahualpa's
general Rumiñahui fortified there, according to Oviedo, with 50,000 soldiers.[3] Benalcázar failed to defeat the native general but managed to proceed further north, encountering continued resistance and slaughtering
many Indians between there and Latacunga. At the end of June 1534 he
reached Quito, only to find that Rumiñahui had overtaken him and reduced the town to ashes. Although Rumiñahui eluded the invaders, he
lacked the political and territorial base from which to organize sustained
resistance. While many caciques, such as those of Latacunga and Chillos,
actively supported Rumiñahui, forming a force of 15,000 men,[4] others to
the north allied with the Spanish, bringing upon themselves the full force
of Inka revenge. At Pomasqui Rumiñahui was said to have put to death
4,000 "Pillaxos, Zámbisa, y Collaguazos" for their betrayal, a figure plausible in the light of the severity of other Inka reprisals.[5] Salomon suggests
the loyalty of groups in the southern part of the Quito Basin may reflect
the greater consolidation of Inka rule in the region, which among other
things was manifest in a more effective military organization.[6] Whatever
the underlying causes, the conquest of the Quito region was complicated
by conflicts between Indian factions supporting or opposing Spanish rule.
(See Map 7.)

Disappointed with the spoils of the Quito region, Benalcázar pushed
north towards Quinche, Cayambe, and Carangue, torturing Indians and
pillaging villages. Frustrated at being unable to find Atahualpa's treasures, he ordered all the women and children at Quinche to be killed; the
men had previously left with the opposing forces.[7] This process was interrupted by Diego de Almagro's call for Benalcázar to return south to forestall the political aspirations of Pedro de Alvarado. Once Santiago de Quito

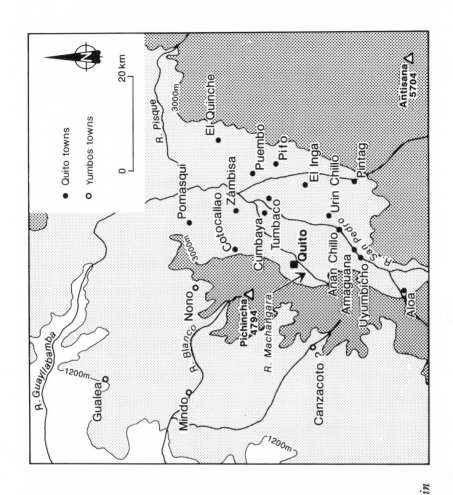

Map 7. The Quito Basin

had been founded at Riobamba and his rights of conquest assured through negotiation, Benalcázar returned to Quito to found the town of San Francisco de Quito on 6 December 1534. Meanwhile, the Inka general Quisquis had retreated from Peru, exacting revenge on those who had betrayed the Inka cause. In the end he failed to make contact with Rumiñahui, and finally both generals were forced to retreat. Rumiñahui's forces retired to the Yumbos, and following his capture and execution, Inka military resistance in the province of Quito came to an end.

The Quito Basin became the focus of Spanish political and economic activities. It is not possible in this short space to review all aspects of colonial rule that affected Indian lives. Instead the chapter will focus on those activities that had the greatest influence on demographic trends. They included Quito's role as expeditionary center; the nature and operation of the encomienda; the establishment of agricultural and textile enterprises; the growth of the city; and the demands that all of these made upon Indian lands, labor, and production.

The first call on Indian labor was for auxiliaries for expeditions that extended Spanish control over the coast, to the north, and to Los Quijos. Although Indian villages in the regions of Otavalo and Latacunga provided substantial numbers of Indians for these expeditions, the area immediately around Quito bore the greatest burden.

Within two years of the foundation of Quito several major expeditions had been dispatched to the southern part of the coast to reinforce the hitherto tenuous control the Spanish possessed over the region. According to Juan de Velasco, Pedro de Puelles's expedition that resulted in the establishment of Puerto Viejo involved 4,000 Indians, of whom nearly all died. This was followed by an expedition of equivalent proportions led by Sebastián de Benalcázar that in 1535 resulted in the establishment of Santiago de Guayaquil. Losses on this expedition mounted to 200 to 300 Indians a day, such that nearly all died—mainly, it was said, because of the change of climate. Finally, Benalcázar's lieutenant, Juan Díaz Hidalgo, dispatched Diego de Tapia and Diego de Daza with 3,000 encomienda Indians to suppress the rebellion of the Chono, none of whom returned.[8] For regions further north, Alcina Franch, Moreno, and Peña list thirty-one expeditions that were conducted to Esmeraldas before 1570, of which at least seven were mounted from Quito and passed either through Sicchos or the Yumbos.[9] Little is known of these early expeditions, which were all military in character, but those that passed through Sicchos led by Gonzalo Díaz de Pineda and Alonso de Rojas involved 800 and 400 Indians respectively.[10] Other early expeditions probably involved several hundred Indians, but toward the end of the sixteenth century expeditions became missionary rather than military in character and smaller numbers were involved, mainly as porters and cooks. The majority were drawn from the highlands. Of thirty-five expeditions to Esmeraldas between 1570 and 1630, at least seventeen were mounted from Quito.[11] Larrain Barros, accepting Velasco's estimates, suggests that up to 1580, expeditions to the coast involved between 16,000 and 20,000 Indians, most of whom came from the sierra.[12]

Meanwhile between 1534 and 1538 large numbers were also involved in expeditions to the north that resulted in the establishment of Pasto, Cali, and Popayán.[13] The first colonizing expedition of Juan de Ampudia in 1534 involved 2,000 Indians, of whom 1,000 proceeded ahead to open up roads and search for provisions, while the rest were employed as porters. This was followed shortly by another expedition of 4,000 Indians led by Benalcázar himself, and it was estimated that of those involved in the two expeditions, not more than 20 returned home.[14] By June 1538 Benalcázar led an even larger expedition of 5,000 Indians to Popayán.[15] Most of those who participated in expeditions never returned, and the continual drain on labor resources in the Quito region began to generate opposition to further levies.[16] The fact that protests continued indicates that Indians were still being recruited, probably most for smaller unauthorized expeditions. Larrain Barros estimates that not less than 15,000 to 18,000 Indians were involved in northern expeditions as porters, cooks, or auxiliaries.[17]

Others expeditions penetrated east. The number involved in Gonzalo Díaz de Pineda's expedition to La Canela in 1538 is not known, but it was clearly substantial, for encomenderos actively resisted its mobilization on the grounds it would provoke a rebellion.[18] Preoccupied with affairs in Popayán, it was not until 1541 that the expedition materialized when Gonzalo Pizarro was finally able to muster a force of 4,000 Indians, which was later joined by troops led by Francisco de Orellana.[19] Over half of those involved in these expeditions died of ill-treatment, cold, and hunger; one account puts the death toll as high as 6,000.[20] Later expeditions to the east were largely concerned with the suppression of revolts. One thousand men and women from the sierra were forcibly recruited by Andrés Contero to suppress the uprising in 1562,[21] and at least 200 Indians from Cayambe were involved in Rodrigo Núñez de Bonilla's suppression of the 1578 rebellion.[22] Larrain Barros suggests that expeditions to the east prior to 1580 may have involved 12,000 to 15,000 Indians.[23]

In summary, Larrain Barros's figures suggest that not less than 50,000 Indians from the northern sierra were involved in expeditions, of whom he estimates 80 percent never returned to their homes.[24] Some were killed in battle; others died of ill-treatment, hunger, cold, or changes in climate; and those who survived were often sold as slaves.[25] On first examination this figure may appear exaggerated, particularly since it is largely based on estimates given by Juan de Velasco, whose works have been heavily criticized for their lack of historical accuracy. However, no movement of

Spaniards through the region, particularly on expeditions, was possible without Indian support in the form of porters, cooks, or troops, and Quito was the center of operations. Also, the figure is based primarily on evidence for the largest expeditions and does not include many smaller ones that were being mounted at the same time. Although Larrain Barros's figures for the numbers involved in individual expeditions need to be used with caution, his total estimate does not appear unreasonable. Not all Indians were recruited from the Quito region, however. It is known that Indians from Latacunga and Cayambe were involved in expeditions to Los Quijos and that the provinces of Carchi and Imbabura supplied larger numbers for expeditions to Esmeraldas and Popayán.[26] Nevertheless, despite some attempts to control the extraction of Indians without license, it was the Quito region that bore the heaviest burden.[27] By 1540 the province of Quito was described as "destroyed and dissipated" and on the verge of rebellion as a consequence of the enslavement of Indians to serve on expeditions.[28] However, complaints from the cabildo were largely overidden by governors and their tenientes hoping to expand their jurisdictions and find new sources of wealth, and it was not until political stability had been achieved and the New Laws effectively introduced that the situation ameliorated. Even so, Indians continued to be employed in the pacification of Los Quijos and Esmeraldas to the extent that during the sixteenth century as many as 30,000 Indians may have been lost from the Quito Basin as a result of expeditions.

The corregimiento, or "five leagues," of Quito broadly covered the sierra to the south of the Guayllabamba River to the Nudo de Tiopullo. It also included a number of villages on the western slope in the Yumbos, such as Mindo, Gualea, Nono, and Canzacoto. Quito was selected as the location of the region's major administrative center, because of its strategic position. The site not only dominated the Quito Basin but controlled the passes that defended the region from dense Indian populations to the north.[29] It had previously been the site of Atahualpa's court.[30]

When Sebastián de Benalcázar founded the city of San Francisco de Quito, he allocated encomiendas to its vecinos.[31] How many were distributed at this time is not known, and undoubtedly more were allocated as new areas were pacified. The initial distribution was made in the name of Francisco Pizarro, who had been given royal authority to allocate encomiendas in his contract for the conquest of Peru. Those who had been allocated encomiendas in the name of Pizarro bitterly defended their rights against the viceroy, Blasco Núñez de Vela, who was encharged with the introduction of the New Laws issued in 1542 and with the confiscation of encomiendas from those involved in the deaths of Diego de Almagro and Francisco Pizarro. With the final defeat of the rebels led by Gonzalo Pizarro in 1548, Licenciado Pedro de La Gasca set about reforming encomiendas within the viceroyalty, distributing to loyal supporters those confiscated from the rebels.[32] About 40 percent of encomiendas in the Quito Basin were reallocated, though they were generally of lesser value than those retained.[33] Subsequently the number of encomenderos in the jurisdiction of Quito fluctuated little.

Prior to the publication of the New Laws and their effective introduction by La Gasca, the exaction of tribute and labor was unregulated. Although the introduction of official tasaciones had been mooted as early as 1535, they were strongly resisted.[34] Evidence exists for a few of the tasaciones ordered by La Gasca for the Quito Basin. Those for the villages of Puembo, Pingolqui, El Inga, Uyumbicho, Anan Chillo, and Urin Chillo indicate that a wide range of items were demanded, including gold or silver pesos, and that despite the New Laws, Indians were still required to provide labor for household service and agricultural tasks.[35] In the late 1550s the viceroy, Antonio de Mendoza, the Marqués de Cañete, continued to commission visitas and tasaciones of villages on a piecemeal basis. Under his orders the aforementioned six villages in the vicinity of Quito were assessed by Gaspar de San Martín and Juan Mosquera.[36] Nevertheless, at that time royal government remained too weak to resist the demands of encomenderos and impose just tasaciones.[37] In 1568 Licenciado Pedro de Hinojosa was encharged with a visita of the audiencia that involved the reassessment of tribute payments and the prosecution of encomenderos for ill-treatment and excessive exactions.[38] Hinojosa, in the company of Licenciado García de Valverde, spent the next two years conducting visitas, and the process was still incomplete in 1570 when Viceroy Francisco de Toledo ordered a visita general of the viceroyalty.[39] Within the following five years most villages were inspected and reassessed, but unfortunately the returns for the audiencia of Quito have not been found.[40] However, an account by Juan Canelas Albarrán in 1586 that purports to be based on the visita general suggests that about two-thirds of the province of Quito was visited.[41] As late as the early 1580s, however, some villages in the Yumbos had never been assessed.[42] It was not until 1624 that the corregimiento of Quito was reassessed on a comprehensive basis.[43] Reassessments were thus piecemeal and took place at extended intervals.

The delay between reassessments meant that tasaciones failed to keep pace with demographic changes, such that Indians were often forced to pay for Indians who were absent or dead.[44] For example, in the 1560s Oidor Salazar de Villasante noted that the extant tasación for the village of Copiz was twenty years out-of-date and that only 20 Indians were left of the 300 for whom it had been assessed.[45] As populations declined, the burden of meeting tribute and mita demands fell on those who remained, encouraging them to migrate to escape registration. As a consequence the visitas conducted in the 1590s were finding only one-half, one-third, or

even one-quarter of the Indians registered in the previous inspection.[46]
The failure of assessments to take account of the downward spiral in the
numbers of tributary Indians actually present resulted in mounting trib-
ute debts. In 1626 the tribute arrears of the villages of Pomasqui, Guay-
llabamba, Tumbaco, Puembo, Pifo, Pinta(g), Sangolquí, Uyumbicho,
Amaguana, Aloa, and Canzacoto, which comprised the encomienda of the
Duque de Uzeda, amounted to 38,799 pesos. As in the corregimiento of
Otavalo, a solution was sought in the establishment of two *obrajes de
comunidad,* one between Sangolquí and Amaguana, and the other near
Tumbaco.[47]

The tribute burden for Indians in the Quito Basin was higher than
suggested by the tasaciones, not only because they failed to keep pace
with demographic changes, but also because of fraud in its collection,
which stemmed in part from the nature of the items levied. In the jurisdiction of Quito each Indian generally paid between one and a half and two
pesos in cash, one manta, a half a *fanega* each of wheat and maize, and one
chicken.[48] The actual value of tribute varied from year to year according
to the state of the harvest and the degree of fraud practiced. In the early
seventeenth century it was judged to be worth between four and six pesos
per tributary Indian.[49] Given that at that time monthly wages for a mitayo
were between nineteen and twenty reals,[50] the levy was equivalent to
about two months' wages. Many considered the level of tribute exaction in
the Audiencia of Quito exorbitant, particularly compared to New Spain,
where it was argued that Indians were richer and yet only paid one peso
and half a fanega of maize; for Indians in the Audiencia of Quito one and a
half silver pesos were considered enough, and anything more, excessive.[51]
The authorities conceded that the Indians paid more tribute than they had
done under the Inka, but it was argued that the overall burden they bore
was lower because they no longer had to provide personal service and
could therefore attend to their lands, and that they lived in greater peace
and security.[52]

Tribute payment and collection provided opportunities for fraud and
exploitation. Indians were required to pay part of their tribute in cash,
which in theory was payable in either silver or gold pesos. The coins that
circulated in Quito were either silver pesos that had come from Potosí or,
given their shortage, gold pesos made of low-grade ore mixed with silver
and sometimes copper. Encomenderos, however, levied cash equivalent to
the value of high-quality gold pesos and in this way made as much as 30
percent profit.[53] Since neither silver nor gold was produced around Quito,
cash had to be acquired through trade or wage labor. Tribute payments
became so dependent on the ability of Indians to earn wages that they
were threatened in 1609 when the mita for servicio ordinario was abolished by the viceroy, the Marqués de Montesclaros.[54] However, in many

cases, wages were only sufficient to buy food, so that many were jailed for debts that they were unable to pay even if they sold their lands.[55] In many cases tribute payments were commuted to personal service.[56]

Tribute payments in agricultural produce presented other problems. Sometimes items were not produced locally and had to be purchased in the marketplace.[57] In other cases, excessive exactions occurred because the dimensions of the cloth to be levied were not specified and crops collected were not weighed. Such practices were so common that it was suggested that tribute would be better paid in cash because at least the Indians would know exactly what they had to pay.[58] However, neither the Indians nor the authorities agreed. The bishop of Quito argued that the commutation of tribute to cash payments would encourage Indians to seek wage labor and abandon their lands. This, he went on to suggest, would create food shortages, cause prices to rise, and would result in Indians' becoming "denaturalized" as they left their villages and became vagrants.[59]

Other intractable problems were associated with the collection of tribute. Many items levied, such as maize, wheat, and salt, were bulky and heavy, and despite orders to the contrary, Indians were generally required to transport them, generally on their backs, to the homes of their encomenderos.[60] In 1577 the archdean of Quito reported that the delivery of tribute items required some Indians to travel fifty leagues, incurring absences of up to four months, from which many failed to return.[61] The alternative of allowing encomenderos or their overseers to collect the tribute themselves offered too many opportunities for fraud; entrusting the task to corregidores did not solve the problem either, since it afforded them opportunities for illegal trade and for coercing Indians to spin and weave cloth.[62]

The tribute burden of Indians in the Quito Basin was one of the highest in the Spanish empire. It constituted a drain on Indian production and encouraged Indians to abandon their lands in search of wage labor. This process was reinforced by demands for mita labor, but before the evolution of labor systems is discussed, it is useful to examine the development of agricultural estates, the textile industry, and the city, all of which generated demands for labor and, in the case of the first, led to the alienation of Indian lands, which in turn further encouraged the emergence of free labor and migration.

Several authors have argued that Spanish interest in agriculture did not develop until the second half of the sixteenth century, when Indian depopulation reduced the availability of produce through tribute payments and marketplace exchange, while demands for supplies rose as the number of Spanish settlers increased. Commercial agricultural production, it is suggested, emerged to fill the vacuum.[63] In the province of Quito evidence from the first distribution of land grants indicates that Spaniards were not only interested in the status they bestowed but developed an earlier than usual interest in agricultural production. What encouraged this interest is not clear. It may have been stimulated by demands for supplies for expeditions or for armies involved in the civil wars at a time when Indian production was declining with the population. Once political stability had been achieved, the lack of alternative sources of income, particularly from mining, left agricultural production aimed at the local market, and possibly a small export market within Spanish America, the main alternative. Agricultural products could not be exported to Spain because of their bulky and perishable nature and high transport costs. The natural fertility of the region and its relatively abundant sources of labor meant that agricultural products could be produced at competitive prices, which, unlike in other regions, such as Mexico, did not rise substantially during the century. However, the absence of a substantial mining sector left the Audiencia of Quito short of coinage, hence an export trade to mineral-producing regions was essential in order acquire the cash needed to purchase European products, such as cloth and wine. These were regarded as vital to sustain a civilized lifestyle, and in the absence of an export trade its citizens were destined for a life of provinciality.[64] At first the export trade centered on the production of livestock and to a lesser extent cereals; later it focused on the textile industry.

The natural fertility of the Quito Basin and its suitability for raising many European crops and animals led to its emergence as a major agricultural region, with an emphasis on cereal production and livestock raising.[65] As one observer noted, there was such a diversity of climates that crops that could not grow in one area could be grown in another.[66] The Valle de los Chillos remained the maize-growing area par excellence, while wheat, barley, and potatoes were raised at more temperate elevations. The area around Pomasqui became noted for the production of vegetables and fruit, as did the hotter, drier Guayllabamba Valley, where sugarcane was also grown. Livestock were to be found throughout the basin, but particularly on the páramo toward Panzaleo.[67] Maize yields in the Valle de los Chillos reached 1:60 or 1:70, comparable with the lower yields produced with modern technology.[68] While wheat yields were much lower—on of the order of 1:10 or 1:20—they were still relatively good compared with other parts of the viceroyalty.[69] Similarly, livestock introduced from New Spain multiplied rapidly, so that by 1573 the price of a cow had fallen from between 80 and 100 pesos to 4 pesos, and the price of sheep and goats had fallen from 50 pesos to 2 tomines.[70] Indeed livestock became so abundant that the slaughter of feral animals found straying on to arable lands was permitted.[71] The low prices of provisions and meat, and hence the cost of living, attracted immigrants to the corregimiento of Quito from as far afield as Colombia, Popayán, and Peru.[72]

Agricultural products could be produced so cheaply that from an early date Spaniards became involved in their production. In 1577 there were said to be 200 Spaniards in the city of Quito who lived by farming.[73] Agricultural production was aimed at two markets: export markets in present-day Peru and Colombia, and a domestic market in the city. Initially Spanish interest focused on the livestock raising, particularly cattle, and on the cultivation of maize, wheat, and barley, the last being used for fattening livestock.[74] Sheep raising did not develop on a large scale until the emergence of the textile industry in the latter part of the century, and even then the major areas of production were outside the Quito Basin. Cattle were raised for meat, horses and mules were exported to Lima and even as far as Charcas, while pigs were marketed to the north in Popayán, Cali, and Anserma.[75] Some animal products such as cheese and ham were also exported.[76] Such products were processed by households from items raised on their smallholdings, but these were probably sold in local markets.[77] Where and by whom the export items were produced and marketed is not clear. Finally, most of the cereals produced were consumed locally, although some flour and *bizcocho* were exported as far as Lima and Panama.[78] Cereal crops were cultivated by all races; other crops were mainly grown by Indians. The latter included vegetables, which, because of their bulky and perishable nature, only catered for a local market. Indians were favored over other racial groups in the marketing of produce, since they were exempt from the *alcabala,* or sales tax. This privilege encouraged Spaniards and mestizos to use Indian agents to sell their goods, and even in some cases to masquerade as Indians.[79]

The development of commercial agriculture necessitated the acquisition of land. With the exception of the subsoil and all lands that had belonged to the Inka state, which passed to the Spanish Crown, pre-Columbian landholding rights were recognized.[80] Nevertheless, it was not long before Indian lands were being alienated by legal and illegal means. These processes involved the issuance of new land grants, transfers by purchase or donation, and usurpation. Legal means were generally preferred as less contentious, but even these transactions often involved covert, and even overt, coercion.

Initially land grants in the Quito region were made by the cabildo. Following the establishment of Quito, lands were granted in Pomasqui and Cumbaya in 1535, in the Valle de los Chillos and Pintag in 1536, and further allocations were made in Cotocallao, Zámbisa, Pifo, and along the route to Panzaleo in 1537.[81] These lands were considered surplus to community needs and therefore appropriate for redistribution. The main beneficiaries were members of the cabildo, many of whom received several parcels of land scattered throughout the Quito Basin. For example, the *regidor* Juan Díaz Hidalgo received an *estancia* on the road to Panzaleo, a garden plot in

Pomasqui, and other lands in Cumbaya and on the road to Pintag.[82] The fragmented nature of many holdings probably reflected the limited availability of land in this densely settled region.

Despite the civil wars the cabildo continued to function, and the allocation of land grants reflected changes in its membership.[83] There are also indications that lands were given to vecinos within the jurisdiction of their encomiendas, in clear contravention of the law.[84] The early monopolization of land by cabildo members meant that by 1540 grants were being made outside the "five leagues" of Quito in the hinterlands of Latacunga, Ambato, and Riobamba.[85] Following the erection of the audiencia in 1563, lands granted by the cabildo had to be approved by the president, but this requirement failed to stem the accumulation of lands in the hands of cabildo members.[86] In the 1580s avowed attempts by President Pedro Venegas de Cañaveral to ensure that Indians possessed sufficient land for their subsistence[87] proved little more than a cover to enable the confiscation of legally held lands. Each tributary Indian was to receive four *cuadras* (about 2.8 hectares), and any surplus land was deemed fit for redistribution.[88] His successor, Dr. Barros, immediately ordered any seized lands to be returned and put a break on the allocation of new grants. Increasingly Spaniards looked to alternative methods of acquiring lands.

In the latter part of the century most lands were acquired by purchase and illegal occupation. Lands might be purchased from individuals or caciques acting on behalf of the community. Indians were often under pressure, particularly from encomenderos, to sell their lands to discharge tribute debts. In order to prevent forced sales, permission for the purchase of land had to be obtained from the Spanish authorities; in practice this regulation also restrained caciques intent on selling community lands for private gain in face of opposition from their subjects.[89] The deeds of sale formed the basis on which a purchaser could then petition for a formal title to the land.

Another means of acquiring land was by declaring a tract unoccupied and requesting a grant. The main stipulation was that the grant should not conflict with the claims of other parties, particularly Indians.[90] Lands claimed had to be surveyed, the boundaries marked, and an inquiry held at which other parties could object; once granted, the land had to be used or cultivated continuously for five years before a formal title was issued.[91] A major problem for Indian communities in the Quito region was that many lands regarded as unoccupied were essential to daily life. They might constitute valuable hunting grounds or sources of fuel, house-building materials, and even water. Particularly vulnerable to alienation were lands left fallow as part of a cycle of cultivation.[92] The acquisition of lands by this method was further encouraged by the program of reducciones between 1570 and 1575, which separated many communities from the lands they had previously cultivated. While Spaniards regarded these lands as ripe for occupation, in many cases Indians continued to exploit them, sometimes because they had not been allocated new lands in their new place of residence.[93] Indian control over land was weakened even further in 1591 by a decisive piece of legislation that consisted of two *cédulas*. The first ordered all lands that had been illegally occupied to be returned to the Crown. This would have dealt a blow to the illegal occupation of Indian land. However, the second cédula declared that anyone who possessed land without legal title could obtain one on payment of a fee, or *composición*. The aim was to raise money for defense; the result was to legitimize the illegal occupation of land.[94] The law not only was retrospective but was to apply to lands that were to be occupied in the future. Henceforth a common means of acquiring land was for an individual to declare a tract unoccupied or uncultivated and then pay the corresponding composición.

Spaniards also acquired Indian lands through marriage and as donations. Spaniards or mestizos marrying Indians not only might acquire any land they possessed but through their Indian spouses could purchase other Indian lands without the transaction having to be sanctioned by the authorities.[95] Others passed into non-Indian hands as donations. Small parcels of land were sometimes given by Indians to individual Spaniards, often under coercion, or as an act of piety to a church or convent.[96]

Despite the fragmentary nature of the evidence, it is clear that the pattern of landholding in the Quito Basin was not one of large estates but one of medium-sized farms. Even though in the 1560s Oidor Salazar de Villasante claimed that the smallest grants owned by Quito's citizens were 100 *fanegadas de tierra* (about 290 hectares), with some as large as 500 and even 1,000 fanegadas,[97] many of the initial grants were small, and the pattern of landholdings was one of scattered parcels that were operated as distinct enterprises. Some consolidation of holdings occurred as a result of purchase, marriage, and other means, but other estates were broken down by inheritance. Over time, the religious orders, a number of whom possessed estates in the Valle de los Chillos, were probably the most successful in consolidating their holdings.[98]

Although the pattern of landholding was unstable, it is clear that there was a drift of properties into non-Indians hands. Particularly vulnerable to alienation were lands in the immediate vicinity of the city and in the fertile Valle de los Chillos. As early as 1574 Indian villages nearest to Quito were said to have insufficient lands to support their populations, with any lands they retained being mountainous, rocky, and impossible to plow or irrigate.[99] At the same time lands were often overrun by straying cattle, despite laws stipulating that estancias should not be established within two leagues of Indian lands or one league from cultivated lands.[100] Even if Indian communities retained their lands, heavy demands for labor limited the time available to work them. Loss of land and high demands for labor encouraged the early proletarianization of the population.[101] To what extent the alienation of Indian lands was conducted with the intention of forcing into the labor market is not clear. My impression is that the need to obtain cash to meet tribute demands or evade the mita acted as a more powerful stimuli in encouraging Indians both to sell their lands and to seek wage labor.[102]

Textile production emerged as a secondary economic activity in the Quito Basin. Its structure and organization was different from that in the rest of the sierra, and it was of secondary importance. A community mill operated at Guápulo for a brief period in the sixteenth century,[103] but the mills established within Quito's "five leagues" were all private mills, the majority of the licensed ones receiving approval from President Ibarra between 1605 and 1607.[104] In 1680 there were twenty licensed mills in the Quito region, only five of which had the authority to use forced labor and then in smaller numbers than similar mills in other regions.[105] Six of these mills were established within the city walls, but the rest were located on haciendas or in Indian villages within the city's "five leagues." The licensed mills, which operated in a similar fashion to those described for Riobamba, Ambato, and Latacunga, were probably the largest in the Quito Basin, but they represented only a fraction of the number that operated there. Most mills were small and operated illegally. They generally employed less than 20 workers and produced coarse woolen cloth primarily for the domestic market, though some was exported to Nueva Granada. Phelan claims that by 1603 there were sixty illegal mills operating in the jurisdiction of Quito employing 1,350 Indians,[106] while at the end of the seventeenth century about 10,000 workers may have been employed in the city's fifty *obrajuelos* alone.[107] If this is correct, then the textile industry was absorbing a sizable proportion of the city's workforce. Unfortunately we know nothing of the wages and working conditions in this sector of the industry.

The urban industry emerged out of household operations. In 1578 the *oficiales reales* in Quito reported that many households in the city possessed looms for the production of coarse cloths.[108] Whether this referred to Spanish or Indian households, or both, is not clear. Spaniards almost certainly maintained looms in their homes that were worked by Indians in their personal service and mitayos, or possibly wage laborers. Certainly there were many complaints from mitayos that, having completed their official duties, they were required to carry out household chores, including weaving.[109] Some Spaniards, particularly encomenderos with greater power to coerce Indian labor, may have established small workshops employing larger numbers of workers; by the mid–seventeenth century it is clear that Indians also owned similar operations.[110] The rapid expansion of the textile industry was seen as a major cause of rural depopulation. In 1660 the procurador of the cabildo of Quito estimated that 20,000 Indians had migrated to Quito, the majority of whom were employed in the manufacturing of textiles, working for either Spaniards or themselves.[111] Although another account put the estimate lower at 10,000, it is clear that the industry employed a significant proportion of the labor force.

Added to labor demands created by the establishment of agricultural and textile enterprises, the city's inhabitants generated demands for a wide range of services. Initially these were met by personal service and the mita, but increasingly they were provided by wage labor. Labor demands encouraged migration and fostered racial mixing. Quito was founded with 204 vecinos,[112] but many were involved in expeditions to other regions where they later became settlers. Others were killed or left the province during the civil wars between 1546 and 1548. However, these losses were made up for by settlers who were attracted to the city by its fertile farmlands and the relative abundance of Indian labor.[113] Most accounts written in the 1560s and 1570s suggest that there were about 300 to 400 Spanish houses in the city.[114] However, in 1577 there were 1,000 Spanish men but only 300 Spanish women.[115] This marked imbalance in the sex ratio gave rise to a large urban mestizo population.[116] Over time, houses belonging to Spaniards ceased to be distinguished but were simply described as belonging to vecinos or *moradores*. In the early seventeenth century Vázquez de Espinosa recorded that the city possessed more than 3,000 vecinos, including mestizos.[117]

No Spanish society could exist without the employment of a subservient class of workers, but "the labor and sweat of the Indians" constituted the wealth of the province of Quito.[118] Various labor systems emerged that were modifications of pre-Columbian practices or local adaptations of those that operated elsewhere in the Spanish empire. In practice they coexisted, though in terms of their contribution to the colonial economy there was a general transition from personal service to forced labor under the mita and then to free labor.

The abolition of personal service ushered in the mita. It became one of the most despised institutions, to the extent that mita evasion was regarded as essential for survival. Increasing tribute burdens, loss of land, and ill-treatment acted as powerful stimuli to migration, but documentary sources suggest that the mita played the most significant role. The impact of different labor systems on Indian populations varied according to the tasks in which they were employed, as well as the extent to which they undermined native subsistence patterns and social relations and provided effective substitutes for them. To different degrees they promoted the maintenance and reproduction of the labor force and encouraged migration and racial mixing.[119]

In the sixteenth century Indians who worked in Spanish households on a permanent basis were often referred to as *yanaconas*. The designation was a corruption of the Inka term *yanakuna,* which was used to identify individuals who had no community affiliation but worked in the service of elites as servants, craftsmen, or agricultural laborers. A visita of villages in the Valle de los Chillos in 1559 recorded the presence of large numbers of yanaconas who at that time were still providing service for their caciques.[120] During the early colonial period the numbers of yanaconas increased, but their origins were diverse. A small proportion had been yanakuna under Inka rule and with Spanish conquest passed directly into the service of Spaniards. Others ended up in their service, either by choice or coercion, having served on expeditions and wars. Yet others were war captives.[121] They worked as household servants, artisans, and agricultural laborers, and many of them were given small subsistence plots.[122] In addition, encomenderos often illegally transferred Indians to their households and haciendas, and sometimes employers retained workers in their service once their mita duties had ended.[123] Some haciendas around the city contained 70 or 80 encomienda Indians,[124] while in 1571 the bishop of Quito reported that one encomendero had taken 50 boys and 69 girls from a single village to work in his service.[125] Sometimes these Indians were also referred to as yanaconas. Yanaconas were exempt from the mita and initially paid no tribute, which encouraged some to seek work as wage laborers or artisans in the hope they might obtain yanacona status. Many women found employment as wet nurses. In 1579 it was claimed that each year 300 Indian women migrated to the city in search of employment as household servants.[126] Some accounts distinguished yanaconas from other Indians working in the service of encomenderos and others. The duties of yanaconas appear to have been more exclusively tied to Spanish households and were said to include tending horses, acting as messengers or pages, and, in the case of women, cooking, washing, and cleaning.[127] Nevertheless, over time distinctions faded, and by the mid–sixteenth century the term "yanacona" had lost any Inka connotations, and Indians with no community affiliation were increasingly referred to as *vagamundos*.

Some indication of the numbers and origins of Indians employed in the service of Spaniards can be gleaned from an examination of the baptismal records of the cathedral church of El Sagrario.[128] This church was the focus of Spanish worship, and large numbers of children born to Indians in the service of Spaniards were baptized there. The records are particularly interesting, since they indicate not only the individual in whose service the parents worked but also in many cases their geographic provenance. The first series runs from April 1566 to November 1569, when, according to Moreno Egas, 1,788 individuals were baptized, of whose parents 1,042 (58 percent) were in the service of Spaniards;[129] the place of employment of other parents is not given, but most likely some worked in Spanish households. During this short period no less than 103 infants were baptized whose parents were in the service of Rodrigo de Salazar, the encomendero of Otavalo, and 74 who were the offspring of parents who worked for Alonso de Bastidas, the encomendero of Cumbaya and Guambahaló.

Quito's vecinos possessed encomiendas as far-flung as Pasto and Cuenca, and Indians were drawn to the city from this broad region, but they came almost exclusively from the sierra and predominantly from Quito's "five leagues" (see Appendix 3).[130] A longer run of baptisms between 1594 and 1605 reveals a similar pattern of provenance of Indian parents. Of 2,516 baptismal entries between August 1594 and December 1600, fully 2,162 give the origins of parents, of which it is possible to locate 2,108. Of the total number listing the place of origin, 65 percent came from Quito and its "five leagues," with 6 percent coming from the northern sierra and 28 percent from the southern sierra. Of those originating within the corregimiento of Quito, only 10 percent came from the city itself, thereby suggesting that newcomers constituted a substantial portion of the city's Indian population. Moreno Egas suggests that the numbers of those baptized should be doubled to give the approximate numbers of Indians in service, but this would give an inflated figure, for some couples would have registered the birth of more than one infant during the period covered by the baptismal registers. However, there were undoubtedly others who baptized their children in the Indian parish churches of San Blas and San Sebastián. What is clear is that the city contained several thousand Indian immigrants who were working in the service of Spaniards. Under what circumstances they were employed is not clear. Some certainly lived in Spanish households and received no pay, but others would have been wage laborers who resided in their own homes.

As early as 1538 there were said to be large numbers of yanaconas around the city, and the *alguacil* was ordered to ascertain how many there were and to whom they belonged.[131] Yanaconas posed a number of legal and administrative problems for the authorities. Their status as permanent household servants contravened laws banning personal service, while their scattered distribution hindered their instruction in the Catholic faith. Perhaps most important, they did not pay tribute.[132] The reiteration in 1563 of the cédula of 22 February 1549 banning personal service prompted Oidor Salazar de Villasante to initiate the formation of two villages composed of Indians who were scattered around the city "wandering like Arabs."[133] These two settlements, Villasante and Velasco, were promptly dismantled by his rival, President Hernando de Santillán, but new efforts to establish Indians in distinct settlements accompanied the Toledo reforms. In 1571 the president of the audiencia, Don López de Almendariz, was ordered to proceed with the reducción of yanaconas, of those who resided permanently in Spanish households, and of others who provided service for the city.[134] In 1573 it was judged that they numbered 2,000.[135] The process was initiated by the next president, García de Valverde, who with Oidor Francisco de Auncibay began settling Indians at Añaquito. The program soon ran into difficulties, since the surrounding lands had been monopolized by cabildo members, and despite exhortations from the Crown that landholdings should be reformed to accommodate the new settlers, little was done, and the process remained incomplete.[136] By the 1590s only sixty houses were left at Añaquito, the rest having been abandoned because of shortages of land or to avoid tribute payment, which the process of settlement implied.[137] One of the main aims of the reducciones was to increase royal tribute income by enrolling Indians who had formerly claimed yanacona status and been exempt from tribute payment. From 1572 a tax of three pesos was imposed on yanaconas.[138] In practice this tax proved impossible to collect because of their scattered locations and the protection from the authorities provided by employers.[139]

The program of reducciones initiated by Viceroy Toledo was conducted by royal officials, but the reforms included incentives to caciques to participate in the process by giving them power over those they settled who became tributary to the Crown.[140] Although many Indians resisted enrollment, it proved increasingly attractive to tributary Indians, who preferred to be registered as Crown Indians who were exempt from the mita and in effect paid a lower rate of tribute. Tributary Indians thus began to drift to other villages, where they became forasteros paying tribute to the Crown rather than to private individuals. Whether by design or not, the effect was to reduce the economic and political power of encomenderos, while it enhanced that of the Crown and of small-time employers who profited from increased access to labor unburdened by the mita.[141]

Despite the ban on personal service and attempts to control Indian residence, many Indians continued to work and live in Spanish households on a permanent basis. Nevertheless, this type of service was overshadowed by the emergence of the mita, which was described as even more prejudicial to Indian survival.[142] It was intended that the abolition of personal service would open the way for the development of a free labor market. However, concerned that if given the freedom to work, the Indians would refuse, the Crown sanctioned the introduction of systems of forced labor that followed the same basic pattern throughout the empire. In essence each Indian community was to make available a quota of its tributary population to work on a rotational basis on approved tasks for limited periods and fixed wages. In the Audiencia of Quito it was known as the mita, taking its name from the forced labor system operated by the Inka. The quota of tributary Indians required to serve at any one time was set at one-fifth, which as far as I am aware is the highest quota demanded anywhere in the Spanish empire. It was justified on the grounds that its large population could easily sustain this levy.[143] The periods for which mitayos worked and the wages they received varied according to the types of activity in which they were employed. Mita labor was allocated for servicio ordinario; to collect wood and fodder; to construct and repair buildings, roads, and bridges; and for agricultural tasks, textile manufacture, and mining. Mines were absent from the Quito region, and mita labor was not employed extensively in the textile industry, so the employment of mitayos in these activities is considered later when regions where they were concentrated are discussed. Although the mita was not supposed to be used for personal gain, it is clear that on many occasions it was. Citizens who were allocated mitayos to collect wood and fodder to support their households, often marketed the items, while others who were assigned mita labor to build and repair their houses, employed them to build sumptuous houses for sale.[144] Other types of forced labor included the supply of eggs, chickens, and game for the city as well as the provisioning of *tambos* and general porterage.

It is not clear when the mita was formally introduced. A rotational system of forced labor operating on a quota basis was used to supply the mines of Cuenca in 1549, though it only affected communities south of the Quito Basin.[145] The development of a more formal system for providing workers for domestic service and agricultural labor was almost certainly delayed in the Quito region by the widespread persistence of personal service. Tasaciones drawn up after 1549 still included the allocation of Indians to serve encomenderos. In 1551 Indian communities in the Valle de los Chillos were each required to supply their encomendero with small numbers of Indians for household service who were changed "por sus mitas," and others were assigned to tend livestock and cultivate gardens.[146] These types of service resembled those rendered to the Inka and local caciques, and elements of the latter still persisted in the 1550s. Evidence from the Quito region suggests that the Spanish mita evolved out of the mit'a operated by the Inka, although the reciprocal benefits that workers had previously enjoyed no longer pertained.

By 1572 it had become "the custom" for the citizens of Quito to enjoy the paid service of Indians distributed on a rotational basis. At that time the allocation of mitayos was undertaken by the city's alcaldes ordinarios.[147] One alcalde was responsible for the allocation of Indians to provide wood and fodder, and the other for construction and agricultural labor.[148] The alcaldes were criticized for levying more mitayos than specified, for receiving bribes for the receipt of mitayos, for allocating Indians to tasks that were ostensibly for private gain, and generally for profiting as intermediaries between employers and employees.[149] Given the potential income to be derived from the posts, conflicts emerged over the appointment of alcaldes, particularly between the cabildo and audiencia. In 1586 the Crown ordered the task to be entrusted to an oidor,[150] and further wranglings occurred at the beginning of the seventeenth century, when the viceroy entrusted the task to the corregidor.[151] Despite changes in official responsibility, the abuses continued.

The Crown stipulated that Indians should not be employed at great distances from their homes. Originally they were employed within a radius of two to three leagues. By 1563 the legal limit over which they could travel was extended to ten leagues, and by 1591 it had risen to twenty-five leagues.[152] In fact the mita within the términos of Quito involved Indians from regions as distant as Pasto and Riobamba.[153] In practice communities around Latacunga and Riobamba provided services for local vecinos, but those to the north commonly serviced Quito and were forced to travel long distances across several climatic zones, despite orders to the contrary.[154]

Other regulations banned the employment of mitayos in a number of arduous and unhealthy tasks. These included sugar milling and porterage. In the sixteenth century a number of sugar estates were established in Quito's warmer valleys, particularly the Guayllabamba Valley. Despite attempts to impose the ban on the employment of mitayos in sugar milling, once they had been assigned, the authorities were unable to control the tasks undertaken.[155] Owners of sugar estates claimed that the Indians were not employed in sugar milling but in the cultivation and harvest of the cane, which was not arduous work.[156] They also maintained that their employees came from villages located in areas with a similar climate. Many of the sugar estates belonged to the missionary orders, and the authorities appear to have been powerless to proceed against them.

During the first two decades of conquest Indians were used extensively for general porterage and to carry supplies on expeditions. From 1549 Indians could not be forced to transport goods against their will, but in recognition of the transitional difficulties this rule posed until roads could be constructed, the Crown allowed it to continue but insisted that Indians were to travel only short distances and that loads were to be moderate.[157] In 1564 President Santillán reported that he had ordered roads to be constructed and had dispensed with Indian porters.[158] By this he must have meant the employment of forced laborers, for Indians continued to form the basis of the transport system, even though by the end of the century it was claimed that horses outnumbered Indians and that human porters were unnecessary.[159] Others continued to justify their employment on the grounds that the terrain was too rugged, that they were accustomed to carrying loads and did so voluntarily, and that it provided them with an income from which they could pay their tribute.[160]

The burden imposed by the mita varied among other things with the tasks mitayos were assigned and the distances they had to travel. The collection of wood and fodder drew many complaints, since it involved carrying heavy loads over long distances, a task that became increasingly burdensome as woodlands close to the city became depleted.[161] Those physically incapable of this heavy work were forced to purchase wood in the marketplace at a cost judged to be twice their wages.[162] Most complaints were directed at this type of service, but construction work was also arduous, and Indians employed in ranching also protested that they were required to tend too many animals and were punished or had to compensate for any losses.[163] All types of personal service were banned in 1601 and 1609, which included the employment of Indians as porters, in construction, and in the collection of wood and fodder. Henceforth mitayos worked primarily in agricultural tasks, though small numbers were also employed in obrajes.[164]

The numbers involved in the mita were considerable, despite avowed attempts to moderate levies.[165] In 1589 President Manuel Barros estimated that within the términos of Quito there were at least 5,300 Indians working on a temporary rotational basis. They comprised 2,000 employed to tend livestock on a yearly basis, 1,000 to collect wood and fodder for periods of two months, 1,000 to work for several months at harvest time, and finally 1,300 to work in construction between July and September.[166] An earlier account suggests that 10,500 Indians were employed in the collection of wood and fodder and in agricultural activities.[167] The discrepancy in the accounts may well reflect differences in the categorization of workers but could be accounted for by population losses associated with the epidemics of the late 1580s. Although mitayos were assigned to work in particular tasks, there was little control over their employment, and having completed their official duties, they were often required to undertake additional tasks such as household chores and weaving.[168]

In addition to providing one-fifth of their tributary populations to serve as mitayos, Indian communities were also required to supply Quito with provisions. Twice a week each community had to provide a fixed number of chickens, eggs, rabbits, and game birds for sale at fixed prices. Indians complained about the operation of this market, called "el gatillo," since the prices set were considerably less than those of the free market.[169] It was claimed that the goods were then resold by the cabildo to the city's most eminent citizens, leaving little for the poor. The requirement of Indian communities to supply these items may have been introduced after the abolition of personal service to ensure a regular supply of cheap provisions for the city. Communities were also required to service the tambos by providing a small number of mitayos, who received the pitiful wage of five tomines a month.[170] However, the system of tambos soon disintegrated, and travelers resorted to extracting provisions from nearby communities.[171]

The wages paid to mitayos in the Audiencia of Quito must have been some of the lowest in the Spanish empire. In 1563 the Crown ordered them to be paid two tomines (about 112 *maravedís*) a day, but this wage was never achieved during the sixteenth century.[172] In 1564 President Santillán reported that he had doubled the monthly wage for mitayos to 1 peso a month, that is, between 15 to 18 maravedís a day, which was less than one-sixth of the recommended rate.[173] He claimed he had been unable to raise it any further because of opposition from vecinos. Although wages rose gradually in subsequent years, so that by the late 1580s they were being paid twenty maravedís a day, this wage was considered inadequate to live on, and in 1588 the Crown ordered it to be raised.[174] In 1591 wages were increased to nineteen or twenty reals a month (about 40 maravedís a day) depending on the distance traveled,[175] but this still fell short of the one tomín a day that the Indians considered to be a fair wage[176] and that the Crown was then recommending, even though it was only half of that originally ordered in 1563.[177] Although mitayos were also to be provided with food, often they were not. In many cases they were supported by their families who accompanied them, or else they took provisions with them or purchased them in the market.[178] Although food was relatively cheap,[179] the pitiful wages earned by mitayos also had to cover tribute payments, which it has been judged were equivalent to two months' income.

The main criticisms of the mita were not dissimilar to those directed at personal service. Both groups complained about the long hours of work, the arduous tasks they were assigned, and the ill-treatment they suffered. Those employed as mitayos raised additional complaints about long traveling distances, poor wages, and lack of food. At the same time the mita rendered them unable to cultivate their own lands. The hardships it imposed were exacerbated during the sixteenth century as demands for labor increased and Indian communities were required to meet their quotas with declining populations. The tours of duty for those who remained came round with increasing frequency,[180] and migration to escape the mita played an increasing role in survival strategies.[181]

It is difficult to ascertain the importance of free labor during the sixteenth century because of confusion in the terms used and the fact that free labor often involved a degree of coercion. In the sixteenth century the term *gañán* was applied to a voluntary farm worker, but a mitayo could also be a gañán, the term being used in this case to specify a general farm laborer.[182] Later the term *concertaje* was employed to describe a labor system whereby individuals freely contracted to work for employers at an agreed rate of pay. This term was not used widely in the sixteenth century, and it probably reflects the limited use of this type of labor.

The origins and conditions of those who worked in Spanish households and haciendas is not clear. Neither was it clear to the authorities at the time.[183] In addition to those who were tied to Spanish households as yanaconas, encomienda Indians, or as mitayos coerced into working for their employers on a permanent basis, others were migrants in search of better wages and living conditions in the city or on haciendas.[184] Others may have remained in their communities but worked voluntarily as day laborers on local haciendas. In the city and on haciendas Indians were generally able to evade the mita, sometimes with the collusion of employers.[185] Most, however, paid tribute, although at a reduced rate and in cash. Tribute payments were generally deducted from workers' salaries, causing some to fall into the debt of employers.[186] To what extent debts acted as a constraint on the mobility of workers is not clear. While Indians did incur debts, they may have been viewed as a benefit rather than a constraint when alternative sources of income to meet obligations were limited and private employment offered the additional attraction of exemption from the mita. President Barros claimed that Indians preferred working for Spaniards on a permanent basis to being subject to the mita.[187] While such claims might be regarded with skepticism, the large numbers employed as free workers provide some supporting testimony. As early as 1589 there were said to be 3,000 gañanes living on haciendas in the términos of Quito.[188] However, not all free labor was as free as its name suggests, for there is some evidence that when cash incentives failed, coercive measures were employed.[189]

Not all Indians sought wage labor. Some were self-employed artisans and tradesmen, while others manufactured cloth and processed food for sale.[190] In the 1590s Licenciado García de Tamayo estimated that there were 2,000 Indians called *peinadillos* who lived in Quito and Añaquito who were employed as servants or were craftsmen such as masons, carpenters, tailors, and blacksmiths.[191] In 1612 there were said to be 4,000 Indian artisans in Quito and its hinterland.[192] Some claimed these Indians had good incomes and that any attempt to enroll them in the mita would cause them to flee and deprive the city of essential services.[193] Others were more concerned about their licentious and criminal lives and the burden their absence posed on their home communities.

The demographic impact of the alienation of Indian lands and demands for labor systems was indirect rather than direct. It is clear that arduous labor contributed to raised mortality rates. These were probably higher among forced laborers who traveled longer distances to work and whose employers had no incentive to treat them well. Documentary sources provide little evidence for differences in the working and living conditions of different types of workers, but one might expect that free workers enjoyed better wages and working conditions than forced laborers. Since no time limits governed the employment of free workers, an employer could build up a more reliable and skilled labor force. The desire of employers to protect the capital invested in their workers and to ensure a future supply of labor constituted added incentives for their better treatment. The fact that many Indians attempted to escape the mita and opted for wage labor suggests that conditions were better for free workers.

This is not to say that conditions were good or did not deteriorate in colonial times particularly for forced laborers. Some Indians died of ill treatment and possibly some of starvation, but the influence of labor systems on demographic trends was generally more subtle. In some cases nutritional levels may have declined sufficiently to increase the susceptibility of Indians to disease and pose a threat to weaned infants, but the Quito Basin was a fertile region for which there is no evidence for chronic food shortages. However, some evidence from the parish of San Sebastián in 1582 suggests that urban Indians were failing to reproduce themselves.[194] The small number of children might be explained by raised mortality rates and/or a real or apparent decline in fertility. Fertility rates may have fallen with the arduous work undertaken and the stresses of colonial life, which induced amenorrhea and resulted in extended birth intervals. Under conditions of urban living, children are often a greater burden, especially in the early years of life, when they are less able to supplement the family income. There is little evidence for infanticide, but baptismal registers indicate that many women abandoned their infants to be brought up in Spanish households.[195] Although this may have enhanced their chances of survival, in many cases it led to their disappearance from official records as they became acculturated to urban living and could pass as non-Indians. It was of concern to the authorities that by "putting on a hat and taking a book in the hand," Indians would become gentlemen who would refuse to serve on the mita.[196] The apparent failure of the Indian population to reproduce itself may have been due in part to reclassification.

Apart from the effects of employment on mortality and fertility rates, the Indian population suffered losses due to racial mixing. Racial mixing was rife in Quito, particularly in Spanish households where Indians came into contact with employers, overseers, and servants of diverse racial origins.[197] While some marriages occurred between Spaniards and Indians, most mestizo offspring were illegitimate. Many were raised as servants in Spanish households. In the 1560s Salazar de Villasante observed that apart from the large numbers of Indians living in Spanish households, each encomendero had eight, twelve, or sixteen mestizas in their service, whom they treated like slaves.[198] In 1577 it was estimated that there were 2,000 mestizos in the Audiencia of Quito, of whom about half lived in the city.[199] The rapid increase in the numbers of mestizos is evident from the baptismal records of El Sagrario at the end of the century. In the register of Spanish baptisms, the total number of non-Indian baptisms recorded between June 1595 and December 1600 was 258.[200] Of this number 66 percent were born to parents who were both Spaniards, but 17 percent were born to an Indian mother and a Spanish father, and another 14 percent, one or both of whose parents were unknown, were probably illegitimate mestizos.[201] The number of mestizo baptisms represents a significant proportion of the total baptized, and interestingly they are entered in the register of Spanish baptisms, rather than that reserved for "Mestizos, Montañeses, Indios," in which during the same period only six mestizo baptisms were registered. This suggests that mestizos were being accepted as Spaniards and that they formed a substantial proportion of the Creole population. The growth in the number of mestizos is even more impressive when it is remembered that most Spanish infants would have been baptized in the cathedral, whereas many mestizos were probably registered in other urban parishes, and even Indian villages.

The growth in the mestizo population was so marked that in 1600 *Fiscal* Torres Altamarino noted that there were four mestizos for every Spaniard,[202] and in 1609 Sancho Díaz de Zurbano claimed that there were more mestizos in the city of Quito than in the rest of Peru.[203] Although the increase was greatest among mestizos, there were also small numbers of zambos, incorrectly called mulattoes. Even though by law blacks were liable for castration for having contact with other races,[204] by 1577 there were 200 mulattoes in the city.[205] Smaller numbers of persons of mixed race were born in or migrated to Indian villages; some may have been involved in the textile industry.[206]

Even if it was possible to obtain an accurate estimate of the numbers of non-Indians in the corregimiento of Quito during the early colonial period, it is difficult to quantify the contribution of racial mixing to Indian population decline. If all those of mixed race were able to escape enumeration as tributary Indians, then clearly the growth in their numbers would have had a considerable impact. However, it is likely that many were registered as Indians, especially those raised in Indian communities. Those who resided in the city, particularly those who worked in the service of Spaniards or as artisans, would have been more rapidly absorbed into Spanish urban society. Most mestizos fell into the latter category, and as such *mestizaje* must have made a significant contribution to the failure of the urban Indian population to maintain itself independent of migration. The process may have even affected regional demographic trends.

The demographic impact of labor systems affected not only those employed in the city or on estates but also the native communities from which they came. While those working in personal service and as free laborers depended on employers for wages and often food, mitayos received pitiful wages, and their survival depended on continued subsistence production, which the mita itself undermined.[207] Licenciado García de

Valverde noted perceptively that the impact of labor service on Indian subsistence was greater for small communities, where relatively higher demands left fewer Indians to continue production.[208] Even so, there are relatively few references to food shortages in the region, which remained better provisioned than many areas in the Spanish empire. The mita more often than other labor systems also involved the separation of spouses for extended periods. Although in many cases mitayos were accompanied by their families, who provided material and moral support, in others extended absences strained relations and contributed to marriage breakdown. In practice they also affected the fertility rate directly by reducing the frequency of sexual intercourse and the probability of conception.[209] For these reasons the mita is likely to have had more adverse effects on demographic trends than other labor systems.

DEMOGRAPHIC TRENDS IN THE QUITO BASIN

The rapid turnover of population in the Quito Basin exacerbates attempts to estimate its Indian population, as it did for the authorities at the time. The turbulent years of conquest and civil war resulted in major social dislocations as soldiers were conscripted for military campaigns, and others fled or returned to communities from which they had been drafted to serve as mitmaq.[210] Once political stability had been achieved, the city of Quito and expanding agricultural enterprises created demands for Indian labor, at the same time as the alienation of Indian land, tribute demands, and the mita encouraged many to migrate in search of wage labor. Over time many migrants were able to escape enumeration as tributary Indians; in some cases their children were mestizos. Others chose to escape registration or pay a reduced tribute levy by moving to other Indian communities. Unfortunately most contemporary population estimates, which were generally based on tribute records, failed to take account of the growing numbers who had left their natal communities. In the seventeenth century greater efforts to register these Indians on tribute rolls created the illusion that the population was increasing rapidly. Any attempt at estimating the Indian population during the sixteenth century must take account of these high levels of mobility and fugitivism.

Before proceeding, it is necessary to comment on the reliability of tribute records and the difficulties involved in making comparisons between different areas over time. Delays between enumerations, the corruption and incompetence of Spaniards in compiling and handling accounts, and the efforts of Indians to avoid registration mean that tribute records are at best highly imperfect. In 1600 President Miguel de Ibarra acknowledged that even if everything was carried out correctly, it was impossible to obtain an accurate list of tributary Indians.[211] These shortcomings are compounded in records pertaining to large administrative units. While such accounts give the impression of being comprehensive and referring to a single date, in practice villages were sometimes omitted, and the dates to which the figures refer are often inconsistent. Because of the rapid turnover in the population, the figures available for the Quito Basin are probably a less accurate reflection of the actual Indian population when it was reported than was the case for other parts of the sierra.

Population trends are also difficult to establish because the data available refer to different administrative units. The region of interest here is the corregimiento, or "five leagues," of Quito, but separate figures for this region are available only from the latter part of the sixteenth century. In their absence, reliance has to be placed on records relating to the gobernación, audiencia, provincia, términos, or distrito of Quito, of which the corregimiento was a part. The Audiencia of Quito established in 1563 was the most extensive administrative unit that formed the basis of independent Ecuador. It included the términos or distrito of Quito, which generally referred to the highland region bounded by Pasto to the north and Cuenca to the south, thereby encompassing what became the corregimientos of Ibarra, Otavalo, Quito, Latacunga, Riobamba, and Guaranda and the *tenientazgo* of Ambato.[212] This broadly corresponded to the original gobernación of Quito, which encompassed the region conquered by Sebastián de Benalcázar. The term "provincia" was used inconsistently. Disaggregating the population of the corregimiento of Quito from estimates for these areas is not an easy task.

Our knowledge of demographic trends in sixteenth-century Ecuador derives largely from tribute records. However, it was not until fifteen years after conquest that the first official tasaciones were drawn up by Licenciado Pedro de La Gasca,[213] by which time the native population had been devastated by wars and epidemics. Unfortunately few details of these tasaciones exist, but one report suggests that the gobernación of Quito contained 27,036 "indios visitados."[214] Later accounts suggest the visita was incomplete. During the 1550s other *visitas* were conducted of different parts of the distrito of Quito,[215] but how comprehensive they were is unknown. Their findings were incorporated into a list of encomiendas in the Viceroyalty of Peru drawn up by the secretary of the Audiencia of Lima, Pedro de Avendaño in 1561. The number of tributary Indians recorded for the gobernación of Quito was 48,134, and this was multiplied by five to give a total population of 240,670.[216] The accompanying list of encomiendas suggests that about 25 percent of the population of the gobernación was to be found in the Quito Basin,[217] which would argue for a tributary population of about 12,000 and a total population of 60,000. Unfortunately these figures are not an accurate reflection of the Indian population in 1561, for the list was compiled from tasaciones drawn up at various times during the previous decade, many of which predated the 1558 smallpox epidemic.

One of the most important sources for the study of the historical demography of the Viceroyalty of Peru is Francisco de Toledo's visita general carried out in the early 1570s.[218] Although the detailed returns for the Audiencia of Quito have not been found, an account by Juan Canelas Albarrán suggests about 60 percent of the province of Quito was visited. The visita general found 78,141 Indians, and it was estimated that another 30,000 had not been included.[219] The former figure may have been the basis of the report by Oidor Licenciado García de Valverde in 1572 that noted the highlands of Quito possessed 70,000 Indians.[220] The visita general was also the source of many figures for individual villages recorded in 1591 by Luis de Morales Figueroa, the secretary of the Audiencia of Lima.[221] His summary figures assign the province of Quito a tributary population of 24,380,[222] which is approximately one-fifth of the total population recorded in the visita general. Since many figures predate the epidemics of the late 1580s, the 1591 list probably overestimates the native population at that time, even though it omits several substantial villages and does not include vagamundos. Figures for Indian villages that can be definitely identified as falling within Quito's "five leagues" produce a minimum total tributary population of 4,467, with a further 1,072 to be found in the Yumbos.[223] A somewhat smaller figure of 4,100 tributary Indians for the corregimiento of Quito can be calculated from the *Relación del distrito del Cerro de Zaruma,* written in the early 1590s, but in this case the villages are not identified and the figures presented in hundreds are clearly broad estimates.[224]

In 1624 it was reported that there had not been a visita for over thirty years.[225] Although one was initiated by Oidor Licenciado Pedro Zorilla in 1591, by 1600 at least it had not been completed.[226] It was later reported that the oidor had found 5,800 tributary Indians in Quito's "five leagues," but on what evidence this comment was based, given the incompleteness of the visita, is unknown. Two accounts from the early seventeenth century claim the region possessed about 8,000 tributary Indians, and it is possible this figure took account of those not enumerated by Zorilla.[227] By 1650, according to Rodríguez Docampo, there were 7,860 tributary Indians in the corregimiento of Quito, of whom 1,200 lived in the Yumbos, added to which there were 700 vagamundos, making 42,950 souls altogether.[228]

Apart from the figures drawn from tributary rolls, there are a number of general estimates of the region's population, though most of these would have been loosely based on tribute records. These estimates are shown in Table 11 and are commented on in Appendix 1. Since all of them refer to administrative units more extensive than the corregimiento of Quito, and since comparisons for similar jurisdictions over time indicate no clear trends, they will not be discussed here in further detail.

Most sixteenth-century accounts of the Indian population do not include those who had left their natal villages and did not pay tribute. During the latter part of the century several attempts were made to register these Indians as tribute payers to the Crown. These attempts were only partially successful. In fact as the century progressed, the numbers of nontributary Indians increased. In 1573 the city of Quito contained 2,000 Indians and "yanaconas de servicio,"[229] and in the late 1570s around Quito, Licenciado Auncibay managed to register at least 1,000 "indios vagantes" who did not recognize a cacique or encomendero.[230] These figures are fairly consistent with a report that in the city and its suburbs there were 1,500 houses belonging to "yanaconas, naturales, y estrangeros."[231] The numbers of Indians not paying tribute or providing service continued to grow. In 1592 there were said to be 3,000 "vagamundos" in the city of Quito and surrounding villages, and by 1622 their number had doubled.[232] In all cases the numbers clearly referred to adult male Indians or Indian heads of households. An estimate of 3,000 vagamundos living in and around Quito at the end of the sixteenth century does not seem unreasonable. This might give a total of 9,000 individuals, including women and children. The smaller multiplication factor of 3 may be justified on the grounds that urban Indians appear to have had smaller families, though there is a suggestion that tradesmen had slightly larger families than those who worked on estates or in flour mills.[233] The origin of those employed in the service of Spaniards suggests that about two-thirds came from Quito's "five leagues" (see Appendix 3), so that to avoid double counting, it would be more accurate to add only 2,000 vagamundos to population estimates for the Quito Basin.

Highland Ecuador is perhaps unique in the demography of sixteenth-century America in that commentators often reported that the population of the sierra was increasing. The tierra fría and tierra templada were often compared with the tierra caliente, where the population was said to be declining. Reasons given for the increase included the healthy climate and the absence of mines and other forms of hard labor.[234] The population of the province of Quito was said to have increased more than in any other part of the Viceroyalty of Peru.[235] These comments generally referred to a wider area than just the corregimiento of Quito, but in 1576 the oficiales reales in Quito noted that the city's population was growing daily.[236]

Several authors have noted that these qualitative accounts are not supported by the quantitative evidence drawn largely from tribute records.[237] The compilations by Avendaño in 1561 and Morales Figueroa in 1591 suggest a decline in the tributary population for the términos of Quito from 48,134 to 24,380, to whom perhaps 3,000 vagamundos should

Table 11. General Estimates for the Indian Population of the Jurisdiction of Quito

Date	Population estimate	Region	Source
1552	50,000 indios	provincia	AGI AQ 81 Father Francisco Morales, Guardián of Quito 13.1.1552
[before 1564]	27,036 indios visitados	gobernación	AGI JU 672 Relación de los vecinos encomenderos, no date; BM Add. 33,983 fol. 236r La tasa y visita de Presidente Gasca, no date
1561	240,670 personas de todas edades; 48,134 tributarios de 16 a 50 años	gobernación	RAHM A/92 fols. 55–77 Relación de los naturales que hay 1561
1561	270,000 personas de todas edades; 54,000 tributarios de 16 a 50 años	gobernación	AGI AL 120 Relación de los naturales del reino del Perú 1561; BM Add. 33,983 fol. 236v La visita y tasa por orden de la Audiencia 1561
1563	16,000 indios tributarios; 80,000 almas	audiencia	AGI AQ 32 Vázquez de Acuña 4.4.1636
[1567?]	35,000 indios	términos	RAHM 9/4664 no. 21 Los pueblos despáñoles que hay, no date
1571–74	42,000 to 43,000 indios tributarios	jurisdicción	López de Velasco, *Geografía*, 217–18
	93,000 indios tributarios	audiencia	
1572	70,000 indios	jurisdicción	AGI PAT 192-1-68 García de Valverde 4.2.1572
1573	50,000 indios tributarios	términos	RGI 2:224 La cibdad de Sant Francisco del Quito 1573
1570–75	108,141 naturales	provincia	BNM 3178 fols. 1–15 Canelas Albarrán 1586
1576	30,000 indios casados	provincia	RGI 2:170 Oficiales reales 30.12.1576
1577	50,000 indios tributarios de 18 a 50 años; 200,000 ánimas	términos	AGI AQ 17 Cabildo of Quito 3.1.1577
[after 1582]	100,000 indios tributarios	audiencia	RGI 2:183 Relación de las cibdades, no date
1591	24,380 indios tributarios	provincia	CDI 6:61 Relación de los indios tributarios que hay 1.11.1591
	4,467 indios tributarios	Quito's five leagues	
	1,072 indios tributarios	Yumbos	
1591	50,000 indios tributarios	provincia	AGI AQ 9 and CDI 19:147–49 Real cédula 19.10.1591
1590s	4,100 indios (but probably ablebodied males)	corregimiento	AGI PAT 240-6 and RGI 2:315–16 Relación del Cerro de Zaruma, no date
1590s	5,800 indios tributarios	Quito's five leagues	AGI AQ 10 Morga 15.4.1624, AQ 31 Sevilla 13.3.1626
1595	200,000 ánimas que confirmar	obispado	AGI AQ 76 Bishop of Quito 20.2.1595
1598	96,000 indios tributarios	obispado	AGI AQ 9 Mejía Mosquera 29.3.1598
1598	29,000 indios tributarios, 105,000 almas	audiencia	AGI AQ 32 Vázquez de Acuña 4.4.1636
1609	8,000 indios tributarios	Quito's five leagues	AGI AQ 27 Díaz de Zurbano 13.2.1609, AQ 9 Recalde and Armenteros y Henao 22.3.1611

be added. Part of the difference in the numbers can be explained in terms of the data themselves, but this would not convert the apparent decline into an increase. The figure of 48,134 tributary Indians for 1561 was probably higher than the number present at that time, for it was almost certainly based on enumerations undertaken prior to the smallpox epidemic of 1558. The same can be said for the 1591 figures, which probably did not take into account of the epidemics of the late 1580s. The figure for 1591, however, omitted a number of substantial villages, and there was extensive tribute evasion. Unfortunately the numerous accounts of the tributary population in the términos of Quito show no clear trend. (See Table 11.)

The discrepancy in the qualitative and quantitative records is difficult to explain. It could be that commentators were impressed by the growth of the city of Quito and erroneously inferred that demographic trends elsewhere in the sierra were similar. The quantitative evidence drawn from tribute records, however, undoubtedly underestimated the numbers present because of high levels of tribute evasion. Indeed, Powers has argued that the apparent increase in the Indian population in the first half of the seventeenth century was a function of the more effective registration of fugitive Indians, some of whom migrated, either voluntarily or under coercion, from the Oriente and Yumbos to the highlands.[238] Unfortunately, it is not possible to disaggregate the figures for the corregimiento of Quito from the rest of the términos of Quito except for the last decade of the century, after which the tributary population appears to have been increasing slightly, though this might be the first reflection of more effective registration.

Whatever the trajectory of demographic trends during the second half of the sixteenth century, it is clear that taken as a whole, the first century of Spanish rule brought a dramatic decline. Although the Quito Basin was not as badly devastated during Inka conquest as other highland regions, large numbers were drafted to serve in Spanish armies, many of whom either died in campaigns or were transferred to other regions. Sebastián de Benalcázar alone was accused of having killed 15,000 Indians of Quito.[239] It has been suggested that possibly 50,000 Indians were involved in subsequent expeditions of conquest and colonization, of whom maybe 30,000 came from the Quito Basin. The Spanish civil wars between 1546 to 1548, which were particularly bloody around Quito, claimed yet further Indian lives, which may be estimated at about 10,000. By this time the region had probably been afflicted by epidemics of smallpox, measles, plague, and possibly typhus,[240] which it has been estimated claimed about 60 percent of the population. By the 1550s therefore the Indian population had fallen from an estimated 190,000 to about 60,000, of whom about 12,000 were tributary Indians.[241] For over two decades after the 1558 smallpox epidemic, in which Cook estimates that native populations suffered a minimum decline of 18 percent,[242] population decline seems to have slowed with the establishment of political stability, the introduction of the New Laws, and as the population developed some immunity to Old World diseases. During this period, however, a new generation emerged that lacked immunity to disease, so that the epidemics of the late 1580s were particularly devastating, wiping out any increase that might have been achieved in the previous two decades.[243] Cook suggests that the epidemic period of the late 1580s may have reduced the population by as much as 30 percent.[244] Assuming, as Browne suggests, that losses sustained in the smallpox epidemic had been made good by the end of the 1580s, this would leave about 8,400 tributary Indians in the early 1590s. Official tribute records suggest that there were just over half that number. The difference between the two estimates may be explained by nature of the data and the methods used. The first estimate is based on numbers lost on expeditions, in battle, and as a result of epidemics and therefore takes no account of other losses due to changes in mortality and fertility rates or racial mixing, which it has been shown were not insignificant. The second estimate is derived largely from tribute records, and it has been demonstrated that there was considerable tribute evasion. A tributary population of 5,500 (see Table 11), which includes an estimate of 1,000 for the Yumbos, with a generous multiplication factor of 4.5, would give a total population of 24,750. To this figure should be added a further 2,000 vagamundos, whose number might be trebled, given their smaller families, to give a total vagamundo population of 6,000. This would give an overall estimate for the corregimiento at the end of the sixteenth century of 30,750, which represents a decline of 84 percent or 1:6.2.

CHAPTER 9

Latacunga and Riobamba

All year they are lacerated by whips and broken by being chained
and shackled in stocks such that the Egyptians did not suffer more
than these Indians in *obrajes,* who for the twelve *patacones* they are
paid each year have received more than 200,000 lashes and each
Indian provided more profit than would be necessary to pay the
tribute of twelve Indians.

Fathers of the convent of Chambo, 25 April 1619[1]

In order to forestall the territorial aspirations of Pedro de Alvarado, on 15
August 1534 Diego de Almagro founded the city of Santiago at Riobamba
in the name of Francisco Pizarro. Once the rival conquistador had agreed
to withdraw, on 6 December the city of San Francisco de Quito was
established, and forty-three of Santiago's original sixty-seven founders
became citizens of the new city.[2] Left with only twenty-two Spanish inhabitants,[3] Santiago ceased to function as an urban center, even though an
important tambo continued to operate there as it had in Inka times. It
was not until 1575 that the town was reestablished with twenty-four
vecinos; later it was named after the current viceroy, the Conde del Villar
Don Pardo.[4] About the same time, the town became the administrative
center of the corregimiento of Riobamba, encompassing within its jurisdiction the town of Ambato.[5] By 1583 corregidores had also been installed
at Chimbo and Latacunga.[6] These four regions—Riobamba, Ambato,
Chimbo, and Latacunga—formed part of the gobernación and later the
términos of Quito, and as such their encomenderos were vecinos of Quito.
(See Map 8.)

Throughout the sixteenth century the central sierra was noted for its
dense Indian population. Indeed in 1604 Chimbo and Latacunga, along
with Otavalo, were regarded as the largest Indian villages in the audiencia.[7] Although Spanish conquest of the central sierra was a bloody affair,
with the exception of Latacunga, the area was not drained by demands for
auxiliaries for expeditions to the same extent as the Quito Basin. However,
in supplying *tamemes,* its Indian communities bore a heavier burden. The
camino real from Quito to Guayaquil via the Desaguadero passed through
these areas, and the provinces of Chimbo and Riobamba in particular
developed as important regions of transit. Later with the development of
sheep raising, they emerged as the audiencia's most important textile-
producing regions.

In his march north through the sierra, Sebastián de Benalcázar met

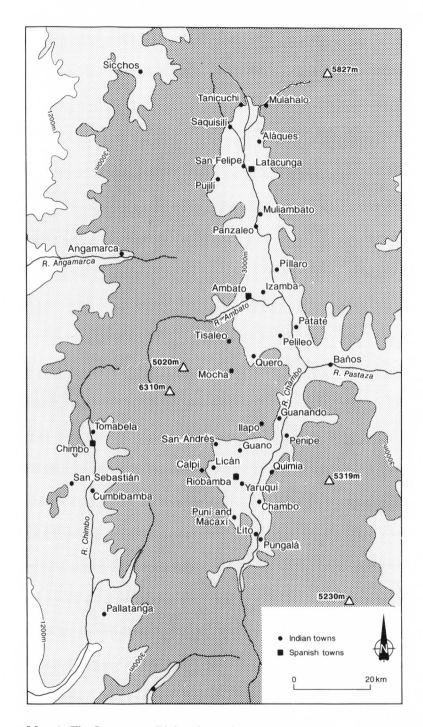

Map 8. *The Latacunga-Riobamba region*

continued resistance, with numerous battles leaving many dead. The most notable was at Teocajas, where a substantial proportion of the 50,000 Indians deployed were killed.[8] Subsequently 5,000 attempted to defend the crossing of the Ambato River, and other battles took place at Latacunga and Panzaleo. The pacification of the region did not bring an end to battle casualties, since those defeated were often conscripted to conquer other regions. Indians from Latacunga were more commonly drafted because of their proximity to Los Quijos, which the Spanish were particularly intent on pacifying, and also because their cacique, Don Sancho Hacho, saw opportunities for personal advancement through providing troops to serve on Spanish expeditions. Don Sancho Hacho participated in the initial pacification of Los Quijos by Gil Ramírez Dávalos that culminated in the establishment of Baeza. On this occasion he mobilized and sustained 200 Indian auxiliaries and provided gifts to buy the allegiance of hostile groups. Following the rebellion in Los Quijos in 1560, he supplied a further 200 Indians to help in the pacification of the province. In the event, both expeditions resulted in little bloodshed, but they were highly disruptive to community life. Don Sancho Hacho also supplied 40 Indians for the pacification of Lita, and 50 to search for gold and silver.[9] Most expeditions to Los Quijos involved Indians from Quito and Latacunga, while those to Yaguarzongo and Pacamoros conscripted Indians from around Cuenca and Loja. Those around Riobamba and Ambato were largely protected from such levies by the absence of large Indian populations immediately to the east and by the more difficult access to the Oriente through the Cordillera Oriental.

While fewer Indians from Latacunga and Riobamba were involved in expeditions than from the Quito Basin, greater demands were made upon them to act as porters on the camino real and to service tambos. The system of tambos established by the Inka survived into the colonial period, although their administration and the relative importance of particular tambos changed under Spanish rule. Previously the main Inka highway to Cuzco had passed through the highlands, but under Spanish rule the route south of Riobamba was redirected to the coast through Chimbo to Guayaquil. Tambos in the Puruhá and Chimbo regions thus assumed greater importance, the major ones being Luisa (probably San Andrés), Riobamba, Los Tambillos, Chimbo, Guapo, and Pucará. Further north other important tambos continued to operate at Mocha, Ambato, Latacunga, Mulahaló, and Panzaleo.[10]

Inka tambos still existed as physical entities in the 1540s,[11] but they were largely deserted, since Indians, having suffered ill-treatment and excessive exactions at the hands of travelers, were reluctant to service them or work as tamemes. Remedial measures were initiated in 1543 by the viceroy, Cristóbal Vaca de Castro, who issued ordinances regulating the servicing of tambos and the size of loads to be carried by Indian porters, anticipating that within two to three years the construction of roads would render tamemes unnecessary. Loads were limited to thirty pounds, and tamemes were not permitted to travel between more than two tambos and were to be paid for their labor. Travelers were allowed to stay only one night at a tambo and forbidden to exact goods from Indian villages along the road.[12]

Encomenderos allocated villages along the camino real were called upon to supply the tambos.[13] It is assumed that this meant providing tribute items for sale at tambos as well as ensuring that Indians in their charge serviced them as mitayos. In 1581 Indians from Chimbo were taking the tribute they paid in maize, barley, salt, chickens, and pigs to the tambo at Chimbo, while Indians from Tomabela were taking salt, chickens, and pigs to that at Ambato.[14] Despite the 1544 ordinances, the abuses continued. In 1549 travelers were still exacting food from communities bordering the camino real and insisting that Indians carry excessive loads, often taking them and their families in chains. As a consequence the cabildo of Quito issued further orders prohibiting the ill-treatment of Indians and setting fixed prices for food and for distances traveled; it also provided alguaciles to inspect the tambos.[15]

Under Spanish rule the former Inka tampu became the property of the city or town within whose jurisdiction they fell. In 1573 the cabildo of Quito, attempting to enhance its income, decided to rent out its tambos and their surrounding lands to private individuals,[16] even though the lands, such as that around the tambo of Guapo, often belonged to local communities. Important tambos such as those at Riobamba and Ambato were leased for periods of several years at biannual rents of between sixty to eighty pesos, but most commanded smaller rates. The cabildo also undertook to supply the tambos with mitayos, who were to be paid five tomines a month, and to establish fixed prices.[17] These more formal arrangements may have eased the burden for some Indian communities, but probably at the expense of those located nearest the camino real. No doubt there were many instances where Indians were still required by travelers to carry excessive loads, for longer distances than permitted, and for inadequate pay.

Associated with the importance of Riobamba and Chimbo as regions of transit and with the development of shipbuilding at Guayaquil was the production of cordage and other rope articles made from cabuya.[18] Some of these items were even exported to Panama.[19] The main center of production was at San Andrés, although the Riobamba region as a whole was renowned for their manufacture, and in 1605 four workshops were in operation around Ambato.[20] The production of cabuya was sufficiently profitable to merit the involvement of the local corregidor, who in the

1570s required caciques to provide fifty mitayos skilled in the manufacture of *alpargates*. They were paid only six tomines a month, when it was estimated that the goods they produced were worth ten pesos.[21] Similar types of exploitation by corregidores were later associated with textile production.

The establishment of textile obrajes was dependent on the availability of wool or cotton and on an abundant supply of labor. The raising of livestock, particularly sheep, was well suited to the cold climate of the páramos where wool production came to dominate. Cotton was cultivated in warmer valleys, where Indian communities paid tribute in cotton cloth.[22] A number of early tasaciones indicate that some highland communities also paid tribute in cotton cloth, the cotton being provided by their encomenderos or obtained through the kamayuq system, which continued to operate in the late sixteenth century.[23] As sheep raising expanded, the manufacture of woolen cloth far outstripped that of cotton, effectively undermining the systems of exchange established between the highlands and lowlands in pre-Columbian times.

As early as the 1570s livestock raising had become the major economic activity in the Puruhá region. Sheep raising expanded on the páramos, particularly around Riobamba, which was described as a "village of shepherds."[24] In 1573 it was claimed that some estancias possessed over 80,000 sheep, and in the early seventeenth century the Puruhá region was said to contain 600,000 sheep, while many merino sheep were being raised around Latacunga.[25] These two regions also supplied the textile mills in Chimbo and Sicchos, where the more humid climate was unsuitable for sheep raising.[26] Some flocks were owned by Indians, particularly caciques. In 1606 the cacique of Latacunga, Francisco Ati, owned no less than 12,000 sheep, but generally cacical flocks were smaller than those of Spaniards.[27] As livestock raising expanded, demands for shepherds increased. Initially these demands were met by the mita. As the textile industry expanded, however, the demand for forced laborers outstripped supply, and sheep raisers resorted to various forms of coercion to retain mitayos in their service or were forced to seek alternative sources of labor.[28]

The textile obrajes became a notorious feature of the colonial economy of highland Ecuador, with the provinces of Riobamba and Latacunga emerging as the most important wool-producing regions. For this reason the operation of the industry is discussed most fully here, even though textile manufacture was a significant employer of Indian labor in the city of Quito and in Otavalo. Within the Viceroyalty of Peru obrajes developed where there were extensive flocks of sheep but, above all, relatively abundant sources of Indian labor.[29] Encomenderos were among the first to become involved in textile production as a means of enhancing their declining incomes from Indian tribute and gold mining. Textile production not only provided an outlet for capital accumulated from mining but constituted an effective mechanism for ensuring and maximizing tribute revenue.[30] Perhaps more important, it provided a means by which scarce coin could be obtained.

Cloth from the Audiencia of Quito was exported all over the Viceroyalty of Peru, from Colombia to Chile, but the main markets were in Lima, from whence cloth was traded in mining areas to the south, and in cattle-raising and mining regions of Nueva Granada. Textiles produced in Ecuador could undercut local production in these areas, despite the high cost of transport, largely because labor costs were lower.[31] The main product exported to Peru was fine blue woolen cloth—*paño azul,* whereas a greater variety of fine and coarse textiles, such as *bayetas* and jergas, was sent north; the latter textiles were also produced for the domestic market. Although the cloth manufactured in Ecuador was finer than that woven in Lima, even the finest cloths were coarse compared to those imported from Europe. As such, it was produced primarily for Indian and mestizo markets.[32] The mills also manufactured shawls, hats, and carpets, among other things.

The first obraje in the Viceroyalty of Peru was probably established in the Jauja Valley in 1545,[33] and the first to be founded in the Audiencia of Quito was at Chimbo. The precise date of its establishment is unknown, but it had been established by 1564, when the obraje at Latacunga was founded.[34] By the 1620s there were at least fifty mills in operation in the Audiencia of Quito, the majority of which were concentrated in the central provinces of Riobamba and Latacunga (see Map 9).[35] There were several kinds of obraje. The most common were those owned by Indian communities—obrajes de comunidad—and those owned by private individuals. The former were more important in the sixteenth century, but burdened by administrative costs, they later declined in the face of competition from private mills. Other mills at Otavalo and Peguchi were owned by the Crown, and these operated in much the same way as obrajes de comunidad. In addition there were a large number of small mills, or chorillos, which were either household operations or workshops employing perhaps ten to twenty people. Most were established without license and were located in and around Quito.

Obrajes de comunidad were the first to be established. They were originally founded by encomenderos interested in increasing or maintaining their tribute income. In theory the mills were owned by Indian communities, since encomenderos were not allowed to own property within the jurisdictions of their encomiendas; in reality encomenderos provided the capital for the construction of mills, as well as the raw materials to produce the textiles, while caciques ensured the supply of labor. Revenue from the sale of the cloth paid the salaries of a mill's administrator and its workers,

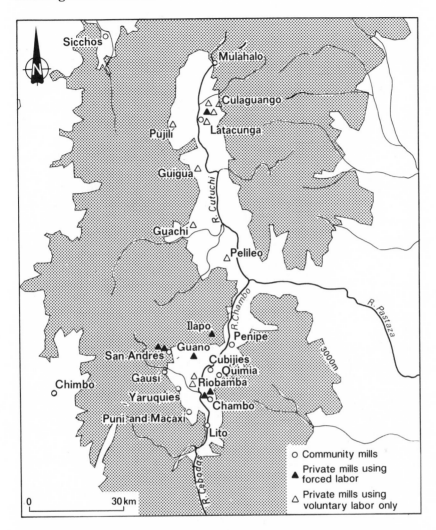

Map 9. Location of textile mills in the central Sierra

and the remaining income met the encomendero's normal obligations and contributed to the payment of Indian tribute; any left over was supposed to go into the *caja de comunidad*. Since the operation of a mill depended on a supply of labor, its foundation depended on the cooperation of the local cacique.[36] In fact caciques often actively supported their establishment, since they held the prospect of facilitating tribute payments, for which they were personally responsible. Furthermore, caciques generally received salaries for their administrative assistance and in some cases shared the profits. The contract made by Cacique Don Sancho Hacho for the establishment of an obraje at Latacunga divided the profits five ways, with one-fifth each going to the obrajero and cacique, and the other three-fifths to the community.[37]

Obrajes de comunidad were not autonomous, however. The Crown was anxious to control the exploitation of Indian labor for private gain and sought to do this by appointing official administrators and by introducing legal codes governing the operation of mills. Initially the administrators were appointed by the viceroy in Lima and were paid salaries between several hundred and a thousand pesos out of obraje profits.[38] Many of those who held office were relatives and friends of the viceroy, and far from improving the economic status of obrajes, many mills slid into bankruptcy as administrators indulged in numerous types of fraud and corruption, particularly in the marketing of textiles, and as their profits failed to reduce tribute debts.[39] The inefficient operation of the mills and the ill-treatment suffered by workers prompted suggestions that the obrajes should be rented out on contract.[40] The viceroy was reluctant to relinquish authority over the obrajes, but pressed by elites in Quito for greater control over their own industry, and possibly concerned at mounting tribute debts, he yielded to local demands. From 1616 obrajes could be rented out.[41] Henceforth, responsibility for the operation of the mills passed to lessees, but the administrative posts remained, performing few functions and becoming the perquisites of corregidores. Most leases went to a small number of elite families, many of whom also possessed private mills. Most were already major landowners, encomenderos, or had kinship ties with persons holding political or religious office. The obrajeros emerged as a small but powerful elite.[42]

Obrajes were generally rented for periods of six years at a cost based on the number of *años de rayas* worked.[43] An año de rayas comprised a work year of 312 days. Obrajes were rented to the highest bidders, and in 1623 the rental value for each Indian working an año de rayas varied between 41 and 74.5 pesos, according to the obraje.[44] The rent was often more than twice the cost of Indian wages, since the excess was needed to pay a mill's high administrative costs. These costs derived from the fact that obrajes de comunidad had been attached to encomiendas, and formerly obraje revenues had been used to meet the financial obligations of encomenderos. These included duties to pay the salaries of caciques and priests, to pay the corregidor for the administration of justice, and to provide items for the church; they also had to pay the salaries of Indians employed in the collection and supervision of workers in the mills. Leasing was not a completely uneconomic proposition, however, since compared with running a private mill, community mills had the advantage of an assured labor force. Nevertheless, because private mills did not have to bear administrative costs unrelated to textile production, their running costs were lower than those of community obrajes, even though they paid higher wages. Private mills were therefore able to attract workers, and during the seventeenth century they flourished as community mills declined.[45]

Obrajes de comunidad were established in the late sixteenth and early seventeenth centuries, reaching their maximum numbers in the 1620s, when there were thirteen in the central sierra. (See Table 12.)[46] The aim of establishing community mills was to facilitate tribute payment, from which the salaries of priests and caciques and contributions to the corregidores for judicial administration were normally paid by the encomendero. Tyrer suggests that in the late seventeenth century only about 30 to 45 percent of obraje revenue went to meet these obligations, and since the profits were used to reduce the tribute payments of communities as a whole, not only those who worked in the mills, the maximum reduction individuals received was 25 percent.[47] In reality, therefore, individuals benefited little from their operation. Meanwhile tribute rates for Indians in textile-producing areas were generally higher than elsewhere, since it was expected the mills would yield high profits. In the jurisdiction of Riobamba, Indians were often forced to make good inevitable shortfalls by selling their possessions or else face imprisonment; many preferred to flee. Others, as will be seen, were forced to work in private mills in order to pay off their debts. For reasons that are unknown, Indians in the jurisdiction of Latacunga were not required to meet tribute obligations not discharged by obraje profits. Even so, in some cases, tribute arrears began to amount to considerable sums, and eventually they became uncollectable. However, the financial viability of obrajes de comunidad seems to have depended largely on the efficiency with which mills were run. Some obrajes, such as those of Latacunga, Chambo, and Lito, amassed assets worth tens of thousands of pesos, which were invested in materials and loans, while others, such as those at Chimbo and Sicchos, accumulated sizable debts.[48]

Obrajes belonging to private individuals were operated for private gain, but they had to be licensed by the Crown. The Crown was ambivalent about the establishment of obrajes. It was opposed to them on the grounds they exploited the Indians and because their products competed with cloth produced in Spain. However, it was prepared to overcome its objections, if it could raise revenue from them. This it did through issuing licenses, both for the establishment of mills and for the employment of forced labor. In the sixteenth century a few licenses had been issued by the viceroy, mainly to encomenderos, but it was not until President Miguel de Ibarra assumed the functions of governor while the position of viceroy was vacant that a large number of licenses began to be issued, mainly to

Table 12. Estimated Number of Textile Mills and Their Labor Forces in the Central Sierra at the Beginning of the Seventeenth Century

Year and region	Mills		Workers				
	Community	Private	Community mills	Private mills (forced labor)	Private mills (voluntary labor)	Total private	All workers
1604[a]							
Riobamba	2	3	302			220	522
Latacunga	2	0	594			—	594
Chimbo	1	0	266			—	266
Total	5	3	1,162			220	1,382
1620[b]							
Riobamba	9	9	2,250	900	400	1,300	3,550
Ambato	0	2	—	0	160	160	160
Latacunga	3	7	750	150	560	710	1,460
Chimbo	1	0	250			—	250
Total	13	18	3,250	1,050	1,120	2,170	5,420

[a] AGI AG 13 Ibarra 4.4.1604.
[b] Landázuri Soto, Régimen laboral, 110–58; Tyrer, "Demographic and Economic History," 161–62. The licence of two mills in Riobamba was disputed, as was that of one mill in Latacunga.

those who held political office in the Audiencia or cabildo of Quito.[49] Between 1601 and 1628, thirty-seven licenses were issued for the establishment of private mills, and many of them, particularly the larger ones, included the assignment of forced laborers. Although over half were established in the corregimiento of Quito, only six had associated labor concessions, whereas six of the eight founded in the jurisdiction of Riobamba obtained permits to use forced labor, and the numbers of workers they were assigned were substantially larger. The rest were established around Latacunga and Ambato. Most of the private mills were owned by a small number of families.[50] Many private obrajes were founded illegally within the jurisdiction of their owners' encomiendas.[51]

In addition to legally established community and private mills, many other illegal obrajes existed. Tyrer suggests that in the Audiencia of Quito at the end of the seventeenth and beginning of the eighteenth centuries, at least fifty-seven obrajes were operating illegally,[52] though most were probably small urban workshops. However, a few illegal obrajes were established in rural areas by corregidores and priests, and haciendas often had small *galpones* attached.[53]

Of the thirty-seven private mills licensed at the beginning of the seventeenth century, only twelve received permits to use forced labor. Others could employ only voluntary labor, or occasionally black slaves. Some obrajeros received licenses to employ forced labor as a favor for services, but others paid substantial sums for permits to employ only a few workers. For example, in 1644 Juan de Santísteban paid 4,000 pesos for a permit to employ twelve mitayos and forty *indios de merced* in his obraje at Yaruquí.[54] The most important mills possessed a nucleus of forced labor. Although some obrajeros obtained permits to employ forced labor, more commonly they made agreements with encomenderos and caciques to supply workers on the pretext it would enable them to discharge tribute debts. If this failed, they resorted to coercion. The idea of voluntary labor was largely a myth.

Indians assigned to work in obrajes de comunidad or by special permit to private mills appear to have been allocated from the quinto, or one-fifth of the tributary population of Indian villages liable for the mita. In the documentary record these Indians are often referred to as "indios de entero," and the maximum number that could be employed at any one time was specified. While most were employed in textile manufacture, small numbers were employed in associated activities such as building work, supplying wood and water, and tending mules that were used for transport.[55] Children over the age of ten, women, and old persons were also employed as forced laborers in both types of mills. For example, in 1564 the cacique of Latacunga agreed to provide 35 Indians and 80 youths to work in the obraje de comunidad,[56] while in 1620 the Duque de Uzeda was granted a permit to employ 150 mitayos and 100 youths in his private mills.[57] Child labor was justified on the grounds that it taught the Indians a useful trade.

Community mills drew their labor from the villages in which they were established, though the larger ones drafted labor from wider regions. For example, the obraje de comunidad at Latacunga drew forced laborers from Saquisilí, Tanicuchí, Aláques, San Sebastián, Pujilí, and San Felipe.[58] Most community mills employed several hundred Indians. In 1581 the obraje at Chimbo employed 200 workers,[59] and in 1605 that at Chambo was worked by 160 Indians from the villages of Chambo and Quimia, while the Lito mill was worked by 130 Indians from that village and another nearby.[60] The Chambo and Lito mills effectively monopolized the local supply of mita labor, for in 1603 only 116 Indians were liable for the mita from Chambo and Quimia, and only 100 from Lito.[61] In 1591 there were said to be 1,350 Indians working in the seven obrajes de comunidad in the términos of Quito,[62] and in 1604 there were 1,162 employed in those of Latacunga, Riobamba, and Chimbo alone. (See Table 12.)[63]

The Crown's attitude toward the employment of forced labor in private mills vacillated, but from 1609 it was permitted under special license, though workers could only be drawn from within a distance of two leagues.[64] In 1680 only about one-third of the licensed mills, though the largest, could employ forced labor.[65] Other mills were only permitted to employ voluntary labor or black slaves. Some obrajeros secured small numbers of convicts from local jails, but most had to rely on attracting voluntary labor through offering higher wages than those paid to forced laborers or to free workers in other enterprises. Tyrer suggests that wages in private mills were between 30 to 50 percent higher than in community mills[66] and were good compared with those of mitayos and agricultural laborers.[67] Increasingly, private mills attracted labor from community mills, and children sometimes worked there to supplement the family income.[68] Even so, there were cases where higher wages had to be accompanied by cash advances or coercion.[69] Agreements were often made between caciques, encomenderos, and obrajeros for the provision of "voluntary" workers ostensibly to pay off tribute debts.[70] Particularly oppressive were corregidores and priests, who often forced Indians to work in small personal obrajes.[71] By this means it was estimated a corregidor could increase his salary of 1,000 pesos to between 15,000 and 20,000 pesos.[72] In addition to "voluntary" labor, some private mills employed black slaves, though their high cost limited their number. In 1604 three private mills were employing black slaves.[73] The largest number were working in the mill of San Ildefonso at Pelileo near Ambato, which in 1605 employed sixty black slaves and some Indians.[74]

In the early seventeenth century the textile mills absorbed a large proportion of the region's labor force. Table 12 indicates that by the 1620s thirteen community mills were in operation. In 1604 the region's five community mills employed 1,162 forced laborers, giving an average per mill of 232. (See Table 12.)[75] Given that most mills would have employed some voluntary workers, particularly in skilled tasks, the average size of a mill's labor force in the 1620s may be estimated at about 250 workers, suggesting that the community mills employed 3,250 Indians. At the same time, there were eighteen licensed private mills, and Tyrer suggests that there were another three whose licenses were in dispute.[76] In 1604 one private mill licensed to use forced labor employed 140 Indians, and in 1680 similar mills were employing over 170 workers.[77] These mills, like community mills, employed a small number of voluntary workers in skilled occupations, so that an average of 150 workers per mill would seem reasonable. This would give a total work force of 1,050 for the seven private mills licensed to employ forced labor. Given that these mills were the largest in the private sector, and given the greater difficulty of securing voluntary labor in the early part of the century, it is not unreasonable to suggest that the average work force of the remaining private mills was about 80 workers and that together they employed 1,120 workers. These calculations suggest that in the 1620s a total of 5,420 Indians were employed in the textile industry in the corregimientos of Riobamba and Latacunga. These figures take no account of illegal obrajes, of which there are likely to have been a small number in the 1620s. About 65 percent of the textile workers worked in mills in the Riobamba region. When the estimate of 3,550 workers employed in the textile industry of the Riobamba region is compared with the tributary population in 1605 of 5,720—a figure that increased only slightly in the subsequent two decades[78]—it is clear that over half of the male labor force was employed in the industry and that textile production touched the lives of most people in the region.

The Ordinances of Toledo of 1577 specified that mill workers were to be paid wages between twenty and twenty-four pesos a year, and women, children, and old persons, thirteen pesos.[79] Wages increased into the seventeenth century, though they varied from mill to mill;[80] continuing abuses in the payment of wages, however, required more effective regulation. In 1621 Oidor Peralta introduced fixed annual minimum wages of between eighteen and ninety patacones according to the tasks performed, which fell into three basic groups.[81] First, basic work such as cleaning the wool, spinning, and weaving was paid at the lowest rate of eighteen patacones, even though weaving was a more skilled occupation. The second group of tasks concerned with dyeing and finishing the cloth were paid at the higher rate of between twenty-four and thirty patacones. The most highly paid workers were carders and fullers and those involved in the running and maintenance of the mill, such as blacksmiths and carpenters.

Over 85 percent of a mill's labor force was employed in basic occupations.[82] Despite these fixed wage scales, they were not always adhered to,[83] and payments were often delayed. Those delayed long after harvest could result in higher food costs and reduced consumption, from which it was said "many Indians and their children die."[84] In 1619 Indians working in obrajes in the jurisdiction of Riobamba were owed four *pagas,* since the corregidor, Martín de Vergara, had pocketed more than 100,000 pesos of their profits.[85]

In the early seventeenth century the tours of duty of forced laborers assigned to obrajes lasted a whole year,[86] except that Peralta's Ordinances specified they were to be free for three weeks in October and two in February to enable them to sow and harvest their crops. To control the exploitation of Indian labor, the same ordinances specified the amount of work to be undertaken in a day by each type of worker.[87] They also reduced the working day from twelve hours, from sunrise to sunset, to nine hours, and insisted that work should be moderate. Mill owners were required to provide workers with food in the form of meat, salt, and ají, as well as medicine and later even a doctor to care for the sick.[88] Despite the existence of ordinances, conditions of work were poor. Most workshops were barnlike structures with small windows, which meant they were poorly lit and ventilated and were bitterly cold in winter. The largest obrajes contained separate buildings for different stages in the manufacturing process, but smaller ones housed all activities. Poor ventilation and the presence of indoor latrines encouraged the spread of disease and made them unhealthful places of work.[89] Indians were often chained to looms or locked in to prevent them from escaping.[90] Despite these poor working conditions, they were not the focus of most Indians complaints. Rather their objections related to the ill-treatment they suffered and the punishments they received for shortcomings that included flogging and imprisonment.[91] Indians fled and practised infanticide rather than subject themselves and their families to work in obrajes. Conditions were sufficiently harsh that it was suggested that convicted criminals should be employed in textile mills rather than sent to work as rowers on board galleys at Cartagena.[92]

Although work in the mills was hard, it was generally less destructive of native communities than other forms of forced labor, which required extended absence. Obrajes were generally constructed within Indian villages, additional workers being drawn from smaller villages located within a few miles; from 1609 forced laborers could not be taken from communities more than two leagues from their place of employment.[93] Most mill workers returned home each night, while those from more distant villages could visit their communities at weekends, and later the authorities permitted the construction of separate galpones in satellite villages.[94] Even though harsh work in the obrajes stimulated some migration, which may have gathered momentum as the seventeenth century progressed, their establishment in Indian villages served to maintain community ties. This was regarded as a particular advantage of community mills, to the extent that residents of villages with obrajes de comunidad were not permitted to work in mills elsewhere, even though they might be offered higher wages as voluntary laborers, for fear they would become "denaturalized."[95] Although labor gradually drifted to private obrajes, and migration may have increased,[96] the social dislocations associated with the textile industry were generally not as great as for other enterprises.

The textile industry dominated the economy of the corregimientos of Riobamba and Latacunga, but it was not the only activity to make demands on Indian labor. Although few mines existed in the region, Indian labor was drafted to work in mining areas to the south. From 1549 Indians from the central sierra, in common with other parts of the province of Quito, were assigned to work in the mines of Santa Barbara near Cuenca. At that time the region supplied 1,730 forced laborers for these mines.[97] The number declined, however, as the deposits became exhausted, though a few Puruhá continued to be employed there on a voluntary basis.[98] In the late sixteenth century the plan to provide 2,000 workers for the mines of Zaruma claimed that the region could supply 1,020 Indians drawn from encomiendas[99] or 750 vagamundos.[100] Although the plan envisaged drawing Indians from the whole of the sierra, attention increasingly focused on the Puruhá region as opposition from other regions mounted. It was one of the closest regions to Zaruma and possessed a similar climate. Moreover it was argued that the labor force was involved in the textile industry, from which the Crown received no material benefit.[101] Such attempts to involve Puruhá Indians in mining at Zaruma and Cuenca were strongly opposed by local encomenderos and vecinos, and there is no evidence they were successful.[102] However, in 1611 the audiencia approved the allocation of 200 mitayos to work in the local Angamarca mines near Latacunga.[103]

Even though the Puruhá and Panzaleo were not involved extensively in the mining mita, by the end of the sixteenth century they were overburdened with supplying labor for a variety of activities that fell under the heading of servicio ordinario. These included tending livestock, provisioning tambos, constructing buildings and roads, and working in obrajes. Demands for these types of service clearly exceeded supply, and conflicts arose between potential employers both within the region and with those in the Quito Basin.[104] The level of service demanded was clearly considerable. In 1592, Oidor Auncibay calculated it would be possible to send one-eighth of the 1,200 tributary Indians in the province of Chimbo to work in the mines of Zaruma. This proportion, he observed, would represent a lighter burden than that currently borne by villages in the region, which were required to supply one-fifth for servicio ordinario, another one-fifth of those remaining to tend livestock, and another one-fifth of those remaining to work in obrajes. He noted that as a consequence two-thirds of families were absent from their homes at one time.[105] Further evidence for excessive levels of service exaction was revealed by an oidor in the early seventeenth century who found 500 more mitayos working on haciendas in Riobamba, Latacunga, and Chimbo than permitted by the mita.[106] Other commentators similarly observed that the level of service demanded was well in excess of that legally permitted[107] and that the wages paid were pitifully low, amounting to only twelve pesos a year for shepherds and agricultural laborers.[108]

The burden of supplying such large numbers of laborers was clearly exacerbated by the expansion of the textile industry and was sufficient to stimulate Indians to abandon their families and communities.[109] As labor shortages developed, employers with access to mita labor began to use force to retain mitayos in their service as "free" workers. In 1631 the bishop of Quito reported that Guaranda (Chimbo) and Tomabela were unable to meet their tribute and mita obligations, since employers in Ambato were forcibly retaining Indians in their service.[110] While permanent absentees evaded the mita, their communities were required to meet their obligations in full until tribute rolls were readjusted during subsequent visitas. A visita of Chambo, Quimia, Puní, Lito, and Penipe undertaken by Muñoa Ronquillo in 1603 registered 33 Indians as absent, and presumably lost to official records, but recorded that a further 185 resided in other communities. Those absent or living elsewhere represented about 10 percent of their total tributary populations, and although they were liable to pay tribute, they were exempt from the mita.[111] However, those who escaped from the mita by working for private employers enjoyed few benefits. They were often treated like slaves and paid derisory salaries on the understanding, often unfulfilled, that their employers would meet their tribute obligations.[112]

High levels of service detracted from subsistence production and encouraged increasing dependence on the market for food.[113] This process was accelerated by the alienation of Indian lands, although this was less advanced in the Riobamba region because of its limited agricultural potential. Livestock raising dominated agricultural activities in the region, but cereal production probably had the greater impact on Indian subsistence. Livestock raising centered on the extensive páramos, which in pre-Columbian times had been used primarily as sources of wood, straw, and game. Indian access to these grasslands continued into the early seventeenth century, though it became more restricted, and Spanish demands for game reduced that available for local needs.[114] However, native demands fell with the population, and the newly introduced livestock partially compensated for reduced access to wild resources. Cereal production had more severe, though possibly more localized, effects, since it competed with native agriculture for land and labor.[115] Some lands were usurped by Spaniards, and others made available to them following the reducciones in the early 1570s. However, the fact that the kamayuq system was still operating in the early seventeenth century suggests that the widespread alienation of Indian lands had not taken place. In 1605 only one village in the Puruhá region, that of Guanando, was described as having insufficient lands to cultivate.[116] Even so, farming in this region was not easy. Crops were often destroyed by frost, particularly at higher elevations, by straying livestock, and occasionally by volcanic ash.[117] Harvest failure, such as occurred in 1628 and 1629, was occasionally so severe as to cause labor services to cease and render the Indians incapable of paying their tribute.[118] In general, cereal yields were said to be better around Ambato than Riobamba, though prices were similar, while Latacunga was well supplied with cheap provisions.[119]

DEMOGRAPHIC TRENDS IN THE CENTRAL SIERRA

The early demographic history of the regions of Riobamba, Chimbo, Ambato, and Latacunga is difficult to trace, since it is not possible to disaggregate figures for these areas from those for jurisdiction of Quito, of which they were a part. The first figures that permit some insight into the size and distribution of population within the jurisdiction are contained in the *Ordenanzas de Minas* of 1549, which assigned Indians from the central and southern sierra to work in the Cuenca mines.[120] From the jurisdiction of Riobamba and Chimbo 820 Indians were drafted, and a further 810 were assigned from around Ambato and Latacunga.[121] It has been suggested that maybe 1 in 10 tributary Indians was drafted,[122] which would argue for a combined total tributary population of about 16,300 (Table 13). What proportion this represented of the total population is difficult to judge. Most contemporary accounts assume a multiplication factor of 5, but as will be shown, late sixteenth-century accounts indicate that the ratio of tributary to nontributary Indians seldom reached that figure, and it is likely to have been even lower in the immediate postconquest period. Multiplying the figure for the total tributary population in 1549 by four and five gives estimates for the total population of the whole region of between 65,200 and 81,500.

During the early 1570s Viceroy Toledo's program of reducciones was put into effect in Latacunga, Ambato, and Riobamba by Antonio de Clavijo on orders from Oidor Licenciado Francisco de Cárdenas. The program involved the establishment of eighteen villages each with 2,000 to 4,000

Table 13. Estimated Indian Population of the Central Sierra in the Sixteenth Century

Region	Tributary population						Total population			
	1549[a]	1581[b]	1591[c]	1590s[d]	1590s[e]	1605[f]	1549[a] × 4	1549[a] × 5	1581[b]	1605[f]
Latacunga	4,900g	3,432g	4,750 (4,750)	3,300	4,700	—	19,600g	24,500g	13,728g	19,000g
Ambato	3,200g	1,761g	3,955g (2,571)	1,200h	1,700h	2,762	12,800g	16,000g	7,044	9,840g
Riobamba	6,000g	4,372g	6,157g (2,709)	4,504g,h	4,500	5,720	24,000g	30,000g	17,487	22,042
Chimbo	2,200g	1,875i	1,481g (474)	—	1,100	—	8,800g	11,000g	8,841i	8,800g
Total	16,300g	11,440g	16,343g (10,504)		12,000	—	65,200g	81,500g	47,100g	59,682g

a AMQ LC 4:228–32 Ordenanzas de minas 7.6.1549. Multiplication factors of 4 and 5 are applied to tributary populations.
b AGI AQ 8 Visita of Riobamba 1581.
c CDI 6:41–63 Relación de los indios tributarios 1591. The numbers in parentheses are the actual figures given in the documentary sources.
d AGI AQ 9 Licenciado Marañón, no date.
e RGI 2:316 Relación del distrito del Cerro de Zaruma, no date.
f CDI 9:452–88 Descripción . . . de la villa del Villar Don Pardo 1605.
g Estimate. See text for calculation.
h Incomplete.
i RGI 2:256–59 Cantos 7.10.1581; the figures exclude Tomabela.

Indians.[123] For example, the village of Ambato was created from six parcialidades—Pacas, Hambatillos, Quizapincha, Tomabela, Angamarcas, and Izambas—which together contained 3,386 Indians.[124] Most of the newly formed villages comprised several ayllus, some of which were former colonies of mitmaq or kamayuq. Each had its own cacique, who was subject to the authority of a *cacique principal* or *gobernador*. Some larger settlements, such as San Andrés, Chambo, Lito, and Puní, comprised over twelve parcialidades,[125] which among other things reflected the degree of depopulation since Spanish conquest.

As part of the program of reducciones, the inhabitants of the newly created communities were enumerated.[126] Figures from these counts together with others undertaken during the 1570s were incorporated into a report of the visita conducted by the corregidor of Riobamba, Pedro de León, in 1581.[127] This visita, which covered the Riobamba and Ambato regions, revealed the presence of 24,531 Indians, while in the same year the corregidor of Chimbo, Miguel de Cantos,[128] enumerated 8,841 Indians in his jurisdiction. So far there is no evidence for a similar visita of Latacunga region. The visita of Riobamba and Ambato does not indicate the number of tributary Indians, but for Chimbo the ratio of tributary to nontributary Indians can be calculated at 1:4.7. Similar details are available only from San Andrés in the corregimiento of Riobamba, and they suggest a ratio of 1:4.3.[129] Using an average multiplication factor of 4.5, the tributary population of the Riobamba-Ambato region can be estimated at about 5,451. This is considerably lower than estimates that can be obtained by other methods. The total numbers of male married Indians, single males, and widowers enumerated in the 1581 visita sum to 7,795. Not all of these Indians would have been tributary Indians. Evidence from the 1581 visita of Chimbo suggests that 20 percent should be deducted for *reservados*,[130] which applied to the corregimiento of Riobamba and Ambato would give an estimated tributary population of 6,236 and a ratio of tributary to nontributary Indians of 1:3.9. Alternatively, Ortiz de la Tabla Ducasse, using evidence for the amount of tribute paid, has estimated that there were 6,336 tributary Indians, giving a ratio of 1:3.87.[131] In the absence of further information, it is not unreasonable to assume an average tributary to nontributary Indian ratio of 1:4 to give an estimate of 6,133. Unfortunately, the 1581 visita did not extend to Latacunga, but if it is assumed that it contained about 30 percent of the population of the region under discussion, as it did in 1549, its tributary population may be estimated at 3,432 and its total population at 13,728.

The list of tributary Indians drawn up by Morales Figueroa for 1591 is clearly incomplete for all jurisdictions under consideration here.[132] For Riobamba it includes only the villages of Chambo, Puní, Macaxí, and Luisa (San Andrés), which together possessed a tributary population of 2,709,

and for the Chimbo region only the villages of Pallatanga and Cumbibamba, which together contained 474 tributary Indians. If it is assumed
those villages excluded accounted for the same proportion of the populations of those regions as they did in 1581, then their total tributary populations may be estimated at 6,157 and 1,481 respectively.[133] The figures are
more complete for the Latacunga region and, unlike the figures for Riobamba, are more complete than those indicated in the *Relación de Zaruma,*
to be discussed below. The Morales Figueroa figures suggest there were
4,750 tributary Indians in and around Latacunga, with another 2,571 in the
Ambato region. Several villages in the latter region are omitted, and the
figures for 1605 suggest that 35 percent should be added to give an estimate for the tributary population of 3,955.[134] What figures these numbers
were based on is not clear, but they are clearly different from those recorded in 1581. Although the combined estimate of 16,343 for 1591 represents an increase over that for 1581, it is unlikely to have reflected the
actual population, since many figures predate the epidemics of the late
1580s.

Probably a better reflection of the general size of the population in the
early 1590s, but lacking in detail, is the list of tributary Indians by encomienda in the province of Quito, from which it was suggested that it would
be possible to extract labor for the mines of Zaruma.[135] Six encomenderos
were listed for the jurisdiction of Riobamba with 4,500 Indians, four for
Latacunga with 4,700 Indians, while the encomienda of Miguel de Sandoval in Chimbo comprised 1,100 Indians; others for the latter jurisdiction
are not included, and the figures recorded for Ambato region are too
incomplete to be of any use in indicating demographic trends. At the same
time, it was suggested that vagamundos and peinadillos might be employed
in the mines. Within the jurisdiction of Quito they numbered 2,000, of
which 800 were found in the regions under discussion. Chimbo in particular was noted as having many vagamundos.[136] These Indians do not appear
to have been included in any earlier enumerations.

A similar account drawn up by President Esteban de Marañón in the
late 1590s that lists the number of tributary Indians in parishes administered by regular clergy gives similar figures.[137] In the jurisdiction of
Riobamba the villages of Calpi, Licán, and Yaruquí were administered by
parish priests, and therefore their populations were not included. In 1581
these villages accounted for 12.6 percent of the total number of Indians
enumerated. This percentage may be added to the total number of 4,000
tributary Indians reported by Marañón to provide a more complete figure
for the region of 4,504, but 200 need to be deducted for Ilapo.[138] The total
of 4,304 tributary Indians compares with the estimate of 4,372 in 1581,
suggesting little change between the two dates. The same is not true of
the Latacunga region. With the exception of Sicchos, all parishes in the

Table 14. Indian Population Estimates for the Central Sierra
at the Beginning of the Seventeenth Century

Region	Tributary population	Total Indian population	Vagamundos	Population resident outside the region	Total
Latacunga	4,750	19,000	900	1,458	21,358
Ambato	2,762	9,840	375	365	10,580
Total	7,512	28,840	1,275	1,823	31,938
Riobamba	5,720	22,042	375	486	22,903
Chimbo	2,200	8,800	750	121	9,671
Total	7,920	30,842	1,125	607	32,574

province of Latacunga were under the administration of Franciscans, and it is assumed that President Marañón's account, which included 3,300 tributary Indians, was complete. If the Sicchos communities are excluded from Morales Figueroa's figures, then by comparison the president's account shows a decline of 11.3 percent between the two dates. Only a few parishes around Ambato were administered by regular clergy, in this case Augustinians, so that the account provides insufficient figures to give an overall estimate for the region; other parishes and those in the province of Chimbo were under secular clergy.

Finally, a detailed description of the corregimiento of Riobamba in 1605 suggests the Riobamba region possessed a tributary population of 5,720 and the Ambato region 2,762.[139] At the same time, the former had a total Indian population of 22,042 giving a tributary to nontributary ratio of 1:3.85.[140] The figure for the Ambato region omitted the populations of Patate and Baños. These communities possessed 340 tributary Indians, and since the average tributary to nontributary ratio for neighboring communities may be calculated at 1:3.56, it is reasonable to apply this ratio to raise the total of 8,630 by 1,210 to give 9,840 for the Ambato region (Table 14).

In estimating the total population of the central sierra at the turn of the century, the figures for 1605 may be used for the Riobamba and Ambato regions. Added to these, two accounts of the tributary population of Latacunga in the 1590s suggest the presence of about 4,750 Indians, which, using a multiplication factor of 4, gives a total population of about 19,000. For Chimbo, the *Relación de Zaruma* indicated that the encomienda of Miguel de Sandoval possessed 1,100 tributary Indians, while the 1581 enumeration indicated that it contained about half of the population of the corregimiento. As such, the tributary population in the 1590s may be calculated at 2,200, giving a total Indian population of about 8,800. The combined Indian population for the four areas may thus be estimated at

Table 15. Estimates of Population Change in the Central Sierra
in the Sixteenth Century

	Aboriginal population	Indian population in 1600	Percent decline	Depopulation ratio
Latacunga-Ambato	160,000	31,938	80.0	5.0:1
Riobamba-Chimbo	131,250	32,574	75.2	4.0:1
Total	291,250	64,512	77.8	4.5:1

59,682. To this figure should be added estimates for those with no community affiliation who lived outside the region and vagamundos resident in the region whose origins are unknown. The account of Indians baptized in the cathedral church of El Sagrario in Quito suggests that many hundreds from these regions, and especially from Latacunga, were living in the city. The baptismal registers suggest that about 27 percent of parents came from the regions under discussion here.[141] Since about 3,000 Indians with no community affiliation were to be found in the Quito Basin at that time, it may be estimated that about 810 came from the central sierra, which, using the same multiplication factor of 3, would argue for an additional 2,430 Indians.[142] The region also contained about 800 vagamundos. While some may have come from other regions, probably most were of local provenance and as such should be included here. Since this number clearly referred to able-bodied males, the figure can be multiplied by three, as for those in the Quito region, which would give a total population of 2,400.

These calculations suggest that, overall, the Indian population of the central sierra declined from an estimated 291,250 at the time of Spanish conquest to 64,512 at the beginning of the sixteenth century. (See Table 15.) This decline appears to have been slightly greater in the Latacunga-Ambato region, where the population fell by 80 percent; in the Riobamba region the loss was in the order of 75 percent. Although this difference could derive from errors of estimation, it is not unexpected. The Latacunga region bore a heavier burden in supplying auxiliaries for expeditions, and located nearer to Quito, it was also more exposed to demands for labor, which expanded with the growth of the city and its textile industry.

Demographic trends during the sixteenth century show a decline until about the 1590s, with a sharp dip in the late 1580s due to epidemics, and then a slow increase. By 1550 the population had fallen to about 81,500, largely as a result of conquest and epidemics. It has been suggested that about 15,000 Indians were lost during conquest or on expeditions.[143] This may be an underestimate, but in any case losses were much smaller than those inflicted by epidemics. It has been estimated that the two preconquest epidemics, probably of smallpox and measles, together with the plague or typhus epidemic of 1546, may have reduced the population by about 60 percent. Further epidemics occurred in 1558 and the late 1580s, and the region may well have participated in the 1582 epidemic that affected the Cuenca region.[144] Apart from epidemics, these regions were generally regarded as healthful, with the most notable illnesses being "headaches, stomach-aches, and colds."[145]

While the direct causes of depopulation were most significant in determining demographic trends, other factors operated to raise mortality levels and suppress fertility rates. Ill-treatment and harsh working conditions among those employed as tamemes and in obrajes elevated mortality rates. In 1603 no less than 13 percent of the combined tributary populations of Chambo, Quimia, Penipe, Puní, and Lito was exempt from the mita because of disablement or sickness.[146] The harsh labor regimes for which the obrajes became so notorious eventually encouraged fugitivism,[147] but in the meantime labor drafts represented a constant drain on native labor resources that may have affected food supplies, particularly in more difficult environments. The lower average adult/child ratio of 1:0.51 for Indian communities in the Riobamba region in 1581, compared with 1:0.60 for those around Ambato, could be attributed to less adequate food supplies in the more difficult environment that affected children disproportionately.[148] Although adult/child ratios seem to have improved slightly into the seventeenth century,[149] the population was still failing to reproduce itself. For example, in 1620 the adult/child ratio for Macaxí was 1:0.83, compared with 1:0.64 in 1581. However, these figures mask considerable demographic instability reflected in large numbers of absentees, many second marriages, and many illegitimate children.[150] Recovery was retarded by low fertility rates associated with arduous female labor, premature weaning and infanticide,[151] and by fugitivism, which strained social relations. Nevertheless, in the early colonial period at least, most large mills were established in Indian villages rather than urban centers. As a consequence, although textile manufacture had adverse effects on demographic trends, in the early colonial period it did not undermine the economic viability of Indian communities or precipitate long-term or wide-scale displacements that were associated with other forms of employment, such as mining and domestic service, which brought high social costs. Not surprisingly, the depopulation ratios for the central sierra of between 4.0:1 and 5.0:1 are lower than for most other highland regions and especially the Quito Basin and mining areas.

CHAPTER 10

Cuenca

The province of Cañares is the key to this land and that which helps
us conquer and sustain this province of Quito and from which
other provinces have been conquered.

Cabildo of Quito, 31 March 1540[1]

In 1557 the city of Cuenca was founded at Tomebamba, and its jurisdiction
broadly corresponded to the pre-Inkan province of Cañar.[2] Despite the
city's relatively late foundation, the surrounding region did not escape the
upheavals associated with Spanish conquest elsewhere in the sierra. Subsequently the Cañar were conscripted for military campaigns and expeditions, while others were involved in the exploitation of gold and silver.
Since the Cañar region fell within the jurisdiction of Quito, many of its
vecinos became the region's first encomenderos, and even after its foundation most of its encomenderos continued to reside in Quito. By the time
Cuenca was founded, its surrounding Indian population had already suffered major losses. Subsequently, mining declined, and Cuenca became
the center of a predominantly agricultural region. (See Map 10.)

Hoping to liberate themselves from Inka rule, the Cañar at first supported the Spanish cause.[3] Indeed 300 Cañar aided Sebastián de Benalcázar in the initial conquest of Quito.[4] The Cañar were first allocated in
encomiendas by Francisco Pizarro. His brother Gonzalo Pizarro, Diego de
Sandoval, and Rodrigo Núñez de Bonilla all received sizable encomiendas
in the region in or before 1540.[5] Others were later assigned by President
La Gasca. Those allocated encomiendas commonly employed their Indians
as soldiers and porters on military expeditions that extended and consolidated conquest. In 1536 Diego de Sandoval drafted 500 Cañar to aid Benalcázar in the conquest of northern Peru.[6] They were also conscripted to
serve in armies during the Spanish civil wars when different groups sometimes found themselves on opposing sides. The Cañar taken by Benalcázar
to Peru to support La Gasca were so numerous that women had to be
drafted to serve as porters.[7] In the meantime others were involved in
expeditions to the east. Cañar Indians were almost certainly employed in
the expeditions to Macas by Rodrigo Núñez de Bonilla and Hernando de
Benavente in 1540 and 1549 respectively.[8] Another expedition proposed by
Pedro de Vergara envisaged the recruitment of 800 Cañar. This was opposed by Indian leaders who made representations to the cabildo of
Quito.[9] The cabildo was sympathetic, for it feared that persistent drafts
would destabilize the region, which was regarded as the key to Spanish

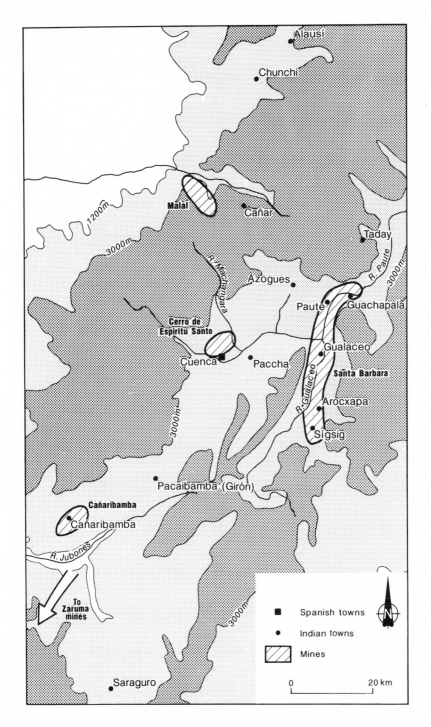

Map 10. The Cuenca region

occupation of the province of Quito and vital in extending control over new territories. The importance of the Cañar region as a source of auxiliaries is evident. Although the outcome of their representations is not known, at least some Cañar probably served on Pedro de Vergara's two-year expedition that from 1541 explored the Upper Zamora.[10] Later expeditions to Yaguarzongo and Pacamoros by Juan de Salinas probably also employed Cañar Indians; certainly at least 300 were involved in the expedition that suppressed the revolt in Logroño in 1580.[11] Altogether during the first fifty years of conquest several thousand Cañar were involved in military campaigns and expeditions that brought battle casualties and severe disruption to the economic and social life of Indian communities.

Demands for Indian labor extended beyond the needs of expeditions to the requirements of miners. Archaeological excavations indicate that the Cañar had a good knowledge of working gold, silver, and copper,[12] and in Inka times local Indians were probably employed to construct the richly adorned palaces of Tomebamba so admiringly described by Cieza de León.[13] Although gold was probably mined in the region in Inka times, to the extent that the gold extracted from the Santa Barbara River was said to have been a cause of dispute between Huascar and Atahualpa,[14] Spanish interest in gold mining did not develop until the 1540s. Cieza de León claimed that gold was discovered in the region in 1544,[15] but evidence exists for the exploitation of deposits at Sangorima before 1539.[16] Prior to the foundation of Cuenca the mines of Santa Barbara, also known as Santa Bárbola, were the most important in the region. Here most gold extracted came from alluvial deposits, although some veins were also worked.[17] The deposits were obviously rich, for treasury officials claimed that in 1544 miners had extracted 300,000 pesos of gold,[18] and this was considerably lower than the estimate of 800,000 pesos recorded by Cieza de León, who himself claimed to have obtained 700 pesos of gold from one pan.[19]

The gold deposits were worked by gangs of encomienda Indians and hired laborers. In 1544 eighteen to twenty *cuadrillas* of between 50 and 80 Indians each were panning gold at Santa Barbara, which implies a labor force of between 900 and 1,600 workers.[20] Forced to work there by encomenderos, they came from villages up to thirty or forty leagues away, many of them from outside the Cañar region. Working conditions were unregulated, so that Indians were often ill-treated and provided with inadequate food; in fact most were required to take food with them. It was to rectify these abuses that mining ordinances were introduced in 1549.[21] These stipulated that cuadrillas were not to exceed 80 Indians and that they were not to be drawn from regions whose climate differed from that which prevailed around the mines.[22] The ordinances also restricted mine labor to six months from August to February and specified that an Indian's weekly provisions were to include two *almudes* of maize, plus some ají and coca, and that 15 Indians were to share one pig. Miners were also required to provide workers with clothes and sleeping quarters, as well as to care for the sick. At that time 2,355 Indians were approved for the next *demora,* the majority of whom were drawn from the central sierra, with only 585 coming from the Cañar region itself. It was noted that these numbers represented a reduction of those formerly assigned. The new ordinances were accompanied by a schedule of fines for infringements, which if they been enforced, would have brought considerable improvements to working conditions. However, Indians continued to be ill-treated and over-worked. It was claimed that most of those who worked in the mines died there and that those who returned to their homes, who did not die on the road, died shortly after. As a consequence, viceregal and presidential decrees occasionally ordered mining to cease.[23]

When Cuenca was founded in 1557 by Gil Ramírez Dávalos under instructions from the viceroy, the Marqués de Cañete,[24] most Indians in the surrounding region had already been distributed in encomiendas to vecinos of Quito. However, it was anticipated that when these encomiendas became vacant, they would be reallocated to citizens of Cuenca.[25] Nevertheless, in the late 1560s or early 1570s the city possessed only two or three encomenderos, even though its original twenty Spanish inhabitants had risen to between sixty and eighty.[26]

Labor shortages retarded the region's economic development and in the latter part of the century contributed to a shift from mining into agricultural production. Five years after Cuenca had been established, its vecinos were complaining they were poor and had no means of existing except by employing a few Indians to mine gold.[27] This was despite the fact that new deposits had been discovered in other parts of the province and a *casa de fundición* established there in 1559.[28] Perhaps most interesting was the exploitation of mercury at Azogues, which was reputedly discovered by Gil Ramírez Dávalos. Mercury production from this source, possibly discovered in 1558,[29] was sufficiently great to enable some to be exported to New Spain.[30] However, beset by flooding and shortages of labor, production was eclipsed by the discovery of mercury at Huancavelica in 1563, such that by 1582 mining had ceased.[31]

More significantly, gold and silver deposits were found at Cerro de Espíritu Santo, within a league of Cuenca.[32] Unlike those at Santa Barbara, which were worked mainly by miners from Quito, these were mined by vecinos who hired local workers.[33] In 1562 they bitterly opposed a royal provision that allowed a local merchant, Manuel de Mondoya, to employ 200 Indians from within the términos of Cuenca in the Santa Barbara mines. They argued that the provision would effectively exhaust the available labor supply, which had recently been severely reduced by an epidemic of smallpox. They also commented that forced labor in the Santa

Barbara mines had been banned as unhealthy and for the same reason no
Indians went there voluntarily.[34] It is not clear whether the provision was
revoked, but subsequently Indians from other regions, rather than local
Cañar, were employed in the Santa Barbara mines, in theory on a voluntary basis.[35] Both Oidor Salazar de Villasante and the *alcalde mayor* of
Zaruma, Rodrigo de Arcos, claimed to have recruited 200 and 300 voluntary workers respectively from the Puruhá region to exploit the deposits
at Santa Barbara.[36] Although this labor was allegedly voluntary, there is
clear evidence that force was applied.[37]

During the latter part of the sixteenth century the mines of Espíritu
Santo, especially those of Todos Santos, continued to be worked only
intermittently because of shortages of labor,[38] and the center of mining
activities shifted to Malal and Cañaribamba. The silver mines at Malal,
located seven leagues from Cuenca, probably entered production about
1575 and were worked irregularly into the seventeenth century.[39] If these
deposits were the same as those discovered by Rodrigo de Paz Maldonado,
in the first years of production their output was said to be better than
those of Guadalcanal in Spain.[40] Various modern authors claim that Juan
de Salinas Loyola was the first to exploit the mineral deposits near Cañaribamba.[41] There is no direct evidence that this was the case, although
he did possess an encomienda in the region and left 4,000 pesos to establish an Indian hospital in the town.[42] Mining operations appear to have
begun in the 1580s, but the ore extracted was of low grade, and production
was hindered by labor shortages.[43] During the second half of the sixteenth century problems of labor recruitment were exacerbated by competition from the newly opened mines of Zaruma, for which mitayos were
drafted from Cañaribamba and Pacaibamba.[44] In 1598 a small number of
black slaves were imported,[45] but by the early seventeenth century, mining in the Cuenca region had effectively ceased because of shortages of
labor, and miners were looking to the Puruhá and the conquest of the
Jívaro to provide the labor necessary for its revival.[46]

Conditions in the mines, particularly those of Santa Barbara, remained
poor, despite the existence of mining ordinances. The Santa Barbara
mines could only be worked twice a year, when the river level was low, and
even then work had to continue through the day and night so that the pits
from which the ore was extracted would not flood and make them impossible to work. Long hours of work, many spent immersed in water, made
mining an unhealthy occupation. Those Indians who did not take food with
them were forced to buy provisions at exorbitant prices and so ate very
little. Their accommodation consisted of poorly constructed huts in which
they slept on the floor.[47] In addition to poor working and living conditions,
they often suffered ill-treatment. Diego de Ortegón was described as an
"enemy of Indians and a friend of gold and silver mines." It was claimed

that within six months, twenty Indians whom he forced to work in the mines of Santa Barbara had died through ill-treatment.[48] Not surprisingly, the mines failed to attract voluntary workers, even though wages in mining were considerably better than in other activities.[49] When they needed ready cash, Indians preferred to trade their produce or seek employment in Cuenca.

Prior to the establishment of Cuenca, mining formed the basis of the region's economy, but as mineral deposits became depleted and labor shortages restricted output, agricultural production played a more significant role. As early as the 1570s Cuenca's vecinos were described as living on the profits from the cereal cultivation and livestock raising; no mention was made of mining.[50] The topography of the Cañar region is rugged, so that only limited stretches of flat land exist. Nevertheless, the valleys were fertile and well watered, and good pastures existed for the raising of livestock. Particularly favored areas were the Machangara Valley, in which Cuenca was located, the valleys around Azogues, and the hinterlands of Cañaribamba and Pacaibamba.[51] Possessing a more temperate climate than regions to the north, the area was particularly well suited for the production of European cereals, vegetables, and fruit. Occasionally, however, frosts resulted in cereal shortages, as in 1563, 1577, and 1586, when bans had to be imposed prohibiting their export without license.[52] Nevertheless, provisions and meat were generally cheap, partly due to the lack of an external market.[53] Most agricultural produce was consumed locally, though wheat and maize were sold in local mining areas and in Zaruma, and some were exported to Guayaquil via the Bola River.[54] The market for cattle was more limited,[55] but horses were sold outside the region.[56]

The establishment of rural estates occurred with the collusion of the cabildo of Cuenca and at the expense of Indian communities. This process was given added impetus by Toledo's program of reducciones, which enabled the cabildo to reserve for itself and its members lands that it claimed that Indians no longer exploited.[57] The lands deemed most attractive were those located near to or belonging to Indian villages, from which encomenderos hoped to recruit labor and even encourage them to become resident peons.[58] As early as 1582 estancias in the Chuquipata Valley were housing workers from neighboring Indian villages.[59] The expansion of Spanish haciendas not only undermined native production but, in areas of restricted cultivable land, brought conflicts between Indian communities.[60] Nevertheless, Albornoz claims that Indian communities in the Cuenca region sought land titles at an early date and as a result remained proprietors of their lands for longer than elsewhere in Ecuador.[61] However, the early acquisition of land titles could also reflect the pressure on Indian lands that was evident in attempts by Spaniards to move boundary markers and in allowing cattle to stray onto Indian lands.[62] Certainly the alienation of Indian lands was a matter of concern to royal officials, who believed that ownership of land was fundamental to the preservation of Indian communities and necessary to facilitate their administration and Christian instruction.[63]

Changes in Indian subsistence patterns arose not only from losses of land and labor resources but also from the introduction of new crops and domesticated animals. Indians in the Cuenca region were quick to adopt chickens, cattle, pigs, sheep, goats, and even horses, even though they continued to hunt deer and rabbits, which were still in plentiful supply. Overall sources of animal protein appear to have improved for Indians in this region during the early colonial period.[64] Wheat and barley were probably grown on a small scale primarily for tribute payment, and in some cases Indians possessed plows and oxen.[65]

Agricultural products figured significantly among the items paid as tribute, though in addition manufactured goods and cash were always levied. The earliest evidence of tribute payments in the Cañar region comes from a tasación for the encomienda assigned to Rodrigo Núñez de Bonilla drawn up by President La Gasca, probably in the late 1540s. The list of items payable by 420 Cañar was enormous and included gold or silver in the form of 1,000 pesos, cotton thread and cloth, pigs, chickens, eggs, deer, partridges, maize, wheat, potatoes, coca, ají, honey, fruit, and articles made of cabuya.[66] In addition they were to supply twelve Indians for servicio ordinario and eight for tending cattle and cultivating their encomendero's lands. Tasaciones for the Cuenca region were drawn up at very irregular intervals. In the early 1570s Licenciado Francisco de Cárdenas was ordered by Viceroy Toledo to undertake a visita of the jurisdiction of Cuenca.[67] Unfortunately no detailed accounts of the visita have been found, but it is known that some consideration was given to raising the level of tribute exaction; in the event, for reasons unknown, this proved impracticable.[68] It was probably according to these tasaciones that Indians were paying in 1582 when the relaciones geográficas were compiled. By then the number of items paid as tribute had been reduced, so that most communities paid in maize, cotton cloth, chickens, sometimes wheat, and silver or cash.[69] Some of these items were raised communally, but the production of cotton cloth, which in pre-Columbian times had been based on cotton obtained by trade or from distant archipelagos, remained dependent on these sources.[70] The persistence of silver or cash as a element of tribute payments may have been a hangover from more prosperous times, when encomenderos commonly employed their Indians in mining. As mining declined, however, the acquisition of silver or cash became more difficult, and inevitably it forced Indians into the market economy as traders or wage laborers.

Indians earned wages as mitayos and free laborers. After Cuenca was founded, Indians were forced to work as mitayos in the construction of the city and as domestic servants or farm laborers.[71] Prior to 1577 Indians from Cañaribamba and Pacaibamba were required to work in the mines of Zaruma, but later the number assigned from Cañaribamba was split between the mines of Zaruma and the town of Cuenca.[72] Those employed to tend cattle and collect wood and straw were paid seven pesos a year, and those working as general farm laborers five and a half pesos. They were also to receive half a fanega of maize a month, which they could commute to a money payment.[73] These wages were pitifully low, especially when it is considered that each Indian needed two pesos to satisfy only the cash element of the tribute due. One account by Hernando Pablos, a vecino of Cuenca, suggests those not wishing to serve as mitayos earned money by trading goods in Cuenca or Zaruma, or by hiring themselves as porters to carry goods to Guayaquil, Zaruma, and towns to the east. Of these activities porterage was considered the most onerous because of the excessive loads that were carried, inadequate resting times, and the changes of climate they experienced, which all contributed to high death rates.[74] Although Pablos states that Indians had some choice as to how they acquired cash, it seems unlikely that, as he implies, they were free to evade the mita.

DEMOGRAPHIC TRENDS IN THE CUENCA REGION

Matovalle claims that the Cañar were better treated than other Indian groups because labor in mining was lighter than in other areas and the region possessed few resident encomenderos and no obrajes.[75] While this conclusion may have some validity for the second half of the sixteenth century, it takes no account of the demographic collapse of the region prior to the establishment of Cuenca. It has been estimated that even before Spanish conquest, the population of the Cañar region may have been reduced to about 58,500 as a result of Inka conquest, the dynastic wars, and preconquest epidemics. Subsequently, Spanish conquest, the demands made by expeditions, and forced labor in the mines took a heavy toll. Even though the latter burden was partly borne by Indians from other provinces, harsh labor together with epidemics were identified as the main causes of depopulation.

The province of Cuenca appears to have participated in most epidemics that ravaged Ecuador during the sixteenth century,[76] and there may have been a more localized outbreak of smallpox in 1562.[77] Albornoz claims that in 1582 there was a smallpox epidemic that resulted in many deaths in Gualaceo, Paute, Azogues, Guachapala, Taday, and Sigsig[78] and stimulated the establishment of the first hospital in Cuenca in 1585.[79] In fact a plot had been designated for the purpose prior to 1582, but its construction had been delayed because of lack of funds.[80] The seasonal occurrence of measles and smallpox claimed large numbers,[81] though their impact was said to have been reduced by the breakup of extended family households. Previously households had contained twenty to thirty inhabitants with their wives and children, and it was said that the formation of dispersed nuclear family residences had reduced personal contact and discouraged the spread of disease.[82] Although this assertion may have been correct, the impact of diseases may also have been moderated by Indians' acquiring some immunity to them through constant exposure. Local inhabitants also suffered from a number of chronic infections related to the region's warmer and more humid climate. Dysentery and other intestinal infections afflicted those who lived in the more humid valleys, while the damp mists that formed from the moist winds passing from the Pacific gave rise to coughs and other respiratory infections. These chronic infections were fairly widespread and took a heavy toll,[83] though some inhabitants were said to live to 80 and even 100 years.[84]

Until 1557 the Cañar region fell under the jurisdiction of Quito, so that population estimates for the area were subsumed in figures for the latter region. The earliest account giving a separate estimate for the Cuenca region probably dates from 1567, when it was said to possess 6,000 tributary Indians.[85] However, the figure of 8,000 tributary Indians recorded by Juan López de Velasco in the early 1570s probably predates this estimate. Nevertheless, its accuracy is questionable, since he noted that no list of villages and encomiendas in the region had yet been compiled.[86] Probably the most accurate estimate of the mid–sixteenth century is that of 5,470 tributary Indians which accompanies a list of sixteen encomiendas compiled in 1576 by the *juez de naturales,* Juan de Balboa, in an attempt to settle disputes between encomenderos.[87] This figure was probably based on the recent visita by Francisco de Cárdenas,[88] which is also the likely source used to compile of some of the relaciones geográficas drawn up in 1582. Unfortunately the demographic details contained in the latter are incomplete, since they omit the villages of Alausí, Chunchi, and Gualaceo, as well as those living in the town of Cuenca itself.[89] For the regions covered the number of tributary Indians sums to 2,250, and about one-third might be added to account for those not listed. A visita conducted by the bishop of Quito in 1581 suggests that in some cases these figures overestimated the number actually present. On his visita of Cañaribamba the bishop had expected to find 600 tributary Indians and 2,100 souls or more, but only encountered 50 "chicos y grandes, niños y viejos,"[90] and for Pacaibamba he reported that similarly many had fled.[91] In both cases flight to escape work in the mines was given as the reason. Since these

Table 16. Indian Population of the Jurisdiction of Cuenca in the Sixteenth Century

Year	Tributary population	Total population	Source
1567	6,000	—	RAHM 9/4664 no. 21 Los pueblos despañoles, no date
1571	8,000	—	López de Velasco, *Geografía*, 220
1576	5,470	—	Albornoz, *Monografía histórica del Girón*, 40–42
1582	—	12,000	RGI 2:268 Pablos 20.9.1582
1591	2,242	—	CDI 6:41–63 Relación de los indios tributarios 1.11.1591
1590s	3,000	—	RGI 2:316 Relación del distrito del cerro de Zaruma, no date

two communities were the main suppliers of mita labor in the province of Cuenca for the mines of Zaruma, this high level of fugitivism cannot be inferred for the whole region. The destination of the fugitives is unknown. Some probably became resident workers on local haciendas or in the town of Cuenca,[92] while others fled to Macas or the region between Piura and Loja or became forasteros in other communities;[93] Quito was too distant to attract many migrants.

In 1582 the province as a whole was said to possess 12,000 Indians, which it is assumed referred to the total population.[94] This figure is almost certainly too low if the figure of 5,470 tributary Indians for 1576 is accepted as the most reliable for the period. Nevertheless, the qualitative evidence confirms the continued decline of the Indian population into the last quarter of the sixteenth century, though some observers suggested that it was occurring less rapidly than previously.[95]

According to the summary list of tributary Indians drawn up by Morales Figueroa in 1591, there were 1,472 in the province of Cuenca.[96] This was clearly an underestimate, for his account omits the villages of Paccha and Alausí, and even his own figures for individual villages in the jurisdiction of Cuenca sum to 2,242. In the early 1590s plans to recruit workers for the mines of Zaruma estimated that there were at least 3,000 tributary Indians in the province, from which it would be possible to draw 200 Indians, and suggested that a further 200 vagamundos could be employed.[97] (See Table 16.) These estimates do not seem unreasonable, although it unclear on what sources they were based, except that they were clearly different from those used in the compilation of the relaciones geográficas. In 1600 President Ibarra claimed that the province of Cuenca had not been inspected for fourteen years, which suggests that a visita was conducted in the mid-1580s.[98] It is possible that accounts written in the 1590s used these sources, in which case they are unlikely to have taken account of the impact of epidemics that afflicted the region in the late 1580s. Without reducing the estimate of 3,000 Indians to take account of the probable impact of epidemics, it reveals the continued decline of the population to the end of the sixteenth century.[99] Employing a multiplication factor of 4, as for other highland regions for the same period, the total population may be estimated at about 12,000, to which a further 600 may be added to take account of the 200 vagamundo families. The resulting figure of 12,600 may be compared with an estimated contact population of 58,500, revealing a decline of 79 percent, or a depopulation ratio of 4.6:1. Although this level of decline is less than that experienced in some regions to the north, it occurred from a lower baseline. While the Cuenca region may have possessed few mines and no obrajes, the impact of mining in the early colonial period was greater than often supposed, and any moderating influences were more than made up for by the disastrous effects of wars, which depleted local populations before colonial rule took its toll.

CHAPTER 11

Loja

With the said diseases and ill-treatment most of these Indians have died, and because of the lack of tribute their *encomenderos* have remained poor and the mines are without investment.

No author, no date[1]

The Loja region was bypassed in the first decade of Spanish conquest as conquistadores sought greater prizes to the north and east. Later its strategic location in controlling access from Lima to Quito and to the region occupied by the Bracamoro and Jívaro, where gold had been discovered, stimulated the establishment of Loja, but only after the cessation of the Spanish civil wars. During these wars Gonzalo Pizarro ordered the town of La Zarza to be established in the Cangochamba (Upper Catamayo) Valley, probably in 1546. Despite being founded by rebel forces, its establishment was approved by President La Gasca, since it was well located for the pacification of the surrounding region and for the protection of travelers on the road from Quito to Lima from attacks by Indians from Garrochamba and Chaparra.[2] Two years later Alonso de Mercadillo moved the town to the more fertile and cooler valley of Cusibamba, renaming it after his home town, Loja.[3] Encomiendas were distributed when the town was first founded by Gonzalo Pizarro, but others were allocated as Mercadillo continued to pacify the surrounding region.[4] Some accounts suggest that originally twenty encomiendas were allocated,[5] but only thirteen encomenderos are included in the list of encomiendas drawn up in 1561.[6] During the second half of the sixteenth century the discovery of mines at Zaruma enabled Loja to emerge as the audiencia's premier mining region, with a subtreasury being established in the city. Some gold was exported via Paita, but most was transported north to Quito before being shipped to Europe via Guayaquil.[7] The wealth generated by the mining industry attracted traders who imported European cloth, luxury items, hardware, and black slaves, while the production process itself created a demand for salt that was imported from the coast.[8] Mining and trade stimulated the growth of haciendas producing provisions and livestock, especially cattle for hides and mules and horses for the transport industry.[9] More than any other highland residents, the life of Loja's inhabitants revolved around the production of minerals. (See Map 11.)

The date of the discovery of gold at Zaruma remains obscure. The most definitive contemporary statements claim that deposits were discovered there in 1560, though other evidence suggests they were being

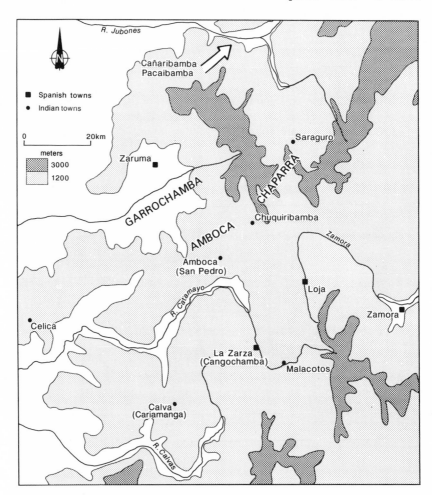

Map 11. The Loja region

exploited in the early 1550s,[10] and more recent writers have claimed they
were worked in pre-Inka or Inka times.[11] Even if mining took place prior to
1560, it clearly failed to take off before that date. The ores at Zaruma were
extensive with some veins estimated as being between four to six leagues
long.[12] However, they were of variable quality, but generally poor, yielding
gold of between fifteen and eighteen carats.[13] Also the veins ran through
parent rock that was hard to mine and difficult to grind into a fine powder
for amalgamation.[14] Hence although the mines yielded about 200,000
pesos a year, production costs were high, and only the *diezmo* was levied.[15]
    In the 1590s there were between fifteen and thirty water-powered ore

crushing plants at Zaruma,[16] each of which required forty Indians to keep it running.[17] At a minimum, therefore, 600 workers were needed. While this number may not appear excessive, in practice local supplies of labor were unable to meet this demand. According to Oidor Francisco de Auncibay, the area had always suffered from labor shortages because of the brutal conquest of the Palta by the Inka,[18] but they were undoubetdly exacerbated by Spanish conquest and epidemics. Indians were drafted from the Loja provinces of Garrochamba, Amboca, Malacatos, Saraguro, Chuquiribamba, Calvas, and Molleturo,[19] but from an early date labor shortages necessitated the recruitment of workers from the neighboring province of Cuenca, most notably from Cañaribamba and Pacaibamba.[20] Different commentators claimed that at its peak the mining mita involved between 300 and 700 Indians,[21] the difference possibly reflecting practice and theory.[22] By the 1590s, however, only 150 and 200 Indians were employed in mining there.[23]

The numbers involved in the mining mita fell, even though the deposits had not been exhausted. Apart from population decline, the poor administration of the mita and growing conflicts with other employers limited the numbers available for mining. Caciques often concealed those liable for the mita—so that, it was claimed, they could employ them themselves.[24] Others assigned to work in the mines never arrived. Some became ill on the journey, others lacking sufficient food to support themselves were forced to return home, and undoubtedly others absconded.[25] At the same time, growing shortages of labor led to increased conflicts between miners and other employers. The allocation of mitayos was undertaken by two officials—one responsible for Palta villages, and the other for Cañaribamba and Pacaibamba. Although miners were supposed to have priority over other employers, in practice they received less than half the mitayos they were allocated. This derived in part from the absolute shortage of workers but also from opposition from encomenderos who wanted to employ the Indians themselves and were reluctant to see them assigned to work in the mines, where high mortality rates posed a threat to their tribute income.[26] In order to gain access to mita labor, employers often petitioned for Indians to work in the mines but then employed them in other tasks, which, according to the cacique of Cañaribamba, were often harder and, in the case of sugar cultivation, prejudicial to their health.[27]

Work in the mines involved some mitayos in traveling up to twenty or twenty-five leagues across rugged terrain dissected by deep valleys.[28] In the absence of bridges, Indians sometimes drowned, particularly in the winter when the rivers were swollen with rain.[29] Particularly hazardous was the deep canyon of the Jubones River, which was known as Tamalaycha, meaning "the river that eats Indians,"[30] but the Girón and Los Naranjos rivers were also regarded as dangerous. A further hazard, particularly for those from Cañaribamba, Pacaibamba, and around Loja, and again in winter, was the journey across the páramo of Girón.[31]

From 1574 the allocation of workers for the mines and working conditions were governed by ordinances introduced by Viceroy Toledo.[32] Mitayos were required to serve on a rotational basis for periods of one month, with each Indian serving two months each year. In practice, however, the two months were served consecutively, and as the population declined and others through favor gained exemption, fewer Indians were involved, but with increasing frequency.[33] In 1580 Toledo's Ordinances were modified by Oidor Diego de Ortegón. Little is known of the changes introduced, but in the absence of evidence to the contrary, it is assumed they were minor, otherwise they would have attracted more contemporary comment, as did the new ordinances introduced in 1588 by Oidor Dr. Moreno de Mera. The latter ordered that no Indians should be sent to the mines for a period of four months during the winter from December to March. Mineowners protested, claiming that these were the months when maintenance work was carried out and that if this did not take place, the mines would flood and it would take 10,000 or 20,000 Indians to clear them before work could begin again. They also objected to Dr. Mera's ban on nightwork in the crushing mills, claiming that it affected only a few Indians who were essential to keep the mills running. Other orders for the construction of a hospital and bridges were regarded by miners in the first instance as unnecessary and in the second as too difficult.[34] The fierce opposition to the new ordinances effectively prevented their implementation. However, in 1593 the Ordinances of San Lorenzo attempted to improve conditions by restricting work to the hours of six to ten and from two to five, while raising the daily wage from one to one and a half tomines. They also banned the use of Indian laborers to carry ore to the crushing mills, a task that henceforth was to be performed by horses and mules.[35]

While the various ordinances tried to bring about improvements in working and living conditions in the mines, they failed to solve the basic problem of the shortage of labor. Several solutions were suggested, but most agreed that the introduction of the mita as it operated in Potosí was undesirable because of the time wasted moving Indians to and from the mines and because it would undermine the viability of Indian communities.[36] From the mid-1580s the best solution was envisaged to be the establishment of two villages near Zaruma each of 1,000 Indians. These were to be either tributary Indians or vagamundos drawn from all highland provinces from Pasto to Loja. It was not anticipated that encomenderos would oppose the proposal, since the wages they earned would improve prospects for maintaining or improving their tribute incomes. The new settlers, who were to be provided with houses and lands, were to work on a rotational basis, providing either one-fifth or one-seventh of their number at a time, for which they were to receive between one and one and a half tomines a day.[37] The general outline of the plan was approved by the Crown in 1590 and 1593,[38] and in anticipation of the growing importance of the mining district, in 1593 Zaruma received the title of *villa* and became the administrative center of a newly created *Alcaldía Mayor*.[39] The plan was imaginative, but it required the cooperation of too many officials and encomenderos, many of whom were opposed to the scheme.[40] By that time, and probably in recognition of the administrative difficulties of putting the scheme into operation, attention focused increasingly on the nearby Puruhá. It was argued that they could easily supply 2,000 Indians, since they were only occupied in textile production, from which the Crown received little profit.[41] This modification to the scheme met opposition from local encomenderos,[42] and by the 1620s it had still not been implemented. Meanwhile, Zaruma's mineowners and vecinos continued to petition in vain for the 2,000 Indians to which the Crown had agreed over thirty years before.[43]

Another solution to the shortage of labor was the introduction of black slaves. Small numbers were employed from the earliest years of mining, but since they cost between 200 and 350 pesos each, their employment on a large scale was not an economic proposition.[44] Black slaves represented considerable investment of capital, and as such they were better treated than Indians, who because "they are defenseless and do not cost them anything, are used like dumb animals."[45] Several petitions urged the importation of black slaves tax-free and on credit over five years,[46] but there is no evidence that large numbers ever arrived. In fact not all officials supported their introduction; some claimed they abused the Indians.[47]

Labor in the mines was harsh to the extent that observers considered it to be one of the two major causes of Indian depopulation, the other being epidemics.[48] Ill-treatment coupled with difficult and harsh working conditions contributed to high mortality rates. The high costs of mining encouraged mineowners to ignore safety precautions and to exact the maximum amount of labor from workers. Pit props that reinforced gallery ceilings were often dispensed with, so that workers were occasionally buried by collapsing tunnels,[49] while others died of exhaustion in carrying ores from the mines to the crushing mills, a task that was meant to be undertaken by mules or horses.[50] Oidores were supposed to inspect the mines regularly to ensure they were worked according to current mining ordinances. Some oidores, such as Dr. Moreno de Mera, tried to improve working conditions in the mines, but tours of inspection were infrequent and irregular, and miners complained, probably with justification, that the oidores knew little about mining.[51] In most cases the ordinances went unobserved.

Initially work in the mines was remunerated at the rate of one tomín a day, or twenty reals a month.[52] It was claimed that wages were low because of high operating costs, but in 1593 the daily wage was raised to one and half tomines.[53] This wage was still low, however, for in 1595 a resident from Chaparra claimed that as a carpenter he could earn as much in a day as a mitayo working in mining earned in a month.[54] A month was calculated on the basis of twenty-six working days, rather than twenty-eight, since Indians were free on Sunday afternoons, when they were permitted to work the mines themselves. Some observers claimed that this privilege attracted workers to the mines instead of serving on other mitas, since it enabled them to enrich themselves, or at least ensure they were well fed and clothed.[55] Other evidence suggests mining held few attractions. The wages paid, which amounted to about three pesos a month, were scarcely sufficient to live on, yet out of them they also had to pay two pesos a year as tribute.[56] The inadequacy of mine wages derived in part from shortages of provisions and hence the high cost of living in the mining areas, particularly in years of bad harvest.[57] Most workers took provisions with them, but to do so they sometimes had to sell their possessions.[58] Oidor Auncibay noted with irony that one fanega of maize, judged necessary to support a miner for a month, was worth three pesos in the mining area, so that it would be better for an Indian to take a fanega of maize and sell it in Zaruma than to consume it and spend twenty-six days working to earn three pesos.[59] In 1619 witnesses in Cuenca testified that Indians who went to work in the mines of Zaruma "fled back to their lands, ill, hungry, badly treated, having lost their homes, and without being paid."[60] The mining mita was sufficiently repellent to encourage fugitivism. By 1581 several hundred Indians had fled from Cañaribamba and Garrochamba,[61] with many from the Palta region seeking refuge in the Lower Calvas River between Loja and Piura.[62]

Mining was not the only economic activity that directly affected Indian lives. The provisioning of the mines, including the supply of mercury and salt for the refining process, and the final export of gold stimulated the development of trade. Furthermore, Loja was on the main route south to the port of Paita and subsequently to Lima. It was also the supply point for Zamora and for Spanish towns in the corregimiento of Yaguarzongo and Pacamoros to the east and south.[63] The high demand for porters was regarded as a significant factor in generating labor shortages in Zaruma.[64] The rugged territory that had to be traversed, the differences in climate Indians experienced, and the heavy loads they were required to carry raised mortality levels. Particularly hazardous was the route across the páramo from Paita to Zamora and Yaguarzongo.[65] Indians not only formed the basis of the transport system, but they were also required to guard, clean, and provision tambos along the major highways.[66]

Like all Indians in highland regions, those of Loja were liable to pay tribute, a proportion of which was payable in gold and the rest as cotton cloth.[67] Remote from the seat of the Audiencia in Quito, the Loja region was rarely inspected, so that tasaciones were often ten to twenty years out of date.[68] Payments for those who were absent or dead sometimes forced Indians to sell their lands.[69] The alienation of Indian lands and demands for agricultural labor were driven by the expansion of haciendas to supply the mining areas of Zaruma and Zamora, particularly with cereals and cattle.[70] Meanwhile, sugar estates developed in the region's warmer valleys.[71]

DEMOGRAPHIC TRENDS IN THE LOJA REGION

The province of Loja was regarded as healthful, with Indians having a relatively long life expectancy.[72] Nevertheless, the early demographic history of the region followed the same downward trend experienced in other highland areas, with the decline being attributed to epidemics and ill-treatment in mining. Indians in the Loja region suffered on a regular basis from dysentery, fevers, and respiratory infections,[73] but it was the major epidemics, in which it was said "always the greater part dies," that decimated the population.[74] Although the first epidemic to be recorded in the Loja region occurred in 1558, when it was hit by smallpox and measles,[75] as a region of transit between Lima and Quito, it is unlikely to have escaped the three pandemics that ravaged the Andean area before 1550. The province also suffered badly during the epidemics of the late 1580s. In 1590 work in the mines had ceased because the Indian population had been "finished off" as a result of the general epidemic of smallpox, measles, and dysentery.[76] Subsequently, in 1606 Loja suffered from an outbreak of garrotillo, but Zaruma does not appear to have been so badly affected.[77] These major epidemics (and there may have been more) undoubtedly reduced the population to a fraction of its former size, but to these should be added the more common illnesses and diseases that Indians contracted under poor working and living conditions. The fact that different schemes for the establishment of two villages in Zaruma stipulated that hospitals should be founded indicates official recognition of the health problems associated with mining and the need to maintain the labor force.

Another factor contributing to Indian population loss was miscegenation. Like most mining areas in the New World, Zaruma developed as a racial melting pot. Loja with 150 Spaniards was the third largest town in the audiencia in the 1580s.[78] Zaruma possessed about 60 Spanish and mestizo men, but they were greatly outnumbered by 300 yanaconas and blacks who were employed in the mining industry and domestic service.[79] The free sexual relationships between the races appalled the bishop of

Quito, who conducted a visita of the region in 1581 and found that only 10 percent of the town's Spanish and mestizo male residents were married.[80]

Although it is clear that Loja's Indian population declined, less information exists to document its decrease in detail. It has been suggested there were about 45,000 Indians in the region prior to the smallpox and measles epidemic of 1558.[81] By the early 1570s the total population of the region was estimated at between 15,000 to 16,000.[82] According to Canelas Albarrán, the latter figure was based on the visita general ordered by Viceroy Toledo. By that time mining was beginning to take its toll, with observers suggesting that previously the population had been increasing.[83] By the 1590s the scale of depopulation caused by hard labor in the mines and epidemics was sufficient to provoke the introduction of new mining ordinances and stimulate attempts to recruit labor from outside the province. The list of tributary Indians compiled by Morales Figueroa in 1591 indicates that the jurisdiction of Loja contained only 2,849 tributary Indians.[84] This figure represents a significant reduction from previous decades, in line with qualitative accounts. Yet the decline is likely to have been even greater than the figure suggests, since it probably predates the epidemics of the late 1580s. In 1616 it was claimed that in the previous fifty years the populations of Cañaribamba and Pacaibamba had fallen by three-quarters as a result of their involvement in the mining mita.[85] While some died, many fled to other provinces. In the absence of more precise information, the total population of the region in the 1590s may be calculated at 11,696. This is achieved by multiplying the tributary population of 2,849 by 4 and adding a further 300 to take account of the 100 vagamundo families who resided there.[86] Since it is assumed that the figure for 1591 overestimated the numbers actually present, no additional numbers will be added to take account of fugitive Indians. The figure of 11,696 represents a decline of 89.6 percent since the time of Spanish conquest and produces the highest depopulation ratio for the sierra of 9.6:1. An interesting feature of the decline is that the trend during the century differed to some extent from other regions. Whereas most highland populations suffered their heaviest losses during the early conquest period, possibly recovering to a degree in the late sixteenth century, in the Loja region the decline, although equally marked in the first half of the century, was more protracted, with mining taking an unusually high toll between 1560 and 1590. Any recovery experienced elsewhere in the sierra was not repeated in the south.

Part Five

SPANISH RULE: THE COAST

CHAPTER 12

Guayaquil and Puerto Viejo

The Indians of the tierra fría and tierra templada are increasing greatly, while those of the tierra caliente are declining, especially those of Guayaquil and Puerto Viejo and the gobernación of Popayán, where it is necessary to relieve them from hard labor for their preservation.

Anonymous, after 1582[1]

Under colonial rule the areas inhabited by the Manta, Huancavilca, Puná, and Chono formed the jurisdictions of Guayaquil and Puerto Viejo. Even though these groups inhabited distinct ecological environments, and their colonial experiences differed to a degree, the two jurisdictions were often considered together by the colonial officials, and their demographic histories were broadly similar. The initial impact of Spanish conquest was most devastating around Puerto Viejo and Manta, but then as permanent settlements were founded and trade developed, demands on those in the vicinity of Guayaquil increased. Even though the lower reaches of the Babahoyo and Daule rivers were explored and the former used as the main artery for commerce between Quito and the coast, the northern part of the region remained largely unknown. This was despite notable expeditions, such as that led by the corregidor of Guayaquil, Andrés Contero, which ascended the Babahoyo and established the short-lived town of Castro.[2]

The coastal area around and to the south of Puerto Viejo was the main entry point for expeditions to the sierra and a supply point for those continuing south to Peru. Even before permanent Spanish settlements had been established, coastal communities had been devastated by the brutal conquest of the region and heavy demands for supplies and for labor to transport goods to and from the highlands. (See Map 12.)

The region was first explored and pacified by Francisco Pizarro and Diego de Almagro in 1531, but no town was founded, since their interests focused further south in Peru.[3] In 1534 Pedro de Alvarado arrived from Nicaragua with an expedition of twelve ships and with the aim of conquering the Quito region. Alvarado's expedition is worthy of extended comment because of the havoc it wreaked on the coast south of the Bahía de Caráquez where he landed. He claimed that at Caráquez the Indians were in rebellion because twenty days before, Hernán Ponce had passed through the area burning and depopulating five villages.[4] This proved to be a foretaste of what Indian villages were to suffer at his hands. Alvarado's expedition comprised 500 soldiers, 2,500 Indians, and 200 black slaves.[5] It

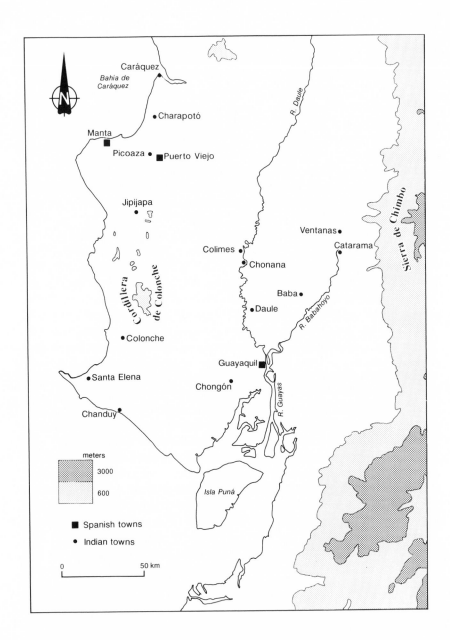

Map 12. The southern Coastal region

was large by any standards and, more significantly, appears unrivaled in the violence it inflicted on local populations. Indians were slaughtered, often in a particularly horrific ways, for failing to cooperate or provide gold, emeralds, or provisions. The cacique of Chonana was torn to pieces by dogs and another member of the same community burned to death. Children were left orphaned as their parents were drafted to carry supplies. Many of those placed in chains died of exhaustion, and others were decapitated when they flagged. Further losses stemmed from the cannibalistic practices of the Guatemalan Indians who accompanied Alvarado. Alvarado's expedition primarily affected the area around Puerto Viejo and Manta, although some of its members explored the coast as far as Santa Elena, where they carried out similar depredations.[6] Following Alvarado's expedition it was said that scarcely an Indian house remained inhabited,[7] and that of 20,000 Indians only a handful were left.[8] The expedition not only devastated the coast, but the route to Quito chosen by Alvarado was appallingly difficult. The expedition passed through the rugged terrain of the Sierra Nevada de Chimbo, where it was lost for six months and many died of cold, hunger, and disease. Loor claims that this disastrous campaign cost the lives of twenty-one Spaniards and 2,000 Indians and blacks.[9] It left the coast severely depopulated and in open rebellion, so that Spaniards on the way to Peru were unable to stop there for provisions.[10]

In order to bring some order to the coast and forestall the political aspirations of others conquistadores, Diego de Almagro commissioned Francisco Pacheco to establish a town in the center of the coastal region. This he accomplished on 12 March 1535, when he founded the town of San Gregorio de Puerto Viejo. Its foundation occurred just prior to the arrival of Pedro de Puelles, who had been sent by Sebastián de Benalcázar with the same objective. Originally founded close to the sea, in the same year its site was moved seven leagues inland.[11] Meanwhile Sebastián de Benalcázar, having pacified the inhabitants of the island of Puná, established the town of Santiago de Guayaquil. However, this settlement was soon destroyed by the Chono, and attempts to reestablish it were thwarted by continued Indian hostility and by the involvement of conquistadores in campaigns elsewhere.[12] It was not until 1547 that the town was established on its present-day site.[13] The constant state of conflict on the southern coast cost many lives and was given by Cieza de León as the reason for the small number of old men around Puerto Viejo.[14]

Since a large proportion of the coastal region remained unexplored, demands for auxiliaries to participate in expeditions did not cease with the establishment of permanent Spanish settlements. Most noteworthy were the expeditions mounted by Andrés Contero and Martín de Carranza, which between 1568 and 1569 explored the Daule and Babahoyo rivers and penetrated Esmeraldas.[15] However, Alcina Franch, Moreno, and Peña list a further six expeditions that were similarly mounted from Guayaquil during the sixteenth century and several others that originated in Manabí.[16] Indians from the southern coast were employed in expeditions not only into the interior, especially north toward Esmeraldas, but also to other regions. There is evidence that Indians from Guayaquil were involved in Andrés Contero's pacification of the Quijos rebellion in 1560 and that many were retained there in the service of local vecinos.[17] Other Indians were required to help defend the coast first from the English and later, in the seventeenth century, from the Dutch.[18] In 1579 Francis Drake appeared in Ecuadorian waters, and in 1587 Thomas Cavendish sacked the island of Puná.[19] Apart from losses sustained on expeditions or in conflict, these activities must have severely disrupted family life and undermined the ability of coastal populations to recover from their brutal conquest and epidemic disease.

The original numbers of Spanish settlers in Guayaquil and Puerto Viejo are not known, though when Guayaquil was destroyed by the Chono in 1536, it contained seventy vecinos, of whom only a few escaped,[20] and later in the century Puerto Viejo was said to have possessed forty encomenderos when it was founded.[21] The number of encomenderos in both towns declined steadily through the middle of the century.[22] In the 1570s Puerto Viejo and Guayaquil purportedly had fourteen and thirteen encomenderos respectively,[23] or ten and fifteen according to officials of the royal exchequer (Table 31).[24] However, the towns were not comparable in size. Puerto Viejo possessed only 17 vecinos, whereas Guayaquil had about 100, who were mostly traders and merchants.[25] This was clear testimony to the latter's growing commercial importance; Puerto Viejo, it was said, never recovered after a fire there in 1541.[26] Indeed in the early 1560s its inconvenient inland location prompted President Hernando de Santillán to order its vecinos to move to the newly established town of Manta. In the event, only 3 of Puerto Viejo's vecinos were persuaded to settle there, because it suffered from shortages of labor and had the reputation of being a "den of thieves."[27]

By the third quarter of the sixteenth century the number and size of encomiendas in both jurisdictions had declined. In 1576 royal officials claimed that the encomiendas around Puerto Viejo had once yielded substantial incomes.[28] The same was probably true of those in the jurisdiction of Guayaquil. There the original encomienda of Yagual comprised 1,000 tributary Indians,[29] and the existence of such large encomiendas is credible, given that Francisco Pizarro pacified thirty caciques and their communities in the valley of Charapotó alone.[30] As early as 1556, however, the governor of Quito, Gil Ramírez Dávalos, was ordered to reform the encomiendas of Guayaquil and Puerto Viejo on account of their small size and the fact that they included unpacified Indians.[31] There is no evidence that a major reform of encomiendas took place, and they continued to decline in size. By 1574 the encomienda of Yagual contained only 110 tributary Indians, and by 1581 only 94.[32] At that time encomiendas in the jurisdiction of Guayaquil averaged just under 100 tributary Indians;[33] by the early seventeenth century they were under half that size.[34]

Indians in both jurisdictions paid tribute in cash and kind, though of greater value to encomenderos was the service they rendered. Prior to the introduction of official assessments encomenderos exacted goods at will and were particularly interested in acquiring gold and emerald jewelery, for which the local inhabitants were famed.[35] Once official tasaciones had been introduced, the items demanded as tribute remained constant throughout the century and included silver pesos, cotton cloth, maize, beans, and chickens; sometimes salted fish was also levied.[36] Despite the existence of official assessments, tribute levies in the jurisdiction of Guayaquil and Puerto Viejo were regarded as excessive. Hence, as part of a proposed reform of encomiendas, in 1557 the governor, Gil Ramírez Dávalos, was commissioned to revise the tasaciones.[37] As indicated, it is not known whether the reform or a visita took place, but in 1572 the region was inspected by Bernardo de Loaysa as part of the visita general ordered by Viceroy Toledo. However, the revised tasaciones based on these enumerations were not drawn up until 1580, by which time many Indians who had been been included in the enumerations were absent or dead. As a consequence it was estimated that the burden of tribute payment amounted to the equivalent of thirteen pesos. This was considered excessive by any standards, but especially for Indians who lived in hot coastal lowlands that were either arid or seasonally flooded.[38] In 1581 the value of tribute paid by each Indian in the jurisdiction of Guayaquil varied between 42 and 60 reals at local market prices.[39] In addition, despite major cultural and demographic changes in the early conquest period, some Indians were still paying tribute to their local leaders as they had done in pre-Columbian times.[40] In 1605 those at Colonchillo paid 60 reals, and those in Chanduy 18 reals.[41] At the same time, the total tribute paid by Indians in the jurisdiction of Puerto Viejo averaged 74 reals. Compared with average wages at the time, these taxes were high. Mitayos employed in agricultural tasks were paid 9.5 reals every fortnight plus food, while yanaconas, who purportedly worked on a voluntary basis, earned 12 pesos a year.[42] The latter appears to have been the minimum wage for agricultural laborers in the jurisdiction of Guayaquil, and more-skilled workers could earn over double that amount. It is clear that mitayos paying 74 reals in tribute would have been contributing the equivalent of nearly four months' wages, although clearly many items they paid as tribute would not have been purchased in the marketplace but produced on their own lands or in their own households.

Tribute constituted a vital source of income for encomenderos, but they probably derived greater benefit from the exploitation of Indian labor. Although a variety of labor systems operated in the jurisdictions of Guayaquil and Puerto Viejo, their encomenderos were notorious for the illegal employment of Indians in their personal service. At the end of the sixteenth century the province of Guayaquil was one of three areas in the audiencia where personal service was still tolerated.[43] The majority of those who worked in personal service worked as household servants or agricultural laborers, but others around Guayaquil were employed in cutting wood and transporting goods on balsas. The employment of Indians in personal service made it impossible for Indian communities to meet their required mita quotas. For this reason, in 1591 the cacique of Charapotó was granted a provision to round up thirty tributary Indians and some youths who were working in the personal service of Spaniards in Puerto Viejo.[44] Like other regions in the audiencia, the mita levy was set at one-fifth, but it is not clear for how long mitayos worked. Most were employed in agricultural tasks and others as messengers, notably between Santa Elena, Chongón, and Guayaquil.[45] Other workers who resided permanently on haciendas or in Spanish households were referred to as yanaconas. Despite their name, their status is unlikely to have originated in pre-Columbian times, since the Inka never effectively controlled the coast. Most likely they were Indians who had been coerced into private employment by encomenderos and others, or by the need to earn cash to meet tribute payments. It is unlikely they worked voluntarily, for the wages they were paid were not significantly greater than those earned by forced laborers. Indeed in the early seventeenth century most of the twenty-eight yanaconas registered as tribute payers in the jurisdiction of Guayaquil did not come from the local area, but from other parts of the audiencia, and even Peru and Colombia.[46]

Indians were employed in a wide range of activities that exploited the region's natural resources and took advantage of its strategic location. Impressed by the ornaments of gold and emeralds possessed by coastal groups, the Spanish embarked on a frenetic search for mineral deposits that proved fruitless but cost many Indian lives.[47] The only precious stones exploited during the sixteenth century were pearls found on the coast from Manta to Santa Elena.[48] Both Indians and blacks were employed in their collection, but on what basis it is not clear. It was a hazardous activity in which divers were exposed to dangerous currents and sharks. In fact it was so hazardous that Indian employment in pearl fishing, whether as forced laborers or on a voluntary basis, was banned.[49] Another activity that exploited the coastal environment around Guayaquil and Puná was the extraction of sarsaparilla. It was used to cure syphilis and exported to Peru. Its reputation drew people from as far afield as Charcas, and it stimulated the early foundation of a hospital in Guayaquil in 1564.[50]

More important in terms of the numbers employed was the extraction of timber. Some Indians were also involved in shipbuilding, but this soon became an industry dominated by blacks and mulattoes.[51] Local demands for timber for the construction of houses were augmented by the needs of residents in Trujillo and Lima on the treeless, arid coast of Peru.[52] Timber was also required for the shipbuilding industry, which began in 1557 when a galley was constructed on the island of Puná.[53] Much of the tackle for vessels was also made there, though some was imported from the highlands.[54] Yaguache was a major source of oak and the highly prized wood of the *guachapelí* (*Lysiloma guachapele* Benth.).[55] Some timber came from the mangrove swamps near Guayaquil, where Indians worked up to their waists in water containing snakes and other poisonous animals.[56] As if this were not enough, the heavy wood then had to be transported several leagues to the coast.[57] These tasks were associated with such high levels of mortality that as early as the 1550s it was anticipated the Indians around Guayaquil would not last long.[58] Meanwhile the "blood and sweat" of the Indians had made many of Guayaquil's citizens wealthy.[59] By the end of the century the audiencia had introduced a number of provisions governing the employment of Indians in this task. They were overruled by the viceroy in Lima, however, who was anxious to protect Peru's supply of timber.[60] By the early seventeenth century, sources of woodlands in vicinity of Guayaquil had been exhausted, and the remaining Indians were involved in yet more arduous labor as they were forced to exploit woodlands further inland.[61]

From the earliest years of conquest the maintenance of Spaniards in the highlands and the export of minerals from the region depended upon good communications with Guayaquil. The first stretch of the journey from Guayaquil to the Desembarcadero, about twenty leagues upriver, involved the use of balsas that were constructed and manned by local populations. Among the villages providing *balseros* were Baba and Daule.[62] Navigation upriver against the current was exhausting work, and operators allowed the rowers little rest, with the result that many died.[63]

The growth of Guayaquil, and to a lesser extent the continuation of Puerto Viejo as a stopping point on the way to Peru, stimulated demands for agricultural products. These demands were met by both Indian and Spanish producers. Since the region was unsuitable for the cultivation of wheat, the main staples raised were maize and beans. Yields were generally high, though harvest failure sometimes occurred around Jipijapa and Picoaza.[64] The needs of the transport industry encouraged the raising of horses and mules, but other livestock were also raised. In the early seventeenth century it was claimed that there was no shortage of land—indeed, it was estimated the region could support 100,000 additional Indians. The availability of land no doubt reflected the decline in the Indian population and the extensive reducciones undertaken in 1572 by the visitador general, Bernardo de Loaysa, which were particularly effective around Manta and Puerto Viejo.[65] Many Indians, especially caciques, owned chacras and estancias to which they had formal title, and many Indians became actively involved in commercial agriculture. Around Guayaquil many opted for livestock raising, with the communities of Chongón and Colonche specializing in the raising of horses and mares, which they hired out to transport goods from Santa Elena to Guayaquil.[66] Indian communities around Puerto Viejo were less involved in raising livestock, but even there each Indian was said to possess at least two horses, and some as many as ten. These were also employed to transport goods to and from the coast or hired out for the same purpose. While these activities may have flourished, considerable strains were placed on community production by excessive tribute demands, and coastal settlements in particular faced continual pressures to supply provisions to passing vessels and their crews, while fishing villages were also required to provide fish for urban markets in the highlands.[67]

DEMOGRAPHIC TRENDS IN THE
SOUTHERN COASTAL REGION

Contemporary observers most commonly attributed the decline in coastal populations to wars, ill-treatment, and disease, though their emphasis on different factors varied. Prior to the mid–sixteenth century the slaughter and ill-treatment of Indians during the pacification of the region was a major factor in its population. Indeed, Cieza de León regarded their impact as more significant than epidemics.[68] The region around Manta that suffered at the hands of Pedro de Alvarado was particularly badly affected. Various commentators noted that "all the coast had been depopulated" and that around Puerto Viejo the number of Indians "could be counted on the fingers."[69] While these observations were clearly exaggerated, the scale of the devastation caused by his expedition seems incontrovertible. More credible is Benzoni's claim that when the Spanish arrived, Manta had possessed 2,000 inhabitants, but in 1546 contained only 50. He further claimed that this level of destruction was characteristic of all villages in the province.[70] Yet it was not confined to Alvarado's expedition or to the Puerto Viejo region. The ill-treatment of Indians around Guayaquil was partially stimulated by the presence of fine jewelery, which erroneously suggested that they possessed mines producing precious metals and stones. The feverish search for these minerals and persistent demands for auxiliaries for expeditions fomented discontent, which served to keep much of the region in a state of rebellion. Cieza de León asserted that by the mid–sixteenth century the greater part of the populations of Guayaquil and Puerto Viejo had died, and undoubtedly a major contributory factor was the constant state of conflict that existed on the coast.[71] Subsequently, the most frequently mentioned cause of the continued depopulation was the employment of Indians in a number of arduous tasks, notably the extraction of timber and the navigation of balsas.[72] These activities primarily affected the jurisdiction of Guayaquil, and it was this region that suffered the greater decline.

Declining sources of Indian labor were compensated for in part by the early importation of black slaves. Many were engaged in arduous activities, such as pearl fishing, in which Indian labor had been banned, and in skilled tasks in shipbuilding, while others were probably employed as overseers of estates and in wealthy merchant households in Guayaquil. The influx of Spanish settlers and black slaves meant that in 1586 over 13 percent of the population of the jurisdiction of Guayaquil was non-Indian, which was the highest proportion anywhere in the audiencia.[73] In 1605 the jurisdiction contained over 350 blacks and mulattoes, who slightly outnumbered whites.[74] Even though blacks and mulattoes were fewer in Puerto Viejo, they still composed about one-third of the non-Indian population.

The introduction of black slaves had several implications for Indian survival on the southern coast. The employment of blacks in arduous tasks relieved the burden of heavy labor falling on Indians, but their presence on the coast threatened their survival in other ways. Although racial mixing was not identified by contemporary observers as a factor contributing to Indian population decline, the presence of relatively large numbers of non-Indians suggest that it must have played a contributory role, albeit a minor one. Second, it seems likely that malaria was introduced to the Ecuadorian coast during the sixteenth century. Anopheline mosquitoes suitable for the propagation of malaria were present on the coast, and theoretically all that was required to begin cycles of infection was a source of infected blood. Since the malaria parasite remains in the blood once it has infected and conferred immunity on a individual, it was probably carried to the New World by apparently healthy individuals.[75] As previously noted, Spaniards may have introduced the benign form of malaria, *Plasmodium vivax,* direct from Europe, but the more acute form *P. falciparum* probably entered with black slaves from Africa, though both parasites might have been carried to the region from other parts of the New World where they had already become established. How quickly malaria may have spread is not clear, particularly given the decline in the Indian population and the growth of the relatively immune black population. While black slaves may have been the original source of malarial

infection, through racial mixing they would have provided local populations with a degree of hereditary immunity.

It is doubtful that malaria had a significant impact on demographic
trends in coastal Ecuador in the sixteenth century, yet most commentators
identified disease as a major cause of the decline in the Indian population.
Many considered that since the coast was hot, it was unhealthy, and that
this was the reason why its population was declining.[76] Diseases common
on the coast were dysentery, *bubas,* and fevers, though the first was said
to result in few deaths.[77] The bubas were treated with sarsaparilla and
were probably associated with syphilis. Fevers, in contrast, were cured by
bleeding or by the use of purgatives made from *michoacán* or canafistula,
though in many cases recovery seems to have followed dietary improvement. Some fevers, such as those suffered by Alvarado's expedition, are
likely to have been induced by malnutrition caused by shortages of supplies and the need to live off the land. Others derived from the bites of
insects, but they were probably not associated with malaria. Elsewhere I
have argued that some of the fevers experienced on the coast were due to
the activities of sandflies (*Phlebotomus* sp.).[78] The bites of these insects
may induce headaches and fevers. They may also be responsible for the
transmission of the leishmaniasis parasite, and possibly the virus associated with Oroya fever and verruga peruana, which are known to have been
present on the coast in pre-Columbian times. A number of observers
reported the existence of a diversity of insects that through their bites
caused infected sores that killed many people.[79] This was almost certainly
verruga peruana, which probably afflicted members of Francisco Pizarro's
third expedition in 1531 and which was contracted by Girolamo Benzoni on
his visit to the coast in 1546.[80] Although these endemic diseases probably
contributed to the unhealthy reputation of the coast, it was the epidemic
diseases introduced from the Old World that were associated with high
levels of mortality that were partially blamed for the depopulation of the
coast.

The heightened impact of Old World diseases on the coast derived
from the constant introduction of new infections by ships that stopped for
provisions or to trade en route to Panama or Peru. Pimental estimates that
twenty-four to thirty ships traded at Guayaquil annually.[81] Even though
levels of disease mortality are likely to have been higher on the coast,
there are few precise references to epidemics there during the sixteenth
century. It has already been shown that the coast was afflicted by diseases
introduced by exploratory expeditions prior to the arrival of large numbers of Spanish settlers. Subsequently the 1558 epidemic of smallpox and
measles, which may have been accompanied by influenza, was probably
partially responsible for the dramatic decline of the encomienda of Yagual
from over 1,000 Indians when it was first allocated to 110 *casados* and

solteros in 1574.[82] At that date other observers testified that, as a consequence of disease, encomiendas in the jurisdictions of Guayaquil and Puerto Viejo comprised less than one-quarter of the Indians they had possessed when originally assigned. According to Campos the next epidemic, which decimated the city of Guayaquil and surrounding villages, occurred in 1589. He suggests the epidemic was smallpox but provides no further details or the source of his information.[83] In fact it could have been any one of a number of epidemics, including smallpox, measles, and typhus, which afflicted the Andean region between 1586 and 1591.[84] It was probably the same epidemic period that was being referred to when in 1605 it was reported that villages around Puerto Viejo had been devastated by measles and typhus.[85] Another unspecified epidemic hit the region in 1609.[86]

High levels of mortality associated with ill-treatment, overwork, and epidemic disease were not compensated for by raised fertility rates. Indeed Benzoni claimed that in some villages around Puerto Viejo Indians were practicing infanticide so that their children would not become Spanish slaves.[87] The psychological impact of conquest and the disruptive effects of expeditions and forced labor on family life and fertility levels would have been particularly acute in this region. This is supported by the low ratio of tributary to nontributary Indians, though there appears to have been a slight upward trend toward the end of the century.[88] Even so, in 1605 ratios of adults to children (under 18) of 1:0.64 and 1:0.50 for Guayaquil and Puerto Viejo respectively suggest alarmingly low levels of natural increase.[89] They indicate clearly that fertility levels were far from compensating for high levels of mortality and that Indian populations were failing to reproduce themselves. (See Table 17.)

Whatever the relative importance of different factors involved in the depopulation of the coast, it is clear that the decline was precipitous. Since the greater part of the decline occurred before official records were kept, the enormity of the decrease is not immediately apparent from the demographic statistics contained in the accompanying table. Nevertheless they do indicate the continued downward trend in the population throughout the century. The pattern appears confused because the figures often refer to dates different from those when they were reported. The figures shown for 1583, 1586, and 1591 were all based on the enumerations conducted as part of Viceroy Toledo's visita general, which was conducted in the early 1570s. Since they are higher than those recorded in the treasury accounts for 1581, they confirm the unrelenting downward trend during the century. It also means the figures for 1605, rather than 1591, reflect the dramatic reduction in the Indian population caused by the epidemics of the late 1580s. The downward trend throughout the sixteenth century is strongly attested by qualitative evidence, and it supports the general observation that these jurisdictions were among the worst affected in the audiencia.[90]

Table 17. Indian Population Estimates for the Jurisdictions of Guayaquil
and Puerto Viejo during the Sixteenth Century

	Guayaquil		Puerto Viejo	
Year	Tributary Indians	Total population	Tributary Indians	Total population
1561(?)[a]	5,000	25,000	5,000	25,000
1561(?)[b]	2,280	4,742	1,377	2,297
Late 1560s[c]	7,000	—	5,000	—
1570s[d]	3,000	—	1,500	—
1576[e]	—	—	1,500	—
1581[f]	1,459	—	—	—
1583[g]	2,192	7,358	1,254	4,159
1586[h]	—	7,355	—	4,102
1591[i]	2,198	—	1,253	—
1605[j]	657	2,576	358	1,461

a RAHM CM 42 fol. 248 and AGI AL 120 Relación de los naturales 1561. Total is "personas de todas edades" and tributary Indians between sixteen and fifty.
b RAHM A/92 fols. 55–77 Relación de los naturales 1561. Total is "personas de todas edades" and tributary Indians between sixteen and fifty.
c RAHM 9/4664 no. 21 Los pueblos despañoles, no date [late 1560s]. Numbers refer to "indios" and, by comparison with other figures for other areas, probably refer to tributary Indians.
d CDI 15:409–572 Demarcación y división, no date; López de Velasco, *Geografía,* 224–25.
e RGI 2:173 Oficiales reales 30.12.1576. Numbers are given in terms of "indios" but, by comparison with other figures for other areas, probably refer to tributary Indians.
f RGI 2:337–40 Razón de los indios tributarios 1581.
g Levillier, *Gobernantes del Perú,* 9:114–230, Relación de los oficios 1583. Numbers refer to "personas."
h BNM 3178 fols. 1–15 Canelas Albarrán 1586.
i CDI 6:41–63 Relación de los indios tributarios 1.11.1591.
j CDI 9:247–309 Descripción de la gobernación 1605.

By the beginning of the seventeenth century the total Indian population for the jurisdictions of Guayaquil and Puerto Viejo had fallen to just over 4,000.[91] This figure is considerably lower than the total of 30,000, including people of all races and ages, that Campos has suggested for the corregimiento of Guayaquil.[92] Of this number he claimed one-third were living in the city of Guayaquil. Unfortunately Campos does not indicate his source. While it is clear that the 4,000 Indians recorded in 1605 underestimated the numbers present, there is no evidence to indicate that they reached the magnitude he suggests.

Official figures fail to take account of those Indians who remained outside Spanish administration, either because they had fled or because they had not been pacified. At the end of the sixteenth century the main area that remained unexplored was the northeast of the jurisdiction around Ventanas and Puebloviejo, just to the west of Chimbo. In the 1560s Oidor Salazar de Villasante maintained that in order to construct a road to Puerto Viejo through this area, which was referred to as the Yumbos, it would be necessary to pacify 12,000 Indians.[93] Whether these Indians were Chono or true Yumbos groups is not clear. Although they had not been pacified, some "indios de guerra" in the eastern foothills had been granted in encomienda although no tribute was collected from them.[94] Some of these Indians, who were also referred to as "jívaros montañeses," voluntarily sought Spanish protection as mulattoes from Esmeraldas began settling at Catarama.[95] How many remained at the end of the century is unknown, but probably at least 1,000. Other "indios de guerra" were to be found to the west of the Daule River on the *lomas* of Chonanas and Colimes and on the slopes of the Cordillera de Colonche,[96] where they were accompanied by Indians who had fled from Spanish control. Their number must have been considerable, for in 1603 Alonso Holguín, an encomendero of Puerto Viejo, claimed that he had captured as many as 400 souls and settled them among converted Tacamaches and Colimes.[97] An estimate of 1,500 Indians outside Spanish administration is proposed for the jurisdiction of Puerto Viejo.

Including the numbers of Indians outside Spanish administration in estimates for the beginning of the seventeenth century raises the population of the southern coast substantially but does not alter the scale of depopulation suffered in both regions. The population of the jurisdiction of Guayaquil had fallen from an estimated 370,230 to a mere 3,530,[98] a decline of 99.0 percent. This converts to a depopulation ratio of about 1:105, which, with exception of the Caribbean, is one of the highest calculated for any region in the New World. The trend in the jurisdiction of Puerto Viejo was similar, though less marked. There the Indian population declined from 120,000 to 2,961,[99] which represents a decline of 97.5 percent and a level of depopulation in the order of 1:41. These exceptionally high levels of decline are dependent on the high estimates for the aboriginal population of the southern coast, which still need to be substantiated. Nevertheless, they suggest that around Guayaquil the level of decline was higher and more sustained, and that most likely this derived from the greater demands placed on Indian communities in this region. The significance of the intensity of Spanish settlement and the development of commercial enterprises on demographic trends may be demonstrated by comparing the experiences of the three ethnic groups that composed the corregimiento of Guayaquil. Table 18 shows that during the sixteenth century the Chono, once the most populous group, declined to a greater degree than their neighbors. Whereas at the time of Spanish conquest they composed over 80 percent of the region's population, by the turn of the century they accounted for under 60 percent. These figures would be modified if the number of Indians outside Spanish control were included, but they would not alter the overall pattern.[100] Such a difference is explicable in terms of the constant introduction of

Table 18. Population Decline among Different Ethnic Groups on the Southern Coast of Ecuador

Ethnic group	Aboriginal population	Percent of total	Population 1581	Percent of total 1581	Population 1605	Percent of total 1605	Percent decline	Depopulation ratio
Chono	302,260	81.6	3,652	62.5	1,462	57.8	99.5	206.7:1
Huancavilca	47,970	13.0	1,480	25.4	880	34.8	98.2	54.5:1
Puná	20,000	5.4	704	12.1	188	7.4	99.1	106.4:1
Total	370,230	100.0	5,836[a]	100.0	2,530[a]	100.0	99.3	146.3:1

Note: Figures for 1581 are taken from RGI 2:339 Razón de los indios tributarios 1581. A multiplication factor of 4 is used to convert tributary populations to total populations. This is based on the ratio obtained from Levillier, *Gobernantes del Perú,* 9:114–230, Relación de los oficios 1583.
[a] Figures do not include Indians outside Spanish administration.

new infections and the greater demands placed on Indian communities around Guayaquil in sustaining the port, in providing workers for the extraction of timber and shipbuilding, and in maintaining an efficient transport system with the highlands. It was here that Spanish conquest took its heaviest toll.

CHAPTER 13

Esmeraldas

> Your majesty has been given an account and long report of the
> expedition to Esmeraldas and Bahía de San Mateo, where more
> than twenty captains have entered on different occasions, and they
> have all been thwarted because they have not found suitable land to
> settle, for it is unhealthy and there are few Indians.
>
> Oidores of the audiencia, 6 April 1588[1]

Apart from the Oriente, Esmeraldas is probably the most difficult region in
the audiencia for which to trace demographic trends during the sixteenth
century. Although Esmeraldas was the focus of a large number of expeditions, many only skirted the region or explored only a limited part of the
interior, so that accounts of their endeavors provide little evidence for the
character and size of Indian populations.

The first expeditions were military in character and were motivated by
the existence of precious jewelery, which raised hopes of finding Indian
treasures or minerals.[2] According to Cabello Balboa, a town was established at an early date between the Pati and San Juan rivers by Juan de
Ladrillero, but following disagreements it was disestablished in favor of
another founded in the Bahía de San Mateo by Captains Garcilaso de la
Vega and Peña. In 1536 this town was abandoned as its citizens left to assist
their compatriots in Peru.[3] The failure of early expeditions to find the
anticipated riches discouraged official support for further expeditions of
conquest. Although entradas continued and some were provided with
mita labor, many later expeditions were privately financed and involved
only small numbers of soldiers, who were often easily routed by equally
small numbers of Indians. By the end of the century over fifty expeditions
had been mounted,[4] but by then Mercedarians were involved, and they
had become missionary rather than military in character.

From the mid–sixteenth century the racial composition and distribution of the population of Esmeraldas began to change. In 1553 seventeen
male and six female black slaves from the Guinea Coast survived a ship-
wreck on the coast at Portete, south of Cabo San Francisco. From the coast
the escaped slaves ventured inland, and after skirmishes with Campaz
Indians, whom they managed to subdue, eleven of them remained. These
blacks intermarried with local Indians, some, it was said, taking fourteen
or fifteen wives. Although the resulting offspring were zambos, they were
generally referred to as mulattoes. The mulattoes extended their domination over neighboring Indian groups and at the end of the century were

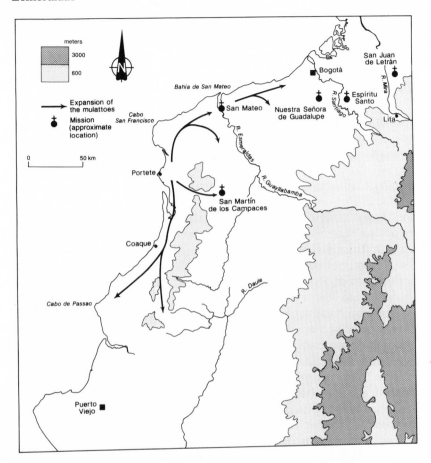

Map 13. The northern Coastal region

concentrated in the mountains of Campaz and the Bahía de San Mateo.[5]
(See Map 13.)

   The arrival of blacks on the coast and their attempts to dominate
neighboring groups resulted in local Indians retreating inland and to the
south. Some were killed in battles with mulattoes, and others were enslaved
by them.[6] Although in 1611 there were only about 200 Indians serving as
slaves in the two mulatto settlements,[7] fear of mulatto domination was
sufficient to encourage Indian groups to retreat inland. As a consequence
in 1600 Captain Pedro de Arévalo found many abandoned settlements and
cultivation plots along the coast.[8] Indians from Coaque and Cabo de Passao
moved inland to the headwaters of the river Daule,[9] and others from the
mountains near Puerto Viejo began descending to Spanish settlements for

protection.[10] The Cayapa and Nigua also became enemies of the mulattoes, and they too retreated inland seeking the help of local caciques against them and their hostile neighbors, who included the Malaba, Ceronda, and Soncón.[11] Against this background of migration and increased hostility, in 1597 the conversion of the Cayapa began.

In the late 1590s the Cayapa sought help from the cacique of Lita against the mulattoes and their hostile neighbors. Oidor Barrio de Sepúlveda together with a Mercedarian friar, Gaspar de Torres, who had been instructing Indians at Lita, were able to establish two settlements and baptize about 1,500 Indians.[12] One settlement, Espíritu Santo, founded four days' journey from Lita, was located at the site where the leader of the Cayapa lived. Further north another settlement, Nuestra Señora de Guadalupe, was established at Çaraha, which was centrally located for groups of Yambas, Lachas, and Aguatene. In the former settlement 781 Indians were baptized, and in the latter 662.[13] A curious feature of the baptismal lists for both settlements is the strong unexplained predominance of men among both adults and children. Somewhat later Chilango Indians were settled at San Juan Letrán near Lita.[14]

These successes prompted other entradas among the "barbacoas, altas, y malabas," which were instigated by the cacique of Tulcán. These expeditions resulted in the establishment of five villages that together possessed 600 Indians, including men, women, and children.[15] By 1601 Indians from the provinces of Mallama and Tusa had been settled in villages, and the village of Guacal had been established near Mira.[16] However, most of the Malaba, who in 1611 were said to number 300 under three caciques, and other neighboring groups, such as the Nurpes, Espies, Pruces, Aguamalabas, Mingas, and Quamingas, remained unpacified and hostile to both their Indian neighbors and Spaniards. As such, they were an obstacle to Spanish plans to open up a road from the sierra to the Santiago River. Nevertheless in 1611 Pablo Durango Delgadillo managed to pacify the Malaba and to found the town of Bogotá six leagues up the Santiago River. The town was served by the port of Santiago, and it was protected by a fort, San Ignacio de Montesclaros.[17] In 1619 there were said to be twenty vecinos in Bogotá and thirty in the port.[18] However, later that year the Malaba rebelled at excessive labor demands for the extraction of timber, to build bridges and roads, and to construct carts to transport salt, goods, and passengers. They burned the town of Bogotá and killed thirty Spaniards, mestizos, mulattoes, and blacks.[19] It was not until earlier this century that a road from the sierra to Santiago was opened.

While the Cayapa were being settled to the west of Lita, attempts were made to convert the mulattoes. In 1570 Andrés Contero established contact with Alonso de Illescas, who was the leader of the mulattoes at Campaz, but the latter escaped.[20] Subsequently in 1577 Cabello Balboa was sent to convert the mulattoes at their request, but no settlements were established there until 1598. At the end of the century there were two concentrations of mulattoes: one at Campaz and the other at the Bahía de San Mateo. The former group, headed by Francisco de Arobe, was established around a church founded in the bay, but the other group, led by Alonso Sebastián de Illescas, the son of Alonso de Illescas, proved more difficult to settle. Finally in 1600 the Mercedarian father, Juan Bautista de Burgos, persuaded them to establish San Martín de los Campaces. Its foundation was accompanied by a fiesta attended by 157 "adults, some children, and a few women."[21] As a token of obedience both leaders went to Quito. This event is depicted in one of the earliest paintings from colonial Latin America.[22]

Although mission settlements had been established, progress was slow. In 1607 Father Hernando Hinacapíe explained that it was difficult to attract Indians to the settlement in the Bahía de San Mateo because the area was so depopulated and the remaining population dispersed. In frustration he passed to San Martín de los Campaces, where he found Illescas dying and the population scattered two, three, and ten leagues apart. He decided to move them to a healthier site at Cabo de Passao, where they could assist travelers along the coast. The new settlement was founded with 50 Indians and mulattoes.[23] In 1611 there were five mulattoes at Cabo de Passao with 100 Indians, whom it was said they used like slaves, while at San Mateo there were said to be 12 to 14 mulattoes and, according to different witnesses, between 80 and 100 Indians.[24] The mulattoes never constituted a significant threat to Spanish control of the region, so the authorities were content to let them exist free of tribute and service. In fact they provided aid to shipwrecked travelers.

By the end of the sixteenth century, and only then in the last three years, the Spanish had managed to convert 5,000 Indians and mulattoes.[25] This was little reward for the considerable effort and money, estimated at 80,000 pesos, that had been expended. The lack of success was attributable in large part to policy conflicts over the region. Phelan argues that the area could have been conquered, despite the difficult topography and hostility of its inhabitants, if sufficient incentives had existed in the form of minerals or large Indian populations.[26] Some individuals who saw opportunities for political and economic advancement were prepared to sacrifice some capital, but generally it was inadequate to support an expedition of the size required to conquer the region effectively. Potential sponsors of expeditions were not encouraged by contradictory official attitudes as to the value of settling Esmeraldas. The main issues of debate were the defense of the coast and the economic benefits to be derived from the opening up of a road from the sierra to the coast; in fact the effective settlement of the region was never considered. Even when the English, and later the Dutch, appeared in Ecuadorian waters, views still differed as to whether the defense of the coast would best be served by effectively colonizing it, or whether the establishment of settlements might not provide further incentive for foreign attack and be costly to defend.[27] Policies generally favored starving the enemy out of the Pacific. Inhabitants of the sierra, however, were anxious for a road to be constructed to the coast at Santiago, since it would reduce transport costs and make their grain more competitive in Panama.[28] Clearly this project would have threatened the economic status enjoyed by more distant ports such as Guayaquil and Callao. As such, there were disputes between the audiencia and Viceroyalty over which policy should be pursued as well as regional conflicts within the audiencia itself. Against this background of conflicting views, no policy could be pursued with vigor, and as such, partly due to indecision, Esmeraldas was to remain a largely unexplored backwater for several centuries longer.

DEMOGRAPHIC TRENDS IN THE
NORTHERN COASTAL REGION

Despite limited Spanish settlement in Esmeraldas during the sixteenth century, its Indian population suffered a marked decline. Much of the blame for the decline must be attributed to epidemics, though Spanish expeditions and the growth of the mulatto population generated conflicts that adversely affected Indian communities. Many comments already made about the impact of Old World diseases in the jurisdictions of Guayaquil and Puerto Viejo apply to Esmeraldas. These include remarks on the absence or late introduction of malaria during the sixteenth century and the hereditary immunity provided to local populations through racial mixing with blacks. However, in Esmeraldas two factors may have moderated the impact of Old World diseases. First, the region's settlement pattern was characterized by small dispersed communities that would have retarded their spread, and probably enabled some to escape infection. Second, contact with passing vessels and hence sources of infection was less intense than in the major ports further south. Even so, disease mortality is likely to have been higher on the Esmeraldas coast than in the sierra and Oriente because of its exposed location.

Other Indians were lost in conflict with Spanish expeditions and with the mulattoes. By the end of the sixteenth century it was said that the coast had been depopulated by the mulattoes as they had extended their domination inland.[29] While the coast had been transformed into a sparsely populated region,[30] some inland areas appear to have retained their populations, perhaps boosted by Indians who had retreated inland. At the beginning of the seventeenth century the area around the Santiago River still possessed "a large number of Indians,"[31] and judging by the numbers baptized at the end of the sixteenth century, the area to the south of the Mira River inhabited by the Cayapa, even though characterized by small, dispersed settlements, must have possessed several thousand inhabitants.[32] To the south of these groups, however, much of the area between the Yumbos and the Bahía de San Mateo appears to have been uninhabited, at least along the Guayllabamba River.[33] Oidor Barrio de Sepúlveda claimed that by 1600 some 5,000 souls had been baptized in Esmeraldas.[34] These must represent only a small proportion of those existing there, for entradas concentrated on the fringes of the region, and many Indians were said to have fled inland. Taking into account the impact of epidemic disease, it is not unreasonable to suggest that the population of Esmeraldas at the end of the century may have been on the order of 20,000. This represents a decline of about 71 percent since the time of Spanish conquest. It is lower than for that for the southern coast, where the greater intensity of non-Indian settlement and frequent introduction of new infections raised mortality rates. It is higher, however, than for lowland regions of the Oriente, which were protected to some extent by their inaccessible location.

Part Six

SPANISH RULE: THE ORIENTE

CHAPTER 14

Los Quijos

Believing it would be a richer land . . . too many people have settled there when there are so few Indians, so that the land has been destroyed and the Indians have fled.

President of the Audiencia,
Licenciado Hernando de Santillán, 15 January 1564[1]

As early as 1535 the Spanish were aware of the existence of the land of cinnamon, which defined the eastern limit of the jurisdiction of Quito.[2] Whether their knowledge was based on information brought back from earlier expeditions or on hearsay is not known. The existence of cinnamon and hopes of discovering gold stimulated early expeditions to and through the region. The first documented entrada was led by Gonzalo Díaz de Pineda, who in 1538 was encharged by Francisco Pizarro with the conquest of La Canela.[3] This expedition, which included 130 Spaniards, reconnoitered the provinces of Hatunquijo and Cosanga and, continuing in search of the province of La Canela, passed through the provinces of Cabi and Guarozta, which reportedly possessed 15,000 Indians. The expedition negotiated rugged terrain, and Indian resistance was fierce. Torrential rains and shortages of food and clothing also contributed to its withdrawal early the following year. Some soldiers were left in Los Quijos in anticipation that a second expedition would be mounted, but because of increased opposition from encomenderos in Quito, who were reluctant to see their dwindling sources of tribute and labor further diminished, it never materialized. (See Map 14.)

In November 1539 Francisco Pizarro named his brother, Gonzalo, as governor of Quito. As soon as he assumed office, he began preparing for another expedition to La Canela. Despite continuing opposition from encomenderos, in February 1541 he finally left Quito with more than 4,000 Indians and over 200 Spaniards, among whom were Gonzalo Díaz de Pineda and a number of those who had taken part in the first expedition.[4] As this force passed over the snow-capped peaks of the Cordillera Oriental, 100 Indians died of exposure. Francisco de Orellana followed closely on Pizarro's heels with the intention of joining him. Orellana's contingent was attacked by Quijo Indians, but it finally rendezvoused with Pizarro, probably in the province of Moti. From here Pizarro and 80 soldiers spent two months exploring the surrounding province of Sumaco.[5] In his desperate search for the land of cinnamon and other riches, the conquistador tortured Indians, burned their homes, and had others torn to pieces by dogs.

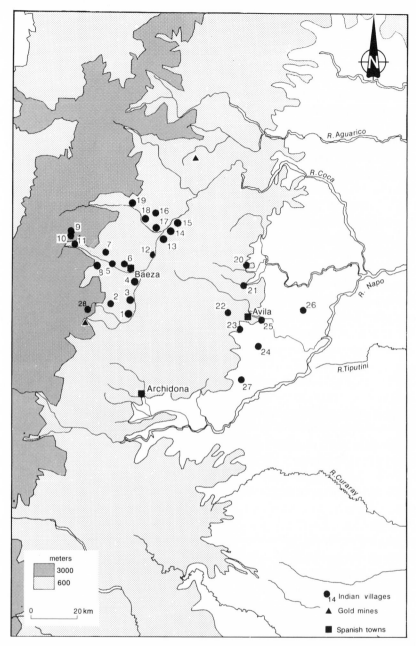

Map 14. The Quijos region (Modified after Porras Garcés, Baeza, 184, 189–90)

District of Baeza	7 Maspa	14 Zanacato	District of Avila	25 Aragua
1 Seteta	8 Maspilla	15 Tangofa	20 Seta	26 Carito
2 Cabi	9 Taçallata	16 Concin	21 Moti	27 Yatso
3 Guarozta	10 Papallacta	17 Anche	22 Sumaco	
4 Coçanga	11 Chimifu	18 Condapa	23 Guacamaya	District of Archidona
5 Hatunquijo	12 Befa	19 Oyacachi	24 Tambiza	28 Conduceta
6 Pachamama	13 Zegui			

He carried out further depredations in villages along the banks of the river Coca, before mustering with the rest of the expedition at Guema, from whence he proceeded downstream, where he encountered the Omagua. Here Gonzalo Pizarro began to construct a brigantine and dispatched Francisco de Orellana downriver in search of provisions. He waited in vain for Orellana to return until shortages of food and arms, and growing discontent among the troops, finally forced the expedition to return to Quito early in 1542.

The impact of Pizarro's expedition on local populations is likely to have been considerable, though localized. Certainly some Indians were killed in skirmishes and others were tortured to death, but probably most fled into the interior. The actions of the conquistadores made it difficult to obtain supplies, which would have been problematic at the best of times because of the large size of the expedition and the small surpluses, if any, produced by local communities. Once the expedition's rations had been exhausted, members were forced to forage for food in plots abandoned by fleeing Indians, such that large numbers starved to death or became ill with dysentery. Of the 230 Spaniards who accompanied Pizarro, only about 100 returned to Quito. Some had continued the journey downriver with Orellana, but 87 had died.[6] Casualties were even higher among the expedition's Indian auxiliaries, most of whom were drawn from the northern sierra. By the time Orellana separated from Pizarro, over 1,000 Indians had died, and after several months searching for provisions while waiting for Orellana to return, only 2,000 remained.[7] Excluding the impact of the expedition on local Indian populations, an early seventeenth-century report claimed it had cost 6,000 Indian lives.[8] The exceptionally high casualty rate was attributed to conflicts with Indians and to starvation and illness because of lack of provisions. There is no evidence that the expedition carried Old World diseases into the region.

Meanwhile in 1541 an expedition under Captain Gonzalo Martín, sent to Los Quijos to locate Gonzalo Pizarro, failed to make contact with him and only managed to penetrate thirty or forty leagues east before it was deterred by the difficult terrain and hostile Indians.[9] During the next sixteen years the Spanish were preoccupied with affairs in the sierra, and although there were plans for further expeditions, none materialized.[10]

Once political stability had been established in the sierra, efforts to bring the Quijo region under Spanish control were renewed. In 1556 the new governor of Quito, Gil Ramírez Dávalos, was encharged by the viceroy, the Marqués de Cañete, to found a town and allocate encomiendas in the province of La Canela.[11] A reluctant conquistador, Gil Ramírez Dávalos determined to bring about the peaceful subjugation of the region. In pursuit of this aim he exploited the kinship ties that existed between the caciques of Latacunga and Hatunquijo.[12] At the invitation of the latter, he left for Los Quijos in March 1558 in the company of thirty-nine soldiers and assisted by Don Sancho Hacho, the cacique of Latacunga, and 200 of his subjects.[13] The villages of Maspa, Maspilla, Atunquijo, Tazallata, and Chimifu were the first to be pacified, and in Hatunquijo Indian leaders from Coca, Sumaco, Ceño, Pachamama, Oyacachi, Cosanga, and many others rendered allegiance. Father Martín de Plasencia, a Franciscan who accompanied Gil Ramírez Dávalos, testified they had seen "all the caciques of the province of Sumaco and Canela and Coca" and estimated that the province of Los Quijos possessed 40,000 Indians; others suggested 50,000.[14] Although these figures may have been exaggerated to magnify the achievements of the governor, the long lists of caciques pacified on this and later occasions, as well as evidence for the existence of substantial villages, such as that of Conchocomi in the province of Sumaco, which possessed 1,000 "indios de visita,"[15] testify to the presence of dense Indian populations. Gil Ramírez Dávalos judged sufficient Indians existed to justify the establishment of four towns, but he waited for reinforcements from Quito, headed by Rodrigo Núñez de Bonilla, before founding the town of Baeza de Nueva Andalucía on 14 May 1559.[16] Accounts of the town's foundation, including a map of the plots assigned to individual vecinos, constitute exceptional records for this early date. The town was founded in the Cosanga Valley, the remains of which were located by Father Pedro Porras in 1957 at La Madrugada, not far from present-day Baeza.[17] At its foundation the town possessed seventy-four vecinos. The number was large compared to other towns in the province, and was excessive, given the size of Indian populations. Many citizens were therefore left without encomiendas, and this became a major source of discontent that threatened Spanish control of the region.[18]

Rodrigo Núñez de Bonilla disputed Gil Ramírez Dávalos's governance of Los Quijos, and in November 1559 the Audiencia in Lima ruled in his favor, ordering the latter to leave the region. Once appointed as governor, Rodrigo Núñez de Bonilla moved the site of Baeza further west, since its original location near the river was regarded as too swampy and unhealthy, and also too close to the powerful caciques of Cosanga and Maspa.[19] Nevertheless, the town's existence continued to be threatened by shortages of provisions and by its restless citizens, who saw the prospects of new encomiendas fade as Indian hostility mounted with excessive demands for tribute and labor.[20] Within a year of Baeza's foundation, Indians in Los Quijos were in rebellion. Alonso de Bastidas, by then interim governor of Quijos, through persuasion and gifts managed to pacify the province of Cosanga and the neighboring caciques of Condapa, Zegui, Tangofa, Anche, Concín, Befa, Zanacato, and Coca. It was not long, however, before the Spanish faced renewed Indian resistance. During the uprising in July 1562, bridges, tambos, and a few houses on the outskirts of Baeza were burned, and crosses destroyed, while Spaniards were attacked both on the road from Quito to Baeza and in Hatunquijo and Pachamama. However, the revolt was not sustained. By October 1562, when Andrés Contero arrived in Baeza as the lieutenant of the newly appointed governor, Melchor Vázquez de Avila, Alonso de Bastidas had managed to reestablish peace.[21]

Alonso de Bastidas had intended to establish two additional towns in the region: one in the province of Sumaco, and the other in the provinces of Atunique and Chumbiyaco. With this intention a group of Spaniards headed by Bartolomé Marín had already started on the journey from Quito to Baeza but were caught up in the uprising in 1562 and did not arrive until after Andrés Contero's contingent. According to Governor Salazar de Villasante, the 200 newly arrived soldiers had been given license by Vázquez de Avila to recruit Indians from the sierra. He reported that 1,000 Indian men and women had been seized, many of whom had died of hard labor, poor food, and ill-treatment, some being torn to pieces by dogs; the more fortunate had fled.[22] Salazar de Villasante was anxious to discredit Vázquez de Avila, but some truth underlay his hyperbolic account. Other reports similarly suggested that large numbers had been taken by force to Baeza; one suggesting that Andrés Contero had drafted Indians from as far afield as Guayaquil.[23] Coercion was also applied by some native leaders. Once again the cacique of Latacunga, Don Sancho Hacho, offered the services of 200 of his vassals, in return for which he received an encomienda of the village of Coxqui in Los Quijos.[24]

In February 1563 the cacique of Sumaco, Jumandi, hearing of the arrival at Guarozta of Andrés Contero and Bartolomé Marín, and learning that Marín had treated those at Hatunquijos kindly, invited the conquistadores to visit him. Jumandi received Marín in peace, after which Indian leaders subordinate to him from Moti, Carito, Seta, Yatso, and Aragua followed his example. However, at the same time he made it clear he could muster 15,000 Indians and that the Spanish might not be so well received in future.[25] After Contero joined Marín in the province of Sumaco, the town of Avila was established on 10 March 1563.[26] Subsequently Marín, accompanied by thirty soldiers, passed to the Loma de las Guabas and called on the surrounding caciques of Tambiza, Ciaque, and Guacamaya and on those of Hipemehene and Tutupambehe to pay allegiance to the Crown.[27] Later the two captains passed to the province of Coca, where they founded the town of Alcalá del Río.[28] Although cabildos were selected for these towns, there is no evidence that encomiendas were distributed. In the autumn of 1563 Marín explored the region of "Los Algodonales," where he established Archidona and discovered gold in its hinterland. He then left for Quito to obtain men and supplies but was retained in Quito to face civil charges and never returned.[29] After it had been abandoned, Vázquez de Avila ordered Juan Mosquera to move the town to a more open site.[30]

For two decades the presence of Spaniards in Los Quijos was strong. The accounts of Contero, Marín, and Vázquez de Avila suggest that the pacification of the region and the establishment of the four towns were brought about peacefully.[31] However, it is clear that all was not well, as finally evidenced by the rebellion of 1578. Salazar de Villasante was highly critical of the activities of Vázquez de Avila's lieutenants. He claimed their expeditions had passed through Indian villages seizing food, so that 5,000 Indians had died of starvation, in addition to which they had committed many atrocities. Indians had been thrown to the dogs, and women who had refused their sexual advances had had their breasts cut off.[32] More dispassionately, President Santillán claimed the problem was that the Quijos region had been considered rich, so that large numbers of Spaniards had settled there who could not be supported by its small population.[33] As a result the land had been destroyed, and the Indians driven to the hills in search of food. Meanwhile settlers, failing to find the hoped-for riches and living a precarious existence dependent on provisions from Quito and the little they could extract from local communities, began to desert the region, leaving the towns of Archidona and Alcalá del Río abandoned.

With the exception of Baeza, which was founded with seventy-four vecinos, the precise number of original settlers in the other three towns is unknown, and even less is known of the number of encomiendas allocated. Even so, by the early 1570s the number of Spaniards in the region had clearly declined. López de Velasco recorded that there were about forty-eight encomenderos in Baeza, Avila, and Archidona together, with a total of 6,000 tributary Indians.[34] Similar numbers were revealed during the visita of Licenciado Diego de Ortegón between 1576 and 1577, when there were forty-one encomenderos in the gobernación, of whom nineteen were in Baeza, twelve in Avila, and ten in Archidona, and together they possessed 6,803 tributary Indians.[35] Up to that time Indians in the Quijo region had not been officially assessed for tribute payment.[36] Encomenderos had levied tribute and services at will, forcing Indians to spin and weave cotton cloth, to manufacture pita, or else to search for gold or transport goods to and from the sierra.[37] Indeed the region's encomenderos were described as having complete control of the Indians, which they exercised by employing dogs to "domesticate" them.[38] Their absolute control was attributed in part to the lack of effective native leadership.[39]

On 6 September 1576 Licenciado Diego de Ortegón was encharged with a visita of the Quijos region. Ortegón initiated a program of reducciones, enumerated the population, and drew up official tasaciones, at the same time fining encomenderos for excessive exactions and for ill-treating Indians. Far from remedying the excesses, the visita resulted in even more oppression as encomenderos increased levies to meet the fines imposed.[40]

Conditions deteriorated, and at the end of 1578 a major rebellion broke out. It was stimulated by two pendes, Beto and Guami, who appear to have functioned as shamans, though they may have also possessed some political power; their status is not clear. Following the destruction of Avila and Archidona and the deaths of between 70 and 150 Spaniards, according to different accounts, Indians under the leadership of Jumandi prepared to attack Baeza. Alerted to this threat, Baeza was reinforced by troops from the sierra led by Rodrigo Núñez de Bonilla that included 200 Indians provided by the cacique of Cayambe, Gieronimo Puento.[41] Large numbers were killed in the suppression of the rebellion. President Barros claimed 800 or more Indians had died, though the cleric Pedro Ordóñez de Cevallos estimated that 5,000 were lost in the battle for Baeza alone.[42] The rebellion was gradually suppressed, its leaders condemned to public hanging, and others exiled to the coast.[43] The severe and public punishment of the rebels was sufficient to deter further uprisings, and Rodrigo Núñez de Bonilla went on to reestablish the towns of Avila and Archidona, naming the latter Santiago de Guadalcanal.[44]

Following the suppression of the rebellion, Viceroy Toledo appointed Agustín de Ahumada as governor of Quijos, even though Melchor Vázquez de Avila still had proprietary rights over the jurisdiction for his life and that of his heir. Governor Ahumada was soon accused of abusing the rights of encomenderos, of conscripting Indians to serve on expeditions, and of forcing them to weave cotton cloth.[45] Subsequently Vázquez de Avila, who resided in Cuzco,[46] appointed various tenientes to administer the region, but they were clearly ineffective, for in 1590 the Crown inquired whether the gobernación should be suppressed and placed under the jurisdiction of the Audiencia of Quito. For reasons unknown, but possibly because Vázquez de Avila possessed friends on the Council of the Indies,[47] or because of conflicts between the Audiencias of Lima and Quito, this proposal was not put into effect. It was only after the death of Vázquez de Avila's successor, Rodrigo Manuel Vázquez, that in 1615 the Crown appointed a new governor, Alonso de Miranda.[48]

DEMOGRAPHIC TRENDS IN LOS QUIJOS

Without exception, observers noted the continued decline of the population through the sixteenth and early seventeenth centuries. The well-known account of the Conde de Lemus y Andrade, written in 1608, attributed the decline to the three uprisings and their suppression, and to "malignant smallpox."[49] The numbers killed in uprisings have already been discussed. As for disease, it seems likely that the smallpox epidemic to which he refers was that of the late 1580s that afflicted other parts of the Audiencia, including the region of Yaguarzongo and Pacamoros to the south. There are no other references to outbreaks of Old World diseases in the region; indeed, the Conde de Lemus y Andrade identifies only dysentery and colds as being common in the area. Nevertheless, the region was probably affected by earlier epidemics. In 1558 a major smallpox epidemic ravaged the Quito Basin, and it was in that year that Gil Ramírez Dávalos's expedition departed the city for Los Quijos. Even so, the only indirect evidence to support the early occurrence of epidemics in this region is the exceptionally high level of decline within the first twenty years of conquest. However, nearly all commentators attributed the decline to excessive exactions of tribute and labor, which maintained high levels of mortality, encouraged forced or voluntary migration, and promoted infanticide and reduced levels of fertility.

During the late sixteenth and early seventeenth centuries the number of Spaniards in the Quijos region never reached the level that had existed prior to the rebellion of 1578. According to Ordóñez de Cevallos, who worked in the region in the 1590s, there were fifty-two vecinos and seventy-four women in the province of Quijos, but the Conde de Lemus y Andrade noted that in addition there were between fifty-four and sixty-eight Spanish forasteros.[50] These figures included the town of Sevilla del Oro, which had been confirmed as part of the gobernación of Quijos and contained over one-third of the Spanish population of the region. Of this number fifty-five were encomenderos, but only two were considered wealthy, and most resided outside the province. When Alonso de Miranda took office as governor of Quijos in 1617, only twenty encomenderos remained, of whom only one-quarter resided there.[51] He blamed absentee encomenderos for continued Indian hostility and the lack of effective Spanish control of the region.[52] Despite the weak Spanish presence Indians enjoyed no respite, for the rights of encomenderos continued to be exercised by their overseers and servants, who exacted additional goods and services for themselves.

Official tasaciones existed, but they were not adhered to or revised for thirty years between Ortegón's visita and that carried out at the very beginning of the seventeenth century. Ordóñez de Cevallos recorded that the annual tribute paid by Indians around Baeza and Avila comprised one *anaco* or manta and two *liquillas* (smaller pieces of cloth), maize, fish, honey, and many other items of lesser importance; those of Archidona paid tribute in gold extracted from the river Napo, or cotton and alpargates.[53] The Conde de Lemus y Andrade valued the tribute at between forty-eight and fifty-six reales.[54] If true, these levels of exaction are higher than those paid by Indians in the more productive basin of Quito. Furthermore, these levels were often exceeded illegally, and in many cases tribute was commuted to personal service. In fact Los Quijos was one of the few areas within the Audiencia where personal service persisted at the end of the sixteenth century,[55] and high levels of service were consistently identified as a major cause of its depopulation.

Most service was exacted illegally, but at the end of the sixteenth century sixty mitayos were allocated to the citizens of Baeza for the collection of wood and water. They were paid the pitiful wage of "una sarta de chaquira" (worth one tomín) a week, which was about one-quarter of the wage paid in Quito, and many were employed illegally in other tasks.[56] At the same time, Indians living around Archidona, who had not been officially assessed, "worked every day in the houses of encomenderos, some extracting pita, others weaving and spinning cotton, others making canvas and cord sandals, and spinning candle wicks." They were also required to sow rice and cotton, and in fine weather they were sent to the river Napo to pan gold. In addition Indians were compelled to construct houses and bridges and to carry goods to and from the sierra, a task that in April and May involved them crossing the freezing páramo.[57] It also seems likely they were used on slave raids into the interior, as several hundred were in the 1620s.[58]

The high levels of service demanded clearly discouraged the peaceful submission of Indians and was a major factor in the depopulation of Los Quijos.[59] As already indicated, the rebellions claimed hundreds, if not thousands, of lives, while many others died because of ill-treatment. Spanish demands for service also undermined subsistence production. Although there is no mention of famines or major shortages of food, Spaniards continually complained about the lack of provisions, and it is unlikely they suffered more than the Indians, on whom they depended. Demands for labor probably also affected subsistence patterns, perhaps resulting in a greater dependence on wild food resources, but details are lacking.

High levels of service also involved the forced removal of Indians from their communities to the sierra or encouraged flight to the interior or the highlands. These movements not only contributed to the depopulation of the region, but it has been suggested by Powers that migration from Los Quijos to the sierra occurred on such a scale that it contributed to the maintenance of the population in the Quito Basin.[60] Two main types of migration may be identified. Some Indians were forcibly transferred to the sierra to work in the personal service of encomenderos, either as household servants or as laborers on haciendas.[61] Young females may have been particularly vulnerable to removal for domestic duties.[62] There is some evidence from the baptismal records of El Sagrario for the late sixteenth century that small numbers of Indians from Los Quijos were working in the service of encomenderos in Quito, though they represented only a tiny percentage of those in service, most of whom came from the highlands.[63] However, those transported to the sierra by encomenderos may have represented only a small proportion of those who migrated. Powers suggests that many were voluntary migrants who were driven from Los Quijos by Spanish abuses and the collapse of the local economy and encouraged to settle in the sierra by offers of land from caciques seeking to enhance their political power. These processes were facilitated by the lack of control exercised by native leaders in Los Quijos and by preexisting kinship ties and trading contacts with groups in the highlands. One account by a vecino of Quito, Alonso de Peñafiel, claimed that Indians from Los Quijos fled to the sierra, preferring to be slaves under caciques in Quito than work for Spaniards.[64] While migration contributed to the depopulation of Los Quijos, as yet insufficient evidence exists to suggest that migration to the sierra occurred on the massive scale Powers suggests. Not all fugitive Indians went to the sierra. Many retreated further east. Following the 1578 rebellion, 200 Quijo Indians sought refuge among the Omagua,[65] and during his visita of Archidona in the mid-1590s, Father Lobato de Sosa estimated that 400 Indians had fled into the interior.[66]

Overwork and ill-treatment not only raised mortality rates and stimulated migration and flight but suppressed fertility levels and undermined the capacity of the population to maintain itself. Women were encouraged to take herbal potions to make themselves sterile and to practice infanticide to liberate their children from servitude.[67] Infanticide had been practiced in pre-Columbian times,[68] but it may have increased in the early colonial period. One reporter suggested that female infants were allowed to live, whereas male offspring were killed so that they would not have to pay tribute.[69] However, if anything Ortegón's visita reveals a shortage of women rather than men.[70] This could derive from the propensity of Spaniards to seize young female Indians for household service, or equally it may be due to inaccurate recording. The Spanish generally showed greater interest in tribute-paying males, and hence their numbers are recorded most consistently; more commonly women and children were underenumerated.[71] Apart from conscious attempts to control fertility, the birthrate would have declined because of disruption to family life caused by death or migration, as well as because of amenorrhea and miscarriages due to stress and heavy labor.

It has been estimated that at the time of Spanish conquest the population of the Quijos region was at least 26,000, and was probably more like 35,000 or more (Table 19). By 1559, when Gil Ramírez Dávalos pacified the region,[72] Indian communities had already sustained major losses through previous encounters with Spanish expeditions, to say nothing of the possible impact of disease. By 1564 the president of the Audiencia, Hernando de Santillán, reported that the population was declining daily because there were too few Indians to support such large numbers of Spaniards.[73] By the early 1570s López de Velasco recorded that the region possessed only a "few" Indians,

Table 19. Estimates of the Indian Population of Los Quijos in the Sixteenth and Early Seventeenth Centuries

Date	Population estimate	Source
At contact	35,000 indios	In the gobernación of Quijos (AGI AQ 31 Alvaro de Cárdenas 2.3.1626); may include Sevilla del Oro
At contact	30,000 indios	BNM 3178 fols. 1–15 Canelas Albarrán 1586
1538	15,000 indios	In the regions of Cabi and Guarozta alone (AGI AQ 20B Información . . . de los servicios de Díaz de Pineda 1539)
1559	40–50,000 indios	In the provinces of Sumaco, Canela, and Coca (AGI PAT 101–19 Información . . . de los servicios de Ramírez Dávalos 25.10.1558)
1559	30,000 indios moradores	In the province of Quijo (RGI 1:77 Lemus y Andrade 16.2.1608); includes Sevilla del Oro
1575	16,000 ánimas	Twenty years ago in Cosanga, Avila, and Archidona; the figure compares with 1,700 in ca. 1595 (AGI AQ 25 Lobato de Sosa, no date)
1577	16,509	Comprising 7,206 converted Indians and 9,183 unconverted around Baeza, Avila, and Archidona. This sums to 16,389, but the summary figures included in the document give 16,509 (AGI AQ 82 Ortegón 1.2.1577).
1586	10,000 naturales de todas edades	BNM 3178 fols. 1–15 Canelas Albarrán 1586.
1590	2,829 indios	Ordóñez de Cevallos, "Viaje del mundo," cap. 29:396; RGI 1:77–78 Lemus y Andrade 16.2.1608. Lemus y Andrade gives fuller details. Since the latter lists the number of tributary Indians as 2,335, it is clear that women and children were not included. The number of children is given as 295, which must be a considerable underestimate and may refer to teenagers about to become tributary Indians.
ca. 1595	8,600 ánimas	AGI AQ 25 Lobato de Sosa, no date
1626	2,250 indios	AGI AQ 31 Cárdenas 2.3.1626; includes Alcalá del Río and Sevilla del Oro and may refer to tributary Indians

Table 20. Indian Population of Los Quijos according to the Visita Conducted by
Licenciado Diego de Ortegón in 1576 to 1577

Status	Baeza	Avila	Archidona	Total
Converted Indians				
Married adults	2,046	212	208	2,466
Unmarried adults	885	29	36	950
Children	2,992	572	226	3,790
Unconverted Indians				
Married adults	4,072	1,224	1,172	6,468
Unmarried adults	969	172	145	1,286
Children	436	404	589	1,429
Total	11,400	2,613	2,376	16,389

Source: AGI AQ 82 Licenciado Diego de Ortegón 1.2.1577.

the rest having died due to ill-treatment.[74] In fact many Indians had probably fled into the interior, only to be reincorporated into formal settlements
during Ortegón's visita in 1577. According to Ortegón's summary figures
rather than those contained in Table 20, the Quijos region possessed 6,803
tributary Indians and a total population of 16,509.[75] Although the majority
who paid tribute had not been converted, these numbers clearly did not
include any outside Spanish control. As such, they provide supporting testimony for the large size of the preconquest population.

In 1577 over 70 percent of the Indians enumerated by Ortegón were
located in villages in and around Baeza. Living close to the sierra, Indians
in this area came into more intense contact with Spaniards and migration
was more easily affected. As such the concentration of population probably
reflected the area's more substantial aboriginal population and the greater
effectiveness of Spanish control in this part of Los Quijos. The jurisdiction
of Baeza seems to have suffered along with other parts of the province;
Father Lobato de Sosa estimated there had been about 4,000 Indians
around Cosanga, but in the mid-1590s there were only 500 souls.[76] At the
same time, there were 8,600 *ánimas* in Los Quijos. This figure is not easy
to compare with that of 2,250 Indians recorded by Governor Alvaro de
Cárdenas in 1626,[77] since the latter included Sevilla del Oro and Alcalá del
Río and, being similar to the number of tributary Indians, is unlikely to
have been an accurate reflection of the total Indian population. Nevertheless, comparisons of the numbers of tributary Indians in Baeza, Avila, and
Archidona between 1577 and 1626 indicate that all declined to less than
one-quarter of their size. (See Table 21.) These dates encompass the smallpox epidemic of the late 1580s, making this order of decline not unreasonable. If Lobato de Sosa's figure of 8,600 ánimas is accepted as the most
accurate for the late sixteenth century, the decline from the time of con-

Table 21. Tributary Population of the Provinces of Los Quijos and Macas in the Sixteenth and Early Seventeenth Centuries

Year(s)	Baeza	Avila	Archidona	Total	Sevilla del Oro
1571–74[a]	2,000	2,000	not given	6,000	not established
1577[b]	5,013	919	871	6,803	not given
ca. 1595[c]	2,000	600	426	3,026	not given
1608[d]	980	240	215	1,435	900
1626[e]	800	200	120	1,120	800

[a] CDI 15:499–500 Demarcación y división, no date; López de Velasco, *Geografía*, 227–28.
[b] AGI AQ 82 Ortegón 1.2.1577.
[c] AGI AQ 25 Lobato de Sosa, no date [ca. 1595].
[d] RGI 1:82–83 Conde de Lemus y Andrade 16.2.1608. Similar figures are found in Ordóñez de Cevallos, "Viaje del mundo," cap 29:396–97.
[e] AGI AQ 31 Cárdenas 2.3.1626. In addition Alcalá del Río had 134 tributary Indians.

quest, given an aboriginal population of 35,000, would be of the order of 75 percent. It would probably be more accurate to increase this figure to 10,000 to take account of fugitives residing within the region and to the east. The number that had migrated to the sierra is difficult to guess but may have been in the order of several thousand. Since these fugitives cannot be clearly separated from other groups in the highlands, to avoid double counting they are not included in the estimate for this region. If the Quijo are estimated to have numbered 10,000 in 1600, the population would have declined by 71 percent since the time of Spanish conquest.

CHAPTER 15

Macas and Canelos

And so [around Sevilla del Oro] the poor Indians and their wives
and children are employed in spinning and weaving without time to
attend to their lands or even eat.
Governor of Quijos, Alvaro de Cárdenas, 2 March 1626[1]

The eastern flanks of the Andes between the Napo and Paute rivers
remained isolated in the early colonial period because of their inaccessibil-
ity and the relative absence of gold and large Indian populations. While the
Upano Valley could be penetrated through Zuña, access from the north
was less easy, and the hostile Jívaro effectively blocked any approach from
the south. In 1540 and 1549 the province of Macas was explored by
Rodrigo Núñez de Bonilla and Hernando de Benavente respectively, but
jurisdictional conflicts between conquistadores and political instability in
the sierra militated against the early consolidation of Spanish control.
Nevertheless, some Spaniards settled there and employed Indian labor to
exploit the gold placers of the Upano and Pastaza.[2] (See Map 15.)

Intent on claiming the area as part of the gobernación of Quijos,
Melchor Vázquez Dávila dispatched his teniente, Juan de Salinas Guinea,
to establish a town in the region. Nuestra Señora del Rosario was founded
at Sumaguallí in 1563, but it gradually lost population. Not until 1575 was
an official Spanish presence established in the area. On returning from
Spain, Juan de Salinas Loyola, anxious to incorporate the province within
the gobernación of Yaguarzongo and Pacamoros, directed his nephew,
José Villanueva Maldonado, to found the town of Sevilla del Oro. Despite
its foundation, his claim over the region was rejected in favor of that of
Vázquez Dávila, who appears to have been supported by relatives on the
Council of the Indies.[3]

Encomiendas were distributed when the earliest expeditions penetrated the area. Rodrigo Núñez de Bonilla was allocated 400 Indians in the
province of Macas and 350 in the province of Quizna.[4] These Indians are
likely to have been reallocated when Sevilla del Oro was established in
1575, if not before.[5] It is not known how many encomiendas were distributed at that time, though it was later said that Sevilla del Oro had originally possessed 3,000 tributary Indians in its jurisdiction.[6] This does not
seem unreasonable, given later observations on the number and size of
encomiendas. In 1584 the town contained twenty encomenderos.[7] One
encomendero, Captain Gabriel Machacón, was said to have possessed
1,000 "indios curicamayos,"[8] and in 1587 Pedro González de Acosta, in a

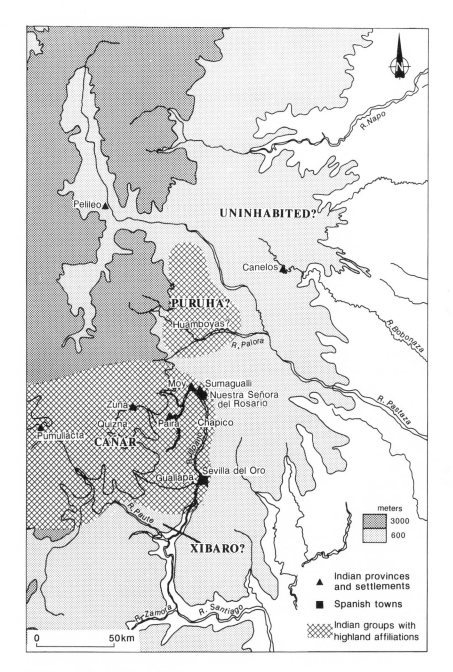

Map 15. The Macas region

dispute with Juan Palomino over rights to certain Indians, claimed that he had been given an encomienda of 260 Indians in the provinces of Coropino, Palora, Lopino, and Guano.[9] Even though the Indians allocated were widely dispersed,[10] these encomiendas were large by the standards of neighboring provinces. By 1608 there were still nineteen encomenderos, whose encomiendas comprised 10 to 120 tributary Indians, and 900 altogether,[11] and in 1626 there were said to be sixteen vecinos in Sevilla del Oro, with 800 tributary Indians.[12]

Despite the presence of gold, like other areas in the gobernación of Quijos, the economy of Macas focused on the production of cotton and cotton cloth. In 1582 the governor of Yaguarzongo and Pacamoros, Juan de Aldrete, explained it was due to the impossibility of organizing mining cuadrillas, since the Indians were not "domesticated."[13] However, small groups of miners far from official surveillance may have preferred to coerce Indians into panning gold illegally rather than see the establishment of greater official control over both Indian labor and the mining industry, which, among other things, would have led to higher taxes. In any event, Macas was known as a textile-producing region.

Cotton cloth was either paid as tribute or produced by forced labor, the precise character of which is not clear, but probably took the form of personal service. From the late sixteenth century at least, each tributary Indian was required to pay thirty *varas* of cotton cloth a year. This was judged as excessive and equivalent of what six tributary Indians should pay. As a consequence, women and children were forced to help in its manufacture, and Indians were left with no time to attend their lands or even eat.[14] In 1626 the governor of Quijos, Alvaro de Cárdenas, fined encomenderos for excessive labor exactions, claiming it was the first time that any such measures had been taken.[15] Having forced the Indians to manufacture so much cotton cloth, encomenderos had to rely on merchants from Sevilla del Oro to trade it in Cuenca, Riobamba, and Guayaquil, since there was only a limited local market for the product.[16] The overproduction of cotton reflected the lack of alternative profitable enterprises in which Indian labor could be employed, and it is not surprising therefore to find many encomenderos transferring their Indians to the sierra. In the 1570s some were servicing the tambo of Hatuncañar,[17] while in 1644 one-fifth of the province's encomienda Indians were registered as being employed in the sierra.[18]

DEMOGRAPHIC TRENDS IN THE MACAS REGION

Despite the relative lack of Spanish interest in the Macas region and the protection its location afforded from epidemics, its population declined.

Even before 1563, when Nuestra Señora del Rosario was founded, the local population had been subjected to overwork and ill-treatment,[19] and demands increased once a permanent Spanish presence was established. Excessive exactions of tribute and labor clearly undermined the native economy and social structure, reducing the capacity of communities to recover from increased mortality levels and compensate for losses associated with forced migrations. Many Indians transferred to the sierra never returned. Nevertheless, Spaniards commonly blamed the decline on attacks by their hostile neighbors, the Jívaro.[20] Whether or not there was a major Jívaro rebellion in 1599 that resulted in the death of thousands, as Velasco suggests, it is clear that Sevilla del Oro was continually assaulted and in 1606 was sacked.[21] How many local Indians fell victim to Jívaro raids is not known, but over fifty years they probably exceeded 1,000.[22]

There is no evidence that epidemics occurred in the region during the sixteenth century, but in the mid–seventeenth century the decline of the Indian population was blamed on "muchas pestes,"[23] and indeed about that time the remnants of Inmunda decimated by a smallpox epidemic joined the mission of Canelos.[24] Most likely this was the epidemic of smallpox that struck Indian groups on the Upper Pastaza in the mid-1650s.[25] Despite the lack of evidence, it seems unlikely that the Macas region escaped the epidemics that ravaged neighboring populations in the sixteenth century.

Unlike most areas during the early colonial period, the region between the Napo and Upper Pastaza rivers attracted fugitive Indians from surrounding regions.[26] Possibly the earliest fugitives came from the highlands, but later they were joined by encomienda Indians from Los Quijos and Gae fleeing from Jesuit control.[27] The history of Dominican missions in the area is full of contradictions, but the first mission was probably not established there until the seventeenth century. In 1624 a Dominican father from the highland parish of Pelileo visited the headwaters of the Bobonaza, where he converted thirty-five Indians, settling them around the church of Santa Rosa de Penday. It was not until 1671, however, that a formal settlement was established and Father Valentín de Amaya began converting Gae Indians on the banks of the Bobonaza. Subsequently Guallinga, Inmunda, and Santi were incorporated into the mission of Canelos, which, taking its name from canela, was officially established in 1684.[28] The Dominicans used the presence of fugitive Gae to argue for an expansion of their jurisdiction to include the wider group. However, in 1683 the Crown insisted that the Dominicans confine their attention to the Canelo and leave the Gae to the administration of the Jesuits.[29] Nevertheless, the presence of Dominicans in this region, albeit weak, effectively blocked the easy passage of Jesuits through the Pastaza Valley to the province of Mainas. Since the history of this region is sketchy and the number of

Table 22. Tributary Population of Macas during the Sixteenth and
Seventeenth Centuries

Year	Tributary Indians	Source
At conquest	ca. 3,330	See the discussion in chap. 4.
1608	900	RGI 1:84 Lemus y Andrade 16.2.1608.
1626	800	AGI AQ 31 Cárdenas 2.3.1626.
1643	400–450	ANHQ Tributos 2 Pérez Navarrete 29.10.1643.
1644	490	AHNQ Tributos 2 Repartición de las alcabalas 6.10.1644.
1662	286	AGI CO 1540 Peñalosa 2.8.1662.

fugitive Indians in the sixteenth century is likely to have been small, they will not enter into calculations attempted as part of this study.

If the size of the tributary population at the time of conquest may be estimated at 3,330,[30] and that of the early seventeenth century at about 900, then the level of decline in the province of Macas was of the order of 73 percent. This is a slightly lower level of decline than that noted for other regions, but it is still high. Although the region may have escaped some epidemics that ravaged other areas, excessive labor demands, the transference of Indians to the sierra, and losses to the Jívaro collectively contributed to high levels of population loss. (See Table 22.)

CHAPTER 16

Yaguarzongo and Pacamoros

Each day, as a result of ill-treatment and continued labor in the mines, the Indians have declined, and each day the few peaceful Indians that are left rebel.

Caciques and Indians of the province of
Yaguarzongo, 10 March 1591[1]

During the sixteenth century the gobernación of Yaguarzongo and Pacamoros was inhabited by the Xíbaro, Bracamoro, and Jívaro, from the river Paute south to the river Chinchipe and east as far as the Santiago River.[2] The gobernación of Yaguarzongo and Pacamoros also included the area inhabited by the Chirino. Part of the region occupied by the Bracamoro, known as the province of Nambija, came under the jurisdiction of Zamora and the corregimiento of Loja. Since these Indians were culturally akin to those in the gobernación of Yaguarzongo and Pacamoros and had a similar experience in mining in the early colonial period, they are considered here. (See Map 16.)

As previously indicated, the Chinchipe Valley was explored three times before the first towns were established.[3] The town of Zamora was founded by Alonso de Mercadillo and Hernando de Benavente in 1549 or 1550, but it took five years before the immediate hinterland was effectively pacified.[4] Between 1557 and 1558 Juan de Salinas explored the gobernación of Yaguarzongo and Pacamoros and founded the towns of Valladolid, Loyola, Santiago de las Montañas, and Santa María de Nieva. Even though the Indian population might have been reduced at an earlier date by epidemics, the foundation of these towns heralded the precipitous decline of the native population as it was drafted to pan gold and as sustained contact with the sierra established channels for the introduction of Old World diseases.

From the beginning, excessive labor demands and ill-treatment provoked unrest that threatened Spanish control of the region. During the 1560s the towns were attacked several times, so that in 1574, when Juan de Salinas returned from Spain, he found Valladolid and Santiago de las Montañas depopulated. He set about reestablishing them and sent his nephew Bernardo de Loyola to rebuild the town of Logroño de los Caballeros and Captain José Villanueva Maldonado to found the town of Sevilla del Oro.[5] The former had been established in 1564 in the region reputed to have the richest mines,[6] but also the most hostile Indians.[7] Jívaro attacks and revolts occurred throughout the region, but it was the town of Logroño that

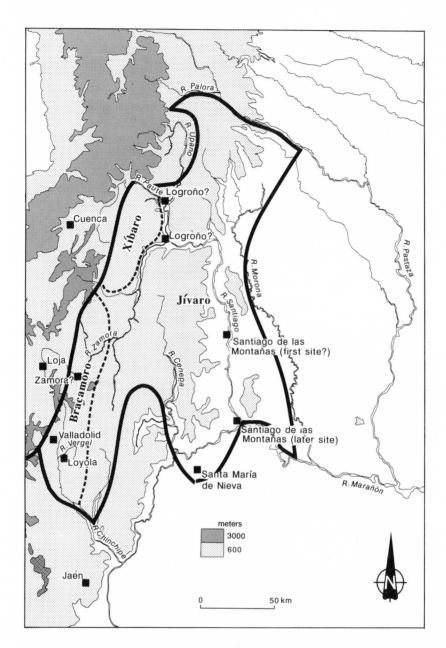

Map 16. The jurisdiction of Yaguarzongo and Pacamoros

suffered most. A major revolt occurred in 1579 when the town was burned and twenty Spaniards killed.[8] Accounts suggest the revolt involved mestizos and converted Indians who had probably been brought from the sierra around Cuenca to work in the mines.[9] Further attacks effectively brought Logroño's existence to an end, so that by the early seventeenth century the area was described as "deserted and depopulated."[10] Having destroyed Logroño, the Jívaro remained unsubdued and throughout the following century continued to attack frontier towns.[11]

Gold was to be found throughout the Jívaro region. Most took the form of alluvial deposits that could be extracted fairly easily from riverbeds and terraces using simple metal tools and wooden pans, but some gold veins were also worked. It was claimed the Inka had obtained much of their gold from the Zamora region,[12] but Juan de Salinas maintained that in pre-Columbian times the Indians had no knowledge of the mines or how to work them.[13] Following the foundation of Zamora and the pacification of the surrounding region, in the mid-1550s extensive gold deposits were found and by 1568 were yielding 100,000 pesos a year.[14] The richest mines were located in the province of Nambija, where it was said that individual grains were worth up to 1,000 pesos.[15] Although other documents testify to large size of some grains, the quality and quantity of the ore was very variable.[16] Other mines were worked at Chupanama and Chungara.[17]

Gold deposits were also worked in the hinterlands of Loyola, Santiago de las Montañas, and Valladolid. The mines of Loyola were located seven leagues from the town and in 1582 were producing 30,000 to 35,000 pesos of gold a year. Those at Congaza and Iranbiza near Santiago de las Montañas do not appear to have been opened until 1567 but in 1582 were yielding 20,000 to 25,000 pesos annually.[18] Although Logroño was established in 1564, it soon fell victim to Indian attacks, and its deposits, which were regarded as the best in that region, were probably not exploited until after it was reestablished in 1575 or 1576.[19] In the first year of production they yielded 30,000 pesos, but by 1582 output had already fallen.[20] Discounting the production figures for Zamora itself and for Valladolid, for which no details exist, in 1582 the total value of gold mined was between 80,000 and 90,000 pesos. Jaramillo Alvarado suggests that the main period of production was between 1577 and 1590, when official treasury receipts in Loja suggest that production did not fall below 150,000 pesos.[21] Indeed in the 1590s it was claimed that once Zamora had been the richest gold mining city in all Peru but later had been deserted because the Indian population had declined and rendered the mines unworkable.[22] By 1618 labor shortages had caused mining to cease, even though the gold deposits had not been exhausted.[23]

Most gold was extracted by panning, but some vein ores were also worked. Black slaves were preferred for underground work,[24] but costing between 250 and 300 pesos each, they were employed only on a small scale.[25] Encomienda Indians constituted the basic source of labor. From the outset, tribute payments in the gobernación of Yaguarzongo and Pacamoros were generally commuted to labor service. In fact it was one of the few areas in the Audiencia where this practice was officially toler- ated.[26] Juan de Salinas argued that its persistence was necessary, since the tribute they could pay in agricultural produce was insufficient to maintain encomenderos in the area, and since the Indians were unfamiliar with such exactions, it was difficult for native leaders to collect it. More- over, labor was essential for the mines.[27] Parts of the gobernación were inspected prior to 1571, but details of the resulting tasaciones are lacking. When Juan de Salinas was appointed governor in 1571, he was ordered to reassess tribute payments in the light of the region's demographic de- cline.[28] However, by 1580 reassessments had not been made, and the Crown reiterated the order for new tasaciones to moderate the excessive exactions.[29]

The tasaciones drawn up by Salinas in 1581 together with the rela- ciones geográficas provide evidence for the organization of mine labor.[30] Indian communities were required to supply one-fifth of those liable for tribute, although only those aged between fourteen and twenty-five. They were assembled by their encomenderos into gangs of twenty, fifty, or eighty *curicamayos*. They worked for seven months, during which time they were supposed to be provided with food, clothing, tools, shelter, and medical care, after which they were to be free to return to their commu- nities to cultivate their lands.[31] Juan de Salinas claimed the Indians were well treated and instructed in the Catholic faith and that they were "richer" than other Indians because they worked with gold and could therefore profit from it, though he did not specify how.[32] Although no details exist of working conditions in the mines or mortality rates sus- tained by the cuadrillas, accounts converge in their condemnation of the hard labor to which they were subjected.

Excessive labor demands were stimulated by the presence of gold and aggravated by the small size of encomiendas. When Zamora was founded, thirty or thirty-five encomiendas were distributed.[33] This number was judged excessive, given the relatively small Indian population, but it was considered necessary to encourage settlers to remain in the region and thereby control an area that was rich in gold. It was anticipated that once the region had been pacified, the number of encomiendas would be re- duced. By 1564 at least the number had not fallen, and most encomenderos possessed fewer than fifty Indians. It was suggested that the number of encomiendas should be limited to twenty-two, even though it was consid- ered the population was really only sufficient for fifteen.[34] No official reorganization of encomiendas occurred, but over time the number gradually fell as the Indian population declined and encomenderos deserted the town. By 1582 there were twenty-one,[35] though in 1590 there were said to be only enough Indians for six or seven encomiendas.[36] The same situation pertained in the gobernación of Yaguarzongo and Pacamoros. When the towns of Valladolid, Loyola, Santiago de las Montañas, and Santa María de Nieva were established, each had possessed about thirty encomenderos.[37] The encomiendas were small, but it was hoped that they would be augmented as yet-unconquered groups were pacified. By 1591, however, the four towns together possessed only fifty encomenderos, and many encomiendas were said to comprise seven, ten, twelve, or twenty Indians often scattered over a wide area.[38]

The Spanish authorities recognized that small encomiendas were undesirable, since they encouraged the overexploitation of Indian labor and had adverse effects on Indian production. Where large encomiendas were large, sufficient numbers remained to continue food production; where encomiendas were small, demands for labor often resulted in lands being left unattended such that the Indians were "always dying of hunger."[39] It was suggested that the minimum size of an encomienda in the province of Zamora should be 200 Indians and that in general they should comprise more than 500 Indians, otherwise within a short time they would become extinct.

Demands for labor were clearly excessive. Apart from work in the mines, official assessments required Indians to provide additional services for encomenderos, such as cultivating plots of maize, manioc, and sweet potatoes; providing fruit, vegetables, and fish, in unspecified amounts; and repairing their houses.[40] Where Indians were not employed in mining, particularly around Santa María de Nieva, they were required to spin and weave cotton, and even manufacture shirts. Here children and old women were also employed on a continual basis.[41]

Apart from these official exactions, encomenderos and priests employed Indians illegally in porterage and to work on a permanent basis on their haciendas.[42] The mining industry attracted traders from distant parts and created high demands for porters. Indians were loaded like horses with goods weighing up to four *arrobas,* when it was considered loads of three arrobas were sufficient to kill a man. They further endangered their health as they journeyed up to 150 leagues, sometimes as far as Chachapoyas, crossing different climatic zones. Not only was labor hard, but there were many instances of cruelty, of which Juan de Salinas and his soldiers in particular were accused. A vecino of Loyola, Juan de Estrada, alleged they had committed many atrocities, including mutilation, throwing Indians bound from high points, and setting dogs upon them. They were also charged with transporting Indians in chains to work in their personal service, decapitating those who flagged, and killing their children.[43]

DEMOGRAPHIC TRENDS IN THE GOBERNACIÓN OF
YAGUARZONGO AND PACAMOROS

There is no doubt that forced labor, particularly in mining, and the ill-treatment that accompanied it were major factors in the depopulation of the province of Zamora and the gobernación of Yaguarzongo and Pacamoros. In 1578 the oidores attributed the region's decline from 20,000 to between 4,000 and 4,500 in the previous twenty years to the diezmo concession on mineral production that had stimulated mining and resulted in the ill-treatment and death of many Indians. They argued that if the concession were to be extended for another twenty years, there would be no Indians left.[44] While forced labor mining was a major factor in the depopulation of the region, other factors, including epidemics, clearly played important roles.

The first documented epidemic to strike the region was smallpox, perhaps accompanied by typhus, which arrived in 1589.[45] It hit the area particularly badly[46] but was not as devastating there as in the province of Jaén.[47] At that time, however, Indians claimed the region had been afflicted by other "pestilencias y enfermedades," suggesting it had previously experienced several epidemics.[48] One unspecified epidemic had occurred a few years earlier. In 1586 testimonies given in the probanza of Bernardo de Loyola, encomendero of Cangasa, in the jurisdiction of Santiago de las Montañas, and of Misalalangui, near Loyola, recorded that in the previous two years the population had declined by more than one-third because of undefined "enfermedades" and "pestilencia."[49] Most likely this was the epidemic of smallpox and measles that broke out in Peru in 1585 and spread north to Ecuador.[50] These epidemics postdate much of the depopulation of the region, and as yet no concrete evidence exists that it was afflicted at an earlier date, though it is probable. As suggested in chapter 6, it is possible that disease was carried there by the "many sick people" who accompanied Juan de Salinas when he founded Santiago de las Montañas in 1557.[51]

While forced labor in mining and epidemics were the most obvious causes of the decline in the Indian population, other processes operated to reduce its ability to maintain and reproduce itself. In pre-Columbian times population levels were low. Food supplies were far from abundant, and Indians relied on game and fish for their protein. In the colonial period the cultivation of maize was probably encouraged by encomenderos as a more acceptable food and item of tribute, while hunting, traditionally a male activity, would have declined as men were employed for extended periods in panning gold. Forced labor undermined subsistence production, and the region as a whole suffered from food shortages. Although maize, beans, and root crops were grown around Zamora, they were not abundant, and in order to support mining activities, food had to be imported from neighboring regions.[52] Few Indians probably starved to death, but low nutritional levels may have heightened the impact of disease.

While the impact of forced labor and epidemics raised mortality rates, and resistance to Spanish rule brought conflict and casualties, in the longer term the introduction of the encomienda brought political stability and led to a reduction in intertribal warfare.[53] However, any positive influence its suppression may have had on mortality levels was insufficient to compensate for other losses. Similarly its influence on fertility levels, together with monogamy, are unlikely to have countered the impact of the prolonged absence of able-bodied men necessitated by forced labor. The few figures available suggest that the fertility rate was low. The woman/child ratios for three groups—the Bolona, Rabona and Gonzaval—calculated from figures supplied by an encomendero of Zamora, Alvaro Núñez, in 1582, indicate small family sizes. The first two groups, with ratios of 1:0.66 and 1:0.60 respectively, were located in the hot humid lowlands, while the lattermost inhabiting the colder sierra had a ratio of 1:1.50.[54] One might suspect underregistration of children, were it not for the fact that Alvaro Núñez drew attention to the small number of children, observing that, except in the higher, colder parts of the province, many children were born, but few survived infancy.[55] This suggests that intestinal infections, more common in warmer climates, may have been a factor in keeping population levels low. Whatever the cause, the population was clearly failing to reproduce itself.

During the sixteenth century the province of Zamora and parts of the gobernación of Yaguarzongo and Pacamoros suffered some of the heaviest population losses in the audiencia. Furthermore, the decline was continuing at the end of the century, while in other regions the population was beginning to stabilize, if not increase.[56] Considering demographic trends in the province of Zamora first, the earliest indications of population levels appear in the list of Indians in the Viceroyalty of Peru drawn up by Pedro de Avendaño in 1561, which recorded that it possessed 11,222 Indians, of whom 6,093 paid tribute. (See Table 23.)[57] Other accounts drawing on information from the 1560s suggest Zamora possessed between 5,000 and 8,000 tributary Indians.[58] By the time of Viceroy Toledo's visita general in the 1570s the province of Zamora possessed only 8,100 Indians of all ages,[59] more than 6,000 of whom were reputedly baptized by the bishop of Quito about the same time.[60] The continuing underlying downward trend is indicated by the fall in the number of tributary Indians from 1,500 in 1582[61] to 685 in 1591.[62] The following year it was reported that around the mines of Zamora only 500 "Indians of all ages" were left because they had been consumed in the mines and by epidemics of "smallpox, measles, and dysentery."[63] By 1622 only 140 Indians remained, the rest having died or fled

Table 23. Indian Population Estimates for the Province of Zamora

Time	Population estimate	Source
At conquest	20,000	Bishop of Nicaragua (RGI 2:308–9 1592)
At conquest	15,000–16,000	Corregidor of Loja, Mexía Sandoval (AGI AQ 30 8.4.1622)
Before 1561	11,222 Indians and 6,093 tributary Indians	RAHM Colección Múñoz A/92 fols. 55–77 Relación de los naturales que hay 1561
1567(?)	8,000 tributary Indians under 27 encomenderos	RAHM 9/4664 no. 21 Los pueblos despanoles que hay, no date
Prior to 1571	5,000 tributary Indans under 28 encomenderos	CDI 15:409–572 Demarcación y división de las Indias, no date; López de Velasco, *Geografía*, 221
1579	more than 6,000 souls baptized by the bishop of Quito in the pro-vince of Zamora	AGI AQ 76 Bishop of Quito 2.4.1579
1586	8,100 Indians of all ages	Canelas Albarrán, Descripción de todos los reinos, BNM 3178 fols. 1–15 1586
No date	8,000 naturales	RGI 3:129 Salinas, no date
1582	1,500 tributary Indians	Estimated by an encomendero of Zamora (RGI 3:136 Núñez 18.12.1582
1591	685 tributary Indians	CDI 6:41–63 Relación de los indios tribu-tarios 1.11.1591
1592	500 Indians of all ages	RGI 2:308–9 Bishop of Nicaragua 1592
1622	140 Indians	AGI AQ 30 Mexía Sandoval 8.4.1622

the province to unspecified locations.[64] If the figure of 20,000 is accepted as a reasonable estimate for the aboriginal population of the province of Zamora, its decline to about 500 in 1600 represents a loss of over 97 percent.[65]

Demographic trends in the gobernación of Yaguarzongo and Pacamoros are less clear because the figures available refer to different areas (Table 24). López de Velasco estimated there were 14,200 tributary Indians in encomiendas in and around the towns of Valladolid, Loyola, and Santiago de las Montañas.[66] His figure was clearly based on estimates predating his 1571 account, and its large size suggests it may relate to the initial distri-bution of encomiendas. A major source of information, though in places difficult to interpret, comprises the testimonies of witnesses to the activ-ities of Juan de Salinas presented in 1577 by Juan de Estrada, a vecino of Loyola.[67] One witness testified that only 8,000 or 9,000 "indios de tributo" remained in the gobernación of Salinas, which had once possessed 25,000.

Table 24. Indian Population Estimates for the Gobernación of Yaguarzongo and Pacamoros

Time	Population estimate	Source
At conquest	30,000 Indians	AGI AQ 23 Caciques of Yaguarzongo and Jaén 10.3.1591
At conquest	20,000 Indians	AGI AQ 8 Oidores 22.1.1578
At conquest	20,000–25,000 Indians approximately, around Valladolid, Loyola, and Santiago de las Montañas	AGI EC 912A Memorial de las cosas 1577
1552	Under 30,000 Jívaros of the Paute	Vacas Galindo, *Límites*, 3:90
1579	Over 15,000 souls baptized by the bishop of Quito	AGI AQ 76 Bishop of Quito 2.4.1579
1582	19,627 "indios e indias," of whom 10,932 were males, in Valladolid, Loyola, and Santiago de las Montañas	RGI 3:145–53 Aldrete 1.12.1582
1586	40,000 Indians of all ages (includes Valladolid, Loyola, Santiago de la Montañas, Santa María de Nieva, Macas, Jívaros, and Logroño)	Canelas Albarrán, Descripción de todos los reinos, BNM 3178 fols. 1–15 1586
1591	3,000 Indians of all ages (includes Yaguarzongo, Jívaros, and Jaén)	AGI AQ 23 Caciques of Yaguarzongo and Jaén 10.3.1591

Other witnesses gave more specific estimates, suggesting there were between 1,000 and 1,500 Indians around Valladolid, between 2,500 and 3,400 around Loyola, and between 3,000 and 4,000 around Santiago de las Montañas (Table 25). It is clear from enumerations made during a visita of the region in 1580 that these figures refer to tributary Indians rather than total populations. The resulting reassessment for Loyola in 1581 indicated the presence of 2,248 tributary Indians between the ages of fifteen and forty-five and, excluding 250 who were absent, 7,248 Indians in total.[68] The latter figure may be compared with that of 6,719 contained in Juan de Aldrete's relación of the gobernación of Yaguarzongo and Pacamoros written in 1582, which also included the results of the 1580 visita.[69] The total populations around Valladolid and Santiago de las Montañas were 2,749 and 10,159 respectively. All three jurisdictions together contained 19,627 Indians, and apparently not all had been pacified and therefore enumerated. These figures give some credence to the bishop of Quito's claim in 1579 that he had baptized 15,000 souls.[70]

Table 25. Indian Population Estimates for Individual Jurisdictions within the
Gobernación of Yaguarzongo and Pacamoros

Time	Population estimate	Source
Valladolid		
At conquest	6,000–7,000 Indians	AGI EC 912A Memorial de las cosas 1577
Before 1571	1,200 tributary Indians	CDI 15:409–572 Demarcación y división de las Indias, no date; López de Velasco, *Geografía*, 229
1577	1,000–1,500 Indians	AGI EC 912A Memorial de las cosas 1577
1582	2,749 "indios e indias," of whom 1,560 were males (the summary figure gives the total as 2,975)	RGI 3:147–53 Aldrete 1.12.1582
1586	4,000 Indians of all ages	Canelas Albarrán, Descripción de todos los reinos, BNM 3178 fols. 1–15 1586
Loyola		
At conquest	8,000–10,000 Indians	AGI EC 912A Memorial de las cosas 1577
Before 1571	6,000 tributary Indians under 31 encomenderos	CDI 15:409–572 Demarcación y división de las Indias, no date; López de Velasco, *Geografía*, 229
1577	2,500–3,400 Indians	AGI EC 912A Memorial de las cosas 1577
1581	7,248 Indians, of whom 2,248 paid tribute	AGI AQ 22 Tasación of Loyola 9.10.1581
1582	6,719 "indios e indias," of whom 3,657 were males (the summary figure gives the total as 6,616)	RGI 3:147–53 Aldrete 1.12.1582
1586	6,500 Indians of all ages	Canelas Albarrán, Descripción de todos los reinos, BNM 3178 fols. 1–15 1586
Santiago de las Montañas		
At conquest	14,000–17,000	AGI EC 912A Memorial de las cosas 1577
Before 1571	7,000 tributary Indians under 22 encomenderos	López de Velasco, *Geografía*, 229

Table 25. *continued*

Time	Population estimate	Source
	Santiago de las Montañas	
1577	3,000–4,000 Indians	AGI EC 912A Memorial de las cosas 1577
1582	10,159 "indios e indias," of whom 5,715 were males (the summary figure gives the number of males as 5,759)	RGI 3:147–53 Aldrete 1.12.1582
1586	15,000 Indians of all ages	Canelas Albarrán, Descripción de todos los reinos, BNM 3178 fols. 1–15 1586

In 1586 Canelas Albarrán claimed that ten years previously he had visited the gobernación and seen for himself that it contained 40,000 Indians.[71] Excluding the regions of Macas and Santa María de Nieva, he lists comparable figures of 4,000 for Valladolid, 6,500 for Loyola, and 15,000 for Santiago de las Montañas, plus 4,000 for Logroño and 3,000 others "en los jívaros." These figures are not substantially different from those revealed by the visita, but they are double those suggested by the testimonies contained in Juan de Estrada's memorial. The higher figures are more detailed and precise, and it is possible the smaller numbers in the memorial were chosen to emphasize the level of depopulation and thereby discredit Juan de Salinas. However, the decline in the Indian population during this period is backed by other documentary evidence already discussed. If the high numbers prove to be more accurate, then the aboriginal population may have been higher than previously suggested.

By 1591 it was estimated there were only 3,000 Indians of all ages in the gobernación of Yaguarzongo, Jívaros, and Jaén.[72] Even though it is clear that the region was ravaged by epidemics in the late 1580s, unless the figure refers only to those existing in encomienda villages, it is clearly an underestimate. At that time there were scarcely fifty encomenderos, each with under twenty Indians. Even though the Indian population may not have declined to the degree reported, in 1593 it was sufficient to persuade the Crown to reduce the status of the gobernación of Yaguarzongo and Pacamoros to that of a corregimiento. At the same time, it was proposed that the small frontier towns should be amalgamated.[73] The proposal envisaged that Santiago de las Montañas and Santa María de Nieva, which between them possessed eighteen vecinos, should be amalgamated and attached to the corregimiento of Jaén, while Valladolid and Loyola with only fifteen moradores should be joined together under the corregimiento of Loja. After considerable debate the proposal was finally approved in 1614, but since it would have abolished the corregimiento of Yaguarzongo and Pacamoros, its implementation was delayed to permit the current corregidor, Diego Vaca de Vega, to proceed with pacification of the Maina and Jívaro.[74] The corregimiento was finally divided between those of Loja and Jaén in 1631.[75]

Estimating the population of the gobernación of Yaguarzongo and Pacamoros in 1600 is not easy. The figure of 3,000 Indians in 1591 has been judged as an underestimate. Perhaps the most reliable figures available for the sixteenth century are those associated with the 1580 visita, which suggest that the region possessed a minimum of about 20,000 Indians. Between 1580 and 1591 the area was hit by two epidemics—one in 1585, and the other in 1589. If it is assumed that each of these epidemics carried off one-third of the population, then about 8,700 may have remained in the early 1590s. While these proportions may be too high, the estimate takes no account of other factors that continued to take their toll. In addition these figures refer essentially to the region under effective Spanish administration.

The numbers outside Spanish control swelled as continued revolts stimulated migration and provided opportunities for fugitivism. In 1606 there were said to be 3,000 to 4,000 warlike Jívaro living thirty leagues to the east of Cuenca.[76] They must have represented only a portion of those outside Spanish administration. An estimate of 5,000 or more might be more realistic. Throughout the seventeenth century these Jívaro remained a constant threat to Spanish settlements and effectively blocked the easy passage of missionaries from the sierra to the Marañón through the Santiago-Paute and Morona rivers. A number of disastrous entradas were conducted among these groups during the century,[77] but they remained unsubdued. By the end of the seventeenth century they were considered to number some 8,000 to 10,000.[78] These numbers appear high, given that they were periodically affected by entradas and most likely epidemics. Nevertheless, it suggests that by effectively resisting Spanish domination, the Jívaro outside Spanish control were able to avoid the precipitous decline experienced by the Bracamoro and Xíbaro, even if they were unable to increase substantially because of intertribal wars and others factors that traditionally maintained their populations at low levels.[79]

Evidence for the gobernación of Yaguarzongo and Pacamoros suggests that the Indian population in 1600 may have been about 8,000, to which another 500 must be added to take account of those in the province of Zamora. A further 5,000 may have existed outside Spanish control. From a total of 50,000 Jívaro and 3,000 Chirino at the time of Spanish conquest, the population had therefore fallen to an estimated 13,500 in 1600, a

Table 26. Estimated Population Decline in Zamora and the Gobernación
of Yaguarzongo and Pacamoros

Ethnic group	Aboriginal population	Estimate for 1600	Percent decline	Depopulation ratio
Zamora	20,000	500	97.5	40.0:1
Yaguarzongo and Pacamoros under Spanish control	23,000	8,000	65.2	2.9:1
Yaguarzongo and Pacamoros outside Spanish control	10,000	5,000	50.0	2.0:1
Total	53,000	13,500	74.5	3.9:1

decline of 74.5 percent (Table 26). However, this statistic masks considerable regional variations. The greatest losses of over 97 percent were sustained in the province of Zamora, where mining activities were
concentrated, while the Jívaro who remained outside Spanish control escaped the worst ravages experienced by their neighbors, but even they
had lost half their populations.[80]

CHAPTER 17

Mainas

It has been the experience that when the Light of Heaven enters their huts, it is followed by the shadowy horrors of plague and miserable death.

Father Francisco de Figueroa, circa 1660[1]

Indian groups along the river Marañón were probably first encountered by Spaniards in 1538, when Alonso de Mercadillo's expedition descended the Huallaga River. However, two decades passed before Juan de Salinas effectively explored the Marañón as far as the Ucayali, venturing up the Pastaza River to Lake Rumachi and south to the river Nieva.[2] In the process he founded Santiago de las Montañas and Santa María de Nieva, and these two towns marked the eastern frontier of Spanish settlement until San Francisco de Borja was established in Maina territory in 1619. Enslaving raids from the frontier towns provoked counterattacks, to which the Spanish responded by dispatching punitive expeditions.[3] An expedition mounted in 1591 by the teniente of Yaguarzongo and Pacamoros, Francisco Pérez de Vivero,[4] failed to prevent further raids, and the viceroy, the Marqués de Montesclaros, was obliged to order the corregidor, then Diego de Tarazón, to send a punitive expedition into Maina territory. In 1616 the expedition headed by his teniente, Luis de Armas, captured some peace-seeking Indians and, on returning to Santiago de las Montañas, reported there were some 8,000 souls wishing to be baptized.[5] News of the existence of such large Indian populations stimulated the experienced soldier Captain Diego Vaca de Vega, who became the next corregidor of Yaguarzongo, to petition the viceroy for permission to found a town in the region explored by Luis de Armas. The *capitulación* he made in 1618 gave him the right to conquer and pacify hostile and heathen Indians in the province of Mainas and also the Cocama, Jívaro, and other Indians nearby, in return for which he was to receive the title of governor and captain general of Mainas with the authority to found a town and distribute encomiendas.[6] The expedition was mounted from Loja and accompanied by three priests: a parish priest, Alonso de Peralta; a Mercedarian, Francisco Ponce de León; and an Augustinian, Lorenzo del Rincón. In 1619 it passed the Pongo de Manseriche, and from there Vaca de Vega sent his son, Pedro Vaca de la Cadena, with his *maestre de campo,* Cristóbal de Saavedra, to pacify Indians on the banks of the Marañón. They returned from the expedition in the company of a number of Indian leaders before exploring the Pastaza. Father Ponce de León reported that 4,000 Indians with their families had been settled at

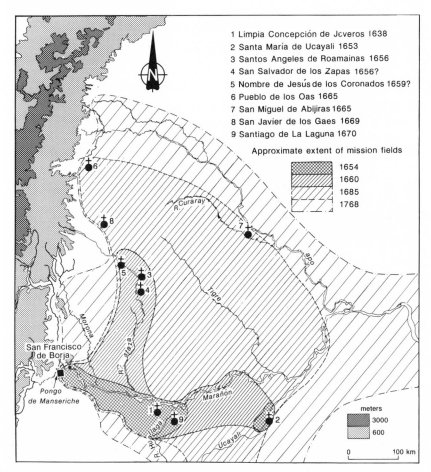

1 Limpia Concepción de Jeveros 1638
2 Santa María de Ucayali 1653
3 Santos Angeles de Roamainas 1656
4 San Salvador de los Zapas 1656?
5 Nombre de Jesús de los Coronados 1659?
6 Pueblo de los Oas 1665
7 San Miguel de Abijiras 1665
8 San Javier de los Gaes 1669
9 Santiago de La Laguna 1670

Approximate extent of mission fields

1654
1660
1685
1768

meters
3000
600

0   100 km

Map 17. The province of Mainas

twenty locations around the projected site of the town, San Francisco de Borja.[7] (See Map 17.)

When San Francisco de Borja was founded on 7 December 1619, Diego Vaca de Vega distributed twenty-one encomiendas, providing 150 Indians for each of its officials and 50, 20, and 15 each to other citizens, while promising to supplement their numbers in the future.[8] Father Francisco de Figueroa later noted that when the city had been founded, the province had possessed 700 tributary Indians,[9] but by 1638, when the Jesuits arrived to initiate their work among the Maina, only 400 remained. The decline was attributed to uprisings, intertribal wars, and disease.[10]

Following the establishment of San Francisco de Borja, further exploratory expeditions were mounted into the interior, many led by Pedro Vaca de la Cadena and involving large numbers of converted Indians.[11] The Maina were regarded as weak and cowardly, so that Indians from around Santiago de las Montañas and Santa María de Nieva, possibly Jívaro, were drafted, and indeed were keen to participate in expeditions because of the opportunities they afforded for pillage.[12] Between 1619 and May 1621 Father Ponce de León claimed to have baptized 2,744 souls.[13]

Vaca de Vega soon left Borja in the charge of his son, Vaca de la Cadena, although the latter did not formally succeed to the office of governor until the death of his father in 1627. During his administration Vaca de la Cadena attempted to establish tobacco cultivation against a background of mounting Indian hostility and frequent revolts. Following the suppression of a major revolt in 1623, some 900 Indians "chicos y grandes" were moved from the Pastaza River and settled on the river Paraná to the south of Borja on the Marañón. Lacking provisions, 500 starved to death; the rest, together with other Maina Indians, fled into the interior, leaving only 370 Indians in the city.[14]

It was the uprising of 1635, however, that precipitated the arrival of Jesuit missionaries. The revolt was provoked by excessive demands for service by Borja's citizens, who had effectively reduced the Indians to little more than slaves. Many were conscripted to serve on expeditions, while others were occupied continuously in hunting and fishing or else employed in spinning and weaving cotton.[15] The uprising involved 1,000 Indians from around Borja and left thirty-four people dead, including twenty-nine Spaniards.[16] To suppress the rebellion Vaca de la Cadena enlisted the help of twenty soldiers and two Jesuit missionaries. In 1638 Fathers Gaspar de Cugía and Lucas de la Cueva arrived in Borja, and the work of Jesuits on the Marañón began.[17] At first they were involved in the pacification of the surrounding region which was accomplished with the help of Jevero Indians. With the exception of several instigators of the revolt, who were executed and their bodies dismembered and displayed in the trees along the banks of the Pastaza and Marañón, those who had participated were pardoned.[18] Many accounts of the province of Mainas begin with the arrival of the Jesuit missionaries, but it will be clear from this short introduction that by that date the Maina and neighboring groups had suffered considerable losses as a consequence of enslaving raids, revolts, and possibly epidemics.

Before examining the expansion of missionary activities in the province of Mainas, it is useful to consider the history of San Francisco de Borja and the process by which the Jesuits established control over Indian populations in the region. After San Francisco de Borja was founded in 1619, the numbers of encomenderos and Indians fluctuated considerably, but both generally followed a downward trend. At its foundation the town contained 700 tributary Indians, but by 1636 they numbered only 400 out of a total population of 2,000. By 1661 both numbers had been halved, though the total number excluded 500 Maina who had fled. By that date the number of encomiendas had fallen from twenty-one to eighteen, and Indians were living scattered around the countryside rather than in formal villages.[19] This was rectified in 1668, when they were congregated into three *anejos* within three leagues of Borja—San Ignacio de Loyola, Santa Teresa de Jesús, and San Luis Gonzaga—that together contained 271 "indios de lanza" and a total population of 1,355.[20]

Because of ill-treatment and food shortages, Indians living in and around Borja continually drifted back to the forest. Each year one or two expeditions were mounted to round up fugitive Indians. In 1660 an expedition captured 340 Indians, among whom were some descendants of those who had fled during the uprising in 1635. However, in the same year the number captured was exceeded by those who died in an epidemic of measles and "mal del valle."[21] Entradas resulted in high mortality and destroyed family life, as captured individuals were allocated to different soldiers and encomenderos, who often transferred them to other regions. It was estimated that within a short time not one-tenth of the captives would remain.[22] Furthermore, missionaries noted that once settled in Borja, the Indians failed to reproduce as they had done in their native lands, and this was attributed to the psychological impact of their loss of liberty, just as "wild birds when captured or caged become sterile."[23] In the longer term, therefore, captives and new converts failed to reverse the downward demographic trend.[24]

From 1638 the arena of Jesuit activity gradually expanded eastward down the Marañón and its tributaries, and later up into the Napo and Aguarico. When the Jesuits were expelled in 1768, the province of Mainas comprised eighty reducciones.[25] But the expansion had not been easy. Among the problems the Jesuits faced was the small number of missionaries available for the huge task at hand, and the lack of trained and effective military support.[26] Moreover the Indians were generally scattered over wide areas and reluctant to settle in the missions without the offer of gifts, particularly metal tools, although a few groups, such as the Jevero and Omagua, actively sought missionary protection from Spanish or Portuguese enslavers. The Jesuits generally employed Indian interpreters, who had been captured on earlier exploratory expeditions and trained at special language schools in Borja and later Santiago de la Laguna.[27] Indian reactions were unpredictable, and as a precautionary measure expeditions were normally accompanied by a few soldiers. Not all entradas went with peaceful intentions, however. Others were associated with the suppression of revolts or the capture of fugitives.

Once Indians had been settled in a mission, the task of retaining them there was no easier. Dissatisfaction with mission life and the desire to return to their native lands encouraged many to avail themselves of the slightest opportunity to flee.[28] Yet constant supervision was impossible. At its peak the vast province of Mainas was divided into ten regions, each theoretically administered by two missionaries, one located in the region's head mission and the other continually moving between its other missions. At best, outlying missions were left unattended for several months, but recruitment difficulties meant they were often unsupervised for longer periods. Between 1661 and the end of the century the number of missionaries working in the field did not exceed twelve, and more commonly there were eight or nine.[29] Individual missions were also distant from any moral, practical, or military support. The Roamaina missions, for example, were located twelve days' journey from San Francisco de Borja, from which the quickest route to Quito through Jaén took three months or more.[30] Even if the Indians remained in the missions, the process of converting them and creating viable communities was hampered by traditional hostilities[31] and the diversity of languages spoken, not only within the region, but sometimes within one mission. The Jesuits made extensive use of interpreters, but they also resorted to the use of Quechua, which the Indians found easier to comprehend than Spanish.[32]

The history of missions in the province of Mainas is difficult to establish in detail. The main sources are the accounts of Jesuits who worked in the region, which were written either as monographs or as letters that were later published in collected volumes or used to compile histories of the Jesuit order.[33] Only for the frontier region do a few secular accounts exist. The sources available are therefore partial in perspective and often frustratingly lacking in ethnographic detail. However, the impact of disease, which clearly threatened the future of the missions, is reported and considered in greater detail than might be expected. The partial record is rendered more difficult to interpret by the multiplicity of names for Indian groups, whose cultural and linguistic affiliations are often uncertain, many of whom migrated during the early colonial period. Similarly, the sites of missions, which often changed over time, are difficult to locate from the vague geographical descriptions contained in accounts. The complete history of Jesuit missions in the province of Mainas still needs to be written, though the studies by Sweet and Grohs represent bold attempts to outline missionary efforts and their demographic effects among different cultural-linguistic groups.[34] As in Sweet's study, the main concern here is with the general impact of missionization on the population of the region. No attempt will be made, therefore, to trace individual mission populations, which in any case probably never represented at maximum more than half the region's total population. For this the reader should refer to the Jesuit histories of the province. However, in order to place the impact of mission-

ization in its temporal and geographical context, a brief outline of the
development of missions fields during the seventeenth century will follow.

At first Jesuit efforts were concentrated around San Francisco de Borja
and to the south of the Marañón. Between 1638 and 1654 five main missions and several anejos were founded in the Huallaga Valley. Meanwhile
in 1653 the mission of Santa María de Ucayali was established among the
Cocama. The latter had been contacted by Jesuit missionaries at least a
decade before, when it was estimated they numbered 10,000 to 12,000.[35]
Although all the missions established prior to 1654 were located on the
right bank of the Marañón and its tributaries, in fact tribes living on the
river Pastaza had had earlier encounters with Jesuits during the punitive
expeditions that followed the Maina revolt of 1635. It was not until 1654,
however, that expeditions among the Roamaina and Zapa resulted in the
establishment of Santos Angeles de Roamainas and San Salvador de los
Zapas, followed shortly by that of Nombre de Jesús de los Coronados.[36]

By 1660 the Jesuits had established missions downriver as far as the
Ucayali on the right bank and as far as the Pastaza on the left bank, and as
such they contained only a small proportion of those who inhabited the
Marañón and its tributaries from the Pongo de Manseriche to its confluence with the Napo. Father Francisco de Figueroa estimated that the
former region contained 60,000 souls divided into forty "provinces," each
containing between 1,000 and 5,000 souls or more.[37] There were undoubtedly many more who had not come to his notice. Father Figueroa claimed
that by 1660 over 6,880 Indians had been baptized, though in the same
year more than 10,000 Indians were receiving Christian instruction.[38]
These figures suggest that only about 10 or 15 percent of the Indian
population was living in the missions. Figueroa stressed that his figures
were not exaggerated. He worked in the province of Mainas for twenty-
four years before his martyrdom in 1666, and his population estimates are
probably a reasonably reliable guide to the size of the population with
which he was familiar. However, his knowledge of populations on the
Lower Marañón and the Tigre, which he included in his estimates, but
where missions were yet to be established, was probably superficial. Juan
de Velasco later made bolder claims for Jesuits efforts. He maintained that
by 1663 the Jesuits had founded sixteen missions, which in 1660 contained
100,000 Indians.[39] This figure appears highly exaggerated, though might
be more acceptable as an estimate for the numbers both inside and outside
the missions for the region as a whole.

In the mid-1660s missions were established among the Oa and Abijira,
but they were short-lived because the former soon passed to secular control and the latter was burned by its inhabitants, who subsequently fled.[40]
The mission of San Javier de los Gaes achieved greater success. Founded
in 1669, it soon had 7,000 inhabitants (according to Velasco's claims), and

by 1686 at least 4,030 Indians had been baptized.[41] Meanwhile Father Juan Lorenzo Lucero consolidated Jesuit control of the Huallaga Valley, so that in 1682 there were nine missions south of the Marañón, to which he had attracted an additional 4,000 souls.[42] The most important of these was Nueva Cartagena de Santiago de la Laguna, which became the residence of the superior of the order and the main base from which missionary expeditions were mounted further down the Marañón.

Velasco claims that by 1683 thirty-three missions had been established, but because 66,000 people, young and old, had recently died in an epidemic in 1680, they contained only 15,000 neophytes and 19,000 who were under Christian instruction but had not been baptized.[43] These figures have been judged by Grohs as highly exaggerated.[44] They suggest individual mission populations averaging between 1,000 and 3,000 Indians, depending on whether or not the impact of the 1680 epidemic is taken into account. While some mission populations did exceed 1,000, most were smaller.[45] However, the average number of about 500 neophytes in each mission in 1683 implied by Velasco's figures appears consistent with the annual number of baptisms revealed in 1686 by a visita ordered by the bishop of Quito, Alonso de la Peña y Montenegro. The visita recorded that since 1638, altogether 107,035 Indians in the region had been baptized, suggesting that individual missions were registering several hundred baptisms a year.[46] Probably most of those who had been baptized would not have been alive in 1686—indeed many would have died in the epidemics of 1660, 1669, and 1680—but given the expansion of the mission field, the number of 15,000 baptized and living in the missions in 1683 is fairly consistent with this visita and, given active recruitment in the interim, is not totally out of line with the Father Figueroa's figure of 3,100 for 1660.[47]

The expansion of Jesuit activities further east was retarded by the shortage of missionaries. Up until 1682 thirty-two Jesuits had worked in the area, the majority for a short time, but in that year only four missionaries were active in the region. Nevertheless, it is clear that by the early 1680s many groups further downriver, such as the Omagua, Urarina, and Yameo, as well as others in the Upper Ucayali, had been contacted, and in anticipation of an expansion in the mission field, small numbers had been transferred to missions in the Upper Marañón, notably to Santiago de la Laguna, for training as interpreters.[48] In 1685 new missionaries arrived, and new mission fields were opened up. One, under the direction of Father Enrique Richter, extended Jesuit control into the Upper Ucayali, where nine reducciones were established.[49] Here he came into conflict with Franciscans, who in 1689 obtained a royal decree giving them jurisdiction of the Upper and Lower Ucayali, and following his martyrdom, Jesuit activities in that area ceased. The other mission field was opened up by Father Samuel Fritz, whose efforts were concentrated among the Omagua and

Yurimagua who in 1681 had sought Jesuit protection from Portuguese enslavers. During his lifetime Father Fritz settled 26,000 Indians in thirty-nine settlements in the lower Marañón, Amazon, and Napo, twenty-eight of them among the Omagua.[50]

The rapid expansion of Jesuit activities in the late seventeenth century undermined the stability of the missions. The continued extension of the mission field in the face of the persistent shortage of priests contributed to the collapse of its organization and the decay of the missions under the strains of epidemics, revolts, and raids by the Portuguese.[51] Chantre y Herrera notes that while in 1656 the Jesuits possessed thirteen villages with about 15,000 families, by the time they were expelled in 1768, they had eighty reducciones with 15,000 souls.[52] By that time, however, the mission field extended into the Lower Marañón, Napo, and Aguarico, which had not been under Jesuit control in the mid–seventeenth century. In 1768 the original mission field of the Upper Marañón and Pastaza contained sixteen reducciones with 8,784 souls, which, if equated with families as implied by Chantre y Herrera's observation, would signify that the mission population in these areas had fallen by nearly one-half during the century.

DEMOGRAPHIC TRENDS IN THE PROVINCE OF MAINAS

While it is clear that the Indian population in the province of Mainas fell during the early colonial period, a quantitative assessment of the decline is fraught with difficulties. Most contemporary accounts provide population estimates for mission populations only, and these are generally given for individual missions for particular dates rather than for the region as whole. As such, it is not easy to obtain a detailed picture of regional demographic trends, given that mission populations, to say nothing of those outside, fluctuated with epidemics, famines, desertions, attacks by hostile neighbors, enslaving raids, and the addition of new converts. The instability of mission populations is particularly characteristic for the late seventeenth and early eighteenth centuries. The few estimates existing for the province of Mainas as a whole are scarcely more helpful, since the extent of the active mission field changed over time. Furthermore, what is of concern here are demographic trends not only in the missions but for the province as a whole, for which little evidence exists. One way forward is to examine the likely impact of epidemics, entradas, and other factors on the estimated aboriginal population and to compare the resulting figures with the few existing contemporary observations.

Missionaries were unanimous in identifying epidemics as the major factor underlying the failure of the missions to prosper. As early as 1661 Father Figueroa judged that since first contact, many Indian groups in the province of Mainas had been reduced to under half their size, largely because of repeated epidemics.[53] The Jesuits were aware of their own role in spreading disease. Father Figueroa commented that missionaries should go equipped not only with axes and knives to help the Indians build their houses and clear the land, but also with hoes to open up graves and bury the dead.[54] The Indians also identified Spaniards with disease to the extent that they were said to fall ill at the mere sound of a gun.[55]

On first contact the Indians suffered from dysentery, catarrh, and colds,[56] but in addition major epidemics assaulted Indian communities at almost regular ten-year intervals, carrying off whole villages like dragnets (Table 27).[57] The first documented epidemic of smallpox to afflict the region struck San Francisco de Borja in 1642, when it raged for six months and 200 or 300 Indians in surrounding villages died.[58] However, it seems likely that by that date the western frontier at least had been affected by disease. The gobernación of Yaguarzongo and Pacamoros was hit by epidemics in the 1580s, and enslaving expeditions from that region may well have carried diseases further east. The fact that children were worst hit by the epidemic in 1642 suggests that the population had been previously affected. Indeed, without specifying particular diseases, Father Figueroa noted that epidemics had contributed to the decline in the Indian population around Borja prior to 1642,[59] and Father Zarate claimed that "within a few years" of the founding of the city its surrounding Indian population had been reduced to one-half or one-third by "catarros y viruelas."[60] Whether he was referring to the 1642 epidemic or an earlier one is not clear.

In 1654 an expedition led by Martín de la Riva Herrera, which will be discussed in more detail below, carried disease into the province of Mainas from Moyobamba.[61] It devastated missions in the Huallaga Valley, where in 1661 only 100 Indians remained in the mission of Santa María of the 600 there had been in 1649.[62] From there the same disease was carried to the Pastaza, where it had equally devastating effects on the Roamaina-Zapa. Between February and July 1656 Father Figueroa baptized 230 children and 125 adults, of whom 60 had died by the end of that period.[63] The missionaries were bewildered by the excessive devastation caused by the epidemic and compiled a special report.[64] They variously thought that it was aggravated by the Indians' diet, their practice of sleeping in damp locations, by the hot, humid climate, and by their attempts to cool the fevers by immersing themselves in the rivers.[65] One account identified the epidemic as one of smallpox and garrotillo, which was said to be raging in the montaña at the time.[66] It was characterized by high fevers, body pains, and vomiting and affected Spaniards as well as Indians. Most likely it was a particularly virulent strain of smallpox, whose effects were exacerbated by food shortages experienced on the expedition.[67] The "garrotillo" identi-

Table 27. Epidemics in the Province of Mainas during the
Seventeenth Century

Date	Epidemic	Impact and Source
Early 1620s	*catarros y viruelas*	Several years after the founding of San Francisco de Borja, the population was reduced by one-half or one-third (Figueroa, *Relación de las misiones*, 15, 384).
1642	smallpox	Rages for six months in San Francisco de Borja (Figueroa, *Relación de las misiones*, 25–26; Jouanen, *Compañía de Jesús*, 1:346).
1645–46	smallpox	Among Omagua villages of the Amazon (Cruz, "Nuevo descubrimiento," 188–89).
1656	smallpox and *garrotillo*	Devastates the Roamaina-Zapa (Figueroa, *Relación de las misiones*, 85, 109; Jouanen, *Compañía de Jesús*, 1:398; "Autos fechos," 436–37, Velásquez de Medrano 22.1.1657).
1660	measles and German measles (*alfombrilla*)	Breaks out in Borja and spreads to the missions. Velasco maintains it killed 44,000 (Figueroa, *Relación de las misiones*, 159; Chantre y Herrera, *Historia de las misiones*, 205–6; Velasco, *Historia del reino*, 3:450).
1660	measles and *mal del valle*	Strikes Roamaina-Zapa (Figueroa, *Relación de las misiones*, 149; Jouanen, *Compañía de Jesús*, 1:399).
Mid-1660s	*recias cuartanas*	Afflict the Oa (Maroni, "Noticias auténticas," 29:119; Jouanen, *Compañía de Jesús*, 1:438; Astrain, *Historia de la Compañía*, 6, lib. 3, cap. 9:609–10).
1669	unidentified epidemic	According to Velasco, kills 20,000; some 6,000 Abijira and Oa die (Velasco, *Historia del reino*, 3:450).
1680	smallpox	Begins in the Upper Huallaga Valley; according to Velasco, kills 66,000 (ARSI NRQ 15 1 fols. 79–80 Lucero 3.6.1681; Figueroa, *Relación de las misiones*, 146; Chantre y Herrera, *Historia de las misiones*, 276; Velasco, *Historia del reino*, 3:369, 450–51).
1689	unidentified epidemic	In the Upper Ucayali (Maroni, "Noticias auténticas," 30:144–45).

fied is unlikely to have been diphtheria, since the latter is generally associated with large urban populations and is not common in the tropics; more likely it was a secondary infection associated with smallpox.[68] After the epidemic the Roamaina were described as suffering continual catarrh, colds, and pains in the side,[69] and in 1660 they were struck by measles and "mal del valle."[70]

In 1660 the province of Mainas was struck by another epidemic, in which Figueroa implies over 3,000 Indians died.[71] This time it was measles and German measles, described as being of a worse kind than in Europe. It broke out in Borja and spread to the missions, killing many adults.[72] Velasco estimated this epidemic claimed 44,000 rather than 3,000 victims.[73] While at first glance Velasco's figure may appear highly exaggerated, the previous year the same epidemic purportedly claimed 15,000 lives in the city of Quito alone.[74] According to Velasco, another unspecified epidemic in 1669 cost a further 20,000 lives.[75] In 1680 another major epidemic, which was described as smallpox "complicadas con otros males," broke out in the Upper Huallaga.[76] There the epidemic lasted from October to the beginning of May, killing Indians of all ages and encouraging 600 to seek baptism and confirmation. Velasco maintains that altogether the epidemic claimed 66,000 lives.[77] Finally, in 1689 another epidemic broke out in the Upper Ucayali.[78] The credibility of these accounts will be discussed more fully below. Before leaving the discussion concerning the incidence of epidemics, it is worth reiterating that it is unlikely that the tropical fevers played a significant role in the depopulation of the Oriente, including the province of Mainas, during the sixteenth and seventeenth centuries.[79]

Old World epidemics took a heavy toll of the Indian population wherever they spread, but their effects were not uniform. Their impact was influenced, among other things, by the size and distribution of the Indian population. Because of the short periods of communicability of most acute infections,[80] "fade-outs" are common where settlements are small and dispersed. Even though a network of communications developed between the missions, for the most part, travel in the Oriente was slow and contacts limited, such that many diseases must have died out before they could reach new hosts. Acute infections thus failed to become endemic diseases of childhood, instead taking a limited but regular toll of the population. Rather, groups in the Oriente remained disease-free for long periods until infections were reintroduced from the outside, when all those who had not been previously infected would be hit, resulting in higher levels of morbidity and mortality that affected adults as well as children. This pattern of infection contrasts with the sierra, where by the early seventeenth century diseases were becoming endemic.

Missionization not only brought disease but heightened its impact. By concentrating Indians in the missions, it brought them into closer, more sustained contact, while the addition of new converts continuously replenished and enlarged the pool of susceptibles. The spread of disease was further enhanced by the propensity of Indians to flee the missions once an outbreak occurred. For example, when the 1680 smallpox epidemic hit Santiago de la Laguna, its inhabitants took to seventy-five canoes and fled downriver, where they probably spread the disease among the Omagua.[81]

Conditions within the missions also amplified the impact of disease. Missions, it will be shown, were constantly fighting food shortages. The sedentary existence imposed on mission Indians led to soil exhaustion and depletion of local game, threatening calorific intake and creating shortages of protein. At the same time sanitary conditions probably deteriorated with the concentration of Indians in large permanent settlements and as social breakdown discouraged attention to personal hygiene. Insanitary conditions would have encouraged the spread of intestinal parasites, and poor-quality diets may have increased susceptibility to disease, particularly among infants.[82] To complete the vicious circle, epidemics in turn affected nutrition. The severest famines followed in the wake of epidemics, when Indians were unable to cultivate the land, and being largely unfamiliar with methods of storing food, were unable to fall back on accumulated surpluses. The Jesuits were well aware of the adverse demographic and psychological effects of disease and did their best to try to cure the sick. They trained some Indians to be surgeons and to let blood, a common prescription at the time.[83] Nevertheless, the medical care available was extremely rudimentary and probably an inadequate substitute for native forms of curing in which the Indians had greater faith. Neither did it compensate for the lack of social support, so critical for survival, that followed from the socially fragmented character of the missions. The "loss of the will to survive" must have hastened the death of many.[84]

Epidemics not only contributed significantly to mortality rates but also affected fertility levels. A group's ability to recover would have depended not only on the numbers dying but also the size of the group and the particular members affected. Pregnancy loss or the death of a child might be compensated for within a short time, perhaps within less than a year, but the loss of an adult usually has a greater impact on fertility, since it results in an immediate reduction in reproductive capacity and the loss of valuable reproductive years as new partners are sought.[85] Adult losses would have been particularly difficult to accommodate in small communities in the Oriente, where the choice of partners was by definition limited. Any cultural restrictions on remarriage and the suitability of spouses would have posed additional obstacles to the formation of new unions. As such, the reproductive lives of some individuals might have been severely curtailed. In preindustrial societies high fertility levels are required to maintain the population in the face of high levels of infant mortality and low life expectancy, so that the loss of reproductive capacity in terms of even a small number of persons or years might prove critical to survival.[86] Once new unions had been formed, the impact of certain diseases, such as smallpox and mumps, would have continued to be felt through their effects on fecundity.[87] As will be demonstrated, these influences often combined with the psychological effects of missionization to induce lower levels of fertility.

There seems no doubt that epidemics were a major factor in the decline of Indian populations in the Oriente. Although Velasco's estimates of mission populations and the numbers killed in epidemics—44,000 in 1660, then 20,000 in 1669 and 66,000 in 1680[88]—appear exaggerated, the *proportions* killed in single epidemics are not impossible,[89] especially given that active recruitment continually supplied the missions with new susceptibles ready for reinfection. Furthermore, the high proportions dying are corroborated by contemporary accounts of the impact of particular epidemics on individual missions. From Velasco's controversial figures, it is possible to calculate that the impact of these three major epidemics on the *total* population may have been to reduce it by 65 percent.[90] Although the dispersed settlement pattern meant that not every mission or Indian community would have been hit by every epidemic, the percentage decline attributed to epidemics will not be reduced, since it is necessary to take account of their impact on fertility levels and the indirect effects of high levels of adult mortality on demographic trends. Indeed, it will be remembered that Father Figueroa judged that as early as 1661 epidemics had reduced the precontact population by half.[91]

After epidemics, the failure of mission populations to expand was blamed on entradas. These were conducted for a variety of reasons. Some sought new converts, others aimed at rounding up fugitive encomienda or mission Indians, while others followed revolts and were primarily punitive in character. In some cases entradas had multiple objectives. Those aimed at suppressing revolts might at the same time result in the punishment of the main instigators, the enslavement of small numbers of fugitive Indians, and the establishment of a new mission. Missionary entradas were generally conducted by one or two missionaries protected by a handful of soldiers, whereas punitive expeditions could involve twenty to fifty soldiers, a missionary, and several hundred converted Indians. In the latter case the plan of campaign had to be approved by the superior of the order, but the missionaries could not refuse to go and were not supposed to intervene in the action.[92] Although they did not always agree with the tactics employed by the secular authorities and were sometimes critical of the less than altruistic motives of the soldiers,[93] they were forced to be pragmatic, given their dependence on them for protection, both from the Indians and from

Portuguese enslavers. Many soldiers, disgruntled by harsh living conditions, poor pay, and being far from home, were only interested in enriching themselves through the acquisition of slaves or other booty. Father Figueroa argued that a permanent *presidio* of twenty-four to thirty skilled, well-armed soldiers paid for by the Crown would significantly advance missionary efforts.[94] In the event, only a few soldiers were provided, and while they wreaked havoc among Indian communities, their limited presence did not deter Portuguese incursions into the Upper Amazon and Lower Marañón.[95]

Apart from entradas involving missionaries, others were conducted by vecinos from frontier towns with the aims of capturing fugitive encomienda Indians or acquiring slaves. Indian groups located nearest the Spanish frontier towns were the worst affected. The Maina were subject to annual enslaving raids by vecinos first from Santiago de las Montañas and Santa María de Nieva, and later from Borja,[96] and the Coronado and Oa were depopulated by raids from Borja and Macas.[97] These periodic entradas were a constant drain on frontier communities, and they gradually retreated eastward where they became acculturated to the Zaparo.[98]

Particularly noteworthy and disruptive to missionary activities in the province of Mainas was the attempt by Don Martín de la Riva Herrera to establish a town within its jurisdiction.[99] He was corregidor of Cajamarca and pretender to the disputed post of governor, left vacant on the death of Pedro Vaca de la Cadena.[100] While the dispute was being resolved, the Crown granted Riva Herrera passage through Maina territory in order to establish a town in the provinces that "bordered upon the Marañón."[101] In 1654 he left Moyobamba, passing through the Jevero missions and those in the Huallaga Valley, where he conscripted Indians to serve on a number of disastrous entradas among the Jívaro in which many Indians were killed.[102] He retreated to Borja in 1656 and from there directed his attention toward the Roamaina and Zapa, among whom he established the town of Nueva Santander half a day's journey up the Pastaza. He ordered the residents of Borja and Santiago de las Montañas to move there, and when it was founded on 25 July 1656, it possessed thirty-three settlers.[103] Most were given encomiendas composed of Indians from the disestablished mission of Santos Angeles de Roamainas, who were settled in four villages around the town.[104] The entradas brought epidemic disease, while ill-treatment by the town's citizens caused many to flee. Hoping to retain control of their jurisdiction, the Jesuits severely criticized Riva Herrera's entradas, which they claimed had undone in one year all that had been accomplished in twenty.[105] Their successful representations resulted in the town being dismantled, in the remaining Indians being returned to the missions, and in Mauricio Vaca de Evan being proclaimed governor.[106]

Punitive entradas were clearly more disruptive to Indian communities than evangelizing expeditions. They involved larger numbers of soldiers and Indian militia, and resulted in more Indians being killed or enslaved. Punitive entradas were announced by the firing of a gun and generally involved combat and considerable loss of life. Occasionally several hundred Indians might be killed or captured, with the instigators of revolts normally being executed.[107] However, the lack of decisiveness in victory might result in many being released subsequently.[108] More often smaller numbers were taken. They often included a few Indians for use as interpreters on future entradas as well as any who were not from the local area.[109] Probably a significant proportion of those captured were taken in small numbers on many small but unrecorded entradas; their numbers are difficult to estimate.

Perhaps more devastating, but limited to the very lower reaches of the Marañón and largely affecting the Amazon and Lower Napo, were the enslaving raids of the Portuguese. From 1640, when Portugal became independent of Spain, Portuguese enslaving raids grew in intensity as demands for labor increased, and in 1686 they were given official sanction.[110] In 1681 the Omagua sought Jesuit protection from Portuguese enslavers, but in the absence of effective military support, the missions failed to stem the raids. Losses were particularly great in the early eighteenth century, when several thousand Omagua and Yurimagua settled in missions were enslaved and the missions forced to relocate further up the Marañón.[111] Since these raids occurred mainly outside the area and period under study, their impact will not be discussed in further detail.

Estimating the numbers directly affected by entradas is not easy, but given that most villages did not exceed several hundred in population and their inhabitants often received prior warning and fled, the numbers killed or enslaved on any one occasion would have rarely exceeded a hundred. Entradas had their most sustained impact on the Maina, Andoa, Murato, Coronado, Oa, and Roamaina, who were located nearest the frontier of Spanish settlement. Groups along the Lower Marañón may have also suffered from raids from Borja, but they were mainly affected at a later date by Portuguese raids up the Amazon. The more populous, concentrated settlements of the Omagua on exposed riverbanks and islands may have suffered greater losses. Indians living closest to the frontier and along the major rivers were the most vulnerable to capture, and as a consequence they began to retreat to less exposed and often interfluvial areas. While some communities were drained almost to the point of extinction, in other areas entradas had more localized and short-lived demographic effects. Sweet argues that the numbers killed or taken as slaves in the whole of the Upper Amazon Valley probably never exceeded 1 percent of the total population per year,[112] which on his estimates suggests annual losses of 1,000 to 2,000. These figures are based largely on the impact of

Portuguese enslaving raids, and it is doubtful that Spanish entradas captured more than 100 or 200 Indians.[113] Nevertheless, the effects of entradas were felt at an early date. From the mid–sixteenth century, expeditions were conducted from the frontier towns, and evidence from 1580 indicates that not insubstantial numbers of Andoa had already been incorporated into encomiendas around Santiago de las Montañas.[114] Most likely they also contained some Maina, although they cannot be identified specifically. Although in reality the enslavement process would have been discontinuous in time and place, between 1560 and 1620 an average of maybe fifty Indians a year may have been captured and transferred to Spanish towns.

After the founding of Borja, raids increased in frequency and extended to more distant groups such as the Coronado, Oa, and Gae.[115] Entradas among the Maina were said to take place every year,[116] in addition to which major punitive entradas were conducted at irregular intervals. Between 1620 and 1700, maybe 100 Indians were captured annually, but some captives would have remained in the region in the service of local vecinos. This suggests that between 1560 and 1700 a total of 11,000 Indians may have been enslaved. The impact of entradas was greatest in the frontier regions, but even in other regions, their cumulative effects might have been substantial. Furthermore, as Sweet recognizes, the direct losses associated with entradas might have been less significant in demographic terms than the indirect effects of the economic and social changes produced by the permanent removal of community members or their temporary employment as conscripts on expeditions. All mission Indians between eighteen and fifty were required to form militias, but the most noteworthy auxiliaries were the Jevero, who sought Jesuit protection from enslaving raids from Moyobamba and remained loyal allies. The Jevero were employed in the suppression of the Maina rebellion,[117] on entradas among the Cocama and Jívaro, and on many other occasions. Friendly Maina and Cocamilla were also involved.[118] The numbers of auxiliaries, particularly on punitive entradas, could run into several hundreds,[119] and expeditions might last several years.[120] They were highly disruptive to subsistence activities and family life, threatening the survival of Indian communities in the same way as epidemics.

Another factor identified as contributing to population decline was intertribal warfare.[121] Warfare among and between tribes in the province of Mainas had been a common feature of life in pre-Columbian times. Hostile relations existed between the Maina and Roamaina,[122] between the Gae and Coronado,[123] and even between factions of the same group. Raids were mounted for revenge or stimulated by the utterances of a shaman, as well as to acquire booty, notably women, and (in the colonial period) metal tools.[124] In the colonial period intertribal wars acquired new dimensions. By employing Indian auxiliaries on entradas, the Spanish not only exploited existing enmities but generated new hostilities. In addition, sickness and death were attributed to sorcery, which required revenge, so that the introduction of Old World diseases substantially increased the potential for conflict.[125] While one might be skeptical of missionary reports identifying tribal wars as a major factor in the decline of the Indian population, there seems little doubt that outside the missions, they increased in intensity.

The process of missionization aimed at restructuring Indian life by creating miniature versions of Spanish towns in which Indians would be taught "civilized" ways and made loyal to church and state. Indians were to live in sedentary communities, practice agriculture or trades, be governed by elected leaders, and adopt the Catholic faith. For those in the missions it spelled the certain destruction of their culture, but for those outside it also heralded major changes, which in both cases had important, but often subtle, demographic consequences.

Social groupings became fragmented as a result of missionization. Missions rarely coincided with former Indian communities but contained individuals drawn from different cultural-linguistic groups often brought into the missions on separate occasions. Sometimes, however, previous conflicts or persistent hostilities necessitated the establishment of separate missions.[126] More often as their populations declined, distinct groups were brought together as missions were amalgamated.[127] The political organization imposed by the Jesuits failed to compensate for the lack of social cohesion. Each mission possessed a gobernador who was normally appointed for life, subject to satisfactory service. Where there was more than one native leader, as was often the case, the leader with the greatest support or with the largest number of subjects was appointed,[128] though for the purpose of organizing the militia, the authority of distinct native leaders continued to be recognized.[129] In addition, a cabildo was normally established in each mission with the avowed aim of training Indians in self-government. However, since elected Indian leaders had to have Jesuit approval and alcaldes could not punish minor offences without permission, they functioned as instruments of Jesuit control rather than expressions of Indian political aspirations.[130] Although little detailed information exists on how life in the missions was organized, it is clear that the rigorous and tedious regimes introduced by the Jesuits were resented to the point that they provoked wholesale revolts.[131] The social cohesion of mission communities was largely artificial, so that when left unsupervised or abandoned, Indians fled to join or establish more viable communities. While this discussion may seem marginal to the consideration of the impact of missionization on demographic trends, it shows how the missions severely eroded native culture but failed to provide a viable substitute that could promote forms social and economic well-being that would enable groups to recover from the effects of epidemics and entradas, and later withstand secularization.

Missionization affected family life and had important but unquantifiable effects on reproduction. Father Figueroa noted that mission families numbered three to five persons, so that 200 families comprised between 800 and 1,000 people.[132] This suggests that the missions were maintaining themselves. However, multiplication factors of 4 or 5 were commonly used to estimate total populations where more detailed information was lacking, and other evidence indicates that fertility levels were low. The Jesuits brought major changes to native marriage patterns, added to which were the indirect effects of epidemics and enslaving raids. Little information exists on the regulation of contact between the sexes, though it is known that the Jesuits encouraged early marriage and attempted to suppress polygamy.[133] Even though polygamy was not widely practiced except among the Maina, its suppression was deeply resented and indeed provoked the Abijira to kill Father Pedro Suárez.[134] Whether or not the imposition of monogamy significantly affected the fertility rate is not clear. Polygamy functioned to promote reproduction and sustain the population where warfare resulted in high levels of male mortality. While monogamy is generally considered to promote higher levels of fertility than polygamy,[135] in such circumstances it would have reduced the reproductive potential of the group, since many women would have been left without partners. However, within the missions tribal warfare was suppressed, so that in theory the sex ratio should have become more balanced and monogamy more practicable. However, because men were more often killed on entradas and more able to escape missionization or subsequently flee, women and children were probably overrepresented in early mission populations. Indeed the sex ratio within the missions may not have been very different from pre-Columbian times, and in these circumstances the imposition of monogamy would have resulted in reproductive resources being underused. As the missions matured, the sex ratio seems to have evened out, with most adults being married, but for reasons that will be explained, the proportion of children declined.[136] Outside the missions the excess of women may well have been inflated further by increased warfare, though compensated for in some cases by the greater likelihood of them being removed to missions. Much of this is reasoned speculation, but it is clear that missionary activity destabilized Indian communities and brought changes to sex ratios and marriage patterns that are likely to have threatened the biological and social reproduction of some groups.

Not only did marriage patterns change, but missionization, entradas, and epidemics broke up family units, often permanently, disrupting reproduction and contributing to lower levels of fertility. To this must be added the psychological impact of the loss of loved ones and the stresses generated by changed economic and social circumstances. We can only infer that the fertility rate of nonmissionized groups fell, but there is more concrete evidence that this was the experience of mission Indians. Missionaries were frustrated to find that whereas in their own communities Indians were very fertile, when moved to the missions, they failed to reproduce. Father Andrés Zarate claimed that women brought into the missions failed to conceive for eight or ten years, a situation he attributed to being removed from their native lands.[137] Most likely he was describing amenorrhea brought on by stress or possibly, though less likely, malnutrition. Increased levels of abortion, practiced in secret in the missions, may also have contributed to low birthrates. Infanticide was also practiced as it had been in pre-Columbian times.[138] Whether by intention or not, it functioned to maintain child spacing. Attempts by missionaries to suppress it had the potential to raise the fertility rate, but not significantly, since infanticide was generally limited to particular situations, such as for deformed children or multiple births.[139] Furthermore, in the missions any increase is likely to have been countered by high levels of infant and child mortality resulting from inadequate food supplies, which among other things may have increased their susceptibility to disease.[140] Whatever the causes, it is clear that many infants failed to reach adulthood. Figueroa maintained that by 1660 some 3,000 children under the age of seven had been baptized, of whom over half had died before they became adult.[141] However, these losses reflected not only adverse conditions for infant survival in the missions but also the impact of epidemics. Most significantly they indicate that high levels of fertility would have been needed to maintain the population. For groups to survive in their new environment, fertility rates needed to increase, but all the evidence suggests that if anything, they declined.

Changes to Indian subsistence patterns brought about directly or indirectly by missionization also influenced demographic trends. While the missions were constantly fighting food shortages, probably few Indians died as a direct result of starvation; rather, the effects of malnutrition were felt indirectly through lowered resistance to disease. The Jesuits considered a sedentary existence based on permanent cultivation to be more "civilized" than a nomadic one based on the exploitation of wild food resources; it also facilitated Indian control and conversion. In pre-Columbian times few, if any, Indian groups in the Oriente were completely sedentary, as most subsisted on a combination of swidden cultivation, hunting, fishing, and collecting, and they shifted their settlements as resources were depleted. Missions, in contrast, were conceived as large permanent settlements around which the Indians would cultivate the land on a permanent basis. The most critical time for the missions was between their foundation and the first harvest.[142] The Jesuits were aware of the need to establish a firm subsistence base and hence ordered lands to be cleared for cultivation as soon as, and even before, missions were founded.[143] The metal tools they introduced made forest clearance easier, and Indians often joined the missions to acquire them. They also introduced cattle, which were said to thrive well and were raised primarily for milk and some cheese.[144] Each mission aimed to possess twelve to twenty cattle. Most crops grown were familiar to the Indians, but the Jesuits were anxious to encourage the cultivation of cotton for the manufacture of "decent" clothing.[145] Despite good intentions, the subsistence base of the missions was ill conceived. Mission settlements were often considerably larger than the communities from which they drew their converts. Given the poor quality of most soils in the region and the consequent need to shift plots regularly, lands around the missions were often insufficient to support them, with the result that food shortages were common.[146] The lack of food stemmed in part from low yields related to the continued cultivation of exhausted lands made necessary by the absence of able-bodied males to clear the land because of the demands of entradas. Low yields contributed to food shortages and possibly famines, particularly in the wake of epidemics, while the suppression of hunting and fishing, which afforded opportunities for fugitivism, may have led to a reduction in the consumption of protein and encouraged malnutrition. Under missionary control, these activities were conducted only by a few specially selected Indians.[147] The Maina, who had previously been heavily dependent on fish as a source of food, may have been particularly adversely affected.

Missionization and entradas affected the subsistence patterns not only of mission Indians but also of those outside. The loss of Indians of a particular sex and age either to the missions or as slaves would have disrupted the allocation of labor to different activities necessary to maintain balanced diets. Raids and entradas also had dramatic short-term effects on production.[148] Clearly raids were not new, though they may have increased in frequency, but expeditions of several hundred people were clearly more than most communities' resources could support, even for short periods. Less dramatically, the retreat of some groups to the less vulnerable interfluvial areas, where soils were less fertile and wild food resources less abundant, would have reduced their productive potential.

By now it will be clear that assessing the overall impact of Spanish settlers, soldiers, and missionaries on the Indian population of the province of Mainas is extremely difficult. The problem stems in part from the inadequacy of the sources and in part from the complexity of the processes at work. Nevertheless, epidemics and entradas clearly had major impacts, although they were not uniform. The accompanying table (Table 28) is a preliminary attempt to assess their impacts by taking into account the location of different Indian groups, the time at which they were subject

Table 28. Population Estimates for the Province of Mainas during the Colonial Period

Ethnic group	Estimated contact population	Lost to entradas	Lost in epidemics to 1700	Assumed percent lost in epidemics post-1660[a]	Estimate for 1700	Estimate for 1800[b]
Maina	12,000	3,000	4,500	50 (pre-1660)	1,575	1,000
			2,925	65		
Andoa-Murato	8,000–10,000	2,000	1,200–1,600	20 (pre-1660)	1,680–2,240	1,000
			3,120–4,160	65		
Roamaina-Zapa	8,000–10,000	2,000	3,900–5,200	65	2,100–2,800	Extinct
Coronado-Oa	8,000–10,000	1,000	4,550–5,850	65	2,450–3,150	1,000–2,000
Abijira	6,000–8,000	1,000	3,250–4,550	65	1,750–2,450	2,000–3,000
Gae-Semigae	6,000–8,000	500	3,575–4,875	65	1,925–2,625	3,000–4,000
Urarina	6,000–8,000	300	3,705–5,005	65	1,995–2,695	2,000–3,000
Yameo	10,000–12,000	300	6,305–7,605	65	3,395–4,095	2,000–3,000
Zapara	3,000–4,000	400	1,690–2,340	65	910–1,260	Not given
Iquito	5,000–6,000	400	920–1,120	20	3,680–4,480	Not given
Pinche	3,000–4,000	50	590–790	20	2,360–3,160	1,000
Payagua	8,000–10,000	50	1,590–1,990	20	6,360–7,960	4,000–6,000
Total	83,000–102,000	11,000	41,820–52,510		30,180–38,490	17,000–24,000

[a] Calculated after the numbers lost in entradas have been subtracted. Percentages for earlier periods are shown for the Maina and Andoa-Murato.
[b] Sweet, "Upper Amazon Valley," 103.

to entradas and missionization, and the intensity of their effects. The average population loss attributable to epidemics has been estimated at about 65 percent,[149] but this needs to be modified in a number of cases. This figure does not take into account any epidemics prior to 1660 that are known to have affected the Maina and possibly the Andoa and Murato, who were subject to entradas prior to that date. For this period an additional loss of 50 percent is estimated for the Maina on the basis of the contemporary observations on the impact of disease, and 20 percent for the Andoa and Murato, with whom there were less intense contacts. Most other Indian groups probably suffered the three major epidemics in 1660, 1669, and 1680. By the latter date not all groups had been settled in missions, but the Urarina and the Yameo are likely to been affected because of easy communications along the Marañón. A lower percentage loss is suggested for the remoter Pinche, Iquito, and Payagua, who were not settled in missions until the late seventeenth and eighteenth centuries.

Losses due to epidemics were highest nearest the frontier of Spanish settlement, as were losses from enslaving entradas. The Maina, Andoa, and Murato were captured to boost encomiendas belonging to citizens of Santiago de las Montañas and later San Francisco de Borja. As these groups were exhausted, raids extended further afield, encompassing the Coronado and Oa, and later the Gae, who were also raided from Macas and Los Quijos. The Roamaina, although located at a greater distance from the frontier, were subject to particularly disastrous campaigns in the 1650s. Similar punitive entradas among the Abijira had equally adverse effects. Although other Indian groups lost members as a consequence of entradas, there is little evidence for the numbers affected, though they are likely to have been smaller than for groups already discussed. The Zapara and Iquito were known to soldiers who participated in expeditions to the Napo Valley in the 1620s,[150] when they are likely to have suffered losses estimated here at maybe 400 for each group. In the absence of evidence to the contrary slightly lower losses of 300 are suggested for the Yameo and Urarina, whose exposed location along the Marañón is likely to have made them more vulnerable to raids from Borja, than the remoter Pinche and Payagua. Although it is possible that Old World diseases preceded entradas, in most cases the reverse was probably true. As such, the numbers lost to entradas have been deducted prior to subtracting losses in epidemics. In reality, of course, the chronologies would have been more complex.

The impact of epidemics and entradas indicate that up until 1700, some 11,000 Indians might have been lost to entradas and between 41,820 and 52,510 to epidemics. These losses represent a 63 percent decline from an estimated aboriginal population of between 83,000 and 102,000. It assumes the losses were not compensated for by natural increase. As yet there is no evidence to suggest that in pre-Columbian times the population was increasing. Even without entradas and the effects of missionization, traditionally low levels of natural increase would have made it extremely difficult for Indian populations to recover from the devastating effects of Old World diseases. As indicated, their effects were amplified and compounded by the activities of Spanish soldiers and missionaries and by the character of the Indian groups themselves. Indian tribes in the Oriente had survived by adapting to the limitations of the tropical forest environment. Although it would be wrong to assume that all had lived in harmony with their environment to the extent that their survival was never threatened and ecological destruction never took place, subsistence activities, social relations, and beliefs often functioned to ensure their survival. Even without epidemic disease, the survival of groups in the Oriente in the face of cultural changes brought by colonial rule was problematic. It is impossible to estimate the losses that might be attributable to factors other than entradas and disease, but the decline was almost certainly greater than their combined effects. While the impact of these two factors suggests a decline to between 31,180 and 38,490 in 1700, in reality the native population at that time is likely to have been even lower.

CHAPTER 18

Napo and Aguarico

> More than another thousand [Omagua and Abijira] have been cap-
> tured and taken to the province of Cofanes, of whom only six re-
> main today, because the rest have died and many of them have been
> taken to the city of Quito, where they have been sold as if they were
> slaves.
>
> Alvaro de Cárdenas, governor of Quijos, 2 March 1626[1]

Following Francisco de Orellana's expedition down the river Napo in 1541, the history of the region during the remainder of the sixteenth century remains obscure. Alcalá del Río was established in Cofán territory in 1563,[2] and the Coca Valley and upper reaches of the Napo were incorporated into the gobernación of Quijos. Nevertheless, the city appears to have been deserted almost as soon as it was founded, and during the sixteenth century attempts to reestablish it were effectively thwarted by Indian hostility.[3] The history of the Aguarico-Napo region is therefore distinct from the rest of the Quijo region in that it was never effectively settled by Spaniards and the main changes to Indian life came with enslaving raids and missionization, but even these were late to materialize.

During the sixteenth century the Spanish were aware that Omagua were living downriver from Los Quijos,[4] and following the uprising in 1578, some 200 Quijo Indians took refuge among them.[5] Meanwhile the Cofán had mounted attacks on the town of Ecija and on villages of converted Indians in the province of Sucumbíos to the north.[6] Attempts to convert Indians in the Coca Valley and further east were therefore forestalled by Indian hostility, and it was not until the late sixteenth century that the first concerted efforts were made to convert Indians in the Aguarico-Napo region. In the 1590s Father Pedro Ordóñez de Cevallos conducted two entradas among the Cofán and managed to establish eight villages with 4,000 souls.[7] At the same time, he noted that further east there were 5,000 converted "Maguas," 200 unconverted "Omaguas," and nearby 3,000 Coronado.[8] Mounting Indian hostility provoked by ill-treatment forced the Spanish to withdraw,[9] and it was not until 1599 that Jesuits began working in the region. Although missionary activities were initiated by the Jesuits, the Aguarico-Napo area alternated between Jesuit and Franciscan control. Between 1599 and 1611 Jesuits headed by Father Rafael Ferrer made six entradas among the Cofán, Omagua, Abijira, and Encabellado, establishing among the Cofán the missions of San Pedro de los Cofanes, Santa María, and Santa Cruz.[10] Whole villages were converted, and the three missions were said to contain 6,500 souls. In 1608 the town of San Pedro de Alcalá del Río was reestablished on its previous site, and it became the base from which entradas were mounted down the Aguarico and Napo rivers.[11] These first missions were destabilized by enslaving raids, especially from Ecija, and finally Jesuit activities lapsed with the martyrdom of Father Ferrer.[12] (See Map 18.)

During his administration as governor of Quijos from 1617 to 1622, Alonso de Miranda commissioned at least four entradas aimed primarily at capturing Indians to boost encomiendas. The governor was convinced that effective control of the region was dependent on a permanent Spanish presence and that this could only be achieved by creating encomiendas of sufficient size to encourage Spaniards to reside there.[13] The entradas launched from Alcalá del Río[14] were accompanied by two Jesuit fathers, Simón de Rojas and Humberto Coronado, with Brother Pedro Limón. They found the province of Abijira comprised "muchos millares de indios," enough to justify the establishment of a new town, and discovered that the Encabellado formed a "gran provincia." In 1621 a total of 100 families were settled at San Juan de los Omaguas, which was located in Omagua territory between the river Quebeno and the confluence of the Napo and Aguarico.[15] However, larger numbers were captured as slaves. It was said that on one entrada 300 Indians were enslaved and divided among the soldiers who had participated in the entrada and the vecinos of Alcalá, with the governor himself taking a quinto.[16] Initially the slaves were taken back to Alcalá to enhance encomiendas, but many died, and others were subsequently transferred to Quito and Sucumbíos. By 1623 only 30 or 40 remained in the town. In 1626 it was estimated that entradas among the Omagua and Abijira had resulted in more than 1,000 being enslaved, of whom no more than 6 remained in the province of Cofanes, the rest having died or been transferred elsewhere.[17] At that time Alcalá's six encomenderos possessed 134 tributary Indians.

What proportion the slaves represented of the total population of the Napo Valley is not clear. Witnesses on the entradas claimed that the whole region, in which they encountered Omagua, Encabellado, Abijira, Iquito, and Zapara, among others, possessed between 100,000 and 150,000 Indians.[18] While descriptions of the Indian culture that accompany this estimate clearly fit the Omagua, it is clear the figure referred to a more extensive area than that considered here and included groups living as far north as the Putumayo, such as the Seño and Becaba. While the estimates were based on firsthand knowledge gained from several years' work in the region, they may have been inflated, since the testimonies were compiled to support the governor's proposal for the creation of a new gobernación.

Initially enslaving activities were concentrated in the Coca and Upper Napo valleys, and many of those captured appear to have been Omagua-

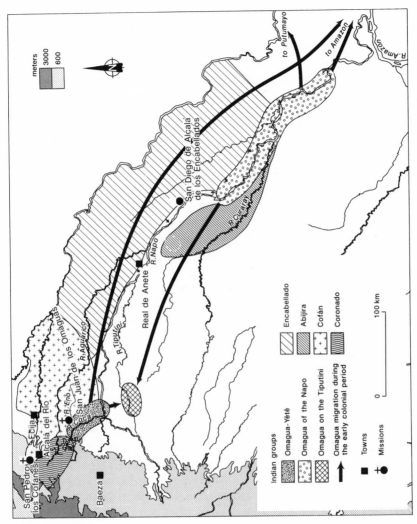

Map 18. *The Napo-Aguarico region*

Yété. The enslaving raids and the subsequent employment of captives in panning gold on the river Sunu sent the Omagua-Yété fleeing to the upper branches of the Tiputini and to the Amazon, where they were encountered by Jesuits in 1638.[19] Not all Omagua fled, however. In 1647 Father Laureano de la Cruz found some living on a tributary of the Napo between the Coca and Aguarico, where small numbers still resided into the eighteenth century.[20]

Jesuit opposition to enslaving raids persuaded the audiencia to suspend their activities in the Napo region in 1630.[21] Two years later the Franciscans were granted permission to work among groups located in the Putumayo Valley. In 1633 and 1635 they accompanied two entradas from Quito through the town of Ecija in the province of Sucumbíos. These entradas among the Seño and Becaba Indians were forced to retreat because of Indian resistance. On returning through Alcalá del Río, they learned that Captain Juan de Palacios had encountered "muchos gentiles" while conducting entradas in search of fugitive encomienda Indians in the Napo Valley. Father Pedro Pecador decided to join Captain Palacios, whom he encountered at the *real* de Anete on the river Napo, where over 8,000 Encabellado were said to have come to meet them to make peace. Father Pecador then returned to Quito, where he obtained permission for some Franciscans to accompany an expedition of thirty soldiers aimed at founding a town in Encabellado territory. In 1637 San Diego de Alcalá de los Encabellados was established, but the ill-treatment of an Indian leader resulted in Captain Palacios being killed and the mission abandoned.[22]

At the same time, two of the seven missionaries involved in the expedition, Fathers Domingo de Brieva and Andrés de Toledo, explored downriver, passing through Omagua territory to Pará. From there in 1638 they returned upriver to Quito with a Portuguese expedition composed of seventy soldiers and about 2,000 Indians. This expedition, led by General Don Pedro de Texeira, clearly had territorial aspirations as evidenced by his act of possession on the return journey. The surprising arrival of the Portuguese in Quito aroused official concern, and when the expedition returned to Brazil, two Jesuit fathers, Cristóbal Vázquez de Acuña and Andrés de Artieda, were ordered to accompany it and record the journey in detail.[23] Acuña's account remains one of the best early ethnographic descriptions of the region. He recorded that not far from the *real* de Anete was the province of the Encabellado, which extended for 180 leagues and was so highly populated that it was prey to Spanish enslaving raids.[24] It was followed by the province of the Omagua, composed of an "infinita multitud" of Indians, whose territory extended for 200 leagues, where the settlements were so continuous that the expedition scarcely lost sight of one village before it came upon another.[25]

Franciscans continued working among the Encabellado through the middle of the seventeenth century, conducting a brief expedition among the Jívaro in 1645.[26] In 1647 four Franciscans left to work among the Omagua. After reaching the island of Piramota, which they called San Pedro de Alcántara, they explored 200 leagues down the Amazon, encountering thirty-four small Omagua settlements.[27] The numbers of houses and inhabitants in a few of the settlements were recorded by Father Laureano de la Cruz, and on the basis of his observations Grohs has suggested that each village probably had about 40 "indios de lança," and each family between 3 and 5 persons, giving an estimated total population for the thirty-four villages of between 4,000 and 7,000.[28] These calculations seem reasonable, but it is necessary to note that at that time many communities had recently suffered or were suffering from smallpox. Father Cruz recorded that this outbreak and other disasters had resulted in some settlements losing one-third of their populations.[29] There is no evidence of further Franciscan activities in the Napo region until 1686, when their work resumed among the Abijira.[30]

Meanwhile the Jesuits, having been refused permission to work in the Napo region in 1630, had directed their efforts toward the gobernación of Mainas. From there they gradually expanded their jurisdiction down the Marañón into the Amazon. In 1645 this region was explored by Father Gaspar de Cugía, who estimated that there were 30,000 Omagua, 15,000 of them living on islands in the major rivers and the other half on their tributaries.[31] It is unlikely that so many inhabited the tributaries, since other evidence suggests they clustered on the banks of the Amazon, though some were probably moving inland to escape enslaving raids.[32] By 1681, however, those on the islands had been reduced to 7,000 as a result of Portuguese enslaving raids and probably disease.[33] These raids prompted the Omagua to seek Jesuit protection, and in 1683 they were given the authority to continue their conversions in the Marañón as far as their "zeal and application" would carry them.[34] This limitless concession enabled the Jesuits not only to move into the Amazon but also, in the eighteenth century, to penetrate the Napo and Aguarico valleys. In 1685 they founded the mission of San Joaquín de Omagua on an island in the Lower Marañón, moving into the Amazon with the founding of Nuestra Señora de las Nieves de Yurimaguas in 1689.[35] Between 1709 and 1769 they established seventeen missions on the Napo and Aguarico rivers.[36]

Meanwhile missionary activity in the Aguarico-Napo had been intermittent. Between 1664 and 1668 Jesuits from the gobernación of Mainas settled some Abijira in missions in the river Curaray.[37] However, the missions came to an abrupt end when an Indian revolt resulted in the death of Father Pedro Suárez and Spanish reprisals claimed the lives of several thousand Abijira.[38] In the absence of Jesuits, in 1686 Franciscans began working among them. They claimed that within three years they had established a number of villages and baptized 6,000 souls;[39] in 1690 the mission of San Francisco de Abijiras on the Curaray was ministering to 3,000 souls.[40] They also established further villages among the Coronado and Encabellado. Drawing attention to the cédula of 1683, the Jesuits complained that Franciscans were working within their jurisdiction, and the latter were forced to withdraw and concentrate their efforts on groups on the Putumayo.[41]

DEMOGRAPHIC TRENDS IN THE
NAPO AND AGUARICO VALLEYS

Spanish entradas, missionary expeditions, and possibly Portuguese slaving raids brought casualties and disease, which not only affected mortality and fertility rates but provoked migrations within and from the area. There is clear evidence that enslaving raids brought casualties among those who resisted, stimulated others to flee, and resulted in the removal of several thousand Indians from the region. Spanish entradas occurred against a background of continued intertribal warfare, in which the Omagua in particular were involved. Tribal warfare may even have increased in intensity as unexplained disasters were attributed to sorcery practiced by enemy neighbors and as the Spanish employed local Indians, such as the Cofán, on their entradas among traditionally hostile groups. Nevertheless, Spanish enslaving raids and their indirect effects were not wholly responsible for the region's depopulation.

Old World diseases had certainly taken their toll by the seventeenth century, but it is not clear when they first arrived. A smallpox pandemic raged in the Peruvian and Ecuadorian sierras between 1558 and 1559, when two expeditions were mounted that could have carried the infection to the region. Smallpox could have been spread by Gil Ramírez Dávalos's expedition to Los Quijos which penetrated the Coca Valley in 1558,[42] or Pedro de Ursúa's expedition down the Marañón between 1559 and 1560 could have carried the infection from the Peruvian sierra to the mouth of the Napo.[43] In both cases, however, no evidence exists that members of the expeditions were afflicted by disease. The first definitely identifiable smallpox epidemic was witnessed in the late 1640s by Father Laureano de la Cruz among the Omagua on islands in the Amazon.[44] During the rest of the century the lower reaches of the Napo are likely to have been affected by the epidemics that ravaged the gobernación of Mainas at almost ten-year intervals.[45] Meanwhile the Encabellado, who lived north of the middle reaches of the Napo, and the Abijira, who were concentrated on the river Curaray, may have been protected to some extent by their remoter locations, and the more dispersed settlement pattern of the Encabellado may have moderated the impact of disease. Old World epidemics apart, the Aguarico-Napo Valley was generally regarded as healthful, even though many observers noted the presence of insects. Soldiers involved in the entradas in the 1620s noted than none of them or their Indian auxiliaries fell ill and that local populations were healthy. They observed there were large numbers of children and that people lived to an old age,[46] which suggests that by the 1630s at least, malaria had not spread to the region.

The indirect effects of enslaving activities and missionization may have also raised mortality rates. Expeditions made demands on local food supplies, which perhaps only the Omagua on the Napo could have met. However, in the seventeenth century the banks of the Napo were less densely settled than when Francisco de Orellana passed down it in 1541. Overall population levels had fallen as a result of enslaving raids and epidemics, and the population had begun to move away from the exposed riverbanks. The Omagua moved toward the Putumayo or fled to join fellow Omagua on the river Tiputini or the Amazon. In some cases retreat meant migration to interfluvial areas, where soils were often less fertile and sources of fish and game less abundant and reliable. Diets may well have deteriorated, but it is not known whether the changes were sufficient to affect mortality or even fertility rates. The direct impact of expeditions on food supplies may have been greater, particularly among the Encabellado and Abijira, whose subsistence bases were inherently more fragile.[47]

The discussion so far has concentrated, as do documentary sources, on the contribution of raised mortality rates to the decline of the Indian population, but it is clear that the effects of enslaving raids, fugitivism, and epidemics also reduced the fertility rate through causing marriage breakdown and interrupting reproduction.[48] The continued practice of infanticide also reduced their ability to rcover.[49] On the whole, missionary activity was not sustained enough to bring about lasting changes to marriage rules that might have affected fertility rates, but it is noteworthy that missionaries tried to suppress polygamy, which functioned to maintain fertility levels in situations of high male mortality.[50] In this context the large number of children noted by soldiers who were involved in entradas in the Napo Valley in the early part of the seventeenth century is surprising.[51] By the middle of the century, however, Father Laureano de la Cruz found only small numbers of children among the Omagua on the Amazon. Although many of their communities had recently been struck by smallpox, even those families in villages that appear to have escaped averaged only three persons.[52] The Omagua located on the Amazon were more exposed to enslaving raids, and these few figures suggest that directly or indirectly they probably contributed to a reduction in fertility levels and to their continued decline.

Demographic trends in the Aguarico and Napo valleys during the early colonial period can be sketched only vaguely. Documentary evidence is very fragmentary, and the picture confused by migrations within and from the region. Since most references to Indian populations refer to cultural groups rather than geographical areas, the following discussion will consider demographic changes for each group before commenting on changes within the region as a whole.

The Cofán, Coronado, and Omagua-Yété located nearest the sierra experienced more intense contact with Spaniards during the early colonial period. Some were allocated in encomiendas, larger numbers were enslaved, and others were brought under missionary control, although not for extended periods. In the 1620s maybe 500 were under the control of encomenderos at Alcalá de Río and another 500 in the Jesuit mission of San Juan de los Omaguas. Nothing is known of the numbers existing in the surrounding region, but the fact that slave raiders were looking further afield to the Omagua, Abijira, and Encabellado suggests that local Cofán and Coronado populations must have been exhausted or at least fairly small. Prior to the entradas conducted between 1617 and 1622, when at least 1,000 Indians were enslaved, larger numbers of Omagua-Yété probably existed outside Spanish control, though smaller enslaving raids from Los Quijos and Ecija, and even by hostile Indian neighbors, continued to drain their populations. While enslaving raids and the conditions to which they were subjected raised mortality rates, the loss in numbers was more apparent than real, since many fled to escape enslavement, and of those enslaved, many were transferred outside the region. About 1630 the Cofán and Coronado together may have numbered about 1,000 and the remaining Omagua-Yété an equivalent number, the latter including any fugitive Indians from Spanish control in Los Quijos or even from the highlands. In addition another 2,000 may have existed outside the region as slaves or fugitives. Certainly the number of Omagua living in the river Tiputini was sufficiently numerous to pose a continual threat to Spanish settlements in Los Quijos into the eighteenth century, though by then their numbers had been boosted by Omagua fleeing from the river Napo and later the Amazon.[53] Of the estimated 28,000 Cofán, Coronado, and Omagua-Yété existing at the time of Spanish conquest, perhaps only 4,000 remained in 1630, a loss of over 85 percent. If only the 2,000 still residing in the region are considered, then level of depopulation would be raised to 93 percent. By 1700 maybe only half that number existed (Table 29). Today there are about 500 Cofán.[54]

With the exception of the Omagua located on the banks of the Lower Napo, losses further downriver were probably not as great. Indeed in 1739 Father Andrés de Zarate regarded the Napo Valley as the most populous part of the gobernación of Mainas.[55] Among groups located further from the sierra, Spanish enslaving raids were less intense, and it was not until

Table 29. Population Decline in the Napo-Aguarico Valley to 1700

Ethnic group	Aboriginal population	Estimated population in
Cofán	15,000	
Coronado	3,000	2,000
Omagua-Yété	10,000	
Omagua of the Napo	15,000	Dispersed
Encabellado	6,000–8,000	4,000

the eighteenth century that the effects of Portuguese raids began to be felt in the Lower Napo. Missionary activities were also less sustained than in the gobernación of Mainas, for after a late beginning in the 1590s, during the first half of the seventeenth century Franciscans and Jesuits operated there only intermittently.

Of the Omagua of the Napo Valley, the Encabellado, and Abijira, the Omagua experienced the greatest decline. Exposed in nucleated settlements on the banks of the Napo and nearest to the Marañón, where Spanish missionary efforts were concentrated, the Omagua fell victim to entradas and epidemics to a greater extent than the Encabellado and Abijira, whose remoter location and more dispersed settlement patterns would have moderated their impact. But not all Indians died. Some fled from the Napo to the river Tiputini or toward the Putumayo, while others left the region for the Amazon. At a guess maybe 1,000 Indians fled to the Amazon, leaving only about 500 Napo Omagua in the region in 1650, after which time there are few references to them. By 1700 the province of Aparia menor, which had contained maybe 15,000 Indians when first contacted, had ceased to exist as a distinct cultural and geographical entity.

The Encabellado and Abijira certainly survived to a greater degree. In the 1720s it was estimated there were about 500 Encabellado in the mission of San Javier de Icaguate and a further 2,000 unconverted Indians outside.[56] These numbers must represent only a proportion of the Encabellado, whose vast territory, which extended from the Napo to the Putumayo, was remote from the arenas of Spanish activity. Maybe 4,000 Encabellado or more still existed in 1700. Fewer Abijira remained. In 1667 Father Lucero reported that he had explored the tributaries of the Curaray and found a total of seventy rancherías, some exceeding 100 people.[57] This suggests that despite entradas from Alcalá del Río, the Abijira could still be numbered in thousands. Nevertheless, many were killed as a consequence of punitive raids that followed the assassination of Father Pedro Suárez in 1667,[58] and Velasco maintains that 6,000 Abijira and Oa died in the epidemics of 1660 and 1669.[59] In 1680 those who had been involved in the entradas estimated that the Abijira and Payagua together numbered 5,000 "indios de guerra."[60] However, in the late 1680s Franciscans claimed to have baptized 6,000 Abijira,[61] and in 1690 there were 3,000 souls being administered to by the mission of San Francisco de Abijiras.[62] These figures may have been exaggerated but are not impossible. Calculations based on the impact of epidemics alone suggest a population in 1700 of between 2,500 and 3,500.[63]

Sweet estimates that at the end of the colonial period, the Encabellado numbered between 6,000 and 8,000, and the Abijira between 2,000 and 3,000.[64] The figure he gives for the Encabellado is considerably higher than that suggested here for 1700, yet recovery on such a scale is unlikely, given the low levels of natural increase that are characteristic of preindustrial societies. Furthermore, it was during the eighteenth century that they were most profoundly affected by missionization and epidemics.[65] Although the Encabellado received some protection from their remote location, the evidence presented here indicates that during the early seventeenth century at least they were focus of entradas and missionary activities, and as such it is unlikely they totally escaped the effects of epidemic disease. Hence the Encabellado may have declined by as much as one-half from an estimated preconquest population of 6,000 to 8,000 to about 4,000 in 1700. Meanwhile the Abijira, despite living further from the direct line of penetration through the Aguarico-Napo, suffered a sharper decline, in common with those of the gobernación of Mainas. Their numbers fell from an estimated aboriginal population of between 6,000 and 8,000 to between 2,500 and 3,500 in 1700. Since the Abijira came under the administration of the Jesuits in the seventeenth century, their numbers will be included in those for the province of Mainas.

Contacts with Spaniards were far from sustained in the Napo Valley, but their impact was nevertheless disastrous. By 1700 the number of Encabellado and Omagua alone had fallen from between 21,000 to 23,000 to about 4,000, a decline of over 80 percent. But clearly Indian fates were different. While the Omagua had been decimated and dispersed, the Encabellado still existed in relatively large numbers. Today the latter number about 1,000.[66]

Part Seven

CONCLUSION

CHAPTER 19

Patterns of Indian Depopulation in Early Colonial Ecuador

> In the lowlands the Indians are declining, and in some parts of the sierra they are maintaining themselves well and are increasing, and in others a large number have been lost such as in the gobernación of Quijos, in that of Zamora, and in the gobernación of Salinas.
>
> Bishop of Quito, 20 March 1598[1]

The impact of Spanish conquest and rule was disastrous for native peoples of Ecuador, yet their demographic experiences differed substantially. Variations in demographic trends reflected the diversity of native cultures, environments, and resources; the depth of Inka rule; the intensity of Spanish settlement; and the institutions used by the new rulers to "civilize" the native population. While the introduction of Old World diseases was the most important factor in Indian depopulation, there were variations in their impact that reflected these diverse cultural and environmental conditions.

At the time of Spanish conquest the Inka were extending their dominion over Andean peoples. Inka rule in Ecuador began seventy to eighty years prior to European contact, and although it had been consolidated in the southern sierra, regions to the north of Quito were still in the process of being incorporated into the empire. As such, Inka influence in the north was of a military character, but in the south administrative centers had been established, and the political economy had been transformed. Colonies of mitmaq had been created, local leaders co-opted into the Inka bureaucracy, lands alienated to provide goods for state and religious purposes, the mit'a introduced, and the vertical archipelago system inaugurated. While these processes may have better prepared southern peoples to weather and respond to the changes demanded under Spanish colonial rule, they had been achieved with considerable loss of life. It has been estimated that about 100,000 Indians lives were lost in Inka conquest and the Inka dynastic wars, with the greatest losses occurring in the south among the Cañar and Palta. Given the low rates of natural increase that are characteristic of preindustrial societies, it is doubtful that, despite Inka policies promoting population increase, even those societies that had the longest experience of Inka rule would have been able to recover to pre-Inka levels by the time the Spanish arrived. Meanwhile in the north heavy losses were still being sustained, particularly by the Caranqui and Cayambe.

Using documentary, archaeological, ethnological, and ecological evidence, the population of Ecuador prior to Spanish conquest has been estimated at about 1.6 million. Of that number about half (51.2 percent) were living in the sierra, slightly more than a third (34.1 percent) on the coast, and the remainder (14.7 percent) in the Oriente. The sierra was the only region to be affected by Inka rule, so that its pre-Inka population is likely to have been both absolutely and relatively more substantial. The densest populations were to be found in the sierra. Here socially stratified polities, which sometimes formed confederacies, comprised populations that ran into tens of thousands. They were supported by intensive forms of agricultural production which involved the construction of raised fields, irrigation, and some terracing. Their diet was supplemented by hunting, and in the north exotic products were obtained by trade and in the south through the vertical archipelago system. The agricultural potential of the Ecuadorian sierra was generally greater than the central Andean high-lands. It contained larger stretches of cultivable fertile land, and its more equable climate rendered it less vulnerable to frosts and droughts. The highland basins of the central and northern sierra appear to have been more densely settled than those to the south, which probably reflected their greater agricultural potential and, with the exception of the Caranqui and Cayambe, the less devastating impact of Inka conquest.

It has been estimated that the pre-Columbian population of the Oriente was between about 230,000 and 250,000. This figure is considerably higher than other estimates for the same area that can be derived from the studies of the aboriginal population of the Amazon headwaters by De-nevan, Sweet, and Taylor.[2] Native groups in this region generally practiced shifting cultivation and to differing degrees relied on hunting and fishing to acquire protein. They were not markedly stratified, though some status was achieved by war leaders and shamans. With the exception of the Omagua, settlements were small and dispersed. Evidence drawn primarily from documentary sources suggests that the Omagua who inhabited the várzea together with groups who lived in the high selva—such as the Quijos, Macas, and some Jívaro—were more populous. These groups exceeded densities of 1.0 person per square kilometer, while those who inhabited the low selva barely achieved densities of 0.5 persons per square kilometer. Even though higher population levels in the high selva generally reflected the greater resource potential of the region, they appear to have varied with the availability of protein, levels of warfare, and the extent of contact with sierran groups. In the low selva resources were more limited, and warfare functioned to keep population levels low.

Aboriginal population estimates for the coast of Ecuador are the most problematic. Despite being the first part of Ecuadorian territory to be reconnoitered by the Spanish, documentary sources for the coast are comparatively few, and greater reliance has to be placed on the archaeological record. Taken together, these sources suggest that the inhabitants of the coast comprised small tribes and chiefdoms, with social stratification and political integration being more highly developed on the coast of Esmeraldas and south of the Chone River. All groups practiced agriculture, but more permanent and intensive forms of production in the southern coastal region suggest the presence of substantial populations. It has been proposed that the aboriginal population of the coast probably exceeded 0.5 million, of whom nearly 90 percent lived in the southern sector. This means that about one-third of Ecuador's total pre-Columbian population may have lived on the coast. Clearly this proportion was slightly inflated by losses resulting from Inka conquest of the sierra, but some readers might consider the absolute figure for the coast and the proportion it represented to be too high. While I would expect the figure to be revised in the light of new research, it is perhaps worth noting that at the same time in neighboring Peru nearly 60 percent of the population lived on the coast.[3] Although one cannot infer too much from this comparison, because native societies and ecological conditions in these neighboring provinces were significantly different, I believe that hitherto the aboriginal population of coastal Ecuador has been considerably underestimated.

The figure of 1.6 million for the aboriginal population of Ecuador cannot be compared easily with previous estimates for the region. Until recently little serious scholarly work has been conducted on Ecuador, and earlier estimates by Steward, Rosenblat, Cisneros Cisneros, and Phelan represent little more than intelligent guesses based largely on analogy with neighboring regions.[4] Their estimates for the Audiencia of Quito range between about 500,000 and a million, of whom the majority lived in the sierra. Unfortunately the more scholarly demographic studies by Tyrer, Browne, Larrain Barros, and Sweet are more limited in geographical scope.[5] The most recent geographically extensive study by Alchon has suggested that the precontact population for the highlands was about 1,080,000, which by the eve of conquest in 1534 had been reduced to between 375,000 and 570,000 as a consequence of two epidemics.[6] In fact her precontact estimate for the highlands should be larger, since the source on which it is based does not include the southern sierran district of Loja.[7] Furthermore, it does not take into account other factors affecting demographic trends or the variable impact of disease. As it stands, her figure of 1,080,000 for the highlands is about 20 percent higher than that suggested here.

The estimate of 1.6 million for the whole of the audiencia may be compared with that of 9 million suggested by Cook for the considerably more extensive region of Peru.[8] While the rugged topography and colder climate in the central Andes restricted agricultural production to narrow valleys, this environmental limitation combined with political pressures to encourage the more extensive development of terracing and irrigation, which could support dense populations. In Ecuador economic and political pressures to intensify and extend cultivation were not as great, and with the exception of raised fields, environmental conditions were generally less favorable for their development.

It has been estimated that during the sixteenth century the Indian population of the sierra declined from about 838,600 to 164,529. This decline represents a depopulation ratio of 5.1:1, which is comparable to Cook's estimate of 5.0:1 for the neighboring Peruvian sierra for the period from 1520 to 1600.[9] Like the latter estimate, the average depopulation ratio for the Ecuadorian sierra masks a degree of regional variation (Table 30). While the figures for individual regions must be considered as estimates that are open to revision, the relative differences in levels of depopulation are not unexpected. These reflected the complex interaction of a number of factors whose relative importance varied from region to region.

Old World epidemics, losses in conflict and on expeditions, and demands on Indian production, labor, and land all affected demographic trends. As yet there is no evidence to suggest that the impact of Old World epidemics differed significantly throughout the highlands, though it is possible that regional differences in working conditions and living standards, particularly nutritional levels, may have exerted some influence. The impact of conquest itself appears to have been more uneven. It took its heaviest toll in the Quito region, though casualties were sustained throughout the sierra as Spanish troops pushed northward. Subsequently it was the Quito Basin that also bore the heaviest burden in providing support for expeditions aimed at exploring and pacifying lowland and northern regions, though the proximity of the provinces of Latacunga and Otavalo to these areas and the collaboration of their native leaders meant their communities were also affected. Communities in the central sierra, however, were partially protected from the demands made by expeditions by the absence of large populations immediately to the east and the more difficult access to the lowlands through the Cordillera Oriental, but those in the Cuenca region, and to a lesser extent around Loja, were not spared.

Once pacified, highland peoples were uniformly subject to the encomienda and systems of forced labor. There appears to have been little difference in the type and amount of tribute demanded from Indians in the sierra. In most cases maize, cotton, wheat, and chickens figured among the items levied, in addition to which two pesos were demanded in cash. Nevertheless the burden that these demands represented was not uniform. The acquisition of cash was a major problem for Indians in all regions, often forcing them into the market economy, but it was particularly acute in nonmining areas such as Otavalo. Similarly the cotton levy appears to have been more difficult to meet in the northern sierra. Even

Table 30. Indian Population Decline in Early Colonial Ecuador

Ethnic group or region	Aboriginal population	End of the sixteenth century	Percent decline	Depopulation ratio
Sierra				
Pasto (Ecuador only)	36,350	15,505	57.3	2.3:1
Caranqui-Otavalo	150,000	29,466	80.4	5.1:1
Panzaleo (Quito Basin)	190,000	30,750	83.8	6.2:1
Panzaleo (Latacunga-Ambato)	160,000	31,938	80.0	5.0:1
Puruhá (Riobamba)	131,250	32,574	75.2	4.0:1
Cañar (Cuenca)	58,500	12,600	78.5	4.6:1
Palta (Loja)	112,500	11,696	89.6	9.6:1
Total	838,600	164,529	80.4	5.1:1
Coast				
Esmeraldas	69,098	20,000	71.1	3.5:1
Puerto Viejo	120,000	2,961	97.5	40.5:1
Guayaquil	357,230–382,730	3,530	99.0	104.9:1
Total	546,828–571,828	26,491	95.3	21.1:1
Oriente—High Selva				
Los Quijos	35,000	10,000	71.4	3.5:1
Macas	10,000	2,700	73.0	3.7:1
Yaguarzongo and Pacamoros	53,000	13,500	74.5	3.9:1
Total	98,000	26,200	73.3	3.7:1
Oriente—Low Selva[a]				
Napo-Aguarico	49,000–51,000	6,000	88.0	8.3:1
Mainas	83,000–102,000	30,180–38,490	62.9	2.7:1
Total	132,000–153,000	36,180–44,490	71.7	3.5:1

[a] Colonial figures for the low selva are for the end of the seventeenth century.

though cotton was levied universally, it could not be cultivated in the cool climate of the sierra but had to be acquired from lowland communities, as it had been in pre-Columbian times. Whether because of the greater inherent robustness of the vertical archipelago system or the less disruptive effects of Spanish conquest and the civil wars on communities in the southern sierra, they appear to have encountered fewer difficulties in supplying this product. In the north exotic items had been acquired by trade, which had depended on political alliances that shifted in the aftermath of Spanish conquest, making the acquisition of both gold and cotton particularly problematic. Even the official tribute burden borne by Indians in the Audiencia of Quito was judged as one of the highest in the Spanish empire. In reality tribute demands were even greater, and in the northern sierra in particular, tribute debts were a major factor encouraging fugitivism and the sale of Indian lands. In addition to legal exactions, unofficial levies by secular officials, encomenderos and priests were most prevalent in the north-central sierra, where Spaniards settled in largest numbers.

From an imperial perspective Ecuador was economic backwater, where agricultural production remained geared to domestic markets in the towns and limited mining regions and later supplied wool for the textile mills. Some encomenderos turned entrepreneurs were able to amass wealth as obrajeros, but the establishment of textile mills began only in the latter part of the sixteenth century. The fact that no great fortunes were to be made was reflected in the delayed foundation and slow growth of towns in the sierra; indeed during the sixteenth century many more towns were founded in the Oriente (Table 31). Yet there were regional variations in demands for labor and land that were highly correlated with the intensity of Spanish settlement and the types of commercial enterprises with which it was associated.

Despite the relatively slow growth of Spanish enterprises, all highland communities were subject to forced labor under the mita. The quota levied was set at one-fifth, which is the highest proportion exacted anywhere in the Spanish empire. However, its impact on native communities varied with the tasks to which mitayos were assigned, the periods for which they were employed, and whether they were required to change their residence or work in regions to which they were not acclimatized. Meanwhile free wage labor emerged in the city of Quito and in regions where mining and textile production effectively monopolized the supply of forced labor. Indians driven by loss of land or tribute debts or desirous of escaping the mita often sought wage labor on nearby estates or in the towns, where many enjoyed better wages and working conditions. Only in the Quito Basin does wage labor appear to have been sufficiently pervasive that it may have had positive effects on demographic trends. This proposition is difficult to substantiate, however, given the region's demographic insta-

Table 31. Non-Indian Population of the Audiencia of Quito in the Early Colonial Period

District and urban center	1570s vecinos (encomenderos)[a]	1560s[?] vecinos (encomenderos)[b]	1576 vecinos (total Spanish males)[c]	1586 Non-Indians[d]	1589 Spaniards[e]	1620s Spanish vecinos[f]
Sierra						
Quito	400 (41)	400	300–400(800)	10,000	1,200	3,000+
Latacunga	—	—	—	—	—	—
Ambato	—	—	—	—	—	—
Riobamba	—	—	—	—	140	400+ and 100 in Chimbo
Cuenca	80 (3)	60 (2)	5–6 vecinos encomenderos 25 vecinos de repartimiento (80–100)	not given	200	500+
Loja	60–70 (12)	—	—	1,000	150 and 40 in Zaruma	300+ and 200 in Zaruma
Total	540–550	—		11,000	1,730	—
Coast						
Guayaquil	100 (23)	25 (14)	15 vecinos encomenderos	1,000	55	400
Puerto Viejo	17 (13)	17 casas (13)	10 vecinos encomenderos	500	35	60
Total	117	—	—	1,500	90	460
Oriente						
Los Quijos	48	—	(100)	500	not given	few
Zamora	28 (ca. 28)	—	20–25	1,000	50	few
Yaguarzongo and Pacamoros (Gobernación de Salinas)	99	—	not given	500	195	few
Total	175	—	—	2,000	—	—

a López de Velasco, *Geografía*, 217–30; CDI 15:409–572 Demarcación y división, no date.
b RGI 1:121–43 Salazar de Villasante, no date.
c RGI 2:169–75 Oficiales de la real hacienda 30.12.1576.
d BNM 3178 fols. 1–15 Canelas Albarrán 1586.
e BM Add. 13,977 fol. 75–v Morales Figueroa 17.5.1589.
f Vázquez de Espinosa, *Compendio*, 254–66.

bility and the fact that racial mixing would have retarded any expansion in the native population.

The intensity of Spanish settlement affected not only demands for tribute and labor but also the alienation of Indian lands, a process that was accelerated by the Toledo reducciones. There is no doubt that the alienation of Indians lands was most widespread in the Quito Basin, which throughout the early colonial period contained considerably more non-Indians than the rest of the sierra put together. At the other end of the spectrum the more limited agricultural potential of the Riobamba region and its focus on livestock production discouraged the extensive alienation of Indian lands. Nevertheless, all regions were affected to some degree. Despite the alienation of community lands, food supplies were generally good. Food shortages were normally attributed to bad weather or to the extraordinary demands generated by expeditions or by nonresident workers, particularly in the mining areas. In the early conquest period food shortages would have occurred in the wake of epidemics, when nutritional levels may have deteriorated sufficiently to affect disease susceptibility. However, most evidence points to some dietary improvement as chickens, pigs, and cattle were widely adopted.

The previous discussion has shown that each of the processes underlying demographic trends varied spatially, but their relative significance varied as did the manner in which they interacted, and these were reflected in the regional differences in levels of decline.

Estimates for the highland regions suggest the highest level of depopulation was experienced by the Palta, who declined by nearly 90 percent from about 112,500 in pre-Columbian times to only about 11,700 at the end of the sixteenth century. The high level of decline may be attributed in large part to the impact of mining on native communities. The correlation between mining and Indian depopulation has long been recognized by colonial historians. It derived from the arduous and hazardous nature of the activity and from the ill-treatment and overwork of the Indians that resulted from the drive to make quick profits. The mining mita also required Indians to leave their communities for extended periods. This not only had adverse effects on subsistence production and fertility levels but encouraged fugitivism and created opportunities for the formations of new unions often with persons of a different race. These processes undermined the ability of the Indian communities to recover from the devastating effects of wars and epidemics. The impact of mining extended beyond mining activities to the stimulation of agricultural production and trade in surrounding areas, where they competed with Indian communities for land and labor. Despite the undeniable impact of mining on Indian communities, the level of depopulation estimated for the Loja region is rather higher than expected. This is especially so when the level of decline is compared to that calculated for the Quito Basin, even taking into account that in the latter region population levels were inflated by immigration. It is particularly surprising, given that the impact of mining was not felt until after 1560 and that losses in conquest and on expeditions were smaller than in regions further north. It is possible that the pre-Columbian population for the Palta region has been overestimated or that figures for some other highland regions have been underestimated.

After Loja, the Quito Basin suffered the greatest level of depopulation of 6.2:1, declining from about 190,000 to about 30,750 at the end of the century. Again this is not unexpected. The effects of conquest itself, the demands of expeditions, and the Spanish civil wars had their greatest impact in this area. It was also here that Spaniards settled in largest numbers, where Indian communities suffered the most extensive alienation of their lands, and where demands for labor were at their greatest. Nevertheless, the tasks in which Indians were employed were not as hazardous or arduous as in some other regions, particularly the southern sierra, where mining and porterage raised mortality rates. Also the mita in the Quito Basin was of shorter duration and generally did not require Indians to cross climatic zones or to change their place of residence. Nevertheless, pressure on Indian lands and demands for labor destabilized Indian communities, encouraging many to seek wage labor, through which many became absorbed in the growing population of mixed races. The level of depopulation in the Quito region would certainly have been greater had not part of the decline been masked by forced or voluntary migration from surrounding regions.

Quito's neighboring provinces of Otavalo and Latacunga experienced similar rates of decline of about 80 percent. Both emerged as important textile-producing regions. Poor working conditions in the textile mills may well have raised mortality rates, and they certainly encouraged fugitivism, but their negative impact on demographic trends was less significant than those experienced in mining. Although periods of work were longer, most obrajes were established in Indian villages so that workers could return home at night or weekends. This meant that subsistence production and social relations could be maintained to a greater degree than where Indians were involved in the mining mita, where, although periods of work were often shorter, they were required to change their place of residence. Indeed the profitability of textile production was dependent on the persistence of Indian communities, which, by bearing the costs of reproduction and maintenance of the labor force, kept wages low and enabled cloth to be produced at competitive prices. The fact that the major textile-producing area of Riobamba registered one of the lowest levels of depopulation (4.0:1) suggests that in the provinces of Otavalo and Latacunga factors other than the presence of obrajes, which were only established at the end of the sixteenth century, had more significant effects on demographic trends. One important difference was that the latter provinces suffered considerably greater losses on expeditions. Comparing the latter two regions, the corregimiento of Otavalo contained no Spanish town. This should have moderated demands for Indian lands and labor. However, Otavalo's communities were sufficiently close to Quito to be drawn into its orbit and required to service the city. The long distances over which Indians traveled to perform required tasks meant that the burden of mita service was greater for them than for communities that served a more local urban center.

The Indian populations of the two predominantly agricultural areas—the regions of Cuenca and the northernmost sierra—experienced lower levels of decline. Among sierran groups the Pasto appear to have suffered the lowest level of depopulation—2.3:1. They sustained losses during Spanish conquest and on expeditions to Colombia and Esmeraldas and, like Otavalo communities, were required to provide service for the city of Quito. In these circumstances the estimated level of decline appears low, even though a lower level of depopulation might be expected, given that their territory was not effectively settled until the end of the sixteenth century. The higher level of decline of 4.6:1 noted for the Cuenca region may be accounted for by heavy losses sustained in conquest and on expeditions, as well as its early role as a major gold-producing region. Indeed a higher level of depopulation might have been expected. It is possible that Inka conquest and the dynastic wars had not reduced the preconquest population to the level suggested here or that the population at the end of the sixteenth century was inflated by migrants from other regions, possibly from the east.

The coast of Ecuador suffered the most dramatic decline. The average depopulation ratio of 21.1:1 is comparable to that estimated for the coasts of central Mexico by Cook and Borah,[10] though it conceals marked differences between its northern and southern sectors. Whereas population decline in Esmeraldas has been calculated at 3.5:1, which was similar to that experienced by groups in the Oriente, the native population around Guayaquil collapsed by the staggering ratio of 104.9:1. This ratio is considerably higher than that for coastal Peru for the same period, which, using Cook's figures, may be calculated at 42.2:1.[11] While this exceptionally high level of depopulation is dependent in part on the presence of an aboriginal population of nearly 0.5 million (which needs further substantiation), there is little doubt that during the early conquest period this region suffered the greatest losses.

High levels of depopulation noted for other tropical coasts have often been attributed to the presence of malaria. Despite the considerable attention to this issue, I have been unable to confirm this proposition for coastal

Ecuador. While I think it unlikely that *Plasmodium falciparum* affected coastal populations during the sixteenth century, the spread of *P. vivax* by Spaniards remains a possibility. Although the latter is normally more benign, its impact on a nonimmune populations might have been more devastating. However, if malaria was a major cause of high levels of depopulation on the coast of Ecuador, it is necessary to explain why there appear to be such significant differences in levels of decline in the northern and southern sectors. Other explanations are more plausible.

One partial explanation also relates to the introduction and spread of Old World diseases. Guayaquil was a major port on the Pacific coast as well as the main entry point for people and goods passing to the sierra. As such, the southern coast was exposed to the constant introduction of new infections by people passing to and from Central America, Peru, and the highlands, and its dense sedentary population facilitated their spread. Fewer vessels stopped in the north, and with the exception of limited stretches of the coast that were rapidly depopulated, settlements were small and dispersed. As such, the introduction and spread of disease occurred less readily, and disease mortality is likely to have been considerably lower than in the south.

In addition to disease, the southern sector of the coast probably suffered more than any other region in Ecuador from the depredations of conquistadores. Here the desperate search for gold resulted in the willful slaughter of thousands and made the Black Legend a reality. Subsequently the growth of the port of Guayaquil generated demands for supplies for passing vessels and travelers and for labor for the extraction of timber, shipbuilding, and transporting goods. Many of these tasks were not only arduous and associated with high levels of mortality, but labor demands coupled with the expanding market economy undermined the viability of native communities. At the same time, the growing commercial importance of the city resulted in an expansion in the numbers of merchants, artisans, and black slaves, such that its jurisdiction contained the largest proportion of non-Indians in the audiencia. Racial mixing was another factor contributing to Indian depopulation.

For the greater part of the century native communities in Esmeraldas were protected by its lack of minerals or large populations. Only at the end of the century did Mercedarian missionaries establish more than a fleeting Spanish presence in the region, and even that was short-lived. Expeditions may have temporarily destabilized native communities, but probably greater effects derived from the presence of the mulattoes, whose hostile stance contributed to increased conflict and caused some groups to move inland. Although Old World diseases took their toll, the lack of a permanent Spanish presence meant that many processes contributing to population decline elsewhere in the audiencia were absent.

Comparisons of demographic trends within the Oriente are made difficult by differences in the timing of contact. During the sixteenth century, groups in the high selva came into sustained contact with Spaniards, but their towns, mines, and haciendas had been abandoned by the time the Jesuits began working in the province of Mainas. Depopulation ratios for different regions within the Oriente are not strictly comparable, therefore, though they are suggestive of demographic trends that might be associated with particular types of activity over a similar time period.

Overall, the depopulation ratios for the Oriente are lower than might be anticipated for all groups and especially those in the province of Mainas. It is possible that native populations were larger than current estimates suggest and that insufficient account has been taken of the impact of epidemics. It is argued here that malaria is unlikely to have spread into the Oriente during the sixteenth century and that the physical barrier of the Andean cordillera may have protected the region from many infections that afflicted the coast. Those epidemics that reached the Oriente caused considerable mortality, but their impact was moderated by the low population density and dispersed settlement pattern. Not only were "fade-outs" common, but diseases failed to become endemic, so that further disease mortality was dependent on the reintroduction of infections, which were generally associated with higher levels of adult mortality. Hence, although low population densities might have moderated disease mortality, the indirect effects of epidemics associated with high levels of adult mortality may have been greater. They often heightened intertribal conflict, damaged fragile subsistence systems, and reduced populations below critical thresholds, from which they were unable to recover without major cultural restructuring.

Among Indian groups in the Oriente, those in the high selva suffered greater depopulation as a consequence of sustained contact with Spaniards during the sixteenth century. The presence of alluvial gold deposits stimulated early expeditions and maintained Spanish interest in the region, despite Indian hostility. In order to maintain political control of the area, an excessive number of towns were founded that generated high demands for tribute and labor, initially for mining, and later for cotton manufacture, which, given the relatively small Indian populations available, resulted in overwork and ill-treatment. Indian resentment was further fostered by their lack of familiarity with tribute payments or forced labor. The results were revolts and fugitivism.

These processes affected all three jurisdictions in the high selva, and the depopulation ratios calculated for them appear fairly similar, ranging from 3.5:1 to 3.9:1. Nevertheless, several spatial differences are worthy of comment. All three regions lost population to the interior or as a result of forced or voluntary migration to the highlands, but the depopulation of

Macas was partially disguised by an influx of fugitive Indians from other regions. Meanwhile the highest levels of decline were associated with mining in the jurisdiction of Yaguarzongo and Pacamoros, where the depopulation ratio was 3.9:1. In reality the decline was greater, since the ratio is depressed by the inclusion of substantial numbers of Jívaro who remained outside Spanish control. It has been estimated that in the province of Zamora, where mining was concentrated, the Indian population suffered a decline in the order of 40:1.

Further east the full impact of enslaving expeditions, missionization, and epidemics was not felt until the seventeenth century. As such, discussions of demographic trends for the gobernación of Mainas and the Napo-Aguarico Valley have been extended to 1700. The levels of depopulation in these regions cannot be compared directly with those for the rest of the audiencia, but extending the time period of analysis enables some discussion of the impact of missionization on native groups and allows comparisons of the fate of tribal groups under the encomienda and mission control, as well as between them and the more highly stratified groups in the highlands.

From the end of the sixteenth century, Indian communities in the Napo-Aguarico region felt the impact of enslaving raids and to a lesser extent missionary expeditions. Those groups located closest to the sierra in the headwaters of the Napo and Coca suffered the most, but by the end of the seventeenth century the whole of the Napo Valley had been affected. Although a few encomiendas were granted and there were intermittent attempts by Franciscan and Jesuit missionaries to convert Indians in this region, the major impact on native communities apart from epidemics came from enslaving raids. These raids were highly disruptive to subsistence activities and social life, to the extent that most opted to flee from exposed locations along the major rivers. Meanwhile those enslaved were generally transferred outside the region. It has been estimated that the population declined by a ratio of 8.3:1. This level of decline is not surprising but is more apparent than real, since many fled to other regions. Importantly, it disguises the virtual disappearance of the once-populous Omagua from Ecuadorian territory and the greater survival of Indian groups in interfluvial areas.

Epidemics, enslaving raids, and missionization were also the major causes of Indian depopulation of the gobernación of Mainas, but there slave raids played a less significant role than missionary activities, whose indirect effects also enhanced the impact of disease. Missionization introduced new diseases and, by continually adding new converts, heightened their impact. It also undermined the subsistence patterns and social systems of Indians both inside and outside the missions. Population losses in turn provided grounds for increased tribal warfare and reduced many

Table 32. Summary Estimates of Indian Population Decline in
Early Colonial Ecuador

Region	Aboriginal population	End of the sixteenth century	Percent decline	Depopulation ratio
Sierra	838,600	164,529	80.4	5.1:1
Coast	546,828–571,828	26,491	95.3	21.1:1
Oriente				
High selva	98,000	26,200	73.3	3.7:1
Total	1,483,428–1,508,428	217,220	85.5	6.9:1
Low selva[a]	132,000–153,000	36,180–44,490	71.7	3.5:1

[a] Colonial figures for the low selva are for the end of the seventeenth century.

groups below the critical size that would enable them to recover. Although these processes can be documented, estimating their quantitative impact is not easy. It has been suggested that by 1700 the region had lost over half of its contact population through epidemics and enslaving raids, the former being about three to four times more significant, and the latter taking their heaviest toll on groups located closest to the sierra. These two factors alone would have been sufficient to reduce the population to between 30,180 and 38,490 in 1700. The operation of other factors suggests that these figures may be overestimates. As they stand, they indicate a depopulation ratio of 2.7:1, which is considerably lower than that calculated for the Napo-Aguarico region. The difference between the ratios may relate in part to the more disruptive effects of enslaving raids compared with missionization, and to the fact that in the extensive gobernación of Mainas some groups were relatively untouched by missionization and able to escape at least some enslaving raids and epidemics.

A superficial comparison between levels of depopulation in the high and low selva suggests that Indian survival depended more on the intensity and nature of Spanish contact than on the character of the Indian groups themselves. Contrary to what might be expected, the more populous groups of the high selva suffered the greater depopulation.

Table 32 shows that the population of the Audiencia of Quito, excluding the Napo and Aguarico valleys and the Jesuit province of Mainas, declined from an estimated population of about 1.5 million at contact to about 217,200 in 1600. This is a decline of about 85 percent, or an average ratio of 6.9:1. As will be apparent from this study, these figures mask considerable regional variations, many of which continue to be concealed when comparisons are made between the coast, sierra, and Oriente. The study shows that levels of depopulation cannot be related simply to differences in elevation. The clear contrast in levels of decline between the lowlands and highlands, which have been noted in other parts of Latin America, cannot be identified for Ecuador. Some lowland groups, such as those in Esmeraldas and the Jívaro, survived better than most highland groups. Indeed differences within lowland areas are as marked as between the highlands and lowlands. Important distinguishing factors included opportunities for the introduction of new infections, which were most marked in Guayaquil and more limited in the Oriente, and also differences in population density and settlement patterns, which affected their spread. But also significant were differences in the intensity of Spanish settlement, the methods used to control and exploit native peoples, and the demands that new commercial enterprises made on Indian lands, labor, and production.

Colonial rule was at its most exploitative around Guayaquil, where the Indian population suffered its greatest decline. The significance of the intensity of Spanish settlement may be seen in the relatively high levels of depopulation in the sierra and high selva. It was not only the number of settlers that was important but, as has been shown, the economic enterprises that they established. The higher mortality levels associated with mining and its more disruptive effects on native communities are apparent in the greater levels of depopulation in the southern sierra, including the province of Zamora, whereas the decline was lower in areas of textile manufacture, where, despite the harsh conditions in the obrajes, the location of the mills in Indian communities minimized disruption to subsistence patterns and family life.

Comparing the demographic impact of the encomienda and the mission as distinct forms of control is not easy. While many processes identified in chapter 1 as being associated with these institutions have been documented, their impact is less clear. If anything, a comparison between the sierra and the gobernación of Mainas suggests a lower level of decline for the latter region that is opposite to what was anticipated. It is important to note, however, that missionary activities did not affect all communities within the area and that in 1700 its population was still declining.

For the most part Ecuador's Indian population did not collapse to the same extent as did native societies in Mexico and Central America. In 1623 the president of the Audiencia of Quito, Antonio de Morga, also judged it had survived to a greater degree than in Peru. He attributed this to the absence of rich gold and silver deposits and wealthy traders. Ecuador's citizens, he observed, were supported by a few agricultural activities and some obrajes and were content to live a life of ease.[12] His observations were almost certainly colored by familiarity with the Ecuadorian sierra, where in the early seventeenth century the Indian population may have appeared to be increasing, while in Peru it was continuing to decline. Nevertheless, Ecuador was not a demographic nirvana, for in common with all native societies in the Americas, contact with Europeans had spelled demographic disaster. By the end of the sixteenth century it had lost about 85 percent of its Indian population. How Ecuador differed was that the population of the sierra appears to have experienced one of the earliest demographic recoveries in the New World, possibly starting at the beginning of the seventeenth century, though the extent to which the recovery was real or reflected migration and/or more effective registration remains an issue of debate. Since this trend is often assumed for Ecuador as a whole, it is important to note that native populations on the coast and in the Oriente continued to decline until at least the second half of the eighteenth century.

General Estimates of the Tributary Population in the Sixteenth Century

Our knowledge of demographic trends in sixteenth-century Ecuador derives largely from tribute records. Although the Crown tried to introduce official tribute assessments from the mid-1530s, they were strongly resisted by local encomenderos, whose opposition grew with the promulgation of the New Laws in 1542. It was not until the ensuing civil wars had ended that in 1549 Licenciado Pedro de La Gasca drew up the first tasaciones for Ecuador. For the first fifteen years after conquest, therefore, no attempts were made to enumerate the Indian population. The only evidence available consists of vague descriptions or at best general estimates of the numbers present or killed in battle generally for ill-defined areas. These accounts are discussed in tracing the demographic history of individual regions.

In theory the introduction of tasaciones should have brought more comprehensive, detailed, and reliable records, but evidence for them is incomplete, contradictory, and difficult to interpret. First, it is not known how much of what became the Audiencia of Quito was actually visited and assessed in 1549. Only a few of La Gasca's tasaciones for Ecuador have been found.[1] However, one account indicates that 27,036 tributary Indians in forty-one encomiendas in the jurisdiction of Quito were enumerated and assessed by the bishop of Lima and Licenciado Ciança.[2] At that time Loja, Zamora, Guayaquil, and Puerto Viejo still needed to be inspected. The figure is surprisingly low compared with later accounts, which suggests that the visita may have been less comprehensive than it appears.

During the following decade some tasaciones were drawn up eliminating personal service banned in 1549, but again the coverage is incomplete.[3] In 1558 the gobernación of Popayán, including the jurisdiction of Pasto, was inspected by Tomás López,[4] and the following year visitas were conducted of villages composing the encomienda of Francisco Ruiz in the Quito Basin[5] and the encomienda of Otavalo belonging to Rodrigo de Salazar.[6] Interestingly, both of these visitas were ordered by Gil Ramírez Dávalos, who used the same instructions as those employed on a visita of a number of Puruhá villages belonging to Juan de Padilla in connection with a lawsuit in 1557.[7] Undoubtedly other communities had been assessed by 1561, when the first comprehensive list of encomiendas within the viceroyalty was compiled.

On orders for the viceroy, Antonio de Mendoza, the secretary of the Audiencia of Lima, Pedro de Avendaño drew up a list of the number and

Table A1. Indian Population according to Pedro de Avendaño, 1561

Region	Total population	Tributary population (age 16–50)	Value of tribute (pesos)
Quito	240,670	48,134	64,800
Loja	9,495	3,647	11,004
Zamora	11,222	6,093	14,000
Guayaquil	4,742	2,280	12,664
Puerto Viejo	2,297	1,377	5,452

Source: RAHM A/92 Colección Múñoz fols. 55–77 Relación de los naturales que hay 1561.

value of encomiendas within the viceroyalty. Unfortunately only summary figures for the tributary and total populations are included in his account. This raises the issue of what enumerations or other information the figures were based upon. No visita general had been conducted in Ecuador prior to this date, though the 1559 inspections may have been more extensive than the remaining tasaciones suggest. The list was probably compiled of tasaciones drawn up at various dates prior to 1561. There is therefore some doubt about the accuracy of the figures as a reflection of the population at that time, particularly since the region was afflicted by a smallpox and measles epidemic in 1558. Most likely his figures were derived from a mixture of pre- and postepidemic tasaciones. The lack of correspondence between the total population, number of tributary Indians, and the amount of tribute payable, observed by Mansilla for Peru, applies equally to Ecuador and, as he suggests, reflects either the arbitrariness of the tasaciones or Avendaño's lack of accuracy.[8] These deficiencies clearly detract from the value of these earliest comprehensive figures, which should be used with caution and if possible in conjunction with other evidence. It is important to note that the list includes no account of Indians in the eastern lowlands, who had not been assessed by that date. (See Table A1.)

The picture becomes more confused when Avendaño's figures are compared with those contained in another document purporting to show the same information, though with rounded estimates. The latter document excludes the jurisdication of Zamora, which it states had not been reassessed. This suggests that it predated Avendaño's list and that the figures it contains may represent provisional estimates entered before more precise ones were known. The enormous discrepancies between the accounts are difficult to explain. (See Table A2.)

Other general accounts are similarly lacking in clarity. Another account lists Quito as having forty encomenderos and 35,000 Indians, clearly tributary Indians, noting that there were a further 6,000 in the jurisdiction

Table A2. Indian Population in the Kingdoms of Perú, 1561

Region	Total population	Tributary population (ages 16–50)	Value of tirbute (pesos)
Quito	270,000	54,000	64,800
Loja	45,000	9,000	14,600
Guayaquil	25,000	5,000	14,160
Puerto Viejo	25,000	5,000	11,600

Source: AGI AL 120 Relación de los naturales de los reinos del Peru 1561, also in RAHM CM 42 fol. 248.

Table A3. Encomenderos and Tributary Indians in Ecuador, ca. 1567

Jurisdiction	Encomenderos	Tributary Indians
Quito	40	35,000
Cuenca	—	6,000
Loja	15	9,000
Guayaquil	18	7,000
Puerto Viejo	15	5,000
Zamora	27	8,000

Source: RAHM 9/4664 no. 21 Los pueblos despañoles que hay, no date.

of Cuenca, which previously had been included in the jurisdiction of Quito.[9] Although undated, this document clearly postdates the erection of the audiencia in 1563 and was possibly written in 1567. (See Table A3.)

In the seventeenth century the corregidor of Quito, Juan Vázquez de Acuña, claimed that in 1563 the audiencia had possessed only 16,000 tributary Indians, who, with their families, numbered 80,000 souls.[10] His figures, which include the whole of the sierra, coast, and Oriente, are clearly underestimates. Most likely they were deliberately depressed so that they could be compared with later figures and reflect favorably on his methods of registering tributary Indians.

The most important source for the study of the historical demography of sixteenth-century Peru is Viceroy Francisco Toledo's visita general initiated in 1570. Unfortunately the only returns available for Ecuador are for Guayaquil and Puerto Viejo.[11] Others have not been found, though there is evidence that visitas were conducted in Pasto,[12] Riobamba, and Ambato.[13] Despite the fact that López de Velasco's description of the region was written between 1571 and 1574, he does not appear to have used the Toledo returns but, rather, relied on earlier figures.[14] While his figure for Pasto was based on the 1558 visita of the region, the sources for his other figures are not clear. (See Table A4.)

Toledo's visitas, however, appear to have formed the basis of Juan

Table A4. Population Estimates of López de Velasco and Canelas Albarrán

Region	López de Velasco			Canelas Albarrán
	Number of encomenderos	Tributary population	Total Indian population	Other races
Pasto	28	23,000–24,000	100,000	4,000
Quito	41	42,000–43,000	108,141	10,000
Cuenca	3	8,000		
Zamora	28	5,000	8,100	1,000
Loja	12–13	6,000	16,000	1,000
Guayaquil	23	3,000	7,355	10,000
Puerto Viejo	13	1,500	4,102	500
Los Quijos	50	6,000	10,000	500
Gobernación of Salinas	120	17,000–18,000	40,000	500
Total	318–19	111,500–114,500	293,698	27,500

Source: López de Velasco, *Geografía*, 204–31; BNM 3178 fols. 1–15 Descripción de todos los reinos del Perú 1586.

Canelas Albarrán's description of the region written in 1586.[15] For most regions he claims the numbers were taken from the visita general. His total Indian populations for Guayaquil and Puerto Viejo are consistent with known tributary numbers for those regions,[16] but the figure for Pasto appears extremely high, given that Valverde's visita in 1570 found only 12,645 tributary Indians. Surprisingly large numbers of Indians are registered for the gobernación of Salinas, but Canelas Albarrán claimed that he had visited the area personally in 1576. Although his account may contain some inaccuracies, in general it appears firmly based on the tasaciones drawn up in the 1570s.

During the 1580s a number of visitas were conducted of different regions within the Audiencia of Quito,[17] but no attempt was made to present a comprehensive picture until 1591, when the introduction of a new tax on tribute income required the drawing up of a list of tributary Indians within the viceroyalty.[18] The lists were compiled by Luis Morales de Figueroa, and it has been judged that his figures were based on the tasaciones ordered by Viceroy Toledo,[19] and certainly those for Guayaquil and Puerto Viejo are the same as those in the latter returns. However, his lists for the jurisdictions of Quito, Cuenca, Loja, and Zamora were drawn from *revisitas,* whose dates are generally unknown. The figure of 2,011 for Otavalo was based on a visita conducted in 1590, but others probably refer to a variety of dates within the previous two decades. Furthermore, many villages appear to have been omitted, and the names of others cannot be identified. Although it was claimed that much effort had been expended in collecting the information, it appears highly inaccurate. Perhaps more significantly, many of the tasaciones predate the major epidemics of the late 1580s, which affected the greater part of the audiencia. As such, the relación is best used, not to provide a comprehensive estimate of the population in 1591, but for tracing the demographic history of individual communities when figures provided can be placed in a better documented local context. No figures are included for Indians in the Oriente. (See Table A5).

In connection with the recruitment of labor for the mines of Zaruma, in the 1590s a list of encomiendas and the numbers of tributary Indians they comprised was drawn up for the province of Quito.[20] The account does not purport to give a comprehensive picture. It only covers the sierra and omits a number of encomiendas, while giving only rounded estimates for those included. Because it covers such a wide area, the relación has been widely used, but the source of the author's information is obscure and, within the broad area covered, appears less complete than the Morales Figueroa list.

The same sources of information formed the basis of general estimates of the Indian population and comments on demographic trends by admin-

Table A5. Tributary Population in the 1590s

Region	Morales Figueroa[a]	Relación de Zaruma[b]
Ibarra	3,464	2,650
Otavalo	2,491	2,500
Yumbos	1,072	—
Quito	4,467	4,100
Latacunga	4,750	4,700
Ambato	2,571	1,700
Riobamba	2,709	4,500
Chimbo	474	1,100
Cuenca	2,242	3,000
Unknown	1,712	—
Total	25,952[c]	24,250
Loja	2,849	
Zamora	685	

[a] CDI 6:43–61 Relación de los indios tributarios que hay 1.11.1591.
[b] RGI 2:315–16 Relación del distrito del cerro de Zaruma, no date.
[c] The summary figure in the document is given as 25,852 (24,380 for Quito plus 1,472 for Cuenca), but this is an arithmetic error by the scribe.

istrators and the clergy. The first estimate was made by the Franciscan Francisco Morales, who in 1552 claimed that the province of Quito possessed over 50,000 tributary Indians.[21] This figure is considerably higher than the 27,306 tributary Indians counted during the visitas initiated by La Gasca,[22] but the latter is generally out of line with most other accounts from the mid-1550s. The figure of 50,000 tributary Indians, and 200,000 souls, for the terminos of Quito reappears in an account of the city written in 1573, and in another by the cabildo of Quito in 1577.[23] By 1591 the same number had been reported to the Crown.[24] According to the cabildo, the figures were based on Toledo's visita general, but the total population does not correspond to that included by Canelas Albarrán, which purports to be based on the same visita. The discrepancy may derive from differences in the boundaries of the jurisdictions being discussed. To add to this confusion, in 1572 Licenciado García de Valverde estimated that the province contained 70,000 Indians.[25] The account by the officials of the royal exchequer written in 1576 gives only 30,000 *indios casados,* but presumably this figure excluded single persons who paid tribute and may have been based on tribute income rather than tasaciones.[26] No estimate for the province of Quito for the period between 1550 and 1580 falls below the latter figure. As such, the estimate of 16,000 tributary Indians and 80,000 souls in 1563 provided by the corregidor Juan Vázquez de Acuña appears to have little foundation.[27]

There are two general estimates of the population for the latter part of the sixteenth century, and they both refer to the Audiencia of Quito, rather than the city's términos, thereby including Guayaquil, Puerto Viejo, Loja, and territories to the east. An anonymous account written in the early 1580s estimated that this broad region contained more than 100,000 tributary Indians,[28] which, if there were 50,000 in the province of Quito, would not be unreasonable. A similar figure of 96,000 tributary Indians for 1598 was estimated for the bishopric of Quito,[29] which in 1595 the bishop himself reported contained over 200,000 souls.[30]

These estimates are of little use in tracing demographic trends, but they are included to show the order of magnitude of the population in the sixteenth century. General commentaries on demographic trends are worth considering briefly here, although detailed discussions of regional trends are considered in the main text. There appears to be no divergence from the view that the Indian population in the lowlands to the east and west continued to decline throughout the sixteenth century. Sometimes the decline in the lowlands is compared with an increase in the sierra.[31] Not all accounts agreed that the population in the sierra was increasing. Views seem to be particularly contradictory for the southern highlands around Cuenca, Loja, and Zamora.[32] Detailed evidence for these regions reveals that in fact their populations declined dramatically, and the confusion seems to have derived in part from comparing conditions with those that prevailed under Inka rule. The Cañar and Palta suffered heavy losses as a result of Inka conquest, such that claims by Spanish officials that the natives lived more leisured, healthier, and longer lives under their administration may have contained a grain of truth for some groups.

A number of observers noted that the Indian population of the highlands was increasing. Many of these accounts were written by officials who resided in Quito, who may have been impressed by the rapid growth of the city. They were probably also correct in stressing that the Audiencia of Quito had not suffered depopulation on a scale found in other parts of the viceroyalty.[33] But did this mean that the Indian population was increasing as they suggested? Meanwhile other observers preferred to distinguish demographic trends in areas with and without mines, rather than between highlands and lowlands.[34] As this study shows, the picture was not as clear as many suggested.

Mitmaq Colonies in Ecuador

Mitmaq Colonies in Ecuador

Destination	Source
Palta region	
General	Collao, near Lake Titicaca
Saraguro, Cariamanga,	Cuzco
Nambacola, Catacocha	
Cañar region	
Cojitambo, Chuquipata,	Cuzco
and possibly Paccha	
Puruhá region	
Chimbo Valley	Cajamarca, Humacucho,
	Guayacondo
Achambo	Cajamarca (Wayacuntu)
San Andrés (Xunxi)	Condesuyo
Quero	Cuzco
Salasaca	Unknown
Latacunga region	
General	Guayacondo
Saquisilí	Unknown
Quito region	
Unknown	Chachapoyas (Chacha)
Uyumbicho?	Huancabamba (from Pampamarca)
	and Ayabaca (Wayacuntu)
Urin Chillo	Unknown
Uyumbicho, Amaguana, El	Multiethnic
Quinche, Pomasqui	
Carapungo, Yaruquí, Zámbiza,	Unknown
Chillogallo, Añaquito, and	
Machangara	
Otavalo-Caranqui region	
Cayambe, Otavalo, Cotacachi,	Unknown
Tontaquí, Intag, Tulla, and San	
Pablo(?)	

Mitmaq Transferred from Ecuador

Ethnic group	Destination
Palta	Collao, near Lake Titicaca
Cañar	Yucay Valley, and later Cuzco; Huancabamba, Cajamarca, Huamacucho, Humanga, and Lima; Yampares, highland Bolivia
Cayambe	Matibamba in Angares; Huánuco, and possibly Cuzco, Copacabana, and Chupaico
Caranqui	Lake Titicaca?
Pasto	Lake Titicaca
Huancavilca	Pachachaca and Amancay

Local Mitmaq Settled in Other Regions of Ecuador

Ethnic group	Destination
Cañar	El Quinche, Pomasqui, Cotocallao in the Quito region
Pasto	Guamote, Alausí, Yaruquies in the Puruhá region
Pasto	Tumbaco in the Quito region, and possibly Cayambe, Tocachí, and Malchinguí.

Origins of Parents of Infants Baptized
in El Sagrario, Quito

Region	1567–68		1594–1600	
	Number	Percent	Number	Percent
Northern sierra				
Colombia	1	0.6	10	0.5
Pasto/Ibarra	7	4.0	31	1.5
Otavalo	5	2.9	77	3.7
Total	13	7.5	118	5.7
Corregimiento of Quito				
Five leagues	72	41.4	1,075	51.0
City of Quito	16	9.2	213	10.1
Yumbos	9	5.1	85	4.0
Total	97	55.7	1,373	65.1
Southern sierra				
Latacunga	31	17.8	360	17.1
Ambato	5	2.9	71	3.4
Riobamba	11	6.3	111	5.3
Chimbo	5	2.9	30	1.4
Cuenca	1	0.6	19	0.9
Loja	0	0.0	3	0.1
Total	53	30.5	594	28.2
Oriente				
Los Quijos	11	6.3	17	0.8
Coast				
Guayaquil	0	0.0	3	0.1
Peru	0	0.0	3	0.1
Grand total	174	100.0	2,108	100.00
Unknown	10		54	

Sources: ASQ, Libro de bautismos de Indios, 1566 to 1568, Libro de bautismos de Mestizos, Montañeses, Indios, 1594 to 1605. Only the two complete years 1567 and 1568 and the period up to 1600 have been analyzed.

Glossaries of Quechua, Spanish, and Other Non-English Terms

Modern Ayacucho Quechua dialect is used, since this is very close to the *lengua general* used by the Inka. Singular forms are employed in the text, since these were commonly used by the Inka and are more familiar to the general reader. Plural forms are shown in parentheses. Old Spanish orthography is used for Inka personal names, since not all were Quechua.

Aklla(kuna)	Chosen, often referred to a woman
Ayllu	Localized kinship group
Chaski(kuna)	Messenger, post runner
Chaskiwasi	Rest house for *chaski*
Chuñu	Freeze-dried potato
Kamayuq(kuna)	Individual residing outside his or her community and specializing in the production or exploitation of exotic goods or resources
Kuraka(kuna)	Local ethnic lord(s)
Mama(kuna)	Chosen woman attached to a temple
Mit'a (Mita)	Inka rotational labor draft. (Ayacucho Quechua is not glottalized, but this form is used here to distinguish it from the Spanish *mita*.)
Mit'ayuq(kuna)	Mit'a worker
Mitmaq(kuna)	An individual transplanted and settled outside his or her area of ethnic origin by the Inka
Qapaq ñan	Inka royal highway
Qumpi	Luxury, fine cloth
Taklla	Foot plow
Tampu(kuna)	Way station along the royal highway
Tawantinsuyu	Inka empire
Tukrikuq	Inka royal official
Yana(kuna)	Servant of Inka nobles or local chiefs

SPANISH AND OTHER NON-ENGLISH TERMS

Ají	Capsicum pepper
Alcabala	Sales tax
Alcalde mayor	Spanish official with political and judicial authority over a district
Alcaldía mayor	Jurisdiction of an *alcalde mayor*

363

Alcalde ordinario	Magistrate attached to a *cabildo*
Alfombrilla	German measles
Alguacil	Constable, police officer
Alma	Soul
Almud	Measure of capacity equivalent to one-twelfth of a *fanega*
Alpargates	Rope sandals
Anaco	Blanket or shawl
Anejo	An annex; a benefice or church dependent on another
Ánima	Soul
Año de raya	A work-year of 312 days in a textile mill
Aposento	Temporary habitation; inn
Arroba	Weight equivalent to 25 pounds or 11.5 kilograms
Audiencia	High judicial court and by extension the region under its jurisdiction
Balsa	Raft or canoe constructed of wood
Balsero	Oarsman of a *balsa*
Barbacoa	Raised wooden platform, on which houses were sometimes built
Barbasco	A fish stupefacient
Bayeta	Baize, or coarse flannel
Behetría	Community or polity, having no legitimate overlord and therefore free to choose its own leader
Bizcocho	Biscuit
Braza	Linear measurement equivalent to two *varas*
Buba	Bubo
Caballería	Area measurement equivalent to 11.3 hectares
Cabildo	Town council
Cabuya	Plant from which cord or rope was made
Cacha.	Messenger (Hispanicized Quechua)
Cacicazgo	Office of a *cacique*, and by extension his or her authority or power
Cacique	Indian leader (Hispanicised Arawak)
Caciquillo	Minor *cacique*
Caja	Strongbox or chest
Caja de comunidad	Community chest
Callejón	Narrow mountain pass or corridor
Camayo	Specialist producer. See *kamayuq*
Camellón	Drained, raised, or ridged field
Camino real	Royal highway
Canela	Cinnamon
Capitulación	Contract for the exploration or pacification of new lands and peoples

Cartas cuenta	Summary account
Casa de fundición	Smeltery
Casado/a	Married person
Cédula	Decree
Ceja de la montaña	Brow of a hill or mountain
Chacra	Smallholding or farm
Chaquira	Small beads of gold, shell or bone used as wealth objects or currency
Chorillo	Small textile workshop
Composición	Payment of a fee to regularize illegal or irregular occupation of land
Concertaje	Contract labor
Consejo de Indias	Council of the Indies
Contador	Treasurer
Corregidor	Royal offical with administrative and judicial authority
Corregimiento	Jurisidiction of a corregidor
Cuadra	Area measurement of about 2.8 hectares. Sixteen cuadras were equivalent to one caballería, or about 11.3 hectares
Cuadrilla	Labor gang
Curicamayo	Forced laborer panning alluvial gold, probably derived from the Quechua *qurikamayuq,* meaning a specialized producer of gold
Demora	Period during which mines were worked
Diezmo	Tithe or tax of one-tenth
Doctrina	Indian parish
Dolor de costado	Pain in the side
Encomendero/a	Holder of an *encomienda*
Encomienda	Grant of Indians to an individual as a personal reward for merits or services that gave the recipient the right to exact tribute in kind or cash and, until 1549, labor services, and who in return undertook to provide Christian instruction
Entrada	Military or missionary expedition into unexplored or unpacified territory
Estancia	Ranch for livestock raising
Fanega	Measure of capacity, about 1.5 bushels
Fanegada de tierra	Area measurement equivalent to about 2.9 hectares
Fiscal	Attorney general
Forastero/a	Indian residing in a community other than that of his or her origin

Galpón	Large shed
Gañán	Wage laborer
Garrotillo	Diphtheria
Gobernación	Jurisdiction of a governor
Guaca	Indian grave or shrine, often with precious items
Guerra florida	Flower war; among the Aztec a prearranged war for the purpose of obtaining prisoners for ritual sacrifice
Hacendado	Owner of a hacienda
Hoya	Mountan basin or valley
Huerta	Large vegetable garden or orchard
Indio de merced	Forced laborer in textile mill assigned by special licence
Jerga	Frieze, a type of coarse cloth
Juez de naturales	Judge of minor Indian offences
Legajo	Bundle; in this book, a bundle of documents
Licenciado	Title given to a person with a degree of bachelor or licentiate
Liquilla	Small piece of cloth
Loma	Small hill; rising ground or slope
Maestre de campo	Campmaster
Mal del valle	Valley sickness; intestinal gangrene caused by amoebic infection
Mano	Pestle for grinding maize
Manta	Blanket or shawl
Maravedí	Coin; in the sixteenth century Ecuador there were 450 maravedís to one peso
Mestizaje	Racial mixing
Metate	Morter for grinding maize
Mindalá(es).	Specialised and privileged long distance trader (Unidentified aboriginal Andean language)
Mita	Spanish forced labor system broadly based on the *mit'a*
Mitayo	Forced Indian laborer working under the colonial *mita*
Montaña	Rain forest on the flanks of the Andes
Morador	Inhabitant
Muchacho/a	Boy/girl
Nudo	Knot, here a transverse ridge separating mountain basins

Obaje de comunidad	Community textile mill
Obraje	Workshop, here a textile mill
Obrajero	Owner of an *obraje*
Obrajuelo	Small textile mill
Oficial real	Royal official
Oidor	Spanish judge and member of an *audiencia*
Orejón.	High-ranking Inka official and imperial advisor
Padrón	Detailed list or census of the inhabitants of a settlement, Indian or Spanish
Paga	Payment
Páramo	Humid upland grasslands characteristic of the northern Andes
Parcialidad	Suburb of a town or village, or a kinship group within an Indian community
Pasto	Pasture
Patacón	Coin equivalent to a peso of one ounce of silver
Peinadillo	An Indian who had left his or her community of origin
Pende	Shaman (aboriginal language)
Peso	Coin of eight reals or *tomines*
Petate	Rush sleeping mat
Pita	Cord or thread extracted from cabuya or an agave
Plaza mayor	Main square
Pochteca	Aztec merchant engaged in foreign trade (Nahuatl)
Presidio	Garrison, fort
Principal	Indian leader, generally with less authority than that of a *cacique*
Probanza	Testimony of merits and services in support of a petition
Procurador	Representative, solicitor, attorney
Puna	Dry highland grasslands characteristic of the southern Andes
Quebrada	Ravine; steep river valley
Quinto	Tax of one fifth the value of an item. Paid on slaves, silver, among other things
Ranchería	Small rural settlement
Real cédula	Royal decree
Reducción	Settlement formed by the amalgamation of several smaller settlements or created by drawing together uncoverted Indians
Regidor	Councilor attached to a *cabildo*
Relación	An account
Relaciónes geográficas	Geographical accounts

Repartimiento	Rotational draft labor system. Alternative name for the *mita*
Reservado/a	Indian exempt from the tribute payment by virtue of age, status or physical disability
Romadizo	Respiratory infection, catarrh, or cold
Salina	Salt deposits
Sayal	Serge or sackcloth, a coarse cloth
Scarlatina	Scarlet fever
Selva	Forest
Servicio ordinario	Domestic service
Soltero/a	Single person
Tabardete	Typhus
Tambo	Colonial way station patterned on the Inka *tanpu*
Tameme	Indian porter
Tapia	Mud wall
Tasación	Official tribute assessment
Teniente	Governor's lieutenant
Tenientazgo	Lieutenantship; office of deputy
Términos.	Limits of jurisdiction
Terra firme	Interfluvial land (Portuguese)
Tierra caliente	Area with a hot climate
Tierra firme	Interfluvial land
Tierra fría	Area with a cold climate
Tierra templada	Area with a temperate climate
Tola	Burial mound
Tomín	Coin equivalent to a real or one-eighth of a peso
Vagamundo	Indian who had left his or her community of origin
Vara	Linear measurement of about 33 inches or 84 centimeters
Várzea	Fertile alluvial bank of river
Vecino	Householder
Visita	Tour of inspection of an area
Visitador	Royal official encharged with conducting a *visita*
Yanacona	Spanish servant

Abbreviations Used in Notes and Bibliography

UNPUBLISHED SOURCES

AGI   Archivo General de Indias, Seville
      AG   Audiencia de Guatemala
      AL   Audiencia de Lima
      AQ   Audiencia de Quito
      ASF Audiencia de Santa Fé
      CO   Contaduría
      EC   Escribanía de Cámara
      IG   Indiferente General
      JU   Justicia
      MP   Mapas y Planos
      PAT Patronato
AGOFM   Archivio Generale dell'Ordine dei Frati Minori, Rome
      M   Misiones
AHBC   Archivo Histórico del Banco Central, Quito
AHG   Archivo Histórico del Guayas, Guayaquil
AMQ   Archivo Municipal, Quito
ANHQ   Archivo Nacional de la Historia, Quito
      PQ   Presidencia de Quito
      RH   Real Hacienda
ARSI   Archivum Romanum Societatis Iesu, Rome
      NRQ Provincia Novi Regni et Quitensis
ASFQ   Archivo Franciscano, Quito
ASQ   Archivo del Sagrario, Quito
BM   British Museum, London
      Add. Additional Manuscripts
BNM   Biblioteca Nacional, Madrid
IOA   Archivo del Instituto Otavaleño de Antropología, Otavalo
      EP/J Escribanía Pública—Juicios
RAHM   Real Academia de la Historia, Madrid
      CM   Colección Muñoz

PUBLISHED SOURCES

AMQ CR 9   *Colección de cédulas reales dirigidas a la Audiencia de Quito, 1538–1601.* Ed. J. A. Garcés. Quito: Archivo Municipal de Quito, 1935.

369

AMQ CR 21	*Colección de cédulas reales dirigidas a la Audiencia de Quito, 1601–1660.* Ed. J. A. Garcés. Quito: Archivo Municipal de Quito, 1946.
AMQ LC 1	*Libro primero de cabildos de Quito. 1534–1543.* Vol. 1. Ed. J. Rumazo Ganzález. Quito: Archivo Municipal de Quito, 1934.
AMQ LC 2	*Libro primero de cabildos de Quito. 1534–1543.* Vol. 2. Ed. J. Rumazo Ganzález. Quito: Archivo Municipal de Quito, 1934.
AMQ LC 3	*Libro segundo de cabildos de Quito. 1544–1551.* Vol. 1. Ed. J. Rumazo Ganzález. Quito: Archivo Municipal de Quito, 1934.
AMQ LC 4	*Libro segundo de cabildos de Quito. 1544–1551.* Vol. 2. Ed. J. Rumazo Ganzález. Quito: Archivo Municipal de Quito, 1934.
AMQ LC 5	*Oficios o cartas al cabildo de Quito por el rey de España o el Virrey de Indias.* Ed. J. A. Garcés. Quito: Archivo Municipal de Quito, 1934.
AMQ LC 6	*Libro de cabildos de la ciudad de Quito. 1573–1574.* Ed. J. A. Garcés. Quito: Archivo Municipal de Quito, 1934.
AMQ LC 8	*Libro de cabildos de la ciudad de Quito. 1575–1576.* Ed. J. A. Garcés. Quito: Archivo Municipal de Quito, 1935.
AMQ LC 10	*Documentos relativos al adelantado capitán don Sebastián de Benalcázar, 1535–1565.* Ed. J. A. Garcés. Quito: Archivo Municipal de Quito, 1936.
AMQ LC 14	*Libro de cabildos de la ciudad de Quito. 1597–1603.* Vol. 2. Ed. J. A. Garcés. Quito: Archivo Municipal de Quito, 1940.
AMQ LC 15	*Libro primero de cabildos de la villa de San Miguel de Ibarra, 1606–1617.* Ed. J. A. Garcés. Quito: Archivo Municipal de Quito, 1937.
AMQ LC 16	*Libro primero de cabildos de la ciudad de Cuenca. 1557–1563.* Ed. J. A. Garcés. Quito: Archivo Municipal de Quito, 1938.
AMQ LC 20	*Libro de cabildos de la ciudad de Quito. 1603–1610.* Ed. J. A. Garcés. Quito: Archivo Municipal de Quito, 1944.
AMQ LC 26	*Libro de cabildos de la ciudad de Quito. 1610–1616.* Ed. J. A. Garcés. Quito: Archivo Municipal de Quito, 1955.
CDI	*Colección de documentos inéditos relativos al descubrimiento, conquista, y organización de las antiguas posesiones españolas de América y Oceanía.* 42 vols. Madrid, 1864–84.
CDIE	*Colección de documentos inéditos para la historia de España.* 112 vols. Ed M. F. Navarrete et al. Madrid, 1842–95.
CDIU	*Colección de documentos inéditos relativos al descubrimiento, conquista, y organización de las antiguas posesiones españolas de Ultramar.* 25 vols. Madrid, 1885–1932.
RGI	*Relaciones geográficas de Indias.* 3 vols. Biblioteca de autores españoles, nos. 183–85. Ed. M. Jiménez Espada. Madrid: Ediciones Atlas, 1965.

Notes

CHAPTER 1

1. See Newson, "Indian Population Patterns," 41–74, for a review of the literature referring to some of these factors.

2. Newson, "Indian Population Patterns"; Newson, *Cost of Conquest;* Newson, *Indian Survival in Colonial Nicaragua.*

3. Cook, *Demographic Collapse,* 70.

4. Cook and Borah, *Indian Population,* 52.

5. Smith, "Depopulation," 459.

6. Borah and Cook, "Conquest and Population," 181.

7. Friedlander, "Malaria and Demography," 217; Cook and Borah, *Essays,* 2:176–79; Denevan, *Native Population,* 41.

8. Brown, "Yellow Fever," 290; Kiple, *Caribbean Slave,* 162–66.

9. Ramenofsky, *Vectors of Death,* 159; Kiple, *Caribbean Slave,* 17, 32.

10. Manson-Bahr, *Tropical Diseases,* 889–90; Rafatjah, "Malaria Vector Control," 1151.

11. Binford et al., "Ecosystems, Paleoecology, and Human Disturbance"; Denevan, "Pristine Myth," 377–78.

12. Molineaux, "Epidemiology of Human Malaria," 941–42; Rafatjah, "Malaria Vector Control," 1152.

13. Although smallpox can survive in a dried form on clothing or bedding for up to eighteen months, its transmission from such sources is not common.

14. Bartlett, "Measles Periodicity," 48–70.

15. Black, "Infectious Diseases, 515–18.

16. Neel, "Health and Disease," 170; Cliff and Haggett, *Atlas of Disease Distributions,* 245–46.

17. Thornton, Miller, and Warren, "Population Recovery," 35–41.

18. Ramenofsky, "Loss of Innocence," 41–42.

19. McFalls and McFalls, *Disease and Fertility,* 60–61, 130, 533.

20. Sweet, "Upper Amazon Valley," 141.

21. Rotberg and Rabb, *Hunger and History,* 305–8; Livi-Bacci, *Population and Nutrition,* 35–39.

22. Sauer, *Early Spanish Main,* 203.

23. Cook and Borah, *Essays,* 3:176; Super, *Food, Conquest, and Colonization,* 28–32, 38, 63, 87–88.

24. Rotberg and Rabb, *Hunger and History,* 305–8; Walter and Schofield, "Famine, Disease, and Crisis Mortality," 17–21.

25. Newson, "Indian Population Patterns," 51–62.

26. Bakewell, *Miners of the Red Mountain,* 149–51; Cole, *Potosí Mita,* 23–24; Bakewell, "Mining," 224, 228.

27. Ruiz Rivera, *Encomienda y mita,* 337; Bakewell, *Miners of the Red Mountain,* 111–13; Cole, *Potosí Mita,* 27.

28. Simpson, *Many Mexicos,* 126; Tyrer, "Demographic and Economic History," 104–5; Cushner, *Farm and Factory,* 94–95; Salvucci, *Textiles and Capitalism,* 106–24.

29. Salvucci, *Textiles and Capitalism,* 97.

30. MacLeod, "Ethnic Relations," 197–205.

31. Villamarin and Villamarin, *Indian Labor,* 2.

32. Gibson, *Aztecs,* 245–46.

33. Simpson, *Many Mexicos,* 22–23; Stern, *Huamanga,* 144; Bakewell, "Mining," 226.

34. Bradby, "Resistance to Capitalism," 99.

35. Newson, "Sistemas de trabajo."

36. Frisch, "Population, Food Intake, and Fertility," 312–20; McKeown, "Food, Infection, and Population," 29–49.

37. Bongaarts, "Does Malnutrition Affect Fertility?" 564–69; Menken, Trussel, and Watkins, "Nutrition-Fertility Link," 426–41.

38. Marcy, "Factors Affecting the Fecundity," 321–22.

39. In colonial Latin America most individuals married in their teens, whereas in Europe at the same time marriages were contracted in the mid to late twenties (Marcy, "Factors Affecting the Fecundity," 309–10).

40. Menken, "Seasonal Migration," 114–15.

41. Newson, "Sistemas de trabajo," 296.

42. Knodel, "Breast Feeding and Population Growth," 1111–15; Marcy, "Factors Affecting the Fecundity," 323.

43. Farriss, *Maya Society,* 277; Saignes, *Caciques, Tribute, and Migration;* Larson, "Bolivia Revisited," 77; Zeitlin, "Ranchers and Indians," 57–60.

44. Tyrer, "Demographic and Economic History"; Larrain Barros, *Demografía;* Ortiz de la Tabla Ducasse, "Población Ecuatoriana"; Alchon, *Native Society and Disease.*

CHAPTER 2

1. AGI AQ 8 Santillán 15.1.1564.

2. For a useful introduction to the physical geography of the Andes and contrasts within it, see Brush, *Mountain, Field, and Family,* 2–6; Molina and Little, "Geoecology of the Andes," 115–44; Parsons, "The Northern Andean Environment," 253–62.

3. For example, Troll, *Culturas superiores andinas,* 39–40.

4. Terán, *Geografía,* 97–99.

5. Knapp, *Ecología cultural,* 22.

6. Holdridge, *Forests of Western and Southern Ecuador,* 16; Acosta-Solís, *Recursos naturales,* 2, vol. 1:111–63; Basile, *Tillers of the Andes,* 5–31.

7. Knapp, *Ecología cultural,* 186.

8. Molina and Little, "Geoecology of the Andes," 131; Knapp, *Ecología cultural,* 18–19.

9. Troll, *Culturas superiores andinas,* 39–40.

10. Gondard and López, *Inventario arqueológico,* 58.

11. Acosta-Solís, *Recursos naturales,* pt. 2, vol. 1:153.

12. Porras Garcés, *Fase Cosanga,* 48–51; Salomon, "Ethnic Lords," 66.

13. Oberem, "Recursos naturales," 51–64. For a contemporary example of the operation of these methods, see Brush, *Mountain, Field, and Family,* 9–15.

14. See chap. 5.

15. Murra, "Control vertical," 59–115.

16. Brush, *Mountain, Field, and Family,* 10–11, 15–16.

17. Murra, "Historic Tribes of Ecuador," 791–802.

18. For brief summaries of Pasto culture, see Romoli de Avery, "Las tribus," 29–30; Uribe, "Comunidades andinas prehispánicas," 9–14; Calero, "Pasto," 35–50.

19. Cieza de León, *Crónica,* cap. 33:47–48, cap. 37:53. In fact the town of Pasto itself was located in the Atris Valley, which was in the territory of the Quillaçinga, who were to be found to the east of the Pasto.

20. AGI AQ 60 Traslado del libro de tasaciones 13.12.1558; Moreno Ruiz, "Primeros asentamientos," 430–31; Romoli de Avery, "Las tribus," 13–14, 44; Larrain Barros, *Demografía,* 1:38.

21. Cieza de León, *Crónica,* cap. 37:53.

22. Martínez, *Pastos,* 55, 101–3; Martínez, *Cacique García Tulcanaza,* 42–43; Espinosa Soriano, *Cayambes y Carangues,* 1:283–84, 291–94. See also chap. 5.

23. AGI AQ 60 Tasación de los tributos . . . García de Valverde 1570–71; Cieza de León, *Crónica,* cap. 33:49, cap. 37:53; Uribe, "Comunidades andinas prehispánicas," 11–12. Much of the following discussion draws on sixteenth-century visitas of the Pasto region, which unfortunately did not extend beyond southern Colombia to northern Ecuador. Nevertheless, at the time of Spanish conquest the two regions formed one cultural area (Uribe, "Asentamientos prehispánicos," 167–72).

24. Uribe, "Asentamientos prehispánicos" 60; Cieza de León, *Crónica,* cap. 34:49, cap. 37:53.

25. RGI 2:252 Borja, no date; Salomon, "Ethnic Lords," 304–6; Salomon, "Status Trader Complex," 65.

26. AGI AQ 60 Tasación de los tributos . . . García de Valverde 1570–71; Salomon, "Ethnic Lords," 297–99.

27. AGI AQ 60 Tasación de los tributos . . . García de Valverde 1570–71; Cieza de León, *Crónica,* cap. 35:50–51.

28. Uribe, "Comunidades andinas prehispánicas," 33–34; Salomon, "Status Trader Complex," 66–67.

29. Salomon, "Ethnic Lords," 299–304; Salomon, "Status Trader Complex," 65; Espinosa Soriano, *Cayambes y Carangues,* 1:160–66. For a comparison of the role of mindaláes and the *pochteca* of central Mexico, see Salomon, "Pochteca and Mindalá."

30. Salomon, "Status Trader Complex," 72–73.

31. Cieza de León, *Crónica,* cap. 33:48.

32. See chap. 7.

33. Calero, "Pasto," 53–56.

34. Uribe, "Documentos del siglo XVIII," 61–62.

35. Cieza de Leon, *Crónica,* cap. 33:48–50; Verneau and Rivet, *Ethnographie ancienne,* 13.

36. Cieza de Leon, *Crónica,* cap. 33:48.

37. CDI 41:447 Escobar, no date.

38. Araníbar, "Necropompa," 115–17; Martínez, *Pastos,* 71–77.

39. Cieza de León, *Crónica,* cap. 33:48.

40. RGI 2:226 Anon. 1573; Cieza de León, *Crónica,* cap. 33:48; Martínez, *Pastos,* 29.

41. Martínez, *Pastos,* 27–30; Uribe, "Comunidades prehispánicas," 11–12; Uribe, "Asentamientos prehispánicos," 165.

42. The visita of Pasto villages by Tomás López in 1558 found 10,241 tributary Indians in twenty-two communities. Although this visita did not extend to Pasto communities in present-day Ecuador, it suggests an average community size of over 400 tributary Indians, which, multiplied by 3 or 4, argues for settlements of well over 1,000 inhabitants (AGI AQ 60 Traslado del libro de tasaciones 9.11.1558; Romoli de Avery, "Las tribus," 32; Larrain Barros, *Demografía,* 1:122).

43. Many of the settlements were not visited by Tomás López in person.

44. RGI 2:240–41 Paz Ponce de León 2.4.1582.

45. In 1570 Valverde's visita revealed 6,032 tributary Indians in the province of Pasto (AGI AQ 60 Tasación de los tributos 1570–71), but by 1590 the *cartas cuentas* indicate there were only 4,671 (Romoli de Avery, "Las tribus," 38–43). An estimate of 5,500 for 1582 assumes greater population losses during the epidemics of the late 1580s.

46. Jaramillo Uribe, "Población indígena," 246, 248; Romoli de Avery, "Las tribus," 17; Calero, "Pasto," 277. Jaramillo Uribe bases his estimate on a ratio of tributary to nontributary Indians of 1:3, thereby implying that there were 50,000 tributary Indians. This is sound in that it takes account of the decline in the population from the time of conquest to the López visita, something that Calero fails to take into consideration, coming up with the same aboriginal population estimate but using a ratio of 1:5. However, the level of decline may not have been as great as Jaramillo Uribe suggests, and his ratio is probably too low. Nevertheless, modifications to take account of these observations would produce a similar estimate of around 150,000. Romoli does not indicate the methods she uses to derive a similar estimate of 140,000 to 150,000. Although the López visita appears detailed and comprehensive and has been widely used, the figures it provides should be used with caution. López claimed that because of the difficult terrain, the lack of roads, and the dispersed nature of the population, he had not been able to count the Indians in their settlements as required by the instructions for the visita (AGI AQ 60 Traslado del libro de tasaciones 9.11.1558). In fact the whole visita took only three weeks, so he would have been unable to visit all of the seventy settlements listed. Instead he relied on information provided by local informants, which probably meant encomenderos and possibly priests. Encomenderos may have exaggerated the numbers of Indians in order to maximize their tribute income. The questionable accuracy of the visita is evident from the rounding of the figures for tributary Indians to the extent that over three-quarters of the figures end in zero (78 percent), and nearly half (46 percent) were multiples of fifty or one hundred. The rounding of figures appears to have been most common for distant parts of the Pasto region and for Sibundoy. Thus the

López visita is far from thorough, and it probably exaggerated the number of Indians present at that time.

47. Cieza de Leon, *Crónica,* cap. 33:48.

48. Of a total of 23,157 tributary Indians, 10,241 were Pasto (AGI AQ 60 Traslado del libro de tasaciones 9.11.1558). In fact the proportion is likely to have been lower, given that the other groups experienced a sharper decline during the early colonial period.

49. See chap. 7.

50. See chap. 5 and RGI 2:210 Anon. 1573; Sarmiento de Gamboa, *Historia índica,* pt. 2, cap. 60:261.

51. Espinosa Soriano, *Cayambes y Carangues,* 1:75–76.

52. Caillavet, "Entre sierra y selva," 86–87.

53. Cieza de León, *Crónica,* cap. 41:58.

54. Caillavet, "Dominación incaica," 418.

55. Verneau and Rivet, *Ethnographie ancienne,* 15; Jijón y Caamaño, *Ecuador interandino,* 1:237–39; Athens, *Proceso evolutivo,* 137; Oberem, "Los Caranquis," 75; Caillavet, "Toponimia histórica," 5–7; Espinosa Soriano, *Cayambes y Carangues,* 1:76–77.

56. RGI 2:248 Borja, no date; Jijón y Caamaño, *Ecuador interandino,* 1:238.

57. There is no evidence for the establishment of the dual division of Hurinsaya and Hanansaya in Quito region. Neither is there much evidence for the redistribution of lands or the reorganization of labor (Caillavet, "Dominación incaica," 412–19). See also chap. 5.

58. AGI EC 922A Visita of Otavalo 11.11.1562; RGI 2:234–35 Paz Ponce de León 2.4.1582. It seems likely that the document meant to say "y" rather than "ni."

59. AGI EC 922A Visita of Otavalo; RGI 2:235, 237–38 Paz Ponce de León 2.4.1582.

60. RGI 2:246 Aguilar 12.11.1582, RGI 2:249 Borja, no date; Oberem, "Recursos naturales," 54.

61. Athens, *Proceso evolutivo,* 122; Gondard and López, *Inventario arqueológico,* 135–44; Knapp, *Ecología cultural,* 123–29. The main areas of terracing in the Otavalo region are to be found at Pinsaquí, Zuleta, Cayambe, and Pimampiro.

62. Myers, "Prehistoric Irrigation," 313; Athens, *Proceso evolutivo,* 122–23.

63. RGI 2:249 Borja, no date; Ordoñez de Cevallos, "Viaje del mundo," lib. 38:418; Espinosa Soriano, *Cayambes y Carangues,* 1:133–34.

64. Knapp, *Ecología cultural,* 122.

65. See chap. 5.

66. Knapp, *Ecología cultural,* 122.

67. Batchelor, "Los camellones," 671–89; Knapp, "Nicho ecológico llanura húmeda," 86–87; Knapp and Denevan, "Use of Wetlands," 188–95; Knapp, *Ecología cultural,* 129–32; Caillavet, "Técnicas agrarias autóctonas," 111.

68. RGI 2:248 Borja, no date.

69. Caillavet, "Toponimia histórica," 14–15; Caillavet, "Técnicas agrarias autóctonas," 112–13.

70. Knapp and Denevan, "Use of Wetlands," 195–98, 202–3; Knapp, *Ecología cultural,* 163.

71. RGI 2:237, 239 Paz Ponce de León 2.4.1582; Jijón y Caamaño, "Provincia de Imbabura," 111.

72. Gondard and López, *Inventario arqueológico,* 65–66; Caillavet, "Técnicas agrarias autóctonas," 117.

73. RGI 2:239–40 Paz Ponce de León 2.4.1582.

74. AGI EC 922A Tasa of Otavalo 8.7.1551 and Visita of Otavalo 11.11.1562.

75. RGI 2:234–35 Paz Ponce de León 2.4.1582; Caillavet, "Caciques de Otavalo," 46.

76. Salomon, "Pochteca and Mindalá," 236; Salomon, "Status Trader Complex," 68–72.

77. RGI 2:240 Paz Ponce de León 2.4.1582; Oberem, "Recursos naturales," 61.

78. Caillavet, "Entre sierra y selva," 86–89.

79. RGI 2:240 Paz Ponce de León 2.4.1582; RGI 2:246 Aguilar 12.11.1582, RGI 2:249 Borja, no date.

80. RGI 2:252 Borja, no date.

81. AGI EC 922A Visita of Otavalo 11.11.1582.

82. RGI 2:207 Anon. 1573; RGI 2:240 Paz Ponce de León 2.4.1582.

83. Caillavet, "La sal," 50–55.

84. RGI 2:177 Valverde and Rodríguez 30.12.1576; Caillavet, "La sal," 53–54.

85. RGI 2:240 Paz Ponce de León 2.4.1582; RGI 2:244 Rodríguez 12.11.1582; Caillavet, "La sal," 52–53.

86. Caillavet, "Entre sierra y selva," 89.

87. Jijón y Caamaño, "Provinica de Imbabura," 183–84. These items may have been obtained through Sicchos and Angamarca, where Indians traded salt for gold, cotton, ají, and dried fish (RGI 3:88 Carranza 1569).

88. Caillavet, "Entre sierra y selva," 83–84.

89. AGI AQ 82 Ortegón 1.2.1577.

90. RGI 2:248–49 Borja, no date; Oberem, "Trade and Trade Goods," 347.

91. Caillavet, "Chefferies préhispaniques," 56.

92. RGI 2:227 Anon. 1573; RGI 2:236–37 Paz Ponce de León 2.4.1582; Espinosa Soriano, "Curaca de los Cayambes," 89–90; Oberem, "Los Caranquis," 77; Caillavet, "Dominación incaica," 409.

93. RGI 2:236 Paz Ponce de León 2.4.1582.

94. Espinosa Soriano, *Cayambes y Carangues,* 1:97.

95. RGI 2:237 Paz Ponce de León 2.4.1582.

96. Caillavet, "Otavalo prehispánico," 110; Caillavet, "Caciques de Otavalo," 39; Espinosa Soriano, *Cayambes y Carangues,* 1:89.

97. Larrain Barros, *Demografía,* 1:114–20; Moreno Yánez, *Pichincha,* 98–103; Espinosa Soriano, *Cayambes y Carangues,* 1:81.

98. AGI AQ 22 Probanza of Geronimo Puento 1583 (testimonies 9.2.1579, 19.5.1579, 20.5.1579); *Documentos para la historia militar* 1:27; Borregán, *Crónica,* 83; Caillavet, "Dominación incaica," 409–10.

99. Salomon, "Status Trader Complex," 72.

100. RGI 2:237 Paz Ponce de León 2.4.1582; RGI 2:246 Aguilar 12.11.1582; RGI 2:251 Borja, no date; Cieza de León, *Crónica,* cap. 39:55–56.

101. Caillavet, "Entre sierra y selva," 86–87. For example, in the early colonial period the cacique of Cayambe, Geronimo Puento, married the daughter of the

cacique of Carangue (Espinosa Soriano, "Curaca de los Cayambes," 104–14; Oberem, "Los Caranquis," 78). Oberem refers to the cacique's being married to his "sister," but the transcript of the document in Espinosa Soriano refers to a "daughter," as does that in *Documentos para la historia militar,* 1:14.

102. Cieza de León, *Señorío,* cap. 66:218. See also AGI AQ 22 Probanza of Geronimo Puento 1583, also in *Documentos para la historia militar,* 1:27.

103. RGI 2:246 Aguilar 12.11.1582; RGI 2:250 Borja, no date; Espinosa Soriano, *Cayambes y Carangues,* 1:177–202.

104. RGI 2:236–37 Paz Ponce de León 2.4.1582; RGI 2:250 Borja, no date; Garcilaso de la Vega, *Comentarios reales,* 2, lib. 8, cap. 7:303.

105. RGI 2:246 Aguilar 12.11.1582; RGI 2:250 Borja, no date.

106. RGI 2:246 Aguilar 12.11.1582.

107. Athens, *Proceso evolutivo,* 145.

108. Knapp and Denevan, "Use of Wetlands," 188; Knapp, *Ecología cultural,* 120, 174.

109. RGI 2:234 Paz Ponce de León 2.4.1582; RGI 2:244 Rodríguez 9.11.1582; RGI 2:248, 252 Borja, no date; Caillavet, "Chefferies préhispaniques," 57.

110. Jijón y Caamaño, *Antropología prehispánica,* 351; Myers, "Prehistoric Irrigation," 313.

111. Athens, *Proceso evolutivo,* 180.

112. RGI 2:240 Paz Ponce de León 2.4.1582.

113. RGI 2:215, 224 Anon., no date; Knapp, *Ecología cultural,* 120.

114. Caillavet, "Chefferies préhispaniques," 43.

115. RGI 2:235 Paz Ponce de León 2.4.1582. "The construction of fields" is translated from "labores de sementeras."

116. See the discussion of the population of colonial Otavalo in chap. 7.

117. Santillán, "Relación del origen," 117.

118. AGI PAT 28-13 Salazar de Villasante, no date.

119. Knapp, *Ecología cultural,* 180. The figure of 4,700 per community is based on the assumption that in the early colonial period there were 2,000 tributary Indians in Otavalo and its associated eight communities and on assumptions that the ratio of tributary Indians to the total population was 1:4.7 and that the population declined by a ratio of 4:1.

120. Knapp, *Ecología cultural,* 180–81. His estimate is based on population densities associated with different forms of cultivation, taking into account the techniques used and crops grown and making assumptions about the length of fallowing periods. Knapp's calculations are summarized in the accompanying table.

Table N1. Forms of Cultivation and Population Densities in Otavalo

Type of area	Crop cultivated	Area cultivated in km²	Estimated density per km²	Estimated population
Upper slopes	Potatoes	230	70	16,100
Lower slopes	Maize	973	125	121,600
Flats (*camellones*)	—	97	750	72,750
Total		1,300		210,450

121. Batchelor, "Los camellones," 686, notes that differences in the style of their construction suggests lapses in building activity and the absence of population pressure.

122. Knapp uses the figures given by Larrain Barros, *Demografía,* 2:147 to give a total of 16,807 Indians in settlements over 2,000 meters for 1582. These figure are found in RGI 2:240–41 Paz Ponce de León 2.4.1582; RGI 2:252 Borja, no date; my own working of them gives a total of 16,975. The total number of Indians in the region in 1582 is estimated at 25,961. (See the discussion of colonial Otavalo in chap. 7.)

123. Knapp, *Ecología cultural,* 181.

124. See chap. 5.

125. Salomon, "Ethnic Lords," 311–15; Moreno Yánez, *Pichincha,* 159–60.

126. Salomon, "Ethnic Lords," 166–67, 312. See also the discussion of the Spanish conquest of the Quito region in chap. 8.

127. Salomon, "Frontera aborigen," 63–67.

128. Cieza de León, *Crónica,* caps. 41–42:58–61.

129. Verneau and Rivet, *Ethnographie ancienne,* 15; Jijón y Caamaño, *Ecuador interandino,* 1:288; Caillavet, "Dominación incaica," 418.

130. Jijón y Caamaño, *Ecuador interandino,* 1:288; Jijón y Caamaño, *Antropología prehispánica,* 79.

131. AGI AQ 82 Father Francisco de Sanctana 1.12.1582.

132. Verneau and Rivet, *Ethnographie ancienne,* 22.

133. Cieza de León, *Crónica,* cap. 41:58.

134. Salomon, "Ethnic Lords," 95–98; Moreno Yánez, *Pichincha,* 89–90.

135. Cieza de León, *Crónica,* cap. 41:58–59.

136. Murra, "Historic Tribes of Ecuador," 807.

137. RGI 2:335–36 Anon., no date; Cabello Balboa, *Obras,* 1:62–63; Cieza de León, *Crónica,* cap. 42:61.

138. Cieza de León, *Crónica,* cap. 41:59.

139. Jijón y Caamaño, *Ecuador interandino,* 1:289–90; Salomon, "Ethnic Lords," 96–97.

140. Porras Garcés, *Fase Cosanga,* 89–98.

141. Salomon, "Ethnic Lords," 96–97; Oberem, *Quijos,* 202–4.

142. Jijón y Caamaño, *Ecuador interandino,* 1:287.

143. AGI AQ 82 Ortegón 1.2.1577; Oberem, *Quijos,* 313–14.

144. AGI JU 683 fols. 817v, 838r, 858r, 869r Visita de la encomienda de Francisco Ruiz 1559; Acosta-Solís, *Fitogeografía y vegetación,* 55. Yields may have been depressed to minimize tribute payments. Spanish accounts indicate higher levels of production of up to 1:100 around Ambato (CDI 9:452 Descripción . . . de la villa del Villar Don Pardo 1605; RGI 2:170 Valverde and Rodríguez 30.12.1576; RGI 2:212 Anon. 1573).

145. RGI 2:212, 227 Anon. 1573.

146. CDI 9:452 Descripción . . . de la villa del Villar Don Pardo 1605; RGI 2:212–13 Anon. 1573.

147. Salomon, "Ethnic Lords," 111–16.

148. RGI 3:75 Docampo 24.3.1650.

149. AGI JU 683 fol. 856r Visita de la encomienda de Francisco Ruiz 1559; RGI 2:212, 226 Anon. 1573; RGI 3:61, 75 Docampo 24.3.1650.

150. CDI 9:459–65 Descripcion . . . de la Villa del Villar Don Pardo 1605.

151. RGI 2:212 Anon. 1573.

152. RGI 3:61, 63 Docampo 24.3.1650; Salomon, "Ethnic Lords," 101–2.

153. RGI 2:214 Anon. 1573; RGI 3:75–76 Docampo 24.3.1650; RGI 3:88 Carranza 1569; CDI 9:453 Descripción . . . de la villa del Villar Don Pardo 1605.

154. AGI JU 683 fols. 817r, 856r, 869r Visita de la encomienda de Francisco Ruiz 1559.

155. AGI AQ 211 Real cédula 21.4.1578.

156. CDI 9:454 Descripción . . . de la villa del Villar Don Pardo 1605; RGI 1:131–32 Salazar de Villasante, no date; RGI 2:220 Anon., no date; Cieza de León, *Crónica,* caps. 41–42:60–61; Cobo, *Historia del nuevo mundo,* 1:289–90.

157. AGI JU 683 fols. 836r, 856v Visita de la encomienda de Francisco Ruiz 1559.

158. AGI JU 683 fols. 803v, 817r–v, 838v, 856r, 869r Visita de la encomienda de Francisco Ruiz 1559; RGI 2:170 Valverde and Rodríguez 1576; Salomon, "Ethnic Lords," 156.

159. RGI 2:259 Cantos 12.9.1581; Salomon, "Ethnic Lords," 100–101. See also the trade of the Otavalo-Caranqui.

160. Cotton was produced only in the Archidona region.

161. AGI AQ 82 Ortegón 1.2.1577; Oberem, "Trade and Trade Goods," 348; Salomon, "Ethnic Lords," 162.

162. RGI 2:252 Borja, no date.

163. RGI 2:256, 259 Cantos 12.9.1581. See also chap. 5.

164. CDI 9:454, 461, 463 Descripción . . . de la villa del Villar Don Pardo 1605. See also chap. 5.

165. Salomon, "Ethnic Lords," 166–67, 312.

166. RGI 2:224 Anon. 1573; CDI 9:462–66 Descripción . . . de la villa del Villar Don Pardo. 1605; Cieza de León, *Crónica,* cap. 41:58.

167. AGI JU 683 fols. 804r, 839r, 869v Visita de la encomienda de Francisco Ruiz 1559; RGI 2:226, 228 Anon. 1573; Salomon, "Ethnic Lords," 175–78, 182.

168. RGI 2:226–27 Anon. 1573; Salomon, "Ethnic Lords," 182.

169. RGI 2:224, 227 Anon. 1573; Salomon, "Ethnic Lords," 175–78, 182.

170. Cieza de León, *Crónica,* cap. 41:60; Salomon, "Ethnic Lords," 175–78, 188.

171. AGI JU 683 fols. 817v, 839r, 856v Visita de la encomienda de Francisco Ruiz 1559; Salomon, "Ethnic Lords," 188–91.

172. See Salomon, "Ethnic Lords," 192–93.

173. Salomon, "Ethnic Lords," 200–201.

174. RGI 2:227 Anon. 1573.

175. For comments on the succession of positions, see AGI JU 683 fols. 804v, 818r, 858r, 870r Visita de la encomienda de Francisco Ruiz 1559; Salomon, "Ethnic Lords," 194–95.

176. RGI 2:227 Anon. 1573; Cieza de León, *Crónica,* cap. 41:60.

177. Verneau and Rivet, *Ethnographie ancienne,* 22.

178. RGI 2:228 Anon. 1573; Cieza de León, *Crónica,* cap. 41:58.

179. Cieza de León, *Crónica,* cap. 41:60.

180. CDI 9:459–60 Descripción . . . de la villa del Villar Don Pardo 1605.

181. RGI 2:225 Anon. 1573.

182. RGI 2:225 Anon. 1573.

183. RGI 2:225–26 Anon. 1573.

184. See chap. 8.

185. See chap. 8.

186. See chap. 6.

187. Cook, *Demographic Collapse,* 70.

188. In his analysis of the 1559 visita of a number of villages in the Valle de los Chillos, Salomon suggests a depopulation ratio for the valley of 3:1, on the basis of the experience of Indians in the central Andes ("Ethnic Lords," 174). This is not dissimilar from that estimated by Cook, given that the 1559 figures take into account the impact of the smallpox epidemic of 1558, which Cook has estimated resulted in a minimum mortality of 18 percent. The impact of this epidemic has not been taken into account in estimating the fall in the Indian population to the level indicated in Avendaño's 1561 summary because it is believed the figures for Quito were compiled mainly on the basis of enumerations made before that date. If the impact of this epidemic was also included, then the depopulation ratio would be 3:1.

189. Avendaño gives the number of people of all ages as 240,670. See app. 1.

190. The visita of the encomienda of Francisco Ruiz indicated that there were 3,567 persons and 824 units, which do not exactly correspond to the number of tributary Indians, because some were exempt. Taking account of this fact, the visita suggests a ratio of about 1:4.5, though it should be remembered that it was conducted the year after the 1558 smallpox epidemic, which probably affected children to a greater degree. Prior to 1558 the ratio was probably higher.

191. RAHM A/92 fols. 55–77 Relación de los vecinos encomenderos que hay, no date. This document gives the value of encomiendas within the jurisidiction of Quito. Some encomiendas comprised villages in more than one region. The whole encomienda has been assigned to the region where it is considered that the largest number of Indians in the encomienda resided. Those in Cuenca, Otavalo, and Pasto are clearly incomplete. The figures in the accompanying table should be regarded as only very rough estimates.

Table N2. Encomiendas in Quito

Region	Number of encomiendas	Total value (pesos)	Percent by value
Otavalo-Pasto	4	4,250	6.6
Quito	18	18,766[a]	29.2
Latacunga-Ambato	8	20,490	31.8
Riobamba-Chimbo	9	19,050	29.6
Cuenca	1	1,800	2.8
Total	40	64,356	

[a] Value is not given for two encomiendas.

192. It will be estimated that between 43,000 and 53,000 Indians were involved in expeditions from the sierra, of which about 30,000 came from the Quito Basin. See chap. 8.

193. Salomon, "Ethnic Lords," 68.

194. Cieza de León, *Crónica,* cap. 42:61.

195. CDI 9:467–88 Descripción . . . de la villa del Villar Don Pardo 1605.

196. Cieza de León, *Crónica,* cap. 43:62.

197. RGI 2:254–60 Cantos 12.9.1581. See chap. 5.

198. Verneau and Rivet, *Ethnographie ancienne,* 24; Haro Alvear, *Puruhá,* 16.

199. RGI 2:286 Gaviria 4.5.1582; RGI 2:288 Italiano 18.10.1582.

200. Salomon, "Ethnic Lords," 274–89.

201. Salomon, "Ethnic Lords," 250; Salomon, "Frontera aborigen," 66.

202. Acosta-Solís, *Recursos naturales,* pt. 2, vol. 1, opp. p. 19.

203. AGI JU 671 fols. 243v, 247v, 249v, 255r Visita de los Puruháes 1557; RGI 2:261 Paz Maldonado, no date; RGI 2:286 Gaviria 4.5.1582; RGI 2:288 Italiano 18.10.1582; CDI 9:468, 470, 478, 485–86, 489–90, 492, 500 Descripción . . . de la villa del Villar Don Pardo 1605; Calancha, "Crónica moralizada," 189–201. Although one account suggests that maize yields could reach 1:100, this seems unlikely, given that those in the more fertile Quito Basin averaged only 1:60.

204. CDI 9:467, 470, 473, 480–81, 491 Descripción . . . de la villa del Villar Don Pardo 1605; RGI 2:261 Paz Maldonado, no date.

205. Salomon, "Ethnic Lords," 278; Oberem, "Recursos naturales," 54–56.

206. AGI JU 671 fols. 245v, 247v, 250r Visita de los Puruháes 1557.

207. ANHQ Indígenas 1 Vergara vs. the corregidor of Riobamba 9.11.1601.

208. RGI 1:127 Villasante, no date; RGI 2:262 Paz Maldonado, no date; CDI 9:470 Descripción . . . de la villa del Villar Don Pardo 1605. The Desembarcadero was located about nineteen leagues upriver from Guayaquil.

209. AGI JU 671 fols. 244r, 247v, 253v Visita de los Puruháes 1557; CDI 9:470, 475–76, 492 Descripción . . . de la villa del Villar Don Pardo 1605.

210. AGI JU 671 fols. 243v, 250v, 252r, 255v Visita de los Puruháes 1557; RGI 2:262 Paz Maldonado, no date.

211. CDI 9:470, 476, 490, 492 Descripción . . . de la villa del Villar Don Pardo 1605.

212. AGI JU 671 fols. 244v, 249v, 252v, 254v Visita de los Puruháes 1557; CDI 9:474, 478, 480, 497 Descripción . . . de la villa del Villar Don Pardo 1605.

213. Probably *cabuyo blanco* (*Fourcroya andina* Trel. and sp.) and *cabuyo negro* (*Agave americana* L. and sp.).

214. CDI 9:467, 470, 473, 486 Descripción . . . de la villa del Villar Don Pardo 1605.

215. RGI 2:261 Paz Maldonado, no date; CDI 9:467, 491 Descripción . . . de la villa del Villar Don Pardo 1605; Salomon, "Ethnic Lords," 286.

216. RGI 2:261 Paz Maldonado, no date; CDI 9:468, 471, 476 Descripción . . . de la villa del Villar Don Pardo 1605.

217. Salomon, "Ethnic Lords," 278.

218. AGI JU 671 fols. 252v Visita de los Puruháes 1557; Salomon, "Ethnic Lords," 200, 277.

219. AGI JU 671 fols. 251v–252r Visita de los Puruháes 1557.

220. AGI JU 671 fols. 252r Visita de los Puruháes 1557.

221. Cieza de León, *Crónica,* cap. 43:62.

222. AGI JU 671 fols. 243r Visita de los Puruháes 1557.

223. Cieza de León, *Crónica,* cap. 43:62.

224. Verneau and Rivet, *Ethnographie ancienne,* 24; Velasco, *Historia del reino,* 2:93.

225. RGI 2:286 Gaviria 4.5.1582; RGI 2:288 Italiano 18.10.1582.

226. Cieza de León, *Crónica,* cap.53:62.

227 RAHM A/92 CM fols. 55–77 Relación de los vecinos encomenderos que hay, no date; RGI 2:215–16 La cibdad de Sant Francisco del Quito 1573.

228. This figure includes only one-half of the population of the encomienda of Puní and Tomebamba, since the latter was in the jurisdiction of Cuenca.

229. RAHM 9/4664 nos. 1–2 fols. 27v–29v Repartimiento de la ciudad de San Francisco de Quito, no date.

230. See chap. 8 and app. 1.

231. See chap. 9.

232 Oberem, "Los Cañaris," 132–33; Salomon, "Cañari 'Inca-ism,'" 211.

233. See chap. 5.

234. Salomon, "Cañari 'Inca-ism,'" 211.

235. RGI 2:286 Gaviria 4.5.1582; RGI 2:288 Italiano 18.10.1582.

236. Cabello Balboa, *Miscelánea antártica,* pt. 3, cap. 16:320; Cieza de León, *Crónica,* cap. 43:63, cap. 56:80; Caillavet, "Grupos étnicos," 128.

237. Cieza de León, *Crónica,* cap. 44:64.

238. Jijón y Caamaño, *Ecuador interandino,* 2:5.

239. See chap. 3.

240. Verneau and Rivet, *Ethnographie ancienne,* 29.

241. RGI 2:266 Pablos 20.9.1582; RGI 2:276 Gallegos 20.9.1582; RGI 2:272 Pereira 1.10.1582.

242. RGI 2:266–67 Pablos 20.9.1582; RGI 2:270 Angeles 12.5.1582; RGI 2:272–73 Pereira 1.10.1582; RGI 2:276–77 Gallegos 20.9.1582; RGI 2:278 Dávila 1.5.1582; RGI 2:281, 284 Gómez, June 1582; RGI 2:286–87 Gaviria 4.5.1582; RGI 2: Italiano 18.10.1582.

243. RGI 2:270–71 Angeles 12.5.1582; RGI 2:273 Pereira 1.10.1582; RGI 2:277 Gallegos 20.9.1582; Garcilaso de la Vega, *Comentarios reales,* 2, lib. 8, cap. 5:298.

244. RGI 2:Pablos 20.9.1582; Cieza de León, *Crónica,* cap. 64:65.

245. RGI 2:271 Angeles 12.5.1582; RGI 2:287 Gaviria 4.5.1582; RGI 2:289 Italiano 18.10.1582.

246. See chap. 5; RGI 2:271 Angeles 12.5.1582; RGI 2:273 Pereira 1.10.1582; RGI 2:278 Gallegos 20.9.1582.

247. RGI 2:280 Dávila 1.5.1582; León, "Cocaismo en el Ecuador," 16; Oberem, "Recursos naturales," 60.

248. See chap. 5.

249. RGI 2:285 Gómez 1582; Oberem, "Recursos naturales," 56.

250. RGI 2:280 Dávila 1.5.1582; RGI 2:276 Gallegos 20.9.1582.

251. RGI 2:270 Angeles 12.5.1582.

252. RGI 2:269 Pablos 20.9.1582; RGI 2:273 Pereira 1.10.1582; RGI 2:278 Gallegos 20.9.1582; RGI 2:285 Gómez June 1582; RGI 2:287 Gaviria 4.5.1582; RGI 2:289 Italiano 18.10.1582.

253. RGI 2:271 Angeles 12.5.1582; RGI 2:287 Gaviria 4.5.1582; RGI 2:289 Italiano 18.10.1582.

254. RGI 1:142 Salazar de Villasante 1571 or 1572; RGI 2:268 Pablos 20.9.1582; RGI 2:270 Angeles 12.5.1582; RGI 2:272–73 Pereira 1.10.1582; RGI 2:283 Gómez June 1582; RGI 2:286 Gaviria 4.5.1582; RGI 2:289 Italiano 18.10.1582; Cieza de León, *Crónica,* cap. 43:63, cap. 44:64.

255. Murra, "Historic Tribes of Ecuador," 799.

256. Cieza de León, *Crónica,* cap. 43:63.

257. RGI 1:142 Salazar de Villasante 1571 or 1572; RGI 2:266 Pablos 20.9.1582; RGI 2:271 Angeles 12.5.1582; RGI 2:273 Pereira 1.10.1582.

258. RGI 2:269 Pablos 20.9.1582; RGI 2:285 Gómez June 1582.

259. RGI 2:272 Pereira 1.10.1582; RGI 2:278 Gallegos 20.9.1582.

260. RGI 2:271 Angeles 12.5.1582; RGI 2:278 Gallegos 20.9.1582.

261. Cieza de León, *Crónica,* cap. 44:65.

262. RGI 2:270 Angeles 12.5.1582; RGI 2:274 Pereira 1.10.1582; RGI 2:278 Gallegos 20.9.1582; RGI 2:280 Dávila 1.5.1582; RGI 2:285 Gómez June 1582.

263. Cieza de León, *Crónica,* cap. 44:65.

264. RGI 2:275 Gallegos 20.9.1582; RGI 2:286 Gaviria 4.5.1582; RGI 2:289 Italiano 18.10.1582.

265. RGI 2:272 Pereira 1.10.1582; RGI 2:275 Gallegos 20.9.1582; RGI 2:283 Gómez June 1582; Cieza de León, *Crónica,* cap. 43:63.

266. See chap. 5.

267. RGI 2:276 Gallegos 20.9.1582; Garcilaso de la Vega, *Comentarios reales,* 2, lib. 8, cap. 4:297.

268. RGI 2:267 Pablos 20.9.1582; RGI 2:276 Gallegos 20.9.1582; RGI 2:283 Gómez June 1582; RGI 2:286 Gaviria 4.5.1582; RGI 2:289 Italiano 18.10.1582; Garcilaso de la Vega, *Comentarios reales,* 2, lib. 8, cap. 4:297.

269. Sarmiento de Gamboa, *Historia índica,* cap. 46:250, cap. 50:263.

270. RGI 2:283 Gómez June 1582; Caillavet, "Grupos étnicos," 129–30.

271. RGI 2:270 Angeles 12.5.1582.

272. RGI 2:270 Angeles 12.5.1582; RGI 2:274 Pereira 1.10.1582.

273. Verneau and Rivet, *Ethnographie ancienne,* 33–34.

274. AHBC Colección Misc. 1 no.1 Instrucción para descubrir todas las guacas, no date [1580s?]; RGI 2:272 Pereira 1.10.1582; RGI 2:275 Gallegos 20.9.1582; RGI 2:283 Gómez June 1582; RGI 2:286 Gaviria 4.5.1582; RGI 2:288 Italiano 18.10.1582; Garcilaso de la Vega, *Comentarios reales,* 2, lib. 8, cap. 5:298.

275. AHBC Colección Misc. 1 no.1 Instrucción para descubrir todas las guacas, no date [1580s?]. This creation myth was described more fully by Sarmiento de Gamboa, *Historia índica,* cap. 6:207–8. He relates that the Cañar were created from Mount Guasano, to which two brothers had fled to escape the Flood. After the Flood the two brothers encountered two women, and after one of the brothers had been drowned, the other took one of the women for his wife and the other for his mistress. By each of the women he had five children, and they gave rise to the provinces of Hanansaya and Hurinsaya. This myth may contain some indigenous elements, but the moiety and decimal systems it embodies clearly indicates Inka influence, while the reference to the Flood reveals the impress of Christianity.

276. RGI 2:276 Gallegos 20.9.1582; Cieza de León, *Crónica,* cap. 44:65.

277. Verneau and Rivet, *Ethnographie ancienne,* plates 23–25; Collier, "Ar-

chaeology of Ecuador," 776–78; Murra, "Historic Tribes of Ecuador," 799–800; Pérez, *Cañaris,* 149, 240, 301; Salomon, "Ethnic Lords," 136.

278. Borregán, *Crónica,* 84.

279. RGI 2:267 Pablos 20.9.1582.

280. Sarmiento de Gamboa, *Historia índica,* pt. 2, cap. 62:264.

281. RGI 2:267 Pablos 20.9.1582.

282. Cook, *Demographic Collapse,* 70.

283. Zarate, "Historia del descubrimiento," lib. 1, cap. 12:478.

284. Cieza de León, *Crónica,* cap. 44:65.

285. RGI 2:267 Pablos 20.9.1582.

286. RGI 2:279 Arias Dávila 1.5.1582.

287. AGI PAT 93-9-3 Services of Diego de Sandoval 19.11.1539.

288. RAHM 9/4664 nos. 1–2 fol. 27v–28v Repartimiento de la ciudad de San Francisco de Quito, no date.

289. AGI PAT 133-3 Información de servicios de Juan de Narváez 14.2.1591.

290. Crespo Toral, "Encomiendas de Cuenca," 26–27.

291. AMQ LC 4:223–32 Ordenanzas de minas 7.6.1549. This figure includes only half of Puní and Tomebamba with eighty Indians, and eighty Indians in Macas and Quizna.

292. See the previous discussion of the Puruhá.

293. This figure is not substantially different from the 50,000 proposed by Alcina Franch ("Tomebamba," 7). His figure is based on the account by Hernando Pablos written in 1582, which reported that at that time the province of Cañares possessed 12,000 *ánimas* (RGI 2:266, 268 Pablos 20.9.1582).

294. Guffroy, "Province de Loja," 281, 283–84, 286.

295. RGI 2:301 Salinas 1571 or 1572; Murra, "Historic Tribes of Ecuador," 801.

296. Cieza de León, *Crónica,* cap. 57:82; Caillavet, "Grupos étnicos," 128; Taylor, "Les Palta," 441–44.

297. Cieza de León, *Crónica,* cap. 56:80.

298. RGI 3 :140–41 Anon., no date.

299. RGI 3 :140–41 Anon., no date; Taylor and Descola, "Conjunto Jívaro," 16–18.

300. Taylor, "Les Palta," 444–46.

301. RGI 3:174 Benavente 25.3.1550. The close relationship between the Palta and Jívaro was confirmed by Juan de Salinas (RGI 2:301 Salinas 1571 or 1572).

302. Caillavet, "Grupos étnicos," 132.

303. ANHQ Presidencia de Quito 3 fol. 3r–v 3.2.1629; RGI 2:301 Salinas 1571 or 1572; RGI 2:315 Anon., no date; RGI 2:321 Auncibay 1592; RGI 3:174 Benavente 23.3.1550; Cieza de León, *Crónica,* caps. 56 and 57:82; Caillavet, "Grupos étnicos," 129–32, 135, 143, 155.

304. RGI 2:294–95 Salinas 1571 or 1572; Caillavet, "Groupes ethniques préhispaniques," 297.

305. RGI 2:295 Salinas 1571 or 1572.

306. RGI 2:302 Salinas 1571 or 1572.

307. RGI 2:294–95 Salinas 1571 or 1572.

308. RGI 2:295–96 Salinas 1571 or 1572.

309. RGI 2:297, 303 Salinas 1571 or 1572.

310. RGI 2:292 Salinas 1571 or 1572.

311 RGI 2; 142 Anon., no date.

312. RGI 2:304–5 Salinas 1571 or 1572.

313. RGI 3:141 Anon., no date; Caillavet, "Grupos étnicos," 134–35.

314. RGI 2:303 Salinas 1571 or 1572; RGI 2:324 Auncibay 1592.

315. RGI 2:304–5 Salinas 1571 or 1572.

316. RGI 2:302 Salinas 1571 or 1572; Caillavet, "Grupos étnicos," 134–35.

317. RGI 2:301–2 Salinas 1571 or 1572; RGI 3:143 Anon., no date.

318. RGI 2:304–5 Salinas 1571 or 1572; Cieza de León, *Crónica,* cap. 56:81.

319. RGI 2:304 Salinas 1571 or 1572.

320. Caillavet, "Groupes ethniques préhispaniques," 293, 305.

321. RGI 2:304 Salinas 1571 or 1572.

322. RGI 2:304–5 Salinas 1571 or 1572.

323. Caillavet, "Groupes ethniques prehispaniques," 304.

324. RGI 2:304–5 Salinas 1571 or 1572.

325. RGI 2:302 Salinas 1571 or 1572; Caillavet, "Grupos étnicos," 142–43.

326. RGI 2:302 Salinas 1571 or 1572; AHBC col. Misc. vol. 1 no. 1 Instrucción para descubrir todas las guacas, no date.

327. Cieza de León, *Crónica,* cap. 56:81.

328. Cieza de León, *Crónica,* cap. 72:81.

329. RAHM A/92 fol. 55–77 Relación de los naturales que hay, no date.

330. AGI AL 120 Relación de los naturales de estos reinos del Perú, no date; RAHM CM 42 fol. 248 Relación de los naturales de estos reinos del Perú, no date; RAHM 9/4664 no. 21 Los pueblos despañoles que hay, no date. See app. 1.

331. RAHM 9/4664 Relación de los encomenderos que hay, no date.

332. Taylor suggests that the aboriginal population was only 20,000 ("Les Palta," 447–48), but this estimate is based on Salinas's account of 16,000 in 1573, and it takes little account of the impact of epidemic disease.

333. Tyrer, "Demographic and Economic History," 3–4; Browne, "Epidemic Disease," 35.

334. Phelan, *Kingdom of Quito,* 45.

CHAPTER 3

1. Cabello Balboa, *Obras,* 1:14.

2. Acosta-Solís, *Recursos naturales,* pt. 2, vol. 1, table opp. p. 19.

3. Murra, "Historic Tribes of Ecuador," 786–87; Bushnell, *Santa Elena Peninsula,* 5; Jijón y Caamaño, *Antropología prehispánica,* map; Estrada, *Culturas preclásicas,* 16–17; Estrada and Evans, "Cultural Development in Ecuador," 85; Borja de Szászdi, "Prehistoria de la costa ecuatoriana," 8–9; Alcina Franch and Peña, "Patrones de asentamiento," 283–84; Palop Martínez, "Mapa étnico."

4. CDI 9:286 Descripción . . . de la gobernación de Guayaquil 1605.

5. Oviedo, *Historia general,* 5, lib. 46, cap. 17:98 says, "tanto que cada población tiene su lengua, e aunque con los vecinos algunos se entienden, es con mucha diversidad de vocablos mezclados con los otros comunes."

6. For example, Cabello Balboa, *Obras,* 1:8; Alcina Franch and Peña, "Patrones de asentamiento," 285.

7. AGI AQ 9 Torres 20.11.1597 and Monroy, *Convento de la Merced,* 331; Jijón y Caamaño, *Ecuador interandino,* 2:540.

8. AGI AQ 9 Torres 20.11.1597 and the accompanying map MP PAN 333 Descripción de la tierra de Cayapa 1597, also in Monroy, *Convento de la Merced,* 333–34.

9. AGI AQ 9 Romero 9.4.1611.

10. AGI AQ 9 Information on the entrada of Captain Arias de Ugarte 11.4.1611.

11. Rumazo González, *Documentos,* 4:40–53, Relación del camino 3.5.1607.

12. AGI AQ 9 Torres 20.11.1597 and Monroy, *Convento de la Merced,* 327.

13. AGI MP PAN 333 Descripción de la tierra de Cayapa 1597.

14. AGI AQ 10 Morga 1.4.1620.

15. Alcina Franch, Moreno, and Peña, "Penetración española," 72; Alcina Franch and García Palacios, "Materias primas," 306, 308; Palop Martínez, "Los Cayapas," 243–44; Palop Martínez, "Mapa étnico."

16. AGI AQ 10 Morga 1.4.1620.

17. AGI AQ 9 Romero 9.4.1611. For a similar assemblage of crops, see Rumazo González, *Documentos,* 4:40–53, Relación del camino 3.5.1607.

18. Nolasco Pérez, *Misiones mercedarias,* 225; Alcina Franch, Moreno, and Peña, "Penetración española," 99.

19. AGI AQ 9 Information on the entrada of Captain Ugarte 11.4.1611; Nolasco Pérez, *Misiones mercedarias,* 222.

20. Rumazo González, *Documentos,* 4:40–53, Relación del camino 3.5.1607.

21. Cabello Balboa, *Obras,* 1:16.

22. RGI 2:335–36 Relación de los indios que hay ca. 1582.

23. AGI AQ 9 Acuerdo de la real hacienda 18.3.1601.

24. Cabello Balboa, *Obras,* 1:62–63.

25. Alcina Franch, Moreno, and Peña, "Penetración española," 73; Palop Martínez, "Mapa étnico."

26. Murra, "Cayapa and Colorado," 278; Jijón y Caamaño, *Ecuador interandino,* 2:417.

27. AGI AQ 9 Torres 20.11.1597 and Monroy, *Convento de la Merced,* 334; AGI AQ 9 Acuerdo de la real hacienda 18.3.1601; ANHQ RH 5 1601–57 fols. 4–7 Acuerdo de hacienda 1601; Rumazo González, *Documentos,* 4:204–7, President of the audiencia 7.11.1622; Jijón y Caamaño, *Ecuador interandino,* 2:108.

28. AGI MP PAN 333 Descripción de la tierra de Cayapa 1597, AQ 9 Torres 20.11.1597 and Monroy, *Convento de la Merced,* 331–32.

29. AGI AQ 25 Arévalo 22.12.1600.

30. AGI MP PAN 333 Descripción de la tierra de Cayapa 1597.

31. Barrett, *Cayapa Indians,* 1:1.

32. Brinton, *American Race,* 196–99; Barrett, *Cayapa Indians,* 1:28.

33. Alcina Franch, Moreno, and Peña, "Penetración española," 72; Alcina Franch and Peña, "Patrones de asentamiento," 284; Palop Martínez, "Los Cayapas," 238–40.

34. Barrett, *Cayapa Indians,* 1:31.

35. Alcina Franch and Peña, "Etnías y culturas," 335; Moreno Navarro, "Ecología y sociedad de las Cayapas," 321–22.

36. Cabello Balboa, *Obras,* 1:16.

37. Verneau and Rivet, *Ethnographie ancienne,* 40; Murra, "Cayapa and Colorado," 277; Jijón y Caamaño, *Ecuador interandino,* 2:348; Jijón y Caamaño, *Antropología prehispánica,* 77.

38. Bernárdez, "Lingüística de Esmeraldas," 350. This seems credible, given that they speak mutually unintelligible languages (Murra, "Cayapa and Colorado," 284).

39. Cabello Balboa, *Obras,* 1:15; Alcina Franch and Peña, "Etnías y culturas," 333–34.

40. Jijón y Caamaño, *Ecuador interandino,* 2:110; Jijón y Caamaño, *Antropología prehispánica,* 77.

41. RGI 3:89 Carranza 1569.

42. AGI AQ 25 Arévalo 22.12.1600; Monroy, *Convento de la Merced,* 368.

43. AGI AQ 25 Medina 30.12.1600 and Monroy, *Convento de la Merced,* 376.

44. Cabello Balboa, *Obras,* 1:15.

45. Cieza de León, *Crónica,* cap. 50:73.

46. Cieza de León, *Crónica,* cap. 46:68.

47. Bushnell, *Santa Elena Peninsula,* 7.

48. Estrada and Evans, "Cultural Development in Ecuador," 82.

49. Rivera Dorado, "Arqueología y etnohistoria," 559.

50. Estrada and Evans, "Cultural Development in Ecuador," 85.

51. Garcilaso de la Vega, *Comentarios reales,* 3, lib. 9, cap. 8:344.

52. Cabello Balboa, *Obras,* 1:16. See also Trujillo, *Relación,* 46–47.

53. AGI AQ 10 Morga 1.4.1620; López de Gómara, "Hispania Victrix," 224–25; Cabello Balboa, *Obras,* 1:16; Trujillo, *Relación,* 46–47; Porras Barrenechea, *Cronistas del Perú,* 113, Account of Ruiz de Arce; Herrera, *Historia general,* 7, dec. 3, lib. 10:432.

54. RGI 3:61 Rodríguez Docampo 24.3.1650; Oviedo, *Historia general,* 5, lib. 46, cap. 17:97.

55. Barrett, *Cayapa Indians,* 1:73; Maestro, "Sistema de alimentación," 335.

56. Sánchez Montañés, "Los ralladores," 252–54; Guinea Bueno, *Patrones de asentamiento,* 113; Rivera et al., *Cultura Tiaone,* 124, 129.

57. Guinea Bueno, *Patrones de asentamiento,* 110.

58. Cabello Balboa, *Obras,* 1:16.

59. RGI 3:89 Carranza 1569; Trujillo, *Relación,* 46; Oviedo, *Historia general,* 5, lib. 43, cap. 3:13; Murra, "Historic Tribes of Ecuador," 802–3; Murra, "Tráfico de mullu," 255–67; Alcina Franch and Peña, "Patrones de asentamiento," 292; Rivera Dorado, "Arqueología y etnohistoria," 549, 551, 554.

60. CDIE 5:196, 198–99 Sámanos 1526.

61. Oviedo, *Historia general,* 5, lib. 43, cap. 3:13.

62. Jerez, "Conquista del Perú," 321.

63. Guinea Bueno, *Patrones de asentamiento,* 158.

64. Estete, *Noticia,* 17; Trujillo, *Relación,* 47–48; Porras Barrenechea, *Cronistas del Perú,* 113, Account of Ruiz de Arce.

65. Guinea Bueno, *Patrones de asentamiento,* 158.

66. RGI 3:89 Carranza 1569.

67. Alcina Franch and Peña, "Patrones de asentamiento," 289.

68. CDIE 5:199–200 Sámanos 1526.

69. AGI AQ 25 Arévalo 22.12.1600 and Rumazo González, *Documentos*, 4:32; Zarate, "Historia del descubrimiento," lib. 1, cap. 4:465; Estete, *Noticia*, 18; Cabello Balboa, *Obras*, 1:14–15; Trujillo, *Relación*, 47; Collier, "Archeology of Ecuador," 781.

70. AGI AQ 9 Torres 20.11.1597 and Monroy, *Convento de la Merced*, 328; Porras Barrenechea, *Cronistas del Perú*, 113, Account of Ruiz de Arce; Alcina Franch and Peña, "Patrones de asentamiento," 289; Rivera et al., *Cultura Tiaone*, 228.

71. Murra, "Cayapa and Colorado," 282.

72. Cieza de León, *Crónica*, cap. 50:72; Cabello Balboa, *Obras*, 1:15.

73. Guinea Bueno, *Patrones de asentamiento*, 147–50.

74. Estete, *Noticia*, 17; Trujillo, *Relación*, 47–48; Porras Barrenechea, *Cronistas del Perú*, 113, Account of Ruiz de Arce.

75. Guinea Bueno, *Patrones de asentamiento*, 151, which gives the area for the estimated 13,000 to 19,000 population as 175 km². Given a similar population density of 91 persons per km², calculated from the mid-estimate of 16,000, the area inhabited by coastal groups may be calculated at 220 km².

76. Oviedo, *Historia general*, 5, lib. 43, cap. 3:13.

77. Cieza de León, *Crónica*, cap. 46:68.

78. CDIE 5:199–200 Sámanos 1526.

79. Cieza de León, *Crónica*, cap. 46:68.

80. Cieza de León, *Crónica*, cap. 46:68.

81. Zarate, "Historia del descubrimiento," lib. 1, cap. 4:465; Benzoni, *Historia del mundo nuevo*, 255.

82. AGI AQ 10 Autos sobre el descubrimiento 5.1.1620.

83. Estrada and Evans, "Cultural Development in Ecuador," 85; Estrada, *Arqueología de Manabí*, 78–80, 87.

84. Holm, *Cultura Manteña-Huancavilca*, 8.

85. CDIE 5:200 Sámanos 1526.

86. Loor, *Indios de Manabí*, 133.

87. Cieza de León, *Crónica*, cap. 46:68.

88. AGI PAT 240-8 Relación de los pueblos de Manta, no date, and RGI 3:90; Garcilaso de la Vega, *Comentarios reales*, 2, lib. 9, cap. 9:344; Lizárraga, *Descripción breve*, cap. 3:4; Cieza de León, *Crónica*, cap. 46:68.

89. Oviedo, *Historia general*, 5, lib. 43, cap. 3:12, and lib. 46, cap. 17:106.

90. Oviedo, *Historia general*, 5, lib. 43, cap. 3:13; Edwards, *Aboriginal Watercraft*, 35–36; Norton, "Señorío de Salangone," 137.

91. West, "Aboriginal Sea Navigation," 133–34.

92. CDIE 5:196–97 Sámanos 1526; Oviedo, *Historia general*, 5, lib. 43, cap. 3:12; Edwards, *Aboriginal Watercraft*, 67–70; Benzoni, *Historia del mundo nuevo*, 256; Lizárraga, *Descripción breve*, cap. 3:4.

93. CDIE 5:196 Sámanos 1526; Oviedo, *Historia general*, 5, lib. 43, cap. 3:12; Cieza de León, *Crónica*, cap. 46:68.

94. Murra, "Historic Tribes of Ecuador," 805.

95. CDI 9:247–309 Descripción de la gobernación 1605.

96. CDIE 5:200 Sámanos 1526.

97. Cieza de León, *Crónica,* cap. 51:74.

98. Zarate, "Historia del descubrimiento," lib. 1, cap. 4:465; Oviedo, *Historia general,* 5, lib. 44, cap. 17:97; Benzoni, *Historia del mundo nuevo,* 254; Cieza de León, *Crónica,* cap. 4:11, cap. 50:72; Loor, *Indios de Manabí,* 106.

99. Benzoni, *Historia del mundo nuevo,* 255; Cieza de León, *Crónica,* cap. 50:72.

100. Estrada, *Arqueología de Manabí,* 81–83, 86.

101. Cieza de León, *Crónica,* cap. 46:69, cap. 50:72.

102. CDIE 5:200 Sámanos 1526.

103. Benzoni, *Historia del mundo nuevo,* 255.

104. Loor, *Indios de Manabí,* 28; Estrada, *Arqueología de Manabí,* 81–82.

105. Loor, *Indios de Manabí,* 142.

106. Estrada, *Arqueología de Manabí,* 82.

107. CDI 41:538–44 Berlanga 26.4.1535.

108. AGI PAT 28-12 Relación de la conquista, no date; Molina, "Relación," 65.

109. Clark and Haswell, *Economics of Subsistence Agriculture,* 37.

110. Benzoni, *Historia del mundo nuevo,* 256–57.

111. Bushnell, *Santa Elena Peninsula,* 4.

112. Estrada, *Huancavilcas,* 18.

113. CDI 9:247–309 Descripción de la gobernación 1605; Lizárraga, *Descripción breve,* cap. 3:4.

114. Cieza de León, *Crónica,* cap. 55:80.

115. Oviedo, *Historia general,* 5, lib. 46, cap. 17:106.

116. Estrada, *Huancavilcas,* 39.

117. Bushnell, *Santa Elena Peninsula,* 3; Estrada, *Huancavilcas,* 87.

118. Bushnell, *Santa Elena Peninsula,* 15–16, 95–96.

119. Benzoni, *Historia del mundo nuevo,* 256–57. See also CDI 9:247–309 Descripción de la gobernación 1605.

120. Cieza de León, *Crónica,* cap. 55:80.

121. Estrada, *Huancavilcas,* 18.

122. RAHM 9/4664 no. 20 Relación de los vecinos encomenderos, no date.

123. RGI 2:339 Razón de los indios tributarios 1581.

124. See chap. 5.

125. CDIE 5:213–14 Pizarro 1571; Bushnell, *Santa Elena Peninsula,* 8: Borja de Szászdi, "Prehistoria de la costa ecuatoriana," 24.

126. Cieza de León, *Crónica,* cap. 54:78. See also CDIE 5:213–14 Pizarro 1571; CDI 9:247–309 Descripción de la gobernación 1605; Zarate, "Historia del descubrimiento," lib. 1, cap. 4:466; Jerez, "Conquista del Perú," 332; Trujillo, *Relación,* 52; Oviedo, *Historia general,* 5, lib. 46, cap. 1:33.

127. Volland, "Los Punaes," 255.

128. Zarate, "Historia del descubrimiento," lib. 1, cap. 4:466; Estete, *Noticia,* 19; Oviedo, *Historia general,* 5, lib. 46, cap. 17:99.

129. CDIE 5:214 Pizarro 1571; Zarate, "Historia del descubrimiento," lib. 1, cap. 4:466; Cieza de León, *Crónica,* cap. 54:78.

130. Zarate, "Historia del descubrimiento," lib. 1, cap. 4:466; Jerez, "Conquista del Perú," 322.

131. Zarate, "Historia del descubrimiento," lib. 1, cap. 4:466; Cieza de León, *Crónica,* cap. 54:78.

132. Cieza de León, *Crónica,* cap. 54:78.

133. Cieza de León, *Crónica,* cap. 54:78. Cieza de León refers to the island as the Isla de la Plata, but he is clearly confusing it with the island of that name that performed a similar function among the Manta (see Cieza de León, *Crónica,* cap. 4:12).

134. Estrada, *Huancavilcas,* 30.

135. Jerez, "Conquista del Perú," 322; Lizárraga, *Descripción breve,* cap. 6:8; Zarate, "Historia del descubrimiento," lib. 1, cap. 4:466.

136. Purchas, *Purchas His Pilgrimes,* 2:163–64.

137. Oviedo, *Historia general,* 5, lib. 46, cap. 17:98.

138. RAHM 9/4664 no. 20 Relación de los vecinos encomenderos, no date. The value of the encomienda of Puná was 1,000 pesos, whereas those containing Huancavilca villages were worth at least 5,000 pesos.

139. Borja de Szászdi, "Prehistoria de la costa ecuatoriana," map opp. p. 388, 400; Espinosa Soriano, "Reino de Chono," 10–16.

140. Lizárraga describes them as "no tan políticos" (*Descripción breve,* cap. 5:8). In the early seventeenth century Montesinos also referred to the province of the Chono as "los de Guayaquil" (*Memorias antiguas,* 145–46, 148).

141. Montesinos, *Memorias antiguas,* 148; Trujillo, *Relación,* 51; Lizárraga, *Descripción breve,* cap. 6:9; Estrada Ycaza, *Fundación de Guayaquil,* 42–43. The abundance of weapons found in archaeological sites is indicative of the warlike nature of the Chono (Estrada, *Culturas pre-clásicas,* 16).

142. Borregán, *Crónica,* 82; Benzoni, *Historia del mundo nuevo,* 257.

143. RGI 2:337–39 Razón de los indios tributarios 1581.

144. Trujillo, *Relación,* 51.

145. Borja de Szászdi, "Reintepretación," 40.

146. Espinosa Soriano, "Reino de Chono," 10–16. Archaeological evidence would extend the southern boundary to Machala.

147. Estrada, *Culturas pre-clásicas,* 11, 17; Estrada and Evans, "Cultural Development in Ecuador," 85–86; Meggers, *Ecuador,* 131–38; Holm, *Cultura Milagro-Quevedo,* 25–26.

148. RGI 3:88 Carranza 1569.

149. "Sobre los tributos," 74, 85 (1579).

150. Holm, *Cultura Milagro-Quevedo,* 10.

151. Rivet, "Indiens Colorados," 208.

152. Murra, "Cayapa and Colorado," 284–85.

153. Bernárdez, "Lingüística de Esmeraldas," 350.

154. Larrain Barros, *Demografía,* 1:164.

155. RGI 3:88 Carranza 1569.

156. Meggers, *Ecuador,* 132.

157. Lizárraga, *Descripción breve,* cap. 5:6; Benzoni, *Historia del mundo nuevo,* 258; Atienza, "Compendio historial," 53–54.

158. Mathewson, "Guayas Wetlands," 222–23, 242–43; Parsons and Schlemon, "Prehistoric Raised Fields," 209; Stemper, "Raised Fields," 314–15.

159. Murra, "Cayapa and Colorado," 285.

160. CDI 9:247–309 Descripción de la gobernación 1605; Lizárraga, *Descripción breve,* cap. 5:6.
161. Rivet, "Indiens Colorados," 194, 197; Murra, "Cayapa and Colorado," 284–85.
162. Espinosa Soriano, "Reino de Chono," 22–23; Holm, *Cultura Milagro-Quevedo,* 10.
163. RGI 3:88 Carranza 1569.
164. Mathewson, "Estimating Labor Inputs," 331.
165. Knapp, *Ecología cultural,* 163.
166. Oviedo, *Historia general,* 5, lib. 46, cap. 17:98.
167. Lizárraga, *Descripción breve,* cap. 5:6.
168. Espinosa Soriano, "Reino de Chono," 21–22.
169. Espinosa Soriano, "Reino de Chono," 22.
170. Denevan, "Hydraulic Agriculture," 190.

CHAPTER 4

1. AGI AQ 88 Fuentes, no date [ca. 1630].
2. Terán, *Geografía,* 175–97.
3. The Pre-Andes or Third Cordillera comprises three cordilleras—Cóndor in the south, Cutucú, and Napo–Las Galeras in the north.
4. Grubb et al., "Comparison of Montane and Lowland Rain Forest," 567–601; Acosta-Solís, *Divisiones fitogeográficas,* 34.
5. The distinction between the two habitats has been stated most clearly by Meggers in *Amazonia* and Denevan in "Aboriginal Population of Western Amazonia." For a brief review of the debate over the significance of soils versus sources of protein, see Hames and Vickers, *Adaptive Responses,* 7–12. In her monograph *Parmana,* Roosevelt combines these two ideas, suggesting that protein-rich maize and beans could be grown only on the alluvial soils of the floodplain.
6. Denevan, "Aboriginal Population of Western Amazonia," 73; Terán, *Geografía,* 142.
7. Dufour estimates that 5 to 7 percent of protein intake among a Tukanoan group in northwest Amazonia comes from insects ("Insects as Food," 393).
8. Denevan, "Aboriginal Population of Western Amazonia," 78.
9. Denevan, "Aboriginal Population of Amazonia," 217–18.
10. Denevan, *Native Population,* xxvi.
11. Sweet, "Upper Amazon Valley," 157.
12. Sweet, "Upper Amazon Valley," 157–59. The recalculations assume 5.3 persons per km^2 for 2 percent of the area, or 10,000 km^2 (53,000); 0.2 persons per km^2 for 78 percent of the area, or 390,000 km^2 (78,000); and 1.0 persons per km^2 for 20 percent of the area, or 100,000 km^2 (100,000).
13. The linguistic affiliation of the Cofán is the subject of dispute. While some see a remote connection with Chibcha, others see no resemblance to any recognized linguistic family (Neumann, "Quijos y Cofanes," 66).
14. ARSI NRQ 12 I fol. 6 Ferrer 27.1.1605.

15. Maroni, "Noticias auténticas," 26:244, 249; Steward and Metraux, "Peruvian and Ecuadorian Montaña," 651; Espinosa Pérez, *Contribuciones lingüísticas,* 45–46; Velasco, *Historia del reino,* 3:257; Costales and Costales, *Amazonia,* 85; Neumann, "Quijos y Cofanes," 67.

16. AGI PAT 111-6 Probanza of Vázquez Dávila 14.8.1563, AQ 31 Cárdenas 2.3.1626; Rumazo González, *Región Amazónica,* 124, 128. Oberem suggests that it was founded between the extreme north of the Coca and Aguarico rivers, on a line with the equator (*Quijos,* 79).

17. Ordóñez de Cevallos, "Viaje del mundo," lib. 2, cap. 29:397, cap. 32:403–04.

18. Ordóñez de Cevallos, "Viaje del mundo," lib. 2, cap. 32:403–4, cap. 35:411.

19. Heredia, *Antigua provincia,* 9–11; Barnuevo, *Relación apologética,* 8–9; Jouanen, *Compañía de Jesús,* 1:100–106.

20. Jouanen, *Compañía de Jesús,* 1:100, 105.

21. Neumann, "Quijos y Cofanes," 71.

22. Jouanen, *Compañía de Jesús,* 1:105; Neumann, "Quijos y Cofanes," 71–72.

23. ARSI NRQ 12 I fol. 6 Ferrer 27.1.1605, fols. 24–35 Letra annua 1606.

24. Friede, "Kofán," 204; Costales y Costales, *Amazonia,* 16.

25. Neumann, "Quijos y Cofanes," 68.

26. ARSI NRQ 12 I fols. 6–11 Ferrer 20.3.1605, fols. 24–35 Letra annua 1606.

27. ARSI NRQ 12 I fols. 6–11 Ferrer 20.3.1605, fols. 24–35 Letra annua 1606; Ordóñez de Cevallos, "Viaje del mundo," lib. 2, cap. 29:397; Steward and Metraux, "Peruvian and Ecuadorian Montaña," 683.

28. RGI 2:248–49 Borja, no date; Oberem, "Trade and Trade Goods," 347.

29. Ordóñez de Cevallos, "Viaje del mundo," lib. 2, cap. 29:397.

30. ARSI NRQ 12 I fols. 6–11 Ferrer 20.3.1605.

31. Ordóñez de Cevallos, "Viaje del mundo," lib. 2, cap. 33:406.

32. ARSI NRQ 12 I fols. 6–11 Ferrer 20.3.1605, fols. 24–35 Letra annua 1606.

33. AGI AQ 8 Santillán 15.1.1564.

34. Porras Garcés, *Baeza,* see map opp. p. 184.

35. AGI AQ 82 Ortegón 1.2.1577; RGI 1:82–83 Lemus y Andrade 16.2.1608; Porras Garcés, *Baeza,* 185–86; Oberem, *Quijos,* 326–30.

36. Oberem, *Quijos,* 330. It is not clear whether the Indians in this region were a sierran group who had migrated to the lowlands or whether they were a lowland group who through contact with the highlands had become acculturated to groups living there.

37. Ordóñez de Cevallos, "Viaje del mundo," 2, cap. 29:397.

38. See chap. 5.

39. RGI 1:78 Lemus y Andrade 16.2.1608; Ordóñez de Cevallos, "Viaje del mundo," lib. 2, cap. 29:296–97; Porras Garcés, *Misaguallí,* 23. Whitten suggests that Quechua may have been spreading into the tropical forests of the Oriente prior to its introduction to the highlands by the Inka ("Amazonia Today," 126–27).

40. Jijón y Caamaño, *Ecuador interándino,* 1:294–95.

41. Oberem, *Quijos,* 313–14.

42. RGI 2:248 Borja, no date [1582?].

43. AGI AQ 82 Ortegón 1.2.1577.

44. AGI AQ 8 Barros 20.3.1588.

45. AGI AQ 82 Ortegón 1.2.1577.

46. Cieza de León, *Guerra de Chupas,* cap. 19:181.

47. AGI AQ 82 Ortegón 1.2.1577; Oberem, *Quijos,* 221.

48. AGI AQ 82 Ortegón 1.2.1577.

49. AGI AQ 82 Ortegón 1.2.1577; Oberem, Quijos, 197.

50. AGI AQ 82 Ortegón 1.2.1577; RGI 1:75, 77, 79 Lemus y Andrade 16.2.1608; Ordóñez de Cevallos, "Viaje del mundo," lib. 2, cap. 33:407; Oberem, *Quijos,* 152–53, 327–29. Although Lemus y Andrade mentions that plantains were grown, it is possible that they were not indigenous to the area in pre-Columbian times (Oberem, *Quijos,* 183).

51. AGI AQ 82 Ortegón 1.2.1577.

52. Oberem, *Quijos,* 153.

53. RGI 1:75 Lemus y Andrade 16.2.1608; Ordóñez de Cevallos, "Viaje del mundo," lib. 2, cap. 38:417.

54. AGI AQ 82 Ortegón 1.2.1577; Ordóñez de Cevallos, "Viaje del mundo," lib. 2, cap. 33:407; Oberem, *Quijos,* 181–82. Oberem suggests that the tobacco used by the Quijo was probably not cultivated but obtained from wild sources.

55. AGI AQ 82 Ortegón 1.2.1577; RGI 1:77 Lemus y Andrade 16.2.1608; Ordóñez de Cevallos, "Viaje del mundo, lib. 2, cap. 31:400, cap. 33:417; Oberem, "Trade and Trade Goods," 249.

56. Ordóñez de Cevallos, "Viaje del mundo," lib. 2, cap. 31:400.

57. AGI AQ 82 Ortegón 1.2.1577; RGI 2:248 Borja, no date [1582?].

58. AGI AQ 82 Ortegón 1.2.1577.

59. AGI AQ 82 Ortegón 1.2.1577.

60. AGI AQ 82 Ortegón 1.2.1577; Ordóñez de Cevallos, "Viaje del mundo," lib. 2, cap. 31:399.

61. Oberem, *Quijos,* 207.

62. AGI AQ 82 Ortegón 1.2.1577.

63. AGI AQ 82 Ortegón 1.2.1577; Oberem, *Quijos,* 203.

64. Oberem, *Quijos,* 50–54; Oberem, "Trade and Trade Goods," 347.

65. Rumazo González, *Región Amazónica,* 87; Oberem, *Quijos,* 203.

66. AGI AQ 82 Ortegón 1.2.1577; Zarate, "Historia del descubrimiento," lib. 4, cap. 2:493–94; Cieza de León, *Guerra de Chupas,* cap. 19:181.

67. AMQ LC 1:107 28.6.1535; Zarate, "Historia del descubrimiento," lib. 4, cap. 2:493–94; Cieza de León, *Guerra de Chupas,* cap. 19:181.

68. AGI AQ 82 Ortegón 1.2.1577.

69. Zarate, "Historia del descubrimiento," lib. 4, cap. 2:494; Oviedo, *Historia general,* 5, lib. 49, cap. 6:244.

70. AGI AQ 82 Ortegón 1.2.1577.

71. AGI AQ 82 Ortegón 1.2.1577; Ordóñez de Cevallos, "Viaje del mundo," lib. 2, cap. 31:402.

72. AGI AQ 82 Ortegón 1.2.1577. Cuduceta was probably Conduceta. See the map of Los Quijos in chap. 14.

73. AGI AQ 20B Probanza de Don Sancho Hacho 1569. The cacique of Latacunga claimed that the cacique of Hatunquijo was his brother-in-law, because he was married to one of the latter's sisters.

74. AGI AQ 82 Ortegón 1.2.1577; Oberem, *Quijos,* 224.

75. Ordóñez de Cevallos, "Viaje del mundo," lib. 2, cap. 31:400.

76. AGI AQ 82 Ortegón 1.2.1577.

77. AGI AQ 82 Ortegón 1.2.1577.

78. AGI AQ 82 Ortegón 1.2.1577.

79. Ordóñez de Cevallos, "Viaje del mundo," lib. 2, cap. 32:403.

80. Ortiguera, *Jornada,* cap. 57:41; Oberem, *Quijos,* 225.

81. Ordóñez de Cevallos, "Viaje del mundo," lib. 2, cap. 31:402.

82. AGI AQ 82 Ortegón 1.2.1577.

83. AGI AQ 82 Ortegón 1.2.1577; Ordóñez de Cevallos, "Viaje del mundo," lib. 2, cap. 31:40, 402, cap. 34:409; Cabello Balboa, *Obras,* 1:72; Ortiguera, *Jornada,* cap. 57:343–46 passim, cap. 58:349.

84. AGI AQ 82 Ortegón 1.2.1577; Ordóñez de Cevallos, "Viaje del mundo," lib. 2, cap. 33:406.

85. AGI AQ 82 Ortegón 1.2.1577; Ordóñez de Cevallos, "Viaje del mundo," lib. 2, cap. 33:406–7.

86. AGI AQ 82 Ortegón 1.2.1577.

87. AGI AQ 82 Ortegón 1.2.1577; Oberem, *Quijos,* 251.

88. AGI AQ 82 Ortegón 1.2.1577.

89. AGI AQ 82 Ortegón 1.2.1577.

90. AGI AQ 82 Ortegón 1.2.1577.

91. Ortiguera, *Jornada,* cap. 57:341.

92. AGI AQ 82 Ortegón 1.2.1577.

93. See chap. 16, which discusses the region of Yaguarzongo and Pacamoros.

94. AGI AQ 20B Información de servicios de Díaz de Pineda 1539; Oberem, *Quijos,* 40.

95. AGI PAT 101-19 Información de servicios de Ramírez Dávalos 25.10.1558, PAT 101-19 Probanza de Ramírez Dávalos, no date.

96. See the discussion of demographic trends in Los Quijos during the sixteenth century in chap. 14.

97. RGI 1:77 Lemus y Andrade 16.3.1608.

98. AGI AQ 31 Cárdenas 2.3.1626.

99. Oberem, *Quijos,* 40, 48. Taylor concurs with Oberem's estimate ("Évolution démographique," 230), although she gives the figure as 28,000 rather than 26,000.

100. The area inhabited by the Quijo has been estimated at about 13,000 km².

101. Denevan, "Aboriginal Population of Western Amazonia," 75.

102. Velasco, *Historia del reino,* 3:281–82; Naranjo, "Zonas de refugio," 135; Taylor and Descola, "Conjunto Jívaro," 46; Taylor, "Versants orientaux," 336.

103. Karsten, *Head-Hunters,* 9–10; Oberem, "Trade and Trade Goods," 347; Naranjo, "Zonas de refugio," 137 ; Costales and Costales, *Amazonia,* 121–22; Whitten, "Amazonia Today," 129–29; Whitten, *Sacha Runa,* 7. See the discussion of this group under colonial rule in chap. 15.

104. Montesinos, *Memorias antiguas,* 138; Garcilaso de la Vega, *Comentarios reales,* 2, lib. 8, cap. 6:299. In fact Montesinos refers to its conquest by Huiracocha.

105. Sarmiento de Gamboa, *Historia índica,* cap. 60:261.

106. Rumazo González, *Region Amazónica,* 133–35, 149; Taylor and Descola, "Conjunto Jívaro," 37.

107. RGI 3:178; Rumazo González, *Región Amazónica,* 136.

108. AGI AQ 20B Benavente 25.3.1550, also in RGI 3:174–77.

109. AGI PAT 97-5 Fundación del pueblo de Nuestra Señora del Rosario 15.8.1563, PAT 111-6 Gaspar de Ulloa, escribano 1.10.1563.

110. Taylor and Descola, "Conjunto Jívaro," 38–41.

111. Harner, *Jívaro,* 13–14; Costales and Costales, *Nación Shuar,* series E, 5:15–79; Taylor and Descola, "Conjunto Jívaro," 41–44, 46.

112. Harner, *Jívaro,* 13–14; Costales and Costales, *Nación Shuar,* series E, 1:40; Taylor and Descola, "Conjunto Jívaro," 46.

113. AGI PAT 97-5 Fundación del pueblo de Nuestra Señora del Rosario 15.8.1563; see the discussion of the Cañar in chap. 2.

114. AGI PAT 93-10-3 Account of an encomienda to Núñez Bonilla 23.11.1550.

115. ANHQ Tributos 2 Pérez Navarrete 29.10.1643. By 1608 there only 900 tributary Indians left (RGI 1:84 Lemus y Andrade 16.2.1608).

116. Accepting that the Indian population had declined to a degree (possibly only 10 percent) before 1575 and that the figure of 3,000 tributary Indians is reliable for that date, a tributary population at conquest of about 3,330 and a multiplication factor of 3 would give 9,990. Those enumerated in the account of Benavente's expedition suggest a minimum of 3,000 Indians, and not all would have been enumerated.

117. Harner, *Jívaro,* 13; Taylor and Descola, "Conjunto Jívaro," 48–49.

118. Taylor and Descola, "Conjunto Jívaro," 51–53.

119. See the discussion of the Palta in chap. 2; Taylor and Descola, "Conjunto Jívaro," 16–17.

120. RGI 3:125 Salinas, no date; Cieza de León, *Crónica,* cap. 56:80; Cieza de León, *Señorío,* cap. 56:206, cap. 64:215.

121. RGI 3:165–66; Rumazo González, *Región Amazónica,* 159.

122. RGI 3:186–87 Palomino, no date; Rumazo González, *Región Amazónica,* 160–61. It was on this expedition that in 1549 the town of Jaén was founded with twenty-six vecinos to the south of the Chinchipe. See the Kandoshi cultural-lingusitic group for a discussion of the Chirino.

123. RGI 3:197–98 Salinas 10.6.1571; see also Anda Aguirre, *Don Juan de Salinas,* 42–44.

124. RGI 3:189–92; Rumazo González, *Región Amazónica,* 155–59.

125. AGI AQ 18 Hernández—Interrogatorio 21.2.1558; RGI 3:179–80 Baraona 24.11.1568; Anda Aguirre, "Origenes de Zamora," 72–75.

126. RGI 3:190.

127. AGI AQ 20B Benavente 25.3.1550 and RGI 3:174–77; Taylor and Descola, "Conjunto Jívaro," 38.

128. AGI PAT 97-5 Fundación del pueblo de Nuestra Señora del Rosario 15.8.1563; Taylor and Descola, "Conjunto Jívaro," 46–47.

129. AGI AQ 20B and RGI 3:174–77 Benavente 25.3.1550 for the Xíbaro region. In 1582 villages around Loyola and Valladolid listed by Aldrete averaged 209 and 78 Indians respectively, but these figures probably reflect a degree of nucleation imposed by the Spanish authorities (RGI 3:150–51 Aldrete 1.12.1582).

130. Karsten, *Head-Hunters,* 94; Stirling, *Ethnographical Material,* 89–90; Meggers, *Amazonia,* 56–58.

131. RGI 3:133 Salinas, no date.

132. RGI 3:150–51 Aldrete 1.12.1582; Karsten, *Head-Hunters,* 94.

133. RGI 3:152 Aldrete 1.12.1582.

134. RGI 3:141 Alvaro Núñez, no date.

135. RGI 3:128 Salinas, no date; RGI 3:151 Aldrete 1.12.1582.

136. RGI 3:133 Salinas, no date.

137. RGI 3:128, 133 Salinas, no date; RGI 3:150, 152 Aldrete 1.12.1582, RGI 3:141 Alvaro Núñez, no date, RGI 3:205 Salinas, no date.

138. RGI 3:127 Salinas, no date, RGI 3:141 Alvaro Núñez, no date.

139. Denevan, "Aboriginal Population of Western Amazonia," 73–74. Although rich in species, there were relatively small numbers of each.

140. RGI 3:129, 133 Salinas, no date; RGI 3:142 Alvaro Núñez, no date; RGI 3:150–51 Aldrete 1.12.1582; RGI 3:197 Salinas, 10.6.1571; RGI 3:205 Salinas, no date.

141. RGI 2:269 Pablos 1582; RGI 3:142 Alvaro Núñez, no date. Otherwise trade appears to have been relatively insignificant to the extent that they possessed no markets but bartered items on an individual basis (RGI 3:134 Salinas, no date).

142. Kroeger and Barbira-Freedman, *Cultural Change and Health,* 9.

143. RGI 3:205 Salinas, no date.

144. ARSI Provincia Peruana 12 fol. 292 Carta annua for 1602, written by Rodrigo de Cabredo 28.4.1603.

145. RGI 3:142 Alvaro Núñez, no date; RGI 3:151 Aldrete 1.12.1582; RGI 3:197–98 Salinas, no date; Maroni, "Noticias auténticas," 30:116; Stirling, *Ethnographical Material,* 38–42; Taylor and Descola, "Conjunto Jívaro," 51.

146. RGI 3:133 Salinas, no date; RGI 3:151 Aldrete 1.12.1582; RGI 3:175 Benavente 25.3.1550; Stirling, *Ethnographical Material,* 79–81; Taylor and Descola, "Conjunto Jívaro," 52.

147. RGI 3:142 Alvaro Núñez, no date; RGI 3:150–51 Aldrete 1.12.1582; RGI 3:204 Salinas, no date.

148. RGI 3:132, 134 Salinas, no date.

149. RGI 3:133 Salinas, no date; RGI 3:197 Salinas 10.6.1571; RGI 3:205 Salinas, no date.

150. RGI 3:141 Alvaro Núñez, no date; Steward and Metraux, "Peruvian and Ecuadorian Montaña," 626.

151. RGI 3:199 Salinas 10.6.1571.

152. RGI 3:199 Salinas 10.6.1571; RGI 3:148 Aldrete 1.12.1582.

153. RGI 3:148 Aldrete 1.12.1582; RGI 3:199–200 Salinas 10.6.1571; Descola, "Scattered to Nucleated Settlement," 621, 623, 633–34; Boster, "Jivaroan Gardens," 48–50.

154. Descola, "Scattered to Nucleated Settlement," 623.

155. Maroni, "Noticias auténticas," 30:112.

156. Descola, "Scattered to Nucleated Settlement," 623.

157. RGI 3:148 Aldrete 1.12.1582; RGI 3:199–200 Salinas 10.6.1571.

158. RGI 3:148 Aldrete 1.12.1582.

159. RGI 3:303 Salinas 1571; RGI 3:149 Aldrete 1.12.1582.

160. RGI 3:148 Aldrete 1.12.1582.

161. RGI 3:148 Aldrete 1.12.1582; RGI 3:199 Salinas 10.6.1571.

162. RGI 3:199 Salinas 10.6.1571.

163. ARSI Provincia Peruana 12 fols. 291–92 Carta annua for 1602, written by Rodrigo de Cabredo 28.4.1603.

164. Descola, "Scattered to Nucleated Settlement," 626–29. See also DeBoer, "Buffer Zones," 365.

165. AGI EC 912A Memorial de las cosas 1577.

166. BNM 3178 fols. 1–15 Canelas Albarrán 1586. The remaining figures were for Macas and Santa María de Nieva, with 4,000 souls each. The figures include small numbers of non-Indians to the total of 500 for the whole gobernación.

167. RGI 3:149–52 Aldrete 1.12.1582. There were 6,719 and 2,749 encomienda Indians around Loyola and Valladolid respectively, with a further 10,159 around Santiago de las Montañas. In addition there were 3,328 Indians around Santa María de Nieva.

168. In fact Stirling suggests that they may represent only one-half of the total number of Jívaro, but the area he includes extends to the Morona and Pastaza, where the Maina and Andoa were living (*Ethnographical Material*, 37).

169. AGI AQ 20B Benavente 25.3.1550.

170. AGI EC 912A Memorial de las cosas 1577.

171. AGI AQ 30 Mexía Sandoval 8.4.1622.

172. RAHM Colección Muñoz A/92 fols. 55–77 Relación de los naturales 1561. The ratio of tributary Indians to the total population is surprisingly high. It may reflect inadequate recording of nontributary Indians.

173. RAHM 9/4664 no. 21 Los pueblos despañoles que hay, no date. Although the document is undated, it says that the gobernación of Yaguarzongo and Pacamoros had been conquered about ten years ago, which allows us to date it at around 1567.

174. CDI 15:409–572 Demarcación y división de las Indias, no date; López de Velasco, *Geografía*, 221.

175. RGI 2:308–9 Escobar 1592.

176. Taylor, "Évolution démographique," 230.

177. RGI 3:199 Salinas 10.6.1571.

178. See chap. 6.

179. The area estimated to have been inhabited by the Jívaro was about 41,570 km², which, at a density of 1.2 persons per km², would give approximately 49,884.

180. With the Jívaro of the low selva inhabiting one-quarter of the total area of 41,570 km², the estimated populations for both groups would be high selva 37,413 (31,177 km² at 1.2 per km²) and low selva 2,079 (10,393 km² at 0.2 per km²), giving a total of 39,492.

181. RGI 3:197 Salinas 10.6.1571.

182. Rivet, "Indiens Jíbaros," 357–58. Their combined populations fell from 255 to less than 100.

183. Kroeger and Barbira-Freedman, *Cultural Change and Health,* 18–20. A study of 471 Shuar adult deaths in 1971 showed that 36 percent were due to accidents and warfare. See also Descola, "Scattered to Nucleated Settlement," 625, and Bennett Ross, "Revenge Hostilities," 96.

184. RGI 3:139–41 Alvaro Núñez, no date; RGI 3:147–53 Aldrete 1.12.1582.

185. Karsten, *Head-Hunters,* 186; Stirling, *Ethnographical Material,* 37, 56, 71, 108.

186. Karsten, *Head-Hunters,* 187; Stirling, *Ethnographical Material,* 114.

187. Karsten, *Head-Hunters,* 229; Meggers, *Amazonia,* 107.

188. Kroeger et al., "Salud y la alimentación," 131–32, 150.

189. Meggers, *Amazonia,* 107; Kroeger and Barbira-Freedman, *Cultural Change and Health,* 14.

190. RGI 3:137–38 Alvaro Núñez, 18.12.1582; RGI 3:142 Alvaro Núñez, no date. See the discussion of the province of Yaguarzongo and Pacamoros in chap. 16.

191. Metraux, "Middle and Upper Amazon," 687.

192. Metraux, "Migrations," 36–41; Lathrap, "Alternative Models of Populations Movement," 14, 19; Chaumeil and Chaumeil, "Canela y El Dorado," 80. On the basis of archaeological investigations on the Napo River, Meggers and Evans postulate a primary movement eastward from the Andean area into the Oriente and a dispersion from there (Meggers and Evans, *Archaeological Investigations,* 108–10). See also Vickers, "Adaptation to Amazonian Habitats," 35–37 for a discussion of the alternative hypotheses.

193. Ortiguera, *Jornada* , 355.

194. Vázquez, "Omagua y Dorado," 429–30; Carvajal, *Descubrimiento del famoso río grande,* 20–29, 41, 43; Metraux, "Middle and Upper Amazon," 689; Oviedo, *Historia general,* 5, lib. 50, cap. 24:383, 385; Ortiguera, *Jornada,* 249; Grohs, *Alto Amazonas,* 22–25; Chaumeil and Chaumeil, "Canela y El Dorado," 81–83.

195. This group of Omagua inhabited the stretch of the Coca River following the site at which a boat was constructed by Gonzalo Pizarro and Francisco de Orellana and before they parted to continue their separate journeys (Carvajal, *Descubrimiento del famoso río grande,* 88, Pizarro to Crown 3.9.1542; see also Heaton, *Discovery of the Amazon,* 246). The latter point has been interpreted by many as the confluence of the Napo and Coca rivers. See Rumazo González, *Región Amazónica,* opp. p. 64; Gil Munilla, *Descubrimiento del Marañón,* 261–67; Chaumeil and Chaumeil, "Canela y El Dorado," 65.

196. Oberem, "Grupo indígena desaparecido," 160–61.

197. Carvajal, *Descubrimiento del famoso río grande,* 13, 17; Rumazo González, *Región Amazónica,* 60; Oviedo, *Historia general,* 5, lib. 50, cap. 24:375–76; Cieza de León, *Guerra de Chupas,* cap. 21:185.

198. Meggers and Evans, *Archaeological Investigations,* 4.

199. Ortiguera, *Jornada,* 245, 355. A similar pattern of subsistence is described by Ordóñez de Cevallos, "Viaje del mundo," lib. 2, cap. 33:407. See also ARSI NRQ 12 I fols. 6–11 Ferrer 20.3.1605.

200. Carvajal, *Descubrimiento del famoso río grande,* 6.

201. AGI AQ 82 Ortegón 1.2.1577; Oberem, "Grupo indígena desaparecido," 152.

202. Ordóñez de Cevallos, "Viaje del mundo," lib. 2, cap. 33:407, cap. 34:408–9.

203. Ordóñez de Cevallos, "Viaje del mundo," lib. 2, cap. 33:406.

204. Grohs, *Alto Amazonas,* 22.

205. Maroni, "Noticias auténticas," 28:190; Oberem, "Grupo indígena desaparecido," 158.

206. ARSI NRQ 12 I fols. 4–6 Ferrer 3.11.1604, NRQ 14 fol. 65 Ferrer 9.7.1608.

207. This figure is not beyond the realms of possibility, given Carvajal's comment that the river was continuously inhabited for fifty leagues.

208. Acuña, *Nuevo descubrimiento,* 124–25; Oberem, "Grupo indígena desaparecido," 158; Chaumeil and Chaumeil, "Canela y El Dorado," 81.

209. Carvajal, *Descubrimiento del famoso río grande,* 13, 17; Rumazo González, *Región Amazónica,* 60; Oviedo, *Historia general,* 5, lib. 50, cap. 24:375–76; Cieza de León, *Guerra de Chupas,* cap. 21:185. As already indicated, the lack of settlement in this region may be due to the lack of suitable lands for cultivation rather than intertribal wars.

210. Carvajal, *Descubrimiento del famoso río grande,* 13, 20–22; Oviedo, *Historia general,* 5, lib. 50, cap. 24:375–77.

211. AGI AQ 50 Información . . . de servicios de Alonso de Miranda 1620, AQ 88 Información sobre las entradas que Alonso de Miranda . . . hizó 1630.

212. Cruz, "Nuevo descubrimiento," 192; Acuña, *Nuevo descubrimiento,* 116, 119; Fritz, *Journal,* 50; Oviedo, *Historia general,* 5, lib. 50, cap. 24; 382; Ortiguera, *Jornada,* 236, 246; Zúñiga, "Relación muy verdadera," 511–12; Metraux, "Middle and Upper Amazon," 694; Oberem, "Trade and Trade Goods," 355.

213. Ortiguera, *Jornada,* 246.

214. Acuña, *Nuevo descubrimiento,* 116, 119; Fritz, *Journal,* 419; Oviedo, *Historia general,* 5, lib. 50, cap. 24:382.

215. AGI AQ 88 Información sobre las entradas que Alonso de Miranda . . . hizó 1630.

216. Some of these methods were used by the Machifaro (Ortiguera, *Jornada,* 247) and are used in the area today (Meggers, *Amazonia,* 141).

217. Maroni, "Noticias auténticas," 28:184.

218. Denevan, *Native Population,* xxvi.

219. Lathrap, "Alternative Models of Populations Movements," 14, 19; Hames and Vickers, *Adaptive Responses,* 12–14.

220. See the discussion of the Omagua.

221. Barnuevo, *Relación apologética,* 9.

222. Steward and Metraux, "Peruvian and Ecuadorian Montaña," 635; Steward, "Western Tucanoan Tribes," 737–38.

223. Cruz, "Nuevo descubrimiento,"155.

224. AGI AQ 50 Información . . . de servicios de Alonso de Miranda 1620, AQ 88 Información sobre las entradas que Alonso de Miranda . . . hizo 1630; AGI AQ 88 Reyes Villalobos 1630, AQ 158 Nieto Polo, no date [1735?]; Jouanen, *Compañía de Jesús,* 1:319–20; Barnuevo, *Relación apologética,* 13.

225. Maldonado, *Descubrimiento del río de las Amazonas,* 15; Espinosa Pérez, *Contribuciones lingüísticas,* 9–17.

226. Cruz, "Nuevo descubrimiento,"157–59; Izaguirre, *Misiones franciscanos,* 1:181–82.

227. Cruz, "Nuevo descubrimiento," 157; Chantre y Herrera, *Historia de las misiones,* 61; Maroni, "Noticias auténticas," 26:245; Steward, "Western Tucanoan Tribes," 738; Espinosa Pérez, *Contribuciones lingüísticas,* 29–32.

228. Espinosa Pérez, *Contribuciones lingüísticas,* 167–69.

229. Cruz, "Nuevo descubrimiento," 157.

230. AGOFM M/42 fols. 151–52 Relación de viaje . . . Domingo de Brieva,

written by Antonio de San Pedro ca. 1647; Cruz, "Nuevo descubrimiento," 157–59; Maroni, "Noticias auténticas," 29:238–40.

231. Steward, "Western Tucanoan Tribes," 742.

232. Vickers, "Adaptation to Amazonian Habitats," 129, Vickers, "Territorial Dimensions," 450, 456.

233. Maroni, "Noticias auténticas," 29:239, Letter from Lucas de la Cueva 22.3.1665.

234. Steward, "Western Tucanoan Tribes," 741, 744; Vickers, "Adaptation to Amazonian Habitats," 96.

235. Velasco, *Historia del reino,* 3:414.

236. AGI AQ 50 Información . . . de servicios de Alonso de Miranda 1620.

237. Acuña, *Nuevo descubrimiento,* 109–10.

238. Izaguirre, *Misiones franciscanos,* 1:334; Maldonado, *Descubrimiento del río de las Amazonas,* 13.

239. Sweet, "Upper Amazon Valley," 71–73.

240. AGOFM M/42 fols. 151–52 Relación de viaje . . . Domingo de Brieva, written by Antonio de San Pedro ca. 1647.

241. Costales and Costales give a much higher figure of 20,000 (*Amazonia,* 16). This includes the Siona and Secoya with 5,000 Indians each, in addition to the Encabellado proper, which they estimate at 10,000.

242. AGI AQ 50 Información . . . de servicios de Alonso de Miranda 1620, AQ 31 Información de las provincias descubiertas 23.6.1623.

243. Maroni, "Noticias auténticas," 29:246.

244. ARSI NRQ 15 I fols. 81–82 Lucero 20.2.1682.

245. Anda Aguirre, *Primeros gobernadores,* 119.

246. Compte, *Varones ilustres,* 2:49. The account is rather ambiguous, but it would appear that the 6,000 baptized were all Abijira and that among them the Franciscans had established the pueblos of Nuestra Señora de Guadalupe, Encarnación de Abijiras, San Buenaventura, and San Francisco. Since they fell under the jurisdiction of the Jesuits, however, Franciscans decided to concentrate their efforts on groups on the Putumayo.

247. AGOFM M/42 fols. 169–72 San Julián 3.2.1694.

248. Sweet, "Upper Amazon Valley," 69, 74.

249. AGI AQ 88 Información sobre las entradas 1630.

250. Taylor, "Versants orientaux," 288–303, 345.

251. Taylor and Descola, "Conjunto Jívaro," 26–27, 48–49.

252. RGI 3:243–44 Saavedra 24.4.1620.

253. Steward and Metraux, "Peruvian and Ecuadorian Montaña," 629.

254. Taylor and Descola, "Conjunto Jívaro," 26–27.

255. RGI 3:200–201 Salinas 10.6.1571.

256. Figueroa, *Relación de las misiones,* 14.

257. RGI 3:243 Saavedra 24.4.1620; Maroni, "Noticias auténticas," 28:191, 193; Figueroa, *Relación de las misiones,* vi–vii; Heredia, *Antigua provincia,* 12.

258. RGI 3:243 Saavedra 24.4.1620; RGI 3:253 Ponce de León 1644.

259. RGI 3:245–46 Saavedra 24.4.1620.

260. RGI 3:243 Saavedra 24.4.1620.

261. AGI AQ 11 Morga 25.4.1629; RGI 3:247 Saavedra 24.4.1620; RGI 3:206 No author, no date.

262. RGI 3:246 Saavedra 24.4.1620.

263. RGI 3:246 Saavedra 24.4.1620.

264. RGI 3:201 Salinas 10.6.1571; RGI 3:206 Salinas, no date; RGI 3:245–46 Saavedra 24.4.1620.

265. RGI 3:246 Saavedra 24.4.1620.

266. RGI 3:246 Saavedra 24.4.1620.

267. RGI 3:245 Saavedra 24.4.1620.

268. RGI 3:201 Salinas 10.6.1571; RGI 3:206 Salinas, no date; RGI 3:245–46 Saavedra 24.4.1620; Figueroa, *Relación de las misiones,* 261–65; Cieza de León, *Guerra de Salinas,* cap. 79:133.

269. RGI 3:246 Saavedra 24.4.1620.

270. RGI 3:201 Salinas 10.6.1571.

271. Anda Aguirre, *Primeros gobernadores,* 33.

272. RGI 3:243 Saavedra 24.4.1620; RGI 3:253.

273. Figueroa, *Relación de las misiones,* 15; see also Maroni, "Noticias auténticas," 28:193.

274. AGI AQ 11 Vaca de la Cadena, April 1629.

275. Rivet, "Province de Jaén," 245–47; Taylor and Descola, "Conjunto Jívaro," 12.

276. RGI 3:187 Palomino, no date.

277. RGI 3:143 Relación de la tierra de Jaén, no date; RGI 3:187 Palomino, no date.

278. RGI 3:143 Relación de la tierra de Jaén, no date; RGI 3:187 Palomino, no date.

279. Viegl, "Gründliche Nachrichten," 47; Maroni, "Noticias auténticas," 26:217, 226–27; 29:261–63; Figueroa, *Relación de las misiones,* 163; Taylor, "Versants orientaux," 289–92.

280. RGI 3:147–48 Aldrete 1.12.1582; Maroni, "Noticias auténticas," 29:261–63; Jouanen, *Compañía de Jesús,* 1:346.

281. Viegl, "Gründliche Nachrichten," 49; Jouanen, *Compañía de Jesús,* 2:533; Velasco, *Historia del Reino,* 3:426.

282. Chantre y Herrera, *Historia de las misiones,* 477; Steward and Metraux, "Peruvian and Ecuadorian Montaña," 628, 632–33.

283. Taylor and Descola, "Conjunto Jívaro," 31–32; Taylor, "Versants orientaux," 292–93.

284. Taylor, "Versants orientaux," 292–94.

285. Sweet, "Upper Amazon Valley," 68.

286. Costales and Costales, *Amazonia,* 15.

287. Jouanen, *Compañía de Jesús,* 1:354.

288. Taylor, "Versants orientaux," 296–97.

289. Maroni, "Noticias auténticas," 28:443–44, 452; Figueroa, *Relación de las misiones,* 135–36, 149; Jouanen, *Compañía de Jesús,* 1:395, 399.

290. ARSI NRQ 14 fol. 150 Razón y noticia de las reducciones 1686, NRQ 15 fols. 135–40 García de Zeares 30.5.1686.

291. Steward and Metraux, "Peruvian and Ecuadorian Montaña," 634–35; Taylor and Descola, "Conjunto Jívaro," 33–34; Taylor, "Versants orientaux," 297–98.

292. Maroni, "Noticias auténticas," 28:448, 452–53.

293. Taylor, "Versants orientaux," 297–98.

294. Sweet, "Upper Amazon Valley," 65; Costales and Costales, *Amazonia,* 15; Taylor, "Versants orientaux," 345.

295. "Autos fechos," 415. This would give each leader about 550 subjects.

296. The detailed figures given by Costales and Costales (*Amazonia,* 15) are as follows: Andoa 2,000, Andoa subgroups 4,000, Murato 4,000, and Roamaina-Zapa 10,000. Sweet ("Upper Amazon Valley", 65, 68) estimates Andoa 3,000–4,000 and Roamaina-Zapa 8,000–10,000.

297. Taylor, "Versants orientaux," 345.

298. Taking account of the fact that Sweet does not include the Murato and that the basis of Costales and Costales's estimate for the same group is not known, a compromise lower figure of 16,000 seems acceptable.

299. Steward and Metraux, "Peruvian and Ecuadorian Montaña," 628.

300. Steward and Metraux, "Peruvian and Ecuadorian Montaña," 639–51; Steward and Metraux, "Peban Tribes," 730–36.

301. Maroni, "Noticias auténticas," 29:86, 246; Chantre y Herrera, *Historia de las misiones,* 207, 214, 249, 307–8; Viegl, "Gründliche Nachrichten," 50; Steward and Metraux, "Peruvian and Ecuadorian Montaña," 631; Amadio, "Los Muratos," 120–21.

302. Maroni, "Noticias auténticas," 29:255; Chantre y Herrera, *Historia de las misiones,* 250, 307; Jouanen, *Compañía de Jesús,* 1:463. This was where the Jesuits established the mission of San Javier in 1669, but in 1672 its site was moved upriver to a northern tributary of the Bobonaza (Taylor, "Versants orientaux," 315).

303. AGOFM M/42 fol. 174 No author, no date; AGI AQ 158 Cabaleyro 27.8.1708; Maroni, "Noticias auténticas," 26:232; 29:230–33, 246; Acuña, *Nuevo descubrimiento,* 113; Taylor, "Versants oreintaux," 314.

304. Taylor, "Versants orientaux," 314.

305. Velasco, *Historia del reino,* 3:384–85, 392, 447; Rodríguez, *Descubrimiento del Marañón,* 511.

306. ARSI NRQ 14 fol. 150 Razón y noticia de las reducciones 1686, NRQ 15 fols. 135–40 García de Zeares 30.5.1686; Jouanen, *Compañía de Jesús,* 1:487–88.

307. Velasco, *Historia del reino,* 3:398, 414.

308. Costales and Costales, *Amazonia,* 15–16.

309. Sweet, "Upper Amazon Valley," 67.

310. ARSI NRQ 15 I fols. 81–82 Lucero 20.2.1682; Rodríguez, *Descubrimiento del Marañón,* 511.

311. Maroni, "Noticias auténticas," 29:118–19.

312. Maroni, "Noticias auténticas," 26:216; 29:85–87; Figueroa, *Relación de las misiones,* 157; Jouanen, *Compañía de Jesús,* 1:401.

313. Astrain, *Historia de la Compañía,* 6, lib. 3, cap. 9:608; Taylor, "Versants orientaux," 299, 302.

314. Maroni, "Noticias auténticas," 29:118; Jouanen, *Compañía de Jesús,* 1:437.

315. Taylor, "Versants orientaux," 303.

316. Maroni, "Noticias auténticas," 29:87; Jouanen, *Compañía de Jesús,* 1:401.

317. ARSI NRQ 15 I fols. 81–82 Lucero 20.2.1682.

318. Sweet, "Upper Amazon Valley," 70; Costales and Costales, *Amazonia,* 15–16. The latter estimate 5,000 for the Coronado, 3,000 for the Oa, and 1,000 for the Chudavinas, who were friends of the Coronado living on the banks of the Upper Bobonaza (Taylor, "Versants orientaux," 299).

319. Taylor, "Versants orientaux," 288, 296.

320. Maroni, "Noticias auténticas," 26:216–17; 29:85–87; Chantre y Herrera, *Historia de las misiones,* 308; Figueroa, *Relación de las misiones,* 297, 395.

321. Maroni, "Noticias auténticas," 29:265.

322. Sweet, "Upper Amazon Valley," 67.

323. AGI AQ 158 Zarate 30.11.1735; Viegl, "Gründliche Nachrichten," 75; Maroni, "Noticias auténticas," 26:236–37; Steward and Metraux, "Peruvian and Ecuadorian Montaña," 636; Velasco, *Historia del reino,* 3:415.

324. Maroni, "Noticias auténticas," 26:236–37; Chantre y Herrera, *Historia de las misiones,* 344–45, 348–49, 544–50; Figueroa, *Relación de las misiones,* 379–82.

325. AGI AQ 50 Información de los servicios de Alonso de Miranda 1620. Velasco also notes they were "bien numeroso" and formed two provinces, but ones of equal size (Velasco, *Historia del reino,* 3:415).

326. Maroni, "Noticias auténticas," 31:69.

327. Costales and Costales, *Amazonia,* 15.

328. Grohs, *Alto Amazonas,* 97–101.

329. Maroni, "Noticias auténticas," 26:233, 236.

330. Steward and Metraux, "Peban Tribes," 727.

331. AGI AQ 158 Zarate 30.11.1735.

332. ARSI NRQ 15 I fols. 81–82 Lucero 20.2.1682; Chantre y Herrera, *Historia de las misiones,* 283.

333. Maroni, "Noticias auténticas," 31:49.

334. AGI AQ 158 Zarate 28.8.1739; Figueroa, *Relación de las misiones,* 373–74.

335. Sweet, "Upper Amazon Valley," 80; Costales and Costales, *Amazonia,* 15. The latter estimate 10,000 for the Yameo and another 4,500 inhabitants of the Nanay and Itatay rivers.

336. Maroni, "Noticias auténticas," 25:231; 27:65; Steward and Metraux, "Peruvian and Ecuadorian Montaña," 556.

337. Steward and Metraux, "Peruvian and Ecuadorian Montaña," 557.

338. RGI 3:254.

339. AGI AQ 158 Zarate 30.10.1736; Maroni, "Noticias auténticas," 26:231; 29:266.

340. Maroni, "Noticias auténticas," 29:266.

341. Velasco, *Historia del reino,* 3:414.

342. Jouanen, *Compañía de Jesús,* 2:484. The misson contained 563 Indians.

343. Sweet, "Upper Amazon Valley," 83. Costales and Costales give an estimate of 5,000 for the Itucale and 3,000 for the Urarina (Shimacos) (*Amazonia,* 15).

344. Phelan, *Kingdom of Quito,* 45.

345. Sweet's figures for groups in this study area are as follows: Encabellado, Abijira, and Payagua, 15,000–20,000; for the Maina, Andoa, Murato, and Roamain-Zapa, 21,000–26,000; for the Gae, Semigae, Coronado, Oa, Pinche, and Yameo, 27,000–34,000; for the Urarina-Itucale 5,000–6,000 (Sweet, "Upper Amazon Valley," 103).

346. Taylor, "Évolution démographique," 230. Although her work is based on excellent ethnohistorical research, Taylor, unlike Sweet, does not examine the evidence for each Indian group separately; rather, she provides a few very general estimates for the major cultural-linguistic groups.

347. Denevan, *Native Population*, xxvi.

348. Sweet, "Upper Amazon Valley," 157–59.

349. Descola suggests that warfare in this region may have been motivated by the desire to maintain control of hunting grounds ("Scattered and Nucleated Settlement," 633).

CHAPTER 5

1. RGI 2:322 Auncibay 1592. These comments were made about the southern highlands of Ecuador.

2. Morris, "Organization and Administration of Tawantinsuyu," 478.

3. Murra, "Estructura política de los inka," 23–43; Spalding, *Huarochirí*, 78; Salomon, "Potential of the Complementarity Concept," 523.

4. Rowe, "Inca Culture," 206–8; Murra, "Guerre et les rébellions," 929–32.

5. Cieza de León, *Señorío*, cap. 56:205–7.

6. Larrea, *Cultura incasica*, 19; Larrea, *Notas de prehistoria*, 167.

7. Cieza de León, *Señorío*, cap. 56:206.

8. Idrovo, "Tomebamba," 96–99.

9. Cieza de León, *Señorío*, cap. 56:206–7. Espinosa Soriano also suggests that there may have been incursions into Guayllabamba Valley on the edge of Caranqui territory (*Cayambes y Carangues*, 1:219).

10. Cabello Balboa, *Miscelánea antártica*, pt. 3, cap. 18:340; Garcilaso de la Vega, *Comentarios reales*, 1, lib. 8, caps. 6–7:299–302; Sarmiento de Gamboa, *Historia índica*, pt. 2, cap. 44:249, cap. 46:250.

11. Oberem, "Quitoloma," 203; Salomon, "Ethnic Lords," 202–4; Idrovo, "Tomebamba," 96.

12. Cabello Balboa, *Miscelánea antártica*, pt. 3, caps. 21–23:364–83; Salomon, "Ethnic Lords," 204–6; Cieza de León, *Señorío*, cap. 67:218–19; Caillavet, "Dominación incaica," 417–18. See Espinosa Soriano, *Cayambes y Carangues*, 1:219–73 for an analytical account of the northern campaigns.

13. Salomon, "Ethnic Lords," 295; Cieza de León, *Crónica*, cap. 34:49; Cieza de León, *Señorío*, cap. 21:170.

14. Larrea, *Cultura incasica*, 19; Salomon, "Ethnic Lords," 206.

15. Meyers, *Die Inka in Ekuador*, 154–55; Salomon, "Ethnic Lords," 296; Salomon, "Systèmes politiques verticaux," 972, 986–87; Espinosa Soriano, *Cayambes y Carangues*, 1:329, 334–35.

16. Cieza de León, *Crónica*, cap. 47:69.

17. Loor, *Indios de Manabí*, 85–87; Cabello Balboa, *Miscelánea antártica*, pt. 3, cap. 17:322–24; Garcilaso de la Vega, *Comentarios reales*, 1, lib. 9, cap. 8:343–44; Sarmiento de Gamboa, *Historia índica*, pt. 2, cap. 46:251; Borja de Szászdi, "Prehistoria de la costa ecuatoriana," 428–30; Cieza de León, *Crónica*, caps. 47–50:69–73 and cap. 53:75–77.

18. Garcilaso de la Vega, *Comentarios reales,* 1, lib. 9, cap. 8:344.

19. Espinosa Soriano, "Mitmas multiples en Abancay," 237.

20. Estete, *Noticia,* 20; Oviedo, *Historia general,* 5, lib. 46, cap. 17:99; Cieza de León, *Crónica,* cap. 48:70.

21. Cieza de León, *Crónica,* cap. 48:70. Garcilaso de la Vega was of the same opinion (*Comentarios reales,* 1, lib. 9, cap. 8:344).

22. Bushnell, *Santa Elena Peninsula,* 9; Borja de Szászdi, "Prehistoria de la costa ecuatoriana," 435–36; Hyslop, "Fronteras estatales," 37–38.

23. Dillehay and Netherly, *Frontera del estado Inca,* 11.

24. Borja de Szászdi, "Prehistoria de la costa ecuatoriana," 433; Meyers, *Die Inka in Ekuador,* 144–46.

25. Murra, "Historic Tribes of Ecuador," 809.

26. Oberem, *Quijos,* 50–64; Chaumeil and Chaumeil, "Canela y El Dorado," 57–61.

27. Montesinos, *Memorias antiguas,* cap. 25:143–45; Oberem, *Quijos,* 51–52.

28. Cieza de León, *Señorío,* cap. 56:206.

29. Sarmiento de Gamboa, *Historia índica,* pt. 2, cap. 60:261; Taylor and Descola, "Conjunto Jivaro," 34–36.

30. Ortiguera, *Jornada,* cap. 51:355; Oberem, *Quijos,* 53.

31. Cabello Balboa, *Miscelánea antártica,* pt. 3, cap. 29:437–38.

32. Cabello Balboa, *Miscelánea antártica,* pt. 3, cap. 29:438.

33. Meggers, "Environmental Limitations," 808.

34. Gade, "Coca Cultivation and Endemic Disease," 263–79.

35. Salomon, "Status Trader Complex," 63, 72–73; Taylor, "Versants orientaux," 251–52. This contrasts with the western flanks of the Andes, where the Inka developed the vertical archipelago system.

36. Salomon, "Ethnic Lords," 311–13; Salomon, "Systèmes politiques verticaux," 985–86; Spalding, *Huarochirí,* 76–79; Morris, "Organization and Administration of Tawantinsuyu," 479–82.

37. See, for example, RGI 2:251 Borja, no date; RGI 2:270 Los Angeles 12.5.1582; RGI 2:275–76 Gallegos 20.9.1582; Cieza de León, *Crónica,* cap. 38:54.

38. Cieza de León, *Crónica,* cap. 38:55.

39. Cieza de León, *Crónica,* cap. 53:77.

40. Garcilaso de la Vega, *Comentarios reales,* 1, lib. 8, cap. 7:301; Cieza de León, *Señorío,* cap. 56:205.

41. Cabello Balboa, *Miscelánea antártica,* pt. 3, cap. 16:320; Cieza de León, *Señorío,* cap. 56:206.

42. Cobo, *Historia del nuevo mundo,* 2, lib. 12, cap. 14:84; Sarmiento de Gamboa, *Historia índica,* pt. 2, cap. 44:249; Cieza de León, *Señorío,* cap. 56:206.

43. Larrea, *Notas de prehistoria,* 179; *Documentos para la historia militar,* 1:132–50 (Puento 1586); Espinosa Soriano, "Curaca de los Cayambes," 91.

44. RGI 2:210 Anon. 1573; RGI 2:238 Paz Ponce de León 2.4.1582; Cieza de León, *Crónica,* cap. 37:53; Cobo, *Historia del nuevo mundo,* 2, lib. 12, cap. 17:92, cap. 35:137; Cieza de León, *Señorío,* cap. 67:219.

45. Sarmiento de Gamboa, *Historia índica,* pt. 2, cap. 60:261.

46. Diez de San Miguel, *Visita hecha a la provincia de Chucuito,* 106.

47. Murra, *Economic Organization,* 99, 102; Murra, "Andean Societies," 75.

48. Murra, "Guerre et les rébellions," 931–34; Murra, "Andean Societies," 75, 87.
49. Cieza de León, *Descubrimiento,* cap. 69:315; Caillavet, "Dominación incaica," 411–12.
50. AGI JU 671 fol. 251v. Visita de los Puruháes 1557, JU 683 fols. 838v, 856v, 869v Visita de la encomienda de Francisco Ruiz 1559.
51. RGI 2:279 Arias Dávila 1.5.1582.
52. Cieza de León, *Señorío,* cap. 72:223.
53. Zarate, "Historia del descubrimiento," lib. 1, cap. 12:478.
54. Herrera, *Historia general,* 10, dec. 5, lib. 3, cap. 17:261; Cieza de León, *Señorío,* cap. 72:223.
55. Zarate, "Historia del descubrimiento," lib. 1, cap. 12:473; Oviedo, *Historia general,* 5, lib. 46, cap. 9:62.
56. RGI 2:267–68 Pablos 1582.
57. Zarate, "Historia del descubrimiento," lib. 1, cap. 12:473; Cabello Balboa, *Miscelánea antártica,* pt. 3, cap. 28:435; Cieza de León, *Crónica,* cap. 44:65.
58. Cieza de León, *Señorío,* cap. 73:224; Herrera, *Historia general,* 10, dec. 5, lib. 3, cap. 17:262–63; Campos, *Compendio histórico,* 23.
59. Larrea, *Notas de prehistoria,* 178.
60. RGI 2:299 Salinas 1571 or 1572; Larrea, *Notas de prehistoria,* 178; Plaza Schuller, *Incursión Inca,* 42–88.
61. Meyers, *Die Inka in Ekuador,* 154, 162.
62. AGI PAT 1-1-14/19 Ramo 12 Probanza de Hernando de la Parra (1560) and *Documentos para la historia militar,* 2:63; Salomon, "Ethnic Lords," 212.
63. Oberem, "Quitoloma," 203.
64. Larrea, *Notas de prehistoria,* 178–79; Salomon, "Ethnic Lords," 210–13; Espinosa Soriano, *Cayambes y Carangues,* 1:296.
65. *Documentos para la historia militar,* 1:35 Puento (1586); Oberem, "Quitoloma," 201; Plaza Schuller, *Incursión Inca,* 42–84; Oberem, "Los Caranquis," 85–87; Gondard and López, *Inventario arqueológico,* 110. Gondard and López (pp. 111, 114) supplement Plaza Schuller's list of thirty-seven forts.
66. Larrea, *Cultura incasica,* 31; Salomon, "Ethnic Lords," 211.
67. Cabello Balboa, *Miscelánea antártica,* pt. 3, cap. 21:368–69; Sarmiento de Gamboa, *Historia índica,* pt. 2, cap. 60:262–63; Gondard and López, *Inventario arqueológico,* 116–17; Espinosa Soriano, *Cayambes y Carangues,* 1:296–304.
68. Salomon, "Ethnic Lords," 155–56; Hyslop, *Inka Road System,* 247.
69. Hyslop, *Inka Road System,* 35.
70. Salomon, "Ethnic Lords," 220–21; Hyslop, *Inka Road System,* 23; Cieza de León, *Crónica,* cap. 37:53.
71. Hyslop, *Inka Road System,* 35–36.
72. Cieza de León, *Crónica,* cap. 45:67.
73. Strube, *Vialidad imperial,* 24; Salomon, "Ethnic Lords," 220–25; Cieza de León, *Crónica,* cap. 56:81.
74. Hyslop, *Inka Road System,* 36.
75. RGI 2:267 Pablos 1582. Hyslop's recent survey of about 100 kilometers of Inka road in Ecuador found that roads varied in width between 2 and 7 meters, being narrower where they negotiated higher slopes and wider in the páramo.

76. Salomon, "Ethnic Lords," 27; Hyslop, *Inka Road System*, 36.

77. Strube, *Vialidad imperial*, 62–66; Hyslop, *Inka Road System*, 279–80.

78. Hyslop, *Inka Road System*, 298, 303.

79. RGI 2:296, 300 Salinas 1571 or 1572; Hyslop, *Inka Road System*, 301–2.

80. Murra, *Economic Organization*, 102–3.

81. Poma de Ayala, *Nueva corónica*, 3:1002–3; Hyslop, *Inka Road System*, 277.

82. Rowe, "Inca Culture," 232; Strube, *Vialidad imperial*, 83; Salomon, "Ethnic Lords," 217.

83. Hyslop, *Inka Road System*, 285–86 (for example, at Paredones, Cuenca [p. 31]); Cieza de León, *Crónica*, cap. 44:63–64.

84. Cieza de León, *Crónica*, cap. 37:54.

85. Garcilaso de la Vega, *Comentarios reales*, 1, lib. 8, cap. 5:298–99, cap. 7:301–3; Salomon, "Ethnic Lords," 207; Cieza de León, *Crónica*, cap. 37:54, cap. 41:59, cap. 44:64; Cieza de León, *Señorío*, cap. 64:216, cap. 67:219.

86. AGI AQ 8 Cabezas de Meneses 1.4.1590; Garcilaso de la Vega, *Comentarios reales*, 1, lib. 3, cap. 8:95.

87. Cieza de León, *Crónica*, cap. 40:57.

88. AGI AQ 8 Cabezas de Meneses 1.4.1590.

89. AGI AQ 8 Cabezas de Meneses 1.4.1590; Cieza de León, *Crónica*, cap. 44:64; Garcilaso de la Vega, *Comentarios reales*, 1, lib. 8, cap. 5:299.

90. Murra, *Economic Organization*, 105, 127.

91. Murra, *Economic Organization*, 48.

92. AGI AQ 8 Cabezas de Meneses 1.4.1590.

93. Rowe, "Inca Policies," 96–97.

94. Espinosa Soriano, "Mitmas Huayacuntu," 351; Murra, *Economic Organization*, 175–82; Cieza de León, *Señorío*, cap. 22:171.

95. Sarmiento de Gamboa, *Historia índica*, pt. 2, caps. 39–40:244–45.

96. Morris, "Organization and Administration of Tawantinsuyu," 482.

97. For example, at Pomasqui (Salomon, "Ethnic Lords," 233–37); Moreno Yánez, "Colonias mitmas," 108–14.

98. Cieza de León, *Crónica*, cap. 41:59.

99. Murra, *Economic Organization*, 180.

100. Poma de Ayala, *Nueva corónica*, 1:164, 171.

101. Espinosa Soriano, "Mitmas Huayacuntu," 360.

102. Cieza de León, *Señorío*, cap. 22:171–72.

103. Spalding, *Huarochirí*, 88.

104. Cobo, *Historia del nuevo mundo*, 2, lib. 12, cap. 25:114.

105. Murra, "Historic Tribes of Ecuador," 810.

106. RGI 2:302 Salinas 1571 or 1572; Cieza de León, *Señorío*, cap. 56:206; Jaramillo Alvarado, *Provinica de Loja*, 36; Caillavet, "Grupos étnicos," 136–37.

107. Cieza de León, *Señorío*, cap. 56:206.

108. Espinosa Soriano, "Mitmas Huayacuntu," 155; Murra, "Guerre et les rébellions," 933; Wachtel, "Nitimas of the Cochabamba Valley," 219; Murra, "Andean Societies," 88; Oberem and Hartman, "Indios Cañaris," 374–75, 386.

109. AGI AL 288 Lib. VI Toledo 1.3.1572.

110. Rowe, "Inca Culture," 270; Espinosa Soriano, "Señoríos étnicos," 25; Miño Grijalva, *Los Cañaris*, 72.

111. Espinosa Soriano, "Mitmas Canar," 153.

112. Murra, "Historic Tribes of Ecuador," 810; Pérez, *Quitus y Caras,* 242; Salomon, "Ethnic Lords," 228–37; Oberem and Hartmann, "Apuntes sobre Cañaris," 10.

113. Mitmaq from Cuzco were probably settled at Cojitambo and Chuquipata (RGI 2:275 Gallegos 20.9.1582; Murra, "Historic Tribes of Ecuador," 810), and there may have been another colony at Paccha to the east of Cuenca (Matovalle, *Cuenca de Tomebamba,* 82).

114. Jerez, "Conquista del Perú," 335; Murra, *Economic Organization,* 174.

115. Oviedo, *Historia general,* 5, lib. 46, cap. 20:115.

116. RGI 2:254–60 Cantos 12.9.1581. In 1581 the corregidor of Chimbo enumerated 11,410 Indians in eight settlements in the valley, of whom 2,018 were mitmaq comprising seven ayllus. Five of the mitmaq ayllus were composed of colonists from northern Peru, notably from Huamacucho, Cajamarca, and Guayacondo. The other two were composed of colonists from a variety of origins.

117. Those at Achambo were Wayacuntu from the Cajamarca region, of whom there were over 300 in 1603, while those at San Andrés reportedly came from Condesuyo (AGI EC 919A Muñoz Ronquillo 31.1.1603; ANHQ Presidencia de Quito 3 fols. 92–188 Cartas cuentas 1642–1644; RGI 2:262 Paz Maldonado, no date; Salomon, "Ethnic Lords," 231). The early seventeenth-century description of the corregimiento of Riobamba, which covers these two villages, makes no mention of mitmaq there, but it notes the presence in Quero of over 1,500 mitmaq and carpenters who had been transferred from Cuzco (CDI 9:452–88 Descripción . . . de la villa del Villar Don Pardo 1605).

118. Guevara, *Puerto de El Dorado,* 50; Albuja Galindo, *Cantón Cotocachi,* 76.

119. Cieza de León, *Crónica,* cap. 41:59.

120. Salomon, "Ethnic Lords," 231–32.

121. ANHQ Cacicazgos 3 5.9.1582–7.12.1613; Pérez, *Los Seudo-Pantsaleos,* 95.

122. CDI 9:452–88 Descripción . . . de la villa del Villar Don Pardo 1605.

123. Salomon, "Ethnic Lords," 226–27.

124. AGI JU 683 fols. 829v–831v, 867r–869r Visita de la encomienda de Francisco Ruiz 1559. While the origin of the mitmaq of Urin Chillo is unknown, some of those at Uyumbicho were Wayacuntu. The visita of 1559 lists 109 mitmaq under Francisco Condor from "Guayacondo," and Espinosa Soriano suggests that 1,000 families were transferred to "Yumbichu" from Pampamarca in the district of Huancabamba and employed as soldiers in the northern campaigns ("Mitmas Huayacuntu," 532–59, 387). However, a later account of the encomiendas of Uyumbicho and Amaguana indicates that a multiethnic group had been established there, but it makes no reference to the Wayacuntu noted in the visita (AGI AQ 82 Father Francisco de Sanctana 1.12.1582). At that time the villages included 418 tributary Indians, of whom it was said that 52 were Sicchos, 12 were from Guamacucho, 20 from Charcas (possibly Lupacas from Lake Titicaca), and 24 from Huánuco. The visita of Chucuito by Diez de San Miguel notes that Lupacas were taken to the province of Quito (*Visita hecha a la provincia de Chucuito,* 81); Espinosa Soriano, "Los Chambillas," 420.

125. Pérez, *Quitus y Caras,* 242; Salomon, "Ethnic Lords," 232–37; Caillavet, "Dominación incaica," 408; Espinosa Soriano, *Cayambes y Carangues,* 1:281–83.

126. Uhle, "Reino de Quito," 10; Salvador Lara, "Quito en la prehistoria," 248; Espinosa Soriano, "Mitmas Huaycuntu," 357; Miño Grijalva, *Los Cañaris,* 22.

127. Espinosa Soriano, "Coca y los mitmas Cayampis," 11, 13–14.

128. Ortiz Zúñiga, *Huánuco,* 1:295; Espinosa Soriano, *Cayambes y Carangues,* 1:286.

129. Espinosa Soriano, "Curaca de los Cayambes," 91; Espinosa Soriano, *Cayambes y Carangues,* 1:287.

130. Ponce, *Cantón de Montúfar,* 37.

131. Martínez, *Pastos,* 103.

132. Espinosa Soriano, *Cayambes y Carangues,* 1:292.

133. Santa Cruz Pachacuti Yamqui, "Antigüedades," 311.

134. Cieza de León, *Crónica,* cap. 37:53–54.

135. Caillavet, "Dominación incaica," 408–9.

136. There were 2,781 "indios tributarios incas" at that time (Espinosa Soriano, *Cayambes y Carangues,* 1:273–79). The document to which he refers is transcribed in Herrera, *Cantón de Otavalo,* 34–56.

137. Salomon, "Frontera aborigen," 67–69.

138. Salomon, "Ethnic Lords," 249–50, 273; Salomon, "Don Pedro de Zámbisa," 292–93; Salomon, "Frontera aborigen," 66–67.

139. Cieza de León, *Crónica,* cap. 43:63; Caillavet, "Grupos étnicos," 137–38. This division is confirmed in an encomienda of Cañares to Gonzalo Pizarro in 1540 (AGI PAT 90A-1-23 15.6.1540).

140. Martínez, *Cacique García Tulcanaza,* 41–42; Caillavet, "Dominación incaica," 415; Espinosa Soriano, *Cayambes y Carangues,* 1:320–21; Salomon, "Ethnic Lords," 273.

141. RGI 2:304 Salinas 1571.

142. Salomon, "Ethnic Lords," 266.

143. Salomon, "Ethnic Lords," 312; Wachtel, *Vision of the Vanquished,* 72–73.

144. Cobo, *Historia del nuevo mundo,* 2, lib. 12, cap. 28:120–22.

145. Murra, "Historic Tribes of Ecuador," 808–10; Kelly, "Land Use Regions," 328; Murra, *Economic Organization,* 15–19.

146. Murra, "Historic Tribes of Ecuador," 799.

147. Albornoz, *Monografía histórica del Girón,* 52; Garcilaso de la Vega, *Comentarios reales,* 1, lib. 8, cap. 5:298.

148. Garcilaso de la Vega, *Comentarios reales,* 1, lib. 8, cap. 7:302.

149. Salomon, "Ethnic Lords," 93, 236.

150. Myers, "Prehistoric Irrigation," 313; Caillavet, "Toponimia histórica," 18–19.

151. Murra, "Mit'a Obligations," 238.

152. For example, at Pomasqui mitmaq appear to have been settled on previously uninhabited lands (Navarro, "Pueblo de Pomasqui," 266; Salomon, "Ethnic Lords," 234–36).

153. ANHQ Cacicazgos 3 Testimony of the principal of Taypacana 2.12.1613.

154. Brush, *Mountain, Field, and Family,* 83.

155. AGI JU 683 fol. 856v Visita de la encomienda de Francisco Ruiz 1559.

156. Polo de Ondegardo, *Religión y gobierno,* 58–60; Wachtel, *Vision of the Vanquished,* 66–67.

157. Murra, "Mit'a Obligations," 248.

158. Murra, *Economic Organization,* 132, 188.

159. AGI JU 671 fols. 245v, 247r–v, 250r Visita de los Puruháes 1557; Salomon, "Ethnic Lords," 279.

160. Salomon, "Ethnic Lords," 280.

161. AGI JU 671 fols. 251v–252r Visita de los Puruháes 1557, JU 683 fols. 817v, 839r, 856v Visita de la encomienda de Francisco Ruiz 1559; RGI 2:275 Gallegos 20.9.1582; RGI 2:286 Gaviria 4.5.1582; RGI 2:288 Italiano 18.10.1582; Salomon, "Ethnic Lords," 117, 189–91, 277, 280–81.

162. RGI 2:275 Gallegos 20.9.1582.

163. AGI JU 683 fols. 817v, 838v, 856v, 869v Visita de la encomienda de Francisco Ruiz 1559.

164. Murra, "Historic Tribes of Ecuador," 811.

165. AGI JU 671 fols. 243v, 249v, 253r, 255r Visita de los Puruháes 1557.

166. Oberem, "Recursos naturales," 54.

167. RGI 2:213 Anon. 1573; Cieza de León, *Crónica,* cap. 40:57.

168. RGI 2:213 Anon. 1573 ; RGI 2:Paz Maldonado, no date; RGI 2: Italiano. 18.10.1582

169. AGI JU 671 fol. 244r Visita de los Puruháes 1557, JU 683 fols. 817v, 838v, 856v Visita de la encomienda de Francisco Ruiz 1559.

170. AGI JU 671 fols. 252r Visita de los Puruháes 1557.

171. See chap. 2.

172. Murra, "Control vertical," 59–115. See also chap. 2.

173. Evidence from the Pasto region is suggestive of the method used to acquire exotic products in pre-Inka times. See RGI 2:252 Antonio Borja, no date; Salomon, "Ethnic Lords," 304–5, and the discussion of the Pasto in chap. 2.

174. Salomon, "Ethnic Lords," 273–74, 314–15.

175. Salomon, "Ethnic Lords," 166–67.

176. AGI JU 671 fols. 243v–254v Visita de los Puruháes 1557.

177. See, for example, RGI 2:289 Italiano 18.10.1582; Salomon, "Ethnic Lords," 286–87.

178. AGI JU 671 fols. 243–54 Visita de los Puruháes 1557; Salomon, "Ethnic Lords," 282. In 1581 fifty Puruhá Indians were still present at Pangor in the jurisdiction of Pallatanga (RGI 2:256–58 Cantos 12.9.1581).

179. AGI JU 683 fol. 869r Visita de la encomienda de Francisco Ruiz 1559; Salomon, "Ethnic Lords," 167.

180. RGI 2:287 Gaviria 4.5.1582; RGI 2:289 Italiano 18.10.1582.

181. RGI 2:273 Pereira 1.10.1582; RGI 2:278 Gallegos 20.9.1582.

182. RGI 2:207 Anon. 1573; RGI 2:177 Valverde y Rodríguez 30.12.1576; Caillavet, "La sal," 51–55 .

183. AGI JU 671 fols. 243v–254v Visita de los Puruháes 1557; RGI 2:259 Cantos 12.9.1581.

184. AGI JU 671 fols. 243v–254v Visita de los Puruháes 1557.

185. See chap. 2.

186. RGI 2:270 Angeles 12.5.1582.

187. León, "Cocaismo en el Ecuador," 9–10; Plaza Schuller, *Incursión Inca,* 16–17; Gade, "Coca Cultivation and Endemic Disease," 264.

188. Salomon, "Ethnic Lords," 131.

189. Oberem, "Recursos naturales," 57.

190. AGI JU 671 fols. 243v–254v Visita de los Puruháes 1557.

191. AGI JU 671 fols. 251v Visita de los Puruháes 1557.

192. CDI 9:452–88 Descripción . . . de la villa del Villar Don Pardo 1605; ANHQ Cédulario 2 fol. 296r–v 17.1.1646. There were 400 in Pelileo, 150 in Patate, 100 in Píllaro, and 40 in Baños. In 1601 the cacique of Chambo possessed three coca chacras in Pelileo (ANHQ Indígenas 1 9.11.1601).

193. RGI 2:271 Angeles 12.5.1582; RGI 2:287 Gaviria 4.5.1582; RGI 2:289 Italiano 18.10.1582.

194. AGI AQ 18 Espinosa 10.4.1606.

195. RGI 2:280 Arias Dávila 1.5.1582; León, "Cocaismo en el Ecuador," 16.

196. AGI JU 683 fols. 803v, 817r–v, 838v, 856v Visita de la encomienda de Francisco Ruiz 1559.

197. Salomon, "Ethnic Lords," 157–59.

198. Salomon, "Ethnic Lords," 153–56, 169–70; Oberem, "Recursos naturales," 59–61. For a full discussion of mindaláes in the northern Andes, see chap. 2 and Salomon, "Pochteca and Mindalá," 234–39; Salomon, "Status Trader Complex," 62–74.

199. Salomon, "Status Trader Complex," 71–72.

200. Salomon, "Status Trader Complex," 72–73.

201. Salomon, "Ethnic Lords," 286–87, 314.

202. Murra, *Economic Organization,* 139.

203. Hartmann, "Mercado y ferias prehispánicos," 214–36. Evidence for the existence of markets in pre-Spanish times needs to be evaluated carefully, for markets may have been established in the early colonial period under Spanish stimulus (Salomon, "Ethnic Lords," 143–50).

204. Kelly, "Inca Land Use," 329, 336–38; Mejía, "Economia de la sociedad 'primitiva,'" 59; Morris, "Organization and Administration of Tawantinsuyu," 487.

205. Murra, *Economic Organization,* 13.

206. Murra, *Economic Organization,* 130–31; Baudin, *Socialist Empire.*

207. Murra, *Economic Organization,* 40–43; Spalding, *Huarochirí,* 88.

208. Murra, "Estructura política de los inka," 42–43; Murra, *Economic Organization,* 132.

209. Murra, "Poblaciones yana," 225–42; Salomon, "Ethnic Lords," 237; Murra, *Economic Organization,* 163–77; Rowe, "Inca Policies," 96–102.

210. Oberem, *Miembros de la familia del Inca,* 40; Salomon, "Ethnic Lords," 243–45.

211. RGI 2:277 Gallegos 20.9.1582.

212. AGI JU 671 fols. 244v, 246v, 249v, 252v, 254v Visita de los Puruháes 1557; CDI 9:452–88 Descripción . . . de la villa del Villar Don Pardo 1605.

213. AGI AQ 8 Oidores 22.1.1578, AQ 8 Real cédula 10.11.1578.

214. Murra, "Poblaciones yana," 235; Salomon, "Ethnic Lords," 185–88.

215. Salomon, "Ethnic Lords," 187–88.

216. RGI 2:204 Salinas 1571 or 1572; Rowe, "Inca Culture," 269.

217. Cieza de León, *Crónica,* cap. 37:54, cap. 41:59, cap. 44:64.

218. Compare Smith, "Depopulation," 458.

219. Cieza de León, *Crónica,* cap. 44:65. A similar imbalance in the sex ratio was also noticeable in the central Andes (Smith, "Depopulation," 457–58).

220. Rabell and Assadourian, "Self-Regulating Mechanisms," 31–32; Cook, *Demographic Collapse,* 25; Silverblatt, *Moon, Sun, and Witches,* 87–100.

221. For example, RGI 2:235 Paz Ponce de León 2.4.1582; RGI 2:270 Angeles 12.5.1582; RGI 2:286 Italiano 18.10.1582; RGI 2:322 Auncibay 1592.

222. For example, the revenge killing of Indians on the island of Puná by Huayna Capac, the massacre at Yaguarcocha at the end of the Caranqui wars, and the devastation wrought by Atahualpa of the Cañar region for its support of Huascar.

223. Cook, "Human Sacrifice," 81–102.

224. Rowe, "Inca Culture" 285; Katz, *Ancient American Civilizations,* 301.

225. Silverblatt, *Moon, Sun, and Witches,* 102.

226. RAHM CM 65 fols. 5–8v Horden que el Ynga tubo, no author, no date; Rowe, "Inca Culture," 285; Rabell and Assadourian, "Self-Regulating Mechanisms," 35, 37.

227. Rabell and Assadourian, "Self-Regulating Mechanisms," 38; Silverblatt, *Moon, Sun, and Witches,* 29–31, 51.

228. Garcilaso de la Vega, *Comentarios reales,* 1, lib. 5, cap. 15:169; Cobo, *Historia del nuevo mundo,* lib. 12, cap. 28:121; Poma de Ayala, *Nueva corónica,* 1:163–64 (fols. 188–89).

229. Garcilaso de la Vega, *Comentarios reales,* 1 lib. 5, cap. 1:150.

230. Silverblatt, *Moon, Sun, and Witches,* 77.

231. Garcilaso de la Vega, *Comentarios reales,* 1, lib. 4, cap. 12:132.

232. Cobo, *Historia del nuevo mundo,* lib. 13, cap. 38:234.

233. Poma de Ayala, *Nueva corónica,* 1:207.

234. RGI 2:225–26 Anon. 1573; RGI 2:246 Aguilar 12.11.1582; RGI 2:288 Italiano 18.10. 1582; Cieza de León, *Crónica,* cap. 41:62, cap. 44:65, cap. 56:81.

235. Araníbar, "Necropompa," 117.

236. RAHM CM 65 fols. 5–8v Horden que el Ynga tubo, no author, no date; Atienza, "Compendio historial," 118; Salomon, "Ethnic Lords," 189; Cieza de León, *Crónica,* cap. 41:60, cap. 44:65.

237. Kelly, "Inca Land Use," 337.

238. AGI JU 671 fols. 243v., 250r, 255r Visita de los Puruháes 1557.

239. Conrad and Demarest, *Religion and Empire,* 183–85.

CHAPTER 6

1. Lizárraga, *Descripción breve,* lib. 1, cap. 54:40.

2. Parts of this chapter have appeared in Newson, "Old World Epidemics."

3. McNeill, *Plagues and Peoples,* 54; Way, "Diseases of Latin America," 261.

4. Oberem, "Recursos naturales," 54. See chap. 5.

5. Way, "Diseases of Latin America," 253–91; Alchon, *Native Society and Disease,* 19–25; Verano, "Prehistoric Disease," 17.

6. Newson, "Old World Epidemics," 85–88.

7. RGI 2:206 La cibdad de Saint Francisco del Quito 1573; RGI 2:266 Pablos

20.9.1582; RGI 2:273 Pereira 1.10.1582; RGI 2:292 Salinas, no date; RGI 2:286 Italiano 4.5.1582; RGI 3:126 No author, no date; CDI 9:452–503 Descripción . . . de la villa del Villar Don Pardo 1605.

8. See Newson, "Old World Epidemics," 88–91. For contemporary comments, see Cabello Balboa, *Miscelánea antártica*, 393; Cobo, *Historia del nuevo mundo*, 1, lib. 12, cap. 17:93; Sarmiento de Gamboa, *Historia índica*, pt. 2, cap. 62:265; Garcilaso de la Vega, *Comentarios reales*, 2, cap. 15:354; Santa Cruz Pachacuti Yamqui, "Antigüedades," 311; Cieza de León, *Señorío*, cap. 67:219; Poma de Ayala, *Nueva corónica* 1:93, 260.

9. Hermida Piedra, "Medicina en el Azuay," 13; Madero, *Historia de la medicina*, 25; Arcos, *Medicina en el Ecuador*, 94; Browne, "Epidemic Disease," app. 3, p. 162. Madero, citing Herrera, says that Huayna Capac contracted malaria while he was in the island of Puná punishing the Indians there for their betrayal, but Herrera's account refers to "una grande enfermedad general de viruelas" (Herrera, *Historia general*, 10, dec. 5, lib. 3, cap. 17:258).

10. Polo, *Epidemias en el Perú*, 5–6; Lastres, *Medicina Peruana*, 1:150; Dobyns, "Andean Epidemic History," 497; Crosby, *Columbian Exchange*, 52–53.

11. Newson, "Depopulation of Nicaragua," 278.

12. Murphy, "Earliest Advances Southward," 20–25.

13. Christie, "Smallpox," 259–60.

14. Sarmiento de Gamboa, *Historia índica*, pt. 2, cap. 62:265.

15. Cieza de León, *Crónica*, cap. 53:77–78.

16. See Newson, "Old World Epidemics," 91, and Chamberlain, *Conquest and Colonization of Honduras*, 28; Dobyns, "Andean Epidemic History," 498; Newson, "Depopulation of Nicaragua," 279–80.

17. Estete, *Noticia*, 17, 19; Cieza de León, *Descubrimiento*, cap. 30:259, cap. 32:262, cap. 47:280.

18. Lizárraga, *Descripción breve*, lib. 1, cap. 54:40.

19. CDIE 26:238 Fray Pedro Ruiz Navarro, no date; Madero, *Historia de la medicina*, 31. The Spanish reads "achaques de viruelas y bubas de que murieron algunos, y otros quedaron hoyosos los rostros y sumamente feos efecto que causan las viruelas."

20. Zarate, "Historia del descubrimiento," lib. 1, cap. 4:465; Estete, *Noticia*, 17; López de Gómara, "Hispania Victrix," 226; Cieza de León, *Crónica*, cap. 46:68; Cieza de León, *Descubrimiento*, cap. 31:260. The Spanish reads "unas berrugas bermejas de granor de nueces, y les nacen en la frente y las narices y en otros partes."

21. Benzoni, *Historia del mundo nuevo*, 256.

22. Cieza de León, *Señorío*, cap. 67:219.

23. RGI 2:267 Pablos 20.9.1582; Morúa, *Historia general*, 1:104.

24. Sarmiento de Gamboa, *Historia índica*, pt. 2, cap. 62:264.

25. Newson, "Old World Epidemics," 94.

26. Herrera, *Historia general*, 16, dec. 8, lib. 2, cap. 16:162; Cieza de León, *Crónica*, cap. 24:26.

27. Dobyns, "Andean Epidemic History," 499.

28. Zinsser, *Rats, Lice, and History*, 183, 256–58; McNeill, *Plagues and Peoples*, 194; MacLeod, *Spanish Central America*, 119; Cook, *Demographic Collapse*, 68, 71.

29. Polo, *Epidemias en el Perú,* 9. See Newson, "Old World Epidemics," 95 for a fuller account of diseases that afflicted domesticated animals about this time.

30. Manson-Bahr, *Tropical Diseases,* 255, 281.

31. Bubonic plague is normally contracted through the bite of a flea that has obtained the disease from an infected rat. The presence of the disease thus depends on a reservoir of infected rats, and its spread tends to be slow and sporadic. Pneumonic plague, however, can be spread from person to person through the inhalation of droplets expelled into the air by the coughing or sneezing of an infected person, and its spread, therefore, tends to be more rapid. The origin of pneumonic plague is uncertain, but it has been suggested that it develops when a person suffering from a respiratory infection, a high possibility in the Andean area, contracts bubonic plague. Plague flourishes between 10°C and 30°C, with pneumonic plague found at the lower end of the temperature range and bubonic plague at the higher end of the range, although not over 30°C or in dry conditions (Pollitzer, *Plague,* 418, 483, 510–13, 535–38).

32. Cook, *Demographic Collapse,* 68, 70–71.

33. RGI 2:292 Salinas 1571 or 1572; Montesinos, *Anales del Perú,* 1:254; Cobo, *Historia del nuevo mundo,* 2, lib. 3, cap. 27:447; Zinsser, *Rats, Lice, and History,* 256.

34. AGI ASF 188 fols. 226r–229r Peñagos 15.9.1559.

35. RGI 2:205 La cibdad de Sant Francisco del Quito 1573; RGI 2:292 Salinas 1571 or 1572; Herrera, *Apunte cronológico,* 50.

36. Browne, "Epidemic Disease," 54.

37. Dobyns, "Andean Epidemic History," 500–501.

38. AMQ LC 16:364–65 Cabildo of Cuenca 10.6.1562.

39. RGI 3:199 Salinas 10.6.1571.

40. Newson, "Old World Diseases," 97.

41. RGI 2:266 Pablos 20.9.1582; Albornoz, *Cuenca,* 111; Hermida Piedra, "Medicina en el Azuay," 76.

42. Dobyns, "Andean Epidemic History," 501–2.

43. Polo, *Epidemias en el Perú,* 11–12; Madero, *Historia de la medicina,* 66.

44. AGI AL 32 Conde de Villar 19.4.1589; RGI 3:70 Docampo 24.3.1650; Simón, *Noticias historiales,* 3:271; Polo, *Epidemias en el Perú,* 15–20; Herrera, *Apunte cronológico,* 57; Castellanos, *Elegías,* 3:733 and 735; Dobyns, "Andean Epidemic History," 504–5; Colmenares, *Historia económica,* 84.

45. Polo, *Epidemias en el Perú,* 16–18, 55–56.

46. Dobyns, "Andean Epidemic History," 504–5.

47. AGI AL 32 Conde de Villar 19.4.1589; RGI 3:70 Docampo 24.3.1650.

48. AMQ LC 26:394–95 Cabildo of Quito 28.7.1614.

49. Velasco, *Historia del Reino,* 3:137.

50. RGI 3:70 Docampo 24.3.1650.

51. AGI PAT 240-4 No author, 1590, PAT 240-6 Lic. Ortegón, no date. The Spanish reads "consumido y acabado."

52. RGI 2:308–9 Bishop of Nicaragua 1592.

53. AGI AQ 8 Barros 28.2.1591, AQ 23 Informe 10.3.1591.

54. Anda Aguirre, *Don Juan de Salinas,* 181–88. Unfortunately Anda Aguirre does not cite his source.

55. Campos, *Compendio histórico,* 46.

56. AGI PAT 118-8 Probanza . . . Ramírez de Guzmán 1574.

57. CDI 9:247–309 Descripción de la gobernación 1605.

58. AGI AL 32 Conde de Villar 19.4.1589. It is described as "romadizo con calentura."

59. AGI AL 33 lib. 1 fols. 25–29 Velasco 16.9.1597.

60. AMQ LC 20:98 Cabildo of Quito 5.2.1604, referred to in Browne, "Epidemic Disease," 69.

61. AGI AQ 19 Aguirre de Ugarte 24.4.1607.

62. AMQ LC 26:107 Cabildo of Quito 10.11.1611; Herrera, *Apunte cronológico,* 73–74; Arcos, *Medicina en el Ecuador,* 108.

63. AMQ LC 26:394 Cabildo of Quito 28.7.1614; Herrera, *Apunte cronológico,* 76–77; Arcos, *Medicina en el Ecuador,* 76–77. Unfortunately Arcos does not provide the source of his information, though the presence of diphtheria seems likely, given that there was an outbreak in the Cuzco region in the same year (Dobyns, "Andean Epidemic History," 508–9).

64. AGI AQ 10 Morga 20.4.1618.

65. Dobyns, "Andean Epidemic History," 509.

66. Alchon, *Native Society and Disease,* 58–60.

67. Brown, "Yellow Fever," 290; Kiple, *Caribbean Slave,* 162–66.

68. Paredes Borja, *Medicina en el Ecuador,* 1:383.

69. Pineo, "Misery and Death," 614.

70. Paredes Borja, *Medicina en el Ecuador,* 1:305.

71. Newson, "Old World Epidemics," 102–3. Descriptions of the most harmful insects responsible suggest that they were sandflies (*Phlebotomus* sp.) rather than *Anopheles* mosquitoes. Sandflies may induce fevers and headaches and can also transmit the leishmaniasis parasite, and possibly the virus associated with Oroya fever and verruga peruana, which are known to have been present on the coast in pre-Columbian times (Manson-Bahr, *Tropical Diseases,* 208, 997).

72. Pineo, "Misery and Death," 611.

73. Ayala Mora, "Epidemiología de la malaria," 31.

74. Zurita et al., "Comportamiento ecológico de la malaria."

75. Newson, "Highland-Lowland Contrasts," 1190–91.

76. Maroni, "Noticias auténticas," 26:233, 422; 29:231; Figueroa, *Relación de las misiones,* 225–27, 397.

77. Kaplan et al., "Infectious Disease Patterns," 304–6.

78. Astrain, *Historia de la Compañía,* 6, lib. 3, cap. 9:609–10; Jouanen, *Compañía de Jesús,* 1:438. The Spanish description is "unas recias cuartanas."

79. Ayala Mora, "Epidemiología de la malaria," 58–59, 65.

80. For example, Crosby, *Columbian Exchange,* 35–63.

81. Dobyns, "Estimating Aboriginal Population," 410–11; Jacobs, "Tip of the Iceberg," 130–32; McNeill, *Plagues and Peoples,* 189–90; Cook, *Demographic Collapse,* 63–66.

82. Cook, *Demographic Collapse,* 70.

83. Shea, "Defense of Small Population Estimates," 161.

CHAPTER 7

1. AGI AQ 12 Suárez de Poago 2.5.1634.

2. AMQ LC 10:579–82 Relación de un testigo, no date; Cieza de León, *Descubrimiento,* cap. 87:339.

3. AMQ LC 1:106 Benalcázar 28.6.1535.

4. Navas, *Ibarra,* 1:83.

5. For example, AMQ LC 2:97–100 Cabildo of Quito 20.2.1540, LC 2:217–221 Cabildo of Quito 21.2.1541; Larrain Barros and Pardo, "Corregimiento de Otavalo," 65.

6. AMQ LC 3:309–10 Cabildo of Quito 10.10.1547.

7. AMQ LC 4:347–48 Cabildo of Quito 22.7.1550.

8. Jaramillo, *Corregidores de Otavalo,* 66.

9. AMQ LC 2:21–25 Cabildo of Quito 26.2.1539.

10. AGI AQ 22 Probanza de Gerónimo Puento 1.9.1586.

11. AGI AQ 10 Audiencia 15.4.1620.

12. See the discussion of the Quito Basin in chap. 8.

13. AGI AQ 9 Father Gaspar de Torres 20.11.1597; Monroy, *Convento de la Merced,* 322, 383–84; Martínez, *Pastos,* 141, 148, 150; Martínez, *Cacique García Tulcanaza,* 5.

14. RAHM CM A/92 fols. 55–77 Relación de los vecinos encomenderos, 1561. At that time the villages that later fell under the jurisdiction of the corregimiento of Otavalo were held by nine encomenderos.

15. AMQ LC 10:345–60 Benalcázar 3.11.1549.

16. RAHM 9/4662 nos. 1–2 fols. 27v-29v Tasación of Otavalo, no date.

17. AGI AQ 20B Tellez 3.1.1552.

18. AGI EC 922A Tasa de Otavalo 30.11.1562.

19. AGI AQ 20B Tellez 3.1.1552.

20. The 1552 visita was conducted by two vecinos of Quito, Pedro Moreno and Pedro Muñoz, and it revealed that the repartimiento Otavalo comprised 2,311 *indios casados tributarios.* A *revisita* in 1559 ordered by the viceroy, the Marqués de Cañete, and conducted by Gil Ramírez Dávalos found a similar number of 2,163 *casados* and 411 *solteros* (AGI EC 922A Tasa de Otavalo 30.11.1562).

21. AGI EC 922A Tasa de Otavalo 30.11.1562.

22. AGI AQ 8 Santillán 15.1.1564.

23. AGI PAT 28-13 Salazar de Villasante, no date.

24. AGI PAT 28-13 Salazar de Villasante, no date.

25. AGI PAT 114-4 Probanza de Diego Méndez 9.2.1566.

26. AGI EC 922A Caciques, principales y indios de Otavalo 13.9.1579.

27. ANHQ Cedulario 1 fol. 365 real cédula 17.11.1602, also in AMQ RC 21:33–34.

28. AGI EC 922A Tasas of Otavalo 4.9.1579, Caciques, principales y indios de Otavalo 13.9.1579. It recorded the presence of 3,135 tributary Indians.

29. AGI EC 922A Ortegón and Auncibay 4.9.1579.

30. Assadourian, "Despoblación indígena," 262–63.

31. The ayllu of Yaçelga was broken up, and its members dispersed among four communities, while that of Camuendo was distributed among three. For a

full discussion of the *reducciones,* see Espinosa Soriano, *Cayambes y Carangues,* 2:102–10.

32. Caillavet, "Chefferies préhispaniques," 47.

33. RGI 2:248 Borja, no date.

34. AGI AQ 9 Moreno de Mera 6.3.1591.

35. AGI AQ 19 Testimonio del acrecimiento 7.11.1612, AQ 9 Zorilla 20.4.1613, AQ 10 Zorilla 15.4.1618.

36. AGI AQ 19 Testimonio del acrecimiento 7.11.1612, Relación sumaria 22.3.1618. It seems that Zorilla had originally tried to impose a tax of six pesos three tomines, but a lawsuit resulted in its being reduced (AGI AQ 61 Mañosca 10.4.1625).

37. AGI AQ 10 Audiencia 15.4.1620.

38. RGI 2:189 Relación de las cibdades, no date.

39. AGI AQ 61 Mañosca 10.4.1625; Tyrer, "Demographic and Economic History," 117.

40. AGI AQ 61 Mañosca 10.4.1625.

41. ANHQ RH 5 Libro de acuerdos de hacienda 1601–57 fols. 14–16v 1602.

42. AGI AG 13 Ibarra 4.4.1604. They came from Otavalo and the neighboring villages of San Pablo, Tontaquí, and Cotacachi.

43. AGI AG 13 Ibarra 4.4.1604.

44. AGI AQ 9 Audiencia 1.4.1599.

45. AGI AQ 9 Oficiales reales 23.3.1609.

46. AGI AQ 10 Audiencia of Quito 15.4.1620; AQ 61 Mañosca 10.4.1625.

47. AGI AQ 31 Balbazil y Rivera 11.9.1626; Ortiz de la Tabla Ducasse, "Obraje colonial," 508; Rueda Novoa, *San Joseph de Peguchi,* 78–80.

48. Tyrer, "Demographic and Economic History," 117.

49. ANHQ Indígenas 5 (1640–50) Cacique of Otavalo 1.2.1648; Landázuri Soto, *Régimen laboral,* 143–44.

50. IOA EP/J 1a (43) C.2 Juicios seguidos por Cristóbal Cuchuango 27.10.1615.

51. AHBC 20a Colección nos. 838 and 839 29.7.1610, 24.10.1614.

52. AHBC 20a Colección no. 839 24.10.1614; IOA EP/J 1a (43) C.2 Juicios seguidos por Cristóbal Cuchuango 27.10.1615.

53. AGI AQ 30 Morga 10.3.1620, AQ 10 Audiencia 15.4.1620.

54. See the discussion of the organization of the mita in the Quito Basin in chap. 8.

55. RGI 2:238 Paz Ponce de León 2.4.1582; AGI AQ 10 Don Francisco Paspuel, cacique of Tuza, no date, AQ 211 Real cédula 2.2.1622; ANHQ Indígenas 5 (1640–50) Cacique of Otavalo 1.2.1648; Ponce, *Montúfar,* 66.

56. ANHQ Cedulario 1 fol. 348 and AMQ CR 9:447–48 Real cédula 13.5.1589.

57. AGI AQ 26 Probanza de Don Pedro Zámbiza 1603 (24.4.1583).

58. AGI AQ 22 Caciques of Tuza, Guaca and Tulcán 19.6.1576, AQ 25 Real cédula 6.4.1588 in letter from the viceroy 4.8.1591, AQ 10 Ibarra 27.11.1600.

59. AGI AQ 32 9.11.1611, 11.2.1633; AMQ LC 15:295–300 Repartición de los indios mitayos 9.11.1611.

60. AMQ LC 15:438–40 Cabildo of Ibarra 16.5.1614; AGI AQ 32 11.2.1633; Martínez, *Pastos,* 128–30.

61. RGI 2:212 La cibdad de Sant Francisco de Quito 1573; RGI 2:235, 238 Paz

Ponce de León 2.4.1582; RGI 2:250 Borja, no date; Calancha, "Crónica moralizada, 189–201; Vázquez de Espinoza, *Compendio,* 256; Caillavet, "Técnicas agrarias autóctonas," 121.

62. Ordóñez de Cevallos, *Viaje del Mundo,* lib. 2, cap. 38:418.

63. AGI AQ 9 Ibarra 25.10.1606, 8.5.1607.

64. AMQ Cedulario 1541–1673 vol. 13 fols. 87–91 21.8.1604, 1.9.1604. They were required to provide 100 for construction and 120 for *servicio personal,* for which they were able to muster only 87 and 100 respectively, of whom 12 and 20 respectively fled before their tour of duty commenced.

65. AGI AQ 22 Caciques of Tuza, Guaca and Tulcán 19.6.1576.

66. AGI AQ 22 Caciques of Tuza, Guaca and Tulcán 19.6.1576.

67. AGI AQ 9 Ibarra 27.11.1600, AQ 31 Balbazil y Rivera, corregidor of Otavalo 11.9.1626.

68. AGI AQ 9 Ibarra 27.11.1600.

69. AGI AQ 9 Zorilla 20.4.1613.

70. AGI 61 Mañozca 10.4.1625.

71. Powers, "Indian Migrations," 313–23; Powers, "Migration and Socio-Political Change," 215–27.

72. AGI AQ 30 Ponce de Castellejo 15.3.1623.

73. Knapp, *Ecología cultural,* 181; Caillavet, "Técnicas agrarias autóctonas," 120–21.

74. RGI 2:253 Borja, no date.

75. RGI 2:235 Paz Ponce de León 2.4.1582.

76. See the discussion of expeditions in chap. 8, where it is suggested that about one-third of the 43,000 to 53,000 that may have taken part in expeditions may have come from the northern sierra.

77. RGI 2:235 Paz Ponce de León 2.4.1582.

78. AGI PAT 28-13 Salazar de Villasante, no date.

79. AGI AQ 20B Tellez 1.2.1552; RGI 2:235, 237 Paz Ponce de León 2.4.1582. See the discussion of the mita for its effects on fugitivism.

80. AGI EC 922A Visita of Otavalo 11.11.1562.

81. AGI EC 922A Tasa de Otavalo 30.11.1562; Mansilla, *Tributo indígena,* 44–47.

82. The tributary population declined from 2,994 to 2,360, a fall of 21.1 percent (AGI EC 922A Visita de Otavalo 11.11.1562; RGI 2:240–41 Paz Ponce de León 2.4.1582). See also Mansilla, *Tributo indígena,* 53.

83. RGI 2:238 Paz Ponce de León 2.4.1582; RGI 2:244 Rodríguez 9.11.1582; RGI 2:248 Borja, no date.

84. AGI AQ 22 Caciques of Tuza, Guaca and Tulcán 19.6.1576.

85. The actual figure based on the estimate of 39,622 is 44,971.

86. AGI AQ 9 Ibarra 27.11.1600, AQ 19 Testimonio del acrecimiento 7.11.1612. This figure is included by Morales Figueroa (CDI 6:41–63 Relación de los indios tributarios 1.11.1591).

87. AGI AQ 9 Ferrer de Ayala and Armenteros y Henao 23.3.1609, AQ 19 Relación sumaria 22.3.1618.

88. AGI AQ 9 Ibarra 27.11.1600. Whether they included fugitives who were living in other regions, notably the city of Quito, or only those within the corregimiento is not clear. Toward the end of the century (between August 1594 and

December 1600) 77 infants born to parents from Otavalo and 31 from the Pasto region were baptized in the Cathedral, El Sagrario (ASQ Libro de bautismos de mestizos, montañeses, indios 1594–1605). These figures underestimate the number of infants born to immigrants from the corregimiento of Otavalo, since others were certainly baptized in local parishes churches in the city.

89. AGI AQ 19 Testimonio del acrecimento 7.11.1612. See also AGI AQ 9 Zorilla 20.4.1613.

90. AGI AQ 61 Mañosca 10.4.1625. He also attempted to raise revenue by increasing per capita tribute payments by over two pesos.

91. Tyrer, "Demographic and Economic History," 378.

92. CDI 6:41–63 Relación de los indios tributarios 1.11.1591.

Table N3. Tributary Population in Selected Villages in the Southern Otavalo Region

Village	1590	1655
Cayambe	442	1,055
Malchinguí	57	47
Tocache	32	29

Source: ANHQ RH 63 fols. 50–83, 104, 216–51; ANHQ Tributos 2 Cartas cuentas 1655–56.

93. Alchon, *Native Society and Disease,* 59.

94. CDI 6:41–63 Relación de los indios tributarios 1.11.1591.

95. See table 9. ANHQ Residencias 1 Residencia of Pedro de Torres 1646; ANHQ Indígenas 10 Cartas cuentas 1666–69; Tyrer, "Demographic and Economic History," 381.

96. AGI AQ 10 Governor of Tuza, Angel and Puntal, no date; AQ 212 Real cédula 2.2.1622.

97. AGI AQ 212 Real cédula 2.2.1622.

98. Larrain Barros, *Demografía,* 2:162–63.

99. See chap. 2. There it was suggested that the Pasto numbered 36,350 and the chiefdoms between the Chota-Mira and Guayllabamba valleys 150,000, of whom 120,000 were living in areas over 2,000 meters and 30,000 at lower elevations.

100. See chap. 5; Larrain Barros, *Demografía,* 1:128–29; Knapp, *Ecología cultural,* 179, 181.

CHAPTER 8

1. AGI AQ 27 Sancho Díaz de Zurbano 13.1.1609

2. Herrera, *Historia general,* 10, dec. 5, lib. 4, cap. 11:330; Oberem, "Los Cañaris," 135–37.

3. Hererra, *Historia General,* 10, dec. 5, lib. 4, cap. 11:332; Oviedo, *Historia General,* 5, lib. 46, cap. 19:111. Hernando de la Parra, a vecino of Quito who was involved in the battle, estimated that Rumiñahui had 30,000 Indians (AGI PAT 103B-12 Información de los servicios de Hernando de la Parra 1560). Other accounts suggest numbers as low as 12,000. For accounts of Sebastián de Be-

nalcázar's defeat of Rumiñahui, see Zarate, "Historia del descubrimiento, 480–81; López de Gómara, "Hispania Victrix," 234; Herrera, *Historia general,* 10, dec. 5, lib. 4, caps. 11–12:327–36, lib. 5, cap. 1:339–44, 11, dec. 5, lib. 6, cap. 5:31–35; Oviedo, *Historia general,* 5, lib. 46, cap. 19:111–13; Rumazo, "Las fundaciones," 180–83; Hemming, *Conquest of the Incas,* 151–68; Borchart de Moreno, "Conquista española," 179–88.

4. Oviedo, *Historia general,* 5, lib. 46, cap. 19:113.

5. Salomon, "Ethnic Lords," 259–61.

6. Salomon, "Ethnic Lords," 213–14; Salomon, "Don Pedro de Zámbisa," 286–89.

7. Herrera, *Historia general,* 11, dec. 5, lib. 6, cap. 5:32–35.

8. Ceballos, *Resumen de la historia,* 1:305–9; Jijón y Caamaño, *Ecuador interandino,* 2:70–71; Velasco, *Historia del reino,* 2:316–19.

9. Alcina Franch, Moreno, and Peña, "Penetración española," 115–17; see also Jijón y Caamaño, *Ecuador interandino,* 2:71–72.

10. González Suárez, *Historia general,* 2:486–87 n. 4.

11. Alcina Franch, Moreno, and Peña, "Penetración española," 116–20.

12. Larrain Barros, *Demografía,* 2:55–56. He suggests an average figure of 1,000 Indians per expedition, but from the table he presents, it is not clear how he estimates between 16,000 and 20,000. These figures do not include those involved in missionary expeditions toward the end of the century.

13. AMQ LC 10:579–82 Relación de las conquistas de Sebastián de Benalcázar, no date; Moreno Ruiz, "Primeros asentamientos," 424–26; Padilla Altamarino, López Arellano, and González, Rodríguez, *Encomienda en Popayán,* 3–7; Larrain Barros, *Demografía,* 2:51.

14. Velasco, *Historia del reino,* 2:324–27; see also Ceballos, *Resumen de la historia,* 1:304, 308, 365, 367.

15. AMQ LC 1:443–48 Cabildo of Quito 30.8.1538.

16. AMQ LC 1:443–48 Cabildo of Quito 30.8.1538, LC 2:29–31, 31–34 Cabildo of Quito 16.5.1539, 17.5.1539; Jijón y Caamaño, *Sebastián de Benalcázar,* 1:155–59; Rumazo González, *Región amazónica,* 31–32; Vargas, *Siglo XVI,* 50. In particular the expeditions to the Yumbos and Popayán proposed by the new teniente, Gonzalo Díaz de Pineda, were strongly opposed by supporters of the deposed governor, Sebastián de Benalcázar, who objected to the new appointment.

17. Larrain Barros, *Demografía,* 2:47, 53.

18. AMQ LC 2:21–25 Cabildo of Quito 26.2.1539.

19. See chap. 14.

20. AGI AQ 85 Díaz Docampo 1605.

21. See chap. 14; RGI 1:139 Salazar de Villasante, no date.

22. See chap. 14; AGI AQ 22 Probanza de Gerónimo Puento 1.9.1586.

23. Larrain Barros, *Demografía,* 2:56.

24. Larrain Barros, *Demografía,* 2:57.

25. Uribe suggests that *yanaconas* found in the Pasto villages of Túquerres, Cumbal, Ipiales, and Pupiales and along the road from Quito to Popayán probably originated as porters on early expeditions ("Documentos del siglo XVIII," 44). Romoli de Avery suggests that the expeditionaries may have been responsible for the expansion of Quechua beyond the region of Inka control ("Las tribus," 15).

26. For example, Cacique García Tulcanaza (Pasto) helped Captain Hernán González de Saa in the conquest of Esmeraldas by supplying 100 Indians from Tulcán (Martínez, *Pastos,* 141; Martínez, "Pastos y Quillaçingas," 661–62).

27. AMQ LC 1:277–78 9.7.1537, LC 1:282–83 29.7.1537.

28. AMQ LC 2:97–101 20.2.1540.

29. RGI 1:132 Salazar de Villasante, no date; RGI 2:221 Anon. 1573; López de Velasco, *Geografía,* 219; Salomon, "Ethnic Lords," 207, 209–10.

30. Salomon, "Ethnic Lords," 238, 241, 251–53.

31. See AMQ LC 1:85–86 Cabildo of Quito 31.5.1535, LC 1:106–8 Términos de San Francisco de Quito 28.6.1535, LC 1:264–65 Cabildo of Quito 18.6.1537.

32. Vargas, *Siglo XVI,* 105–8.

33. A list of forty encomiendas in the jurisdiction of Quito in 1561 lists nineteen that had been distributed by Pizarro or Vaca de Castro and thirteen allocated by La Gasca (RAHM A/92 Relación de los vecinos encomenderos que ay, no date, reproduced in Hampe, "Relación de los encomenderos," 75–117). Of those in the corregimiento of Quito only, which numbered eighteen, seven were distributed by Pizarro or Vaca de Castro and seven by La Gasca, the average values of which were 1,260 pesos for the former and 1,050 pesos for the latter.

34. Mansilla, *Tributo indígena,* 28–31.

35. AGI JU 683 fols. 798r–874v Visita de la encomienda de Francisco Ruiz 1559.

36. AGI JU 683 fols. 798r–874v Visita de la encomienda de Francisco Ruiz 1559. For the instructions used in the visita, see AGI JU 671 fols. 235v–238r Visita de los Puruháes 1557.

37. AGI AQ 8 Santillán 15.1.1564.

38. AGI JU 639 Hordenanzas hechas 9.11.1569; see also AGI AQ 22 Commission for the visita of Quito 19.7.1567, 7.12.1567; Padilla Altamarino, López Arellano, and González Rodríguez, *Encomienda en Popayán,* 31–33. The latter book discusses Popayán, but the order applied to the whole audiencia.

39. AGI AQ 21 Zúñiga 15.12.1574. See AQ 8 Toledo 17.11.1570 for instructions on the conduct of the visita.

40. AGI CO 1786 Tasa de la visita general ca. 1582. See also Cook, *Tasa de la visita general*; Cook, *Demographic Collapse,* 77–78.

41. BNM 3178 fols. 1–15 Canelas Albarrán 1586. Canelas Albarrán records that the visita of the province of Quito undertaken by Licenciado Francisco de Cárdenas enumerated 78,141 ánimas but estimates that 30,000 were not enumerated.

42. RGI 2:335–36 Provincia de los Yumbos, no date.

43. AGI AQ 10 Morga 15.4.1624. Licenciado Pedro de Zorilla began a visita in 1591, but by 1600 it was still incomplete (AGI AQ 9 Ibarra 27.11.1600). In 1609 royal attempts to enforce a visita general were opposed by the viceroy, the Marqués de Montesclaros, on the grounds that it would provoke unrest (Mansilla, *Tributo indígena,* 76).

44. For example, AGI EC 912A Los capítulos que su señoría presentó 7.8.1570, AQ 76 Bishop of Quito 12.3.1598; ANHQ Cedulario 1 fol. 514 Real cédula 6.6.1609.

45. AGI PAT 28-13 Salazar de Villasante, no date.

46. AGI AQ 9 Ibarra 27.11.1600.

47. ANHQ Tierras 2 Caciques of the encomienda of the Duque de Uzeda 1626.

48. AGI JU 672 Relación de los vecinos encomenderos, no date; RGI 2:182 Relación de las cibdades, no date; RGI 2:227–28 La cibdad de Sant Francisco de Quito 1573; AGI AQ 17 Cabildo of Quito 23.1.1577, AQ 23 Probanza of Galarraga 2.7.1590.

49. AGI AQ 9 Torres Altamarino 9.4.1604, AQ 31 Sevilla 13.3.1626.

50. AGI AQ 25 Audiencia 25.9.1591, AQ 8 Barros, Mera, and Cabezas de Meneses 2.5.1592.

51. ANHQ Cedulario 1 fol. 489 Real cédula 29.11.1563; AGI AQ 76 Herrera 1570, EC 912A Los capítulos que su señorío presentó 7.8.1570, AQ 18 Los naturales de la provincia de Quito, no date [ca. 1571].

52. RGI 2:227–28 La cibdad de Sant Francisco del Quito 1573.

53. AGI AQ 18 Los naturales de la provincia de Quito, no date [ca. 1571]; AGI PAT 28-13 Salazar de Villasante, no date; RGI 2:170 Oficiales reales 30.12.1576.

54. AGI AQ 17 Cabildo of Quito 30.5.1615, AQ 212 and AMQ Cedulario 1567–1680 vol. 11 fol. 41 Real cédula 2.9.1617, AQ 30 Quiros 22.4.1622.

55. AGI AQ 18 Los naturales de la provincia, no date [ca. 1571], AQ 8 Marañón 1.5.1594.

56. ANHQ Cedulario 1 fol. 492 28.12.1563; AGI AQ 18 Los naturales de la provinica, no date [ca. 1571].

57. ANHQ Cedulario 1 fol. 489 Real cédula 29.11.1563; AGI AQ 18 Los naturales de la provincia, no date [ca. 1571].

58. AGI AQ 24 Freire 31.5.1593.

59. AGI AQ 76 Bishop of Quito 12.3.1598.

60. ANHQ Cedulario 1 fol. 492 28.12.1563; AGI AQ 18 Los naturales de la provincia, no date [ca. 1571].

61. AGI AQ 80 Archdean of Quito 1577.

62. AGI AQ 24 Freire 31.3.1593, AQ 10 Morga 20.4.1616.

63. Borchart de Moreno, "Período colonial," 223. For the same arguments, see Borah, *Century of Depression,* 32–33; Frank, *Mexican Agriculture,* 21.

64. Tyrer, "Demographic and Economic History," 96–97.

65. AGI AQ 8 Santillán 15.1.1564; RGI 2:183 Relación de las cibdades, no date; Vázquez de Espinosa, *Compendio,* 254–55; Cieza de Leon, *Crónica,* cap. 40:56–57.

66. RGI 2:212 La cibdad de Sant Francisco del Quito 1573.

67. For example, AGI AQ 17 Cabildo of Quito 23.1.1577; RGI 2:201–2 Aguayo, no date; RGI 2:210–14 La cibdad de Sant Francisco del Quito 1573; RGI 3:61–64 Rodríguez Docampo 24.3.1650; Salomon, "Ethnic Lords," 82–83.

68. AGI JU 683 fols. 817r, 838r, 856r, 869r Visita de la encomienda de Franisco Ruiz 1559; RGI 2:170 Oficiales reales 1576; RGI 2:212 La cibdad de Sant Francisco del Quito 1573; Salomon, "Ethnic Lords," 82–83.

69. RGI 2:212 La cibdad de Sant Francisco del Quito 1573; RGI 1:132 Salazar de Villasante, no date.

70. RGI 2:213 La cibdad de Sant Francisco del Quito 1573.

71. AGI PAT 28-13 Salazar de Villasante, no date; RGI 2:213–14 La cibdad de Sant Francisco del Quito 1573.

72. RGI 2:319 Relación del distrito del cerro de Zaruma, no date. The prices

given in different accounts vary, the reasons for which are unknown. Nevertheless, food prices were generally considered to be low, with wheat being about double the price of maize (for example, RGI 1:132 Salazar de Villasante, no date; RGI 2:212–13, 220 La cibdad de Sant Francisco del Quito 1573; RGI 2:170 Oficiales reales 30.12.1576).

73. AGI AQ 17 Cabildo of Quito 23.1.1577.

74. RGI 2:212 La cibdad de Sant Francisco del Quito 1573.

75. RGI 1:124, 132 Salazar de Villasante, no date; RGI 2:213 La cibdad de Sant Francisco del Quito 1573.

76. RGI 2:218 La cibdad de Sant Francisco del Quito 1573; Vázquez de Espinosa, *Compendio,* 261, 264.

77. RGI 2:220 La cibdad de Sant Francisco del Quito 1573; Minchom, "Urban Popular Society," 169–72.

78. RGI 2:212 La cibdad de Sant Francisco del Quito 1573; Vázquez de Espinosa, *Compendio,* 261.

79. Minchom, "Urban Popular Society," 166–67, 171–73.

80. Rowe, "Inca under Spanish Colonial Institutions," 180.

81. AMQ LC 1:108–15 Cabildo of Quito 22.7.1535, LC 1:116–18 Cabildo of Quito 23.7.1535; Schottelius, "Fundación de Quito," 202–3.

82. Borchart de Moreno, "Período colonial," 228 gives this and other examples.

83. Borchart de Moreno has calculated that of the thirty-one beneficiaries between 1544 and 1551 only three were not members of the cabildo ("Período colonial," 228). See also AGI PAT 28-13 Salazar de Villasante, no date.

84. AMQ Cedulario 1 fol. 320 Real cédula 2.6.1573; Borchart de Moreno, "Período colonial," 229–30.

85. AMQ LC 2:135 Cabildo of Quito 24.6.1540; Schottelius, "Fundación de Quito," 203.

86. AGI AQ 21 Zúñiga 15.12.1574.

87. AGI AQ 8 Venegas de Cañaveral 20.8.1584, 26.3.1585.

88. AGI AQ 211 Real cédula 12.8.1587, AQ 8 Dr. Barros 12.5.1589; González Suárez, *Historia general,* 2:457; AMQ CR 9:546–48 and ANHQ Cedulario 1 fol. 358 Real cédula 23.12.1596 give an account of some of the lands distributed. Sixteen cuadras were equivalent to one *caballería;* one cuadra was equivalent to the size of the *plaza mayor* (AMQ LC 6:26–27 Cabildo of Quito 17.4.1573).

89. AGI PAT 28-13 Salazar de Villasante, no date; Borchart de Moreno, "Período colonial," 232.

90. *Recopilacion,* 2, lib. 4, tit. 12:41, ley 7 6.4.1588 and ley 9 11.9.1594.

91. Cushner, *Farm and Factory,* 26.

92. AGI AQ 211, AMQ CR 9:400, and ANHQ Cedulario 1 fol. 339 Real cédula 22.8.1584.

93. AGI AQ 25 Los indios de Pintag, no date [after 1573], ASF 8–8 fols. 1–8 Autos de la población del pueblo de Tanicuchi 21.10.1597.

94. Ots Capdequí, *Estado español,* 36.

95. Borchart de Moreno, "Período colonial," 234–35.

96. For example, AMQ CR 9:435–36 and ANHQ Cedulario 1 fol. 343 6.4.1588; ANHQ Indígenas 1 Testament of Juan Zimbana 11.5.1592, 6.10.1609. The transfer of lands to the Jesuits is exemplified well in Cushner, *Farm and Factory,* 41–56.

97. AGI PAT 28-13 Salazar de Villasante, no date. One fanegada de tierra was approximately 2.9 hectares (Cushner, *Farm and Factory,* 193).

98. Borchart de Moreno, "Período colonial," 236–39; Cushner, *Farm and Factory,* 60–65; Vargas, *Economía política,* 137–43.

99. AGI PAT 28-13 Salazar de Villasante, no date, AQ 21 Zúñiga 15.12.1574, AQ 8 Oidores 22.1.1578.

100. ANHQ Cedulario 1 fol. 320 2.6.1573.

101. AGI AQ 27 Sancho Díaz de Zurbano, 13.1.1609.

102. AGI AQ 21 Zúñiga 15.12.1574, AQ 8 Barros 12.5.1589, AQ 27 Sanchez Díaz de Zurbano 13.2.1609; AMQ RC 21:137 and ANHQ Cedulario 1 fol. 374 Real cédula 15.3.1609; AGI AQ 9 Testimonio del padrón de los indios mitaios 16.3.1611, AQ 10 Zorilla, no date [ca. 1619].

103. AGI AG 13 Ibarra 4.4.1604.

104. Landázuri Soto, *Régimen laboral,* 110–58.

105. Between them, the five mills in the Quito region could employ 245 indios and *muchachos de merced,* and in addition 28 mitayos.

106. Phelan, *Kingdom of Quito,* 69.

107. Tyrer, "Demographic and Economic History," 173, 317. In 1680 President Munive claimed that there were 30,000 Indians in the city employed in the manufacture of textiles, most of them in small operations (Landázuri Soto, *Régimen laboral,* 110–58). This figure may have been exaggerated, for he goes on to suggest that they could be employed in forty mills that could be established in rural areas to stem depopulation. Given that rural mills generally employed only several hundred Indians, forty mills would have accounted only for approximately 10,000 workers. Apparently he had private motives for exaggerating the number of workers.

108. AGI AQ 19 Oficiales reales 6.2.1578.

109. See the discussion of the mita.

110. Minchom, "Urban Popular Society," 105.

111. Tyrer, "Demographic and Economic History," 173.

112. AMQ LC 1:45–48 Foundation of Quito 6.12.1534.

113. RGI 2:170 Oficiales reales 30.12.1576; AGI AQ 8 Barros 12.5.1589, AQ 9 Crown to the Audiencia 19.10.1591. Other immigrants to the city were black slaves, though they were small in number, given their cost and the availability of Indian labor (AGI AQ 17 Cabildo of Quito 23.1.1577; Minchom, "Urban Popular Society," 93, 117–18).

114. RGI 1:132 Salazar de Villasante, no date; RGI 2:221 La cibdad de Sant Francisco del Quito 1573; RGI 2:169 Oficiales reales 30.12.1576; López de Velasco, *Geografía,* 218.

115. AGI AQ 17 Cabildo of Quito 23.1.1577.

116. AGI AQ 76 Bishop of Quito 12.3.1598; RGI 2:203 Rodríguez Aguayo, no date.

117.. Vázquez de Espinosa, *Compendio,* 254.

118. AGI AQ 9 Barros 12.5.1589.

119. For the differential impact of labor systems on Indian populations, see Newson, "Indian Populations Patterns," 52–57; Newson, "Sistemas de trabajo."

120. AGI JU 683 fols. 798r–874v Visita de la encomienda de Francisco Ruiz 1559.

121. Legally, Indians were not to be held against their will, and they were to be paid for their labor (AMQ CR 9:136–37 and ANHQ Cedulario 1 fol. 328 Real cédula 23.11.1536).

122. ASF 7-1 no. 6 fols. 13–18 Jorge de la Cruz, no date [ca. 1570]; AGI AQ 19 Oficiales reales 30.12.1576, AQ 8 Oidores 22.1.1578; Borchart de Moreno, "Período colonial," 252–54.

123. AGI AQ 8 Santillán 15.1.1564, PAT 28-13 Salazar de Villasante, no date, AQ 18 Los naturales de la provincia, no date [ca 1571].

124. AGI AQ 25 Commission to Joan Pardo, no date.

125. AGI AQ 76 Bishop of Quito 1.12.1571.

126. Compte, *Varones ilustres,* 1:53, Zúñiga 15.7.1579.

127. RGI 2:226 La cibdad de Sant Francisco del Quito 1573.

128. ASQ Libro de bautismos de indios 1566–69, Libro de bautismos de mestizos, montañeses, indios 1594–1605.

129. Moreno Egas, "Apuntes para el estudio de la población," 75–77.

130. These figures exclude ten individuals whose provenance is unknown. Others were from Los Quijos (6 percent). The figure excludes thirty-seven from Guano, many of them adults, who came or were brought to the city to be baptized as a group.

131. AMQ LC 1:380–81 Cabildo of Quito 22.3.1538.

132. BNM 3035 fols. 82–87 Instruction to Santillán 1563; AGI JU 681 no. 11 Crown to Santillán 27.9.1563.

133. AGI PAT 28-13 Salazar de Villasante, no date; RGI 1:134–35 Salazar de Villasante, no date; RGI 1:44. The latter document gives the number established in the two villages as 500 and 400 respectively, but the former figure may have been an error of transcription. Minchom suggests that these settlements may have constituted the parishes of San Blas and San Sebastián ("Urban Popular Society," 96 n.18), which were apparently established by the Dominican bishop Pedro de la Peña in 1565 or 1566 (Vargas Ugarte, *Iglesia en el Perú,* 1:153; Albuja Mateus, "Obispado de Quito," 165).

134. AGI AQ 8 Francisco de Toledo 7.12.1571.

135. RGI 2:225 La cibdad de Sant Francisco del Quito 1573.

136. AGI AQ 8 Oidores 22.1.1578; ANHQ Cedulario 1 fols. 519–22 and AMQ CR 9:334–36 Real cédula 10.11.1578; ANHQ Cedulario 1 fol. 467 and AMQ CR 9:368 Real cédula 1.5.1581.

137. RGI 2:319 Relación del distrito del cerro de Zaruma, no date.

138. AGI AL 20B vol. 2 fol. 332 Toledo 24.9.1572.

139. AGI AQ 19 Oficiales reales 30.12.1576, AQ 9 Bedón 10.3.1598.

140. AGI AQ 8 Instrucción a . . . Licenciado Francisco de Cárdenas 17.11.1571, AQ 8 Toledo 7.12.1571.

141. Powers, "Indian Migrations," 316, 322.

142. AGI AQ 8 Santillán 15.1.1564.

143. Memorias de los virreyes, 1:89, Borja 1621.

144. AMQ CR 9:404–5, ANHQ Cedulario 1 fol. 340 and AGI AQ 211 Real cédula 10.1.1586; AGI AQ 8 Barros 12.5.1589, AQ 9 Crown to the Audiencia 19.10.1591.

145. AMQ LC 4:223–32, Ordenanzas de minas 7.6.1549.

146. AGI JU 683 fols. 798r–874v Visita de la encomienda de Francisco Ruiz 1559. The tasaciones were drawn up in 1551, and similar stipulations were included in those drawn up for Otavalo, Chambo, and Cañares (RAHM 9/4664 nos. 1–2 fols. 27v–29v, no date).

147. AGI AQ 18 Los naturales de la provincia, no date [ca. 1571], AQ 17 Cabildo of Quito 20.5.1572.

148. RGI 2:183 Relación de las cibdades, no date.

149. RGI 2:186 Relación de las cibdades, no date. AGI AQ 211 Real cédula 10.1.1586.

150. AGI AQ 211 Real cédula 10.1.1586.

151. AGI AQ 9 Torres Altamarino 15.4.1600; AMQ RC 21:67 and ANHQ Cedulario 1 fol. 366 Real cédula 25.4.1605; AMQ RC 21:138 and ANHQ Cedulario 1 fol. 375 Real cédula 15.3.1609.

152. AMQ CR 9:78–94 and ANHQ Cedulario 1 fols. 323–24 Real cédula 2.12.1563; AGI AQ 25 Viceroy 4.8.1591, Audiencia 25.9.1591.

153. AGI AQ 86 Villanueva February 1612.

154. AGI AQ 18 Los naturales de la provincia, no date [ca. 1571], AQ 21 Zúñiga 15.12.1574, AQ 22 Caciques of Tuza, Guaca, and Tulcán 19.6.1576. See the discussion of the Otavalo region in chap. 7.

155. AGI AQ 18 Los naturales de la provincia, no date [ca 1571].

156. AGI AQ 83 Convent of Dominicans 1592.

157. AMQ CR 9:71–76 Real cédula 2.12.1563.

158. AGI AQ 8 Santillán 15.1.1564.

159. AGI AQ 24 Freire 31.3.1593. For similar observations, see AGI AQ 20B Tellez 3.1.1552.

160. AMQ LC 20:100–103 Cabildo of Quito 18.2.1604; AMQ Cédulas y provisiones vol. 14 fols. 20–51 Procurador 1604.

161. ANHQ Cedulario 1 fols. 325–26 and AMQ CR 9:71–76 2.12.1563; AGI AQ 21 Zúñiga 15.12.1574; ANHQ Cedulario 1 Real cédula fol. 342 6.4.1588.

162. Compte, *Varones ilustres,* 1:55, Zúñiga 15.7.1579.

163. AGI AQ 82 Memorial de las cosas, no date; Compte, *Varones ilustres,* 1:54, Zúñiga 15.7.1579.

164. ANHQ Autos acordados 1 libro 1578 fol. 7 7.6.1630, includes the royal cédulas for 24.11.1601 and 26.5.1609 (also contained in *Recopilación,* 2, lib. 6, tit. 12, leyes 1 and 9, pp. 285, 290); AMQ Cédulas y provisiones 14 fol. 20–51 1604, Cedulario 11 f.41 2.9.1617.

165. AGI AQ 8 Santillán 15.1.1564, AQ 8 Venegas de Cañaveral 20.8.1584, AQ 8 Barros 12.5.1589.

166. AGI AQ 8 Barros 12.5.1589. Slightly different figures are given in another account, although their source is not known:1,000 for the collection of wood and fodder for the city of Quito and 500 for other towns; 2,000 for tending livestock (including those employed in Riobamba), 1,200 for public works, and an unspecified number for the harvest (AGI AQ 25 Viceroy 4.8.1591). Another account gives similar numbers but specified 600 for the harvest (RGI 2:319 Relación del distrito del cerro de Zaruma, no date). Although the figures are slightly different, the overall pattern of employment is similar.

167. RGI 2:183 Relación de las cibdades, no date.

168. AGI AQ 82 Memorial de las cosas, no date, AQ 8 Venegas de Cañaveral 20.8.1584, AQ 9 Bedón 10.3.1598; Compte, *Varones ilustres,* 1:54, Zúñiga 15.7.1579.

169. RGI 2:220 La cibdad de Sant Francisco del Quito 1573; AGI AQ 18 Los naturales de la provincia, no date [ca. 1571].

170. AMQ Cedulario 13 fols. 91v–118v Real cédula 1573.

171. See the discussion of the tambo system in the Riobamba region in chap. 9.

172. ANHQ Cedulario 1 fols. 323–24, AMQ CR 9:78–84, and *Recopilación,* 2, lib. 6, tit. 12, ley 3:241, 2.12.1563.

173. AGI AQ 8 Santillán 15.1.1564.

174. ANHQ Cedulario 1 fol. 342 and AMQ CR 9:434–35 Real cédula 6.4.1588. For the wages paid to mitayos, see: RGI 2:183 Relación de las cibdades, no date; RGI 2:226 La cibdad de Sant Francisco del Quito 1573; AGI AQ 8 Barros, Auncibay, and Mera 6.4.1588, AQ 9 King to Audiencia 19.10.1591.

175. AGI AQ 25 Audiencia 25.9.1591, AQ 8 Barros, Mera, and Cabezas de Meneses 2.5.1592.

176. AGI AQ 18 Los naturales de la provincia, no date [ca. 1571]; ANHQ Cedulario 1 fol. 342 and AMQ CR 9:434–35 Real cédula 6.4.1588.

177. AMQ CR 9:468–69 Real cédula 22.9.1590; AGI AQ 8 Barros 12.5.1589; Pérez, *Las mitas,* 98.

178. AGI AQ 22 Caciques of Tuza, Guaca, and Tulcán 19.6.1576.

179. RGI 1:132 Salazar de Villasante, no date; RGI 2:212–13, 220 La cibdad de Sant Francisco del Quito 1573; AGI AQ 76 Bishop of Quito 28.1.1580.

180. AGI AQ 22 Caciques of Tuza, Guaca, and Tulcán 19.6.1576, AQ 86 Villanueva February 1612.

181. AGI AQ 18 Los naturales de la provincia, no date [ca. 1571], AQ 8 Barros 12.5.1589, AQ 76 Bishop of Quito 10.4.1603; ANHQ PQ 1 fols. 28r–28v 1.11.1608.

182. For example, AGI AQ 8 Venegas de Cañaveral 20.8.1584.

183. For example, AGI AQ 8 Santillán 15.1.1564; RGI 2:319 Relación del distrito del cerro de Zaruma, no date.

184. AGI AQ 21 Zúñiga 15.12.1574, AQ 8 Barros 12.5.1589, AQ 27 Sanchez Díaz de Zurbano 13.2.1609; AMQ RC 21:137 and ANHQ Cedulario 1 fol. 374 Real cédula 15.3.1609; AGI AQ 9 Testimonio del padrón de los indios mitaios 16.3.1611, AQ 10 Zorilla, no date [ca. 1619].

185. AGI AQ 9 Testimonio del padrón de los indios mitaios 16.3.1611, AQ 32 Vázquez de Acuña 4.4.1636.

186. RGI 2:183 Relación de las cibdades, no date; Cushner, *Farm and Factory,* 123–29.

187. AGI AQ 8 Barros 12.5.1589.

188. AGI AQ 8 Barros 12.5.1589. The Indians are described as "de asiento," and they included some *encomienda* Indians and others whose origin was not known. Another account the following year gives the number of gañanes as 1,400, but in this case their employment status is not clear. They may have been mitayos, for the same figure appears in a letter written in 1591, when they are described as providing *servicio de gañanes* (AGI AQ 55 Cabrera 1621, includes a letter from Lima dated 12.11.1590, AQ 25 Viceroy 4.8.1591).

189. AGI AQ 10 Caciques of Sangolquí 1623.

190. AGI PAT 28-13 Salazar de Villasante, no date, AQ 9 Recalde and Armenteros y Henao 22.3.1611; RGI 2:183 Relación de las cibdades, no date; RGI 2:220 La cibdad de Sant Francisco del Quito 1573; Minchom, "Urban Popular Society," 92–93. A padrón of the parish of San Sebastián in 1582 indicates the presence of large numbers of artisans (77). They included carpenters, masons, blacksmiths, tailors, hatters, a buttonmaker, a shoemaker, a tanner, saddlers, muleteers, silversmiths, potters, a musician, a singer, and a painter (ASFQ 8-1 fols. 55–65 Padrón de los parroquianos . . . San Sebastián, no date [ca. 1582]). Some of these artisans—notably the silversmiths, potters, and carpenters—may predate Spanish rule and may have been installed in the city by the Inka.

191. AGI PAT 240-6 García de Tamayo, no date; RGI 2:319 Relación del distrito del cerro de Zaruma, no date.

192. AGI AQ 86 Villanueva February 1612.

193. RGI 2:183 Relación de las cibdades, no date.

194. ASFQ 8-1 fols. 55–65 Padrón de los indios parroquianos . . . San Sebastián 1582. See n. 233.

195. ASQ Libro de bautismos de indios 1566–69, Libro de bautismos de mestizos, montañeses, indios 1594–1605.

196. AGI AQ 76 Bishop of Quito 10.4.1603. See also Powers, "Migration and Socio-Political Change," 102.

197. AGI PAT 28-13 Salazar de Villasante, no date, AQ 24 Freire 31.3.1593.

198. AGI PAT 28-13 Salazar de Villasante, no date.

199. AGI AQ 17 Cabildo of Quito 3.1.1577. There were 400 mestizas in the city, so it is not unreasonable to suppose that there were equal numbers of mestizos.

200. ASQ Libro de bautismos de españoles 1595–1649, Libro de bautismos de mestizos, montañeses, indios 1594–1605.

201. The remainder comprised other racial groups.

202. AGI AQ 9 Torres Altamarino 15.4.1600.

203. AGI AQ 28 Díaz de Zurbano 22.3.1609, cited in Minchom, "Urban Popular Society," 120; AGI AQ 27 Díaz de Zurbano 13.2.1609.

204. AMQ LC 4:386–88 Cabildo of Quito 26.1.1551.

205. AGI AQ 17 Cabildo of Quito 23.1.1577.

206. AGI AQ 9 Torres Altamarino 15.4.1601.

207. AGI AQ 18 Los naturales de la provincia, no date [ca. 1571]; AMQ Cedulario 1 fol. 320 Real cédula 2.6.1573.

208. AGI PAT 192-1-168 García de Valverde 4.2.1572.

209. Recent studies of the impact of seasonal migration on fertility levels have shown that it may reduce the probability of conception by 11.2 percent in the case of workers who are absent for three months each year, rising to 43.3 percent for those absent for eight months (Menken, "Seasonal Migration," 114–15).

210. The varied origins of Indians enumerated in early visitas of Indian communities in the Quito Basin is testimony to the instability of the early years (AGI JU 683 fols. 794r–874v Visita de la encomienda de Francisco Ruiz 1559; ASFQ 8-1 fols. 55–65 Padrón de los indios parroquianos . . . San Sebastián, no date [ca. 1582]; Salomon, "Ethnic Lords," 238–41). Their diverse origins are demonstrated in the padrón of the parish of San Sebastián dating probably from 1582. Some Indians whose role derived from pre-Spanish times were mindaláes and

carpenters; others were distinguished as yanaconas, some of whom had been in the service of the Inka; while others were probably Indians with no community affiliations who had migrated to the city and should have been more accurately called vagamundos. Other Indians were mitmaq. In addition to those whose presence in the city predated Spanish rule, there were large numbers whose presence was related to Spanish demands for labor. There were four mills belonging to Spaniards that employed 38 resident adults, and twenty-five estancias and *huertas* that employed another 149 residents. In addition there were nine ayllus, many of which possessed Indians whose names suggest that they were not of local origin; the ayllu of Pedro Caxas is particularly noteworthy in possessing a large number of artisans, including many silversmiths.

211. AGI AQ 9 Ibarra 27.11.1600.

212. The audiencia embraced these areas as well as the corregimientos of Cuenca, Loja, Guayaquil, and Puerto Viejo and the gobernaciones of Los Quijos, Yaguarzongo, and Pacamoros.

213. See app. 1.

214. BM Add. 33,983 fol. 236r La visita y tasa de Presidente Gasca, no date. The same figures appear in AGI JU 672 Relación de los vecinos encomenderos, no date.

215. See app. 1. For those in the Quito Basin, see AGI JU 683 fols. 798r–874v Visita de la encomienda de Francisco Ruiz 1559.

216. RAHM A/92 fols. 55–77 Relación de los naturales que hay 1561.

217. See the discussion of the Panzaleo in chap. 2.

218. See app. 1.

219. BNM 3178 fols. 1–15 Canelas Albarrán 1586. The summary gives 118,141 naturales, but this figure included 10,000 Spaniards.

220. AGI PAT 192-1-68 García de Valverde 4.2.1572.

221. CDI 6:41–63 Relación de los indios tributarios 1.11.1591.

222. This summary figure is incorrectly calculated by Morales Figueroa. The figures for individual villages sum to 23,710 (see app. 1).

223. This figure differs from the 3,777 calculated by Tyrer ("Demographic and Economic History," 349–50). Tyrer incorrectly assigns Calicali a figure of 770 rather than 270 and does not include Panzaleo within Quito's five leagues.

224. AGI PAT 240-6 and RGI 2:315–16 Relación del distrito del cerro de Zaruma, no date.

225. AGI AQ 10 Morga 15.4.1624.

226. AGI AQ 9 Ibarra 27.11.1600.

227. AGI AQ 27 Díaz de Zurbano 13.2.1609, AQ 9 Recalde and Armenteros y Henao 22.3.1611.

228. RGI 3:62–64 Rodríguez Docampo 24.3.1650.

229. RGI 2:225 La cibdad de Sant Francisco del Quito 1573.

230. RGI 2:319 Relación del distrito del cerro de Zaruma, no date.

231. AGI AQ 8, AMQ CR 9:334–36, and ANHQ Cedulario 1 fols. 519–20 Real cédula 10.11.1578.

232. AGI PAT 240-5 Vecinos and moradores of Zaruma, seen in Madrid 22.5.1592, AQ 30 Quiros 22.4.1622.

233. This is suggested by the population for the parish of San Sebastián. A

padrón of different Indians groups—tributary Indians, yanaconas (these included pre-Spanish yanaconas and vagamundos), and those working on estates and in mills—suggests the population was failing to reproduce itself, with a ratio of couples to children of only 1:1.02. However, it was slightly higher among those who were tradesmen (1:1.09) than those who were residing on estates (1:0.81). See ASFQ 8-1 fols. 55–65 Padrón de los indios parroquianos . . . San Sebastián, no date [ca. 1582].

234. For example, AGI AQ 8 Santillán 15.1.1564; RGI 2:224 La cibdad de Sant Francisco del Quito 1573; RGI 2:183 Relación de las ciudades, no date; AGI AQ 76 Bishop of Quito 20.3.1598, AQ 10 Morga 20.4.1616, 15.4.1623.

235. RGI 2:202 Rodríguez Aguayo, no date.

236. RGI 2:169 Oficiales reales 30.12.1576.

237. Tyrer, "Demographic and Economic History," 6–22; Ortiz de la Tabla Ducasse, "Población ecuatoriana," 269.

238. Powers, "Migración vertical," 107; Powers, "Migration and Socio-Political Change," 72–78.

239. AGI AQ 20B and AMQ LC 10:586–90 Instructions given to Lica. Briceño on the residencia of Sebastián de Benalcázar, no date [ca. 1549].

240. See chap. 6 and the discussion of the Panzaleo population in chap. 2.

241. For the calculation of these figures, see the discussion of estimates of the Panzaleo at the time of Spanish conquest.

242. Cook, *Demographic Collapse,* 70.

243. Browne, "Epidemic Disease," 48, 139.

244. Cook, *Demographic Collapse,* 70.

CHAPTER 9

1. AGI AQ 87 Memorial de los agravios que Martín Vergara . . . hace 25.4.1619.

2. AMQ LC 1:25–29 Act of foundation of Santiago 15.8.1534, LC 1:33–35 Padrón of Santiago 17.8.1534, LC 1:45–48 Act of foundation of San Francisco de Quito 6.12.1534; Cieza de León, *Crónica,* cap. 42:61; Rumazo, "Las fundaciones," 191.

3. Rumazo, "Las fundaciones," 191.

4. AMQ LC 8:101–23 Act of foundation of Riobamba 9.7.1575.

5. RGI 2:180 Oficiales reales 30.12.1576; CDI 9:489–53 Descripción . . . de la villa del Villar Don Pardo 1605. In 1605 Riobamba contained 314 inhabitants and Ambato 97 Spaniards.

6. Levillier, *Gobernantes del Perú,* 9:114–230.

7. AGI AQ 9 Memorial de avisos . . . Torres Altamarino 9.4.1604.

8. Herrera, *Historia general,* 10, dec. 5, lib. 4: cap. 11:332; Oviedo, *Historia general,* 5, lib. 46, cap. 19:111; Rumazo, "Las fundaciones," 182–83.

9. AGI AQ 20B Probanza of Don Sancho Hacho 1569, also in *Documentos para la historia militar,* 2:122–46; Rumazo, *Región amazónica,* 98–99; Oberem, *Quijos,* 75, 78. Other caciques who cooperated with the Spanish in supplying auxiliaries for expeditions were the cacique of Punín, who supported Díaz de

Pineda, and the cacique of Gualsaquí, who aided Gonzalo Pizarro (Deler, *Ecuador,* 55).

10. AMQ LC 6:55–92 Organización de los tambos 7.10.1573; AMQ Cedulario 13 fols. 91v–118v 1573; Poma de Ayala, *Nueva corónica,* 3:1002–3.

11. Cieza de León, *Crónica,* cap. 41:58–59, cap. 42:61, cap. 43:62.

12. Vaca de Castro, "Ordenanzas de tambos," 427–92 (31.5.1543). These ordinances were echoed in orders issued by the cabildo of Quito in 1544 (AMQ LC 3:79–80 28.7.1544, LC 3:86–88 26.8.1544, LC 3:123–26 29.12.1544).

13. AMQ LC 3:223–24 13.7.1546.

14. RGI 2:256, 259 Cantos 7.10.1581.

15. AMQ LC 4:214–22 20.5.1549.

16. AMQ LC 6:15–17 11.3.1573.

17. AGI AQ 17 Cabildo of Quito 1573; AMQ LC 6:15–17 11.3.1573, LC 6:55–92 Organización de los tambos 1573; AMQ Cedulario 13 fols. 91v, 118v 1573.

18. Early tasaciones such as those for Chambo and Luisa (probably San Andrés) include a large range of products made from cabuya (RAHM 9/4664 nos. 1–2 fols. 27r–29v Repartimientos de la ciudad de San Francisco de Quito, no date; AGI JU 672 Doña Pascuala de la Calle 1564).

19. AGI PAT 28-13 Salazar de Villasante, no date.

20. RGI 1:130 Salazar de Villasante, no date; RGI 2:261–62 Paz Maldonado, no date; CDI 9:452–88 Descripción . . . de la villa del Villar Don Pardo 1605.

21. AGI AQ 18 Los naturales de la provincia, no date [ca. 1571].

22. For example, RGI 2:258–59 Cantos 7.10.1581.

23. See chap. 2.

24. CDI 15:409–572 Descripción y demarcación, no date.

25. RGI 2:212 Anon, 1573; Vásquez de Espinosa, *Compendio,* lib. 3, caps. 8–9:257–58. In 1597 the cabildo reported that there were 150,000 head of sheep and other livestock in the *pastos* and páramos around Riobamba (ANHQ Gobierno 1 fol. 98 Cabildo of Riobamba 1.5.1597).

26. AGI AG 13 Ibarra 4.4.1604.

27. Ortiz de la Tabla Ducasse, "Obraje colonial," 496–97. In 1601 the cacique of Chambo died intestate, leaving, among other things, 540 sheep (ANHQ Indígenas 1 Vergara 9.11.1601).

28. AMQ RC 21:199–200 and ANHQ Cedulario 2 fols. 77–78 8.3.1631.

29. Silva Santísteban, *Los Obrajes,* 7–8.

30. Tyrer, "Demographic and Economic History," 111.

31. Tyrer, "Demographic and Economic History," 95–96, 102.

32. Silva Santísteban, *Los Obrajes,* 11; Phelan, *Kingdom of Quito,* 68, 70; Tyrer, "Demographic and Economic History," 278–80; Ortiz de la Tabla Ducasse, "Obraje colonial," 506–7.

33. Silva Santísteban, *Los Obrajes,* 18.

34. AGI AQ 20B Probanza of Don Sancho Hacho 1569; RGI 1:129 Salazar de Villasante, no date; Silva Santísteban, *Los Obrajes,* 50–52; Vargas, "Cacicazgos," 261–63.

35. Landázuri Soto, *Régimen laboral,* 108–58; Tyrer, "Demographic and Economic History," 163.

36. Pérez, *Las mitas,* 178.

37. AGI AQ 20B Probanza of Don Sancho Hacho 1569; Vargas, "Cacicazgos," 261.

38. Silva Santísteban, *Los Obrajes,* 96.

39. AGI AQ 9 Audiencia 1.4.1599. For further complaints about obraje administrators, see AGI AQ 211 and ANHQ Cedulario 1 fol. 354 20.5.1592, AQ 8 Marañón and Zorilla 7.4.1594, AQ 9 Memorial de avisos . . . Torres Altamarino 8.4.1605, AQ 10 Morga 20.4.1616; ANHQ Morga Cedulario fol. 40 and pp. 48–49 17.3.1619.

40. AGI AQ 9 Audiencia 1.4.1599.

41. Phelan, *Kingdom of Quito,* 72–74; Ortiz, "Obraje colonial," 512–15. In fact some obrajes had been rented out illegally before this date.

42. Tyrer, "Demographic and Economic History," 123.

43. Tyrer, "Demographic and Economic History," 123–24.

44. AGI AQ 10 Valencia León 26.4.1623.

45. Powers, "Migration and Socio-Political Change," 169–87; Tyrer, "Demographic and Economic History," 124–25, 136–38.

46. AGI AQ 10 Valencia León 26.4.1623; Landázuri Soto, *Régimen laboral,* 110–58.

47. Tyrer, "Demographic and Economic History," 128–33. Tyrer suggests that reductions may have been greater at other times when textile production was more profitable.

48. Ortiz de la Tabla Ducasse, "Obraje colonial," 507–9.

49. Landázuri Soto, Régimen laboral, 110–58; Ortiz de la Tabla Ducasse, "Obraje colonial," 512.

50. Ortiz de la Tabla Ducasse, "Obraje colonial," 521–28. The main families were Ramírez de Arellano, Galarza, Villacis, Londoño, Carrera, and Martínez de Aibar.

51. AGI AQ 30 Caciques of San Andrés 20.2.1620, 28.2.1620, 1.2.1625. For example, in 1610 the Duque de Uzeda obtained licences to establish mills at Guano, Ilapo, and San Andrés employing Indians, some of whom came from his own encomienda.

52. Tyrer, "Demographic and Economic History," 160.

53. ANHQ PQ 1 fol. 28r–28v Caciques of Latacunga 1.11.1608; Tyrer, "Demographic and Economic History," 160.

54. Landázuri Soto, *Régimen laboral,* 126.

55. AGI AG 13 Ibarra 4.4.1604; Landázuri Soto, *Régimen laboral,* 110–58.

56. AGI AQ 20B Probanza of Don Sancho Hacho 1569; Vargas, "Cacicazgos," 261.

57. AGI AQ 30 Caciques of San Andrés 1.2.1625.

58. Landázuri Soto, *Régimen laboral,* 114.

59. RGI 2:259 Cantos 7.10.1581.

60. AGI AG 13 Ibarra 4.4.1604; CDI 9:470 Descripción . . . de la villa del Villar Don Pardo 1605.

61. AGI EC 919A Visita of Muñoa Ronquillo 31.1.1603.

62. AGI AQ 25 Virrey 4.8.1591, AQ 55 Cabrera 1621 (includes an account for 6.4.1588). In 1589 it was estimated that in the jurisdiction of Quito there were approximately 2,000 Indians working in all mills, both communal and private (AGI AQ 8 Dr. Barros 12.5.1589).

63. AGI AG 13 Ibarra 4.4.1604. In 1680 the fourteen community mills that still existed could employ 2,586 Indians and 50 boys, of which 1,888 Indians and the 50 boys were employed in the jurisdictions of Riobamba, Ambato, and Latacunga (Landázuri Soto, *Régimen laboral,* 110–58).

64. Silva Santísteban, *Los Obrajes,* 25, 28, 38; Tyrer, "Demographic and Economic History," 149; Villalaba, "Obrajes de Quito," 53, 57.

65. Landázuri Soto, *Régimen laboral,* 110–58.

66. Tyrer, "Demographic and Economic History," 137.

67. AGI AQ 25 Virrey 4.8.1591; CDI 9:470 Descripción . . . de la villa del Villar Don Pardo 1605; Ortiz de la Tabla Ducasse, "Obraje colonial," 495, 498.

68. Cushner, *Farm and Factory,* 103; Powers, "Migration and Socio-Political Change," 174–75.

69. Cushner, *Farm and Factory,* 103–5.

70. Tyrer, "Demographic and Economic History," 153–54; Cushner, *Farm and Factory,* 101–2.

71. AGI AQ 8 Venegas de Cañaveral 20.8.1584; AMQ LC 20:54–56 Cabildo of Quito 26.9.1603; ANHQ PQ 1 fol. 28r–v Cabildo of Latacunga 1.11.1608; ANHQ PQ 1 fols. 82–84 Peralta 18.7.1614; AGI AQ 28 Memoria de los agravios . . . de Gabriel Villafuerte 1613, AQ 77 Bishop of Quito 15.12.1628.

72. AGI AQ 9 Memorial de avisos . . . Torres Altamarino 9.4.1604.

73. AGI AG 13 Ibarra 4.4.1604.

74. CDI 9:470 Descripción . . . de la villa del Villar Don Pardo 1605. This mill was later acquired by the Jesuits (Cushner, *Farm and Factory,* 93).

75. AGI AG 13 Ibarra 4.4.1604. In 1680 the existing twelve community mills employed 1,888 forced laborers (Landázuri Soto, *Régimen laboral,* 110–58), giving an average of 157 per mill, although the four that had been established by 1604 averaged 276 forced laborers, suggesting that the earliest established mills were the largest and that the numbers of forced laborers they employed increased slightly during the century.

76. Landázuri Soto, *Régimen laboral,* 110–58; Tyrer, "Demographic and Economic History," 161–62.

77. AGI AG 13 Ibarra 4.4.1604. In 1680 the seven mills permitted to employ forced labor possessed licences for the employment of 1,242 mitayos, giving an average of 177 forced laborers per mill (Landázuri Soto, *Régimen laboral,* 110–58). Unfortunately it is not always clear whether the numbers of forced laborers included in the licences refer to those specified in the original licences or the number actually employed at that time.

78. See table 13 and CDI 9:470 Descripción . . . de la villa del Villar Don Pardo 1605.

79. Levillier, *Gobernantes del Perú,* 8:400–406; Villalaba, "Obrajes de Quito," 49–56.

80. In 1605 workers in the obrajes de comunidad in Chambo and Lito were paid between 12 and 30–40 pesos (CDI 9:470 Descripción . . . de la villa del Villar Don Pardo 1605); in Latacunga in 1611 Indians were paid between 18 and 32 pesos (ANHQ Obrajes 1 fols. 43–58 1611); and in 1619 those employed in a private mill at Panzaleo were paid between 14 and 32 pesos (Cushner, *Farm and Factory,* 92).

81. AGI AQ 69 Ordenanzas de obrajes 15.8.1621; Ortiz de la Tabla Ducasse, "Ordenanzas de obrajes," 22–23, 52–53.

82. Ortiz de la Tabla Ducasse, "Obraje colonial," 490. Of 250 Indians employed in Latacunga in the early seventeenth century, 217 (87 percent) were employed in basic tasks. Cushner provides a similar breakdown of mill tasks for the Jesuit mill at Chillo in 1767 (*Farm and Factory,* 100) and it is likely to have been fairly constant across the industry.

83. AGI AQ 30 Caciques of San Andrés 1.2.1625.

84. AGI AQ 87 Memorial de los agravios . . . Martín de Vergara 25.4.1619.

85. AGI AQ 87 Memorial de los agravios . . . Martín de Vergara 25.4.1619; AMQ Morga Cedulario p. 106 fol. 20 11.6.1621.

86. In 1674 the Santísteban ordinances reduced the tour of duty to six months (Silva Santísteban, *Los Obrajes,* 81; Villalaba, "Obrajes de Quito," 121–22).

87. AGI AQ 69 Ordenanzas de obrajes 15.8.1621; Ortiz de la Tabla Ducasse, "Ordenanzas de obrajes," 21–24, 41–57.

88. Silva Santísteban, *Los Obrajes,* 69, 82–83; Villalaba, "Obrajes de Quito," 51–52, 128–31, 135.

89. Silva Santísteban, *Los Obrajes,* 54; Tyrer, "Demographic and Economic History," 104–5; Cushner, *Farm and Factory,* 94–95.

90. AGI AQ 87 Memorial de los agravios . . . Martín de Vergara 25.4.1619.

91. For example, AMQ LC 20:54–56 Cabildo of Quito 26.9.1603; ANHQ PQ 1 fol. 28r–v Caciques de Latacunga 1.11.1608; AGI AQ 28 Memorial de los agravios . . . de Gabriel Villafuerte 1613, AQ 87 Memorial de los agravios . . . Martín de Vergara 25.4.1619; ANHQ PQ 1 fol. 102r–v Centeno Maldonado 4.10.1619; AGI AQ 30 Caciques of San Andrés 1.2.1625.

92. AGI AQ 10 Audiencia 29.4.1615.

93. Landázuri Soto, *Régimen laboral,* 155.

94. Landázuri Soto, *Régimen laboral,* 134.

95. Landázuri Soto, *Régimen laboral,* 151.

96. Powers, "Migration and Socio-Political Change," 174–75.

97. AMQ LC 4:228–32 Ordenanzas de minas 7.6.1549. This figure includes half of those assigned from the encomienda of Francisco Campos of the communities of Puní and Tomebamba. In 1557 there were 95 miners from the encomienda of Puruháes possessed by Juan de Padilla who were still being sent to the mines of Santa Barbola (Barbara) (AGI JU 671 fols. 243r–256v Visita de los Puruháes 1557).

98. See the discussion of mining in the Cuenca region.

99. RGI 2:316 Relación del distrito del cerro de Zaruma, no date.

100. AGI PAT 240-6 Cerro de Zaruma, no author, no date.

101. AGI AQ 9 Aguirre de Ugarte 6.11.1611.

102. AGI AQ 19 Oficiales reales of Loja 1.11.1611, AQ 9 Aguirre de Ugarte 6.11.1611; AMQ LC 21:172–73 and ANHQ Cedulario 2 fol. 58 15.9.1612.

103. AGI AQ 28 Soravia 10.3.1611; Zúñiga, *Significación de Latacunga,* 2:389.

104. For example, AGI AQ 28 Memorial de los agravios . . . Gabriel Villafuerte 1613.

105. RGI 2:329 Auncibay 1592.

106. AGI AQ 28 Soravia 10.3.1611.

107. For example, AGI AQ 28 Memorial de los agravios . . . Gabriel Villafuerte 1613, AQ 55 Cabrera 1621, AQ 22 Reales cédulas 29.3.1621, 10.5.1621.

108. CDI 9:497 Descripción . . . de la villa del Villar Don Pardo 1605.

109. AMQ LC 20:54–56 Regidor of Quito 26.9.1603; ANHQ PQ 1 fol. 28r–v Caciques of Latacunga 1.11.1608; AGI AQ 25 Cabrera 1621, AQ 30 Caciques of San Andrés 1.2.1625.

110. AMQ RC 21:199–200 and ANHQ Cedulario 2 fols. 77–78 8.3.1631.

111. AGI EC 911A Visita of Muñoa Ronquillo 31.1.1603.

112. ANHQ Indígenas 171 Caciques of Aloasí and Quisapincha 1600.

113. AGI AQ 9 Memorial de avisos . . . Torres Altamarino 9.4.1604, AQ 87 Memorial de los agravios . . . Martín Vergara 25.4.1619, AQ 211 Real cédula 29.3.1621, AQ 77 Bishop of Quito 15.12.1628.

114. AGI AQ 211 Real cédula 21.4.1578.

115. RGI 1:129–30 Salazar de Villasante, no date.

116. CDI 9:452–93 Descripción . . . de la villa del Villar Don Pardo 1605; see also the discussion of cultivation under the Puruhá in chap. 2.

117. ANHQ Indígenas 1 Cacique of Guanujo 9.5.1596; Calancha, "Crónica moralizada," 189–201: CDI 9:453–93 Descripción . . . de la villa del Villar Don Pardo 1605; Cieza de León, *Crónica,* cap. 41:59.

118. AGI AQ 11 Morga 30.4.1629.

119. CDI 9:453–93 Descripción . . . de la villa del Villar Don Pardo 1605; Calancha, "Crónica moralizada," 189–201: Cieza de León, *Crónica,* cap. 41:59.

120. AMQ LC 4:228–32 Ordenanzas de minas 7.6.1549.

121. The latter figure includes only half of the population of the encomienda of Puní and Tomebamba, since the latter was in the jurisdiction of Cuenca.

122. See the discussion of the Puruhá population in chap. 2.

123. CDI 9:452–88 Descripción . . . de la villa del Villar Don Pardo 1605; Guevara, *Puerto de El Dorado,* 94–96; Zúñiga, *Significación de Latacunga,* 2:365.

124. AGI AQ 8 Visita of Riobamba 1581.

125. In 1605 the eighteen villages in the corregimiento were made up of 123 parcialidades (CDI 9:452–88 Descripción . . . de la villa del Villar Don Pardo 1605).

126. For example, AGI AQ 22 Tasa of Ambato 8.2.1575.

127. AGI AQ 8 Visita of Riobamba 1581; Ortiz de la Tabla Ducasse, "Corregimiento de Riobamba," 23–87.

128. RGI 2:256–59 Cantos 7.10.1581.

129. RGI 2:261 Paz Maldonado, no date. Paz Maldonado estimates that there were about 3,000 souls and 700 tributary Indians.

130. RGI 2:256–59 Cantos 7.10.1581. There were 2,630 tributary Indians and 521 reservados.

131. Ortiz de la Tabla Ducasse, "Corregimiento de Riobamba," 21–26.

132. CDI 6:41–63 Relación de los indios tributarios 1.11.1591.

133. In 1581 the villages of Chambo, Puní, Macaxí, and San Andrés accounted for 44 percent of the population of Riobamba, and Pallatanga and Cumbibamba 32 percent of the population of Chimbo.

134. In 1605 the missing villages of Píllaro, Quero, Tisaleo, Mocha, and Baños accounted for 35 percent of the tributary population of the Ambato region (CDI 9:452–88 Descripción . . . de la villa del Villar Don Pardo 1605).

135. RGI 2:316 Relación del distrito del cerro de Zaruma, no date.

136. RGI 2:320 Relación del distrito del cerro de Zaruma, no date. The breakdown was 300 from Latacunga, 250 from Riobamba and Ambato, and 250 from Chimbo. The status of these Indians is unclear.

137. AGI AQ 9 Marañón, no date.

138. President Marañón's list does not record the populations of Puní and Guanando, which are included in the 1581 visita, but in this case they were probably included in other parishes—Puní probably with Macaxí, and Guanando probably with San Andrés.

139. CDI 9:452–88 Descripción . . . de la villa del Villar Don Pardo 1605. A few of the figures appear to have been based on a visita conducted by Muñoa Ronquillo in 1603 (AGI EC 919A Visita of Muñoa Ronquillo 31.1.1603).

140. CDI 9:452–88 Descripción . . . de la villa del Villar Don Pardo 1605. Although the figures for the number of tributary Indians around Ambato are clear enough, the total figures should be used with caution, since the terms in which they are expressed are often ambiguous, and the arithmetic is sometimes faulty. For Riobamba the populations of Macaxí and Licán were not specified, but the former was probably included with Puní and the latter with San Andrés or Calpi. A slightly larger ratio of 1:4.8 can be calculated for the five villages of Chambo, Quimia, Penipe, Puní, and Lito in 1603 (AGI EC 919A Visita of Muñoa Ronquillo 31.1.1603).

141. See app. 3.

142. Their distribution throughout the region is based on the relative numbers recorded in the baptismal records for El Sagrario, which suggest that about 60 percent came from Latacunga, 15 percent from Ambato, 20 percent from Riobamba, and 5 percent from Chimbo.

143. See the discussion of the Panzaleo and Puruhá in chap. 2.

144. See the discussion of epidemics in chap. 6.

145. CDI 9:52–88, 489–503 Descripción . . . de la villa del Villar Don Pardo 1605.

146. AGI EC 919A Visita of Muñoa Ronquillo 31.1.1603.

147. Powers, "Migration and Socio-Political Change," 169–87.

148. AGI AQ 8 Visita of Riobamba 1581. For Ambato the numbers were 3,921 adults and 2,350 children under fifteen years old, and for Riobamba the corresponding figures were 11,604 and 5,883 respectively. Parcialidades for Ambato for which the numbers of children are not known have been excluded from the calculations. Unfortunately, the figures do not permit the calculation of woman/child ratios.

149. Comparing the accounts of five villages that were subject to visitas in both 1581 and 1603, the adult/child ratio increased from 1:0.45 to 1:0.59, despite differences in the classification of children that favored a slightly higher ratio at the earlier date. In the 1581 visita children were classified as such if they were under fifteen years old, whereas in 1603 females under fourteen and males under seventeen years old were regarded as such (AGI AQ 8 Visita of Riobamba 1581, EC 919A Visita of Muñoa Ronquillo 31.1.1603).

150. ANHQ Indígenas 1 Visita de Macaxí 14.10.1620.

151. Harsh working conditions in the private obraje of San Andrés drove Indians to practice infanticide (AGI AQ 30 Caciques of San Andrés 1.2.1625).

CHAPTER 10

1. AMQ LC 2:110–13 Cabildo of Quito 31.3.1540.

2. López de Velasco, *Geografía,* 220.

3. Salomon, "Cañari 'Inca-ism,'" 211–12.

4. Herrera, *Historia General,* 10, dec. 5, lib. 4, cap. 11:330; Oberem, "Los Cañaris," 135–37.

5. AGI PAT 90A-1-23 Pizarro 15.6.1540, PAT 93-9-3 Services of Sandoval 19.11.1539; RAHM 9/4664 nos. 1–2 fols. 27v–29v, no date; Crespo Toral, "Encomiendas de Cuenca," 26.

6. AGI PAT 93-9-3 Services of Sandoval 19.11.1539.

7. Oberem, "Los Cañaris," 139; Cieza de León, *Crónica,* cap. 44:65.

8. RGI 3:176 Benavente 25.3.1550; RGI 3:178 Jiménez Espada; Rumazo González, *Región Amazónica,* 136, 138.

9. AMQ LC 2:110–13 Cabildo of Quito 31.3.1540; Rumazo González, *Región Amazónica,* 156–58.

10. RGI 3:190.

11. See the discussion of the Yaguarzongo and Pacamoros region in chap. 16; AGI AQ 22 Sánchez de la Parra 1584.

12. See the discussion of the Cañar in chap. 2.

13. Cieza de León, *Crónica,* cap. 44:64.

14. AGI IG 2987 Auncibay, no date.

15. Cieza de León, *Crónica,* cap. 44:64.

16. Navarro Cárdenas, *Minería en el Ecuador,* 8, refers to cabildo records of 20.1.1539.

17. See AMQ LC 16:365 Cabildo of Cuenca 10.6.1562.

18. RGI 2:174 Oficiales reales 30.12.1576.

19. Cieza de León, *Crónica,* cap. 44:66.

20. RGI 2:174 Oficiales reales 30.12.1576.

21. AMQ LC 4:212–14 Cabildo of Quito 8.5.1549.

22. AMQ LC 4:223–32 Ordenanzas de minas 7.6.1549.

23. AGI IG 2987 Auncibay, no date; RGI 1:142 Salazar de Villasante, no date.

24. AGI PAT 101-1-19 Información de servicios de Gil Ramírez Dávalos 25.10.1558; RGI 1:142 Salazar de Villasante, no date; RGI 2:265 Pablos 20.9.1582; RGI 2:173 Oficiales reales 30.12.1576.

25. AGI PAT 101-1-19 Información de servicios de Gil Ramírez Dávalos 15.9.1556; Rumazo González, *Región Amazonica,* 152.

26. CDI 15:409–572 Demarcación y división, no date; RGI 1:141 Salazar de Villasante, no date; RGI 2:265 Pablos 20.9.1582; RGI 2:282 Gómez et al. June 1582; López de Velasco, *Geografía,* 220.

27. AMQ LC 16:364–65 Cabildo of Cuenca 10.6.1562.

28. AMQ LC 16:227–29 Cabildo of Cuenca 20.10.1559.

29. AGI IG 1530 Relación de minas, no date; Chacón, *Minería de Cuenca,* 18.

30. RGI 1:141 Salazar de Villasante, no date.

31. RGI 2:269 Pablos 20.9.1582; RGI 2:275, 277 Gallegos 20.9.1582.

32. RGI 1:141 Salazar de Villasante, no date.

33. AGI AQ 22 Santillán 27.2.1565; Paniagua Pérez, *Plata labrada,* 69, 71–72.

34. AGI PAT 188-38 Real provisión 7.4.1562; AMQ LC 16:364–65 Cabildo of Cuenca 10.6.1562.

35. RGI 1:141 Salazar de Villasante, no date.

36. RGI 3:81–82 Arcos 13.12.1586; RGI 1:141 Salazar de Villasante, no date.

37. AGI AQ 8 Barros 26.4.1591. This must have been between 1573 and 1583, when Ortegón was oidor.

38. RGI 2:269 Pablos 20.9.1582; Chacón, *Minería de Cuenca,* 42–51.

39. RGI 3:81 Arcos 13.12.1586; Chacón, *Minería de Cuenca,* 58–72.

40. AGI IG 1530 Relación de minas, no date.

41. Crespo Toral, "Encomiendas de Cuenca," 29; Albornoz, *Monografía histórica del Girón,* 51; Albornoz, *Cuenca,* 91–92; Chacón, *Minería de Cuenca,* 53; Paniagua Pérez, *Plata labrada,* 59.

42. Anda Aguirre, *Don Juan Salinas Loyola,* 83, 171; Crespo Toral, "Encomiendas de Cuenca," 26.

43. RGI 2:269 Pablos 20.9.1582; RGI 3:81–82 Arcos 13.12.1586; AGI PAT 240-8 Arias Pacheco 1594; Chacón, *Minería de Cuenca,* 54–56.

44. See the discussion of the Loja region in the following chapter.

45. Paniagua Pérez, *Plata labrada,* 72.

46. AGI AQ 18 Espinosa 10.4.1606, AQ 26 Ocampo 20.4.1606; ANHQ Cedulario 2 fol. 58 15.9.1612.

47. AGI IG 2987 Auncibay, no date.

48. AGI AQ 8 Barros 26.4.1591.

49. In 1623 wages for miners averaged 40 reals a month, whereas workers in other activities earned only 16 reals (AGI AQ 30 Espinosa 28.3.1623).

50. RGI 1:141 Salazar de Villasante, no date; RGI 2:173 Oficiales reales 30.12.1576.

51. RGI 2:266, 269 Pablos 20.9.1582; RGI 2:277 Gallegos 20.9.1582; RGI 2:278–79 Arias Dávila 1.5.1582; RGI 2:284 Gómez et al. June 1582.

52. AMQ LC 16:412–13 Cabildo of Cuenca 22.1.1563; ANHQ Indígenas 1 Caciques of Paute 1603; Albornoz, *Cuenca,* 102.

53. AGI AQ 26 Ocampo 20.4.1606, IG 1530, no date; Paniagua Pérez, *Plata labrada,* 59.

54. AGI PAT 240-8 Arias Pacheco 1594; RGI 1:141 Salazar de Villasante, no date; RGI 2:285 Gómez et al. June 1582.

55. AGI AQ 26 Ocampo 20.4.1606.

56. RGI 2:269 Pablos 20.9.1582.

57. AGI AQ 21 Zúñiga 15.12.1574; Albornoz, *Cuenca,* 123–24.

58. For example, AMQ Tierras de Cuenca, Alausí 1611–1762 fols. 1–6 Cacique of Gualaceo 1611.

59. RGI 2:277 Gallegos 20.9.1582.

60. For example, AMQ Tierras de Cuenca, Alausí 1611–1762 fols. 1–6 Cacique of Gualaceo 1611.

61. Albornoz, *Cuenca,* 123–24.

62. AGI AQ 21 Zúñiga 15.12.1574.

63. AGI AQ 21 Zúñiga 15.12.1574.

64. RGI 2:270–71 Los Angeles 12.5.1582; RGI 2:272 Pereira 1.10.1582; RGI 2:276–77 Gallegos 20.9.1582; RGI 2:284 Gómez et al. June 1582; RGI 2:287 Gaviria 4.5.1582.

65. RGI 2:269 Pablos 20.9.1582; RGI 2:276–77 Gallegos 20.9.1582.

66. RAHM 9/4664 nos. 1–2 fols. 27v–29v, no date.

67. AGI AQ 8 Toledo 17.11.1570, AQ 8 López de Herrera 22.10.1575.

68. AGI AQ 21 Zúñiga 15.12.1574, AQ 8 López de Herrera 22.10.1575.

69. RGI 2:271 Los Angeles 12.5.1582; RGI 2:274 Pereira 1.10.1582; RGI 2:278 Gallegos 20.9.1582; RGI 2:287 Gaviria 4.5.1582.

70. RGI 2:271 Los Angeles 12.5.1582.

71. AMQ LC 16:209–12 Cabildo of Cuenca 11.9.1559, LC 16:227–29 Cabildo of Cuenca 20.10.1559, LC 16:272–73 Cabildo of Cuenca 31.5.1560.

72. Albornoz, *Cuenca,* 98.

73. AMQ LC 16:209–12 Cabildo of Cuenca 11.9.1559.

74. AGI EC 912A Memorial de las cosas 1577; AMQ LC 16:291–93 Cabildo of Cuenca 22.10.1560; RGI 2:269 Pablos 20.9.1582. For different means by which Indians obtained cash with which to meet tribute demands, see RGI 2:274 Pereira 1.10.1582; RGI 2:278 Gallegos 20.9.1582; RGI 2:280 Arias Dávila 1.5.1582; RGI 2:284 Gómez et al. June 1582).

75. Matovalle, *Cuenca de Tomebamba,* 143.

76. See chap. 6.

77. AMQ LC 16:364–65 Cabildo of Cuenca 10.6.1562.

78. Albornoz, *Cuenca,* 111; Hermida Piedra, "Medicina en al Azuay," 76. Unfortunately, Albornoz does not indicate the source of his information, and not one of the relaciones geográficas for the Cuenca area written in 1582 makes reference to a smallpox epidemic. Neither is there any evidence for its presence in other regions of Ecuador at that time. It is clear, however, that the Cuenca region participated in the epidemics that ravaged Ecuador in the late 1580s (see chap. 6; AGI AL 32 Conde de Villar 19.4.1589).

79. Albornoz, *Cuenca,* 112; Hermida Piedra, "Medicina en al Azuay," 17.

80. RGI 2:270 Pablos 20.9.1582.

81. RGI 2:266 Pablos 20.9.1582.

82. RGI 2:286 Gaviria 4.5.1582.

83. RGI 2:286 Gaviria 4.5.1582; RGI 2:270 Los Angeles 12.5.1582. For other accounts of intestinal and respiratory infections, see RGI 2:266 Pablos 20.9.1582; RGI 2:281–82 Gómez et al. June 1582; RGI 2:273 Pereira 1.10.1582.

84. RGI 2:273 Pereira 1.10.1582; RGI 2:286 Gaviria 4.5.1582.

85. RAHM 9/4664 no. 21 Los pueblos despanoles, no date. The document must have postdated the establishment of the audiencia in 1563, and the account says that ten years before, the province of Yaguarzongo had been conquered, thereby suggesting it was written about 1567.

86. CDI 15:409–572 Demarcación y división, no date; López de Velasco, *Geografía,* 220.

87. Crespo Toral, "Encomiendas de Cuenca," 27; Albornoz, *Monografía histórica del Girón,* 40–42. The former gives the number of Indians as 5,460, which was apparently extracted from the fourth *Libro de Cabildo* of Cuenca.

88. AGI AQ 21 Zúñiga 15.12.1574, AQ 8 Herrera 22.10.1575.

89. It is also assumed that the figure for Pacaibamba was 500 tributary Indians, but as already indicated, what this figure refers to is unclear. The figures are Pacaibamba 500 (RGI 2:279 Arias Dávila 1.5.1582), Cañaribamba 700 (RGI

2:282 Gómez et al. June 1582), Paccha 200 and Arocxapa 190 (RGI 2:270–71 Los Angeles 12.5.1582), Paute 200 (RGI 2:271 Pereira 1.10.1582), and Azogues 460 (RGI 2:274 Gallegos 20.9.1582). In the last case the transcriber noted the actual figures were uncertain, being difficult to read in the original document).

90. AGI AQ 76 Bishop of Quito 28.10.1581.

91. RGI 2:279 Arias Dávila 1.5.1582.

92. Powers, "Indian Migrations," 317–20.

93. See chap. 11 for the migration of Indians to the region between Loja and Piura.

94. RGI 2:268 Pablos 20.9.1582.

95. RGI 2:270 Los Angeles 12.5.1582; RGI 2:276 Gallegos 20.9.1582.

96. CDI 6:41–63 Relación de los indios tributarios que hay 1.11.1591. Those identifiable as being in the jurisdiction of Cuenca are Paute, Azogues, Cañaribamba, Hatuncañar, Gualaceo, Pacaibamba, Chunchi, and Saraguro (of which only half of the population is included in the figure for this region).

97. RGI 2:316, 320 Relación del distrito del cerro de Zaruma, no date; see also AGI PAT 240-6 No author, no date, though this source gives only 150 vagamundos.

98. AGI AQ 9 Ibarra 27.11.1600.

99. This is also suggested by the trajectory of the population of Pacaibamba, which in 1550 included 1,000 Indians; in 1582 it had 500, and in 1591 there were 400 (AGI PAT 133-3 Información de los servicios de Juan de Narváez 14.2.1591; RGI 2:279 Arias Dávila 1.5.1582). The decline continued into the seventeenth century, with increasing numbers of Indians being recorded as absent (AGI AQ 18 Espinosa 10.4.1606, AQ 26 Ocampo 20.4.1606).

CHAPTER 11

1. RGI 2:309 Relación de lo que es el asiento del cerro de Zaruma 1592.

2. RGI 2:291 Salinas 1571 or 1572; Cieza de León, *Crónica,* cap. 56:82.

3. RGI 2:297 Salinas 1571 or 1572; Anda Aguirre, *Mercadillo,* 19–28; Jaramillo Alvarado, *Provincia de Loja,* 73, 85; Caillavet, "Grupos étnicos," 131.

4. Anda Aguirre, *Mercadillo,* 32.

5. RGI 2:297 Salinas 1571 or 1572; López de Velasco, *Geografía,* 221.

6. RAHM A/92 fols. 55–77 and 9/4664 no. 20 Relación de los vecinos encomenderos, no date.

7. RGI 2:308, 313 Relación de lo que es el asiento del cerro de Zaruma 1592.

8. RGI 2:301 Salinas 1571 or 1572; Caillavet, "Echanges et crédit," 35–38.

9. AGI AQ 19 Ugarte 24.4.1607; RGI 2:295–97 Salinas 1571 or 1572; Cieza de León, *Crónica,* cap. 56:82.

10. AGI PAT 240-1 Vecinos and moradores of Zaruma 13.8.1580, PAT 240-6 Bishop of Nicaragua 1592; RGI 2:292–93 Salinas 1571 or 1572; Caillavet, "Exchanges et crédit," 33. Salinas claims that they had been discovered twenty years previously, which would argue for a date of 1551 or 1552.

11. Jaramillo Alvarado, *Provincia de Loja,* 121–22; Anda Aguirre, *Zaruma,* 48.

12. AGI PAT 240-4, No author, no date; RGI 2:307 Relación de lo que es el asiento del cerro de Zaruma 1592; RGI 2:330 González Mendoza, no date.

13. AGI PAT 240-6 Bishop of Nicaragua 1592; RGI 2:308 Relación de lo que es el asiento del cerro de Zaruma 1592.

14. RGI 2:322 Auncibay 1592; RGI 2:330 González Mendoza, no date.

15. AGI PAT 240-1 Vecinos of Zaruma 30.9.1580, PAT 240-6 Cerro de Zaruma, no date; RGI 2:307 Relación de lo que es el asiento del cerro de Zaruma 1592; RGI 2:330 González Mendoza, no date.

16. AGI AQ 22 Ciança 1.3.1583, PAT 240-5 Vecinos of Zaruma 22.5.1592, PAT 240-6 Cerro de Zaruma, no date; RGI 2:308 Relación de lo que es el asiento del cerro de Zaruma 1592; RGI 2:330 González Mendoza, no date.

17. RGI 2:330 González Mendoza, no date.

18. RGI 2:322–23 Auncibay 1592.

19. AGI AQ 211 Real cédula 15.11.1576, PAT 240-3 Arcos 19.8.1592, PAT 240-6 Ortegón, no date; RGI 2:309 Relación de lo que es el asiento del cerro de Zaruma 1592; RGI 2:323 Auncibay 1592; RGI 2:315 Relación del distrito del cerro de Zaruma, no date; AGI AQ 10 Zorilla 26.11.1617; ANHQ PQ 3 fol. 3r–v 3.2.1639.

20. See chap. 10.

21. RGI 2:309 Relación de lo que es el asiento del cerro de Zaruma 1592. In 1582 Cañaribamba was sending sixty to seventy Indians to Zaruma (RGI 2:285 Gómez et al. 5.6.1582).

22. RGI 2:323 Auncibay 1592.

23. RGI 2:310 Relación de lo que es el asiento del cerro de Zaruma 1592; RGI 2:315 Relación del distrito del cerro de Zaruma, no date; RGI 2:330 González Mendoza, no date. In 1620 there were 247 Indians assigned (AGI AQ 30 Escribano público of Zaruma and Loja 8.4.1620).

24. AGI PAT 240-6 González Mendoza, no date.

25. Anda Aguirre, *Zaruma,* 66–67.

26. RGI 2:309–10 Relación de lo que es el asiento del cerro de Zaruma 1592; RGI 2:322–23 Auncibay 1592.

27. Anda Aguirre, *Zaruma,* 69.

28. AGI AQ 211 Real cédula 15.11.1576; RGI 2:315 Relación del distrito del cerro de Zaruma, no date.

29. AGI PAT 240-6 Ortegón, no date; RGI 2:315 Relación del distrito del cerro de Zaruma, no date; Anda Aguirre, *Zaruma,* 56, 57, 67.

30. RGI 2:280 Arias Dávila 1.5.1582.

31. RGI 2:332 González Mendoza, no date: RGI 2:322 Auncibay 1592.

32. Levillier, *Gobernantes del Perú,* 8:143–240, Ordenanzas del Virrey Don Francisco de Toledo 7.2.1574.

33. AGI PAT 240-5 Vecinos of Zaruma 22.5.1592; RGI 2:309 Relación de lo que es el asiento del cerro de Zaruma 1592.

34. AGI PAT 240-5 Vecinos of Zaruma 22.5.1592; RGI 2:309 Relación de lo que es el asiento del cerro de Zaruma 1592.

35. Anda Aguirre, *Zaruma,* 111–13.

36. RGI 2:325 Auncibay 1592; RGI 2:330 González Mendoza, no date.

37. For different variations of this scheme, see AGI AQ 8 Auncibay and Venegas de Cañaveral, no date; PAT 240-6 Cerro de Zaruma, no date; PAT 240-6 Ortegón, no date; RGI 2:310–13 Relación de lo que es el asiento del cerro de

Zaruma 1592; RGI 2:316–18 Relación del distrito del cerro de Zaruma, no date; RGI 2:325–28 Auncibay 1592; RGI 2:330–31 González Mendoza, no date.

38. ANHQ Cedulario 1 fol. 544 31.1.1590, fol. 469 17.10.1593.

39. AGI PAT 240-9 Instrucción to Figueroa 29.11.1594; Anda Aguirre, *Zaruma*, 130; Andrade, *Provincia de El Oro*, 19. In fact the title "villa" was not confirmed until 1606 because of opposition from vecinos in Loja and Cuenca.

40. AGI AQ 19 Aguirre de Ugarte 24.4.1607.

41. AGI AQ 19 Aguirre de Ugarte 24.4.1607.

42. AGI AQ 9 Aguirre de Ugarte 26.11.1611, AQ 19 Oficiales reales of Loja 1.11.1611.

43. AGI AQ 30 Espinosa 28.3.1623, AQ 212 Miners of Zaruma 10.4.1624, AQ 30 Villa and miners of Zaruma 1624.

44. RGI 2:302 Salinas 1571 or 1572; AGI PAT 240-5 Vecinos of Zaruma 29.1.1578, AQ 76 Bishop of Quito 28.10.1581.

45. AGI PAT 240-6 Bishop of Nicaragua 1592.

46. AGI AQ 22 Cianca 1.3.1583, PAT 240-4 No author 1590, AQ 8 Oidors 18.4.1590, PAT 240-6 González Mendoza, no date (also RGI 2:331–32), PAT 240-6 Cerro de Zaruma, no date.

47. AGI PAT 240-6 Ortegón, no date, PAT 240-6 Cerro de Zaruma, no date; RGI 2:312 Relación de lo que es el asiento del cerro de Zaruma 1592.

48. ANHQ Cedulario 1 fol. 469 Real cédula 17.10.1593; RGI 3:310 Relación de lo que es el asiento del cerro de Zaruma 1592.

49. AGI PAT 240-6 Ortegón, no date, PAT 240-6 Cerro de Zaruma, no date; RGI 2:324 Auncibay 1592; RGI 2:310 Relación de lo que es el asiento del cerro de Zaruma 1592.

50. RGI 2:310 Relación de lo que es el asiento del cerro de Zaruma 1592.

51. ANHQ PQ 2 fol. 152 Rodríguez 11.6.1636.

52. AGI AQ 211 Real cédula 15.11.1576; RGI 2:285 Gómez et al. 5.6.1582; AGI PAT 240-5 Vecinos of Zaruma 22.5.1592; RGI 2:323 Auncibay 1592.

53. RGI 2:313 Relación de lo que es el asiento del cerro de Zaruma 1592; Anda Aguirre, *Zaruma*, 112.

54. ANHQ Indígenas 171 Juan Cumbinama 29.8.1595.

55. RGI 2:323 Auncibay 1592.

56. RGI 2:311 Relación de lo que es el asiento del cerro de Zaruma 1592; RGI 2:317 Relación del distrito del cerro de Zaruma, no date.

57. AGI AQ 11 Morga 30.4.1629; RGI 2:315 Relación del distrito del cerro de Zaruma, no date.

58. RGI 2:323 Auncibay 1592; Anda Aguirre, *Zaruma*, 67.

59. RGI 2:323 Auncibay 1592; RGI 2:315 Relación del distrito del cerro de Zaruma, no date.

60. Anda Aguirre, *Zaruma*, 67.

61. AGI AQ 76 Bishop of Quito 28.10.1581. See the discussion of the population of the Cuenca region in chap. 10.

62. AGI AL 29 Relación de los indios de guerra, no date.

63. Caillavet, "Echanges et crédit," 35–38.

64. AGI AQ 30 Villa and miners of Zaruma 1624.

65. AGI EC 912A Memorial de las cosas 1577; Anda Aguirre, *Zaruma*, 38.

66. RGI 2:300 Salinas 1571 or 1572.

67. AGI AQ 211 Real cédula 10.8.1592; RGI 2:298 Salinas 1571 or 1572.

68. For example, AGI AQ Ibarra 27.11.1600, AQ 9 Relación . . . en razon de las visitas 25.4.1602; ANHQ PQ 2 fol. 163r–163v Cañizares 1.10.1637.

69. ANHQ PQ 3 fol. 3r–v 3.2.1639.

70. ANHQ PQ 2 fols. 98–99 14.12.1630.

71. Anda Aguirre, *Zaruma,* 69–70.

72. RGI 2:302 Salinas 1571 or 1572; RGI 2:322 Auncibay 1592; RGI 2:330 González Mendoza, no date; Cieza de León, *Crónica,* cap. 56:81.

73. RGI 2:292 Salinas 1571 or 1572.

74. RGI 2:309 Relación de los que es el asiento del cerro de Zaruma, no date.

75. RGI 2:292 Salinas 1571 or 1572.

76. AGI PAT 240-5 No author 1590.

77. AGI AQ 19 Ugarte 24.4.1607.

78. BM Add. 13,777 fol. 75r–v Relación de las ciudades, Morales Figueroa 17.5.1589.

79. AGI AQ 76 Bishop of Quito 28.10.1581; Caillavet, "Echanges et crédit," 36–37.

80. AGI AQ 76 Bishop of Quito 28.10.1581.

81. See chap. 2.

82. RGI 2:302 Salinas 1571 or 1572; BNM˙3178 fols. 1–15 Canelas Albarrán 1586.

83. RGI 1:174 Oficiales reales 30.12.1576; RGI 2:302 Salinas 1571 or 1572.

84. CDI 6:43–61 Relación de los indios tributarios que hay 1.11.1591.

85. Anda Aguirre, *Zaruma,* 58–61 refers to a real cédula of 6.2.1616.

86. RGI 2:320 Sobre la cantidad de los peinadillos que hay en Quito, no date.

CHAPTER 12

1. RGI 2:183 Relación de las cibdades, after 1582.

2. RGI 3:87–88 Carranza 1569; Cabello Balboa, *Obras,* 1:26.

3. Estete, *Noticia,* 17–19; Cieza de León, *Descubrimiento,* cap. 30–32:259–62.

4. CDI 41:513–18 Alvarado 10.3.1534.

5. Estrada Ycaza, *Puerto de Guayaquil,* 1:38.

6. AGI PAT 185-I-7 Información que va de tierra firme 7.4.1534, PAT 185-1-8 Testimonio de una carta escrita en Jauja 25.5.1534, PAT 185-1-9 and CDI 10:152–237 Almagro 12.10.1534 Información hecha a pedimiento . . . de Almagro 12.10.1534; CDI 42:104–13 Almagro 8.5.1534.

7. AGI PAT 185-1-9 and CDI 10:152–237 Almagro 12.10.1534.

8. AGI PAT 28-12 Relación de la conquista, no date; Molina, "Relación," 65.

9. AGI PAT 103B-1-11 Información de los servicios de Cap. Antonio Morán 10.8.1558; Loor, *Españoles en Manabí,* 46–47.

10. AGI PAT 185-1-8 Testimonio de una carta escrita en Jauja 25.5.1534; CDI 42:104–13 Ayuntamiento of Jauja 20.7.1534.

11. Cieza de León, *Crónica,* cap. 51:73; Loor, *Españoles en Manabí,* 49–50, 55; Rumazo González, "San Gregorio de Puerto Viejo," 68–70.

12. Campos, *Compendio histórico,* 27; Borja de Szászdi, "Reinterpretación," 39.

13. Acounts of the dates and locations of the various foundations of Guayaquil differ substantially. The most definitive account appears to be that of Borja de Szászdi. See Aspiazu, "Santiago de Guayaquil," 143–79; Estrada Ycaza, *Fundación de Guayaquil,* 55–65; Borja de Szászdi, "Reinterpretación," 40; Cieza de León, *Crónica,* cap. 55:79.

14. Cieza de León, *Crónica,* cap. 46:67–68.

15. RGI 3:87–90 Carranza 1569.

16. Cabello Balboa, *Obras,* 1:24; Alcina Franch, Moreno, and Peña, "Penetración española," 115–20; González Suárez, *Historia general,* 2:482–507.

17. BNM 3044 fols. 9–10 Advertencias de Francisco de Toledo 7.8.1569.

18. AGI AQ 31 Cacique of Daule 20.10.1626.

19. Purchas, *Purchas His Pilgrimes,* 2:163–65; Clayton, "Defensa de la hegemonía española," 27–29; Estrada Ycaza, *Puerto de Guayaquil,* 3:57–78.

20. Loor, *Españoles en Manabí,* 61; Borja de Szászdi, "Reinterpretación," 40.

21. RGI 2:173 Oficiales reales 30.12.1576.

22. In the early 1560s there were twenty-two encomenderos in Puerto Viejo and sixteen in Guayaquil (RAHM 9/4664 no. 20 Relación de los vecinos españoles, no date). Another document, probably written a few years later, gives the number of encomenderos as eighteen for Guayaquil and fifteen for Puerto Viejo (RAHM 9/4664 no. 21 Los pueblos despanoles, no date [probably late 1560s]).

23. RGI 1:126, 136 Villasante, no date.

24. RGI 2:172–73 Oficiales reales 30.12.1576.

25. CDI 15:409–572 Demarcación y División, no date; López de Velasco, *Geografía,* 224–25.

26. Loor, *Españoles en Manabí,* 62.

27. AGI AQ 20B Vecinos of Puerto Viejo 6.2.1566; RGI 1:136–37 Villasante, no date.

28. RGI 2:173 Oficiales reales 30.12.1576.

29. AGI 118-8 Probanza de Ramírez de Guzmán 1574.

30. CDI 41:538–44 Father Berlanga 26.4.1535.

31. AGI PAT 101-1-19 Información de servicios de Gil Ramírez Dávalos 25.10.1558 (contains a cédula 18.9.1556).

32. AGI 118-8 Probanza de Ramírez de Guzmán 1574; RGI 2:339 No author 1581.

33. RGI 2:337–40 No author 1581. The summary figure for the *doctrinas* is 1,459 tributary Indians, but the individual figures give only 1,457. All encomiendas, except that of the island of Puná, where the Indians paid tribute to the Crown, were allocated to private individuals.

34. In 1605 there were thirteen encomenderos in the jurisdiction of Guayaquil who together possessed 657 tributary Indians, and ten or twelve in Puerto Viejo with only 358 tributary Indians (CDI 9:247–309 Descripción de la gobernación 1605).

35. RGI 2:173 Oficiales reales 30.12.1576.

36. RGI 1:127 Villasante, no date; RGI 2:173 Oficiales reales 30.12.1576; RGI

2:337–40 No author 1581; CDI 9:247–309 Descripción de la gobernación 1605; Espinosa Soriano, "Reino de Chono," 17; "Sobre los tributos," 73–75, 85–86.

37. AGI PAT 101-1-19 Información de los servicios de Gil Ramírez Dávalos 25.10.1558, commissioned 8.4.1557.

38. AGI AQ 8 Auncibay 20.2.1580.

39. RGI 2:337–40 No author 1581.

40. CDI 9:247–309 Descripción de la gobernación 1605.

41. CDI 9:247–309 Descripción de la gobernación 1605.

42. CDI 9:247–309 Descripción de la gobernación 1605.

43. AGI AQ 9 Bedón 10.3.1598. The other two regions were in the Oriente— in Los Quijos and in Yaguarzongo and Pacamoros.

44. AGI AQ 24 Cacique of Charapotó 27.10.1591.

45. AGI AQ 31 Cacique of Daule 20.10.1626; CDI 9:247–309 Descripción de la gobernación 1605; Rumazo González, *Documentos,* 4:120–33, Martin de Fuica 9.11.1619.

46. AGI CO 1575 fols. 183–85 Cuentas de los oficiales reales 1600–1611.

47. RGI 2:173, 177 Oficiales reales 30.12.1576; CDI 9:247–309 Descripción de la gobernación 1605; Cieza de Leon, *Crónica,* cap. 55:79.

48. RGI 2:177 Oficiales reales 30.12.1576; RGI 3:90 No author, no date.

49. *Recopilación,* 2, lib. 4, tit. 25, ley 31:102 2.6.1585.

50. AGI AQ 8 Santillán 15.1.1564; RGI 1:126–27 Villasante, no date; Benzoni, *Historia del mundo nuevo,* 259; Lizárraga, *Descripción breve,* cap. 5:6; Estrada Ycaza, "Hospital de Puerto Viejo," 14; Cieza de León, *Crónica,* cap. 54:78–79.

51. Pimental, "Los árboles," 8–9; Clayton, "Guayaquil Shipyards," 176.

52 RGI 1:127 Villasante, no date; Calancha, "Crónica moralizada," 189–201; Pimental, "Los árboles," 8–9, 12–13.

53. Clayton, "Guayaquil Shipyards," 20. For a discussion of shipbuilding activity through the sixteenth century, see pp. 57–63 and 126–28.

54. RGI 1:126 Villasante, no date; RGI 2:178 Oficiales reales 30.12.1576. See also the discussion of Riobamba.

55. Clayton, "Guayaquil Shipyards," 116–18.

56. AGI AQ 9 Torres Altamarino 15.4.1601; ANHQ Cedulario 1 fol. 365 Real cédula 17.11.1602.

57. AGI PAT 28-12 Relación de la conquista, no date; Calancha, "Crónica moralizada," 189–201; RGI 1:126–27 Villasante, no date; Molina, "Relación," 66.

58. AGI PAT 28-12 Relación de la conquista, no date; Molina, "Relación," 66.

59. BNM 3044 fols. 366–67 President of Quito, no date.

60. AGI AQ 9 Torres Altamarino 15.4.1601; ANHQ Cedulario 1 fol. 365 Real cédula 17.11.1602.

61. Clayton, "Guayaquil Shipyards," 145, which refers to AGI AQ 10 Morga 20.11.1615.

62. CDI 9:247–309 Descripción de la gobernación 1605; AGI AQ 31 Cacique of Daule 20.10.1626.

63. RGI 2:128–29 Villasante, no date; RGI 2:173 Oficiales reales 30.12.1576; Rumazo González, *Documentos,* 4:109–18, Illescas et al. 1617.

64. AGI AQ 10 Autos sobre el descubrimiento 5.1.1620; CDI 9:247–309 Descripción de la gobernación 1605.

65. CDI 9:247–309 Descripción de la gobernación 1605.

66. CDI 9:247–309 Descripción de la gobernación 1605.

67. RGI 1:126 Villasante, no date; CDI 9:247–309 Descripción de la gobernación 1605.

68. Cieza de León, *Crónica,* cap. 46:67–68, cap. 55:80.

69. AGI PAT 28-12 Relación de la conquista, no date, PAT 185-1-8 Testimonio de una carta 25.5.1534, PAT 185-1-9 Información . . . contra Alvarado 12.10.1534.

70. Benzoni, *Historia del mundo nuevo,* 255.

71. Cieza de León, *Crónica,* cap. 55:80.

72. AGI PAT 28-12 Relación de la conquista, no date; BNM 3044 fols. 366–67 President of Quito, no date; AGI AQ 9 Bedón 10.3.1598, AQ 9 Torres Altamarino 15.4.1601; ANHQ Cedulario 1 fol. 365 Real cédula 17.11.1602; Rumazo González, *Documentos,* 4:109–18, Illescas et al. 1617.

73. BNM 3178 fol. 1–15 Canelas Albarrán 1586.

74. CDI 9:247–309 Descripción de la gobernación 1605.

75. Kiple, *Caribbean Slave,* 17.

76. RGI 1:126–27, 129 Villasante, no date; RGI 2:173 Oficiales reales 30.12.1576; RGI 2:183 Relación de las ciudades, no date.

77. CDI 9:247–309 Descripción de la gobernación 1605; "Sobre los tributos," 81; Lizárraga, *Descripción breve,* cap. 5:6.

78. Newson, "Old World Epidemics," 102–4.

79. RGI 1:129 Villasante, no date; Lizárraga, *Descripción breve,* cap. 5:6.

80. Zarate, "Historia del descubrimiento," lib. 1, cap. 4:465; Estete, *Noticia,*17; López de Gómara, "Hispania Victrix," 226; Benzoni, *Historia del mundo nuevo,* 256; Cieza de León, *Crónica,* cap. 46:68.

81. Pimental, "Los árboles," 10.

82. AGI PAT 118-8 Probanza of Ramírez de Guzmán 1574.

83. Campos, *Compendio histórico,* 46.

84. Newson, "Old World Epidemics," 97–100.

85. See chap. 6; CDI 9:247–309 Descripción de la gobernación 1605.

86. AGI AL 43 Meritos de Amores Herrera 18.4.1610.

87. Benzoni, *Historia del mundo nuevo,* 254.

88. Figures for 1561, 1583, and 1606 give ratios of tributary to nontributary Indians of 1 to 2.1, 3.3, and 3.9 for Guayaquil, and 1 to 1.7, 3.3, and 4.1 for Puerto Viejo (RAHM A/92 fols. 55–77 Relación de los naturales 1561; Levillier, *Gobernantes del Perú,* 9:114–230; CDI 9:247–309 Descripción de la gobernación 1605).

89. CDI 9:247–309 Descripción de la gobernación 1605.

90. RGI 3:183 Relación de las ciudades, no date.

91. CDI 9:247–309 Descripción de la gobernación 1605.

92. Campos, *Compendio histórico,* 53.

93. RGI 1:137 Villasante, no date.

94. CDI 9:247–309 Descripción de la gobernación 1605.

95. CDI 9:247–309 Descripción de la gobernación 1605.

96. Espinosa Soriano, "Reino de Chono," 15.

97. AGI AQ 211 Real cédula 24.1.1603.

98. This figure is based on the total for individual communities contained in CDI 9:247–309 Descripción de la gobernación 1605, rather than the summary of

2,576 that it includes, with a further 1,000 added for those outside Spanish administration.

99. This is based on the summary figure for the jurisdiction contained in CDI 9:247–309 Descripción de la gobernación 1605, with an additional 1,500 for those outside Spanish administration.

100. If all the estimated 1,000 Indians outside Spanish control in 1605 were Chono, the corresponding breakdown for the different ethnic groups would be Chono 69.7 percent, Huancavilca 24.9 percent, and Puná 5.3 percent.

CHAPTER 13

1. AGI AQ 8 Oidores 6.4.1588.

2. AGI PAT 28-9 Relación de Fuenmayor, no date; Cieza de León, *Crónica,* cap. 50:73.

3. Cabello Balboa, *Obras,* 1:5.

4. Cabello Balboa, *Obras,* 1:23–24; Estrada, *Relaciones históricas,* 1:47–50; González Suárez, *Historia general,* 2:486–87 n. 4; Alcina Franch, Moreno, and Peña, "Penetración española," 115–20.

5. AGI AQ 10 Morga 1.4.1620; RGI 1:138 Villasante, no date; Cabello Balboa, *Obras,* 1:18–20.

6. AGI 9 Barrio de Sepúlveda, no date.

7. AGI AQ 9 Información sobre las malabas 9.4.1611.

8. AGI AQ 25 Arévalo 22.12.1600; see also AQ 10 Morga 1.4.1620.

9. Rumazo González, *Documentos,* 4:109–18, Illescas et al. 1617.

10. CDI 9:247–309 Descripción de la gobernación 1605.

11. AGI AQ 9 Descripcion de los indios infieles 31.5.1597, AQ 10 Morga 1.4.1620.

12. The procurador of the Mercedarians suggested that they had baptized 1,800 Indians, but only 1,443 are included in the baptismal register. Detailed lists of those baptized are included in AGI AQ 9 Torres 20.11.1597 and Monroy, *Convento de la Merced,* 334–63.

13. AGI AQ 211 Real cédula 11.8.1596, AQ 9 Descripción de los infieles 31.5.1597 (includes map), AQ 25 González 11.4.1600, AQ 9 Barrio de Sepúlveda 20.7.1600, AQ 84 Procurador of the Mercedarians 15.3.1601; Monroy, *Convento de la Merced,* 314–67. Among adults there were only 58 women for every 100 men.

14. AGI AQ 9 Barrio de Sepúlveda 20.7.1600, AQ 9 and ANHQ RH 5 fols. 4r–7v Acuerdo de la real hacienda 18.3.1601.

15. ANHQ RH 2 fol. 71r–v 2.8.1598; AGI AQ 9 Barrio de Sepúlveda 20.7.1600, AQ 25 González 11.4.1600, AQ 9 and ANHQ RH 5 fols. 4r-7v Acuerdo de real hacienda 18.3.1601.

16. AGI AQ 9 Barrio de Sepúlveda 20.7.1600, AQ 9 and ANHQ RH 5 fols. 4r–7v Acuerdo de real hacienda 18.3.1601.

17. AGI AQ 9 Recalde 20.3.1612, AQ 10 Morga 1.4.1620.

18. AGI AL 38 and Rumazo González, *Documentos,* 4:229–30, Viceroy to the Crown 29.4.1619; AGI AQ10 Morga 1.4.1620; Phelan, *Kingdom of Quito,* 18.

19. AGI AQ 10 Morga 1.4.1620.

20. Cabello Balboa, *Obras,* 1:24.

21. Monroy, *Convento de la Merced,* 377 refers to AQ 25 Medina 30.12.1600; see also Nolasco Pérez, *Misiones mercedarias,* 209–15. The latter gives the number participating in the fiesta as 135.

22. AGI AQ 25 Arévalo 22.12.1600; ANHQ RH fols. 4r–7v and AGI AQ 9 Acuerdo de real hacienda 18.3.1601; Mörner, *Race Mixture,* 20.

23. ANHQ PQ 1 fols. 15–16 Hinacapíe 23.3.1607.

24. AGI AQ 9 Información de los indios malabas 9.4.1611.

25. AGI AQ 9 Barrio de Sepúlveda 20.7.1600.

26. Phelan, *Kingdom of Quito,* 21.

27. For examples of these views, see AGI AQ 8 Oidores Barros, Auncibay, Moreno de Mera 6.4.1588, AQ 10 Morga 1.4.1620.

28. For example, ANHQ Cedulario 3 lib. 1 fol. 128 Real cédula 13.7.1627.

29. AGI AQ 9 Barrio de Sepúlveda, no date, AQ 10 Morga 1.4.1620.

30. AGI AQ 8 Oidores 6.4.1588, AQ 8 Auncibay 18.2.1587; Cabello Balboa, *Obras,* 1:19.

31. Rumazo González, *Documentos,* 4:53–74, Troya Pinque 19–23.4.1607.

32. AGI AQ 9 Descripción de los indios infieles 31.5.1597.

33. AGI AQ 25 Arévalo 22.12.1600.

34. AGI AQ 9 Barrio de Sepúlveda 20.7.1600.

CHAPTER 14

1. AGI AQ 8 Santillán 15.1.1564.

2. AMQ LC 1:106–8 Terminos de la ciudad de San Francisco de Quito 28.6.1535.

3. AGI AQ 20B Probanza of Díaz de Pineda 28.1.1539; AMQ LC 2:21–25 Cabildo of Quito 26.2.1539; Cieza de León, *Guerra de Chupas,* cap. 18:179–80; Rumazo González, *Región Amazónica,* 34–43; Porras Garcés, *Baeza,* 27–31; Oberem, *Quijos,* 62–65.

4. Heaton, *Discovery,* 245–50 includes a letter from Pizarro 3.9.1542; López de Gómara, "Hispania Victrix," 243–44; Zarate, "Historia del descubrimiento," lib. 4, caps. 1–3:493–94; Oviedo, *Historia general,* 5, lib. 49, cap. 2:236–37, cap. 6:244–45; lib. 50, cap. 24:374; Garcilaso de la Vega, *Comentarios reales,* 3, lib. 3, caps. 2–4:172–77; Cieza de León, *Guerra de Chupas,* caps. 19–22:180–87. A detailed account of 495 Indians supplied by vecinos of Quito is contained in AMQ LC 2:217–21 21.2.1541.

5. It is not clear why the expedition tarried so long; it is possible that Pizarro was purposely misled by his Indian guides (Oberem, *Quijos,* 67).

6. Oviedo, *Historia general,* 5, lib. 49, cap. 2:239.

7. Garcilaso de la Vega, *Comentarios reales,* 3, lib. 3, cap. 4:175, 177.

8. AGI AQ 85 Díaz Docampo 1605.

9. Oberem, *Quijos,* 70; Vaca de Castro, *Cartas de Indias,* 469; Rumazo González, *Región Amazónica,* 65.

10. Oberem, *Quijos,* 70.

11. AGI PAT 101-19 Fundación de la ciudad de Baeza 1559, commission and instructions issued 15.9.1556; RGI 3:109.

12. Oberem, *Quijos,* 73–74.

13. AGI PAT 101-19 Probanza de Ramírez Dávalos 28.5.1559, AQ 20B Probanza of Don Sancho Hacho 1569.

14. AGI PAT 101-19 Probanza de Ramírez Dávalos—Interrogatorio 1559.

15. AMQ LC 5:232–34; Oberem, *Quijos,* 76.

16. AGI PAT 101-19 Fundación de la ciudad de Baeza 14.5.1559, PAT 97B Información . . . de los servicios de Alonso de Bastidas 1562. Other useful accounts of its foundation are contained in Rumazo González, *Región Amazónica,* 88–99; Porras Garcés, *Baeza,* 55–70; Oberem, *Quijos,* 73–75.

17. Porras Garcés, *Misaguallí,* 144–47.

18. AGI PAT 97B-5 Información . . . de los servicios de Alonso de Bastidas 1562.

19. Rumazo González, *Región Amazónica,* 104–5; Porras Garcés, *Misaguallí,* 27.

20. AGI PAT 97B-5 Información . . . de los servicio de Alonso de Bastidas 1562; Porras Garcés, *Baeza,* 77–78.

21. AGI PAT 97B-5 Información . . . de los servicios de Alonso de Bastidas 1562; Rumazo González, *Región Amazónica,* 106–9; Porras Garcés, *Baeza,* 77–78, 84–86; Oberem, *Quijos,* 76–78.

22. AGI PAT 28-13 Salazar de Villasante, no date, reproduced in Salazar de Villasante, "Exposición," 198–99; RGI 1:139 Salazar de Villasante, no date.

23. BNM 3044 fols. 9–10 Avertencias de Francisco de Toledo 7.8.1569.

24. AGI AQ 20B Probanza of Don Sancho Hacho 1569.

25. AGI AQ 22 Probanza of Bartolomé Marín 2.6.1563.

26. AGI PAT 111-6 Fundación de la ciudad de Avila 8.4.1563. For the foundation of Avila and other towns in the Quijos region, see Szászdi, "Documentos relativos," 264–66.

27. AGI AQ 22 Probanza of Bartolomé Marín 2.6.1563.

28. AGI PAT 111-6 Fundación de la ciudad de Alcalá del Río 14.8.1563. The valley was known by the Indians as Maça, and the principal cacique was called Taxe.

29. Porras Garcés, *Baeza,* 93; Oberem, *Quijos,* 79.

30. AGI AQ 82 Ortegón 1.2.1577.

31. AGI PAT 111-6 Fundación de la ciudad de Alcalá del Río 16.8.1563, AQ 22 Probanza of Bartolomé Marín 2.6.1563; Ortiguera, *Jornada,* cap. 56:339.

32. RGI 1:139 Salazar de Villasante, no date.

33. AGI AQ 8 Santillán 15.1.1564.

34. López de Velasco, *Geografía,* 227–28; CDI 15:499–500 Demarcación y divisón, no date. The source of his information is not clear, but according to López de Velasco, Baeza had eighteen encomenderos, and Avila and Archidona possessed fifteen each.

35. AGI AQ 82 Ortegón 1.2.1577.

36. RGI 2:175 Oficiales reales 30.12.1576.

37. AGI AQ 82 Ortegón 1.2.1577; RGI 2:175 Oficiales reales 30.12.1576; Ortiguera, *Jornada,* cap. 56:340, cap. 58:348–49.

38. Rumazo González, *Región Amazónica,* 189. Ortegón apparently put large packs of dogs to death.

39. AGI AQ 82 Ortegón 1.2.1577.

40. AGI AQ 76 Bishop of Quito 28.1.1580; BNM 3044 fols. 171–72 Archdean of Quito 6.12.1581; AGI AQ 8 Barros 20.3.1588; Compte, *Varones ilustres,* 1:50, includes Zúñiga 15.7.1579; Ortiguera, *Jornada,* cap. 56:340. The fines amounted to the enormous sum of 8,000 pesos.

41. Compte gives the numbers killed as 70 (*Varones ilustres,* 1:50, includes Zúñiga 15.7.1579); Ordóñez de Cevallos gives 93 ("Viaje del mundo," cap. 30:398); and Dr. Barros gives 150 (AGI AQ 8 20.3.1580). For details of the rebellion, see AGI AQ 22 Probanza de Hieronimo Puento 10.2.1578, 19.5.1579; Rumazo González, *Región Amazónica,* 191–216; Ordóñez de Cevallos, "Viaje del mundo," caps. 30–31:379–99; Ortiguera, *Jornada,* caps. 57–60:340–53.

42. AGI AQ 8 Barros 20.3.1588; Ordóñez de Cevallos, "Viaje del mundo," cap. 30:398.

43. AGI AQ 8 Auncibay and Hinojosa 20.2.1580.

44. AGI AQ 8 Auncibay and Hinojosa 20.2.1580.

45. Rumazo González, *Región Amazónica,* 235–36; Oberem, *Quijos,* 90–91.

46. RGI 2:175 Oficiales reales 30.12.1576.

47. Anda Aguirre, *Don Juan de Salinas,* 132.

48. Rumazo González, *Región Amazónica,* 235–42.

49. RGI 1:77 Lemus y Andrade 16.2.1608. The Spanish reads "unas viruelas malinas."

50. RGI 1:82–84 Lemus y Andrade 16.2.1608; Ordóñez de Cevallos, "Viaje del mundo," cap. 29:396–97. Although Ordóñez de Cevallos worked in Los Quijos from 1590, his account was completed in 1614, some years after he returned to Spain. The date and origin of the figures he includes in his account are unknown, but they are the same as those found in Lemus y Andrade's account written in Spain in 1608. They may have copied from one other or from a third unknown source. The figures given by Lemus y Andrade appear in the accompanying table.

Table N4. Lemus y Andrade Population Figures for Spanish Towns in Los Quijos

Classification	Baeza	Avila	Archidona	Sevilla del Oro	Total
Adult males	20	8	4	20	52
Adult females	20	10	14	30	74
Forasteros	10–12	20	12–16	20	54–68
Encomenderos	20	9	7	19	55

Source: RGI 1:82–84 Lemus y Andrade 16.2.1608.

51. AGI AQ 10 Miranda 15.3.1617.

52. AGI AQ 10 Miranda 25.4.1621.

53. Ordóñez de Cevallos, "Viaje del mundo," cap. 29:397.

54. RGI 1:78 Lemus y Andrade 16.2.1608.

55. AGI AQ 9 Bedón 10.3.1598.

56. AGI AQ 25 Lobato de Sosa, no date. In Los Quijos, mitayos received four

to five tomines a month, and it was suggested that they should be paid one peso, since in Quito they received two pesos a month.

57. AGI AQ 25 Lobato de Sosa, no date; Ordóñez de Cevallos, "Viaje del mundo," cap. 31:399–400.

58. AGI AQ 30 Cárdenas 20.4.1623. See chaps. 4 and 18.

59. Ordóñez de Cevallos, "Viaje del mundo," cap. 31:399–400. This is demonstrated by the contract drawn up by Father Ordóñez de Cevallos and the cacique of Coca, Quispa Senacato, for their peaceful submission.

60. Powers, "Migración vertical," 107, 116–26.

61. AGI AQ 25 Lobato de Sosa, no date; AMQ Morga cedulario pp. 194–95 (fol. 240) 13.7.1627.

62. Powers argues than the underrepresentation of women in Ortegón's visita may reflect this process ("Migración vertical," 118). However, the greater number of men recorded could also reflect a greater concern with tribute payers, or simply inaccurate recording.

63. See chap. 8. The source provides information of the origins of the parents of infants being baptized. Of 2,162 examined for the period August 1594 to December 1600, only 17 came from Los Quijos (0.8 percent), while 92.5 percent came from the sierra.

64. BNM 3044 fol. 478 Alonso de Peñafiel, no date [ca. 1569–70]; Oberem, *Quijos,* 82; Powers, "Migración vertical," 116–17; Powers, "Migration and Socio-Political Change," 72–78, 102, 216–27.

65. Ordóñez de Cevallos, "Viaje del mundo," lib. 2, cap. 34:409

66. AGI AQ 25 Lobato de Sosa, no date.

67. AGI AQ 25 Lobato de Sosa, no date, AQ 31 Cárdenas 2.3.1626.

68. AGI AQ 82 Ortegón 1.2.1577. See also chap. 4.

69. RGI 3:29 Rodríguez Docampo 1650.

70. It is not clear whether Ortegón included single females in the category "solteros." Certainly there are a large number of solteros, which would suggest that he probably did. They could have been included, however, in the category of "muchachos y muchachas." Even if a significant proportion of the latter category were single women, in the case of Baeza there would still be a shortage of adult females (See Powers, "Migración vertical," 118).

71. Ortegón's visita shows that of 16,389 Indians, only 5,219 were "muchachos y muchachas" (AGI AQ 82 Ortegón 1.2.1577). Although less than one-third of the total population may have been children, the picture may not have been as desperate as may first appear, for the ratios for the different jurisdictions are highly variable; the smallest number of children appear among unconverted groups, for which records are likely to have been less accurate. Among the converted Indians children composed just over 50 percent of the total. The picture would be improved even further if the category of "muchachos y muchachas" did not include infants.

72. See chap. 4; AGI PAT 101-19 Probanza of Gil Ramírez Dávalos 1559.

73. AGI AQ 8 Santillán 15.1.1564.

74. López de Velasco, *Geografía,* 228.

75. AGI AQ 82 Ortegón 1.2.1577.

76. AGI AQ 25 Lobato de Sosa, no date.

77. AGI AQ 31 Cárdenas 2.3.1626.

CHAPTER 15

1. AGI AQ 31 Cárdenas 2.3.1626.

2. Taylor and Descola, "Conjunto Jívaro," 37; Taylor, *Versants orientaux,* 323–24, 334–35.

3. Anda Aguirre, *Don Juan de Salinas,* 132; RGI 3:177–84.

4. AGI PAT 93-10-3 Account of an encomienda given to Núñez Bonilla 23.11.1550.

5. A reallocation may have occurred when Nuestra Señora del Rosario was founded.

6. ANHQ Tributos 2 Pérez Navarrete 29.10.1643. In 1586 Canelas Albarrán said he had visited the region in 1576, when he found 4,000 ánimas (BNM 3178 fols. 1–15 1586). This is likely to have been an underestimate, given the size of the encomiendas and the number of tributary Indians present at the end of the century.

7. RGI 3:183 Villanueva 7.2.1584.

8. ANHQ Tributos 2 Pérez Navarrete 29.10.1643.

9. ANHQ Oriente 1 González de Acosta 1587.

10. RGI 2:153 Aldrete 1.12.1582.

11. RGI 1:84 Lemus y Andrade 16.2.1608.

12. AGI AQ 31 Cárdenas 2.3.1626. By 1643 their number had fallen by half, to between 400 and 450 tributary Indians (ANHQ Tributos 2 Pérez Navarrete 29.10.1643), and the decline continued unabated, leaving only 286 tributary Indians in 1662 (AGI CO 1540 Peñalosa 2.8.1662).

13. RGI 3:153 Aldrete 1.12.1582. The Spanish reads "no estar los indios domésticos."

14. RGI 1:84 Lemus y Andrade 16.2.1608; AGI AQ 31 Cárdenas 2.3.1626.

15. AGI AQ 31 Cárdenas 2.3.1626.

16. ANHQ Tributos 2 Pérez Navarrete 29.10.1643.

17. AGI AL 29 Relación de los indios de guerra, no date.

18. ANHQ Tributos 2 Repartición de las alcabalas 6.10.1644. There were seventeen encomenderos in the region with 490 Indians, of whom 98 were employed in the sierra.

19. Taylor and Descola, "Conjunto Jívaro," 37.

20. ANHQ Tributos 2 Pérez Navarrete 29.10.1643.

21. Velasco, *Historia del reino,* 3:287–95; Anda Aguirre, *Don Juan Salinas Loyola,* 334; Taylor and Descola, "Conjunto Jívaro," 44–45; Taylor, *Versants orientaux,* 331–34.

22. This would imply a loss of twenty Indians a year, which seems a reasonable minimum.

23. AGI CO 1540 Peñalosa 2.8.1662.

24. Vacas Galindo, *Exposición sobre los límites,* 3:25.

25. See the discussion of epidemics in chap.17.

26. See the discussion of the Macas in chap. 4.

27. Taylor, *Versants orientaux,* 318.

28. Vacas Galindo, *Exposición sobre los límites,* 3:24–26; Costales and Costales, *Amazonia,* 121–22; Naranjo, "Zonas de refugio," 131–34; Taylor, *Versants*

orientaux, 316–19. Unfortunately, I have been unable to consult the Dominican sources on which these comments are based, but by consensus it appears that the mission was not founded in 1581, as suggested by Father Pierre, *Voyage d'explorations* (1889) and widely quoted.

29. Jouanen, *Compañía de Jesús,* 1:466.

30. See the discussion of the Macas in chap. 4.

<h3 style="text-align:center">CHAPTER 16</h3>

1. AGI AQ 23 Caciques and Indians of the province of Yaguarzongo 10.3.1591.

2. The Jívaro also extended south of the Marañón around Santa María de Nieva, but this region is outside the study area.

3. It was explored by Alonso de Alvarado in 1535, by Juan Porcel in 1545–46, and by Diego de Palomino in 1548. See chap. 4.

4. AGI AQ 18 Hernández—Interrogatorio 21.2.1558; RGI 3:180 Baraona 24.11.1568; Anda Aguirre, "Origenes de Zamora," 72–75.

5. RGI 3:216 Loyola 26.1.1586; RGI 3:216–17 Villanueva Maldonado 7.2.1584; Anda Aguirre, *Don Juan de Salinas,* 57–58, 268. See the discussion of Macas for the establishment of Sevilla del Oro.

6. RGI 3:216 Loyola 26.1.1586; RGI 3:216–17 Villanueva Maldonado 7.2.1584; RGI 3:217 Montesinos, no date, but refers to 1564; RGI 3:218 Salinas 4.2.1577.

7. RGI 3:153 Aldrete 1.12.1582.

8. AGI AQ 8 Auncibay and Hinojosa 7.2.1580, AQ 8 Auncibay 20.2.1580, AQ 18 Espinosa 10.4.1606. One account suggests that sixty Spaniards were killed in the 1579 revolt, but this figure seems high, given the number of Spanish residents (AGI AQ 22 Probanza of Sánchez de la Parra 1584).

9. Taylor and Descola, "Conjunto Jívaro," 44–45.

10. AGI AQ 18 Espinosa 10.4.1606, AQ 32 Cañizares 10.5.1640; AHBC 2a Colección vol. 1 doc. 3 Ocampo, no date; Anda Aguirre, *Don Juan de Salinas,* 316–18. Apparently Captain Francisco Pérez de Vivero attempted to reestablish the town of Logroño but was prevented by the superior forces of the Jívaro (Conde, *Yaguarzongos,* 42).

11. For example, ANHQ Presidencia de Quito 1 fol. 98 Peñalosa 30.1.1616; ANHQ Tributos 2 Navarrete, on behalf of the vecinos of Sevilla del Oro 29.10.1643. The history of the frontier towns of Santiago de las Montañas and Santa María de Nieva is discussed in the next chapter.

12. AGI PAT 240-6 Mendoza, no date.

13. RGI 3:126 Salinas, no date; RGI 3:197 Salinas 10.6.1571.

14. RGI 3:180 Baraona 24.11.1568.

15. RGI 3:137 Alvaro Núñez 18.12.1582; Jaramillo Alvarado, *Historia de la provincia de Loja,* 110.

16. RGI 3:126 Salinas, no date; RGI 3:141 No author, no date.

17. Garcés, *Minas de Zamora,* throughout.

18. RGI 3:149, 150, 152 Aldrete 1.12.1582; Jaramillo Alvarado, *Historia de la provincia de Loja,*146.

19. RGI 3:217 Montesinos, no date; Taylor and Descola, "Conjunto Jívaro," 41.

20. RGI 3:137 Núñez 18.12.1582; RGI 3:153 Aldrete 1.12.1582.

21. Jaramillo Alvarado, *Historia de la provincia de Loja,* 146. This is considerably higher than during the 1560s, when diezmo receipts in the *caja* of Zamora averaged 4,800 pesos. In his *capitulación* for the conquest of Yaguarzongo and Pacamoros, Salinas Loyola had been granted the concession of having to pay only the diezmo on gold and silver produced for twenty years, and this concession was prolonged in subsequent years (AGI AQ 8 Oidores Valverde, Ortegón and Hinojosa 22.1.1578; RGI 3:211 Consejo de Indias 22.1.1571). According to Garcés, *Minas de Zamora,* entries into the *caja* of Zamora for complete years were as follows:

Year	Pesos
1561	3,338
1562	6,780
1563	4,322
1564	4,624

22. AGI PAT 240-6 and RGI 2:332 González Mendoza, no date.

23. AGI AQ 10 Zorilla 15.4.1618.

24. AGI PAT 240-8 Arias Pacheco 1594.

25. RGI 3:135 Salinas, no date.

26. AGI AQ 9 Father Bedón 10.3.1598.

27. AGI AQ 22 Salinas 12.9.1581.

28. AGI AQ 22 Real cédula 7.5.1571.

29. AGI AQ 9 Real cédula 23.5.1580.

30. See AGI AQ 22 Salinas tasaciones from 12.9.1581; Anda Aguirre, *Don Juan de Salinas,* 142–49.

31. AGI AQ 22 Salinas tasaciones from 12.9.1581; RGI 3:134 Salinas, no date; RGI 3:136 Núñez 18.12.1582; RGI 3:149–50 Aldrete 1.12.1582; AGI AQ 31 Velasco 8.2.1627.

32. AGI AQ 22 Salinas 12.9.1581; RGI 3:134 Salinas, no date.

33. RGI 3:129 Salinas, no date; AGI AQ 18 Hernández—Interrogatorio 24.1.1564, AQ 18 Cabildo of Zamora 4.12.1565.

34. AGI AQ 18 Hernández, no date, AQ 18 Cabildo of Zamora 4.12.1565, AQ 211 Real cédula 29.11.1566.

35. RGI 3:129 Salinas, no date.

36. AGI AQ 8 Oidores 18.4.1590.

37. The actual numbers allocated were Valladolid, thirty; Loyola and Santiago de las Montañas, thirty-one each; and Santa María de Nieva, twenty-seven (RGI 3:198–200 Salinas 10.6.1571).

38. AGI AQ 23 Caciques of Yaguarzongo and Jaén 10.3.1591.

39. AGI PAT 192-1-68 Valverde 4.2.1572.

40. For example, see the tasaciones of Salinas from 12.9.1581 in AGI AQ 22.

41. AGI AQ 23 Caciques of Yaguarzongo and Jaén 10.3.1591.

42. AGI EC 912A Memorial de las cosas 1577, AQ 8 Auncibay and Hinojosa

7.2.1580; ANHQ Cedulario 1 fol. 504 Real cédula 26.2.1582; AGI AQ 23 Caciques of Yaguarzongo and Jaén 10.3.1591.

43. AGI EC 912A Memorial de las cosas 1577.

44. AGI AQ 8 Oidores de la Audiencia 22.1.1578.

45. Newson, "Old World Epidemics," 99–100.

46. AGI AQ 8 Dr. Barros 28.2.1591.

47. AGI AQ 23 Caciques of Yaguarzongo and Jaén 10.3.1591.

48. AGI AQ 23 Navarro Biamonte 21.4.1589.

49. Anda Aguirre, *Don Juan de Salinas,* 181–88. Unfortunately Anda Aguirre does not cite his source.

50. Dobyns, "Andean Epidemic History," 501–2.

51. RGI 3:199 Salinas 10.6.1571. See chap. 6.

52. RGI 3:128 Salinas, no date.

53. It is surprising, therefore, to find an excess of males in the order of 20 percent in 1582. Figures provided by an encomendero of Zamora, Alvaro Núñez, for fourteen individual villages in 1582 show a clear predominance of males (100 men : 83 women; RGI 3:136 Núñez 18.12.1582). Governor Aldrete's figures for Yaguarzongo and Pacamoros also show an unexpected predominance of men, in this case an average ratio of 100:80 (RGI 3:147–53 Aldrete 1.12.1582). Most likely the predominance derived from women being underrecorded, but it could have reflected the preferential removal of females from their communities for domestic service.

54. RGI 3:139–41 Relación . . . Nambija, no date. No author is given, but it probably was written by Alvaro Núñez (p. 142n).

55. RGI 3:137–38 Núñez 18.12.1582; RGI 3:142 Relación de Nambija, no date.

56. AGI AQ 76 Bishop of Quito 20.3.1598.

57. RAHM Colección Muñoz A/92 fols. 55–77 Relación de los naturales 1561. The ratio of tributary Indians to the total population is surprisingly high. It may reflect inadequate recording of nontributary Indians.

58. A list of towns in the Audiencia of Quito and the number of Indians in their jurisdictions, possibly drawn up in 1567, recorded that Zamora had twenty-seven encomenderos and 8,000 tributary Indians (RAHM 9/4664 no. 21 Los pueblos despanoles que hay, no date). Although the document is undated, it says that the gobernación of Yaguarzongo and Pacamoros had been conquered about ten years ago; it can therefore be dated at around 1567. López de Velasco suggests that there were 5,000 "indios tributarios" (CDI 15:409–572 Demarcación y división de las Indias, no date; López de Velasco, *Geografía,* 221).The source and date of his information is unknown, but it is likely to have referred to the 1560s.

59. RGI 3:129 Salinas, no date; BNM 3178 fols. 1–15 Canelas Albarrán 1586.

60. AGI AQ 76 Bishop of Quito 2.4.1579.

61. RGI 3:136 Núñez 18.12.1582. It is assumed that his figure included the doctrina of Nambija, which comprised fourteen villages with a total of 1,600 Indians, including men, women, and children. Unfortunately the number of tributary Indians is not recorded (RGI 3:139–41 Relación . . . Nambija, no date).

62. CDI 6:41–63 Relación de los indios tributarios 1.11.1591. The figure almost certainly relates to an earlier date and therefore does not reflect the impact of the epidemics of the late 1580s.

63. RGI 2:308–9 Bishop of Nicaragua 1592.

64. AGI AQ 30 Mexía Sandoval 8.4.1622.

65. See chap. 4.

66. López de Velasco, *Geografía, 229.* There were 1,200 around Valladolid, 6,000 around Loyola, and 7,000 around Santiago de las Montañas.

67. AGI EC 912A Memorial de las cosas 1577. The information on Santiago de las Montañas is much more sketchy.

68. AGI AQ 22 Tasación of Loyola 9.10.1581.

69. RGI 3:147–53 Aldrete 1.12.1582. In fact the document gives 6,616, but the figures for the individual encomiendas sum to 6,719, of whom 3,657 were men.

70. AGI AQ 76 Bishop of Quito 2.4.1579.

71. BNM 3178 fols. 1–15 Canelas Albarrán 1586. He includes 4,000 each for Macas and Santa María de Nieva.

72. AGI AQ 23 Caciques of Yaguarzongo and Jaén 10.3.1591.

73. AGI AQ 23 Caciques of Yaguarzongo and Jaén 10.3.1591, AQ 9 Marañón 1.5.1597.

74. ANHQ Cedulario 1 fol. 391 29.8.1598; AGI AQ 9 Ribero Pacheco 27.3.1612; BNM 2351 fol. 359r–v Viceroy to Crown 16.4.1618.

75. Anda Aguirre, *Don Juan de Salinas,* 316.

76. AGI AQ 18 Espinosa 10.4.1606, AQ 26 Martin de Ocampo 20.4.1606. Not all witnesses testified to the presence of these numbers of Indians. One witness suggested that there were 1,000, not counting those that were in the "comarca," and another that there were 2,000 "indios de pelea sin la otra chusma."

77. Figueroa, *Relación de las misiones,* 92.

78. Jouanen, *Compañía de Jesús,* 1:517.

79. See chap. 4.

80. If it is accepted that at the time of Spanish conquest there were 23,000 Indians (20,000 Jívaro and 3,000 Chirino) in the gobernación of Yaguarzongo and Pacamoros and 10,000 Indians who did not come under permanent Spanish control, then the decline for the two populations between conquest and 1600 was 65 percent for the gobernación and 50 percent for those outside Spanish control.

CHAPTER 17

1. Figueroa, *Relación de las misiones,* 182.

2. RGI 3:200–201 Salinas 10.6.1571; Anda Aguirre, Don Juan de Salinas, 41–50.

3. RGI 3:251 Carvajal 7.10.1591; Figueroa, *Relación de las misiones,* 14; Jouanen, *Compañía de Jesús,* 1:335.

4. RGI 3:251 Carvajal 7.10.1591; Anda Aguirre, *Primeros gobernadores,* 33; Anda Aguirre, *Don Juan de Salinas,* 264.

5. Anda Aguirre, *Primeros gobernadores,* 33. Anda Aguirre's account is based on original documents contained in a private archive in Loja—the Archivo Gongoteña y Jijón—which it has not been possible to consult.

6. For the capitulacíon, see Anda Aguirre, *Primeros gobernadores,* 34–42.

7. Anda Aguirre suggests that twenty-one tribes were settled within ten to

eighteen leagues of the camp on the banks of the Marañón and that 141 Indians came from the Pastaza region giving accounts of large numbers of villages and tribes who wished to recognize royal authority (*Primeros gobernadores,* 44). For accounts of these expeditions, see RGI 3:242–47 Saavedra 24.4.1620; RGI 3:253 Ponce de León 1644; Nolasco Pérez, *Misiones mercedarias,* 239–46.

8. AGI AQ 11 Núñez Castaño 1623; Figueroa, *Relación de las misiones,* 14, 18; Jouanen, *Compañía de Jesús,* 1:335–36; Anda Aguirre, *Primeros gobernadores,* 52. The account by Núñez Castaño suggests that forty-two encomiendas were distributed, though most other accounts suggest that Vaca de Vega was given the right to distribute twenty-four, but in the event, only twenty-one were allocated.

9. AGI AQ 158 Zarate 28.8.1739; Figueroa, *Relación de las misiones,* 15.

10. Figueroa, *Relación de las misiones,* 15.

11. In one case 400 Indians were employed in an expedition among the Cocama, and another 800 accompanied exploratory expeditions along the Marañón and its tributaries (RGI 3:254 Ponce de León 1644; Anda Aguirre, *Primeros gobernadores,* 57–65).

12. AGI AQ 10 Vaca de Vega 1.10.1620. The Maina were described as "flojos y cobardes."

13. RGI 3:254 Ponce de León 1644; Nolasco Pérez, *Misiones mercedarias,* 245.

14. AGI AQ 11 Núñez Castaño 1623; Anda Aguirre, *Primeros gobernadores,* 78–79.

15. Figueroa, *Relación de las misiones,* 10–11.

16. ARSI NRQ 14 fols. 151–52 Gaspar Sobrino 25.10.1640; Chantre y Herrera, *Historia de las misiones,* 47; Figueroa, *Relación de las misiones,* 4, 10–11; Anda Aguirre, *Primeros gobernadores,* 84–87.

17. Chantre y Herrera, *Historia de las misiones,* 48; Figueroa, *Relación de las misiones,* 9; Heredia, *Antigua provincia,* 14; Anda Aguirre, *Primeros gobernadores,* 87.

18. Chantre y Herrera, *Historia de las misiones,* 131; Figueroa, *Relación de las misiones,* 9–10; Jouanen, *Compañía de Jesús,* 1:361–62.

19. Figueroa, *Relación de las misiones,* 15–16, 32–33.

20. Maroni, "Noticias auténticas," 28:202.

21. Figueroa, *Relación de las misiones,* 20.

22. Figueroa, *Relación de las misiones,* 10–11.

23. Figueroa, *Relación de las misiones,* 10–11, 22–23; Jouanen, *Compañía de Jesús,* 1:346, 396.

24. Grohs, *Alto Amazonas,* 37.

25. Chantre y Herrera, *Historia de las misiones,* 578–80.

26. Figueroa, *Relación de las misiones,* 169, 172; Chantre y Herrera, *Historia de las misiones,* 403.

27. Jouanen, *Compañía de Jesús,* 1:404–5.

28. ARSI NRQ 15 I fols. 135–140 García de Zeares 30.5.1686; Figueroa, *Relación de las misiones,* 50, 55, 97.

29. ARSI NRQ 3 Catologi triennales 1610–88, NRQ 5 Catologi breves 1654–87, NRQ Catologi triennales 1690–1756.

30. Figueroa, *Relación de las misiones,* 172, 189; Jouanen, *Compañía de Jesús,* 1:403.

31. Chantre y Herrera, *Historia de las misiones,* 89–90; Jouanen, *Compañía de Jesús,* 1:403.

32. Figueroa, *Relación de las misiones,* 24, 187–88; Jouanen, *Compañía de Jesús,* 1:404–5; Phelan, *Kingdom of Quito,* 33.

33. The most important firsthand accounts for the seventeenth century are those of Figueroa and Fritz, who both worked as missionaries in the province of Mainas. Later important histories and compilations based on these acccounts and other Jesuit letters are those by Velasco, Maroni, Chantre y Herrera, and Jouanen.

34. Sweet, "Upper Amazon Valley"; Grohs, *Alto Amazonas.*

35. Figueroa, *Relación de las misiones,* 33–135; Jouanen, *Compañía de Jesús,* 1:363–94. In 1638 the mission of Limpía Concepción de Jeveros was founded, and subsequently three anejos of Cutinanas, Pambadeques, and Ataguates were established, the last in 1648. Shortly after Santa María de Guallaga was founded among the Cocamillas in the Huallaga Valley, while further upriver the mission of Nuestra Señora del Loreto de Paranapura was established, containing the remnants of the Paranapura, Chayabita, and Muniche, who had been decimated by enslaving raids from Moyobamba. Subsequently two further missions of Barbudos (also called Mayorunas) and Aguanos were established in the Huallaga Valley in 1654.

36. Figueroa, *Relación de las misiones,* 135–59; Jouanen, *Compañía de Jesús,* 1:395–401.

37. Figueroa, *Relación de las misiones,* 164–65.

38. Figueroa, *Relación de las misiones,* 161–62; Jouanen, *Compañía de Jesús,* 1:402. The epidemic of 1661 reduced their numbers to 7,000, of whom 3,100 had been baptized.

39. Velasco, *Historia del reino,* 3:369, 450.

40. AGOFM M/42 fols. 173, 174 No author, no date; Maroni, "Noticias auténticas," 29:119, 244–46; Chantre y Herrera, *Historia de las misiones,* 236, 240–41; Jouanen, *Compañía de Jesús,* 1:438; Astrain, *Historia de la Compañía,* 6, lib. 3, cap. 9:608–10.

41. ARSI NRQ 14 fol. 150 Razón y noticia de las reducciones 1686, NRQ 15 I fols. 135–40 García de Zeares 30.5.1686; Chantre y Herrera, *Historia de las misiones,* 250; Jouanen, *Compañía de Jesús,* 1:488; Velasco, *Historia del reino,* 3:385, 392. The figure of 4,030 refers to baptisms between 1669 and 1686.

42. Chantre y Herrera, *Historia de las misiones,* 280; Jouanen, *Compañía de Jesús,* 1:475–78.

43. Velasco, *Historia del reino,* 3:369–70, 450–51.

44. Grohs, *Alto Amazonas,* 34.

45. Grohs, *Alto Amazonas,* 33–113 passim.

46. ARSI NRQ 14 fol. 150 Razón y noticia de las reducciones 1686, NRQ 15 I fols. 135–40 García de Zeares 30.5.1686; Jouanen, *Compañía de Jesús,* 1:487–88, p. 488n.

47. Figueroa, *Relación de las misiones,* 161–62; Jouanen, *Compañía de Jesús,* 1:402.

48. Chepeo, Urarina, Payagua, and Yameo were taken to Santiago de la Laguna for use as interpreters (Maroni, "Noticias auténticas," 30:130–31; Chan-

tre y Herrera, *Historia de las misiones,* 283), while Roamaina and Gae were taken to Borja (Figueroa, *Relación de las misiones,* 136–37, 141, 156–57).

49. Chantre y Herrera, *Historia de las misiones,* 292–96; Vacas Galindo, "Misiones de Mainas," 15–17; Grohs, *Alto Amazonas,* 72–75.

50. Fritz, *Journey,* 132. Heredia, maintains there were forty settlements with 40,000 Indians (*Antigua provincia,* 23).

51. Phelan, *Kingdom of Quito,* 34.

52. Chantre y Herrera, *Historia de las misiones,* 580, 582–83.

53. Figueroa, *Relación de las misiones,* 165. For example, by that date the population of the Jevero missions had fallen from 1,600 to 800 (Figueroa, *Relación de las misiones,* 72, 266), while only 1,500 souls remained of the 9,000 to 10,000 Roamaina-Zapa who had been pacified (Figueroa, *Relación de las misiones,* 149–50).

54. Figueroa, *Relación de las misiones,* 183.

55. Figueroa, *Relación de las misiones,* 121.

56. Figueroa, *Relación de las misiones,* 121, 143.

57. Chantre y Herrera, *Historia de las misiones,* 580.

58. Figueroa, *Relación de las misiones,* 25–26; Jouanen, *Compañía de Jesús,* 1:346. It also struck the Upper Huallaga Valley and Huánuco, where it was said to have killed 10,000 Indians ("Autos fechos," 326–27, Petition by Hazana on behalf of Riva Herrera 22.12.1653).

59. Figueroa, *Relación de las misiones,* 15.

60. Figueroa, *Relación de las misiones,* 384.

61. Figueroa, *Relación de las misiones,* 84–85, 266; Jouanen, *Compañía de Jesús,* 1:392.

62. Figueroa, *Relación de las misiones,* 81, 84–85.

63. Jouanen, *Compañía de Jesús,* 1:398.

64. "Autos fechos," 469–76, Testimonio de las enfermedades que ha padecido el General Don Martín de la Riva Herrera en la pacificación de las provincias de los infieles 17.10.1656.

65. Figueroa, *Relación de las misiones,* 85, 109.

66. "Autos fechos," 436, Velásquez de Medrano 22.1.1657. See also pp. 469–76, Testimonio de las enfermedades 17.10.1656. Polo, *Epidemias en el Perú,* 23–25, and Browne, "Epidemic Disease," app. 3, p. 162, list a number of epidemics in the sierra in the 1640s and 1650s.

67. "Autos fechos," 437, Velásquez de Medrano 22.1.1657.

68. Manson-Bahr, *Tropical Diseases,* 49.

69. Figueroa, *Relación de las misiones,* 149; Jouanen, *Compañía de Jesús,* 1:399

70. Figueroa, *Relación de las misiones,* 149, 271; Jouanen, *Compañía de Jesús,* 1:399.

71. Figueroa, *Relación de las misiones,* 161–62.

72. Chantre y Herrera, *Historia de las misiones,* 205–6; Velasco, *Historia del reino,* 3:450. Figueroa notes only the presence of measles (*Relación de las misiones,* 159).

73. Velasco, *Historia del reino,* 3:450.

74. ARSI NRQ 13 I fol. 14 Relación annua 1655–60 written 20.2.1661. The epidemic in Quito was identified as "sarampión, alfombrilla, y viruelas."

75. Velasco, *Historia del reino,* 3:450.

76. ARSI NRQ 15 I fols. 79–80 Lucero 3.6.1681; Chantre y Herrera, *Historia de las misiones,* 276; Figueroa, *Relación de las misiones,* 416; Velasco, *Historia del reino,* 3:450–51.

77. Velasco, *Historia del reino,* 3:369, 451.

78. Maroni, "Noticias auténticas," 28:144–45.

79. See chap. 6.

80. Ramenofsky, *Vectors of Death,* 146–48.

81. Figueroa, *Relación de las misiones,* 414–17, Father Lucero 3.6.1681; Jouanen, *Compañía de Jesús,* 1:477.

82. Neel, "Health and Disease," 161, 163; Polunin, "Tribal Peoples," 14.

83. Chantre y Herrera, *Historia de las misiones,* 176.

84. Sweet, "Upper Amazon Valley," 135; Polunin, "Tribal Peoples," 14, 18.

85. Sweet, "Upper Amazon Valley," 141.

86. Harvey, "Cahuilla Indians," 195–96.

87. McFalls and McFalls, *Disease and Fertility,* 534.

88. Velasco, *Historia del reino,* 3:450–51.

89. Ramenofsky, *Vectors of Death,* 170. In fact in the absence of immunity and medical attention the mortality level in a smallpox epidemic may be as high as 100 percent.

90. This figure may be reached by accepting Sweet's assumption that about half of the Indian population of the province of Mainas was contained in the missions in the late seventeenth century (Sweet, "Upper Amazon Valley," 129), together with Velasco's figures for the numbers killed in epidemics and in the missions at that time, and assuming that mission populations were sustained by new recruits rather than natural increase. Assuming that there were 100,000 Indians in the missions and 100,000 outside prior to the epidemic in 1660 and that the three specified epidemics did result in the loss of 44,000, 20,000, and 66,000 missionized Indians respectively, and that the losses were made up to 80,000 in 1669 and 100,000 in 1680 by recruiting 24,000 and 40,000 respectively from the nonmissionized population, that would leave 34,000 Indians in the missions and 36,000 outside, of the original total of 200,000.

91. Figueroa, *Relación de las misiones,*165.

92. Chantre y Herrera, *Historia de las misiones,* 609–10.

93. Figueroa, *Relación de las misiones,* 138; Jouanen, *Compañía de Jesús,* 1:396, 484; Anda Aguirre, *Primeros gobernadores,* 88.

94. Figueroa, *Relación de las misiones,* 173–74.

95. Phelan, *Kingdom of Quito,* 36.

96. Figueroa, *Relación de las misiones,* 14, 22; Jouanen, *Compañía de Jesús,* 1:346.

97. Figueroa, *Relación de las misiones,* 157; Jouanen, *Compañía de Jesús,* 1:401.

98. See the discussion this process in chap. 4.

99. This episode is described in Morton, "Spanish Exploratory and Missionary Activity," 69–101, 146–56. Many of the documents that form the basis of this study have been published in *Revista de los Archivos y Bibliotecas Nacionales* (Lima) 3 (1899). See also Maroni, "Noticias auténticas," 29:100–102; Figueroa,

Relación de las misiones, 84–85, 148–49, 170–72; Jouanen, *Compañía de Jesús,* 1:417–22, 426.

100. At that time the post was in dispute between Mauricio Vaca de Evan, the original governor's second son, and the *corregidor* of Quito.

101. "Autos fechos," 43–49, 17.4.1650; p. 340, Real acuerdo 3.12.1654.

102. For an account of these entradas by Riva Herrera, see "Autos fechos," 483–520, Diligencias fechas . . . Don Martín de la Riba 30.11.1657; Morton, "Spanish Exploratory and Missionary Activity," 78–82.

103. A later account suggested there had been forty-six settlers.

104. "Autos fechos," 415–56, Fundación de la ciudad de Santander, various testimonies 1656–57.

105. "Autos fechos," 517–20, Cueva to the Viceroy 30.11.1657.

106. The Jesuits supported the aspirations of Mauricio Vaca de Evan, since it was under his father's governorship that the Jesuits had been invited to work in the region, and they felt their position might be threatened by Riva Herrera or the corregidor of Quito, Gonzalo Rodríguez de Monroy. The former was supported by the other missionary orders, who hoped to expand their jurisdictions. Although the bitter attack on Riva Herrera's expeditions was probably justified, it should be seen in the context of this rivalry between the missionary orders.

107. Maroni, "Noticias auténticas," 29:92–95, 224–26; Chantre y Herrera, *Historia de las misiones,* 131, 234–35; Figueroa, *Relación de las misiones,* 9–10; Jouanen, *Compañía de Jesús,* 1:361–62, 449–55, 458–59.

108. In 1641, for example, 100 Roamaina were captured but had to be released under threat of attack by larger numbers of Indians (Figueroa, *Relación de las misiones,* 140–41; Jouanen, *Compañía de Jesús,* 1:396–97).

109. For example, in 1664 the expedition among the Cocama returned to Borja with a number of Chepeo from the Upper Ucayali (Jouanen, *Compañía de Jesús,* 1:449).

110. Phelan, *Kingdom of Quito,* 32; Porras, *Gobernación y obispado de Mainas,* 70.

111. Sweet, "Upper Amazon Valley," 96–97; Phelan, *Kingdom of Quito,* 37; Grohs, *Alto Amazonas,* 75–77.

112. Sweet, "Upper Amazon Valley," 122.

113. In 1660 an exceptional number of 340 fugitive Indians were rounded up and brought back to Borja (Figueroa, *Relación de las misiones,* 22).

114. RGI 3:147 Aldrete 1.12.1582; Taylor, "Versants orientaux," 287.

115. Maroni, "Noticias auténticas," 29:87; Jouanen, *Compañía de Jesús,* 1:401.

116. Figueroa, *Relación de las misiones,* 22; Jouanen, *Compañía de Jesús,* 1:346.

117. Figueroa, *Relación de las misiones,* 9–10; Jouanen, *Compañía de Jesús,* 1:361–62.

118. Jouanen, *Compañía de Jesús,* 1:377, 380–82, 449–55.

119. For example, 320 were used to pacify the Aguano (Jouanen, *Compañía de Jesús,* 1:392–93), 200 in the suppression of the revolt of the Cocama (Jouanen, *Compañía de Jesús,* 1:454), and 300 and 800 on different entradas among the Jívaro (Jouanen, *Compañía de Jesús,* 1:481–83, 506, 515).

120. For example, Father Enrique Richter conducted a two-year expedition among the Jívaro on which he took 100 Cunivo (Maroni, "Noticias auténticas," 30:151; Grohs, *Alto Amazonas,* 115).

121. Figueroa, *Relación de las misiones,* 15, 109, 157, 400; Jouanen, *Compañía de Jesús,* 1:404.

122. Figueroa, *Relación de las misiones,* 136; Jouanen, *Compañía de Jesús,* 1:395.

123. Figueroa, *Relación de las misiones,* 157.

124. Figueroa, *Relación de las misiones,* 21.

125. ARSI NRQ 15 I fols. 79–80 Lucero 3.6.1681.

126. Jouanen, *Compañía de Jesús,* 1:403.

127. Amalgamations were often precipitated by an epidemic, revolt, or hostile attack. For example, the final blow to the mission of Santa María de Guallaga, which had been attacked by the Cocama, came with the 1680 epidemic, when it was dissolved and the remaining Indians moved to Santiago de la Laguna (Maroni, "Noticias auténticas," 28:418).

128. Chantre y Herrera, *Historia de las misiones,* 585.

129. Chantre y Herrera, *Historia de las misiones,* 606–7.

130. Chantre y Herrera, *Historia de las misiones,* 586, 594, 597; Figueroa, *Relación de las misiones,* 82.

131. Maroni, "Noticias auténticas," 30:135, 143; Chantre y Herrera, *Historia de las misiones,* 211.

132. Figueroa, *Relación de las misiones,* 166.

133. Maroni, "Noticias auténticas," 29:244–46; Chantre y Herrera, *Historia de las misiones,* 244; Figueroa, *Relación de las misiones,* 401; Jouanen, *Compañía de Jesús,* 1:404.

134. Maroni, "Noticias auténticas," 29:244–46; Chantre y Herrera, *Historia de las misiones,* 240–41, 244.

135. Krzywicki, *Primitive Society,* 201–2.

136. See Sweet's figures for the eighteenth century, "Upper Amazon Valley," apps. B and C, pp. 373–74.

137. Figueroa, *Relación de las misiones,* 400.

138. ARSI NRQ 15 I fols. 79–80 Lucero 3.6.1681; Chantre y Herrera, *Historia de las misiones,* 72–77, 274–75; Figueroa, *Relación de las misiones,* 111.

139. Taylor, "Evolution démographique," 235–36.

140. Neel, "Health and Disease," 156–58, 162–63 discusses this issue for the Yanomama.

141. Figueroa, *Relación de las misiones,* 161; Jouanen, *Compañía de Jesús,* 1:402.

142. Figueroa, *Relación de las misiones,* 218; Jouanen, *Compañía de Jesús,* 1:404.

143. Figueroa, *Relación de las misiones,* 183.

144. Figueroa, *Relación de las misiones,* 75, 135, 218; Jouanen, *Compañía de Jesús,* 1:377.

145. Figueroa, *Relación de las misiones,* 48.

146. Jouanen, *Compañía de Jesús,* 1:403.

147. Figueroa, *Relación de las misiones,* 73, 83, 369, 377.

148. Maroni, "Noticias auténticas," 27:84.

149. See n. 90.

150. See chap. 18; AGI AQ 88 Información sobre las entradas que Alonso de Miranda . . . hizo 1630.

CHAPTER 18

1. AGI AQ 31 Cárdenas 2.3.1626.

2. AGI PAT 111-6 Dávila 14.8.1563; Rumazo González, *Región Amazónica,* 124–25.

3. AGI AQ 8 Santillán 15.1.1564; ARSI NRQ 14 fol. 65 Ferrer 9.7.1608; López de Velasco, *Geografía,* 228.

4. AGI AQ 82 Ortegón 1.2.1577.

5. Ordonez de Cevallos, "Viaje del mundo," lib. 2, cap. 34:409; Oberem, "Grupo indígena desaparecido," 152–54.

6. Friede, "Kofán," 203; Velasco, *Historia del reino,* 3:257.

7. Ordonez de Cevallos, "Viaje del mundo," lib. 2, cap. 29:397, cap. 32:403–4.

8. Ordóñez de Cevallos, "Viaje del mundo," lib. 2, cap. 33:406.

9. ARSI NRQ 12 I fols. 24–35 Letra annua 1606.

10. Maroni, "Noticias auténticas," 28:178; Chantre y Herrera, *Historia de las misiones,* 28–31; Barnuevo, *Relación apologética,* 8–9; Heredia, *Antigua provincia,* 9–11; Jouanen, *Compañía de Jesús,* 1:100–103; Velasco, *Historia del reino,* 3:256–61.

11. ARSI NRQ 14 fol. 65 Ferrer 9.7.1608; Maroni, "Noticias auténticas," 28:173–76.

12. Jouanen, *Compañía de Jesús,* 1:103–6.

13. AGI AQ 10 Miranda 25.4.1621; Phelan, *Kingdom of Quito,* 26.

14. Referred to in the documents as San Pedro de Alcalá del Río Dorado.

15. Maroni, "Noticias auténticas," 28:182–84; Jouanen, *Compañía de Jesús,* 1:319–20; Barnuevo, *Relación apologética,* 19. Quebeno was the name given to the *quebrada* de Eno.

16. AGI AQ 31 Información . . . de los Cofanes 23.6.1623.

17. AGI AQ 31 Cárdenas 2.3.1626.

18. AGI AQ 88 Información sobre las entradas que Alonso de Miranda . . . hizo 1630. Other groups mentioned included Coporates, Urasunis (Yurusunis), Mires, Peguas, Ocayures (Ucayares), Seños, Becabas, Mancosales, Amantios (Amanantios, Aguantios), and Ocochas.

19. Acuña, *Nuevo descubrimiento,* 116, 125; Maroni, "Noticias auténticas," 28:190; Oberem, "Grupo indígena desaparecido," 158; Grohs, *Alto-Amazonas,* 22.

20. Cruz, "Nuevo descubrimiento," 185; Oberem, "Grupo indígena desaparecido," 158–64.

21. Figueroa, *Relación de las misiones,* 346, Zarate 28.8.1739; Barnuevo, *Relación apologética,* 14.

22. Cruz, "Nuevo descubrimiento," 148–61; Maldonado, *Relación del descubrimiento,* 7, 16; Rumazo González, *Región Amazónica,* 255–61.

23. AGOFM M/42 fols. 144–45 Real cédula 31.12.1642, fols. 151–52 Relación del viaje . . . Domingo de Brieva, no date; Acuña, *Nuevo descubrimiento,* 12–18, 24–33; Chantre y Herrera, *Historia de las misiones,* 49–52; Izaguirre, *Misiones franciscanos,* 1:182, 334–36; Jouanen, *Compañía de Jesús,* 1:349. It has been suggested that the Jesuits were favored over the Franciscans because of personal contacts the former possessed with colonial officials (Izaguirre, *Misiones franciscanos,* 1:182; Rumazo González, *Región Amazónica,* 270). Accounts vary as to the number of Indians that accompanied the expedition upriver.

24. Acuña, *Nuevo descubrimiento,* 109–10.

25. Acuña, *Nuevo descubrimiento,* 115, 117.

26. Cruz, "Nuevo descubrimiento," 178.

27. Cruz, "Nuevo descubrimiento," 186–91, 195.

28. Grohs, *Alto Amazonas,* 25.

29. Cruz, "Nuevo descubrimiento," 188–89.

30. AGOFM M/42 fols. 169–72 San Julián 3.2.1694; Compte, *Varones ilustres,* 2:49.

31. Heredia, *Antigua provinica,*15; Velasco, *Historia del reino,* 3:367.

32. Sweet, "Upper Amazon Valley," 92–93.

33. AGI AQ 158 Father Thomas Nieto, no date [1735?]; Heredia, *Antigua provinica,* 21; Velasco, *Historia del reino,* 3:430. For the spread of disease from Santiago de la Laguna in 1680, see chap. 17.

34. AGOFM M/41 fols. 451–52 Rodríguez 1780; Chantre y Herrera, *Historia de las misiones,* 316. The former gives the date of the real cédula as 18.6.1686 rather than 18.6.1683.

35. Maroni, "Noticias auténticas," 26:260, 30:206; Jouanen, *Compañía de Jesús,* 1:499.

36. Vickers, "Adaptation to Amazonian Habitats," 40–46.

37. Maroni, "Noticias auténticas," 29:223–27, 236, 246.

38. Anda Aguirre, *Primeros gobernadores,* 119; Velasco, *Historia del reino,* 3:445–46.

39. Compte, *Varones ilustres,* 2:49. The account is rather ambiguous, but it would appear that the 6,000 baptized were all Abijira and that among them the Franciscans had established the pueblos of Nuestra Señora de Guadalupe, Encarnación de Abijiras, San Buenaventura, and San Francisco.

40. AGOFM M/42 fols. 169–72 San Julián 3.2.1694.

41. Compte, *Varones ilustres,* 2:49.

42. See chap. 14.

43. Vázquez, "Omagua y Dorado," 431.

44. Cruz, "Nuevo descubrimiento," 188–89.

45. See chap. 17.

46 AGI AQ 88 Información sobre las entradas que Alonso de Miranda . . . hizo 1630.

47. See chap.4.

48. Sweet, "Upper Amazon Valley," 143–45.

49. Cruz, "Nuevo descubrimiento," 192. See also chap. 4.

50. For example, among the Abijira (Maroni, "Noticias auténticas," 29:244–46; Chantre y Herrera, *Historia de las misiones,* 240–41, 244).

51. AGI AQ 88 Información sobre las entradas que Alonso de Miranda . . . hizo 1630.

52. Cruz, "Nuevo descubrimiento," 186–89. San Pedro de Alcántara had 80 "indios de lanzas" and 250 "almas"; Sacayey, 30 Indians with few women and children; and Carante, 40 vecinos and altogether 120 "almas."

53. Oberem, "Grupo indígena desaparecido," 162–64.

54. Friede, "Los Kofán," 210; Neumann, "Quijos y Cofanes," 66, 76 n. 7.

55. Figueroa, *Relación de las misiones,* 309–10.

56. Sweet, "Upper Amazon Valley," 72.

57. Maroni, "Noticias auténticas," 29:246. The first seven rancherías he visited had 800 Indians.

58. Velasco, *Historia del reino,* 3:445–46.

59. Velasco, *Historia del reino,* 3:450.

60. Anda Aguirre, *Primeros gobernadores,* 119. The figure could refer to warriors and hence able-bodied males, but the large number suggests this is unlikely.

61. Compte, *Varones ilustres,* 2:49. The account is rather ambiguous, but it would appear that the 6,000 baptized were all Abijira.

62. AGOFM M/42 fols. 169–72 San Julián 3.2.1694.

63. See chap. 17.

64. Sweet, "Upper Amazon Valley," 103.

65. Grohs, *Alto Amazonas,* 101–10.

66. Vickers, "Territorial Dimensions," 453.

CHAPTER 19

1. AGI AQ 76 Bishop of Quito 20.3.1598.

2. Denevan, "Aborginal Population"; Sweet, "Upper Amazon Valley"; Taylor, "Évolution démographique."

3. Cook, *Demographic Collapse,* 96.

4. Steward, "Native Population," 660, 663; Rosenblat, *Población indígena,* 1:102; Cisneros Cisneros, *Demografía,* 110; Phelan, *Kingdom of Quito,* 45.

5. Tyrer, "Demographic and Economic History"; Browne, "Epidemic Disease"; Larrain Barros, *Demografía;* Sweet, "Upper Amazon Valley."

6. Alchon, *Native Society and Disease,* 47. Some care is needed in interpreting the figures, for the arithmetic is slightly faulty, and the figures are inconsistently related to the whole of Ecuador and the highlands. Compare pp. 18 and 47.

7. AGI AL 120 Relación de los naturales de los reinos del Perú 1561.

8. Cook, *Demographic Collapse,* 114.

9. Calculated from Cook, *Demographic Collapse,* table 18 (p. 94) and table 19 (p. 96).

10. Cook and Borah, *Essays,* 2:82.

11. Calculated from Cook, *Demographic Collapse,* table 18 (p. 94) and table 19 (p. 96).

12. AGI AQ 10 Morga 15.4.1623.

APPENDIX 1

1. RAHM 9/4664 nos. 1–2 fols. 27v–29v Tasaciones for the province of Cañar, Chambo, and Otavalo, no date; AGI JU 683 fols. 817v, 839r, 856v Visita de la encomienda de Francisco Ruiz 1559, PAT 133-3 Información de servicios de Juan de Narváez 14.1.1591.

2. AGI JU 672 Relación de los vecinos encomenderos e indios visitados, no

date, and BM Add. Mss 33,983 fol. 236 La visita y tasa de Presidente Gasca, no date.

3. Otavalo was reassessed in 1552 by Pedro Muñoz and Pedro Moreno, vecinos of Quito (AGI EC 922A Tasa de Otavalo 30.11.1562).

4. AGI AQ 60 Traslado del libro de tasaciones 13.12.1558.

5. AGI JU 683 fols. 798r–874v Visita de la encomienda de Francisco Ruiz 1559.

6. AGI EC 922A Tasa de Otavalo 30.11.1562.

7. AGI JU 671 fols. 242r–257r Visita de los Puruháes 1557.

8. Mansilla, *Tributo indígena,* 50 n. 50.

9. RAHM 9/4664 no. 21 Los pueblos despañoles que hay, no date. The document notes that the province of Yaguarzongo had been conquered ten years previously, which was in 1557.

10. AGI AQ 32 Vázquez de Acuña 4.4.1636.

11. Mansilla, *Tributo indígena,* 263–64; CDI 6:47–48 Relación de los indios tributarios que hay 1.11.1591.

12. AGI AQ 60 Tasación de los tributos 1570–71.

13. AGI AQ 22 Tasa of Ambato 8.2.1575; CDI 9:452–88 Descripción . . . de la villa del Villar Don Pardo 1605.

14. López de Velasco, *Geografía,* 204–31. His figure for Pasto is similar to López's visita of 1558.

15. BNM 3178 fols. 1–15 Descripción do todos los reinos del Peru 1586.

16. The tributary populations taken from CDI 6:61 are 2,198 for Guayaquil and 1,253 for Puerto Viejo.

17. For example, of Riobamba (AGI AQ 8 Visita of Riobamba 1581), Chimbo (RGI 2:256–59 Cantos 7.10.1582), and the gobernación of Salinas (AGI AQ 22 Tasas for the gobernación of Salinas 12.9.1581).

18. CDI 6:43–61 Relación de los indios tributarios que hay 1.11.1591. The summary figures are Quito, 24,380; Cuenca, 1,474; Loja, 2,849; Zamora, 685; Guayaquil, 2,198; and Puerto Viejo, 1,253.

19. Cook, *Demographic Collapse,* 51, 78–79; Mansilla, *Tributo indígena,* 165.

20. RGI 2:315–16 Relación del distrito del cerro de Zaruma, no date.

21. AGI AQ 81 Fr. Francisco Morales 13.11.1552.

22. BM Add. Mss. 33,983 fol. 236 La visita y tasa de Presidente Gasca, no date.

23. RGI 2:224 La cibdad de San Francisco del Quito 1573; AGI AQ 17 Cabildo of Quito 23.1.1577.

24. AGI AQ 9 Crown to Audiencia 19.10.1591, also in AMQ CR 9:489–91 and CDI 19:147–49.

25. AGI PAT 191-1-68 Valverde 4.2.1572.

26. RGI 2:169 Officials of the royal exchequer 30.12.1576.

27. AGI AQ 32 Váquez de Acuña 4.4.1636.

28. RGI 2:183 Anon. no date.

29 AGI AQ 9 Mejía Mosquera 29.3.1598.

30. AGI AQ 76 Bishop of Quito 20.2.1595.

31. For example, RGI 2:183 Anon., no date.

32. RGI 2:276 Arias Dávila 1.5.1582; RGI 2:283 Gómez et al. June 1582; RGI

2:286 Gaviria 4.5.1582; RGI 2:288 Italiano 18.10.1582; RGI 2:302 Salinas 1571 or 1572.

33. For example, AGI AQ 20B Tellez 3.1.1552, AQ 8 Santillán 15.1.1564; RGI 2:169 Officials of the royal exchequer 30.12.1576; RGI 2:202 Rodríguez Aguayo, no date; RGI 2:224 La cibdad de Sant Francisco del Quito 1573; AGI AQ 10 Ibarra 20.4.1616, AQ 10 Morga 15.4.1623, AQ 34 Suárez de Poago 2.5.1634.

34. AGI AQ 24 Freire 30.3.1593, AQ 10 Morga 20.4.1616, AQ 10 Morga 15.4.1623.

Bibliography

ARCHIVAL SOURCES

Archival research on sixteenth-century Spanish America necessarily involves piecing together evidence from a wide variety of sources. When I started this project in 1980, I envisaged it would be a short one, but the sources proved richer than expected. Colonial research benefits from both local and colonial perspectives. The most important archives for this research were the Archivo General de Indias (AGI) in Seville and the Archivo Nacional de la Historia (ANHQ) and the Archivo Municipal (AMQ) in Quito. The AGI is particularly important for the sixteenth century, for which fewer documents have survived in Quito. The most important sections researched for this study were the Audiencia of Quito, Patronato, and Escribanía de Cámara. Demographic materials for Ecuador are fragmentary, and tribute lists and visitas do not exist on the same scale as for Peru. Documents in the AGI are currently being digitalized for viewing by computer. As of September 1993 about 10 percent of its total collection had been computerized. The ability to transform computer images facilitates the reading of sixteenth-century documents, while the rudimentary indexing makes it easier to locate relevant materials by date, name, place, or subject. During the process of computerization a few documents have been transferred to different *legajos*. This should not pose a significant problem, but in tracing materials referred to here, readers may find that a few documents have been moved. The main legajos used for this study that have been computerized are Audiencia of Quito 6–26, 45–61, 329–46, and all of Patronato. In Madrid two other archives providing additional information were the Real Academia de la Historia (RAHM), which houses the Colección Muñoz, comprising important early transcripts of sixteenth-century documents, and the Biblioteca Nacional (BNM), which contains a small number of essential documents, mainly geographical descriptions.

In Ecuador the two most important archives researched in were the Archivo Nacional de Historia and the Archivo Municipal, though the former contains relatively few documents from the sixteenth century. Although all sections were investigated, those of most relevance to this study were those entitled Presidencia de Quito and Real Hacienda. The Archivo Muncipal contains an excellent series of cabildo records from the sixteenth century, many of which have been published by the archive. The archives of the missionary orders proved frustratingly uninformative. It was not possible to gain access to the Mercedarian archive, and it was possible to view only a few documents in the Jesuit archive at Cotocallao. The Dominican archive contains the collection of Spanish transcripts made by E. Vacas Galindo. These are generally unreliable; if possible, researchers should use alternative copies. The Franciscan archives proved the most rewarding, containing a small number of sixteenth-century documents relating mainly to the Quito Basin. Evidence for missionary activities was also sought at the headquarters of the Jesuit and Franciscan orders in Rome. The Archivum Romanum Societatis Iesu (ARSI) and Archivio Generale dell'Ordine dei Frati Minori (AGOFM) provided information on their activities in the Oriente. Many of the documents they contain have been transcribed or paraphrased in histories of the respective orders, notably in those of Astrain, Barnuevo, Chantre y Herrera, Jouanen, and Maroni for the Jesuits, and Compte and Izaguirre for the Franciscans.

Only a few collections of published documents exist for early colonial Ecuador. Undoubtedly the most useful, particularly for the sierra, were the transcriptions of sixteenth-century documents by M. Jiménez Espada contained in the *Relaciones geográficas de Indias* (RGI). Another similar collection referring exclusively to Ecuador has recently been published by P. Ponce Leiva in *Relaciones histórico-geográficas*. For the early history of Esmeraldas the *Colección de documentos para la historia de la audiencia de Quito* compiled by J. Rumazo González was particularly useful, but the volumes are not readily available. As for most studies of the early colonial period, two Spanish collections of unedited documents (CDI) and (CDIU) contained some essential materials. The Archivo Histórico del Banco Central (AHBC) in Quito contains some original manuscripts and a large number of transcripts and microfilm from many of the archives mentioned above, and it is an important source particularly for those unable to visit archives in Europe.

PUBLISHED WORKS

Acosta-Solís, M. *Divisiones fitogeográficas y formaciones geobotánicas del Ecuador.* Quito: Casa de la Cultura Ecuatoriana, 1968.

———. *Fitogeografía y vegetación de la provincia de Pichincha.* Plan piloto del Ecuador, sección geografía, publicaciones no. 249. Mexico City: Instituto Panamericano de Geografía e Historia, 1962.

———. *Los recursos naturales del Ecuador y su conservación.* 2 pts., 3 vols. Mexico City: Instituto Panamericano de Geografía e Historia, 1965.

Acuña, C. de. *Nuevo descubrimiento del gran río de las Amazonas.* Colección de libros que tratan de América raros o curiosos, vol. 2. Madrid: Imp. J. C. García, 1891.

Albornoz, V. M. *Cuenca: Monografía histórica.* Cuenca: Editorial Austral, 1948.

———. *Monografía histórica del Girón.* Cuenca: Casa Editora de J. M. Asterdillo Regalado, 1935.

Albuja Galindo, A. *Estudio monográfico del cantón Cotocachi.* Quito: Talleres Gráficos Minerva, 1962.

Albuja Mateus, A. E. "El obispado de Quito en el siglo XVI." *Misionalia hispánica* 18, no. 53 (1961): 161–209.

Alchon, S. A. *Native Society and Disease in Colonial Ecuador.* Cambridge: Cambridge University Press, 1991.

Alcina Franch, J. "Tomebamba y el problema de los indios cañaris de la sierra sur del Ecuador." *Anuario de estudios americanos* 37 (1980): 403–33.

Alcina Franch, J., and M. C. García Palacios. "Materias primas y tecnología en

Esmeraldas." In *Proceedings of the Forty-second International Congress of Americanists* (Paris), 9A:303–18. 1979.

Alcina Franch, J., E. Moreno, and R. de la Peña. "Penetración española en Esmeraldas (Ecuador): Tipología del descubrimiento." *Revista de Indias* 36 (1976): 65–121.

Alcina Franch, J., and R. de la Peña. "Etnías y culturas en el área de Esmeraldas durante el período colonial español." In *Actas del primer congreso español de antropología,* 2:327–41. Barcelona: Departamento de antropología cultural, Universidad de Barcelona, 1977.

———. "Patrones de asentamiento indígena en Esmeraldas durante los siglos XVI y XVII." In *Proceedings of the Forty-second International Congress of Americanists* (Paris), 9A:283–301. 1979.

Amadio, M. "Los Muratos: Una síntesis histórica." *Amazonia peruana* 6, no. 12 (1976): 117–31.

Anda Aguirre, A. *El Adelantado Don Juan de Salinas Loyola y su gobernación de Yaguarzongo y Pacamoros.* Quito: Casa de la Cultura Ecuatoriana, 1980.

———. *El capitán Mercadillo y el IV centenario de la fundación de Loja.* Quito: Editorial "Fr. Jodoco Ricke," 1948.

———. "Orígenes de Zamora: Rasgos biográficos de Mercadillo." *Museo histórico* 8, no. 24 (1956): 66–86.

———. *Primeros gobernadores de Mainas.* Quito: Editorial Santo Domingo, 1955.

———. *Zaruma en la colonia.* Quito: Casa de la Cultura Ecuatoriana, 1960.

Andrade, M. J. A. *Provincia de El Oro: Monografías cantonales.* Quito: Tip. Escuela de Artes y Oficios, 1923.

Araníbar, C. "Notas sobre la necropompa entre los Incas." *Revista del Museo Nacional* (Lima) 36 (1969–70): 109–42.

Arcos, G. *Evolución de la medicina en el Ecuador.* Quito: Casa de la Cultura Ecuatoriana, 1979.

Aspiazu, M. *Las fundaciones de Santiago de Guayaquil.* Guayaquil: Casa de la Cultura Ecuatoriana, 1955.

Assadourian, C. S. "La despoblación indígena en Perú y Nueva España durante el siglo XVI y la formación de la economía colonial." In *Historia e populaçao: Estudos sobre a América Latina,* ed. S. O. Nadalin, M. L. Marcilio and A. P. Balhana, 253–64. São Paulo: Fundaçao Sistema Estadual de Análise de Dados, 1990.

Astrain, A. *Historia de la Compañía de Jesús en la asistencia de España.* 7 vols. Madrid: Sucesores de Rivadeneyra, 1902–25.

Athens, J. S. *El proceso evolutivo en las sociedades complejas y la ocupación del período tardío: Cara en los andes septentrionales del Ecuador.* Colección Pendoneros, no. 2. Otavalo: Instituto Otavaleño de Antropología, 1980.

Atienza, L. de. "Compendio historial del estado de los indios del Perú." In *La religión del imperio de los incas,* ed. J. Jijón y Caamaño, Appendix 1. Quito: Escuela Tipográfica Salesiana, 1931.

"Autos fechos y actuados por el general D. Martín de la Riva Herrera." *Revista de los archivos y bibliotecas nacionales* (Lima) 3, no. 3–4 (1899): 1–632.

Ayala Mora, T. "Epidemiología de la malaria en el Ecuador y su evaluación en la campana de eradicación." *Revista ecuatoriana de higiene y medicina tropical* (Guayaquil)14, no. 4 (1957): 29–86.

Bakewell, P. *Miners of the Red Mountain: Indian Labor in Potosí, 1545–1650.* Albuquerque: University of New Mexico Press, 1984.

———. "Mining." In *Colonial Spanish America,* ed. L. Bethell, 203–49. Cambridge: Cambridge University Press, 1987.

Barnuevo, R. *Relación apologética asi del antiguo como nuevo descubrimiento del río de las Amazonas hecho por los religiosos de la Compañía de Jesús de Quito.* Biblioteca Amazonas VI. Quito: Imp. del Ministerio de Gobierno, 1942.

Barrett, S. A. *The Cayapa Indians of Ecuador.* Indian Notes and Monographs, no. 40. 2 vols. New York: Museum of the American Indian, Heye Foundation, 1925.

Bartlett, M. S. "Measles Periodicity and Community Size." *Journal of the Royal Statistical Society,* ser. A, 120 (1957): 48–70.

Basile, D. G. *Tillers of the Andes: Farmers and Farming in the Quito Basin.* Studies in Geography, no 8. Chapel Hill: University of North Carolina, Department of Geography, 1974.

Batchelor, B. "Los camellones de Cayambe en la sierra de Ecuador." *América indígena* 40 (1980): 671–89.

Baudin, L. *A Socialist Empire: The Incas of Peru.* Princeton, N.J.: Van Nostrand, 1961.

Bennett Ross, J. "Effects of Contact on Revenge Hostilities among the Achuarä Jívaro." In *Warfare, Culture, and Environment,* ed. R. B. Ferguson, 83–109. New York: Academic Press, 1984.

Benzoni, G. *La historia del mundo nuevo.* Biblioteca de la academia nacional de la historia, Caracas, no. 86. Caracas: Academia Nacional de la Historia, 1967.

Bernárdez, E. "Lingüística de Esmeraldas: Relaciones sincrónicas y diacrónicas." In *Proceedings of the Forty-second International Congress of Americanists* (Paris), 9A:343–50. 1979.

Binford, M. W., M. Brenner, T. J. Whitmore, A. Higuera-Gundy, E.S. Deevey, and B. Leyden. "Ecosystems, Paleoecology, and Human Disturbance in Subtropical and Tropical America." *Quaternary Science Reviews* 6 (1987): 115–28.

Black, F. L. "Infectious Diseases in Primitive Societies." *Science* 187 (1975): 515–18.

Bongaarts, J. "Does Malnutrition Affect Fertility? A Summary of the Evidence." *Science* 208 (1980): 564–69.

Borah, W. *New Spain's Century of Depression.* Ibero-Americana, no. 35. Berkeley and Los Angeles: University of California Press, 1951.

Borah, W., and S. F. Cook. "Conquest and Population: A Demographic Approach to Mexican History." *Proceedings of the American Philosophical Society* 113, no. 2 (1969): 177–83.

Borchart de Moreno, C. "La conquista española." In *Pichincha: Monografía histórica de la región nuclear ecuatoriana,* ed. S. Moreno Yánez, 177–91. Quito: Consejo Provincial de Pichincha, 1981.

———. "El período colonial." In *Pichincha: Monografía histórica de la región nuclear ecuatoriana,* ed. S. Moreno Yánez, 193–274. Quito: Consejo Provincial de Pichincha, 1981.

Borja de Szászdi, D. L. "Prehistoria de la costa ecuatoriana." *Anuario de estudios americanos* 21 (1964): 381–436.

———. "Reinterpretación de las fuentes relativas a la fundación de Guayaquil." *Boletín de la academia nacional de historia* 107 (1966): 17–41

Borregán, A. *Crónica de la conquista del Perú.* Sevilla: Escuela de Estudios Hispanoamericanos, 1948.

Boster, J. "A Comparison of the Diversity of Jivaroan Gardens with That of the Tropical Rain Forest." *Human Ecology* 11, no. 1 (1983): 47–68.

Bradby, B. "'Resistance to Capitalism' in the Peruvian Andes." In *Ecology and Exchange in the Andes,* ed. D. Lehmann, 97–122. Cambridge: Cambridge University Press, 1982.

Brinton, D. G. *The American Race.* New York: N. D. C. Hodges, 1891.

Brown, A. W. A. "Yellow Fever, Dengue, and Dengue Haemorrhagic Fever." In *A World Geography of Human Diseases,* ed. G. M. Howe, 271–317. London: Academic Press, 1977.

Browne, S. A. "The Effects of Epidemic Disease in Colonial Ecuador." Ph.D. diss., Duke University, 1984.

Brush, S. B. *Mountain, Field, and Family: The Economy and Human Ecology of an Andean Valley.* Philadelphia: University of Pennsylvania Press, 1977.

Bushnell, G. H. S. *The Archaeology of the Santa Elena Peninsula in South-west Ecuador.* Cambridge: Cambridge University Press, 1951.

Cabello Balboa, M. *Miscelánea antártica.* Lima: Instituto de Etnología, Universidad de San Marcos, 1951.

———. *Obras.* Vol. 1. Quito: Editorial Ecuatoriana, 1945.

Caillavet, C. "La adaptación de la dominación incaica a las sociedades autóctonas de la frontera septentrional del imperio (territorio Otavalo-Ecuador)." *Revista andina* 3, no. 2 (1985): 403–23.

———. "Caciques de Otavalo en el siglo XVI. Don Alonso Maldonado y su esposa." In *Miscelánea antropológica ecuatoriana,* 2:38–55. Guayaquil: Banco Central del Ecuador, 1982.

———. "Les chefferies préhispaniques du nord de l'Equateur: Formes d'habitat et organisation territoriale." *Bulletin de l'institut français d'études andines* 17, no. 2 (1988): 41–59.

———. "Entre sierra y selva: Las relaciones fronterizas y sus representaciones para las etnías de los Andes septentrionales." *Anuario de estudios americanos* 46 (1989): 71–91.

———. "Etnohistoria ecuatoriana: Nuevos datos sobre el Otavalo prehispánico." *Cultura* 11 (1981): 109–27.

———. "Les groupes ethniques préhispaniques selon les sources ethnohistoriques." In *Loja préhispanique,* 289–310. Paris: Editions recherche sur les civilisations, 1987.

———. "Los grupos étnicos prehispánicos del sur del Ecuador según las fuentes etnohistóricas." In *Memorias del primer simposio europeo sobre antropología del Ecuador,* ed. S. E. Moreno Yánez, 127–157. Quito: Ediciones Abya-Yala, 1985.

———. Les rouages économiques d'une société minière: Echanges et crédit. Loja: 1550–1630. *Bulletin de l'institut français d'études andines* 13, no. 3–4 (1984): 31–63.

———. "La sal de Otavalo-Ecuador: Continuidades y rupturas coloniales." *Sarance* 9 (1981): 47–81.

————. "Las técnicas agrarias autóctonas y la remodelación colonial del paisaje en los Andes septentrionales (siglo XVI)." In *Ciencia, vida, y espacio,* 3:109–26. Madrid: Consejo Superior de Investigaciones Científicas, 1989.

————. "Toponimia histórica, arqueología, y formas prehispánicas de agricultura en la región de Otavalo-Ecuador." *Bulletin de l'institut français d' études andines* 12, no. 3–4 (1983): 1–21.

Calancha, A. de. "Crónica moralizada de la orden de San Agustín en el Perú (1575)." *Museo histórico* 12 (1960): 189–201.

Calero, L. F. "Pasto, 1535–1700: The Social and Economic Decline of Indian Communities in the Southern Colombian Andes." Ph.D. diss., University of California, Berkeley, 1987.

Campos, F. *Compendio histórico de Guayaquil desde su fundación hasta el año 1820.* Guayaquil: Filantrópica, 1894.

Carvajal, G. de. *Relación del nuevo descubrimiento del famoso río grande que descubrió por muy gran ventura el capitán Francisco de Orellana.* Biblioteca Amazonas 1. Quito: Imp. del Ministerio de Educación, 1942.

Castellanos, J. de. *Elegías de varones ilustres.* 4 vols. Bogotá: Editorial A.B.C, 1955.

Ceballos, P. F. *Resumen de la historia del Ecuador desde su origen hasta 1845.* 6 vols. Lima: Imp. del Estado, 1870–73.

Chacón, J. *Historia de la minería de Cuenca.* Cuenca: Universidad de Cuenca, 1986.

Chamberlain, R. S. *The Conquest and Colonization of Honduras, 1502–1550.* Carnegie Institution of Washington Publication 598. Washington, D.C.: Carnegie Institution, 1953.

Chantre y Herrera, J. *Historia de las misiones de la Compañía de Jesús en el Marañón español.* Madrid: Imp. de A. Avrial, 1901.

Chaumeil, J.-P., and J. Fraysse-Chaumeil. "'La Canela y El Dorado': Les indigénes du Napo et du Haut-Amazone—au XVIᵉ siècle." *Bulletin de l'institut français d' études andines* 10, no. 3–4 (1981): 55–86.

Christie, A. B. "Smallpox." In *A World Geography of Diseases,* ed. G. M. Howe, 255–70. New York: Academic Press, 1977.

Cieza de León, P. *Obras completas.* 3 vols. Madrid: Consejo Superior de Investigaciones Científicas, Instituto Gonzalo Fernández de Oviedo, 1984.
  Crónica del Perú, 1:1–144.
  Descubrimiento y conquista del Perú, 1:225–357.
  Guerra de Chupas, 2:155–289.
  Guerra de Quito, 2:290–590.
  Guerra de Salinas, 2:1–154.
  Relación de la sucesión y gobierno de los Incas Yupanques [Señorío], 1:148–222.

Cisneros Cisneros, C. *Demografía y estadística sobre el indio ecuatoriano.* Quito: Talleres Gráficos Nacionales, 1948.

Clark, G., and M. Haswell. *The Economics of Subsistence Agriculture.* London: Macmillan, 1966.

Clayton, L. A. "The Guayaquil Shipyards in the Seventeenth Century: History of a Colonial Industry." Ph.D. diss., Tulane University, 1972.

————. "Guayaquil y la defensa de la hegemonía española en el Pacífico Oriental durante los siglos XVI y XVII." *Revista del archivo histórico del Guayas* 4 (1973): 27–46.

Cliff, A., and P. Haggett. *Atlas of Disease Distributions*. Oxford: Blackwell, 1988.

Cobo, B. *Historia del nuevo mundo*. 2 vols. Biblioteca de autores españoles, nos. 91 and 92. Madrid: Real Academia de Historia, 1956.

Cole, J. *The Potosí Mita, 1573–1700*. Stanford, Calif.: Stanford University Press, 1985.

Collier, D. "The Archeology of Ecuador." In *Handbook of South American Indians*, Smithsonian Institution, Bureau of American Ethnology Bulletin 143, ed. J. H. Steward, 2-767–84. Washington D.C., 1946.

Colmenares, G. *Historia económica y social de Colombia, 1537–1719*. Medellín: Editorial La Carreta, 1975.

Compte, F. M. *Varones ilustres de la orden seráfica en el Ecuador desde la fundación de Quito hasta nuestros días*. 2 vols. Quito: Imp. del Clero, 1885–86.

Conde, T. *Los Yaguarzongos: Historia de los Shuar de Zamora*. Quito: Mundo Shuar, 1981.

Conrad, G. W., and A. A. Demarest. *Religion and Empire: The Dynamics of Aztec and Inca Expansionism*. Cambridge: Cambridge University Press, 1983.

Cook, N. D. *Demographic Collapse: Indian Peru, 1520–1620*. Cambridge: Cambridge University Press, 1981.

———, ed. *Tasa de la visita general de Francisco de Toledo*. Lima: Universidad Nacional de San Marcos, 1975.

Cook, S. F. "Human Sacrifice and Warfare as Factors in the Demography of Pre-Colonial Mexico." *Human Biology* 18, no. 2 (1946): 81–102.

Cook, S. F., and W. Borah. *Essays in Population History*. 3 vols. Berkeley and Los Angeles: University of California Press, 1971–79.

———. *The Indian Population of Central Mexico, 1531–1610*. Ibero Americana, no. 44. Berkeley and Los Angeles: University of California Press, 1960.

Costales, A., and P. Costales. *Amazonia: Ecuador-Perú-Bolivia*. Quito: Mundo Shuar, 1983.

Costales, P., and A. Costales. *La Nación Shuar*. Serie E. 5 parts. Documentación etnohistórica, quinta parte. Sucúa, Ecuador: Centro de Documentación e Investigación Cultural Shuar, 1978.

Crespo Toral, R. "Encomiendas de Cuenca: Siglo XVI." *Revista del centro de estudios históricos y geográficos de Cuenca* 5 (1921): 25–30.

Crosby, A. W. *The Columbian Exchange: Biological and Cultural Consequences of 1492*. Westport, Conn.: Greenwood Press, 1972.

Cruz, L. de. "Nuevo descubrimiento del Marañón año 1651." In *Varones ilustres de la orden seráfica en el Ecuador*, ed. F. M. Compte, 1:148–204. Quito: Imp. del Clero, 1885–86.

Cushner, N. P. *Farm and Factory: Jesuits in the Development of Agrarian Capitalism in Colonial Quito, 1600–1767*. New York: SUNY Press, 1982.

DeBoer, W. R. "Buffer Zones in the Cultural Ecology of Aboriginal Amazonia: An Ethnohistorical Approach." *American Antiquity* 46, no. 2 (1981): 364–77.

Deler, J. P. *Ecuador del espacio al estado nacional*. Quito: Banco Central del Ecuador, 1987.

Denevan, W. M. "The Aboriginal Population of Amazonia." In *The Native Population of the Americas in 1492*, 2d rev. ed., ed. W. M. Denevan, 205–34. Madison: University of Wisconsin Press, 1992.

———. "The Aboriginal Population of Western Amazonia in Relation to Habitat and Subsistence." *Revista geográfica,* no. 72 (1970): 61–86.

———. "Hydraulic Agriculture in the American Tropics: Forms, Measurements, and Recent Research." In *Maya Subsistence: Studies in the Memory of Dennis E. Puleston,* ed. K. Flannery, 181–97. New York: Academic Press, 1982.

———. "The Pristine Myth: The Landscape of the Americas in 1492." *Annals of the Association of American Geographers* 82, no. 3 (1992): 369–85.

———, ed. *The Native Population of the Americas in 1492.* 2d rev. ed. Madison: University of Wisconsin Press, 1992.

Descola, P. "From Scattered to Nucleated Settlement: A Process of Socio-economic Change among the Achuar." In *Cultural Transformations and Ethnicity in Modern Ecuador,* ed. N. Whitten, 614–46. Urbana: University of Illinois Press, 1981.

Diez de San Miguel, G. *Visita hecha a la provincia de Chucuito en el año 1567.* Documentos regionales para la etnología y etnohistoria andina, vol. 1. Lima: Casa de la Cultura del Perú, 1964.

Dillehay, T. D., and P. Netherly eds. *Frontera del estado Inca.* Proceedings of the Forty-fifth International Congress of Americanists, Bogotá, 1985. British Archaeological Reports, International Series 442. Oxford, 1988.

Dobyns, H. F. "Estimating Aboriginal Population." *Current Anthropology* 7 (1963): 395–449.

———. "An Outline of Andean Epidemic History." *Bulletin of the History of Medicine* 37 (1963): 493–515.

Documentos para la historia militar. 2 vols. Quito: Casa de la Cultura Ecuatoriana, 1974–75.

Dufour, D. L. "Insects as Food: A Case Study from the Northwest Amazon." *American Anthropologist* 89 (1987): 383–97.

Edwards, C. R. *Aboriginal Watercraft on the Pacific Coast of South America.* Ibero-Americana no. 47. Berkeley and Los Angeles: University of California Press, 1965.

Espinosa Pérez, L. *Contribuciones lingüísticas y etnográficas sobre algunos pueblos indígenas del Amazonas peruano.* Vol. 1. Madrid: Consejo Superior de Investigaciones Científicas, Instituto Bernardino de Sahagún, 1955.

Espinosa Soriano, W. *Los Cayambes y Carangues: Siglos XV–XVI. El testimonio de la etnohistoria.* 3 vols. Otavalo: Instituto Otavaleño de Antropología, 1988.

———. "Los Chambillas y mitmas Incas y Chinchasuyos en territorio Lupaca, siglos XV—XIX." *Revista del museo nacional* (Lima) 46 (1982): 419–506.

———. "La coca y los mitmas Cayampis en el reino de Ancara. Siglo XVI." *Anales científicos de la Universidad nacional del centro del Perú* (Huancayo) 2 (1973): 7–67.

———. "Colonias mitmas multiples en Abancay." *Revista del museo nacional* (Lima) 39 (1973): 225–99.

———. "El curaca de los Cayambes y su sometimiento al imperio español. Siglos XV y XVI." *Bulletin de l'institut français d'études andines* 9, no. 1–2 (1980): 89–119.

———. "Los mitmas Cañar en el reino de Yaro (Perú). Siglos XV y XVI." In *Amerikanistische Studien, Festschrift für Hermann Trimborn,* Collectanea Instituti Anthropos 20, ed. R. Hartmann and U. Oberem, 1:153–62. St. Augustin: Hans Vöker und Kulturem, Anthropos-Institut, 1978.

———. "Los mitmas Huayacuntu en Quito o guarniciones para la represión armada. Siglos XV y XVI." *Revista del museo nacional* (Lima) 41 (1975): 351–94.

———. "El reino de Chono, al este de Guayaquil (siglos XV–XVII): El testimonio de la arqueología y la etnohistoria." *Revista de historia y cultura* (Lima), nos. 13–14 (1981): 7–60.

———. "Los señoríos étnicos del valle de Condebamba y provinica de Cajabamba." *Anales científicos de la universidad nacional del centro del Perú* (Huancayo) 3 (1974): 5–371.

Estete, M. *Noticia del Perú, o el descubrimiento y la conquista del Perú.* Quito: Imp. de la Universidad Central, 1918.

Estrada, T. *Relaciones históricas y geográficas de Manabí.* 9 vols. Guayaquil: Talleres de la Opinión Pública, 1930–39.

Estrada, V. E. *Arqueología de Manabí central.* Guayaquil: Museo V. E. Estrada, 1962.

———. *Las culturas pre-clásicas, formativas o arcaicas del Ecuador.* Publicaciones del Museo V. E. Estrada, no. 5. Guayaquil, 1958.

———. *Los Huancavilcas: Ultimas civilizaciones pre-históricas de la costa del Guayas.* Publicaciones del Museo V. E. Estrada, no. 3. Guayaquil, 1957.

Estrada, V. E., and C. Evans. "Cultural Development in Ecuador." In *Aboriginal Cultural Development in Latin America: An Interpretative Review,* Smithsonian Miscellaneous Collections 146, no. 1, by B. J. Meggers and C. Evans, 77–88. Washington, D.C., 1963.

Estrada Ycaza, J. "Antecedentes sobre el hospital de Puerto Viejo." *Revista del archivo del Guayas* (Guayaquil) 1 (1972): 14–21.

———. *La fundación de Guayaquil.* Guayaquil: Publicaciones del Archivo Histórico del Guayas, 1974.

———. *El puerto de Guayaquil.* 3 vols. Guayaquil: Publicaciones del Archivo Histórico del Guayas, 1972.

Farriss, N. M. *Maya Society under Colonial Rule: The Collective Enterprise of Survival.* Princeton, N.J.: Princeton University Press, 1984.

Figueroa, F. de. *Relación de la misiones de la Compañía de Jesús en el país de los Maynas.* Madrid: V. Suarez, 1904.

Frank, A. G. *Mexican Agriculture, 1521–1630: Transformation of the Mode of Production.* Cambridge: Cambridge University Press, 1981.

Friede, J. "Los Kofán: Tribu de la alta Amazonia colombiana." In *Proceedings of the Thirtieth International Congress of Americanists* (Cambridge, England), 202–59. 1952.

Friedlander, J. "Malaria and Demography in the Lowlands of Mexico: An Ethnohistorical Approach." In *Forms of Symbolic Action,* ed. R. F. Spencer, 217–33. Seattle: American Ethnological Society.

Frisch, R. E. "Population, Food Intake, and Fertility." *Science* 199 (1978): 22–30.

Fritz. S. *Journal of the Travels and Labours of Father Samuel Fritz in the River of the Amazons between 1686 and 1723.* Hakluyt Society, 2d ser., no. 51. London, 1922.

Gade, D. W. "Inca and Colonial Settlement, Coca Cultivation, and Endemic Disease in the Tropical Forest." *Journal of Historical Geography* 5 (1979): 263–79.

Garcés, J. *Las minas de Zamora: Cuentas de la real hacienda, 1561–1565.* Quito: Imp. Municipal, 1957.

Garcilaso de la Vega, "El Inca." *Comentarios reales de los Incas.* 3 vols. Biblioteca de autores españoles, nos. 133–35. Madrid: Gráficas Orbe, 1960.

Gibson, C. *The Aztecs under Spanish Rule.* Stanford, Calif.: Stanford University Press, 1964.

Gil Munilla, L. *Descubrimiento del Marañón.* Sevilla: Escuela de Estudios Hispanoamericanos, 1954.

Gondard, P., and F. López. *Inventario arqueológico preliminar de los Andes septentrionales del Ecuador.* Quito: MAG PRONAREG ORSTOM, 1983.

González Suárez, F. *Historia general de la república del Ecuador.* 3 vols. Quito: Casa de la Cultura Ecuatoriana, 1970.

Grohs, W. *Los indios del Alto Amazonas del siglo XVI al XVIII.* Bonner amerikanistische Studien no. 2. Bonn, 1974.

Grubb, P. J., J. R. Lloyd, T. D. Pennington, and T. C. Whitmore. "A Comparison of Montane and Lowland Rain Forest in Ecuador." Part 1, "The Forest Structure, Physiognomy, and Floristics." *Journal of Ecology* 51 (1963): 567–601.

Guevara, D. *Puerto de El Dorado: Monografía del Cantón Pelileo.* Quito: Editorial Moderna, 1945.

Guffroy, J. "Implantations humaines et ocupation l'espace dans la province de Loja à l'époque préhispanique." In *Equateur 1986,* ed. D. Delaunay and M. Portais, 277–90. Paris: Editions de l'ORSTOM, 1989.

Guinea Bueno, M. *Patrones de asentamiento en la arqueología de Esmeraldas, Ecuador.* Madrid: Ministerio de Asuntos Exteriores, 1984.

Hames, R. B. and W. T. Vickers, eds. *Adaptive Responses of Native Amazonians.* New York: Academic Press, 1983.

Hampe, T. "Relación de los encomenderos y repartimientos del Perú en 1561." *Historia y cultura* (Lima) 12 (1979): 75–117.

Harner, M. *The Jívaro: People of the Sacred Waterfalls.* New York: Doubleday Natural History Press, 1972.

Haro Alvear, S. L. *Puruhá: Nación guerrera.* Quito: Editora Nacional, 1977.

Hartmann, R. "Mercado y ferias prehispánicos en el área andina." *Boletín de la academia nacional de historia* 54, no. 118 (1971): 214–35.

Harvey, H. R. Population of the Cahuilla Indians: Decline and Its Causes." *Eugenics Quarterly* 14, no. 3 (1967): 185–98.

Heaton, H. C., ed. *The Discovery of the Amazon.* New York: American Geographical Society, 1934.

Hemming, J. *The Conquest of the Incas.* London: Abacus, 1972.

Heredia, J. F. *La antigua provincia de Quito de la Compañía de Jesús y sus misiones entre infieles.* Guayaquil: Imp. Gutenberg de E. A. Uzcátegui, 1940.

Hermida Piedra, C. "Apuntes para la historia de la medicina en el Azuay." *Anales de la universidad de Cuenca* 7, no. 2–3 (1951): 5–155.

Herrera, P. *Apunte cronológico de las obras y trabajos del cabildo y municipalidad de Quito desde 1534 hasta 1714.* 2 vols. Quito: Imp. Municipal, 1916.

———. *Monografía del cantón de Otavalo.* Quito: Tip. y Enc. Salesiana, 1909.

Herrera y Tordesillas, A. de. *Historia general de los hechos de los castellanos en las islas i tierra firme del Mar Océano.* 17 vols. Madrid: Real Academia de la Historia, 1934–57.

Holdridge, F. L., et al. *The Forests of Western and Southern Ecuador.* Washington, D.C.: Forest Services, U.S. Department of Agriculture, 1947.

Holm, O. *Cultura Manteña-Huancavilca.* Guayaquil: Banco Central del Ecuador, 1985.

———. *Cultura Milagro-Quevedo.* Guayaquil: Banco Central del Ecuador, 1983.

Hyslop, J. "Las fronteras estatales extremas del Tawantinsuyu." In *Frontera del estado Inca,* Proceedings of the Forty-fifth International Congress of Americanists, Bogotá, 1985, British Archaeological Reports, International Series 442, ed. T. D. Dillehay and P. Netherly, 35–57. Oxford, 1988.

———. *The Inka Road System.* New York: Academic Press, 1984.

Idrovo, J. "Tomebamba, primera fase de conquista incasica en los Andes septentrionales: Los Cañaris y la conquista incasica del austro ecuatoriano." In *Frontera del estado Inca,* Proceedings of the Forty-fifth International Congress of Americanists, Bogotá, 1985, British Archaeological Reports, International Series 442, ed. T. D. Dillehay and P. Netherly, 87–104. Oxford, 1988.

Izaguirre, B. *Historia de las misiones franciscanos y narración de los progresos de la geografía en el oriente del Perú, 1619–1921.* 14 vols. Lima: Tipográficos de la Penitencia, 1922–26.

Jacobs, W. R. "The Tip of the Iceberg: Pre-Columbian Demography and Some Implications for Revisionism." *William and Mary Quarterly,* 3d ser., 31 (1974): 123–32.

Jaramillo, V. A. *Corregidores de Otavalo.* Brevianos de cultura: Serie Historia no. 1. Otavalo: Instituto Otavaleño de Antropología, 1972.

Jaramillo Alvarado, P. *Historia de la provincia de Loja.* Quito: Casa de la Cultura Ecuatoriana, 1955.

Jaramillo Uribe, J. "La población indígena de Colombia en el momento de la conquista y sus transformaciones posteriores." *Anuario colombiano de historia social y de la cultura* 1 (1964): 239–93.

Jerez, F. de. "Verdadera relación de la conquista del Perú y provincia del Cuzco." In *Historiadores primitivos de Indias,* vol. 2, Biblioteca de autores españoles, no. 26, ed. E. de Vedia, 320–46. Madrid: Imp. Los Sucesores de Hernando, 1962.

Jijón y Caamaño, J. *Antropología prehispánica del Ecuador.* Quito: La Prensa Católica, 1952.

———. *El Ecuador interandino y occidental antes de la conquista española.* 4 vols. Quito: Editorial Ecuatoriana, 1941–47.

———. "Nueva contribución al conocimiento de los aborigenes de la provincia de Imbabura de la república del Ecuador." *Boletín de la sociedad ecuatoriana de estudios históricos americanos* 6, nos. 10 and 11 (1920): 1–120, 184–224.

———. *Sebastián de Benalcázar.* 2 vols. Quito: Imp. del Clero (vol. 1) and Editorial Ecuatoriana (vol. 2), 1936–38.

Jouanen, J. *Historia de la Compañía de Jesús en la antigua provincia de Quito, 1570–1774.* 2 vols. Quito: Editorial Ecuatoriana, 1941–43.

Kaplan, J. E., J. W. Larrick, J. Yost, L. Farrell, H. B. Greenberg, K. L. Herrmann, A. J. Sulzer, K. W. Walls, and L. Pederson. "Infectious Disease Patterns in the

Waorani, an Isolated Amerindian Population." *American Journal of Tropical Medicine and Hygiene* 29, no. 2 (1980): 298–312.

Karsten, R. *The Head-Hunters of Western Amazonas.* Commentationes Humanarum Litterarum vol. 7, no. 1. Helsingfors: Soc. Sci. Fennica, 1935.

Katz, F. *The Ancient American Civilizations.* London: Weidenfeld and Nicolson, 1969.

Kelly, K. "Land Use Regions in the Central and Northern Portions of the Inca Empire." *Annals of the Association of American Geographers* 55 (1965): 327–38.

Kiple, K. *The Caribbean Slave: A Biological History.* Cambridge: Cambridge University Press, 1984.

Knapp, G. *Ecología cultural prehispánico del Ecuador.* Biblioteca de geografía ecuatoriana 3. Quito: Banco Central del Ecuador, 1988.

———. "El nicho ecológico llanura humeda, en la economía prehistórica de los Andes de altura: Evidencias etnohistóricas, geográficas, y arqueológicas." *Sarance* 9 (1981): 83–99.

Knapp, G., and W. M. Denevan. "Use of Wetlands in the Prehistoric Economy of the Northern Ecuadorian Andes." In *Prehistoric Intensive Agriculture in the Tropics,* British Archaeological Reports, International Series 232, ed. I. Farrington, 185–207. Oxford, 1983.

Knodel, J. "Breast Feeding and Population Growth." *Science* 198 (1977): 1111–15.

Kroeger, A., and F. Barbira-Freedman. *Cultural Change and Health: The Case of Southamerican Rainforest Indians.* Medizin in Entwicklungsländen Band 12. Frankfurt: Verlag Peter Lang, 1982.

Kroeger, A., H. Heyna, G. Pawelzig, and E. Ilecková. "La salud y la alimentación entre los indígenas Schuaras del Ecuador." *Revista ecuatoriana de higiene y medicina tropical* 30, no. 2 (1977): 119–67.

Krzywicki, L. *Primitive Society and Its Vital Statistics.* London: Macmillan, 1934.

Landázuri Soto, A. *El régimen laboral indígena en la real audiencia de Quito.* Madrid: Imp. de Aldecoa, 1959.

Larrain Barros, H. *Demografía y asentamiento indígenas en la sierra norte del Ecuador en el siglo XVI: Estudio etnohistórico de las fuentes tempranas (1525–1560).* 2 vols. Colección Pendoneros, nos. 11 and 12. Otavalo: Instituto Otavaleño de Antropología, 1980.

Larrain Barros, H., and D. Cruz Pardo. "Apuntes para un estudio de la población del corregimiento de Otavalo a fines del siglo XVI." *Sarance* 3 no. 1 (1977): 63–95.

Larrea, C. M. *La cultura incasica del Ecuador: Notas históricas y cronológicas.* Publication 253. Plan piloto del Ecuador, sección antropología. Mexico City: Instituto Panamericano de Geografía e Historia, 1965.

———. *Notas de prehistoria e historia Ecuatoriana.* Quito: Corporación de estudios y publicaciones, 1971.

Larson, B. "Bolivia Revisited: New Directions in North American Research in History and Anthropology." *Latin American Research Review* 23 (1988): 63–90.

Lastres, J. B. *Historia de la medicina peruana.* 3 vols. Lima: San Marcos, 1951.

Lathrap. D. W. "Alternative Models of Populations [*sic*] Movements in the Tropical Lowlands of South America." In *Proceedings of the Thirty-ninth International Congress of Americanists* (Lima), vol. 4, *Historia etnohistoria y etnología de la selva sudamericana,* 13–23. Lima: Instituto de Estudios Peruanos, 1972.

León, L. A. "Historia y extinción del cocaismo en el Ecuador." *América indígena* 12 (1952): 7–32.

Levillier, R. *Gobernantes del Perú.* 14 vols. Madrid: Sucesores de Rivadeneyra, 1921–26.

Livi-Bacci, M. *Population and Nutrition: An Essay on European Demographic History.* Cambridge: Cambridge University Press, 1991.

Lizárraga, R. de. *Descripción breve, de toda la tierra del Perú, Tucumán, Río de la Plata, y Chile.* Biblioteca de autores españoles, no. 216. Madrid: Ediciones Atlas, 1968.

Loor, W. *Los españoles en Manabí.* Portoviejo: Talleres Tip. Diario Manabita, 1935.

———. *Los indios de Manabí.* Quito: Editorial Ecuatoriana, 1937.

López de Gómara, F. "Hispania Victrix: Historia general de las Indias." In *Historiadores primitivos de Indias,* vol. 1, Biblioteca de autores españoles, no. 22, ed. E. de Vedia, 155–455. Madrid: Imp. Los Sucesores de Hernando, 1918.

López de Velasco, J. *Geografía y descripción universal de las Indias.* Biblioteca de autores españoles, no. 248. Madrid: Ediciones Atlas, 1971.

McFalls, J. A., and M. H. McFalls. *Disease and Fertility.* New York: Academic Press, 1984.

McKeown, T. "Food, Infection, and Population." In *Hunger and History,* ed. R. I. Rothberg and T. K. Rabb, 29–49. Cambridge University Press: Cambridge, 1985.

MacLeod, M. J. "Ethnic Relations and Indian Society in the Province of Guatemala, ca. 1620–ca. 1800." In *Spaniards and Indians in Southern Mesoamerica: Essays on the History of Ethnic Relations,* ed. M. J. MacLeod and R. Wasserstrom, 189–214. Lincoln: University of Nebraska Press, 1983.

———. *Spanish Central America: A Socioeconomic History, 1520–1720.* Berkeley and Los Angeles: University of California Press, 1973.

McNeill, W. H. *Plagues and Peoples.* Penguin: Harmondsworth, 1979.

Madero, M. *Historia de la medicina en la provincia del Guayas.* Guayaquil: Casa de la Cultura Ecuatoriana, 1955.

Maestro, Y. "El sistema de alimentación de los Cayapas de Esmeraldas (Ecuador)." In *Proceedings of the Forty-second International Congress of Americanists* (Paris), 9A (1979): 335–41. 1979.

Maldonado, J. *Relación del descubrimiento del río de las Amazonas llamado Marañón.* Biblioteca Amazonas 5. Quito: Imp. Ministerio de Gobierno, 1942.

Mansilla, R. E. *El tributo indígena en el Perú: Siglos XVI y XVII.* Pamplona: Universidad de Navarra, 1979.

Manson-Bahr, P. H. *Manson's Tropical Diseases.* 11th ed. London: Cassell, 1941.

Marcy, P. T. "Factors Affecting the Fecundity and Fertility of Historical Populations." *Journal of Family History* 6 (1981): 309–26.

Maroni, P. "Noticias auténticas del famoso río Marañón y misión apostólica de la Compañía de Jesús de la Provinica de Quito, en los dilatados bosques de dicho río." Ed. M. Jiménez de la Espada. *Boletín de la Sociedad Geográfica de Madrid* 26–33 (1889–92).

Martínez, E. N. *Cacique García Tulcanaza:* Quito: Editora Andina, 1983.

———. *Etnohistoria de los Pastos.* Quito: Editorial Universitaria, 1977.

———. "Pastos y Quillaçingas." *América indígena* 34, no. 3 (1974): 651–62.

Mathewson, K. "Estimating Labor Inputs for the Guayas Raised Fields: Initial Considerations." In *Pre-Hispanic Agricultural Fields in the Andean Region,* British Archaeological Reports 359 (ii), ed. W. M. Denevan, K. Mathewson, and G. Knapp, 321–36. Oxford, 1987.

———. "Landscape Change and Cultural Persistence in the Guayas Wetlands, Ecuador." Ph.D. diss., University of Wisconsin, Madison, 1987.

Matovalle, J. M. *Cuenca de Tomebamba.* Cuenca: Imp. de la Universidad, 1921.

Meggers, B. J. *Amazonia: Man and Culture in a Counterfeit Paradise.* Chicago: Aldine-Atherton, 1971.

———. *Ecuador.* London: Thames and Hudson, 1966.

———. "Environmental Limitations on the Development of Culture." *American Anthropologist* 56 (1954): 801–24.

Meggers, B. J., and C. Evans. *Archaeological Investigations on the Río Napo, Eastern Ecuador.* Smithsonian Institution, Smithsonian Contributions to Anthropology no. 6. Washington D.C., 1968.

Mejía, L. "La economia de la sociedad 'primitiva' ecuatoriana." In *Ecuador: Pasado y presente,* ed. L. Mejía, 11–60. Quito: Universidad Central, 1982.

Memorias de los virreyes que han gobernado el Perú. 6 vols. Lima: Librería Central de Felipe Bailly, 1859.

Menken, J. "Seasonal Migration and Seasonal Variation on Fecundability: Effects on Birth Rates and Birth Intervals." *Demography* 16 (1979): 103–19.

Menken, J., J. Trussel, and S. Watkins. "The Nutrition-Fertility Link: The Evidence." *Journal of Interdisciplinary History* 11 (1981): 425–41.

Metraux, A. "Migrations historiques des Tupi-Guarani." *Journal de la société des americanistes de Paris* 19 (1927): 1–45.

———. "Tribes of the Middle and Upper Amazon River." In *Handbook of South American Indians,* Smithsonian Institution, Bureau of American Ethnology Bulletin 143, ed. J. H. Steward, 3:687–712. Washington D.C., 1948.

Meyers, A. *Die Inka in Ekuador: Untersuchungen anhand ihrer materiellen Hinterlassenschaft.* Bonner americanistische Studien no. 6. Bonn, 1976.

Minchom, M. "Urban Popular Society in Colonial Quito, c. 1700–1800." Ph.D. diss., University of Liverpool, 1984.

Miño Grijalva, M. *Los Cañaris en el Perú: Una aproximación etnohistórica.* Quito: PUCE, 1977.

Molina, C. de. "Relación de muchas cosas acaecidas en el Perú." In *Crónicas peruanas de interés indígena,* Biblioteca de autores españoles, no. 209, ed. F. Esteve Barba, 56–96. Madrid: Ediciones Atlas, 1968.

Molina, E. G., and A. V. Little. "The Geoecology of the Andes: The Natural Science Base for Research Planning." *Mountain Research and Development* 1, no. 2 (1981): 115–44.

Molineaux, L. "The Epidemiology of Human Malaria as an Explanation of its Distribution, Including Some Implications for Its Control." In *Malaria: Principles and Practice of Malariology,* ed. W. H. Wernsdorfer and I. McGregor, 2:913–98. New York: Longman, 1988.

Monroy, J. L. *El convento de la Merced de Quito de 1534 a 1617.* 2d ed. Quito: Editorial Laboral, 1938.

Montesinos, F. *Anales del Perú.* 2 vols. Madrid: Imp. Gabriel L. y del Horno, 1906.

———. *Memorias antiguas, historiales, y políticas del Perú.* Madrid: Imp. de Miguel Ginesta, 1882.

Moreno Egas, J. "Apuntes para el estudio de la población del siglo XVI de la real audiencia de Quito." *Museo histórico,* year 28, no. 56 (1978): 71–87.

Moreno Navarro, I. "Ecología y sociedad de los Cayapas de Esmeraldas: Los patrones de asentamiento." *Proceedings of the Forty-second International Congress of Americanists* (Paris), 9A: 319–33 1979.

Moreno Ruiz, E. "Noticias sobre los primeros asentamientos españoles en el sur de Colombia." *Revista española de antropología americana (trabajos y conferencias)* 6 (1971): 423–37.

Moreno Yánez, S. E. "Colonias mitmas en el Quito incaico: Su significación económica y política. In *Contribución a la etnohistoria ecuatoriana,* Collección Pendoneros, no. 20, ed. S. E. Moreno Yánez and U. Oberem, 103–27. Otavalo: Instituto Otavaleño de Antropología, 1981.

———, ed. *Pichincha: Monografía histórica de la región nuclear ecuatoriana.* Quito: Consejo Provincial de Pichincha, 1981.

Mörner, M. *Race Mixture in the History of Latin America.* Boston: Little, Brown, 1967.

Morris, C. "From Principles of Ecological Complementarity to the Organization and Administration of Tawantinsuyu." In *Andean Ecology and Civilization,* ed. S. Masuda, I. Shimada, and C. Morris, 477–90. Tokyo: University of Tokyo Press, 1985.

Morton, D. G. "Spanish Exploratory and Missionary Activity in the Province of Mainas, Audiencia de Quito, 1618–1686." M.A. thesis, University of California, Berkeley, 1948.

Morúa, M. de. *Historia general del Perú, origen y descendencia de los Incas (1590–1611).* 2 vols. Ed. M. Ballesteros-Gabrois. Madrid: Instituto Gonzalo Fernández de Oviedo, 1962–64.

Murphy, R. C. "The Earliest Advances Southward from Panama along the West Coast of South America." *Hispanic American Historical Review* 21 (1941): 2–28.

Murra, J. V. "Andean Societies before 1532." In *The Cambridge History of Latin America,* ed. L. Bethell, 1:59–90. Cambridge: Cambridge University Press, 1984.

———. "The Cayapa and Colorado." In *Handbook of South American Indians,* Smithsonian Institution, Bureau of American Ethnology Bulletin 143, ed. J. H. Steward, 4:277–91. Washington D.C., 1948.

———. "El control vertical de un máximo de pisos ecológicos en la economia de las sociedades andinas." In *Formaciones económicas y políticas del mundo andino,* ed. J. V. Murra, 59–115. Lima: Instituto de Estudios Peruanos, 1975.

———. *The Economic Organization of the Inka State.* Greenwich, Conn.: JAI Press, 1980.

———. "En torno a la estructura política de los inka." In *Formaciones económicas y políticas del mundo andino,* ed. J. V. Murra, 23–43. Lima: Instituto de Estudios Peruanos, 1975.

———. "La guerre et les rébellions dans l'expansion de l'état Inka." *Annales: economies, sociétés, civilisations* 33, no. 5–6 (1978): 927–35.

———. "The Historic Tribes of Ecuador." In *Handbook of South American*

Indians, Smithsonian Institution, Bureau of American Ethnology Bulletin 143, ed. J. H. Steward, 2:785–821. Washington D.C., 1946.

———. "The Mit'a Obligations of Ethnic Groups to the Inka State." In *The Inca and Aztec States, 1400–1800: Anthropology and History,* ed. G. A. Collier, R. I. Rosaldo, and J. D. Wirth, 237–62. New York: Academic Press, 1982.

———. "Nueva información sobre las poblaciones yana." In *Formaciones económicas y políticas del mundo andino,* ed. J. V. Murra, 225–42. Lima: Instituto de Estudios Peruanos, 1975.

———. "El tráfico de mullu en la costa del Pacífico." In *Formaciones económicas y políticas del mundo andino,* ed. J. V. Murra, 255–67. Lima: Instituto de Estudios Peruanos, 1975.

Myers, T. P. "Evidence of Prehistoric Irrigation in Northern Ecuador." *Journal of Field Archaeology* 1, no. 3–4 (1974): 309–13.

Naranjo, M. F. "Zonas de refugio y adaptación étnica en el oriente: Siglos XVI-XVII-XVIII." In *Temas sobre la continuidad y adaptación cultural ecuatoriana,* 2nd ed., M. F. Naranjo, J. L. Pereira V., and N. E. Whitten, 97–153. Quito: Ediciones de la Universidad Católica, 1984.

Navarro, J. G. "Fundación del pueblo de Pomasqui." 1573. *Boletín de la academia nacional de historia* 21, no. 58 (1941): 265–66.

Navarro Cárdenas, M. *Investigación histórica de la minería en el Ecuador. Vol. 1, Siglos XVI–XVII.* Quito: Instituto Ecuatoriano de Minería, Ministerio de Energía y Minas, 1986.

Navas, J. de D. *Ibarra y sus provincias.* 2 vols. Quito: Imp. del Clero, 1934–35.

Neel, J. V. "Health and Disease in Unacculturated Amerindian Populations." In *Health and Disease in Tribal Societies.* Ciba Foundation Symposium 49, 155–77. Amsterdam: Elsevier, 1977.

Neumann, S. "Los Quijos y Cofanes del nororiente ecuatoriano: Apuntes etnohistóricos." *Antropología* 2 (1984): 57–78.

Newson, L. A. *The Cost of Conquest: Indian Decline in Honduras under Spanish Rule.* Boulder, Colo.: Westview Press, 1986.

———. "Depopulation of Nicaragua in the Sixteenth Century." *Journal of Latin American Studies* 14 (1982): 253–86.

———. "Highland-Lowland Contrasts in the Impact of Old World Diseases in Early Colonial Ecuador." *Social Science and Medicine* 36 (9) (1993): 1187–95.

———. "Indian Population Patterns in Colonial Spanish America." *Latin American Research Review* 20, no. 3 (1985): 41–74.

———. *Indian Survival in Colonial Nicaragua.* Norman: University of Oklahoma Press, 1987.

———. "Old World Epidemics in Early Colonial Ecuador." In *"Secret Judgments of God": Old World Disease in Colonial Spanish America,* ed. N. D. Cook and W. G. Lovell, 84–112. Norman: University of Oklahoma Press, 1992.

———. "Los sistemas de trabajo y demografía en América española durante la colonia." In *Historia e populaçao: Estudos sobre a América Latina,* ed. S. O. Nadalin, M. L. Marcilio, and A. P. Balhana, 289–97. São Paulo: Fundação Sistema Estadual de Análise de Dados, 1990.

Nolasco Pérez, P. *Historia de las misiones mercedarias en América.* Madrid: Revista "Estudios," 1966.

Norton, P. "El señorío de Salangone y la liga de mercaderes." In *Arqueología y etnohistoria del sur de Colombia y norte del Ecuador,* Miscelanea antropológica ecuatoriana, no. 6, ed. J. Alcina Franch and S. E. Moreno Yánez, 131–43. Quito: Banco Central–Abya-Yala, 1986.

Oberem, U. "El aceso a recursos naturales de diferentes ecologías en la sierra ecuatoriana (siglo XVI)." In *Proceedings of the Forty-second International Congress of Americanists* (Paris), 4:51–64.

———. "Los Cañaris y la conquista española de la sierra ecuatoriana: Otro capítulo de las relaciones interétnicas en el siglo XVI." In *Contribución a la etnohistoria ecuatoriana,* Colección Pendoneros, no. 20, ed. S. E. Moreno Yánez and U. Oberem, 129–52. Otavalo: Instituto Otavaleño de Antropología. Also in *Journal de la Société des Americanistes* 63 (1974–76): 263–74 and *Cultura* 7 (1980): 137–51.

———. "Los Caranquis de la sierra norte del Ecuador y su incorporación al Tahuantinsuyu." In *Contribución a la etnohistoria ecuatoriana,* Colección Pendoneros, no. 20, ed. S. E. Moreno Yánez and U. Oberem, 73–101. Otavalo: Instituto Otavaleño de Antropología, 1982.

———. "La fortaleza de montaña de Quitoloma." *Boletín de la academia nacional de historia,* no. 114 (1969): 196–204.

———. "Grupo indígena desaparecido del oriente ecuatoriano." *Revista de Antropología* (São Paulo), nos. 15 and 16 (1967–68): 149–70.

———. *Notas y documentos sobre los miembros de la familia del Inca Atahualpa en el siglo XVI.* Estudios etnohistóricas del Ecuador no. 1. Guayaquil: Casa de la Cultura Ecuatoriana, Núcleo del Guayas, 1976.

———. *Los Quijos: Historia de la transculturación de un grupo indígena en el oriente ecuatoriano.* Colección Pendoneros, no. 16. Otavalo: Instituto Otavaleño de Antropología, 1980.

———. "Trade and Trade Goods in the Ecuadorian Montaña." In *Native South Americans,* ed. P. J. Lyon, 346–57. Boston: Little, Brown, 1974.

Oberem, U., and R. Hartmann. "Apuntes sobre Cañaris en el Cuzco y en otras regiones del altiplano peruano-boliviano durante la colonia." In *Memorias del primer congreso ecuatoriano de arqueología, Ibarra, 1976,* 106–23. Quito, 1979.

———. "Indios Cañaris de la sierra sur del Ecuador en el Cuzco del siglo XVI." *Revista de la universidad complutense* (Madrid) 18, no. 117 (1980): 373–90.

Ordóñez de Cevallos, P. "Viaje del mundo." In *Autobiografías y memorias,* Nueva biblioteca de autores españoles, no. 2, ed. D. Serrano y Sanz, 271–476. Madrid: Casa Editorial Bailly Bailliere, 1902.

Ortiguera, T. de. *Jornada del Marañón.* Biblioteca de autores españoles, no. 216. Madrid: Ediciones Atlas, 1968.

Ortiz de la Tabla Ducasse, J. "El obraje colonial ecuatoriano: Aproximación a su estudio." *Revista de Indias,* nos. 149–50 (1977): 471–541.

———. "Las ordenanzas de obrajes de Matías de Peralta para la audiencia de Quito 1621." *Anuario de estudios americanos* 33 (1976): 875–931.

———. "La población ecuatoriana en el siglo XVI: Fuentes y cálculos." In *Memorias del primer simposio europeo sobre antropología del Ecuador,* ed. S. E. Moreno Yánez, 159–73. Quito: Ediciones Abya-Yala, 1980.

—. "La población ecuatoriana en la época colonial." *Anuario de estudios americanos* 37 (1980): 235–77.

—. "La población indígena del corregimiento de Riobamba (Ecuador), 1581–1605: La visita y numeración de Pedro de León." *Historiografía y bibliografía americanistas* 25 (1981): 19–87.

Ortiz de Zúñiga, I. *Visita de la provincia de León de Huánuco.* 2 vols. Ed. J. V. Murra. Huánuco: Universidad Hermilio Valdizán, 1967–72.

Ots Capdequí, J. M. *El estado español en América.* México City: Fondo de cultura económica:, 1941.

Oviedo y Valdés, G. Fernández de. *Historia general y natural de las Indias, islas, y tierra firme del Mar Océano.* 5 vols. Biblioteca de autores españoles, nos. 117–21. Madrid: Ediciones Atlas, 1959.

Padilla Altamarino, S., M. L. López Arellano, and A. L. González Rodríguez. *La encomienda en Popayán.* Sevilla: Escuela de Estudios Hispanoamericanos, 1977.

Palop Martínez, J. "Los Cayapas en el siglo XVI." In *Arqueología y etnohistoria del sur de Colombia y norte del Ecuador,* Miscelanea antropológica ecuatoriana, no. 6, ed. J. Alcina Franch and S. E. Moreno Yánez, 231–52. Quito: Banco Central–Abya-Yala, 1987.

—. "Mapa étnico del sur de Colombia y norte del Ecuador durante los siglos XVI–XVII." Paper presented at the Forty-seventh International Congress of Americanists, New Orleans, 1990.

Paniagua Pérez, J. *La plata labrada en la audiencia de Quito (La provincia de Azuay): Siglos XVI–XIX.* León: Universidad de León, 1989.

Paredes Borja, V. *Historia de la medicina en el Ecuador.* 2 vols. Quito: Casa de la Cultura Ecuatoriana, 1963.

Parsons, J. J. "The Northern Andean Environment." *Mountain Research and Development* 2 no. 3 (1982): 253–62.

Parsons, J. J., and R. Schlemon. "Mapping and Dating the Prehistoric Raised Fields of the Guayas Basin, Ecuador." In *Pre-Hispanic Agricultural Fields in the Andean Region,* British Archaeological Reports 359 (ii), ed. W. M. Denevan, K. Mathewson, and G. Knapp, 207–16. Oxford, 1987.

Pérez, A. R. *Los Cañaris.* Quito: Casa de la Cultura Ecuatoriana, 1978.

—. *Las mitas en la real audiencia de Quito.* Quito: Imp. del Ministerio del Tesorero, 1947.

—. *Quitus y Caras.* Llacta no. 10. Quito, 1960.

—. *Los Seudo-Pantsaleos.* Quito: Talleres Gráficos Nacionales, 1962.

Phelan, J. L. *The Kingdom of Quito in the Seventeenth Century.* Madison: University of Wisconsin Press, 1967.

Pimental Carbo, J. "Más altos que ellos, los árboles." *Cuadernos de historia y arqueología* 6 (1956): 13–17.

Pineo, R. F. "Misery and Death in the Pearl of the Pacific: Health Care in Guayaquil, Ecuador, 1870–1925." *Hispanic American Historical Review* 70, no. 4 (1990): 609–37.

Plaza Schuller, F. *La incursión Inca en el septentrión andino ecuatoriano.* Serie Arqueología 2. Otavalo: Instituto Otavaleño de Antropología, 1976.

Pollitzer, R. *Plague.* World Health Organization Monograph Series, no. 22. Geneva, 1954.

Polo, J. T. *Apuntes sobre las epidemias en el Perú.* Lima: Imp. Nacional de Federico Barrionuevo, 1913.

Polo de Ondegardo, J. *Informaciones acerca de la religión y gobierno de los incas.* Vol. 1. *Colección de libros y documentos referentes a la historia del Peru.* Eds. H. Urteaga and C. A. Romero, Vol. 3. Lima: Sanmarti y Ca, 1916.

Polunin, I. "Some Characteristics of Tribal Peoples." In *Health and Disease in Tribal Societies.* Ciba Foundation Symposium, no. 49, p. 5–20. Amsterdam: Elsevier, 1977.

Poma de Ayala, F. G. *El primer nueva corónica y buen gobierno.* 3 vols. Ed. J. V. Murra and R. Adorno. Mexico City: Siglo Ventiuno, 1980.

Ponce, Z. *Monografía del cantón Montúfar.* Quito: Talleres Gráficos Nacionales, 1955.

Ponce Leiva, P. *Relaciones histórico-geográficas de la audiencia de Quito (Siglos XVI–XIX).* Vol. 1. Madrid: Consejo Superior de Investigaciones Científicas, 1991.

Porras, M. E. *La gobernación y el obispado de Mainas. Siglos XVII y XVIII.* Quito: Abya-Yala, 1987.

Porras Barrenechea, R. *Los cronistas del Perú (1526–1650).* Lima: Gracel, 1962.

Porras Garcés, P. I. *Contribución al estudio de la arqueología e historia de los valles Quijos y Misagualli (Alto-Napo).* Quito: Editora Fenix, 1961.

———. *Fase Cosanga.* Estudios científicos sobre el oriente ecuatoriano, vol. 2. Quito: Centro de Publicaciones de la Pontífica Universidad Católica del Ecuador, 1975.

———. *Historia y arqueología de la ciudad española Baeza de los Quijos.* Estudios científicos sobre el oriente ecuatoriano, vol. 1. Quito: Centro de Publicaciones de la Pontífica Universidad Católica del Ecuador, 1974.

Powers, K. M. "Indian Migration and Socio-Political Change in the Audiencia of Quito." Ph.D. diss., New York University, 1990.

———. "Indian Migrations in the Audiencia of Quito: Crown Manipulation and Local Co-optation." In *Migration in Colonial Spanish America,* ed. D. J. Robinson, 313–23. Cambridge: Cambridge University Press, 1990.

———. "Migración vertical en la Audiencia de Quito: El caso de los Quijos en el siglo XVI." *Revista ecuatoriana de historia económica* 2 (1987): 103–30.

Purchas, S. *Purchas His Pilgrimes.* 20 Vols. Glasgow: MacLehose, 1905–8.

Rabell, C. A., and C. S. Assadourian. "Self-Regulating Mechanisms of the Population in a Pre-Columbian Society: The Case of the Inca Empire." In *International Population Conference* (Mexico, 1977), 3:25–42. Liège: Deronaux, 1977.

Rafatjah, H. A. "Malaria Vector Control: Environmental Management." In *Malaria: Principles and Practice of Malariology,* ed. W. H. Wernsdorfer and I. McGregor, 2:1135–72. New York: Longman, 1988.

Ramenofsky, A. F. "Loss of Innocence: Explanations of Differential Persistence in the Sixteenth-Century Southeast." In *Columbian Consequences,* ed. D. H. Thomas, Washington, D.C.: Smithsonian Institution Press, 1990.

———. *Vectors of Death: The Archaeology of European Contact.* Albuquerque: University of New Mexico Press, 1989.

Recopilación de los leyes de los reynos de las indias. 3 vols. Madrid: Gráficas Ultra, 1943.

Rivera, M., E. Sánchez, A. Ciudad, A. Rodríguez, and A. Colón. *La cultura Tiaone.*

Memorias de la misión arqueológica española en Ecuador, no. 4. Madrid: Ministerio de Asuntos Exteriores, 1984.

Rivera Dorado, M. "Arqueología y etnohistoria de la costa norte del Ecuador." *Revista de Indias* 38 (1978): 546–62.

Rivet, P. "Les indiens Colorados." *Journal de la société des americanistes* 2 (1905): 177–208.

———. "Les indiens Jibaros: Étude geographique, historique, et ethnographique." *L'anthropologie* 18 (1907): 333–68, 583–618; 19 (1907): 69–87, 235–59.

———. "La population de la province de Jaén, Equateur." *Congrès international des sciences anthropologiques et ethnologiques* (London), 254–57. 1934.

Rodríguez, M. *El descubrimiento del Marañón.* Ed. A. Durán. Madrid: Alianza Editorial, 1990.

Romoli de Avery, K. "Las tribus de la antigua jurisdicción de Pasto en el siglo XVI." *Revista colombiana de antropología* 21 (1977–78): 11–55.

Roosevelt, A. *Parmana: Prehistoric Maize and Manioc Subsistence along the Amazon and Orinoco.* New York: Academic Press, 1980.

Rosenblat, A. *La población indígena y el mestizaje en América.* 2 vols. Buenos Aires: Editorial Nova, 1954.

Rotberg, R. I., and T. K. Rabb. *Hunger and History.* Cambridge: Cambridge University Press, 1983.

Rowe, J. H. "Inca Culture at the Time of Spanish Conquest." In *Handbook of South American Indians,* Smithsonian Institution, Bureau of American Ethnology Bulletin 143, ed. J. H. Steward, 2:183–330. Washington D.C., 1946.

———. "Inca Policies, and Institutions Relating to the Cultural Unification of the Empire." In *The Inca and Aztec States, 1400–1800: Anthropology and History,* ed. G. A. Collier, R. I. Rosaldo, and J. D. Wirth, 93–118. New York: Academic Press, 1982.

———. "The Inca under Spanish Colonial Institutions." *Hispanic American Historical Review* 37, no. 2 (1957): 15–99.

Rueda Novoa, R. *El obraje de San Joseph de Peguchi.* Quito: Abya-Yala and Taller de Estudios Históricos, 1988.

Ruiz Rivera, J. B. *Encomienda y mita en Nueva Granada.* Sevilla: Escuela de Estudios Hispanoamericanos, 1975.

Rumazo González, J. "La ciudad de San Gregorio de Puerto Viejo." *Boletín de la academia nacional de historia* 16, nos. 46–49 (1937): 67–85.

———. *Colección de documentos para la historia de la audiencia de Quito.* 8 vols. Madrid: Afrodisio Aguado, 1948–49.

———. "Las fundaciones de Santiago y San Francisco de Quito." *Boletín de la academia nacional de historia* 44, no. 100 (1962): 179–93.

———. *La región Amazónica en el siglo XVI.* Quito: Banco Central del Ecuador. Reprint of *Anuario de estudios americanos* 3, no.1 (1946): 1–268.

Saignes, T. *Caciques, Tribute, and Migration in the Southern Andes.* University of London, Institute of Latin American Studies, Occasional paper no. 15. London, 1985.

Salazar de Villasante, J. "Exposición que hace el visitador de la Audiencia, Licenciador Salazar de Villasante, sobre su obra realizada en la cuidad y provinicia de Quito." *Museo histórico* 10, no. 32 (1960): 187–205.

Salomon, F. L. "Ancestors, Grave Robbers, and the Possible Antecedents of Ca-
    ñari 'Inca-ism.'" In *Natives and Neighbors in South America: Anthropological
    Essays,* Ethnologiska Studier 38, ed. H. O. Skar and F. L. Salomon, 207–32.
    Göteborg: Göteborgs Ethnografiska Museum, 1987.
———. "Don Pedro de Zámbisa, un varayuj del siglo XVI." *Cuadernos de historia
    y arqueología,* no. 42 (1975): 285–315.
———. "The Dynamic Potential of the Complementarity Concept." In *Andean
    Ecology and Civilization,* ed. S. Masuda, I. Shimada, and C. Morris, 511–31.
    Tokyo: University of Tokyo Press, 1985.
———. "Ethnic Lords of Quito in the Age of the Incas: The Political Economy of
    North-Andean Chiefdoms." Ph.D. diss., Cornell University, 1978. Published in
    1986 as *Native Lords of Quito in the Age of the Incas: The Political Economy of
    Northern Andean Chiefdoms.* Cambridge: Cambridge University Press.
———. "Frontera aborigen y dualismo Inca en el Ecuador prehispánico: Pistas
    onomásticas." In *Frontera del estado Inca,* Proceedings of the Fofty-fifth Interna-
    tional Congress of Americanists, Bogotá, 1985, British Archaeological Reports,
    International Series 442, ed. T. D. Dillehay and P. Netherly, 59–86. Oxford, 1988.
———. "Northern Andean Status Trader Complex under Inka Rule." *Ethnohis-
    tory* 34, no. 1 (1987): 63–77.
———. "Pochteca and Mindalá: A Comparison of Long-Distance Traders in Ec-
    uador and Mesoamerica." *Journal of the Steward Antropological Society* 9, no.
    1–2 (1978): 231–46.
———. "Systèmes politiques verticaux aux marches de l'empire Inca." *Annales:
    Economies, Sociétés, Civilisations* 33, no. 5–6 (1978): 967–89.
Salvador Lara, J. "Quito en la prehistoria." *Revista de la universidad católica del
    Ecuador* 1 (1972): 231–75.
Salvucci, R. J. *Textiles and Capitalism in Mexico: An Economic History of the Ob-
    rajes, 1539–1840.* Princeton, N.J.: Princeton University Press, 1987.
Sánchez Montañés, E. "Los ralladores en la arqueología de Esmeraldas: Ti-
    pología y función." In *Actas del primer congreso español de antropología,* 2:443–
    55. Barcelona: Departamento de antropología cultural, Universidad de Bar-
    celona, 1977.
Santa Cruz Pachacuti Yamqui, J. de. "Relación de antigüedades del Perú." In *Cró-
    nicas peruanas de interés indígena,* Biblioteca de autores españoles, no. 209,
    ed. F. Esteve Barba, 279–319. Madrid: Ediciones Atlas, 1968.
Santillán, H. de. "Relación del origen, descendencia, política, y gobierno de los
    Incas." In *Crónicas peruanas de interés indígena,* Biblioteca de autores es-
    pañoles, no. 209, ed. F. Esteve Barba, 97–150. Madrid: Ediciones Atlas, 1968.
Sarmiento de Gamboa, P. de. *Historia índica.* Biblioteca de autores españoles,
    no. 135. Madrid: Gráficas Orbe, 1960.
Sauer, C. O. *The Early Spanish Main.* Berkeley and Los Angeles: University of
    California Press, 1966.
Schotellius, J. W. "La fundación de Quito: Plan y construcción de una ciudad
    hispano-americana." In *Libro de proveimientos de tierras, cuadras, solares,
    aguas, etc., por los cabildos de la ciudad de Quito 1583–1594,* Libros de Cabil-
    dos de Quito 18, ed. J. A. Garcés, 163–230. Quito: Talleres Tipográficas Mu-
    nicipales, 1941.

Shea, D. S. "A Defense of Small Population Estimates for the Central Andes." In *The Native Population of the Americas in 1492,* 2d rev. ed., ed. W. M. Denevan, 157–80 Madison: University of Wisconsin Press, 1992.

Silva Santísteban, F. *Los obrajes en el virreinato del Perú.* Lima: Museo Nacional de Historia, 1964.

Silverblatt, I. *Moon, Sun, and Witches: Gender Ideologies and Class in Inca and Colonial Peru.* Princeton, N.J.: Princeton University Press, 1987.

Simón, P. *Noticias historiales de las conquistas de Tierra Firme en las Islas Occidentales.* 5 vols. Bogotá: Imp. de Medardo Rivas, 1882–92.

Simpson, L. B. *Many Mexicos.* Berkeley and Los Angeles: University of California Press, 1966.

Smith, C. T. "Depopulation of the Central Andes in the Sixteenth Century." *Current Anthropology* 11 (1970): 453–64.

"Sobre los tributos de los indios de Yaguachí." *Revista del archivo histórico del Guayas* 1 (1972): 70–97.

Spalding, K. *Huarochirí: An Andean Society under Inca and Spanish Rule.* Stanford, Calif.: Stanford University Press, 1984.

Stemper, D. M. "Raised Fields and Agricultural Production, A.D. 1400–1600, Río Daule, Guayas, Ecuador." In *Pre-Hispanic Agricultural Fields in the Andean Region,* British Archaeological Reports 359 (ii), ed. W. M. Denevan, K. Mathewson, and G. Knapp, 297–319. Oxford, 1987.

Stern, S. *Peru's Indian Peoples and the Challenge of Spanish Conquest: Huamanga to 1640.* Madison: University of Wisconsin Press, 1982.

Steward, J. H. 1949. "The Native Population of South America." In *Handbook of South American Indians,* Smithsonian Institution, Bureau of American Ethnology Bulletin 143, ed. J. H. Steward, 5:655–68. Washington D.C., 1949.

———. "Western Tucanoan Tribes." In *Handbook of South American Indians,* Smithsonian Institution, Bureau of American Ethnology Bulletin 143, ed. J. H. Steward, 3:737–48. Washington D.C., 1948.

Steward, J. H., and A. Metraux. "The Peban Tribes." In *Handbook of South American Indians,* Smithsonian Institution, Bureau of American Ethnology Bulletin, 143, ed. J. H. Steward, 3:727–36. Washington D.C., 1948.

———. "Tribes of the Peruvian and Ecuadorian Montana." In *Handbook of South American Indians,* Smithsonian Institution, Bureau of American Ethnology Bulletin 143, ed. J. H. Steward, 3:535–656. Washington D.C., 1948.

Stirling, M. W. *Historical and Ethnographical Material on the Jivaro Indians.* Smithsonian Institution, Bureau of American Ethnology Bulletin 117. Washington D.C., 1938.

Strube, L. *Vialidad imperial de los Incas.* Serie histórica, no. 33. Córdoba, Argentina: Instituto de Estudios Americanistas, Facultad de Filosofía y Humanidades, Universidad Nacional de Córdoba, 1963.

Super, J. *Food, Conquest, and Colonization in Sixteenth-Century Spanish America.* Albuquerque: University of New Mexico Press, 1988.

Sweet, D. G. "The Population of the Upper Amazon Valley in the Seventeenth and Eighteenth Centuries." M.A. thesis, University of Wisconsin, 1969.

Szászdi, A. "Documentos relativos a ciudades que existieron en Quijos y Bracamoros." *Boletín de la academia nacional de historia* 48, no. 106 (1965): 259–70.

Taylor, A.-C. "L'évolution démographique des populations indigènes de la Haut Amazonie, du XVIe au XXe siècle." In *Equateur 1986,* ed. D. Delaunay and M. Portais, 179–96. Paris: Editions de l'ORSTOM, 1989.

———. "Les Palta-les Jívaro andins précolumbiens à la lumière de l'ethnographie contemporaine." *Bulletin de l'institut français d'études andines* 20, no. 2 (1991): 439–59.

———. "Les versants orientaux des Andes septentrionales: De Bracamoro aux Quijos." In *L'inca, l'espagnol, et les sauvages,* ed. F. M. Renard-Casevitz, T. Saignes, and A. C. Taylor-Descola, 213–352. "Synthèse" no. 21. Paris: Recherches sur les Civilisations, 1986.

Taylor, A.-C., and P. Descola. "El conjunto Jívaro en los comienzos de la conquista española del Alto Amazonas." *Bulletin de l'institut français d' études andines* 10, no. 3–4 (1981): 7–54.

Terán, F. *Geografía del Ecuador.* 10th ed. Quito: Ediciones Libreria "Cima," 1979.

Thornton, R., T. Miller, and J. Warren. "American Indian Population Recovery Following Smallpox Epidemics." *American Anthropologist* 93 no. 1 (1991): 28–45.

Troll, C. *Las culturas superiores andinas y el medio geográfico.* Serie 1. Monografías y ensayos geográficos. Lima: Instituto de Geografía, Facultad de Letras, Universidad Nacional Mayor de San Marcos, 1958.

Trujillo, D. de. *Relación del descubrimiento del reyno del Perú.* Ed. R. Porras Barrenechea. Sevilla: Escuela de Estudios Hispanoamericanos, 1948.

Tyrer, R. B. "The Demographic and Economic History of the Audiencia of Quito: Indian Population and the Textile Industry, 1600–1800." Ph.D. diss., University of California, Berkeley, 1976.

Uhle, M. "El reino de Quito." *Boletin de la academia nacional de historia* 10, nos. 27–29 (1930): 1–17.

Uribe, M. V. "Asentamientos prehispánicos en el altiplano de Ipiales, Colombia." *Revista colombiana de antropología* 21 (1977–78): 57–195.

———. "Documentos del siglo XVIII referentes a la provincia de los Pastos: Problemas de interpretación." *Revista colombiana de antropología* 19 (1975): 39–63.

———. "Etnohistoria de las comundiades andinas prehispánicas del sur de Colombia." *Anuario colombiano de historia social y de la cultura,* nos. 13–14 (1985–86): 5–40.

Vaca de Castro, C. Letter 15.11.1541. In *Cartas de Indias,* 2:465–73. Biblioteca de autores españoles, no. 265. Madrid: Ediciones Atlas, 1974.

———. "Ordenanzas de tambos (31.5.1543)." *Revista histórica* 3 (1909): 427–92.

Vacas Galindo, E. *Exposicion sobre los límites Ecuatoriano-Peruanos.* 3 vols. Quito: Tip. de la Escuela de Artes y Oficios, 1902–3.

———. "Misiones de Mainas." *Boletín del archivo nacional de historia* 8, no. 13 (1964): 12–17.

Vargas, J. M. 1970 "Los cacicazgos." *Boletín de la academia nacional de historia* 56, no. 116 (1970): 250–64.

———. *La economia política del Ecuador durante la colonia.* 2d ed. Quito: Banco Central del Ecuador, n.d.

———. *Historia de la provincia de Santa Catalina virgen y mártir de Quito de la orden de predicadores.* Quito: Tip. y Enc. Salesiana, 1942.

———. *Historia del Ecuador: Siglo XVI.* Quito: Ediciones de la Pontífica Universidad Católica, 1977.

Vargas Ugarte, R. *Historia de la iglesia en el Perú.* 5 vols. Lima and Buenos Aires: Imp. Santa María, 1953–62.

Vázquez, F. "Relación verdadera de todo lo que sucedió en la jornada de Omagua y Dorado." In *Historiadores de Indias II,* Nueva biblioteca de autores españoles, no. 15, ed. D. Serrano y Sanz, 423–84. Madrid: Bailly Bailiere e Hijos, 1909.

Vázquez de Espinoza, A. de. *Compendio y descripción de las Indias Occidentales.* Biblioteca de autores españoles, no. 231. Madrid: Ediciones Atlas, 1969.

Velasco, J. de. *Historia del reino de Quito en la América meridional.* 3 vols. Quito: Casa de la Cultura Ecuatoriana, 1977–79.

Verano, J. W. "Prehistoric Disease and Demography in the Andes." In *Disease and Demography in the Americas,* ed. J. W. Verano and D. H. Ubelaker, 15–24. Washington, D.C.: Smithsonian Institution Press, 1992.

Verneau, R., and Rivet, P. *Ethnographie ancienne de l'Equateur.* Paris: Ministère de l'Instruction Publique, 1912.

Vickers, W. T. "Cultural Adaptation to Amazonian Habitats: The Siona-Secoya of Eastern Ecuador." Ph.D. diss., University of Florida, 1976.

———. "The Territorial Dimensions of Siona-Secoya and Encabellado Adaptation." In *Adaptive Responses of Native Amazonians,* ed. R. B. Hames and W. T. Vickers, 451–78. New York: Academic Press, 1983.

Viegl, F. X. "Gründliche Nachrichten über die Verfassung der Landschaft von Maynas in Süd-Amerika bis zum Februar 1768." In *Reisen einiger Missionarien der Gesellschaft Jesu in Amerika,* ed. C. Gottlieb von Murr, 1–450. Nuremberg, 1785.

Villalaba, J. "Los obrajes de Quito en el siglo XVII y la legislación obrera." *Instituto de historia eclesiástica ecuatoriana* 8 (1986): 43–212

Villamarin, J. A., and J. E. Villamarin. *Indian Labor in Mainland Colonial Spanish America.* Newark: University of Delaware Press, 1975.

Volland, M. "Los Punaes: Una jefatura del período tardio de integración." In *Relaciones interculturales en el área ecuatorial del Pacífico durante la época precolombina,* Proceedings of the Forty-sixth International Congress of Americanists, Amsterdam, 1985, British Archaeological Reports, International Series 503, ed. J. F. Bouchard and M. Guinea, 247–58. Oxford, 1989.

Wachtel, N. "The nitimas [*sic*] of the Cochabamba Valley: The Colonization Policy of Huayna Capac." In *The Inca and Aztec States, 1400–1800: Anthropology and History,* ed. G. A. Collier, R. I. Rosaldo, and J. D. Wirth, 199–236. New York: Academic Press, 1982.

———. *The Vision of the Vanquished: The Spanish Conquest of Peru through Indian Eyes, 1530–1570.* Hassocks: Harvester Press, 1977.

Walter, J., and R. Schofield. "Famine, Disease, and Crisis Mortality in Early Modern Society." In *Famine, Disease, and the Social Order in Early Modern Society,* ed. J. Walter and R. Schofield, 1–73. Cambridge: Cambridge University Press, 1989.

Way, A. B. "Diseases of Latin America." In *Biocultural Aspects of Disease,* ed. H. Rothschild, 253–91. New York: Academic Press, 1981.

West, R. C. "Aboriginal Sea Navigation between Middle and South America." *American Anthropologist* 61 (1961): 133–35.

Whitten, N. E. "Amazonia Today at the Base of the Andes: An Ethnic Interface in Ecological, Social, and Ideological Perspectives." In *Cultural Transformations and Ethnicity in Modern Ecuador,* ed. N. Whitten, 121–61. Urbana: University of Illinois Press, 1981.

————. *Sacha Runa: Ethnicity and Adaptation of Ecuadorian Jungle Quichua.* Urbana: University of Illinois Press, 1976.

Zarate, A. de. "Historia del descubrimiento y conquista de la provincia del Perú." In *Historiadores primitivos de Indias,* Biblioteca de autores españoles, no. 26, ed. E. de Vedia, 2-450–574. Madrid: Imp. Los Sucesores de Hernando, 1906.

Zeitlin, J. F. "Ranchers and Indians on the Southern Isthmus of Tehuantepec: Economic Change and Indigenous Survival in Colonial Mexico." *Hispanic American Historical Review* 69, no. 1 (1989): 23–60.

Zinsser, H. *Rats, Lice, and History.* New York: Bantam, 1960.

Zúñiga, G. de. "Relación muy verdadera de todo lo sucedido en el Marañón, en la provincia del Dorado, hecha por el gobernador Pedro de Orsúa." In *Colección de documentos inéditos sobre la geografía y la historia de Colombia,* ed. A. B. Cuervo, 2:506–38. Bogotá: Zalamea Hermanos, 1892.

Zúñiga, N. *Significación de Latacunga en la historia del Ecuador y de América.* 2 vols. Quito: Instituto Geográfico Militar, 1982.

Zurita, L. J., A. M. Mestanza, C. Zurita, and C. Paz y Miño. "Comportamiento ecológico de la malaria en dos regiones del Ecuador: Atacames y Borbón." *Boletín Científico* 1, no. 1 (1987): 1–8.

Index